Managing Corporate Information Systems Evolution and Maintenance

Khaled M. Khan
University of Western Sydney, Australia

Yan Zhang
University of Western Sydney, Australia

IDEA GROUP PUBLISHING
Hershey • London • Melbourne • Singapore

Acquisitions Editor:	Mehdi Khosrow-Pour
Senior Managing Editor:	Jan Travers
Managing Editor:	Amanda Appicello
Development Editor:	Michele Rossi
Copy Editor:	Ingrid Widitz
Typesetter:	Sara Reed
Cover Design:	Lisa Tosheff
Printed at:	Yurchak Printing Inc.

Published in the United States of America by
Idea Group Publishing (an imprint of Idea Group Inc.)
701 E. Chocolate Avenue, Suite 200
Hershey PA 17033
Tel: 717-533-8845
Fax: 717-533-8661
E-mail: cust@idea-group.com
Web site: http://www.idea-group.com

and in the United Kingdom by
Idea Group Publishing (an imprint of Idea Group Inc.)
3 Henrietta Street
Covent Garden
London WC2E 8LU
Tel: 44 20 7240 0856
Fax: 44 20 7379 3313
Web site: http://www.eurospan.co.uk

Library of Congress Cataloging-in-Publication Data

Managing corporate information systems evolution and maintenance / Khaled Khan, editor, Yan Zheng, editor.
p. cm.
Includes bibliographical references and index.
ISBN 1-59140-366-9 (hardcover) -- ISBN 1-59140-367-7 (pbk.) -- ISBN 1-59140-368-5 (ebook)
1. Information resources management. I. Khan, Khaled, 1959- II. Zheng, Yan, 1962-
T58.64.M353 2004
004'.068--dc22

2004003747

British Cataloguing in Publication Data
A Cataloguing in Publication record for this book is available from the British Library.

Managing Corporate Information Systems Evolution and Maintenance

Table of Contents

Preface

In the past decade, three developments have brought the issues of information systems maintenance and evolution to the fore. First, the creation of large-scale distributed systems, which are dynamically configured and re-configured, and running over global networks. Second, abetted by Internet technologies, the whole business model for many enterprises has been significantly changed. Third, global business competitiveness and complexities have been increased dramatically. Computing technologies, tools, and systems platforms are changing rapidly; so are the business strategies, scope and dimensions. In the past, enterprises could only do business in a particular geographical area. Today, organizations are increasingly becoming location independent and heavily depend on new distributed technologies such as the Internet. Enterprises are finding themselves to be strategically disadvantaged if they do not take advantage of the new technology. The consequence of advances in technologies and the changing business needs have virtually forced the organizations to let their legacy systems evolve more rapidly than they anticipated a few years ago.

In this rapidly evolving world, a corporate information system that interacts with its environment is inevitably required to evolve and to be maintained in order to keep its business competitiveness with others. Information systems (IS) always change and evolve; some more frequently, some are less frequently. System evolution refers to a process of continual change in systems functions and non-functional properties. Evolution of information systems is unavoidable, and organizations need to support and manage systems evolution to take advantage of the new technology and to address the changing business rules. The evolutionary nature of IS products, in fact, leaves us with two options: either maintain the products with their continual changing nature, or accept the degrading performance of the product. In this ever-increasing competitive business environment, the latter one would hardly be an option for most enterprises. A corporate system evolution process often requires managerial and technical skills in order to manage and control system evolution.

Managing systems evolution is generally considered to be complex. This complexity could be further compounded by growing connectivity and integration with other systems such as distributed applications. The rapidly emerging technologies put further pressures on the management task of systems evolution. The ever-dependence of business and enterprises on legacy systems makes the search for effective and viable solutions to the problems of systems evolution and maintenance more urgent. In order to find an effective solution, we need to achieve a deeper and wider understanding of the managerial and technological issues related to the systems evolution.

The importance of IS evolution and maintenance is being increasingly recognized. Global business competitiveness is dependent on the continuous maintenance and evolution of operational legacy systems. In the era of Web-based systems and *e*business, organizations need appropriate maintenance processes and resources that are required to migrate their aging legacy information systems to Web-enabled contemporary systems—for example.

Virtually every organization has to go through some sorts of maintenance and evolution of its systems. The need for a system evolution emerges from various issues such as changes of business rules, emergence of new technology, introducing new functionality, or fixing defects in the systems and so on. Managing system evolution and maintenance involves a great deal of technical, financial and management issues. One of the major concerns of any organization is how to manage the evolution process with minimum cost for maximum benefits. IS maintenance process involves multi-dimensional activities. Very few organizations adopt a separate process for system maintenance because they cannot distinguish the maintenance process from the new development process. The procedures followed in IS evolution and maintenance by practitioners are not well defined. Current practices of system maintenance activities revolve around ad hoc patching that does not follow any defined methodology. A more defined formalism describing various tasks, tools and methods is required to enable a clear understanding of the IS evolution and maintenance activities. The goal of this book is to examine key IS evolution and maintenance issues facing the IS community.

THE CHALLENGES

Any attempt to deal with the management of system evolution and maintenance requires an adequate understanding of the challenges that exist. Such challenges can be classified into different categories:

- The challenge of understanding the existing legacy systems—its architecture, its formation, its use context, and its business values
- The challenge of defining and managing the various tasks of the maintenance process, its resources, and people involved
- The challenge of controlling and containing the impact of changes that are introduced to the legacy system
- The challenge of selecting techniques and methodology to transform the legacy system to a newer form and structure
- The challenge of supporting continuous evolution of large-scale distributed systems that are dynamically self-configured and running over global networks
- The challenge of balancing the business needs and technical requirements of systems evolution
- The challenge of not creating chaos by building overly complex and large systems that we are unable to control the evolution of
- Finally, the challenge of keeping the business goals of the system in an advantageous position in an ever-increasing competitive and complex business environment.

There are no simple solutions to the problems of the topic, and we need a wide spectrum of management and technical approaches to address the challenges.

SEARCHING FOR A SOLUTION

To address the challenges, the approach that we take in this book is to present a broad perspective on systems maintenance and evolution. The focus in this book is, therefore, on the managerial and technical issues related to IS evolution and maintenance to prevent the decay of operational IS products while enhancing their business value and adapting them to a new, rapidly changing environment. The book documents some technical and managerial aspects of systems evolution, providing insights into how a modification to a system could be initiated, managed and technically achieved. The book also addresses how the system evolution has considerable impact on the corporate business process, personnel management, and the technological advantages.

We understand that problem and solution for two legacy systems cannot be the same, but there is an underlying commonality in managing the maintenance tasks from system to system. A general consensus is that a maintenance and evolution process must be manageable and adaptive, the system architecture should be recovered and recreated using defined techniques, the change impact should be controlled and tested, and finally, the business goal should be preserved.

Most books on systems evolution concentrate either on technical aspects or the management issues of the topic. In this book we try to address both issues in a balanced way. The purpose of this book is to disassemble the complex process of information system evolution and maintenance into related managerial and technical tasks so as to aid in the allocation of resources, acquisition of appropriate toolsets, distribution of responsibilities and management of the entire complex process. The book is intended to convey a high-level understanding of managing IS maintenance process and its dimensions. In this book we are particularly interested in exchanging concepts, new ideas, research results, experience and other related issues that could contribute to the academic arena and also benefit the corporate business community.

READERSHIP

The book is primarily aimed at information systems practitioners and researchers. More specifically, the book will suit:

- Researchers who like to keep track of "what is going on" in systems evolution research around the globe
- Practitioners such as systems managers, designers, architects, and planners, who may find the book to be a means of updating their knowledge on the topic
- Graduate students with the goal to acquire the knowledge and skills to manage and understand systems evolution and maintenance process and techniques.

We assume that readers have a basic understanding of general concepts in systems design, programming, and management.

ORGANIZATION OF THE BOOK

Although we have not formally divided the book into parts, each group of related chapters has a different focus on information systems evolution and maintenance. The book is organized into 15 chapters.

Chapter I identifies various issues in the management of information systems evolution and maintenance. The chapter sets the scene for discussions presented by authors in later chapters. In particular, the chapter identifies the global orientation of managing systems evolution and the related issues. Fifteen of the many concerns arising from the interests of the stakeholders of information systems are introduced in this chapter to provide context for the subsequent chapters in this book. This chapter concludes by noting the critical success factor role of leadership in the management of information systems evolution and maintenance.

Chapter II highlights the pervasiveness of change in most developed systems, and the resulting implications on development practice. The chapter emphasizes that the system continuity and evolution require a way of distinguishing between systems that can be assumed to remain stable and those that continuously "live" and evolve in their environment. Developing systems that are expected to evolve calls for a dynamic activity of design that is responsive to changes in the environment. The chapter highlights the implications for the adoption of adaptive design in dynamic environments, thereby justifying the move from discrete and project-based software engineering to a more strategic, continuous and evolving discipline of adaptive design.

Chapter III examines the differences between software maintenance and software development from a service point of view, and the consequences thereof for the maturity of software maintenance organizations. The chapter argues that software maintenance can be seen as providing a service, whereas software development is primarily concerned with the development of products. Differences between products and services affect the way in which customers assess their respective quality. Consequently, customers will judge the quality of software maintenance differently from that of software development. This in turn means that to deliver high quality results in software maintenance, both the functional quality and the technical quality dimensions are important.

Chapter IV presents the process of upfront corrective maintenance at the front-end support level. The chapter is logically divided into two parts. The first part introduces the domain of the upfront corrective maintenance process, and presents its current status within the industry. It lists the problems encountered by the front-support organizations today. The second part provides a glimpse into the Corrective Maintenance Maturity Model (CM^3): a process model specialized in upfront corrective maintenance. The goal of this chapter is to provide detailed insight into the domain of upfront corrective maintenance.

Chapter V reports the development of a novel evolution methodology that integrates the concepts of features, regression testing, and component-based software engineering. The chapter states that regression test cases are untapped resources, full of information about system features. By exercising each feature with its associated test cases using code profilers, code can be located and refactored to create components. These components are then inserted back into the legacy system, ensuring a working system structure. The approach is validated on the evolution of a real-world legacy system to reduce the costs of future maintenance of the system.

Chapter VI provides techniques to re-engineer stand-alone legacy systems into Web-enabled environments. Specifically, it aims for a framework that allows for the identification of reusable business logic entities in large legacy systems in the form of major legacy components, the migration of these procedural components to an object oriented design, the specification of interfaces of these identified components, the automatic generation of CORBA wrappers to enable remote access, and finally, the seamless interoperation with Web services via HTTP based on the SOAP messaging mechanism.

Chapter VII examines the use of patterns for reengineering legacy systems to Web. To address these issues, many different concepts and frameworks need to be well understood, especially legacy system wrapping, connection handling, service abstraction, adaptation techniques, dynamic content generation, and others. In this chapter, we present patterns from different sources that resolve these issues. We integrate them to a pattern language operating in the context of reengineering to the Web, and present pattern variants and examples in this context.

Chapter VIII presents an approach to supporting change impact analysis at the architectural level of software systems based on the architectural slicing and chopping technique. The main feature of the approach is to assess the effect of changes in a software architecture by analyzing its formal architectural specification. The chapter argues and shows that separation of change impact analysis of a system from code level to architectural level is an efficient step to reduce the cost of change impact analysis during software evolution, because this allows a maintenance programmer to assess the effect of changes of the system at the architectural level so that many implementation details of the system need not to be considered.

Chapter IX discusses the requirements that an open architecture for software visualization tools should meet, and details the implementation of such an architecture. The focus in this chapter is on reverse engineering, although the proposed technique could be applicable to forward engineering activities as well. The material presented in this chapter both serves the software architects who are looking for a flexible visualization tool and provides a starting point for the tool designer.

Chapter X addresses the research challenges in the area of software architecture reconstruction and discusses the state-of-the-art solutions to these challenges. The chapter argues that the importance of architecture analysis and reconstruction of a large and complex software system stems from the need to perform continuous maintenance activities, such as migration of a legacy system to a new platform, in which the architectural reconstruction constitutes the major part of these activities. The chapter exposes a systematic approach to the important issues, alternative solutions, and future research in the field of software architecture analysis and reconstruction.

Chapter XI describes the notion of product line models and how to apply them for developing and evolving Web products. A product line captures the common and variable aspects of software systems as key assets under a common architecture. Software companies are increasingly adopting this approach in order to accelerate the development of families of similar software products. The chapter argues that new techniques to engineer Websites are needed in order to reduce the time to market of Web products.

Chapter XII provides insight into the software maintenance process, its features, actors, activities and results, with the emphasis on the importance and complexity of this kind of maintenance. The chapter shows how the software maintenance process is modeled in the form of the queuing network with the applied simulation. Method implementation is described with a case study of telecommunication maintenance. The results of the method show how the process bottlenecks are formally identified and how new proposals for the improved process design are applied.

Chapter XIII proposes a strategy for extracting the requirements for a legacy system evolution from the requirements of the *e*Business evolution. The strategy includes a toolkit composed of a set of decision tables and a measurement framework, both referring to the organization, business processes, and legacy information systems. The decision tables allow the identification of the processes to be evolved, the actions to be performed on them and their activities, and the strategies to be adopted for evolving the embedded software systems. The measurement framework proposed in the chapter aims at achieving a greater understanding of the processes and related problems, taking into account organizational and technological issues.

Chapter XIV discusses some of the common problems in maintenance. The chapter contains a management model for solving these problems, based on theoretical research and practical experience. The central theme of the model is the connection between business and IT in maintenance, and the connected responsibilities of these two. This is achieved by maintaining maintenance objects rather than the system, establishing micro organizations for each maintenance object where business processes are represented. The model is used in more than 50 organizations in Sweden.

Chapter XV concludes the book with a review of a variety of IS quality-oriented approaches based on research findings and dispassionate practitioner accounts, and an indication of their advantages and weaknesses, and the development environments and contexts for which they are most suited. These techniques are available to systems developers to be used individually or in synergistic combinations to confront the prevalent problem of poor system quality and reduce its unfavorable impact on information systems maintenance.

Khaled M. Khan
Yan Zhang, Ph.D.
November 2003

Acknowledgments

The editors would like to acknowledge the help of all involved in the collation and review process of the book, without whose support the project could not have been satisfactorily completed. We are immensely grateful to our friends, well-wishers and fellow professionals who were of great help to us in bringing out this book. We have many people who deserve our thanks. A very special thank you goes to Mehdi Khosrow-Pour of Idea Group Inc., whose enthusiasm and encouragement motivated us to initially accept his invitation for taking on this endeavour. A further special note of thanks goes also to all of the staff at Idea Group Inc., whose contributions throughout the whole process from inception of the initial idea to final publication have been invaluable.

We are very pleased to mention that the book documents contributions from many leading researchers who have been working on systems evolution and maintenance for a long time. Deep appreciation and gratitude is due to Dr. Ned Chapin, co-editor of the *Journal of Software Maintenance and Evolution: Research and Practice,* for accepting our invitation to contribute the introductory chapter of the book.

Most of the chapters have been reviewed and revised twice in order to maintain the quality of this book. Some of the authors of chapters included in this book also served as referees for articles written by other authors. Thanks go to all those who provided constructive and comprehensive reviews; however, some of the reviewers must be mentioned as their reviews set the benchmark. Reviewers who provided the most comprehensive, critical and constructive comments include: Dr. George Heineman of Worcester Polytechnic Institute Computer Science department; Dr. Alok Mehta of American Financial Systems Inc.; Dr. Mira Kajko-Mattsson of Stockholm University; Dr. Jianjun Zhao of Fukuoka Institute of Technology; Dr. Evan Duggan of University of Alabama; Ron Schmid and Narendra Gangavarapu of University of Western Sydney. The editors are thankful to these reviewers for their prompt and constructive review of the chapters.

There have been many discussions of ideas and content that have helped us refine the chapter review process.

Special thanks also go to the publishing team at Idea Group Inc, in particular to Michele Rossi, who continuously prodded via e-mail for keeping the project on schedule.

In closing, we wish to thank all of the authors for their insights and excellent contributions to this book. We also want to thank all of the people who assisted us in the reviewing process. In addition, this book would not have been possible without the ongoing professional support from Mehdi Khosrow-Pour and Jan Travers at Idea Group Inc.

Khaled M. Khan & Yan Zhang, Ph.D.
Editors
November 2003

Chapter I

Managing Corporate Information Systems Evolution and Maintenance

Ned Chapin, InfoSci Inc., USA

ABSTRACT

Five key management considerations center on a basic fact—managers manage people in getting things done. As they manage the people in getting information systems evolution and maintenance done, the managers address many concerns arising from the interests of the corporation and the stakeholders involved in the information systems. One of the two major groups of stakeholders is the people who use and work with the information systems, that is, the systems' customers. The suppliers are the other group and consist of the corporation's information systems personnel and the supporting vendors. Fifteen of the many concerns arising from the interests of the stakeholders are introduced in this chapter to provide context for the subsequent chapters in this book. This chapter concludes by noting the critical success factor role of leadership in the management of information systems evolution and maintenance.

CHAPTER OBJECTIVES

The main objective of this chapter is to provide a foundation and context for the subsequent chapters in this book. This objective is actualized through a set of secondary objectives. They are to introduce at a high level:

- Five key management considerations,
- Fifteen relevant management concerns, and
- Leadership in information systems evolution and maintenance.

Subsequent chapters in this book address at a more detailed level selected aspects of some of these considerations and concerns, and some of the connections among them.

In this chapter, the terms "corporate" and "corporation" are used more broadly than fit the strict legal definitions. Instead, they are used as a brief way of referring to any human organization of people operated by those same people to accomplish some human objectives or goals, and using a computer for implementing at least one information system. Thus for example in this chapter, a "corporation" might be a governmental taxing agency, or a manufacturer, or a barber shop, or a multinational financial institution, or the Red Cross, or a grocery retailer, or the European Union (EU), or an auditing firm, or a coffee plantation, and so forth.

KEY MANAGEMENT CONSIDERATIONS

Information Systems

Managing corporate information systems evolution and maintenance is a major variant of the more general process of managing systems evolution and maintenance, or of managing information and communication technologies and their use. Managing corporation information systems evolution and maintenance includes major aspects of computing management and software management. This *key management considerations* section of this chapter overviews the general process of managing systems evolution and maintenance. With some specific attention to information systems, this major section is organized around five key management considerations:

- Who or what is doing the managing?
- When and where is the management done?
- What is being managed?
- Why is the management done? That is, what are the goals or ends of the management?
- How is the management done?

A non-rigorous definition of "information systems" can help bound the domain of discourse. Information systems are a form of systems. In general, a system is an interacting combination of components. An example of a natural system is the solar system. For our purposes here, natural systems are of less interest than systems created by human beings (people) for human purposes. An example is the system of justice under the Napoleonic code. Because of the historic advances in technology, the human-created systems of current interest have machine or hardware components. An example is the television system used in the United Kingdom.

Because people use languages and have implemented ways of writing those languages using symbols as a way of expressing information, of special interest here are information systems. An example is an inventory control system. To be a little more rigorous for context in this book, an information system is a deliberate human-created combination for handling symbols of the services of people, materials, hardware and methods (Chapin, 1971). While some of the materials may be consumed by the information system as people use it, such as paper and ink, in general the components of information systems survive usage and hence the information system can provide continuing performance over the passage of time. An example is a payroll system that weekly produces paychecks for employees and labor cost reports for financial executives. However, information systems do evolve as people make changes in them—that is, normally as people maintain the information systems.

Of the five key considerations noted above, the "how" one, will garner the most attention in this chapter and in this book. General coverage from a chief information or technology officer (CIO or CTO) perspective can be a useful supplement (Lane, 2003). The subsections following take up in order the five key management consideration.

Who or What is Doing the Managing?

Self-managing information systems share a critically important attribute with self-documenting source code—both are extremely rare. While it is possible to create computer programs that can modify themselves permanently or temporarily, and computer programs that can learn from experience, both are still quite limited. Those capabilities still are far short of what people expect for accomplishing information systems evolution or maintenance. Hence, as a practical matter now and in the foreseeable future, the burden (and opportunity) of managing information systems evolution and maintenance falls to people.

But which people? Interacting are five primary roles for the people:

- Persons or entities (such as corporations) composed of persons, whose performance or well-being is affected by the performance of the information system. Let us call persons or entities in this role as stakeholders.
- Persons or entities who are suppliers of data used as input by the information system, such as a buyer who places an order with a corporation.
- Persons who receive data produced as output from the information system, such as a client who receives a bill from a corporation for services rendered.
- Persons or entities who are involved with other persons' information systems, such as a financial auditor or a tax collector.
- Persons whose jobs are to make changes to information systems, such as programmer-analysts and the chief technology officer (CTO). These persons can have many detailed and specific roles. However, those roles can be classified into two main groups—managing and doing. The "doing" group includes such activities as studying documentation, preparing test data, interpreting requests for changes, drawing UML (Booch, 1999) sequence diagrams, and so forth. The "managing" group includes such activities such as planning, assessing tasks, changing the available resources, making personnel decisions, and so forth. Since this book is focused on managing, the chapters in this book speak relatively little about activities in the "doing" group.

When and Where are the Management Done?

Management is both event driven and time driven. The time driven basis rests on a summarization and expectation of events. Events are changes in the state of something. For example, a corporation ships an order to a buyer. The occurrence of the shipment triggers changes in the corporation's financial status, such as inventory values, accounts receivable amounts, cost of packing materials used, accounts payable amounts (such as for transportation costs), and so forth. Since a major group of information systems are effectively models in symbol form of the corporation, an event recognized by the corporation is also an event recognized by the information systems. And therein lies a potential stumbling block—the link between the occurrence of events for the corporation and for the corporation's information systems.

What events (changes in conditions or states) does the corporation elect to recognize, and what events does it either ignore deliberately, or to neglect to recognize? It is one of the tasks of managers to determine which events to recognize, and what to do about them when they occur. Whenever managers change either what events are to be recognized or what is to be done when events occur, then the information systems have to be changed to preserve their fidelity as models. That itself is an event triggering information systems maintenance. That maintenance sometimes takes the form of or results in information systems evolution.

Information systems maintenance involves a complex of activities, both of the "doing" and of the "managing" character (Chapin et al., 2001). Making changes in the existing information systems usually is information systems maintenance. An example is changing the format of a report to include a new product. When the information systems maintenance changes made are sufficiently extensive to result in a new version of the system, then the result is information systems evolution. An example is a budgeting system that now includes the effects of using a new manufacturing process in producing one of the corporation's product lines. The distinction between information systems maintenance and information systems evolution is neither sharp nor universal. Different corporations distinguish among them differently.

What is the same, however, is the link between the model that the performance of the information systems provides and the functioning of the corporation. As managers change the corporation, they must also change the information systems by having information systems maintenance done, or the information systems lose fidelity and usefulness. An example is expanding the geographic area served by the corporation, such as by adding an overseas distribution point. As managers change their skills and their preferences, they typically also make supportive changes in the information systems by having information systems maintenance done. An example is adding an interactive "what if" capability to an existing financial planning system.

Since the value to managers of having an information system depends upon both its fidelity as a model of some part or function of the corporation, and its acceptability (its interface with people), maintenance is needed whenever either has a change recognized by the managers. Since managers like to protect their "turf", managers prefer to feel that they own the information systems with which they interact or use. Decentralized local ownership implies decentralized local maintenance. An example is a local sales office's prospects system established and run by and for that local office alone. Information systems that model corporate functions broadly typically have centralized ownership and centralized maintenance. An example is an enterprise resource planning system that is used corporation-wide for financial and human resource functions.

What is Being Managed?

Information systems are not only models of functionalities in the corporation; they also are usually the actual means by which many of those functionalities are accomplished. For example, information systems in use do not act the way that sulfuric acid acts in an inorganic chemical processing operation, but information systems can be used to run that inorganic chemical processing operation. And for example, information systems are not flows of money into or out of a corporation's bank account, but information systems can determine and represent the amounts flowing, monitor the timing of the money flows, and apply business rules to determine the consequences of the flows.

For these reasons, managing information systems evolution and maintenance is actually managing changes in the way the corporation does business (Chapin, 2003). A change in an information system usually is also a change in either what business the corporation does, or when it does it, or how it does it. Usually, a change in a corporation's information systems accomplishes all three sorts of changes in the corporation. Under the best of circumstances, the changes in the information systems and in the corporation are carried out in concert. Less desirable (but common) is having the changes in the information system lead the changes in the corporation. Least desirable is having changes in the corporation lead to changes in the information systems. At a general level in all three of the circumstances, what is being managed is a combination of changes in the corporation and changes in the corporation's information systems. A later chapter in this book covers an approach to managing change.

Managing change requires resolving the mix of what can be changed by people and to what extent and by what means, and what cannot be changed. In general, people cannot change things just by "managing" but can change things by combining "managing" and "doing". The things may be inanimate objects, such as doorways, milling machines, sheet steel, warehouses, and so forth. The things may be intangible, such as the corporate image, computer software, human resource policy, and so forth. The things can be animate, such as horses, cornfields, people, and so forth. A person in the "managing" group may decide where and when to plant corn, but a person in the "doing" group has to do the work of tilling and planting. A person in the "managing" group may decide to stamp 50 automobile door panels from sheet steel, but deciding is not enough. The actual work of moving the steel and operating the stamping machine requires work from people in the "doing" group.

At a more detailed level, what is being managed ultimately is people, for it is people who as a practical matter accomplish the "doing". Typically a member of the "managing" group (i.e., a manager) in a corporate environment reports to and is a subordinate of someone higher in the organization. A manager also almost always has subordinates. The subordinates may be lower-level managers (people who are also in the "managing" group) and non-management personnel (people in the "doing" group).

Managing change in the organization and its information systems is fundamentally managing people—who is to do what, where they do it, when they do it, how they do it, and why. The "why" aspect involves more than the basic human resource considerations such as hiring, training, assigning, compensating, transferring, and terminating personnel. For information systems personnel, it also importantly involves motivation and morale. As has been pointed out by Colter, Couger and others, motivation and morale considerations are different for information systems personnel (Couger, 1985).

Why is the Management Done?

Management is done in corporate environments fundamentally because of the worldwide custom of suppliers serving customers through a process of voluntary exchanges. (Involuntary processes of exchange, such as slavery, confiscation and theft, are not covered in this chapter). Each of the two parties in a voluntary exchange supplies value to the other party on an agreed upon basis. In law, that agreement is usually termed a contract. For example, a cobbler repairs shoes in exchange for money from a customer. Or for example, an airline carries a container of tropical flowers from Caracas to London in exchange for the customer's promise to pay later. Or for example, a chemical company trades today a surplus railroad tank car of ammonia to a petrochemical supplier, for a railroad tank car of ammonia to be delivered six months from now. Note that exchanges may be settled transaction by transaction, or grouped, or cover a time period such as a year. Note also that a customer may "pay" a supplier in any of a variety of ways acceptable to both parties, such as by barter, by cash, by budget transfer, by credit, by a charge to corporate overhead, and so forth. A dissatisfied customer or supplier may try to refuse to complete an exchange, or may refuse to make exchanges in the future, or insist on different terms of exchange (such as at a higher or lower price or a lower or higher quality, or on a different delivery schedule).

Are information systems and the services of information systems things of value that have suppliers and customers? A close examination shows that the answer to that question is a very strong yes. That means that the managers responsible for or charged with information systems have both suppliers and customers to satisfy. And whether they want to or like it or not, it means that the managers are participants in customer relationship management (CRM) activities and are participants in supply chain management activities. In both directions, some of the people to be satisfied are employees of the same corporate entity that the manager is, and some are outside stakeholders, such as tax collectors, investors, stockholders, bankers, regulators from government agencies, auditors, and so forth. Sometimes the same people operate in both roles as customers and suppliers. An example is tax collectors.

Strangely, many managers charged with information systems in corporations seem unaware of the identity, number, variety, and needs of their customers. Some systems may have tens of thousands of former, current and potential customers (for example, a Spanish version of the corporation's online order system); others may have only one or a few (for example, an advertising manager's decision support system). "Know the customer" is a timeworn old adage, but still a vital foundation of customer relationship management. What does the customer get from the information system's performance, and on what does that depend, and when? What is the value to the customer of the information system's performance, expressed both qualitatively and quantitatively? What would improve the value of the information system to the customer? Could that improvement be achieved by doing software maintenance activities, or would it take software evolution? What would be the effects of the improvement on the customers of other information systems and upon the corporation?

Most managers charged with information systems in corporations seem quite aware of who their suppliers are (a common example is an employee working as an information systems analyst), and their diversity. Examples of the diversity of outside suppliers are vendors of materials (such as paper), of equipment (such as of client computers), and of services (such as air conditioning repair). But some outside suppliers may be suppliers of data, such as government agencies (such as regulatory authorities), trade associations, and even the corporation's competitors (as when they make changes in their product lines, prices, delivery terms, etc.). Suppliers have diverse capabilities and their own needs and agendas. Ignoring those or giving them short shrift typically decreases either the quantity or the quality of the suppliers' performance. As noted earlier, motivation and morale are matters of special importance affecting the performance of information systems personnel as suppliers.

More distant stakeholders of a corporation's information systems are rarely as significant for the corporation as the information systems' customers and suppliers, but always present. For example, most countries have privacy regulations that affect how some information systems must perform. And for example, a local government where a corporation has a facility may be concerned with traffic abatement, and as such becomes a customer of a corporation's information systems, as well as a data supplier to some corporate information systems. Meeting the demands of such stakeholders may require doing software maintenance on corporate information systems. Then also, the corporation itself is a stakeholder. However, the demands of the corporation are almost always interpreted and expressed through the demands of the higher executives that serve as managers in the corporation, and hence as customers of and as suppliers to the performance of some of the information systems.

In summary, the goals and ends of managing a corporation's information systems evolution and maintenance arise from the recognition of and response to the needs of the information system customers and suppliers. Most of the customers and of the suppliers are themselves employees of the corporation, but outside customers and suppliers, and other outside stakeholders are always an influence on corporate information systems evolution and maintenance.

How is the Management Done?

A manager is a person who does two jobs:

- The manager self-manages—that is, the manager manages the on-the-job performance of himself/herself, and
- The manager manages part of the on-the-job performance of other persons assigned for that manager to manage.

Usually those other persons being managed are identified as being members of an organization unit (such as of a department), or of a team drawn from the personnel of one or more organizational units. Managers typically have hierarchal assignments, so that managers at the top of the hierarchy manage mostly other managers, while at the bottom of the hierarchy, the first line supervisors manage only people in the "doing" group (other than themselves, of course). The size of the management span (how many persons the manager manages) is a measure of the flatness or height of the management hierarchy in a corporation, with bigger spans resulting in flatter organizations with less height (fewer levels of management), and a lower ratio of "managing" to "doing" personnel.

Although a manager may be said to "manage information technology" or "manage the raw material inventory", or "manage accounts receivable", or "manage software maintenance", what is really being said is that the manager manages the people who do the function or work associated with the thing. The people in the "doing" group engage in varying amounts of self-management as they do their jobs. If it is the "doing" group that actually gets the function or work done, how do managers earn their keep?

While the boundary line between the "managing" and the "doing" is neither sharp nor immutable, some activities are distinguishing and dominant in the managing. Among those activities are communicating and decision making, and especially, planning, organizing, directing, monitoring, supervising, evaluating, and coordinating the work of subordinates, and receiving direction from superiors in the hierarchy and taking care of administrative matters. The "doing" activities also involve many of these same activities, but they are focused on the managing the performance of the self (not on managing the performance of subordinates) during the process of doing the work. An example is the work of a truck driver.

The distinguishing activities of management are about how management is done both in general and in the management of information systems evolution and maintenance (Drucker, 1974):

- *Communicating.* The manager is a selective communicator. The manager receives many messages from customers, suppliers, other stakeholders and other sources. The manager stores them, filters and edits them, and forwards them as and when the manager deems appropriate to destinations selected by the manager. The manager also initiates messages and delivers messages. Example: a manager receives and studies a request from a manager of a system user asking for a new function to be added to an existing information system.
- *Decision-making.* The manager is a decision maker within a defined or authorized scope or domain. The manager combines experience, skills and training with the data received via communications to choose or select among alternatives. The manager may create new alternatives. Having made a decision, the manager then communicates it as the manager deems appropriate. Example: a manager decides to shift a programmer-analyst from one maintenance project to a different one where the manager believes the person's skills are more needed.
- *Planning.* The manager visualizes alternative future courses of action and their consequences. The visualization may be at any level of detail, cover any time period, rest upon any assumptions, and be expressed in any from hazy, sketchy qualitative terms to specific, detailed quantitative terms. Example: a manager has been asked by a higher level manager, "What additional software maintenance resources would be needed and when to have systems modified to support a contemplated possible addition of product "X" to the corporation's product line six months from now?"
- *Organizing.* The manager arranges, marshals, schedules and deploys the system resources to support work in progress or work planned. While the human resources are especially important, the equipment and material resources are also involved, as are the methods that are used to get the system to function. Example: a manager

forms a two-person team to use pair programming methods in designing and implementing a minor addition of functionality to an existing information system that will require database access and a protected testing environment during off-peak production times.

- *Directing.* The manager provides the context for work to be done, and points the direction or course the work is to follow. While directing is mostly done at the start of a project, it is sometimes redone, especially when changes have been decided upon. Example: a manager reminds a programmer-analyst working on a project that future maintainability is one of the corporate objectives for information systems, even though it was not explicitly specified in the maintenance project's list of requirements.
- *Monitoring.* The manager gathers data about the quantity and quality of the work being done, relates it to customer and supplier needs, and uses it to the plan for that work, together with any revisions made to the plan. The mechanics of the data gathering depend upon local conditions, customs, and project management methods (e.g., waterfall). Example: a manager finds that the test case preparation step was skipped, but one team member has already started to write source code to implement the one part of the design that has reached the detail stage.
- *Supervising.* Management supervision of subordinates varies greatly in Information Technology work, depending upon local customs and personnel skills and experience. Sometime it can be left largely to self-management; other times it merits frequent interactions during the work period between the manager and the subordinate. Example: a manager points out to the team leader than the test case preparation step was skipped, and asks to see the test cases as soon as they have been prepared.
- *Evaluating.* The manager measures the work that has been done against some performance yardstick. To be effective, this requires the manager to have set in advance an expected amount of performance to have been accomplished by some specific time. As a practical matter, it also requires the manager to have chosen in advance what shall be treated as evidence of the accomplishment, both in qualitative and quantitative terms. Example: a manager checks a programmer-analyst's UML (Booch, 1999) class diagram as the programmer-analyst walks the manager through it.
- *Coordinating.* The manager has to balance conflicting demands in an environment that rarely has all the desired resources available at the times, quantities and qualities the manager would like. The manager is almost always competing with other managers for access to some of the resources. Compromises, tradeoffs and work-arounds are commonly necessary, as the manager strives to provide the information system customers with the requested results. Example: a manager has a maintenance project that is running ahead of schedule and under budget, but agrees to slow down and delay its completion in order to shift a Web security specialist and some computer test time to a different manager's maintenance project that is to interact in use with the manager's project.
- *Receiving direction.* The manager has a critically important customer, the person to whom the manager reports in the corporation. Dealing with this customer requires more than just the usual communication work that the manager does. The received messages from this customer are of special importance to the manager, and

their import has to be reflected in how the manager works and on what and when. Example: a manager passing his "reports to" person in the hall on the way to the lunch room is asked by the "reports to" person, "Why is Janet in marketing telling me that last week's release is producing some garbage for her EU agents?"

- *Administrating*. The administrative workload on managers varies greatly for different corporations, but "paperwork" is notoriously worse in bureaucratic ones. Some of the work is inevitable, such as periodic reviews of personnel performance, annual budget preparation, recommendations for promotions, approval of vacation and training schedules, interviewing job candidates, revising authorized access to resources, making charity collections, and so forth. But some of the work may be burdensome ways of handling communication or coordination, or be reflective of outmoded ways of doing business. Example: a manager is required to fill in by pen and ink a requisition form to get ink cartridges for a subordinate's computer printer.

The "how" of management is fundamentally the management of the work of other persons. While a manager is typically assigned a function or kind of work in the corporation to manage, the manager accomplishes the management mostly by managing people. At the same time, there are concerns or issues and environmental factors that may affect that management process. A selection of those in software evolution and maintenance are described in the next major section of this chapter, and later chapters give more details and present additional approaches to handling some of them and the contexts in which they occur.

RELEVANT MANAGEMENT CONCERNS

Overview

In carrying out the management functions summarized above, managers of information systems evolution and maintenance have many competing concerns. Some of these concerns arise from the particular corporate environment in which the manager operates. Some others arise from the unique capabilities and roles of the information systems in the corporate environment. A few are self-nurtured by the manager. This major section of this chapter introduces the reader to a selection of these concerns, with emphasis on those of particular importance for information systems evolution and maintenance: reducing firefighting, knowing subordinates' work, keeping systems alignment, documenting the information systems, servicing information systems customers, facilitating belonging and teamwork, taking care of suppliers, providing system interoperability, choosing technologies, measuring and tracking, converting and re-engineering systems, architecting information systems, improving evolution and maintenance processes, globalizing information systems, and being promotable. A later chapter in this book offers a taxonomy of activities involved in information systems evolution and maintenance.

Reducing Firefighting

For the manager, the least burdensome way of managing information systems evolution and maintenance is to be reactive, putting out "fires" as and when they are reported to the manager. By putting the emphasis on responding with software maintenance to customer requests that are accompanied by adequate funding, the manager can demonstrate that he did what the information system customers wanted when they wanted it enough to pay for it by the usual means used in the corporation.

While much of corrective maintenance requests can appropriately be handled in a reactive firefighting modus operandi, it rarely is appropriate for systems evolution (Chapin et al., 2001). Pro-active scheduled maintenance procedures handle more effectively most enhancive, reductive, adaptive, performance and preventive maintenance tasks, as well as the larger corrective maintenance assignments. Getting most software evolution and the higher types of software maintenance tasks into a pro-active mode does not happen automatically. Instead, it requires concerted effort by the manager to know the information system customers' current and future needs, to communicate frequently and extensively with the customers and with suppliers, to plan well in advance of the desired completion dates, and to organize to have the resources available when needed.

The effective manager is not just an order taker, but also an initiator who opens and actualizes channels of opportunity to help make others in the organization become more effective in accomplishing their work. In managing systems evolution and maintenance, the manager is at the helm of corporate change. How well people perform in a corporation depends a lot on how current and supportive are the information systems the people use. The firefighting manager of information systems evolution and maintenance takes the heat for delay in getting improvements in place in systems; the pro-active manager of information systems evolution and maintenance clears and smoothes the path of progress for others in the corporation.

Knowing Subordinates' Work

Some managers move into the "managing" group from the "doing" group. That is, previously they worked as analysts, programmers, analyst-programmers, database specialists, software quality assurers, and so forth. Such managers bring with them knowledge and experience gained from their time spent in the "doing" group. If it has sufficient breadth, this knowledge and experience can serve them in managing the subordinates assigned to them in information systems evolution and maintenance work (Chapin, 1987,1988; Kitchenham et al., 1999; Chapin et al., 2001). For example, in helping customers set expectations, in selecting the personnel to assign to a task, and in supervising and evaluating the work of the assigned personnel, knowing what is involved in doing the work can help the manager in being regarded by subordinates and superiors as being realistic, fair and dependable.

Even these managers who come from the "doing" group need to keep up an adequate breadth and currency to their "doing" knowledge because of the continued rush of technological advance in Information Technology. Managers and personnel from other areas who are laterally transferred into managing information systems evolution and maintenance face this situation initially in a serious form. They have to climb a learning curve. For handling this situation, a mentor or the availability of technical resource persons are valuable aids to the newly assigned manager. Also the online courses available from some of the professional associations may help the new manager fill in knowledge gaps.

Keeping Systems Alignment

Information systems can give strategic value to the corporation, for information systems are an important part of the intellectual property of a corporation. Taken together, the information systems and how they are used represent what is unique about how a corporation gets its work done. Changing an information system or changing the use of information systems in a corporation, as in information systems evolution and maintenance, changes the content and value of the corporation's intellectual property.

Managers of information systems evolution and maintenance usually are keenly aware of the importance of keeping information systems aligned with information system customer expectations of where they (the customers) and the corporation are going, especially in the near future. Information system customers have different expectations of what they want to be able to do and not do in the near future. Unfortunately, nearly always, the different customers have competing and incompatible expectations, and see proposed changes as opportunities to expand their respective turfs or to improve some characteristics of their respective turfs. What is best for the corporation as a whole on a strategic or tactical basis may not be the best for some information system customers within the corporation. This can put the manager of information systems evolution and maintenance in what appears as a no-win situation, facing charges of disloyalty, abuse, incompetence, playing politics and mismanagement from the information system customers likely to suffer turf reductions. A task for the manager is to find "win-win" compromises or politically acceptable alternatives that put the corporation first.

To help keep the manager of information systems evolution and maintenance from being a victim in such crossfire, the manager can give particular attention to keeping systems alignment. This spreads across customer relationship management, communicating, reducing firefighting, monitoring the costs and values of information systems usage, prioritizing projects, and planning. The manager of information systems evolution and maintenance has to earn the confidence and ear of the information systems customers to learn from them where they want to go, when, and how. In turn, the manager can provide consultative maintenance to make available to the information system customers guidance about what information systems can and cannot do and help them evaluate the practicalities and the economics of alternative forms and ways of meeting customer desires (Sambamurthy, 2003). The manager of information systems evolution and maintenance also has to communicate with the corporate superiors of those customers, and sometimes with the outside suppliers to those customers. This is in order to identify potential incompatibilities in what different stakeholders want, and to try to guide those stakeholders in order to help them avoid being later snagged or blind-sided. Some later chapters in this book cover maintenance models and strategic uses of information systems.

Documenting the Information Systems

The manager of information systems evolution and maintenance is in practice accountable for creating and updating minimal documentation for the use of each system in the corporation's inventory of information systems. In some countries and jurisdictions such as in the USA, this accountability is mandated on most medium-sized or larger corporations by laws or regulations. An example in the USA is SOX (Moore & Schwartz, 2003). In other countries or jurisdictions, it is simply expected by outside stakeholders as a part of prudent management of all but small-sized corporations. All systems from small through large are covered, but in practice the larger information systems are usually the ones required to have their use the most fully documented.

Briefly stated, the minimal documentation consists of a symbolic model of how what can be done with an information system can affect the assets, liabilities and equity of the corporation. The model can be in annotated graphics, such as in UML (unified modeling language) or in ISO or ANSI standard charts, or in an annotated spreadsheet, or in expository text or an equivalent form. In any case, the model has to provide (at least potential) traceability from what the people using the information system may do, to the running object code, with people's roles in the system clearly presented as specific actions or failures to act. This is usually more of a concern to information systems customers and the corporation's employees than to outside suppliers. The usual focus in the documentation is on the ways the procedures work in the information system to assure the integrity of the data and their processing, and the security of the information system. For those reasons, any time that an information system is changed, as through maintenance or evolution, the existing documentation must be updated (updative), and the corporation's auditing and security personnel normally check the updated documentation for continued conformance with corporate policies.

Servicing Information System Customers

On what terms should a manager of information systems evolution and maintenance provide service and support to the customers of information systems evolution and maintenance? The answers given in practice vary widely, including providing training and "help desk" support, as do the results. For example, a user might telephone in a request or a complaint about an existing system. Or, a manager of an information system customer unit using a system might initiate a service request, as by a "Request for System Change" form, that goes to the manager of information systems evolution and maintenance. Or the manager of information systems evolution and management might send a project leader to confer with the personnel of an information system customer to find out what changes may be in order, to prioritize them, and to make a guess at what the benefit/cost ratios might be if they were done. Payment alternative may be also varied, and run from treating evolution and maintenance as chargeable against a budgeted flat overhead (burden) amount, or budget transfers based on time and materials used, or as payment checks written, or as specific projects that must be approved and funded in advance by some senior executive or committee.

Some of the combinations typically result in more harmonious relationships between information systems customers and the manager of information systems evolution and maintenance. One component is a service request for each project or task requested. A written version prepared in advance that bears the approval of an authorized customer manager appears to work the best, provided it includes the customer's quantitative estimate of the benefit and a specific, detailed function-oriented specification of what the customer wants. For example, a request that says, "Fix the layout to be whatever Gerald wants" is not an adequate service request. In general, time and materials direct payments by the customer give a less political and a more business-oriented flavor to the services provided to the customer. In this book, a later chapter on corrective maintenance notes the importance of identifying what the customer's problem is.

Service Level Agreements (SLA) help avoid controversies and aid planning. The SLA is effectively a written contract specifying the level of effort and work quality in quantitative terms that information systems evolution and maintenance are to supply to the customer, and the form and content of the specifications of the requirements the customer is to supply, and how and when services are to be provided and compensation paid. Even when the manager assigns a specific team of information systems personnel for whatever may come in a succession of projects to meet the needs of a specific information systems customer, an SLA is still helpful in making the services provided more visible and measurable. The SLA is used primarily within the corporation for the major customers of systems evolution and maintenance, and secondarily outside the corporation with suppliers. The use of the SLA helps avoid getting the manager of information systems evolution and maintenance embroiled in disputes among customers or suppliers on information systems matters.

Facilitating Belonging and Teamwork

In managing information systems evolution and maintenance, the manager can try to build communities of interest among the systems customers. These help keep strong feelings of belonging and of loyalty among customers and employees. These communities of interest can aid in providing support for planning and direction in prioritizing both system evolution and the between-time maintenance tasks. That support is especially helpful in securing the funding for system evolution projects.

Team building among the information systems personnel assigned to evolution and maintenance can help identify early on developing weaknesses in the skills complements available for deployment, and identify training and hiring needs. Common weakness areas are in quality assurance, regression testing and version control. Better project management for teams may also be needed. Sometimes teams get co-opted, and instead of building feelings of belonging among the personnel involved, they serve as ways of defending turf or asserting domination. Team building also can help strengthen relationships with the system customers. Customer representatives or contact persons appreciate and usually work more smoothly with established teams of information systems personnel. Later chapters in this book cover some aspects of quality assurance.

Taking Care of Suppliers

As noted previously, the most critical suppliers to information systems evolution and maintenance are the corporation's information systems personnel. Prominent and common outside suppliers are vendors of computer hardware, computer software, communications, supplies (such as of paper), and service contractors (such as air conditioning repair) and information systems outsourcing contractors (such as running a telephone "help desk" from India). Major corporate personnel matters were presented earlier in this chapter. In most corporations, contractual relationships with outside suppliers (vendors) are concentrated in a particular unit, such as Purchasing. However, quality and acceptability ratings from managers of information systems evolution and maintenance are normally taken into account in the contracting process with outside suppliers.

This leaves open the opportunity for managers of information systems evolution and maintenance to work closely with existing current outside suppliers and to keep abreast of developments in the fast moving information technology field. When the manager can make a strong case for changing outside suppliers or establishing a relationship with a new outside supplier, the corporation normally goes along with the change. In addition, many managers are permitted discretion in supplier selection and retention or are granted contracting authority up to corporate-specified levels of annual purchases. Communicating and cooperating with all suppliers can be beneficial in both directions. Most suppliers are aware that by helping their customers, they are also usually helping themselves.

Providing Systems Interoperability

One of the more troublesome difficulties faced by managers of information systems evolution and maintenance involves reconciling relationships with information systems customers and relationships with suppliers. It is meeting the corporate demand for systems interoperability. This process typically generates strong reactions among the information systems customers and supplier personnel because of the ways they are affected.

At a high level, systems interoperability involves how the corporation meets its goals as it carries out its mission and performs its functions. As noted earlier, systems are the means by which the corporation gets the work of producing its products and supplying its services done. Each system plays a role. The typical corporation has and uses many systems, yet the effectiveness of each system depends in part on each system's interactions with other systems used by the corporation. Interactions among them have historically become more complicated by a diversity of methodologies and architectures embodied in the software, such as object-oriented (OO) technology, client/server (C/S) architecture, Web services and e-business, AOP (aspect-oriented programming), relational databases, agile methods, distributed systems architecture, embedded systems, COTS (commercial of-the-shelf) software components, packaged software, programming languages, operating systems, hardware platforms, and so forth. In other words, each system has to have an interface with some other systems, and for information systems, data must flow across the interfaces in the forms, contents, and timings needed by the receiving information systems with scant human intervention and irrespective of the hardware and software technologies employed in the respective systems. This is systems interoperability.

The lure of an enterprise information system is providing those interfaces built-in among the component subsystems that comprise the enterprise system. Examples of some of the component systems are human resources systems, inventory systems, production control systems, general ledger systems, accounts payable systems, and so forth. The corporation can create its own combination of interacting systems to serve as a locally created enterprise information system. Then the corporation has to provide each and every needed interface. When the corporation opts to acquire from an outside supplier an enterprise information system, the corporation accepts the supplier-provided interfaces that the supplier has built into the system. The corporation still must provide interfaces between the enterprise information system and the other information systems that the corporation uses. In doing so, the corporation can incorporate some minor interface tailoring (Light, 2001).

One of the barriers to an outside supplier-provided enterprise information system is that it forces the corporation to use the supplier-provided systems to accomplish major parts of the work of the corporation. In other words, it replaces the corporation's former ways of doing business with generic ways set by the outside supplier. Some customization is possible by minor customization of some of the enterprise system's interfaces. More frequently, the corporation can attempt to use existing or custom interfaces to new corporation-provided software to enhance the enterprise system's features and facilities (Light, 2001). The most common motivation for such customization is to try to approximate the corporate customers' former workflow and reports. But in general, the use of the outside supplier's ways sticks in the throat for many ambitious information systems customers and supplier personnel, who believe they know of customizations or other systems that would better distinguish the corporation from its competition. They want to ride their ownership of data and information systems to advance mutually the goals of the corporation and their own personal goals. Ownership of data and custom information systems are two very strong ways of defining and defending personal turf within the corporation, since the corporation is critically dependent upon information systems usage.

The information system interfaces can be and often are used as facilitators in collaborating with other organizational units within the corporation, or as weapons in bullying them. The choice and the difference largely hinge on how personal status, privilege and power are handled in the corporation. When "win-win" compromises cannot be arranged in managing the interface changes in information systems that arise from evolution and maintenance, the personnel associated with some systems lose some status or privilege or power, and the personnel associated with other systems win additional status or privilege or power. The gains and losses are usually in relative, not absolute, terms except in reorganizations, mergers, acquisitions, retirements and terminations. For example, the chief financial officer of a corporation approves the modification of the purchase request system to include a running 15-month total of requests by requestor. Also, the changed system interface shows individual ceilings on each requestor's 15-month total that, if exceeded, result in an automatic request denial and an automatic notice to a corporate purchasing agent. The net result is shifts in the empowerment both of individual personnel and of organizational units.

In managing systems interoperability, tradeoffs have to be made between teamwork and collaboration on the one hand, and entrepreneurship and competition on the other. Improving interoperability smoothes the functioning of the interacting parts of the corporation and enables the corporation to do faster, better and more efficiently what it normally does. But innovation as in meeting changes triggered by the corporation's competition requires changes to what a corporation normally does. Initially, such changes decrease systems interoperability because the corporate response is ad hoc. Maintenance or evolution is required to incorporate in the corporate systems the ripple effects of the initial changes, and do it in ways that allow the corporate systems to act responsively and effectively in serving the corporate needs.

Choosing Technologies

Making changes to the use of the Information Technology resources is part of managing information systems evolution and maintenance. Four of the ways (they can also change systems interoperability) are to:

- change the methods and techniques used by the information systems personnel;
- replace the licensed or purchased software portions of the information systems;
- install enhanced or upgraded releases of outside suppliers' packaged software; and
- select hardware that implements either different technologies or the same technologies in different ways.

Training, supervising, hiring, transferring, terminating, contracting and outsourcing are common means of changing the methods and techniques used in the corporation by the information systems personnel. Making available software tools and training in the use of the methods can additionally support the use of changed methods and techniques.

Increasingly, because of cost and quality considerations, managers of information systems evolution and maintenance are weighing the use of outside-supplier provided software for their needs. COTS (commercial off-the-shelf software) components and software packages can sometimes be used. Reuse of the corporation's own software has potential, but few corporations have done the preparation to be able to reuse software when doing evolution or maintenance.

Outside suppliers of packaged software provide patches and service packs for supplier-originated corrective maintenance, but the installation of the patches and packs is up to the manager of information systems evolution and maintenance. Installing these patches and packs in a timely and uniform manner helps avoid security and interoperability shortfalls. This is especially important for operating system software, enterprise software systems, and packaged software widely used in the corporation, such as for word processing, spreadsheets, email, instant messaging, and portable digital assistant (PDA) support.

In addition, suppliers of packaged software offer upgrades to new releases of their software. Installing these is nearly always enhancive maintenance, and may result in software evolution (Chapin et al., 2001). The questions if, when and how to install the upgrades are affected by the license contact terms, for those may dictate the support available from the outside supplier. Furthermore, and just as for in-house developed information systems, the balance of advantage and disadvantages that new versions offer have to be weighed both by the corporation and the system's users in the corporation. Currently, most software evolution and enhancive maintenance work to install new versions, whether of in-house or packaged software, is done by the corporation's own personnel or less commonly, by outside contractors. When outside contractors are the suppliers and are left to their own devices, their use of information systems technologies may result in impairments in interoperability when the modified versions of the software systems are installed by the corporation.

In the fast moving field of information technology, outside suppliers' new hardware offerings that offer for the money invested faster speed, greater capacity, additional features and facilities, and more comfortable usability are frequently available. A common issue in managing information systems evolution and maintenance is whether or not the hardware advances alone are a sufficient basis for making changes in the corporate information systems. Sometimes, the hardware advances plus the packaged software upgrades, while separately are insufficient, together provide a sufficient justification for doing adaptive maintenance.

Measuring and Tracking

Given the roles and activities of the manager of information systems evolution and maintenance as noted earlier in this chapter, the manager has to have some way of finding out what situations are and what is going on. Walking around, observing, asking questions, reading memos and mail and manuals, attending meetings, and talking on the telephone are some of the traditional ways of keeping informed. But the manager of information systems evolution and maintenance can also install and operate means of measuring attributes of software maintenance that are of interest to the manager. This is often done with software metrics. Since tastes and situations differ, measuring with one set of metrics does not meet all managers' needs all of the time (Munson, 2003).

Also, just gathering data about events, conditions and situations is not enough. Those data have to be organized and processed in order to serve as intelligence for the manager. Tracking the status and progress of situations, conditions or maintenance helps give the manager a time-oriented picture so that trends can be more easily spotted. Software metrics and tracking are the focus of several chapters in this book.

Converting and Re-engineering Systems

Very rarely are corporate resources sufficient for the corporation and all of its constituent organizational units to do everything that every manager wants to do whenever the managers individually want to do it. In well-managed corporations, even when corporate resources are not plentiful, information systems evolution and maintenance are not deferred (Chapin, 1993). But in stringent circumstances with only paltry resources, only a few things can be done, usually the ones near the top of a prioritized list. In such environments, many proposed or needed information systems evolution and maintenance projects are not done, and hence information systems gradually become increasingly obsolete in meeting current corporate needs.

When the systems have become sufficiently obsolete so that the cost of continuing to have to use them gets high, corporate management may see value in trying to play "catch up" or trying to replace systems that it has allowed to become noticeably obsolete. When hardware is a limitation, migrating the systems to a different platform may be tried. Since new systems development efforts are risky (Jones, 1993; Metricnet, 2003) and often require a significant up-front investment, corporate management may opt to try less risky systems evolution projects, typically by converting legacy information systems or by re-engineering them. Later chapters in this book cover some aspects of these processes. Interoperability concerns are typically of critical importance in making conversion and re-engineering projects successful. Later chapters in this book cover aspects of re-engineering and legacy systems.

Architecting Information Systems

In many corporations, the information systems evolution and maintenance work is done by a rush to coding. Coding can be easily measured and source lines of code (SLOC) are a popular metric, but are of limited usefulness. However, the most critical parts of most information system evolution and maintenance projects are the analysis and design phases, since they set the course in determining the resulting characteristics of the information system (Chapin, 1988). Currently during analysis and design, increasing recognition is being given to the architecture of the information system, and how to evolve it during evolution and how to improve it during maintenance. Providing or improving system scalability is sometimes a major concern. These processes are closely tied to the choice of technologies and to process improvement. As such, they are focused on activities within the information systems unit in the corporation. They are mostly unseen and hence unappreciated by customers and outside suppliers, even though they can result in information systems that operate faster, more reliably, and at a lower cost, and/or are more maintainable. Some aspects of systems architecture are covered in later chapters in this book.

Improving Evolution and Maintenance Processes

Processes used in the development of information systems have received significant attention through the Capability Maturity Model Integration (CMMI) work of the Software Engineer Institute (SEI) at Carnegie Mellon University (Sheard, 2002). Unfortunately, the SEI has not yet extended its efforts to give equivalent attention to processes used in the evolution or maintenance of information systems. Other sources have acted to compensate partially for this lack of attention. Two examples are the efforts of Kajko-Mattsson (2001) and Niessink (2000).

Process improvement in the maintenance of information systems has gotten attention for more than two decades. While favorable results in practice have been achieved, they have been widely scattered and not generally copied. Partly this has arisen from many managers trying to manage information systems evolution and maintenance as if they were managing the development of information systems (Chapin, 1987, 1988). That is like trying to manage goats as if they were mules. The corporation does not get the full value.

Two important general processes in evolution and maintenance are understanding the existing system and regression testing. More specialized processes, such as slicing, may be used. Whether specialized or general, they illustrate the similarity of process improvement with architecting the information system and converting and re-engineering the information system. They typically involve the efforts of in-house suppliers and sometimes contractors, but are largely unseen and unappreciated by customers and outside suppliers. Improving the information evolution and maintenance processes is largely internal to the information systems organizational unit of the corporation. Later chapters in this book provide some coverage of process improvement generally, of some specialized processes such as slicing, and of maturity and process models.

Globalizing Information Systems

While the majority of corporations do not operate outside of the country where their headquarters are located, an increasing proportion of corporations operate internationally. All corporations that operate internationally have to modify their information systems because of differences in:

- laws and regulations;
- personnel policies and practices;
- customs of the trade or usual business practices;
- supplier and customer availability and expectations;

- monetary and language conventions; and
- social and cultural norms.

To provide information systems that work satisfactorily to meet the needs at diverse places across the globe, the manager of information systems evolution and maintenance faces an array of choices, typically like but more difficult to implement than those in most mergers and acquisitions. Straightforward conversions of systems usually are not possible because of hardware differences and differences in the personnel skills repertoires at the different sites. In addition, what is acceptable input data and output data to go across the system interfaces at the sites usually have to be changed, with no two sites being identical in content and language on all of the information systems. Furthermore, the personnel at each site usually have needs and capabilities unique to the site. These usually require not only different interfaces but also site-unique systems that have a family resemblance to systems at other sites. Supplier costs including the corporation's personnel costs change at different rates at different sites. Currency exchange rates keep fluctuating so information systems that include comparative data have to be modified to handle multiple and changing rates. Complicating this is that communication with suppliers and customers is more difficult because unstated assumptions are tacitly made about policies, practices, customs and conventions, and the language used for the communication may not be one in which both parties are fluent and comfortable. The overall effect for the manager usually is more information systems to evolve and to maintain under a greater variety of conditions and with more differing requirements.

Being Promotable

While many of the work stimuli for managers of information systems evolution and maintenance come from the corporation and the stakeholders involved in information systems, some come from within the manager himself/herself. The big majority of those are the same character traits that result in the on-the-job behaviors that employers prize in employees in general. The list is long and includes such traits as dependability, honesty, intelligence, persistence, emotional stability, initiative, patience, social graces, common sense, tolerance, consistency, adaptability, and so forth. A minority of the character traits have particular importance for employees in the role of managers, such as self-confidence, ambition, drive, vision, low risk-aversion, people-oriented, dedication, flexibility, willingness to listen and to learn, tolerance of ambiguity, entrepreneurial stance, and so forth.

Career paths differ among corporations, although in most, high-level managers receive the most pay (mostly salaries and bonuses). In some corporations, middle levels of pay can be earned in either management roles or in non-management ("doing") roles and by some commission employees. In most corporations, middle and higher levels of pay are only available to persons in management roles, and moving up the management ladder brings the manager more pay. If the manager wants to move up and be paid more, then the manager has to be open to job transfers that offer more management growth opportunity, and to be promotable out of every job the manager holds. The usual three general guides for promotability are to 1) do the current management job to the satisfaction of that job's current supervisor and that job's customers, 2) groom and prepare at least one current subordinate to take over the current job, and 3) seek an opportunity to be groomed and prepared as by a mentor or supervisor to take over a higher-level management job. Just as much as elsewhere, these three general guides apply to persons seeking and holding jobs in the management of information systems evolution and maintenance.

LEADERSHIP IN EVOLUTION AND MAINTENANCE

In concluding this chapter's overview of managing systems evolution and maintenance, a critical success factor emerges. However, first is the question of what indicates success in managing information systems evolution and maintenance. A common measure of success in a corporate management position is the general agreement among co-managers and superiors in the corporation that the manager contributes more value than that manager's cost to the corporation. The more the value consistently exceeds the cost, the greater is the success. While this measure normally applies to managers in line functions such as sales or manufacturing, it is hazy for managers in staff functions such as human resources or information systems. The exception of course is where information systems or software are the corporate product. In the staff area, the costs are more easily quantified than are the values, because staff functions are commonly regarded as overhead functions. This is because the common view in corporate management is that staff functions are necessary overhead but should be minimized.

A less common measure of success in a corporate manager is that the manager accomplishes what no other manager in the corporation could accomplish. The practical difficulty here is that these tend to be one-time feats, rather than a consistent stream of net value for the corporation. However, this is where the manager of information systems evolution and maintenance has an edge and an opportunity, because of the manager's skills, experience and knowledge in information technology. Those can enable and empower the manager to provide value to the corporation that others in the organization are unable to provide. Even so, the difficulty still exists of quantifying that value and making sure it is visible to and recognized by co-managers and superiors in the corporation. The most workable technique for quantifying the value has two parts:

- The first part is to have information systems customers assign in writing an estimated value as a part of every request for change in any information system.
- The second part is to do a follow-up subsequently, preferably by an independent third party but with the assistance of the information systems customer, about a year after installation or deployment of the requested change, to try to measure to what extent the customer's estimate of the value has actually been realized.

Another well-regarded measure of success is promotion up the management ladder. As noted earlier, to accomplish that takes more than technical proficiency in information systems. It also takes people skills, social skills, and the manager's recognition of opportunities beyond a manager's current job assignment.

Leadership is a critical success factor in managing information systems evolution and maintenance. Is the manager along for the ride, or is the manager making a positive difference for the corporation? Is the manager just following orders, filling requests, and keeping things running in information systems? Or is the manager also breaking path for information systems customers, providing opportunities, and coordinating change in the corporation? Leadership is a component of management that gets increasingly important the higher the manager goes up the management ladder (Kotter, 1990).

People working in and with information systems sometimes get sucked in by the challenge of the technology involved. In a research environment, leadership can be in terms of creating innovations in the technology. Things are typically different in the common corporate environments, however. In those, leadership in the management of information systems evolution and maintenance involves working with people to help them benefit by changing their use of information systems.

REFERENCES

Booch, G., Rumbaugh, J., & Jacobson, I. (1999). *The Unified Modeling Language user guide*. Reading, MA: Addison Wesley Longman, Inc.

Chapin, N. (1971). *Computers: A systems approach*. New York, NY: Van Nostrand Reinhold Co.

Chapin, N. (1987). The job of software maintenance. In *Proceedings Conference on Software Maintenance–1987* (pp. 4–12). Los Alamitos, CA: IEEE Computer Society Press.

Chapin, N. (1988). Software maintenance life cycle. In *Proceedings Conference on Software Maintenance–1988* (pp. 6–13). Los Alamitos, CA: IEEE Computer Society Press.

Chapin, N. (1993). Software maintenance characteristics and effective management. *Journal of Software Maintenance*, *5*(2), 91–100.

Chapin, N. (2003). Software maintenance and organizational health and fitness. In M. Polo, M. Piattini & F. Ruiz (Eds.), *Advances in software maintenance management* (pp. 1–31). Hershey, PA: Idea Group Publishing.

Chapin, N., Hale, J.E., Khan, K.M., Ramil, J.F., & Tan, W.-G. (2001). Types of software evolution and maintenance. *Journal of Software Maintenance and Evolution*, *13*(1), 3–30.

Couger, J.D., & Colter, M.A. (1985). *Maintenance programming: Improved productivity through motivation*. Englewood Cliffs, NJ: Prentice-Hall Inc.

Drucker, P.F. (1974). *Management*. New York, NY: Harper & Row Publishers.

Jones, T.C. (1993). *Assessment and control of software risks*. Upper Saddle River, NJ: Prentice Hall PTR.

Kajko-Mattsson, M. (2001). *Corrective maintenance maturity model: Problem management*. Stockholm, Sweden: Stockholm University/Royal Institute of Technology.

Kitchenham, B.A., Travassos, G.H., Mayrhauser, A.V., Niessink, F., Schneidewind, N.F., Singer, J., Takada, S., Vehvilainen, R., & Yang, H. (1999). Toward an ontology of software maintenance. *Journal of Software Maintenance, 11*(6), 365–389.

Kotter, J.P. (1990). *A force for change*. New York, NY: The Free Press.

Lane, D. (Ed.). (2003). *CIO wisdom*. Upper Saddle River, NJ: Prentice Hall PTR.

Light, B. (2001). The maintenance implications of the customisation of ERP software. *Journal of Software Maintenance and Evolution*, *13*(6), 415–429.

Metricnet. (2003). *Metricnet.* Stamford, CT: META Group, Inc. Available: *http://www.metricnet.com*

Moore, C., & Schwartz, E. (2003). Sorting through SarbOx. *InfoWorld, 25*(27), 53–56.

Munson, J.C. (2003). *Software engineering measurement.* Boca Raton, FL: Auerbach Publications.

Niessink, F. (2000). *Perspectives on improving software maintenance.* Amsterdam, the Netherlands: Vrije Universiteit.

Sambamurthy, V., Bharadwaj, A., & Grover, V. (2003). Shaping agility through digital options: Reconceptualizing the role of Information Technology in contemporary firms. *MIS Quarterly, 27*(2), 237–263.

Sheard, S.A. (2002). How do I make my organization comply with yet another new model? *CrossTalk: The Journal of Defense Software Engineering*, *15*(2), 15–20.

Chapter II

Design for Evolution: Fostering Continuity and Responding to Change

Darren Dalcher, Middlesex University, UK

ABSTRACT

This chapter highlights the pervasiveness of change in most developed systems, and the resulting implications on development practice. A key problem with developed software systems is the focus on discrete one-off development. Emphasising continuity and evolution requires a way of distinguishing between systems that can be assumed to remain stable and those that continuously "live" and evolve in their environment. Developing systems that are expected to evolve calls for a dynamic activity of design that is responsive to changes in the environment. The chapter concludes by discussing the role of design in such environments and characterising design as a complex, responsive and negotiated search for an acceptable, yet changeable trade-off. This is taken forward by highlighting the implications for the adoption of adaptive design in dynamic environments, thereby justifying the move from discrete and project-based software engineering to a more strategic, continuous and evolving discipline of adaptive design.

INTRODUCTION: THE PROBLEM OF CHANGE

Software systems are often designed using the assumptions of "fixed" reality and a process that freezes out change and sees little need for allowing alterations. In fact, such a process typically assumes that once the requirements are "objectively" understood and fixed, the rest of the process can be rigorously engineered, or even described through a set of (formal) transformational implementations. Proponents of this approach often cite bridges and buildings as proof that formal engineering can be utilised independently from the need to consider change. This enables optimisation with respect to a specific equilibrium point in an effort to maximise potential gains. Maintenance and adaptation occur post-design and construction and thus fail to be considered during these activities. However, change appears to be an inevitable facet of reality and thus a major issue in the context of development for future use.

The chapter focuses on some of the implications of change (and the need to address it) in the context of software development and evolution. It begins by highlighting some of the problems associated with the view of a fixed and change-free reality. Software cannot be designed independently from its environment and will require a capacity to evolve and adapt in order to deal with change in its environment. The rapid rate of change requires a continuous focus capable of dealing with open-ended change and responding to and evolving as a result of new knowledge. The discussion is then re-focused to the context of different software development environments, thereby emphasising the continuous nature of development in most environments. This provides the foundation for developing a framework of software development domains that also highlights the different modes of problem resolution required to populate each of the domains. The interest in the continuous nature of development evolves into a discussion of design as a resolution approach, and more particularly, to the identification of adaptive, dynamic design as the approach that needs to be adopted in evolving and change-intensive environments. The penultimate section highlights the implication of dynamic design in change-intensive and evolving environments by outlining the special characteristics of adaptive design, thereby leading the way to defining the broader context of software development in Domain III. The final section rounds off the discussion by developing the characterisations into a set of implementation issues that enable designers to start taking account of change and foster continuity in an effort to design living and evolutionary information systems that can continue to grow and adapt in response to change.

Traditional software development has attempted to freeze out change. However, empirical evidence presented by Lehman and others (see for example, Lehman, 1985,1994, 1998, 2000; Rajlich, 2000; Pereira, 2001) demonstrates in general that a program that is used, regardless of the original assumptions, must be continually adapted or otherwise it will become progressively less satisfactory. The implicit assumption that an agreed specification will remain valid and offer a solid basis for all subsequent work is unrealistic, as observed by Lehman (1985, 1998), Wand (1995), and Pereira (2001), as complete and final requirements are seldom available at the start of a project (Cave, 1978; Distaso, 1980; Brooks, 1986; Parnas, 1986; Yourdon, 1993; Schneider, 1998; Pressman, 2000), and are likely to change, with their impacts rippling through all parts of the system (Gibson, 1989; Littlewood, 1992). In reality, software is often forced to adapt to various changes (Land, 1982; Longworth, 1985; Cleland, 1998; Rajlich, 2000), including to the evolving requirements and tastes of users, to new regulations, to the developing capabilities of machines, and to the rising level of expectations. This often calls for constant refinement and gradual modification and reshaping of function in response to context. The need to maintain the fit rather than the initial manifestation of structure forces developers to mature from being artists of shape and structure to artists of time and adaptation (see for example Brand, 1997; Rechtin, 2000).

Change occurs during development but also during operation. The main area that addresses the need for change in operational systems (i.e., post-development) is maintenance. Maintenance, or evolution, consumes anything between 70-90 percent of the total development cost (see for example Schach, 1996; Pressman, 2000), and can account for 90 percent of the intellectual effort (Giddings, 1984). The Quality Assurance Institute estimates that the figure for maintenance rose from 30 percent in 1963 to 65 percent in 1980, and again, to 80 percent in 1985 (Andriole, 1986). These figures are interesting as they address the period of almost total domination by the Waterfall approach. A large proportion of the maintenance effort (around 70-90 percent) involves adaptations to accommodate changes in the specifications, adaptations to the external environment and enhancement requested by users (see for example Shemer, 1987; Fitzgerald, 1990; Avison, 1995; Pressman, 2000).

Many of the maintained systems were developed using a sequential approach. With up to 90 percent of cost, effort and time spent on maintenance, and a large proportion of that on perfective and adaptive maintenance, the effectiveness of this method has been seriously questioned. In addition, hidden as well as visible backlogs resulting from these problems have been identified (see for example Shemer, 1987; Fitzgerald, 1990; Avison, 1995; Grindley, 1986). Requests for change can therefore occur before, during and after development.

Project work, it would thus appear, cannot be shielded from change: The assumption of stability and structure resulting from the tendency to freeze out change does not eliminate the need to deal with change. Indeed, Cusumano (1995) observed that features may change by at least 30 percent as a direct result of learning during a single iteration. Moreover, even when a formal attempt is made to define all functional requirements, 35 percent are unlikely to be identified during the first attempt (Charette, 1990). This is supported by the emerging recognition among project managers that a project is conceived, born, lives and expires in change (Gilbreath, 1988; Rajlich, 2000). In many projects, the combination of induced and incurred change is therefore likely to lead to ongoing adjustments to specifications and plans, as change appears to be a permanent feature of systems and also of any attempt to improve or deal with them.

In practice, development is not purely concerned with the fabrication of the initial artefact. Systems respond to changes and adapt. Development therefore needs to adopt a continuous perspective that justifies the survival and prosperity of the artefact, and its longevity and continued relevance. The focus of development is to ensure that the product, when delivered, fulfils a need expressed by the users. In fact, users play a critical part in shaping and maintaining the fit, as their perception of problems triggers new action cycles to address challenges and opportunities. Focusing on time and adjusted needs and perceptions makes functionality more multi-dimensional. As users and developers learn to work with time, it becomes possible to enhance the value of artefacts (or any other capital goods) through improvement and growth. Change becomes the facilitator of continuity, growth and re-organised re-emergence of knowledge and potential.

Given that change is likely to affect most systems and that developers need to be able to accommodate change both in the product and the development process, there would appear to be a greater need to appreciate the rate of inherent change. Stacey divided situations according to the degree of inherent change they embodied (see for example, Stacey, 1991, 1992, 1996).

- Closed change situations occur when the system is well understood and there is little, if any, that is left to learn. Problem resolution methods rely on structure and rationality and therefore support prescriptive control measures (i.e., damping control loops). The principal feature of closed change is that "the consequences of events are clearly understandable in their past form and accurately predictable in their future forms" (Stacey, 1991).
- Contained change situations are partly understood and the rest is obtained by purposeful adaptation (learning is still minimal). Partial understanding requires a greater reliance on probabilistic interpretation of events and potential outcomes.
- Open-ended change situations occur in complex environments. In these environments learning is equated with discovery and is part of the process of dealing with change. Reliance on rationality or anticipation is inadequate, as the key lies in spontaneity, informality and difference. Each situation is new and requires a new conceptual model. The inherent uncertainty and the multiplicity of options lead to increasing returns perspective with multiple equilibrium points and randomness and accidents that can get magnified. Long-term objectives have to be discovered and cannot be tightly defined in advance of action. Learning is viewed as a political process that depends on the initial conditions and the initial steps taken.

Which of the change scenarios should concern developers? Very few systems can survive as closed change situations. Most design problems are open-ended and reside in change-ridden environments. The environment is responsible for generating new circumstances, change and other perturbations and irregularities. This implies that detailed planning is practically impossible (Stacey, 1991, 1992). Instead, complex feedback loops pervade and drive such systems. See for example Prigogine (1980), Smith (1984), Stacey (1991), Waldrop (1992), Wheatley (1992), Coveney and Highfield (1995), Kauffman (1995), Rescher (1995), Bak (1996) and Pool (1997). Lehman has shown that these characteristics apply to most software development environments (Lehman, 1998, 2000). In this type of environment, opportunities, problems, challenges and aspirations, as well as visions are continuously explored (Stacey, 1991; Parker & Stacey, 1994). Such exploration leads to new changes, and to the creation of new agendas and new issues. The key to success lies in a spontaneous and on-going learning, experimentation and rapid feedback process that discovers new meanings, hence revealing new potential. Processes designed for such environments must match the tendency (and need) to change and facilitate effective design.

In an ever-changing environment that characterises typical design problems, change appears inevitable. Indeed, the figures given earlier point to high rates of change in software development environments. Moreover, part of the change may be generated by the development effort itself as artefacts, including working programs, shape perceived function. In such a transitive relationship, software designed to address a particular need shapes the business, and life cycles designed to facilitate certain features shape operations. This leads to an ever-changing and ever-adapting environment. Given the dynamic nature of software development, the direct implication is that as functional needs change with time, design should address the tendency to grow and evolve. Design is therefore aimed at growth and functional correctness (rather than absolute correctness) on a continuing basis.

Growth, however, may be countered by a tendency towards disorganisation. Over time, entropy and decay will combine with the environment to make artefacts less useful (hence the maintenance problem and the backlogs described above). Maintaining the value of an asset will thus require an additional input of resources. Rather than allow the process to be function-driven, this suggests that in maintenance, form follows funding—when available!

Neither perfection nor correctness is attainable in the long term. Brand pointed out that in reality, finishing is never finished (1997). The focus on completing to deadline and budget often excludes user and time continuity considerations (ibid.). Generally, therefore, there is a need to convert from design based on a static representation to one based on continuity, process and adaptability. The following section explores continuity and adaptation and the relationship between "what happens next" and "what happened before".

ISSUES: CONTINUITY AND EVOLUTION

"Since fitness is always fitness relative to the environment, an organism (or a firm) can grow unfit simply by virtue of standing still in a changing world" (Elster, 1989).

Change is inevitable: indeed, many systems reflect open-ended change. Continuity suggests a responsive perspective that takes in changes. The environment, the organism and all other connected parts continuously interact, and therefore change, adjust, and co-evolve. Fitness (and the task of selection) is therefore a set of interacting and re-adjusting moving targets. Gould asserted that regardless of the constraint of fitness, evolution offers a rich source of endless form (1996). This form represents potential for growth, survival and excellence. "What is" is in fact only a poor subset of "what could be".

In systems theory, ecopoiesis is the process by which a system makes a home for itself, by means of continuous, mutual adaptation between itself and the environment (including other systems), in search of an acceptable fit. Such adaptation will result in the establishment of new interaction patterns and feedbacks. Gradual fine-tuning allows change to accumulate over time (while making obsolete needs disappear) (Brand, 1997). In this fashion, successful designs grow and adapt over time (ibid.).

Mutual adaptation occurs in small steps. Alexander accordingly proposed the replacement of a comprehensive master plan with a meta-plan composed of: a philosophy of piecemeal growth, a set of patterns or shared design principles governing growth, and local control of design for the stakeholders (1979). In this way, different components are allowed to evolve through a series of small steps, while respecting the shared principles and retaining a harmony of vision, as advocated in Alexander (1979) and Weick (1984).

Weick similarly discussed the value of concentrating on modest achievable step targets rather than focusing on the full scale of problems, in order to achieve small wins and encourage further exploration (Weick, 1984). This entails a shift from a focus dominated by outcomes to one driven by adjustment to inputs (and the identification of opportunities). Small (and moderate) wins provide experimental building blocks couched in terms of limited commitment that can often overcome cognitive limitations and barriers. One advantage from the position advocated by Alexander and by Weick is the ability and the willingness to deviate from prescriptive plans and to be adaptive and responsive to the unexpected as part of the effort to improve the mutual fit between perceived need and a changing reality. However, it is the effort to improve the fit that also plays a crucial role in changing the nature of reality and adding new knowledge as a result of that effort. The small steps effecting the mutual adaptation thus get to play a role in making possible the next step and everything else that ultimately follows.

Steps are often understood in the context of knowledge. Knowledge grows through critical selection, as understanding is synonymous with the process of problem-solving (Popper, 1972). As identified problems qualify for tentative solutions, they open themselves up to the discovery of faulty assumptions, which in turn lead to the next cycle of problems. Indeed, Plato was perhaps the first to be troubled by the fact that applying conception to a class of things,always resulted in the identification of exceptions, differences and dilemmas (Polanyi, 1962). Criticism becomes the main instrument of learning and further growth as new problems lead to new creations, which are helpful in discovering new facts, which in turn lead to new problems. They emerge from the field of new relationships, which problem solvers cannot help but bring into existence when they attempt to acquire new knowledge to solve a current problem (as part of the continuing adaptation). In order to solve the newly created problems, one needs new knowledge—new theories and tools. The process thus continues ad infinitum. A simplified schema based on Popper (1972) follows:

Problem(1)→Tentative Solution→Error Elimination→Problem(2)

Thomas Huxley similarly commented that *"The rung of a ladder was never meant to rest upon, but only to hold a man's foot long enough to enable him to put the other somewhat higher"* (1946). This reflects the observations on development offered in Section 1. Development needs to be responsive to changing needs. Good design therefore can transcend the boundaries of time by always resonating from what came before in light of new perspectives and change. Adaptation thus builds on what already exists. In fact, conceptualisation approaches such as prototyping attempt to provide a framework for speeding up this process by providing a working short cut that will enable developers and users to conceptualise and experiment with designs in order to conceive the next step.

Design patterns are likewise structured on the basis of what came before (and the response patterns it evoked) (Alexander, 1979; McMaster, 1996). Holyoak (1990) suggested that problem-solving was intimately connected with learning. *"An intelligent problem solver uses the results of solution attempts to acquire new knowledge that will help solve similar problems more readily in the future"* (ibid.). It appears, therefore, that unsuccessful attempts are thus responsible for the acquisition of new and valuable knowledge. This suggests a double loop learning process that is used to update the implicit skillset available to the problem solver. These skills form part of the tacit knowledge set that is rarely specified, stated or even acknowledged explicitly.

Failure offers a good learning tool, as it often identifies the next "rung on the ladder"; an opportunity to eliminate an error and improve the available knowledge. Rather than expand excessive effort on perfect pre-planning, it becomes possible to make small adjustments (as proposed by Weick) and observe their effects and the resulting adaptations. In organisations, evolution can thus be confined to taking a short-term perspective for control purposes and attempting to generate a future that is a little better than the present (as opposed to a major effort that attempts to remedy the effects of development). This becomes the starting point for the next short-term perspective assessment. As a system progressively changes with the passage of time, the strengths and orientation of the controls will also need to be altered (Waddington, 1977). In this way, change triggers changes in roles, internal variety, range of responses and required intervention modes. The adjustments, however, can be made in a gradual and continuous manner.

This enables the process to benefit from exploiting the fluidity of reality through the avoidance of an optimised single equilibrium (i.e., a single snapshot of reality). The development of order and the imposition of structure reduce the behavioural variety by forcing the system towards one stable equilibrium point (leading to more drastic structural adjustments at intervals). This robs the system of an entire dimension of potential meaning and responses, leaving it impoverished in terms of its ability to adopt different responses and adapt to changing situations and forces. The dynamic balance between opposites is nature's way of introducing variation and forcing differentiation, which encourages creative responses and the establishment of a reservoir of resilience. By avoiding optimisation in either direction, it opens a potential for great variation through a fluidly alternating balance between opposite states, thereby enabling design and creativity. The following section links the discussion of continuity and change back to the domain of software development.

THE DYNAMIC ECOLOGY OF COMPUTER PROGRAMS

Software programs are created in response to conceptualisations of perceived problem situations. Typically, the surrounding environment, the emergent uncertainty and the complexity of interactions result in certain characteristics that define and distinguish both problem and solution. This section focuses on the interaction between software and the environment and the ecological implications of change and adaptations in computer systems.

The type of solution process applied to simple problems (especially those entailing closed-change situations) tends to be a rigid normative process, as they are particularly amenable to sequential resolution. With the exception of the most trivial specifiable programs, most problems can be said to depend on their external environment. Their utility, usability and relevance are therefore strongly dependent on change, the environment, the interactions, and their ability to adapt; in other words, change and continuity. Blum (1996) suggested that most computing problems are and will continue to be evolving problems due to the need to respond to changing and uncertain needs. Paul (1993) also reasoned that systems are created in dynamic, turbulent and fast-changing contexts that cannot support an obsession with a "fixed point" and a temporal view. Instead, such systems need to embrace a living, growing and changing perspective (ibid.).

Many real-world problems are characterised by ambiguity, uncertainty and complexity. The behaviour of developers therefore defies sequential resolution due to the need to obtain understanding and feedback from multiple, and sometimes conflicting, levels of the problem. The inherent complications with such problems may lead developers to address simpler problems that tackle preferred portions that seem amenable to treatment (defined as soluble problems in science). Moreover, changes and adaptations provide the next rung on the ladder, ready to support the next stage.

Software, in common with other artefacts, embodies within it assumptions regarding relevance and interactions that relate to the external environment. Giddings (1984), for example, reported that most software was domain dependent; yet, the life cycle models could not address the needs of such software. Giddings divided software applications into three types:

- *Domain Independent software.* The class of software where the problem statement is independent from the universe of discourse. The main focus centres on proving the correctness of the solution through verification. This class includes deterministic problems like numerical algorithms and can even be extended to include contracted software developed under a pre-determined and "fixed" specification.
- *Domain Dependent Experimental software.* The class of software characterised by an intrinsic uncertainty about the universe of discourse. The development process is embedded within a search for knowledge about the universe of discourse. The development of software in this domain may eventually lead to the development of a specification for software with other uses.
- *Domain Dependent Embedded software.* The class of software where the universe of discourse and the software are interdependent. The use of the software may change both the form and substance of the universe of discourse and subsequently, the nature of the problem itself. This class includes business systems, office automation systems, software engineering systems and design automation systems. The essential difficulty lies in anticipating the impact of changes on the environment. In fact, Brooks maintained that *"both the actual need and the user's perception of that need will change as programs are built, tested and used"* (1975).

Domain Independent software, as defined by Giddings, does not rely on the provision of feedback as it is assumed that all information is available upfront. It thus conforms to the "fixed point" notion and makes little attempt to justify learning or improvement. Work is conducted according to a pre-defined specification and correctness can subsequently be proven. The work is thus limited to a single optimised pre-determined effort. As a result, quality is limited to the correctness of the resulting product. Domain Dependent Experimental software allows some learning but still reflects a move towards the general preparation of a specification.

However, many real projects are not about well-understood problems that can be analysed and optimised, but have to do with knowledge that is elusive, tacit, incomplete, ephemeral and ambiguous. A sequential approach does not work for domain dependent software due to the inherent uncertainty and the lack of information, which forces developers to experiment within the environment and iterate (Giddings, 1984). The main approach to addressing this dependence is through experimentation and the resulting reduction of the cycle time (i.e., speeding up the feedback from the conceptual stages). Delaying commitment and closure would require a careful balance, continuing experimentation and an active provision of requisite variety. In other words, such systems rely on learning and the adjustment that follows in its wake (i.e., "finding the next rung on the ladder"). The overall level of uncertainty can only be reduced through an iterative process of experimentation and discovery that results in feedback that leads to direct learning. Feedback mechanisms are therefore crucial to learning, adjusting, adapting, and surviving in an evolving real-time world.

Most significant software cannot be represented as a pre-defined and "fixed" specification and therefore requires a strong degree of interdependency between the software, its environment and the relevant stakeholders. In complex situations (i.e., Domain Dependent Embedded software), life cycles need to be living and evolving constructs; see for example Paul (1993), Corbato (1979), Birrell (1985), Andriole (1991), and Arthur (1992). In fact, the metaphor of "building" systems may no longer be appropriate for most systems, as the conceptual structures are too complicated to be accurately specified in advance and faultlessly built (Brooks, 1986). The metaphor of organic growth of software in increments that add functionality (Paul, 1993; Brooks, 1986; Andriole, 1991, 1992) may indeed be better, as it allows easy backtracking, lends itself to prototyping, and offers a tremendous morale boost. Such an approach could be based on agreement on a minimum deliverable for a cost and an intention to add the rest in future, as software has to be given a chance to grow and evolve (Brooks, 1997).

Moreover, development concerns extend beyond the delivery of a product that is subsequently assumed to contain a derived quality. Systems deliver satisfaction of a need, which in many cases will extend beyond a simplistic measure of correctness. Cosgrove noted that satisfaction therefore relates to a need (Cosgrove, 1971) which may be adapting and changing through the use of the program (Lehman, 1994). Functional correctness can thus become a continuous measure of how satisfactory a system is to its users (Lehman, 1985; Truex, 1999).

Unlike the notion of absolute correctness, function in a design sense must be allowed to evolve. If one adopts a long-term perspective, an additional reason for evolving software stems from the need to maintain the value of (and the knowledge embedded in) the product. Satisfaction, knowledge and value are dynamic and relative constructs. One therefore maintains the (shifting level of) user satisfaction, alongside available knowledge and the inherent value of the asset whilst searching for the "next rung".

The focus on knowledge and change introduces a continuous design perspective. As stability and equilibrium become less crucial, the main focus shifts to emergence in the face of constant change (Truex, 1999). (Ill-structured) systems therefore need to be developed using a totally different set of goals that would support emergence, growth and change (ibid.).

More specifically, for such systems:

- lengthy analysis represents a poor investment;
- user satisfaction with a stable system is improbable;
- stable sets of requirements are largely imaginary;
- complete and unambiguous specs are largely ineffectual; and
- pressure for new systems stifles adaptation, emergence and maintenance (ibid.).

Instead, the analysis must be continuous (dynamic requirements would benefit from negotiation) and redevelopment must be embraced as a continuous strategy and adopted by introducing an adaptability orientation (ibid.). Systems should therefore be under constant development (i.e., between equilibriums), which reflects constant adjustments and adaptations in their parent organisations. This perspective complements the view of development and maintenance as an investment in organisational resources. In this way they incorporate continuous change and adaptability, embrace emergence, and generally support organisational survival and improved performance. The following section attempts to map the different assumptions in terms of domains of suitability that characterise particular problem-solving approaches according to expectation of change and the corresponding level of adaptation required to cope with it and emphasises the need to focus on evolutionary approaches that allow adjustment and adaptation in the wake of change.

SOLUTIONS: TOWARDS A FRAMEWORK OF SOFTWARE DEVELOPMENT DOMAINS

Resolution styles depend on the problem at hand. Figure 1 emphasises some of the differences between the assumptions and the operating modes of different domains (cf. Lehman, 1985).

- *Domain I - Sequential resolution.* The domain of application for this type of approach is characterised by well-defined, predictable, repeatable and stable situations, reasonably devoid of change (in the sense described by Stacey) that can be specified in full due to a low level of inherent uncertainty. The domain can also be characterised as dealing with routine design problems (Dym, 1994) that are well structured under the assumption of an optimised closed system (i.e., closed change situations). Typical decisions can be described as programmed (Simon, 1965, 1979) and "rational", and are made under conditions of virtual certainty. Problem resolution is carried out sequentially from the fixed initial definition of the start-state to the envisaged final outcome under the assumption of total anticipation. The main emphasis revolves around the transformation and fixed initial parameters to ensure that the end product is directly derivable from the initial state. Traditional approaches to quality assurance likewise depend on the belief that a sequence of structured transformations would lead to a high quality result, that is, S-type assumptions (Lehman, 1985a, 2000). Resolution in this domain can often be viewed as a search for an optimal solution. Repeatable and well-understood problems will thus benefit from this approach, assuming little scope for risks and surprises.
- *Domain II - Incremental resolution.* The middle ground (Domain II) is occupied by situations characterised by higher levels of uncertainty that cannot be fully specified. Despite a reasonable knowledge of the domain, there is still a degree of uncertainty as to the solution mode, making them more amenable to incremental resolution. Quality is also created and maintained incrementally but requires on-going effort (and organisation). Decision-making is conducted under conditions of risk in contained change situations (Stacey, 1991), leading to what can be described as variant design (Dym, 1994) in Domain Dependent Experimental software (Giddings, 1984).
- *Domain III - Evolutionary resolution.* Domain III situations represent the world of creative design (Dym, 1994) characterised as *ill-structured problems*, *wicked*

problems or *messes* that encompass a complex of relationship between technological and social elements. Planning tends to be opportunistic to cope with high levels of ambiguity and ignorance (Hogarth, 1995) and open-ended change situations (Stacey, 1992). The environment, like the systems within it, is open, requiring a focus on resilience and adjustment. Decision-making in this domain implies nonprogrammed decisions (Simon, 1965, 1979) suggesting Domain-Dependent Embedded software (Giddings, 1984) or evolving (E-type) systems (Lehman, 1985, 2000).

Software engineering, as traditionally perceived, appears to relate to the resolution of Domain I problems. Indeed, many of the issues discussed in Section 1 and the figures used to illustrate them refer to resolution methods that are amenable to this type of problem. However, most problems require a continuous attention to change and the ability to adapt. Far from being a structured, algorithmic approach, as is often advocated, software engineering in Domain III is a continuous act of social discovery, experimentation and negotiation performed in a dynamic, change-ridden and evolving environment. This continuity acknowledges the evolving nature of reality (in terms of meanings and perceptions) and the fact that absolute and final closure in Domain III is not attainable. However, discovery and the concern with knowledge (see Section 2) enable a new focus on the long-term implications of development in terms of assets, improvement and growth. This view underpins the new emphasis on the growth of organisational resources, including knowledge, experience, skills and competencies, and on the improvement that it promises. (The shift therefore is not only from product to process, but also from discrete to continuous-and-adaptive.)

Generally, the temporal and discrete focus of software engineering for Domain I does not justify a long-term view. Rather than create assets for the long run, software engineering is concerned with optimising new undertakings that are viewed as single and discrete projects and ignoring the long-term perspective. As a result, investment in quality and improvement is difficult to justify on a single project basis. Furthermore, no

Figure 1: Selecting a Life Cycle Approach.

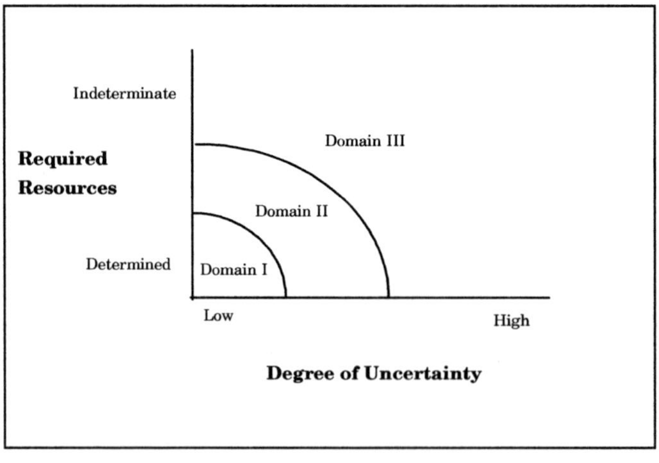

specific mechanisms are introduced to capture and record knowledge. Software engineering for Domain III should be concerned with the longer-term, where justification of resources extends beyond single projects. Investment in tools, improvement and new skills are therefore viewed against corporate targets of improvement and future performance levels that span multiple projects. Significant assets can thus be created in the form of knowledge, skills and competencies, thereby serving the business and providing a competitive edge. Indeed, fostering a strategic view enables one to view all projects as strategic (as part of an asset portfolio). Maintenance becomes a part of normal protection, improvement and growth of assets, which also incorporates initial development.

A long-term perspective views design as an on-going balance between concerns, constraints, challenges and opportunities. Problem-solving in Domain III involves continuous trade-offs in search of constraint satisfaction and opportunity maximisation. A unique feature of this perspective is the focus on the problem in terms of bi-directional adjustment of the starting position and expectations (rather than a uni-directional optimised process towards a static target). The main implication is that users need to be involved throughout as their needs are likely to evolve as a result of the interaction between plan, action and reality. Customer interaction becomes ongoing throughout the evolution of the system and the growth of the resource. Indeed, participation itself can be viewed as a growing asset that offers competitive advantages.

As highlighted, the type of thinking required for Domain III situations relies on embracing a continuity dimension that enables long-term strategic thinking. The general conceptual shift therefore is from discrete software development (in Domain I) to problem-solving in the continuous sense (in Domain III). A long-term perspective can account for knowledge through the required infrastructure supported by the adoption of the growing-asset perspective, thus underpinning normal development and evolution of values, assets, and satisfaction levels (assets in themselves). This allows for the fostering and improvement of expertise, skills and competencies offering a competitive edge through value-driven and experience-based improvement.

Domain III systems are closely entwined with their environment, as they tend to co-evolve with other systems, and with the environment itself. Such systems affect the humans that operate within them (see for example Brand, 1997; Alexander, 1964; Cross, 1981; Simon, 1996) and the overall environment within which they survive, thereby affecting themselves. Many modern applications of technology often realised by computers fall into this category.

Domain III problems extend beyond the limits and boundaries of science (i.e., invoking post-normal science). The process of resolution is a truly multi-disciplinary effort that involves all participants in learning, discovery and negotiation activities. Systems operating within this domain are faced with extremely high levels of complexity, and constant change. The environment in such systems is larger than the humans who try to alter it to suit their own interests. Domain I problems, in contrast, exist within closed environments that enable localised optimisation and resolution, while Domain II problems influence the participants who interact with the problem to some limited extent. Figure 2 offers a simplified depiction of the repeating nature of such situations in relation to their environment (cf. Lehman, 1985). Note that Domain III systems affect the people interacting with them as well as the greater environment within which they operate, as part of the continuous interaction and negotiation at the boundary of social and technical

Figure 2: Systems Types and their Relationships.

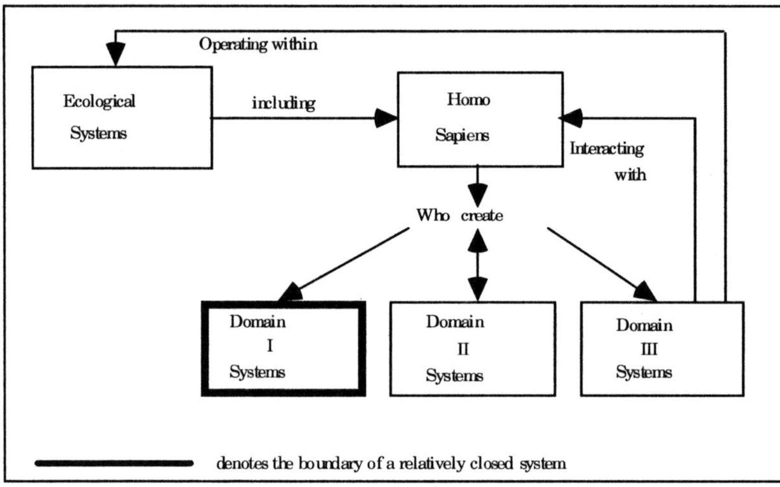

systems. Resolving a problem is linked to the domain within which it exists. Resolution approaches in different domains are explored further in the next section.

DESIGNING IN DIFFERENT DOMAINS

Due to the difference in their nature and relationship to the environment, development in each of the domains is predicated on different assumptions. This section explores the implications of these differences.

Domain I resolution methods reflect the short-term focus on the solution (and the assumption of complete knowledge). Bazjanac argued that all early models of the design process had one characteristic in common: they all viewed the design process as a sequence of well defined activities and were all based on the assumption that the ideas and principles of the scientific method can be applied to it (Bazjanac, 1974). The main criticisms of the early models were: a) that design is not a strictly serial activity driven by technical rationality—in practice, you go around several times; and, b) that design problems are not tame and a linear procedure applied to them cannot yield meaningful solutions (Rittel, 1972; Bazjanac, 1974). Such implied directionality and causality and the separation of analysis from synthesis (and design) disenchanted many practitioners (see for example the comments by Esherick, 1963; Gragg, 1964; Nadler, 1967; Archer, 1979; Nadler, 1985).

Domain III problems, in contrast, start with a limitation on what is, and what can be, known at present. Learning is thus at a premium, as is the need to balance different perspectives and operate in a dynamic and responsive fashion. Such situations combine dynamic complexity with multiple interactions, frequent change and inherent ambiguity. Domain III problems require understanding that is often obtained through learning and continuous experimentation and adjustment. Resolution approaches therefore require a long-term framework to allow for controlled learning and feedback through on-going interaction with the situation. The continuously adapting and evolving nature of such situations defies the notion of optimality in problem-solving. It thus opens the way to the development of a plurality of approaches for addressing the pervasive characteristics of Domain III situations.

Ferguson asserted that design is a contingent process, subject to unforeseen complications and influences as the design develops (Ferguson, 1992); that is, it fits the characteristics of Domain III problems. It is rarely convergent in the sense of being able to direct a designer towards a single preferred solution or approach. The precise outcome of the process cannot be deduced from its initial goal as design is not a formal sequential process, as is often pointed out (see for example Ferguson, 1992; Dym, 2000). Indeed, as noted by both Ferguson and Mann, the orderly pattern (process) is quite unlike the usual chaotic growth of a design (Ferguson, 1992; Mann, 1989).

In fact, as complete knowledge is impossible in any but the simplest task in Domain I, design in Domain III encourages iteration between problem and solution, thus highlighting difficulties (of the type put forward by Page, 1963; Coyne, 1990; Adams, 1991 and Voland, 1999), assumptions and constraints. Indeed, any dynamic and non-trivial system cannot be pre-known and hence, must almost by definition, rely on continuous discovery. Moreover, Rittel was instrumental in confirming that design and analysis, understanding and solving are inextricably linked and only artificially separable (Rittel, 1973; Peters, 1981), as each iteration identifies the next "rung on the ladder". Archer proposed that the "problem" was in the misfit between the requirements and the provision, or in the understanding of either element, while the solution was the acceptable match between the two (Archer, 1979). The essence of design is thus reflected by its commutative nature that allows attention to oscillate between the emerging requirements and the developing provision in an effort to illuminate obscurity and reduce the misfits (ibid.). One should note, however, that in social systems this oscillation is continuous, as the system is constantly adjusting to shifting perceptions and environment (which is also likely to encompass continuous negotiation).

Alexander asserted that design can be described as an activity made of two symmetrical parts, the form and the context (Alexander, 1964). The form refers to the solution to the problem that is being constructed by the designer, while the context is the domain—the setting that defines the problem. The "search for fitness" between the two parts is the essential balancing process suggesting a mutual acceptability, or frictionless co-existence as the two adapt towards one another (ibid.).

Finding a good fit can be achieved through the neutralisation of misfits, the incongruities, irritants and forces that cause clashes that stand out and violate fitness (ibid.). The design problem is therefore a **continuous** effort to achieve fitness between the form and its context. However, this entails finding harmony between a form that is yet to be designed and a context that cannot be properly described (ibid.). Moreover, it also entails re-discovering the new fit at regular intervals. Ultimately, Domain III systems are not searching for the stability of a permanent solution, but rather for a flexible and negotiated co-existence between the form and context that will provide the basis "for climbing to the next rung" as part of evolution and adaptation, in an attempt to "maintain" fitness.

DESIGN IN DOMAIN III

Domain III problem resolution requires dynamic interaction with the environment (see Figure 2). This section focuses on adaptive design, in contrast with comprehensive analysis, as the problem-solving strategy in Domain III problems. Domain III design occurs in change-rich environments. Continuous change points to an open system in continuous interaction with its external environment enabled through the permeable boundaries. Imported inputs will include some known and some unknown properties along with noise and environmental disturbances. The system of interest is thus assumed to be closely interlinked with its universe (external environment).

"Design activity is being increasingly considered in relation to the environment in which it takes place, the participants and elements in the process, the interaction and the dynamics of the process, etc." (Bessant, 1979).

Open systems depend upon the environment and are capable of adapting their behaviour in order to continue to exist in a changing environment (see for example discussion in Peters, 1981; Davis, 1984 and Morgan, 1986). Interaction with the external environment suggests that open systems, in effect, interact with other systems outside themselves. While invisible from within the system itself, systems form complex chains and webs of interaction that may be difficult to recognise or understand.

Daellenbach (1994) observed that all too often emergent properties are not desirable or even planned; yet as Tully (1993) points out, emergence is the central and most pervasive characteristic invoked in systems thinking. Predicting emergence is therefore critical to the engineering professions, yet extremely difficult to perform, as noted by Gosling (1962) and Thome (1993). Indeed, the notion of emergence as proposed by Hopper (1987) and used by Truex (1999, 2000) views emergence not as a sequence of succeeding structures, but rather as a continual movement towards structure without ever attaining a steady state (i.e., a combination of irregular periods with relative periods of emergent regularities during which continuous evolution, growth, adjustment and negotiation are ongoing). True stability is never reached as a result of the deferral of structure via a set of interim agreements.

Behaviour represents a dynamic entity that emerges as a property in response to system stimuli (Kronlof, 1993). Such patterns represent both desirable and undesirable properties that require management (Thome, 1993). The effective use of a systems approach enables better prediction, planning for desirable interactions and the exclusion or mitigation of undesirable consequences. A particular effort needs to be invested in planning, understanding and designing for the emergent effects of systems and their continuous impact on the product, the organisation, and the environment. Systems engineers need to minimise unperfected emergent behaviour while seeking an understanding that will enable them to focus on structures that maximise the effect of "predictable" emergent behaviour (Tully, 1993). Emergent properties thus include desired effects, surprises and newly emerging patterns. Indeed, Winograd suggested that there are no clear problems: Action needs to be taken in situations of irresolution, thereby opening up new opportunities for action (Winograd, 1986).

Purcell (1974) noted that "it is by design that man adapts to, and learns to control, his environment". Unlike the sequential resolution in well-structured problems and permanent structures, design must focus on external factors and interactions. In its broadest context, the goal of design is to alter the environment (Blum, 1996). Afterwards (Winograd, 1986), society engenders inventions whose very existence then alters that society and its environment. The basis of responding and building systems is in attaining a continuous transition under constant development, as proposed by Truex (1999).

Simon (1996) extended the concept of design to include any process of changing from an existing state of affairs to a preferred state (i.e., movement to the next rung). As proposed by Truex (1999), when the design is used to support organisations that cannot help but emerge, it needs to be adaptable and thus incorporate continuous changes. The system is therefore under constant development; constantly growing, improving and responding to emergent patterns through adjustment and adaptation.

Identifying the "next rung" may not be simple. Design appears to be ill structured, as there is no straightforward process to follow and several acceptable solutions may exist (see for example discussion in Klein, 1987; Coyne, 1990; Dym, 2000). Furthermore, as identified by Carroll (1980), the process is radically transformational, involving the development of partial and interim solutions that may ultimately play no role in the next level of "final" design. The direction adopted is random, as design appears to be a process of exploration in which partial responses lead to redefinition of goals, as observed by Bijl (1987), and to the re-negotiation of decisions and trade-offs on the basis of new knowledge.

Problems, it would appear, emerge, unfold, and evolve as participants' knowledge interacts with reality and opportunities. Problem gaps are frequently dynamic, as both the actual state and the desired situation are subjective conceptualisations and hence influenced by each other, the environment, the resolution effort, and most prominently by the observer's perceptions. Progress towards resolution can thus come from dynamic adjustments to either actual state, desired position, or indeed, both. Problem-solving and design are therefore concerned with a perception gap that may represent perceptions, threats, and opportunities. Perceptions, threats and opportunities change, adapt and co-evolve with time, resulting in constantly altered configuration states of such variables. Indeed, as suggested by Carroll (1980), design is therefore an on-going process in the sense that it is not a state and cannot be adequately represented statically. The next section attempts to characterise the adaptive and continuous process of design as it manifests itself in Domain III situations.

FUTURE TRENDS: CHARACTERISING ADAPTIVE DESIGN IN DOMAIN III

The design process requires numerous iterations between the future and the present. The process involves the generation of a basic abstraction and the gradual testing of the abstraction whilst additional details and refinements are being added to maintain the evolving fit with reality. The projection of new concepts to the future and return visits to the original model result in a complex design environment. Problems, opportunities and newly discovered unpredictability result in return visits to the present in order to "improve" the future. This section highlights the implication of dynamic design in change-intensive and evolving environments by outlining the special characteristics of adaptive design, thereby leading the way to defining the broader context of software development in Domain III. In particular, it enumerates the specific characteristics required to effectively design in such environments:

Design is Learning

Holyoak (1990) made the convincing case that problem-solving is intimately connected with learning. The search for a solution is based on the search for a definition that best fits current knowledge. The inevitable result of solution attempts is the acquisition of new knowledge (see for example discussion in Rzevski, 1984 ; Holyoak, 1990). The added insight pertaining to the environment or the problem normally comes from tinkering with a solution, as proposed by Rittel (1972, 1973). As well as the learning itself, intensive, continuous exploration is responsible for the development of appreciation of the beauty, functionality, utility or some other inherent attributes that complement the acquired knowledge. Knowledge is generated, enacted and reflected on in an ongoing process between the materials and the participants' intentions and attached meanings, so that learning occurs when concrete things based on the knowledge are created and evaluated (Gal, 1996). Design is therefore a tool for understanding, as the act of design involves reconciling different perspectives, concepts and viewpoints and making trade-offs. The process of design evolves through the identification of emerging new questions to address that extend beyond the bounded personal world. Learning thus occurs when solutions generate new questions (ibid.).

Design is Trial-and-Error

"In a sense, all problem-solving is trial-and-error, because all problem-solving is thinking, and all thinking involves a search for possibilities, each of which is evaluated in terms of evidence and goals. When a possibility is first thought of, it is a 'trial' possibility, and possibilities that are rejected are 'errors'" (Baron, 1988).

Design is a continuous effort to learn and respond. Learning (by doing) is facilitated by discovery, which in turn relies on experimentation. An understanding of the problem and the potential solutions emerges over time through a trial-and-error process. The design process is concerned with trade-offs between different concerns and constraints. The implications of most trade-offs are not fully appreciated until different options have been explored. By adding and dropping constraints, sampling new perspectives, and exploring new avenues it becomes possible to gain a deeper understanding of the problem through a process of non-binding experimentation. This results in a negotiated process of learning and compromise to arrive at a richer solution that satisfies more of the actual constraints and resolves a greater proportion of the problem.

Design is Negotiation

Balancing perspectives and interests is a critical part of the design process, as all parties have perspectives, opinions and interests that need to be addressed. The raw material, knowledge, required for understanding these problems and forging solutions is dispersed among all the parties. Trade-offs between perspectives and views must legitimately address the problem from all concerned viewpoints and strive to attain a balanced negotiated solution. The design process thus aims to represent and reconcile multiple stakeholders' perspectives and rationales through the introduction of intermediate artefacts that link mental concepts with practical provisions.

Design is a Valued Activity

The design process as described by Alexander (1977) can be viewed essentially as the process of acquiring knowledge and then making decisions that reflect that knowledge. As the design process unfolds, it intrinsically involves the discovery of new goals (Carroll, 1980). This growth enables on-going improvement, as each position becomes a stepping-stone for a fresh design activity (Simon, 1996). Each step along the way creates a new situation, thus providing a new starting point. Goals can thus motivate activity, which in turn will ultimately lead to the generation of new goals (ibid.). Good design practice is therefore an enriched form of directed evolution (Stevens, 1998) exploring new patterns (Alexander, 1979).

Design is Invention

"To design is to invent" (Ferguson, 1992). Designers mentally formulate a particular alternative. The mode of non-verbal thinking employed by engineers and designers is crucial to how outlines are fixed and details of the material surroundings filled in. The variety offered by a virtually "limitless" set of combinations opens the way to originality, experimentation, and innovation through the utilisation of a known set of elements. Novel results and the need for a good fit with environmental and contextual characteristics promote the creative aspect of "innovating with the known".

Design is Satisficing

Exact solutions to large real-world problems are simply not within reach, as explained by Simon (1996). *Satisficing* means finding a satisfactory rather than an optimal course of action. As the designer, user and stakeholders learn more about the problem and as the solution becomes clearer, more and more design decisions are negotiated. In the face of uncertainty, complex projects, multiple participants and various trade-offs, chosen solutions represent local optimisation and simplification, as they are simply good enough to enable progress to the next stage.

Design is an Artefact and an Interface

Design is clearly concerned with and is often measured in reference to the creation of artefacts. Artefacts represent an understanding and agreement between different domains and interests.

"An artefact can be thought of as a meeting point—an interface ... between an 'inner' environment, the substance and organisation of the interface itself, and an 'outer' environment, the surroundings in which it operates" (Simon, 1996).

Artefacts are, in effect, more than a meeting between an inner and an outer environment. As artefacts embody the understanding and agreement of all participants, design becomes an interface of generated wisdom. The artefact thus grows and evolves with time. The representation of the state of negotiation, value and understanding is embodied in the artefact (the design model). It can only be judged in terms of the richness and variety.

The different perspectives can account for a wide variety of factors, which may include: entangled causes, webs of consequences, multiple users, a changing environment, contingent alternatives, use/application domain, developer's domain, the move from a systems model of a problem to a new solution system, changing perspectives, shifting time horizon, altering preferences, ranges of alternatives, satisficing strategies, limited resources, cognitive limitations, attention in fire-fighting mode, nested and conflicting constraints, various hierarchies of politics, and altering dynamics. The design can only make sense with the benefit of hindsight and the understanding that emerges after the fact, reflecting the view of design evoked by Parnas (1986) as a kind of ex-post rationality.

The emerging picture of the nature of design in complex, evolving Domain III environments is of a designer constantly arguing towards a solution with himself, his perceptions and models, and a multitude of other concerned parties in a process that helps the exploration of the design artefact. The parties gradually commit themselves to a particular course of action and subsequently respond to the results of exploring that avenue. The emerging design grows and emerges with time. The essence of the design activity is therefore in the continuous reconciliation and resolution of multi-issue, multi-disciplinary dilemmas, decisions and trade-offs. Political, cultural, social, aesthetic, ecological and ethical perspectives add additional dimensions to what is essentially the human activity of design. This helps to shift design from a stable, problem-oriented field to a dynamic and evolving solution-oriented discipline steeped in fluidity and change. The next section rounds off the discussion by developing the characterisations into a set of implementation issues.

CONCLUSIONS: TOWARDS CONTINUOUS DEVELOPMENT

Many modern problem situations are characterised by high levels of uncertainty, ambiguity and ignorance requiring dynamic resolution approaches. Rather than expend a large proportion of work on the initial analysis of needs and expectations, such situations require openness to different domains and perceptions (rather than a search for optimality) and a recognition of the effect of time. As modern development focus moves from conventional commodities to a knowledge-based economy, intellectual capital becomes a primary resource. The main output of software development can be viewed as the accumulation of knowledge and skills embedded in the new emergent social understanding (see Figure 3). Rather than acting as input, knowledge emerges continuously from the process of development and learning. Continuous discovery and experimentation persist through the development, utilisation and maintenance phases. In addition to this primary output, the process may also create an artefact, which will represent a simplified, negotiated and constrained model of that understanding. Change combines with inputs of varying perspectives, and personal biases, attitudes, values and perceptions to offer the raw materials requiring constant compromise. The resolution process will thus result in a continuous output of understanding and insight that can replenish organisational skill and asset values. In change-rich environments, this output

Figure 3: Development and Learning Process.

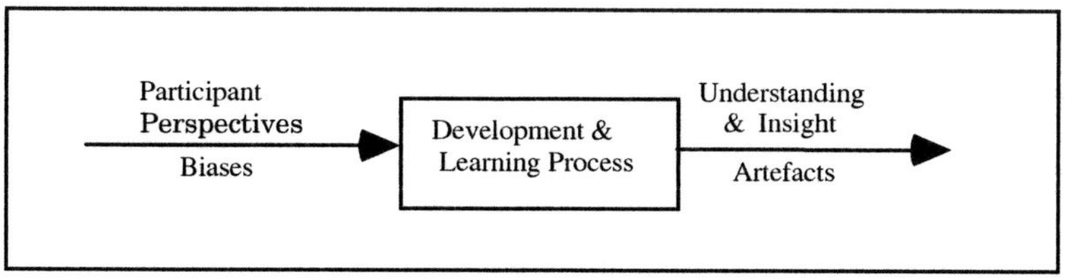

plays a far more crucial role to the future of the organism than the partial artefact whose construction fuelled the enquiry process. In the long run, the intellectual asset defines the range of skills, resilience, competencies and options that will become available.

Engineering a focus shift from delivering to discovering allows for continuous exploration rather than focusing on temporal targets. Changing perceptions, needs, new learning and continuous experimentation will thus involve designers beyond discrete projects and fixed specifications.

Design as a mode of resolution is hardly ever optimal. The act of design itself is neither orderly nor linear. The rest of this section focuses on highlighting the major practical issues emerging from the conceptualisation put forward in this chapter:

- *The Need for Knowledge.* Complete a priori knowledge is not attainable. New informational input will continuously emerge throughout the development, utilisation and maintenance phases.

Given that perfect and absolute knowledge is elusive and that an informational description as an absolute input is not attainable, the issue of knowledge acquisition assumes a critical priority. Furthermore, given continuous change within the environment, this knowledge needs to be continuously refreshed to maintain its utility and relevance. Dynamic resolution through iterations between problem and solution concepts further emphasises the need to revisit and update available knowledge on a progressive basis. Rather than focus on knowledge as a static and discovered input parameter established at the outset, this requires on-going discovery (trial-and-error) through the recognition of the dynamic and adaptive properties of knowledge and their continuous roles. It also places direct emphasis on the tasks of knowledge acquisition, accumulation and consolidation.

The required change in attitude extends not only to the timing of information inputs but also to their completeness and utility levels. Discovery suggests at least a partial incompleteness or ignorance at some early point in time. Design environments and models therefore need to tolerate the essential incompleteness, ambiguity, informality and partiality of knowledge (and given specifications).

- *Beyond the Product Focus.* The process of problem solving leads to improved understanding of the situation through discovery, experimentation and interaction with the problem domain.

Given the inadequacy of the main focus on the production of a working product, there appears to be a need to look at the continuous nature of design, beyond the production of a single work product. This replaces the focus on the notion of efficiency through the elimination of waste and the need for rework. Unlike traditional commodities, software development, and for that matter most knowledge generating activities, are concerned with discovery achieved through iteration cycles and feedback. These entail the need for improvement, rework and re-adjustment in light of discovery. The product emphasis on static properties can thus become limiting and constraining.

As the act of software design is concerned with the generation of understanding and knowledge, the main transformation is likewise concerned with on-going exploration rather than temporal targets. Ill structured problem-solving is thus carried out through open-ended design, which entails experimentation with and within the environment. The main purpose of the design act is to attain understanding (which is a continuous rather than a one-off process) rather than merely deliver a single product. The focus shift therefore is from delivering to discovering.

- *The Persistence of Change.* The design effort evolves and adapts to changing perceptions (including those resulting from discovery, learning and experimentation) and interactions.

Change is all-pervasive. Throughout the life of a system, there will be a continuous stream of changes requiring a continuous effort to adjust and accommodate the new knowledge attained through on-going interaction.

- *The Need for a Process Driver.* Maintaining the evolving focus, value, relevance and satisfaction levels requires a dynamic mechanism for conducting trade-offs as part of the sense-making process.

In light of the continuous nature of design and development, designers need to obtain perspectives that are tolerant of change and do not assume pre-determinism or strict causality. Such a perspective needs to support the discovery of opportunities and emerging knowledge and allow for the distributed nature of such knowledge. Design entails rework and iteration as part of the continuous effort to deal with change and adaptation. The general development model thus needs to display flexibility and diversity to a range of approaches extending beyond the traditional resolution approach.

- *Beyond Quality as a Correctness Measure.* Design of software is problem-focused. Satisfaction is measured with respect to relevant perceptions of the problem. (Continuously evolving) customer focus and satisfaction provide the on-going success measures for determining achievement and utility.

Design is primarily concerned with the perception of a problem and the act of reducing the gap between the current state and the desired position. Measurement of success is likewise based on the perception of this gap (rather than on the satisfaction of pre-agreed and signed-off criteria). In a changing environment, quality is a moving target. Quality cannot be simply perceived as a passive quantity that is acquired through the design and implementation process. Value, especially in terms of the external user, needs to be based on utility and user satisfaction (Cosgrove, 1971; Lehman, 1994), which may become the target. The quality domain thus becomes primarily concerned with the acceptance, quality, usability, usefulness and utility of the resulting artefacts. It encompasses the notions of fitness for purpose, perceived acceptability, and conformance to requirements (or perhaps needs) on a continuous basis. Change and the lack of a static specification permit the view of customer satisfaction as an evolving level that is allowed to grow and improve alongside other assets. (This stems from the recognition that satisfaction is neither a fixed nor a negotiated construct.) The customer focus therefore extends beyond the product development view to incorporate usage and adaptation (of the product to the user rather than the other way around).

Working in ill structured environments (Domain III situations) calls for continuous and adaptive design rather than complete and optimal analysis. The act of design is assumed to be a creative, experimental, argumentative and negotiation-based discovery effort. The process of problem solving leads to improved understanding of a situation through discovery, experimentation and interaction with the problem domain. Above all, the development effort needs to be continuous to reflect the changing nature of reality and to allow for adaptation, survival and growth.

The proposed interpretation of growth and improvement is thus concerned with:

- *Building Intellectual Assets.* Focused primarily on generating a strategic view of development that accounts for long-term investment in, and growth of, intellectual assets.
- *Fostering Continuous Learning.* Grounded in a systematic and multi-disciplinary perspective that is responsive to the results of continuous learning to enable such improvement.
- *Balancing Satisfaction and Utility Trade-offs.* Concerned with the trade-offs and their implication on the resulting outputs and the emerging satisfaction and utility.
- *Monitoring Feedback.* Based on constant monitoring and feedback, which play a part in driving the process and directing the shifting of perceptions and values.

Adoption of the new perspective enables developers to refocus the process around emerging knowledge and its value, to re-emphasise continuity and change and to balance the new values in a dynamic, responsive and evolving fashion. This notion appears to represent a distinct departure from the traditional Domain I focus on discrete and limited efforts viewed in isolation. It also re-emphasises human issues and attention to social and political constraints, issues and processes. Furthermore, a long-term view justifies the adoption of multiple perspectives, the reuse of knowledge and the utilisation of a dynamic perspective, which underpin feedback and improvement. Taken together, this points to a move from a structured engineering to a growing design perspective, and a move from discrete and project-based Domain I software engineering to a strategic, continuous and evolving Domain III discipline of software design. More specifically, it enables designers to start taking account of change and foster continuity in an effort to design living and evolutionary information systems that can continue to grow and adapt.

This interpretation is not proposed as a final answer, but as an intermediary step—an opening of a new perspective on lifelong, long-term development and improvement.

REFERENCES

Adams, J.L. (1991). *Flying buttresses, entropy, and o-rings: The world of the engineer*. Cambridge, MA: Harvard University Press.

Alexander, C. (1964). *Notes on the synthesis of form*. Cambridge, MA: Harvard University Press.

Alexander, C. (1979). *The timeless way of buildings*. Oxford: Oxford University Press.

Alexander, C. et al. (1977). *A pattern language*. Oxford: Oxford University Press.

Andriole, S. J. (1986). *Software validation, verification, testing and documentation*. Princeton, NJ: Petrocelli Books.

Andriole, S. J. (1991). Flexible life cycle for multidisciplinary C2 information systems engineering. In S.M. Halpin (Ed.), *Information Technology for command and control: Methods and tools for systems development and evaluation* (pp. 107-136). Los Alamitos, CA: IEEE Computer Society Press.

Archer, B.L. (1979). Design as a discipline: Whatever became of design methodology. *Design Studies, 1*(1), 17-18.

Archer, B.L. (1979). The three Rs. *Design Studies, 1*(1), 18-20.

Arthur, L.J. (1992). *Rapid evolutionary development: Requirements, prototyping and software creation.* New York: John Wiley and Sons.

Avison, D.E., & Fitgerald, G. (1995). *Information systems development: Methodologies, techniques and tools.* London: McGraw-Hill.

Bak, P. (1996). *How nature works: The science of self-organised criticality*. New York: Copernicus.

Baron, J. (1988). *Thinking and deciding*. Cambridge: Cambridge University Press.

Bazjanac, V. (1974). Architectural design theory: Models of the design process. In W.R. Spillers (Ed.), *Basic questions of design theory* (pp. 3-20). New York: North Holland.Bessant, J.R., & McMahon, B.J. (1979). Participant observation of a major design decision in industry. *Design Studies, 1*(1), 21-28.

Bijl, A. (1987). An approach to design theory. In E.A. Warman (Ed.), *Design theory in CAD* (pp. 3-25). Amsterdam: North Holland.

Birrell, N.D., & Ould, M.A. (1985). *A practical handbook for software development.* Cambridge: Cambridge University Press.

Blum, B.I. (1996). *Beyond programming: To a new era of design*. New York: Oxford University Press.

Brand, S. (1997). *How buildings learn: What happens when they fail*. London: Phoenix.

Brooks, F.P.J. (1975). *The mythical man-month*. Reading, MA: Addison Wesley.

Brooks, F.P.J. (1986). No silver bullet: Essence and accident in software engineering. *Information processing*. Elsevier Science.

Brooks, F.P.J. (1997). *The mythical man-month revisited*. Talk given at the IEE, 2.12.97.

Carroll, J.M., & Thomas, J.C. et al. (1980). Presentation and representation in design problem solving. *American Journal of Psychology*, (93), 269-284.

Cave, W.C., & Salisbury, A.B. (1978). Controlling the software life cycle-The project management task. *IEEE Transactions on Software Engineering, SE-4*(4), 326-334.

Charette, R.N. (1990). *Applications strategies for risk analysis*. New York: Intertext/ McGraw-Hill.

Cleland, D.I. (1998). *Strategic planning. Field guide to project management*. D. I. Cleland, Van Nostrand Reinhold: 3-12.

Corbato, F.J., & C. T. Clingen, C.T. (1979). A mangerial view of the multics system development. In P. Wenger (Ed.), *Research directions in software technology* (pp. 139-160). Cambridge, MA: MIT Press.

Cosgrove, J. (1971). Needed: A new planning framework. *Datamation, 17*(23), 37-39.

Coveney, P., & Highfield, R. (1995). *Frontiers of complexity: The search for order in a chaotic world.* London: Faber and Faber.

Coyne, R.D. et al. (1990). *Knowledge based design systems.* Reading, MA: Addison Wesley.

Cross, N., Naughton, J. et al. (1981). Design method and scientific method. *Design Studies, 2*(4), 195-201.

Cusumano, M.A., & Selby, R.W. (1995). *Microsoft secrets: How the world's most powerful company creates technology, shapes markets, and manages people.* New York: Free Press.

Daellenbach, H.G. (1994). *Systems and decision making; A management science approach.* Chichester: John Wiley and Sons Inc.

Davis, G.B., & Olson, M.H. (1984). *Management information systems, conceptual foundations, structure and development.* New York: McGraw-Hill.

Distaso, J.R. (1980). Software management- A survey of the practice in 1980. *Proceedings of the IEEE Computer Society, 68*(9), 1103-1119.

Dym, C.L. (1994). *Engineering design: A synthesis of views.* New York: Cambridge University Press.

Dym, C.L., & Little, P. (2000). *Engineering design: A project based introduction.* New York: John Wiley.

Elster, J. (1989). *Nuts and bolts for the social sciences.* Cambridge, MA: Cambridge University Press.

Esherick, J. (1963). *Problems of the design of a design system.* Conference on Design Methods. Macmillan.

Ferguson, E.S. (1992). *Engineering and the mind's eye.* Cambridge, MA: MIT Press.

Fitzgerald, G. (1990). Achieving flexible information systems: The case for improved analysis. *Journal of Information Technology, 5*(1): 5-11.

Gal, S. (1996). Footholds for design. In T. Winograd (Ed.), *Bringing design to software* (pp. 215-227). Reading, MA: Addison Wesley.

Gibson, V.R., & Senn, J.A. (1989). System structure and software maintenance performance. *Communications of the ACM, 32*(3), 347-358.

Giddings, R.V. (1984). Accommodating uncertainty in Software Design. *Communications of the ACM, 27*(5), 428-434.

Gilbreath, R.D. (1988). Working with pulses, not streams: Using projects to capture opportunity. In W.R. King (Ed.), *Project management handbook* (p. 3-15). New York: Van Nostrand Reinhold.

Gosling, W. (1962). *The design of engineering systems.* London: Heywood.

Gould, S.J. (1996). *Life's grandeur: The spread of excellence from Plato to Darwin.* London: Jonathan Cape.

Gragg, C.I. (1964). Whose fault was it? *Harvard Business Review,* 42, 107-110.

Grindley, K. (1986). *Fourth generation languages (Vol.1), A survey of best practice. The Grindley report.* IDPM Publications.

Hogarth, R.M., & Kunreuther, H. (1995). Decision making under ignorance: Arguing with yourself. *Journal of Risk and Uncertainty, 10,* 15-36.

Holyoak, K.J. (1990). *Problem solving thinking*. E. E. Smith. Cambridge, MA: MIT Press. 117-146.

Hopper, P. (1987). Emergent grammar. *Berkley Linguistics Society, 13*, 53-79.

Kauffman, S. (1995). *At home in the universe: The search for laws of complexity*. New York: Oxford University Press.

Klein, G.A. (1987). Analytical versus recognitional approaches to design decision making. System Design. K. R. Boff. Amsterdam: North Holland: 175-188.

Kronlof, K. (Ed.). (1993). *Method integration, concepts and case studies*. Chichester: John Wiley and Sons.

Land, F.F. (1982). Adapting to changing user requirements. *Information and Management, 5*(2), 59-75.

Lehman, J.D., & Yavneh, N. (1985). The total life cycle model. *Proceedings of the Third International Workshop on Software Specification and Design,* Los Alamitos, CA: IEEE Computer Society Press.

Lehman, M.M. (1994). Some characteristics of S-, E- and P- type programs. *Proc. Feast Workshop II,* Imperial College of Science and Technology, London, Imperial College.

Lehman, M.M. (1998). Software's future: Managing evolution. *IEEE Software, 15*(1), 40-44.

Lehman, M.M. (2000). *Rules and tools for software evolution planning and management*. FEAST 2000, London, Imperial College.

Lehman, M.M., & Belady, L.A. (1985). *Program evolution: Processes of software change*. London: Academic Press.

Littlewood, B. (1992). The risks of software. *Scientific American*, 271(3), 38-43.

Longworth, G. (1985). *Designing systems for change*. NCC Publications.

Mann, R.W. (1989). Engineering design. *McGraw-Hill encyclopaedia of science and technology*, 6.

McMaster, M.D. (1996). *The intelligence advantage: Organising for complexity*. Boston: Butterworth Heinemann.

Morgan, G. (1986). *Images of organisation*. London: Sage Publications.

Nadler, G. (1967). An investigation of design methodology. *Management Science, 13*(10), B642-B655.

Nadler, G. (1985). Systems methodology and design. *IEEE Transactions on Systems, Man, and Cybernetics, 15*(6), 685-697. Los Alamitos, CA: IEEE Computer Society Press.

Page, J.K. (1963). A review of the papers presented at the conference. *Conference on Design Methods*, Pergamon, Oxford.

Parker, D., & Stacey, R.D. (1994). *Chaos, management and economics.* Institute of Economic Affairs.

Parnas, D.L., & Clements, P.C. (1986). A rational design process: How and why to fake it. *IEEE Transactions on Software Engineering, 12*(2), 251-257. Los Alamitos, CA: IEEE Computer Society Press.

Paul, R.J. (1993). Why users cannot 'get what they want'. *ACM SIGIOS Bulletin, 14*(2), 8-12.

Pereira, R.E. (2001). A model of factors affecting an information system's change in state. *Journal of Software Maintenance and Evolution: Research and Practice, 13*, 245-261. John Wiley and Sons.

Peters, L.J. (1981). *Software design: Methods and techniques*. New York: Yourdon Press.

Polanyi, M. (1962). Tacit knowing: Its bearing on some problems of philosophy. *Review of Modern Physics, 34*(4), 601-616.

Pool, R. (1997). *Beyond engineering: How society shapes technology*. New York: Oxford University Press.

Popper, K.R. (1972). *Objective knowledge: An evolutionary approach*. Oxford: Oxford University Press.

Pressman, R.S., & Ince, D. (2000). *Software engineering: A practitioner's approach*. Maidenhead: McGraw-Hill.

Prigogine, I. (1980). *From being to becoming*. New York: W. H. Freeman.

Purcell, P.A., & Mallen, G.L. et al. (1974). A strategy for design research. In W.R. Spillers (Ed.), *Basic questions of design theory* (pp. 75-93). New York: North Holland.

Rajlich, V.T., & Bennett, K.H. (2000). The staged model for the software life cycle. *IEEE Computer, 33*(7), 66-71.

Rechtin, E. (2000). *The art of systems architecting*. CRC Press.

Rescher, N. (1995). *Luck*. New York: Farrar Straus Giroux.

Rittel, H.W. (1972). On the planning crisis: Systems analysis of the 'first and second generations'. *Bedriftsokonomen, 8*),390-396.

Rittel, H.W., & Webber, M.M. (1973). Dilemmas in a general theory of planning. *Policy Sciences, 4,* 155-169.

Rzevski, G. (1984). *Prototypes versus pilot systems: Strategies for evolutionary information systems development. Approaches to prototyping* (pp. 356-367). Berlin: Springer-Verlag.

Schach, S.R. (1996). *Classical and object-oriented software engineering*. Chicago: Irwin.

Schneider, F.B. (1998). *Trust in cyberspace*. Washington, D.C.: National Academy Press.

Shemer, I. (1987). Systems analysis: A systematic analysis of a conceptual model. *Communications of the ACM, 30*(6), 506-512.

Simon, H.A. (1965). Administrative decision making. *Public Administration Review*, 31-37.

Simon, H.A. (1979). Rational decision making in business organisations. *American Economic Review,* 493-513.

Simon, H.A. (1996). *Sciences of the artificial*. Cambridge, MA: MIT Press.

Smith, K.K. (1984). Rabbits, lynxes, and organisational transitions. In R.E. Quinn (Ed.), Managing organisational transitions (pp. 267-294). R. E. Quinn. Homewood, Ill., Richard D. Irwin: 267-294.

Stacey, R.D. (1991). *The chaos frontier: Creative strategic control for business*. Oxford: Butterworth Heinemann.

Stacey, R.D. (1996). *Strategic management and organisational dynamics*. London: Pitman Publishing.

Stevens, R. et al. (1998). *Systems engineering, Coping with complexity*. London: Prentice Hall.

Thome, B. (Ed.). (1993). *Systems engineering, principles and practice of computer-based systems engineering*. Chichester: John Wiley.

Truex, D., & Baskerville, R. et al. (1999). Growing systems in emergent organisations. *Communications of the ACM, 42*(8), 117- 123.

Truex, D., & Baskerville, R. et al. (2000). A methodical systems development: The deferred meaning of systems development methods. *Accounting Management and Information Technology, 10,* 53-79.

Tully, C. (1993). System development activity. In B. Thome (Ed.), *Systems engineering, principles and practice of computer-based systems engineering* (pp. 45-80). Chichester: John Wiley and Sons Inc.

Voland, G. (1999). *Engineering by design.* Reading, MA: Addison Wesley.

Waddington, C.H. (1977). *Tools for thought.* London: Jonathan Cape.

Waldrop, M.M. (1992). *Complexity: The emerging science at the edge of order and chaos.* New York: Simon & Schuster.

Wand, Y., & Weber, R. (1995). On the deep structure of information systems. *Information Systems Journal, 5*(X), 203-223.

Weick, K.E. (1984). Small wins: Redesigning the scale of social problems. *American Psychologist, 39*(1), 40-49.

Wheatley, M.J. (1992). *Leadership and the new science: Learning About organisation from an orderly universe.* San Francisco: Berret-Koehler.

Winograd, T., & Flores, F. (1986). *Understanding computers and cognition; A new foundation for design.* Reading, MA: Addison Wesley.

Yourdon, E. (1993). *Decline and fall of the American programmer.* Englewood Cliffs, NJ: Yourdon Press.

Chapter III

On the Maturity of Software Maintenance and Other IT Services

Frank Niessink, Software Engineering Research Centre, The Netherlands

ABSTRACT

In this chapter, we examine the differences between software maintenance and software development from a service point of view, and the consequences thereof for the maturity of software maintenance organizations. We argue that software maintenance can be seen as providing a service, whereas software development is primarily concerned with the development of products. Differences between products and services affect the way in which customers assess their respective quality. In particular, service quality is assessed in two dimensions: the technical quality — what the result of the service is — and the functional quality — how the service is delivered. Consequently, customers will judge the quality of software maintenance differently from that of software development. This in turn means that to deliver high quality results in software maintenance, both the functional quality and the technical quality dimension are important.

INTRODUCTION

In order to provide high-quality software *maintenance*, different and additional processes are needed than provided by a high-quality software *development* organization. These processes are derived from the gap model of service quality. This model of service quality explains the difference between expected quality and perceived quality, which in turn, determine customer satisfaction.

If we look at software maintenance and software development from a service perspective, we see that software maintenance is all about sustaining the software system, that is, sustaining the service; whereas software development is about building products. In this chapter, we argue that the processes for high maturity software maintenance are different than those needed for high maturity software development. Consequently, a maturity model for software maintenance organizations needs to be different from a maturity model for software development organizations. This chapter describes the IT Service Capability Maturity Model (CMM[1]), which aims to capture the processes needed for high maturity Information Technology (IT) service provision, including software maintenance.

SOFTWARE MAINTENANCE FROM A SERVICE PERSPECTIVE

In this section we discuss the differences between products and services in general. We translate the gap model to the software maintenance domain to see what processes can be used to minimize the gap between expected service quality and perceived quality in a software maintenance environment.

Service versus Product

A wide range of definitions exists in the marketing literature of what a service actually entails (Grönroos, 1990). Usually, a service is defined as an essentially intangible set of benefits or activities that are sold by one party to another. The main differences between products and services are (Zeithaml, 1996):

- *Intangibility.* This is considered to be the most basic difference between products and services. Services — being benefits or activities — cannot be seen, felt, tasted, or touched, like products can. Consequently:
  - services cannot be inventoried,
  - services cannot be patented,
  - services cannot be readily displayed or communicated, and
  - pricing of a service is more difficult.

- *Heterogeneity.* Because services are created by activities, and activities are performed by humans, services tend to be more heterogeneous than products. Consequently:
  - service delivery and customer satisfaction depend on employee actions,
  - service quality depends on factors that are difficult to control, such as the ability of the customer to articulate his or her needs, the ability and willingness of personnel to satisfy those needs, the presence or absence of other customers, and the level of demand for the service, and
  - these complicating factors make it hard to know whether the service was delivered according to plan or specifications.

- *Simultaneous Production and Consumption.* Services are produced and consumed simultaneously, whereas for products, production and consumption can be separated. For example, a car can be produced first, sold a few months later, and then be consumed over a period of several years. For services, on the other hand, the

production and consumption have to take place in parallel. The production of the service creates the 'set of benefits', whose consumption cannot be postponed. For example, a restaurant service — preparing a meal, serving the customer — has largely to be produced while the customer is receiving the service. Consequently:
- customers participate in and affect the transaction,
- customers may affect each other,
- employees affect the service outcome, and
- centralization and mass production are difficult.

- *Perishability.* Services cannot be saved or stored. Consequently:
  - it is difficult to synchronize supply and demand with services, and
  - services cannot be returned or resold.

The difference between products and services is not clear-cut. Often, services are augmented with physical products to make them more tangible; for example, luggage tags provided with travel insurance. In the same way, products are augmented with add-on services, for example a guarantee, to improve the quality perception of the buyer. In the service marketing literature (e.g., Berry, 1991), a product-service continuum is used to show that there is no clear boundary between products and services. This product-service continuum is a spectrum with pure products on one end and pure services on the other end, and product-service mixtures in between. Figure 1 shows some example products and services positioned on the product-service continuum.

As Figure 1 shows, products and services can be intertwined. In the case of fast food, both the product -the food itself- and the service -fast delivery- are essential to the customer. This means that the quality of such a product-service mix will be judged on both product and service aspects: whether the food is quickly served, and whether it tastes well.

If we turn to the software engineering domain, we see that a major difference between software development and software maintenance is the fact that software development results in a *product*, whereas software maintenance results in a *service* being delivered to the customer. Software maintenance has more service-like aspects

Figure 1: Product-Service Continuum (adjusted from Berry et al., 1991).

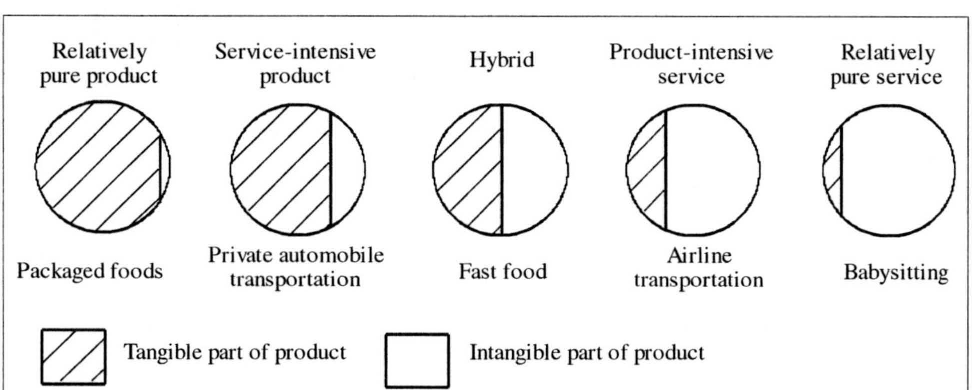

Figure 2: Product-Service Continuum for Software Development and Maintenance.

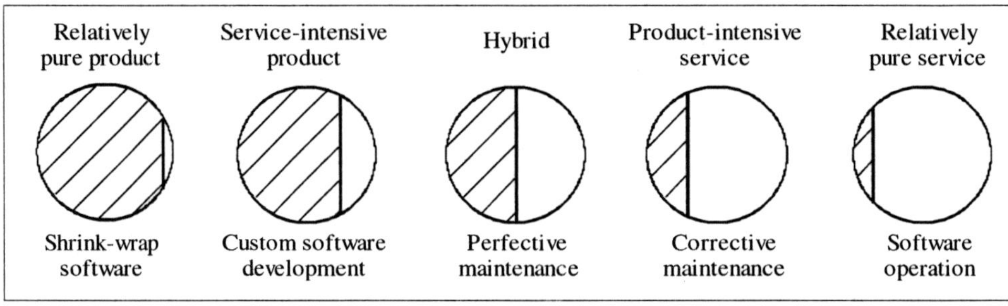

than software development, because the value of software maintenance is in the activities that result in benefits for the customers, such as corrected faults and new features. Contrast this with software development, where the development activities themselves do not provide benefits for the customer, but instead it is the resulting software system that provides the benefits.

As said above, the difference between products and services is not clear-cut. Consequently, this goes for software development and software maintenance as well. Figure 2 shows the product-service continuum, as displayed in Figure 1, but with examples from the software engineering domain.

Services and Quality

Though we argued in the previous section that we can view software maintenance as a service and software development as product development, we did not yet discuss why this would be beneficiary. In order to do so, we again turn to the literature in the area of service management and marketing. Grönroos (1990) states that there are two dimensions that determine the experienced quality of services:

- The technical quality of the outcome. This dimension is formed by the result of the service, *what* the customer is left with when the service has been delivered.
- The functional quality of the process. This dimension is determined by the way in which the customer receives the service; in other words, *how* the service is delivered.

Service marketeers often use the gap model to illustrate how differences between perceived service delivery and expected service can come about (see Figure 3). The net difference between the perceived quality of the services and the expected quality (gap 5) is caused by four other gaps (Zeithaml, 1996):

Gap 1

The expected service as perceived by the service provider differs from the service as expected by the customer.

Due to inadequate market research, lack of communication between contact employees and management, and insufficient relationship focus, the service provider has a perception of what the customer expects, which differs from the real expected service.

Figure 3: Gaps Model of Service Quality (adapted from Zeithaml, 1996).

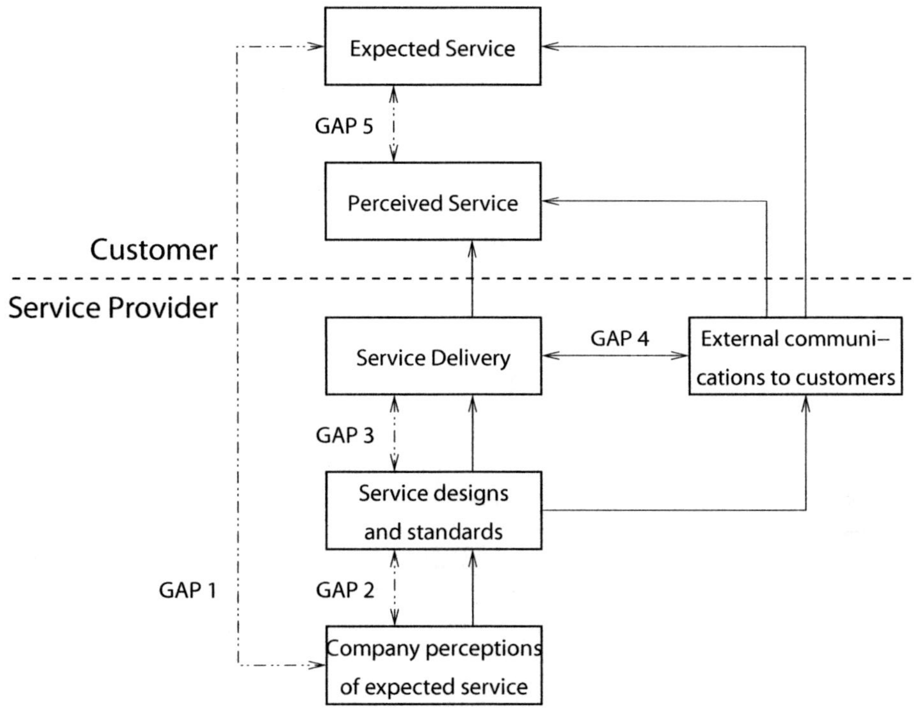

For example, the service organization aims to satisfy certain availability constraints (e.g., 99% availability), while the actual customer concern is with maximum downtime (e.g., no longer than one hour per failure).

Gap 2

The service specification as used by the service provider differs from the expected service as perceived by the service provider. Caused by a lack of customer-driven standards, absence of process management, lack of a formal process for setting service quality goals, poor service design and inadequate service leadership, the service designs and standards will not match the service requirements as perceived by the provider.

For example, the customer expects a quick restart of the system, while the standard procedure of the maintenance organization is focused on analysing the reason for the crash.

Gap 3

The actual service delivery differs from the specified services.

Service delivery does not follow the service designs and standards because of deficiencies in human resource policies, failures to match demand and supply, and customers not fulfilling their role.

For example, customers bypass the help desk by phoning the maintainer of their system directly, and thus hinder a proper incident management process.

Gap 4

Communication about the service does not match the actual service delivery.

Communication by the service provider about its delivered services does not match the actual service delivery because of ineffective management of customer expectations, over-promising, and inadequate horizontal communications (i.e., insufficient communication between sales and operations and between advertising and operations and differences in policies and procedures across the organization).

For example, a customer is not informed about the repair of a bug he or she reported.

The fifth gap is caused by the four preceding gaps. Hence, perceived service quality can be increased by closing the first four gaps, thus bringing the perceived service in line with the expected service.

To summarize so far, we see that two quality dimensions determine the quality of services: the technical quality — what the result is — and the functional quality -how the result is reached. We also showed how the gap between the perceived service delivery and expected service delivery is caused by several other gaps in the service provider's organization.

The question is, how does this all translate to the area of software engineering? Our argument is that since software maintenance organizations are essentially service providers, they need to consider the issues mentioned in this section. They need to manage their product -software maintenance- as a service to be able to deliver high quality software maintenance.

Looking at the gap model presented in Figure 3 we notice a number of processes emerge that pertain to the quality of the delivered services. To close the gaps a service provider needs to:

- Translate customer service expectations into clear service agreements (gap 1).
- Use the service agreements as a basis for planning and implementing the service delivery (gap 2).
- Ensure that service delivery is done according to planning and procedures (gap 3).
- Manage communication about the services delivered (gap 4).

BRIDGING THE GAPS

In this section, we discuss four processes that may help bridge the gaps identified in the previous section. Obviously, these processes were not derived straightforwardly from these gaps. What we report on here is the a posteriori justification of characteristics that distinguish a successful software maintenance organization from a less successful one, based on many discussions with maintenance managers, experiences with successful and less successful case studies (Niessink et al., 1998), and a critical look at the Software Capability Maturity Model from a maintenance perspective (Drew, 1992).

Gap 1 - Management of Commitments

It is important that maintenance commitments be planned and documented. This works best if the maintenance organization and customer work together towards the specification of relevant and realistic maintenance service commitments (often called service level agreement - SLA), based on the needs of the customer. The actual maintenance services delivered, the specified service levels and the customer's service needs are reviewed with the customer on a regular basis. As a result of this evaluation, the service level agreement may have to be adjusted to stay in line with possibly changing maintenance needs.

There are two basic issues involved here: first, the maintenance service to be delivered is specified in a contract — the service level agreement — containing *measurable* service levels. Second, the service levels specified should address the business needs of the customer.

The service level agreement documents the maintenance services to be delivered. It covers the purpose, scope and goals of the services, their specification, and other agreements. The service level agreement functions as a means to close gap 1 by setting expectations for the maintenance service. It should at a minimum specify:

1. The maintenance services themselves, i.e., a specification of the services to be delivered.
2. With what levels of service, that is, how fast, how reliable, and so forth, specified in a measurable manner. Service levels need to be measurable because the organization has to report the realized service levels.
3. The conditions the customer should obey. Examples of such conditions could be that the customer should use a certain format for documenting change requests or, in case of a bug, provide the maintenance department with the input that caused the fault to manifest itself.
4. What happens if the maintenance organization does not reach the agreed upon service levels while the customer did not violate the customer conditions.
5. When and what will be reported to the customer regarding the actual delivered maintenance services.
6. When and how the service level agreement will be reviewed.
7. Under which circumstances (calamities) service is not guaranteed.

The service commitments as documented in the service level agreement should be derived from the maintenance needs of the customer (as opposed to just the capabilities of the maintenance organization). These maintenance needs should be related to the business processes of the customer, its Information Technology, its business strategy, and so forth. This ensures that the maintenance organization thinks about what the customer needs and thus helps to close gap 1.

Gap 2 - Maintenance Planning

The maintenance activities as specified in the service level agreement have to be planned. This includes the planning of the maintenance activities themselves, the transfer of the results thereof to the customer, the estimation of resources needed, the scheduling of maintenance activities, and the identification of possible risks.

In a normal, non-emergency situation, changes are often bundled into releases. There are various ways of deciding on the contents and timing of the next release. For example, releases may be scheduled at fixed time intervals, while there also is a fixed number of people available for doing maintenance. The next release will then contain all changes that could be handled within that time frame. One may also negotiate and fix the contents of the next release in advance, and allocate the number of maintenance engineers accordingly. This planning of releases is part of the maintenance planning process. See Stark and Oman (1997) for an observation of several strategies applied in practice.

Explicitly basing the planning of maintenance activities on the commitments as agreed upon with the customer helps to close gap 2.

Gap 3 - Maintenance Activity Tracking

The service level agreement states which maintenance activities are to be carried out, and how fast, reliable, and so forth this should be done. In order to be able to report on the performance of the maintenance organization in this respect, information about the actual maintenance activities is to be gathered. The purpose of the maintenance activity tracking process is to provide this information, monitor maintenance activities, and take corrective actions if necessary.

For example, when the customer reports a bug, information about the bug itself (originator, type, etc.) is recorded, as well as the reporting time, the time when corrective action was started and ended, and the time when the bug was reported fixed. If these data indicate that the average downtime of a system exceeds the level as specified in the service level agreement, the maintenance organization might assign more maintenance staff to this system, put maintenance staff on point-duty at the customer site, renegotiate the agreed upon service level, or take any other action to realign agreement and reality.

Keeping a strict eye upon the performance of the maintenance organization, and adjusting the maintenance planning and/or renegotiating the commitments with the customer when required, narrows gap 3.

Gap 4 - Event Management

Event management concerns the management of events that cause or might cause the maintenance activities carried out to deviate from the agreed upon levels of maintenance service. Events can be either:

- Requests for changes from users or other stakeholders. For example, requests for a new feature in the software;
- Incidents that cause or will cause service levels to be lower than agreed upon if no action is being taken. For example, a server that is down might cause the specified maximum downtime to be exceeded if it is not restarted quickly enough.

The main purpose of event management is to manage all events that occur during software maintenance. Event management encompasses a number of activities that should ensure that incidents and change requests are resolved in time and that affected groups, including the customer, are kept informed. These activities thus contribute to both the functional as well as the technical quality of software maintenance. A subset of the event management activities is:

- An event management library system is established as a repository for the event records. This event management library system (often in the form of a "help desk system") should provide for the storage, update, and retrieval of event records, the sharing and transfer of event records between affected groups, and should help in the use of event management procedures.
- The event management library system also supports communication with the customer about the maintenance services delivered. In addition, it supports the maintenance department itself in its role of a historical database of incidents and change requests. The event management system thus helps to close gap 4.
- Events are identified, recorded, reviewed, and tracked according to a documented procedure. Each event is recorded in the library system, the impact of the event is assessed and documented, and "action items" are formulated and initiated to resolve the event. This activity reinforces that the maintenance activities carried out are kept in accordance with the maintenance commitments and the maintenance planning, thus helping to close gap 3.
- Standard reports documenting the event management activities and the contents of the event repository are developed and made available to affected groups and individuals. This activity helps keep the customer informed about the progress of activities to resolve incidents or process change requests. The communication with the customer not only pertains to individual change requests, but also their bundling into releases. There thus is a relation with the maintenance planning process. Keeping the customer informed will help manage customer expectations, again narrowing gap 4.

RELATED WORK

In his book *Practical Software Maintenance*, Thomas Pigoski laments that software maintenance organizations need to realize that they are in the customer service business (Pigoski, 1996, pp. 171-172). Apparently, this is not widely recognized yet. Within the software engineering domain, including software maintenance, the focus is on product aspects. The final phases of software development supposedly concern the delivery of an operations manual, installing the software, handling change requests and fixing bugs. In practice, the role of the IS department is much broader during the deployment stage, as illustrated by the ubiquitous help desk. Also, Finkelstein and Kramer (2000) identify the service view on software engineering as one of the main research challenges for the software engineering discipline.

Published evaluations of software maintenance practices tend to concentrate on the narrow issue of efficiently handling change requests and bug fixes (Briand et al., 1998; Onoma et al., 1995; Singer, 1998; West, 1996). For example, a common denominator in these papers is the emphasis that is placed on a presence of what is termed a bug tracking system, historical data-base of changes, or change management. The wording is such that the *internal* use of this information gets emphasized. The information is considered important for the maintainers: they must be able to track similar bugs, they must be able to retrieve the status of each change, and so on. By taking a service perspective, we additionally stress the *external* use, that is, in the communication with the customer, of essentially the same information in what we call event management.

Stålhane et al. (1997) did a survey to find those aspects of quality that customers consider most important. The most important result of their study is the strong emphasis customers place on service quality. The top five factors found in their study are: service responsiveness, service capacity, product reliability, service efficiency, and product functionality. They also quote an interesting result from a quality study in the telecommunications domain. On the question "Would you recommend others to buy from this company?", a 100% yes was obtained for the category of users that had complained and got a satisfactory result. For the category of users that had not complained, this percentage was 87%. Apparently, it is more important to get a satisfactory service than to have no problems at all.

Pitt et al. also argue that software maintenance has a significant service component. They have used SERVQUAL, an instrument developed in the marketing area, as a measure of IS service quality (Pitt et al., 1995; Watson et al., 1998).

One method that does provide an overall approach to implementing a service-oriented organization is the IT Infrastructure Library (CCTA, 2000; OGC, 2001). ITIL has a scope that is wider than mere software maintenance. An IT service organization may also maintain hardware configurations, handle software distribution, run a computer centre, and so on. Hence the use of the term service, rather than software maintenance, in the remainder of this section. The IT Infrastructure Library essentially is a set of best practices. ITIL was originally developed by the British government through their Central Computer and Telecommunications Agency (CCTA), now incorporated in the Office of Government Commerce. The library consists of two core sets of processes that contain those 'best practices' in IT service delivery. These two core sets (Service Delivery and Service Support) contain the following practices:

- The Service Support set covers the Service Desk, Incident Management, Problem Management, Configuration Management, Change Management, and Release Management.
- The Service Delivery set covers Service Level Management, Financial Management for IT Services, Capacity Management, IT Service Contingency Management, and Availability Management.

Each process is described in terms of planning; implementation; audits; benefits, cost and possible problems; and tool support. Attention is given to operational procedures, roles, responsibilities, dependencies, support processes, training, and so forth.

Although the best practices cover a wide range of issues regarding IT services, there are a number of important issues that need more attention. Examples are:

- The specification of service level agreements (SLAs). Although ITIL does promote the use of SLAs, it does not provide much help on how to develop them.
- The use of service catalogs. ITIL does promote the use of a service catalog to facilitate the communication with the customers, but again does not say much about the contents or how to develop it.

- ITIL implementation. ITIL itself does not provide much information on the best way to implement the different processes and on how to decide on the best order of implementation.
- The distinction between service producing processes and service support processes. In our opinion, ITIL does not clearly distinguish between those two types. For example, the ITIL service desk is both used for communication with the end-users (needed for incident handling) and for user support (a service).

While over the years, different companies have been selling services that complement ITIL, such as education, training, and consulting on ITIL implementation, ITIL still lacks an overall approach to the improvement of service processes. Improvement is not an integral part of the library.

THE IT SERVICE CMM

This section describes the IT Service Capability Maturity Model. The IT Service CMM is aimed at providing a maturity growth model for organizations providing IT services. We have argued that this includes software maintenance. Also, we have derived a number of processes from the gap model of service quality that are important to minimize the gap between expected service quality and perceived service quality. In this section we present the IT Service CMM as a means to improve the maturity of IT service organizations, an overview of the model and we describe the key process areas of level two and three. We also briefly describe our practical experiences with the IT Service CMM.

Overview of the IT Service CMM

The objective of the IT Service CMM is twofold:

- to enable IT service providers to assess their capabilities with respect to the delivery of IT services,
- to provide IT service providers with directions and steps for further improvement of their service capability.

The IT Service CMM aims to fulfil these goals by measuring the capability of the IT service processes of organizations on a five level ordinal scale. Each level prescribes certain key processes that have to be in place before an organization resides on that level. Key processes implement a set of related activities that, when performed collectively, achieve a set of goals considered important for enhancing service process capability. Hence, organizations can improve their service capability by implementing these key processes.

We measure the service process maturity of organizations on a five level ordinal scale. The first - initial - level has no associated key process areas. This is the level where all IT service organizations reside that have not implemented the level two key process areas. Level two is the repeatable level. Organizations that have reached level two will be able to repeat earlier successes in similar circumstances. Thus the emphasis of level two is on getting the IT services right for one customer. On level three, the defined level, the service organization has defined its processes and is using tailored versions of these standard processes to deliver the services. By using common organization-wide standard processes, the process capability to deliver services consistently is improved. At level four, the managed level, organizations gain quantitative insight into their service processes and service quality. By using measurements and an organization-wide measurement database, organizations are able to set and achieve quantitative quality goals. Finally, at level five, the optimizing level, the entire organization is focused on continuous process and service improvement. Using quantitative measurements, the organization prevents problems from recurring by changing the processes. The organization is able to introduce new technologies and services into the organization in an orderly manner.

The IT Service CMM is still being developed (see the IT Service CMM Website (SERC, 2003) for the current status), so what we present here is work in progress. At the time of writing, levels two and three have been fully specified and level four is being developed. The following two sections provide an overview of the level two and three key process areas. Note that the IT Service CMM has been based on the Software CMM, version 1.1 (SEI, 1995) and thus is very similar to the Software CMM in some respects. The five maturity levels are the same and there is some overlap in the key process areas. The advantage of this is that methods that were developed to apply the Software CMM, such as assessment approaches, can be used to apply the IT Service CMM as well.

Level Two

Level two of the IT Service CMM is aimed at repeatable service provision. We give an overview of the level two key process areas, purpose and goals of each key process area.

Overview of the Level Two Key Process Areas

The key process areas for level two are concerned with establishing the processes that enable the organization to repeat earlier successful services in similar situations. We distinguish between two kinds of processes that an organization has to implement on this level. The first category deals with service management: the planning, specification, tracking and evaluation of services. The second category is concerned with service support: processes that support the activities that actually deliver the services.

The management processes on this level look as follows. First, the service provider and the customer draw up an agreement about the services to be delivered, the quality of the services — specified in terms of service levels — and the costs of the services (Service Commitment Management). To ensure that the service levels are realistic, the service provider draws up a service plan that shows the feasibility of the service levels (Service Delivery Planning). During service delivery, the service provider tracks the realized service levels and reports these to the customer on a regular basis to demonstrate that the provider has indeed delivered the services against the promised service levels (Service Tracking and Oversight).

After a period of service provision, the customer and the service provider review the service level agreement to see whether it still conforms to the IT needs of the customer (Service Commitment Management again). Just like the organization draws up a service level agreement with its customer, the organization should also use service level agreements when it delegates parts of the service delivery to third parties (Subcontract Management).

We identify three support processes that a level two organization needs to implement. First, almost all IT services concern the management, operation or maintenance of hardware and software components. Therefore, where necessary for consistent service delivery, these components are put under configuration control. This ensures that at all times the status and history of these components is known, and that changes are controlled (Configuration Management). Second, during the period that the services are delivered, events can occur that need to be resolved by the service provider. These events range from simple requests for service to serious incidents that prevent the customer from using its Information Technology. All these events need to be identified, tracked, resolved and reported to the customer (Event Management). To service the request and to resolve incidents, changes to the configuration may be necessary. The change requests are evaluated by the configuration control board with respect to the service level agreement and risk for the integrity of the configuration. Only after a change request has been approved by the configuration control board will the configuration be changed (Configuration Management again). Finally, to ensure the quality of the services, the service provider deploys quality assurance techniques, such as reviews and audits (Service Quality Assurance).

Purpose and Goals of the Level Two Key Process Areas

This section provides an overview of the purpose and goals of the level two key process areas.

Service Commitment Management

The purpose of Service Commitment Management is that services are specified and realistic service levels are negotiated with the customer in order to deliver services that satisfy the customer's need for IT services. The delivered services, the specified service levels and the customer's service needs are reviewed with the customer on a regular basis. When necessary, the service level agreement is adjusted.

There are two basic issues targeted by this key process area: first, the service to be delivered is specified in a contract — the service level agreement — containing *measurable* service levels. Second, the service levels specified should address the business needs of the customer.

- *Goal 1.* Service commitments are documented.
- *Goal 2.* Service commitments are based on current and future IT service needs of the customer.

Service Delivery Planning

The service delivery is planned in order to ensure that the specified services can indeed be delivered according to the agreed upon service levels. The service delivery planning forms the basis for delivering the services.

- *Goal 1.* Service estimates are documented for use in planning and tracking the actual service delivery.

- *Goal 2.* Service delivery activities and internal commitments are planned and documented.
- *Goal 3.* Affected groups and individuals agree to their commitments related to the service delivery.

Service Tracking and Oversight

Service delivery is being tracked. The realized service levels are compared with the specified service levels and are reported to the customer and management on a regular basis. Corrective actions are taken when actual service delivery deviates from the specified service levels.

The service provider reports to the customer the actual services delivered, the actual service levels, and, when relevant, calamities that hindered accurate service delivery. The service level reports are used as input for the evaluation of service level agreements (see Service Commitment Management).

- *Goal 1.* Actual service delivery is tracked against the specified service levels and reported to the customer.
- *Goal 2.* Corrective actions are taken and managed to closure to prevent actual service delivery from deviate from the specified service levels.
- *Goal 3.* Changes to the service delivery planning are agreed to by the affected groups and individuals.

Subcontract Management

The purpose of Subcontract Management is to select qualified IT subcontractors and manage them effectively.

The service provider can select and hire subcontractors to delegate parts of the service. If this is the case, the service to be delivered by the subcontractors is laid down in a service level agreement. The service provider keeps track of the actual services delivered by the subcontractor and takes corrective actions when the actual service levels deviate from the specified service levels.

- *Goal 1.* The prime contractor selects qualified subcontractors.
- *Goal 2.* The prime contractor and the subcontractor agree to their commitments to each other.
- *Goal 3.* The prime contractor and the subcontractor maintain ongoing communications.
- *Goal 4.* The prime contractor tracks the subcontractor's actual results and performance against its commitments.

Configuration Management

The purpose of Configuration Management is to establish and maintain the integrity of products that are subject to or part of the IT services.

Configuration Management involves the identification of the relevant hardware and software components that need to be put under configuration control. This includes components owned by the customer that are being managed by the service provider, components owned by the provider that are used by the customer and components owned by the provider that are used to deliver the service. Changes to the configuration are evaluated with respect to the service level agreement and with respect to possible risks for the integrity of the configuration.

- *Goal 1.* Selected hardware and software products are identified, controlled, and available.
- *Goal 2.* Changes to the identified hardware and software products are controlled.
- *Goal 3.* Affected groups and individuals are informed of the status and content of configuration baselines.

Event Management

The purpose of Event Management is to identify, register, track, analyze, and resolve events regarding the service delivery. The status of events is communicated with the customer and reported to management.

This key process area concerns the management of events that causes or might cause service delivery to deviate from the agreed upon service levels. Events can be either:

- *Requests for service from users.* For example, requests for a new feature in the software;
- *Incidents that cause or will cause service levels to be lower than agreed upon if no action is being taken.* For example, a server that is down might cause the specified maximum downtime to be exceeded if it is not restarted quickly enough.

To resolve requests for service and incidents, changes to the configuration might be necessary. The decision whether to implement the change request that results from a service request or incident is the concern of configuration management.

- *Goal 1.* Event Management activities are planned.
- *Goal 2.* Events are identified, recorded, analyzed, tracked, and resolved.
- *Goal 3.* Affected groups and individuals are informed of the status of events and action items.

Service Quality Assurance

The purpose of Service Quality Assurance is to provide management with the appropriate visibility into the processes being used and the services being delivered.

Service Quality Assurance involves the reviewing and auditing of working procedures, service delivery activities and work products to see that they comply with applicable standards and procedures. Management and relevant groups are provided with the results of the reviews and audits. Note that whereas Service Tracking and Oversight is concerned with measuring service quality in retrospect, from an external point of view, Service Quality Assurance is concerned with measuring quality in advance, from an internal point of view.

- *Goal 1.* Service quality assurance activities are planned.
- *Goal 2.* Adherence of services and service activities to the applicable standards, procedures and service commitments is verified objectively.
- *Goal 3.* Affected groups and individuals are informed of service quality assurance activities and results.
- *Goal 4.* Non-compliance issues that cannot be resolved within the service delivery group are addressed by senior management.

Level Three

Level three of the IT Service CMM is aimed at standardization of services and processes. We give an overview of the level three key process areas, the purpose and goals of each key process area.

Overview of the Level Three Key Process Areas

An IT service provider at level three has a general description of the services he/she can provide. This description is called a service catalog. This service catalog contains a specification of the services in terms of benefits for the customer. The service catalog also includes the service levels that the provider can guarantee and the price of the services. The decision *what* services to include in the catalog is based on issues external to the IT Service CMM, such as marketing research or contractual obligations (in case of in-house IT service providers). The service catalog is continuously updated with experiences from the actual delivery of services. The key process area that covers these activities is called 'Organization Service Definition'.

At level three, the organization uses standard processes for delivering IT services. The actual development and maintenance of the standard process is the goal of the key process area Organization Process Definition. Which processes the organization needs depends on the services defined in the Organization Service Definition key process area. The aim of organization Process Focus is to make sure that all organizational units are using (a possibly tailored version of) the standard processes, and to improve the standard processes. These two key process areas (Organization Process Definition and Organization Process Focus) are similar to their counterparts in the Software CMM.

Each service delivered in the IT Service CMM follows a tailored version of the standard process. This tailoring is necessary to adapt the standard process to the service commitments at hand. For example, choosing a particular methodology is part of this tailoring step. Tailoring is done in Integrated Service Management key process area. This is the counterpart of the Software CMM key process area Integrated Software Management.

The tailored process is input for the Service Delivery key process area, together with the service commitments and service delivery planning. The purpose of Service Delivery is to execute the tailored process and thus deliver the service to the customer. This is the counterpart of the Software CMM key process area Software Product Engineering.

Because a level three organization uses standard processes, it is necessary to train employees to perform their roles. This is not possible at level two, when standard organization-wide processes are not yet in place. The key process area Training Program is aimed at this. This key process area is similar to the one in the Software CMM, although we place more emphasis on service attitude than the Software CMM does.

At the third level, the organization has implemented organization-wide Resource Management. This key process area is aimed at maintaining control of the resources, hardware, software, and human capacity needed to deliver the services. Before commitments are made to customers, resources are checked. This key process area also assigns responsibility for monitoring resources and trends.

The key process area Problem Management implements the organization-wide investigation of events that occur during service delivery. Practices like root-cause analysis are used to determine underlying problems. Problems are solved by changing either the infrastructure (through Configuration Management), the processes (through Organization Process Definition) or training (through Training Program). The goal of Problem Management is to prevent incidents. Service requests are also subject to investigation in order to detect patterns and trends. Problem Management plays a remotely similar role to that of Peer Reviews in the Software CMM. Both are aimed at removing defects from the 'product'. However, because of the different nature of products and services, Peer Reviews can be used to remove defects before the product is handed over to the customer. With services, this is much more difficult, if not impossible, because services are produced and consumed in parallel.

Intergroup Coordination is similar to the Software CMM counterpart. Its aim is to establish means for communication between the different groups involved in delivering the services to the customer.

Purpose and Goals of the Level Three Key Process Areas

This section provides an overview of the purpose and goals of the level three key process areas.

Organization Service Definition

The Organization Service Definition key process area is aimed at developing and maintaining a description (service catalog) of the services that an organization is able to provide. The services are to be described in terms of benefits for the customer, not in technical terms. The service catalog should also include typical service levels the service provider can deliver and an indication of the price of the services. Which services are in the service catalog largely depends on factors outside the scope of the IT Service CMM. For in-house service providers this may be dictated by the business of the customer; for other service providers this may depend on the mission, business strategy and marketing information. The processes needed to deliver the services in the service catalog are developed by Organization Process Definition. So Organization Service Definition describes the services in terms of benefits for the customer, while Organization Process Definition describes which activities are needed to create the services. Information about the actual delivery of the services is collected and made available to guide in establishing realistic service commitments with customers (Service Commitment Management).

- *Goal 1.* Standard services of the organization are documented.
- *Goal 2.* Information related to the delivery of services is collected, reviewed, and made available.

Organization Process Definition

The purpose of Organization Process Definition is to develop and maintain a usable set of service process assets that improve process performance across services and customers and provide a basis for cumulative, long-term benefits to the service organization. Organization Process Definition involves developing and maintaining the organization's standard service processes, along with related process assets, such as descriptions of process tailoring guidelines and criteria, the organization's service process database[2] and a library of service process-related documentation.

The organization's service process assets are available for use in developing, implementing, and maintaining the services' defined service processes. (Practices related to the development and maintenance of the services' defined service process are described in the Integrated Service Management key process area.)

- *Goal 1.* Standard service processes for the organization's standard services are developed and maintained.
- *Goal 2.* Information related to the use of the organization's standard service processes in delivering services is collected, reviewed, and made available.

Organization Process Focus

The purpose of Organization Process Focus is to establish the organizational responsibility for process activities that improve the organization's overall service process capability.

Organization Process Focus involves developing and maintaining the understanding of the organization's and services' processes and coordinating the activities to assess, develop, maintain, and improve these processes.

The organization provides the long-term commitments and resources to coordinate the development and maintenance of the service processes across current and future service delivery via a process improvement group. This group is responsible for the organization's service process activities. It is specifically responsible for the development and maintenance of the organization's standard service process and related process assets, and it coordinates the process activities.

- *Goal 1.* Service process development and improvement activities are coordinated across the organization.
- *Goal 2.* The strengths and weaknesses of the service processes used are identified relative to a process standard.
- *Goal 3.* Organization-level process development and improvement activities are planned.

Integrated Service Management

The purpose of Integrated Service Management is to integrate the service delivery and management activities into a coherent, defined service process that is tailored from the organization's standard service process and related process assets, which are described in Organization Process Definition.

Integrated Service Management involves developing the service's defined service process and managing the service using this defined service process. The service's defined process is tailored from the organization's standard service process to address the specific characteristics of the service to be delivered.

The service delivery plan (see the key process area Service Delivery Planning) is based on the service's defined service process and describes how the activities of the service's defined service process will be performed and managed. The management of the service levels, effort, cost, schedule, staffing, and other resources is tied to the tasks of the service's defined service process. Since the service's defined service processes are all tailored from the organization's standard service processes, services can share process data and lessons learned.

The basic practices for estimating, planning, and tracking service delivery are described in the Service Delivery Planning and Service Tracking and Oversight key process areas. They focus on recognizing problems when they occur and adjusting the plans and/or performance to address the problems. The practices of this key process area build on, and are in addition to, the practices of those two key process areas. The emphasis of Integrated Service Management shifts to anticipating problems and acting to prevent or minimize the effects of these problems.

- *Goal 1.* The service's defined service process is a tailored version of the organization's standard service process.
- *Goal 2.* Service delivery is planned and managed according to the service's defined service process.

Service Delivery

The purpose of Service Delivery is to consistently perform a well-defined service process that integrates all the service activities to deliver correct and consistent IT services effectively and efficiently.

Service Delivery involves performing the service activities to operate, manage and maintain the IT using the service's defined service process (which is described in the Integrated Service Management key process area) and appropriate methods and tools. Documentation needed to perform the service delivery activities (e.g., service commitments and service delivery planning) is developed and reviewed to ensure that each task addresses the result of predecessor tasks and the results produced are appropriate for the subsequent tasks. When changes are approved, affected work products, plans, commitments, processes, and activities are revised to reflect the approved changes.

- *Goal 1.* The service delivery activities are defined, integrated, and consistently per formed to deliver the service.
- *Goal 2.* Service work products are kept consistent with each other.

Intergroup Coordination

The purpose of Intergroup Coordination is to establish a means for the service groups to participate actively with each other so service delivery is more likely to satisfy the customer's needs effectively and efficiently.

Intergroup Coordination involves the service delivery groups' participation with other service groups to address the service commitments, service schedule and other issues. Representatives of the service groups participate in establishing the service commitments and plans by working with the customer and end users, as appropriate. These commitments and plans become the basis for all service activities.

The technical working interfaces and interactions between groups are planned and managed to ensure the quality and integrity of all delivered services. Technical reviews and interchanges are regularly conducted with representatives of the service groups to ensure that all service groups are aware of the status and plans of all the groups and that service and intergroup issues receive appropriate attention.

- *Goal 1.* The service commitments are agreed to by all affected groups.
- *Goal 2.* The commitments between the service groups are agreed to by all affected groups.
- *Goal 3.* The service groups identify, track, and resolve intergroup issues.

Training Program

The purpose of the Training Program key process area is to develop the attitude, skills, and knowledge of individuals so they can perform their roles effectively and efficiently.

Training Program involves first identifying the training needed by the organization, services, and individuals, then developing or procuring training to address the identified needs.

For each service, the current and future skill needs are evaluated and it is determined how these skills will be obtained. Some skills are best imparted through informal vehicles (e.g., on-the-job training and informal mentoring), whereas other skills need more formal training vehicles (e.g., classroom training and guided self-study) to be effectively and efficiently imparted. The appropriate vehicles are selected and used. This key process area covers the practices for groups performing the training function. The practices identifying the specific training topics (i.e., attitude, knowledge, or skills needed) are contained in the ability to perform common feature of the individual key process areas.

- *Goal 1.* Training activities are planned.
- *Goal 2.* Training for developing the attitude, skills, and knowledge needed to perform service management and technical roles is provided.
- *Goal 3.* Individuals in the service delivery and service groups receive the training necessary to perform their roles.

Problem Management

The purpose of the Problem Management key process area is to remove problems from the IT that is managed, maintained or operated by the service provider.

Problem Management analyzes the incidents and service requests that occur during service delivery for patterns. Underlying causes for the incidents and service requests are identified and analyzed. Changes to the IT are submitted to Configuration Management to solve the problems. Problem Management maintains a list of known errors and work-arounds to be used by Event Management.

- *Goal 1.* Problem management activities are planned.
- *Goal 2.* Problems that occur during service delivery are identified, recorded, analyzed, tracked, and resolved.
- *Goal 3.* Affected groups and individuals are informed of the status of problems.

Resource Management

The purpose of Resource Management is to provide pro-active organization-wide management of resources needed to provide the IT services. This means that based on the service catalog, resources are established (such as network infrastructure and computing capacity). Before service commitments are made to the customer, the needed resources are checked. If not enough resources are available, either the commitments are adapted or extra resources are installed. During service delivery, the amount and availability of resources is tracked to ensure that enough capacity is available to deliver the services.

- *Goal 1.* Resource management activities are planned.
- *Goal 2.* The amount and availability of resources needed for service delivery is identified, planned, and tracked.
- *Goal 3.* Affected groups and individuals are informed of the status of resources.

The IT Service CMM Applied

The IT Service CMM is a description of the processes IT service providers need to implement in order to reach a higher maturity level. The real value of the IT Service CMM has to be proved in practice, by means of applying the model to improve IT service organizations. So far, we have done eight assessments in seven different organizations in the United States and the Netherlands. In each of these assessments, software maintenance and IT service organizations were compared with the IT Service CMM. Two of these assessments are described in Niessink (2000). Unfortunately, due to issues of confidentiality we cannot discuss these assessments in great detail here.

In each of the assessments we compared the organization with level two of the IT Service CMM. The organizations assessed varied from a maintenance team of 15 people to an organization of about 500 IT professionals. Two of the organizations assessed are IT organizations, two are government organizations, two are financial service providers and one of the organizations is an energy corporation.

During all but one of these assessments we used a lightweight self-assessment approach, similar to Wiegers et al. (2000), called A2I: *Assess to Improve*. See the IT Service CMM Website (SERC, 2003) for more information about the A2I method.

Each of these eight assessments confirmed the suitability of the level two key process areas and none of the assessments led to any substantial adjustments of the model itself.

CONCLUSIONS

In this chapter we have described the differences between products and services in general, and between software maintenance and software development in particular.

We have shown how the differences between services and products affect the way in which customers judge the quality of products and services and hence how these differences affect organizations that maintain software. From these differences we have deduced four processes that pertain to the quality of software maintenance:

- Translate customer expectations with respect to maintenance into clear service agreements.
- Use these service agreements as a basis for planning and implementing maintenance activities.
- Ensure that maintenance is done according to planning and procedures.
- Manage the communication about the maintenance activities carried out.

Software maintenance organizations can improve the quality of their services, not only by improving the technical quality of their work -less faults, better functionality- but also by improving the functional quality of software maintenance -that is, by implementing the above processes.

The IT Service CMM is a maturity model that aims to describe the key processes needed for software maintenance and other IT service organizations to reach a higher level of maturity. The IT Service CMM is derived from and similar to the Software CMM, but is aimed at IT service providers instead of software development organizations. Despite the fact the IT Service CMM is still under development, the model can already be used to assess and improve software maintenance organization. We have performed eight assessments in seven different organizations and have found the model a useful tool to determine the current process maturity of software maintenance organizations and suggest ways to improve these organizations.

ACKNOWLEDGMENTS

This research was partly supported by the Dutch Ministry of Economic Affairs, project 'KWINTES', No. ITU 96024. Partners in this project were Cap Gemini, Twijnstra Gudde, the Tax and Customs Computer and Software Centre of the Dutch Tax and Customs Administration, the Technical Universities of Delft and Eindhoven, and the Vrije Universiteit Amsterdam. The IT Service CMM is an idea from Prof. Hans van Vliet. We gratefully acknowledge the support of the companies and employees that performed the assessments. Finally, we thank the anonymous reviewers for their suggestions and Professor Khaled Khan at the University of Western Sydney for his support in finalizing this chapter.

This chapter is based on work published in Niessink (2000) and Niessink et al. (1998, 2000, 2002) and on work done in the DOCIS project (SERC, 2003).

ENDNOTES

1 CMM® is registered in the U.S. patent and Trademark Office. Accuracy and interpretation of this document are the responsibility of Software Engineering Research Centre. Carnegie Mellon University has not participated in this publication.

2 The service process database contains data on the execution of processes, such as estimates on workload, effort, and costs, productivity data, service level measurements, number of incidents, and so forth.

REFERENCES

Berry, L., & Parasuraman, A. (1991). *Marketing services: Competing through quality.* The Free Press, Macmillan Inc.

Briand, L., Kin, Y., Melo, W., Seaman, C., & Basili, V. (1998). QMOPP: Qualititative evaluation of maintenance organizations, processes and products. *Journal of Software Maintenance: Research and Practice*, *10*(4), 249-278. John Wiley & Sons.

Central Computer and Telecommunications Agency (CCTA). (2000). *Best practice for service support. IT infrastructure library.* London: The Stationary Office.

Drew, D. (1992). Tailoring the Software Engineering Institute's (SEI) Capability Maturity Model (CMM) to a software sustaining engineering organization. *Proceedings of the Conference on Software Maintenance*, IEEE Computer Society, 137-144.

Finkelstein, A., & Kramer, J. (2000). Software engineering: A roadmap. The future of software engineering. *22nd International Conference on Software Engineering*, 5-22. ACM Press.

Grönroos, C. (1990). *Service management and marketing: Managing the moments of truth in service competition.* Lexington, MA: Lexington Books.

Niessink, F. (2000). *Perspectives on improving software maintenance.* Ph.D. Thesis, Division of Mathematics and Computer Science, Faculty of Sciences, Vrije Universiteit Amsterdam, The Netherlands.

Niessink, F., & van Vliet, H. (1998). Towards mature IT services. *Software Process – Improvement and Practice*, *4*(22), 55-71.

Niessink, F., & van Vliet, H. (2000). Software maintenance from a service perspective. *Journal of Software Maintenance: Research and Practice*, *12*(2),103-120.

Niessink, F., Clerc, V., & van Vliet, H. (2002). *The IT service Capability Maturity Model* (Technical Report Model version L2+3-0.3). Software Engineering Research Centre.

Office of the Government Commerce (OGC). (2001). *Best practice for service delivery. IT infrastructure library.* London: The Stationary Office.

Onoma, A., Tsai, W., Tsunoda, F., Suganuma, H., & Subramanian, S. (1995). Software maintenance — An industrial experience. *Journal of Software Maintenance: Research and Practice*, *7*, 333-375.

Paulk, M., Weber, C., Curtis, B., & Chrissis, M. (1995). The Capability Maturity Model: Guidelines for improving the software process. *SEI series in software engineering.* Reading, MA: Addison-Wesley Publishing Company.

Pigoski, T. (1996). *Practical software maintenance: Best practices for managing your software investment.* John Wiley & Sons.

Pitt, L.F., Watson, R.T., & Kavan, C.B. (1995). Service quality: A measure of information systems effectiveness. *Management Information Systems Quarterly*, *19*(2),173-187.

Singer, J. (1998). Practices of software maintenance. *Proceedings of the International Conference on Software Maintenance*, 139-145. IEEE Computer Society.

Software Engineering Research Centre (SERC). (2003). The IT service CMM website: *http://www.itservicecmm.org*

Stålhane, T., Borgersen, P., & Arnesen, K. (1997). In search of the customer's quality view. *The Journal of Systems and Software, 38*(1), 85-93.

Stark, G., & Oman, P. (1997). Software maintenance management strategies: Observations from the field. *Journal of Software Maintenance: Research and Practice*, *99*(6), 365-378.

Watson, R.T, Pitt, L.F., & Kavan, C.B. (1998). Measuring information systems service quality: Lessons from two longitudinal case studies. *Management Information Systems Quarterly*, *22*(1), 61-79.

West, R. (2000). Improving the maintainability of software (book review). *Journal of Software Maintenance: Research and Practice, 8*(5), 345-356.

Wiegers, K., & Sturzenberger, D. (2000). A modular software process mini-assessment method. *IEEE Software*, *17*(1), 62-69.

Zeithaml, V., & Bitner, M. (1996). Services marketing. *McGraw-Hill series in marketing.* McGraw-Hill.

Chapter IV

Upfront Corrective Maintenance at the Front-End Support Level

Mira Kajko-Mattsson
Stockholm University/Royal Institute of Technology, Sweden

ABSTRACT

This chapter presents the process of upfront corrective maintenance at the front-end support level. The chapter is logically divided into two parts. The first part introduces the domain of the upfront corrective maintenance process, and presents its current status practised in the industry. It first describes the process, places it within a global virtual IT enterprise and explains its role within the enterprise. It then puts the process in the context of a total front-end support process, the process performing a multitude of diverse types of support activities. Finally, it lists the problems encountered by the front-support organisations today. The second part provides a glimpse into Corrective Maintenance Maturity Model (CM^3): Upfront Maintenance, a process model specialised in upfront corrective maintenance. It describes its process phases, maturity levels, and collaboration with the CM^3: Problem Management model, a problem management process model at the back-end support level. The goal of this chapter is to provide a detailed insight of the process of upfront corrective maintenance.

INTRODUCTION

Recently, one has realised that the value of the IT (Information Technology) business does not only lie in the products it offers, but also in the needs it serves (Kalakota, 2001; Nelson, 2002). Service quality has become a critical survivability factor.

Figure 1: CM³ Roadmap — Organisational Perspective (Kajko-Mattsson, 2003a).

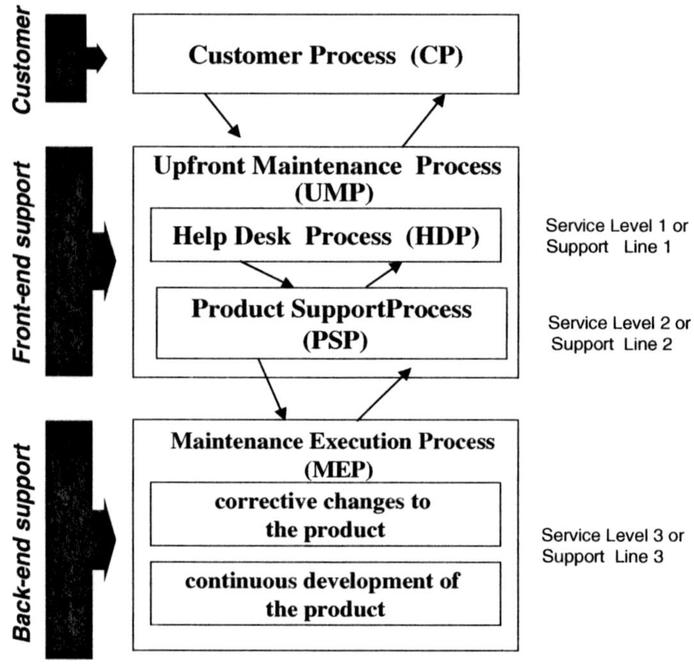

More and more customers require that the IT companies continuously improve the overall quality of the service they provide. They count service as a key reason for doing business.

With the shared objective of pleasing customers and providing high quality service, the collaborating IT companies organise themselves into so-called virtual IT enterprises, acting as single confluent units handling both B2B[1] and B2C[2] operations. By integrating their processes and applications, they strive to achieve a global inter-organisational co-operation, which in turn would help them to provide their customers with timely, seamless and effective supports on a specific software product or a group of products.

The *CM³ Organisational Roadmap* in Figure 1 depicts the most common constellation of the virtual IT enterprises. This constellation encompasses three groups of organisational levels: (1) customer, (2) front-end support, and (3) back-end support. These three levels play different roles within the enterprise. The customer uses software products and states new requirements for evolving and maintaining them. The front-end support assists the customer in the daily operation of the software products (Kriegsman et al., 1993; Niessink, 2000). The back-end support evolves and maintains the products according to the requirements as requested by the customer.

The front-end support organisations play an important role within corrective maintenance. They receive reports on different types of software problems from customers, transfer them on to the back-end support, and deliver problem solutions from the back-end support to the customers. We say that they conduct upfront corrective maintenance. Their main role is to relieve the back-end support from communicating with customers, thus helping it concentrate on the actual development, evolution, and maintenance work (Kajko-Mattsson et al., 2000).

The front-end support organisations substantially contribute to the efficiency of the IT enterprise. They are very important from the perspective of product quality and enterprise productivity and survivability. By keeping track of the customers, their products, and problems, they contribute to the optimisation of the product, optimisation of the customer satisfaction, and optimisation of the overall development and maintenance processes (Hart, 1993). The customer profits from the front-end maintainers' know-how and the back-end support gains data on product quality, adherence to user expectations, product use patterns, the requirements for future enhancements/adaptations, and design improvements (Hart 1993; Zuther, 1998). Finally, the enterprise gains feedback on upfront maintenance processes, which is, in turn, pivotal for understanding the overall scope and dimension of the enterprise-wide corrective maintenance.

The front-end support process is important for achieving global process maturity within the whole IT enterprise. If well-defined and adhered to, it contributes to its overall efficiency. If run in an ad-hoc manner, it may substantially undermine and even contaminate other healthy processes within the enterprise. Despite this importance, however, the front-end support has been hitherto strongly neglected. It is under-researched and immature in comparison with other software engineering disciplines. The standard process models barely touch on this subject. To our knowledge, there are only two support process models today (Kajko-Mattsson et al., 2001a; Niessink, 2000). One of them is *CM³: Upfront Maintenance*, to be presented in this chapter.

Recently, the front-end support has grown in importance. This is due to its immense cost and the desire to increase customer satisfaction. It is estimated that to give support to the customers worldwide costs about 80% of the enterprises' IT-related investments (Bouman et al., 1999). This very high cost is due to many reasons. The main ones are fast globalisation of the markets, worldwide geographical distribution of customers, rising dependency on exports, increasing complexity of new products, increasing frequency of new releases, and immaturity of the front-end support processes (Bouman et al., 1999; Nihei et al., 1998; Zuther, 1999).

This chapter presents upfront corrective maintenance at the front-end support level. It is logically divided into two parts. The first part introduces the domain of the upfront corrective maintenance, and presents its current status within the industry. It consists of the sections: *Virtual IT Enterprise, Diversity of Front-End Support* and *Problems within Support. Virtual IT Enterprise* describes the front-end support process, places it within a global virtual IT enterprise, and explains its role within the enterprise. It also describes different constellations of the virtual IT enterprises and co-operation amongst them. *Diversity of Front-End Support* identifies the diverse types of activities conducted at the front-end support level. *Problems within Support* points out the problems encountered by the front-end support organisations today.

The second part of this chapter provides a glimpse into an upfront corrective maintenance process model. It consists of one section, *CM³: Upfront Maintenance.* This section presents *Corrective Maintenance Maturity Model (CM³): Upfront Maintenance,* a constituent process model of *Corrective Maintenance Maturity Model (CM³).*

It describes its process phases, suggests issues that are important for achieving an efficient process, presents its maturity levels, and depicts a collaboration with *CM³: Problem Management* — a corrective maintenance process model at the back-end support level (Kajko-Mattsson, 2001c, 2002a).

VIRTUAL IT ENTERPRISE

Corrective maintenance may be conducted by one or several organisations, departments, teams and/or even individuals. Usually, it is performed by several co-operating organisations, building a so-called virtual IT enterprise (Kajko-Mattsson, 2003a). Such an enterprise is logically divided into three organisational levels, where each level plays a clearly defined role within corrective maintenance. *Upfront Maintenance within a Virtual IT Enterprise* describes the role of each level within corrective maintenance. This description is based on the most common constellation of the virtual IT enterprises, as depicted in Figure 1. The constellations of the enterprises may differ widely within the industry. *Infrastructures of Virtual IT Enterprises* shows these differences. Finally, *World-wide Global Co-operation* briefly describes how the organisations belonging to the same virtual IT unit collaborate worldwide.

Upfront Maintenance within a Virtual IT Enterprise

As depicted in Figures 1 and 2, a virtual IT enterprise consists of customer, front-end support and back-end support levels. The customer is the service acquirer. It may be a person or an organisation. The support is the service provider. It is a software

Figure 2: Visualising the Co-Operation in the Virtual IT Enterprise.

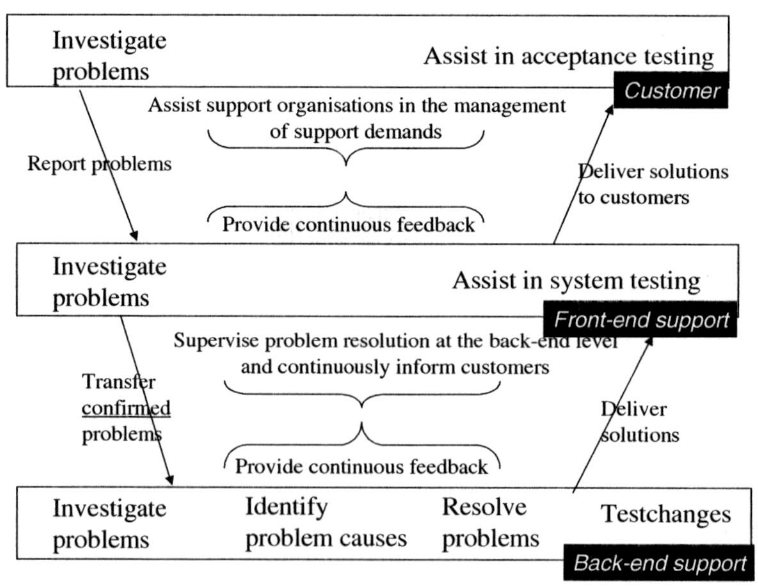

organisation. It performs development and maintenance for the customer. The actual development and maintenance is conducted by the back-end support level. Within corrective maintenance, we call it *Maintenance Execution Process level (MEP).* The communication between the customer and back-end support is managed by the front-end support. Within corrective maintenance, we call it *Upfront Maintenance Process* level *(UMP).*

The front-end support further consists of two levels: *Help Desk Process level (HDP)*, and *Product Support Process level (PSP).* The *Help Desk Process* level, usually denoted as *Service Level 1* or *Support Line 1,* is the customers' first and preferably the only point of contact. Its main role is to guarantee the continuity of customers' daily business operation. At this level, the engineers support a wide range of customers and products.

The support engineers at this level possess a general knowledge of the software products they are supporting. Hence, they may not always be competent enough to attend to all the customer demands. Usually, they are able to attend to 70-80% of all the demands requested by the customer. The remaining demands, those requiring further attention and higher expertise (due to their complex character) or those concerning corrective maintenance are channelled to the *PSP* process level.

Regarding the corrective maintenance demands (reported software problems), the *HDP* organisations are obliged to first investigate the reported software problems, confirm that they are in fact problems and that they are unique (unknown)[3] before transferring them on (or escalating them in the industrial parlance) to the next service level, that is, the *PSP* level. If a software problem is already known to the organisation (the problem is a duplicate), then the *HDP* level should not further report it to the *PSP* level. It may, however, complement the original problem description with the additional information elicited from the recent duplicate problem report. This complementary addition might substantially help resolve the problem.

At the *PSP* process level, usually denoted *as Service Level 2* or *Support Line 2,* the support engineers are more competent with respect to the supported products. Their main role is to assist the *HDP* engineers in attending to more difficult tasks. Within corrective maintenance, they should repeat the same tasks of the *HDP* level; that is, they should investigate the reported software problems, confirm that they are problems, that they are unique problems, and make decisions whether to escalate them to the *MEP* level at the back-end support level. If they encounter a duplicate software problem, then they should not further report it to the *MEP* level. However, they should check whether the description of the duplicate might be used to complement the original description of the problem.

At the *MEP* level, denoted as *Service Level 3* or *Support Line 3,* the maintainers should first investigate and confirm the reported software problem and make decisions whether to resolve it or not. If yes, then they should design one or several problem solutions, evaluate these solutions, choose the most optimal one, implement and test it. Meanwhile, the front-end support supervises the problem resolution at the *MEP* level and continuously informs the customers about its progress. If necessary, the customers should provide feedback to the *MEP* process via the front-end support.

As soon as the system is tested, the *MEP* level delivers the releases containing the problem solutions to the customers affected by the resolved software problem(s). They do it via front-end support, that is, via the *PSP* and *HDP* levels. The front-end support delivers the corrected releases. It also announces them as available for use to all other customers. It does so in order to make the customers conscious of the problems in the product, and prevent them from encountering them.

The astute reader has probably noticed that all the service levels, including the customer level, are obliged to investigate the software problem before reporting it to the next service level. The reason for this is the fact that many problems encountered by customers today are not always software problems. They may be operational mistakes, or duplicate problems. Their management implies additional workload at each subsequent support level and distracts its engineers from concentrating on other important activities. One way of saving resources and decreasing the workload is to require that each service level makes sure that they report on unique software problems to the next service level.

Infrastructures of Virtual IT Enterprises

The constellations (or infrastructures) of the virtual IT enterprises may vary widely within the industry today, especially the three service level constellations (see Service Levels 1-3 in Figure 1) of the front-end and back-end support levels. In this section, we show some examples of different infrastructures that have been built by various enterprises. These infrastructures were elicited in a study of 37 virtual IT enterprises (Kajko-Mattsson, 2003a). In most of our examples below, we exclude the customer level. We only show the differences of the constellations of the Service Levels 1-3.

Figure 3: Infrastructure 1 and Its Six Variants (Kajko-Mattsson, 2003a).

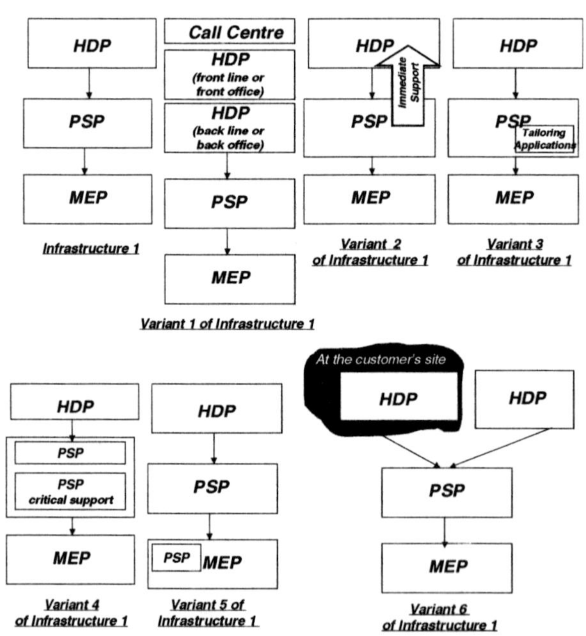

Common Infrastructure

Many large enterprises follow *Infrastructure 1*, the infrastructure suggested by the *CM³: Roadmap: Organisational Perspective,* presented in Figure 1. Their constellations may differ somewhat. The differences, however, are minute. Below, we list all the variants of *Infrastructure 1* and briefly describe their differences. The variants are presented in Figure 3.

- *Variant 1* of *Infrastructure 1:* All the support demands are first registered at the *Call Centre* level, to be immediately dispatched to the *HDP* level. The *HDP* level consists of two sub-levels: the front office and back office. The demand first arrives at the front office, where the engineers attempt to attend to all kinds of problems and difficulties. If it is impossible within the time limit designated for the demand, then the demand escalates to the back office of the *HDP* level. Usually, the same engineer continues with the same demand, but this time, she dedicates more personnel resources to it.
- *Variant 2* of *Infrastructure 1:* The support engineers at the *PSP* level are easily available to the support engineers at the *HDP* level. They often belong to the same department. If the demand is urgent and/or complex and cannot be attended to at the *HDP* level, then the *PSP* engineers immediately set about it.
- *Variant 3* of *Infrastructure 1:* The *PSP* organisations may make minor adaptations of the system to the customer needs, usually with the purpose of knitting together its inherent applications.
- *Variant 4* of *Infrastructure 1:* The *PSP* level may encompass two sub-levels: *Ordinary Support* and *Critical Support*. If the demand is very urgent and critical for the customer's business, then it automatically escalates to the *PSP - Critical Support* level. The main task of this level is to get the system back in business within a predetermined period of time of, for instance, four hours.
- *Variant 5 of Infrastructure 1:* Some *MEP* organisations (at the back-end support level) may conduct additional tasks of the *PSP* level. They provide additional front-end support despite the fact that the customer demands have already been examined at the *HDP* and *PSP* levels. These *MEP* organisations claim that still extra control must be made. They do not rely on their collaborating *HDP* and *PSP* organisations. This is because too many duplicate problems have been unnecessarily escalated to them.
- *Variant 6* of *Infrastructure 1:* Some *HDP* organisations may be situated at the customer's site. The customer's end users should contact the customer *HDP* organisations first. If the demand cannot be attended to at the customer's site, then it is escalated to the organisation providing the *PSP* support.

Other Infrastructures

Many medium-sized and small companies organise themselves, their departments or individuals in other ways. They do not follow the three service level constellation described in the former section. As depicted in Figure 4, most of them follow a two service level constellation instead. Below, we list their infrastructures and briefly describe their differences.

Figure 4: Other Types of Infrastructures (Kajko-Mattsson, 2003a).

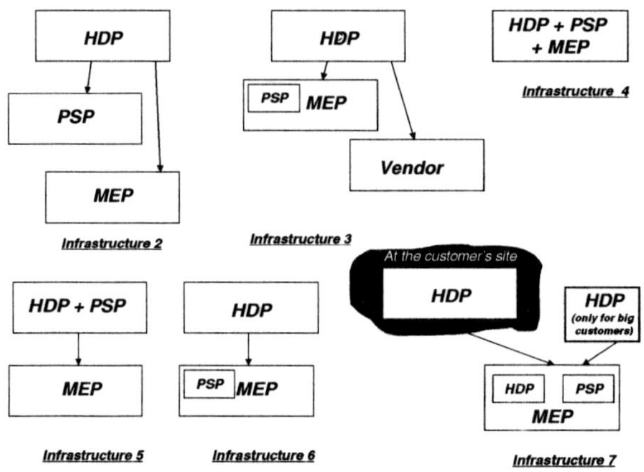

- *Infrastructure 2:* The customer demands are escalated from the *HDP* level either to the *PSP* level or directly to the *MEP* level. This choice is strongly dependent on the demand. If it is a difficult technical problem, then the demand is transferred to the *PSP* level. If it is a suspected software problem then it is immediately escalated to the *MEP* level.
- *Infrastructure 3:* The demands are transferred from the *HDP* level to either a separate vendor, if one discovered a flaw in their products or sub-products, or to an organisation/department executing the combined role of the *PSP* and *MEP* service levels.
- *Infrastructure 4:* This infrastructure reflects the original state of the software organisations at the beginning of the software era. In these years, the software organisations and even individuals executed the varying tasks of all the service levels. Today, the organisations following *Infrastructure 4* are usually small organisations. In our case, they constitute the smallest example of a virtual IT enterprise.
- *Infrastructures 5 and 6:* Some organisations conduct the combined tasks of the *HDP* and *PSP* levels or the combined tasks of the *PSP* and *MEP* levels.
- *Infrastructure 7:* This infrastructure varies depending on the customer. It may execute a combined process of the *HDP*, *PSP* and *MEP* levels, as described in *Infrastructure 4*. For some customers, its *HDP* process may be executed by either the *HDP* organisations placed at the customers' site, or specially created *HDP* departments/teams within their own organisation.

WORLDWIDE GLOBAL CO-OPERATION

Large virtual IT enterprises may support thousands of customers geographically dispersed all over the world. All these customers should have easy access to the *HDP* organisations. To efficiently provide support, many enterprises ascertain that at least

Figure 5: Illustrating a World-Wide Distribution of a Virtual IT Enterprise.

one *HDP* organisation is placed in a vicinity of the customer. For instance, if an enterprise has a customer in Argentina, then it places one *HDP* organisation in Argentina. The enterprise may however increase the number of *HDP* organisations in a certain country. This would depend on the number of customers, their needs, and the complexity and severity of the supported product.

Some very big enterprises may encompass hundreds of *HDP* organisations spread all over the world. These *HDP* organisations should in turn have easy access to the *PSP* organisations at the next support level. Usually, one places at least *one PSP* organisation within one and the same time zone and/or continent. The number of *PSP* organisations depends on the amount and frequency of support as required by the *HDP* organisations.

Let us have a look at Figure 5, showing a worldwide distribution of a virtual enterprise supporting one specific software product or group of products developed in Sweden. The enterprise encompasses the organisations at all three service levels: the *HDP*, *PSP* and *MEP* levels. As can be seen in Figure 5, a product that has been developed and maintained by one organisation in Sweden (identified with a bull's eye) may be attended to by many support organisations in the world, sometimes more than 100 organisations, as is the case of ABB (Kajko-Mattsson et al., 2001a). The *HDP* organisations (identified with a hollow circle) are distributed all over the world. They are placed in every country where first line support is required. Their supporting *PSP* organisations (identified with a hollow circle with a plus inside), on the other hand, are geographically distributed according to a time zone. Within some time zones, there may be need for several *PSP* organisations, as is the case of the European time zone in Figure 5.

DIVERSITY OF FRONT-END SUPPORT

Front-end support is one of the most diverse processes within an enterprise. It typically manages diverse customers, where each customer requires a different degree of support. This degree usually depends on factors such as varying service level

Table 1: Types of Front-End Support Activities (Kajko-Mattsson, 2003b).

• *Software problem management*	• *Self Education and Training*
• *Testing*	• *Preventive maintenance activities*
• *Participation in the change management process*	• *Passive requirements elicitation*
• *Quality management*	• *Active requirements elicitation*
• *Consultation*	• *Various monitoring activities*
• *Technical support*	• *Management of customer profile*
• *Education and Training of Customers*	• *Measurement of customer satisfaction*
	• *Emergency corrective maintenance*

agreements (SLAs), and varying packages of product applications that are, in turn, implemented in a great variety of different environments.

It is not only customers, their products and product environments that vary. The support demands and the ways of attending to them may vary as well. The character of the demands ranges from simple requests for help to problem management within corrective maintenance. These demands may be communicated via a tool, email, telephone, Internet, and other media. Table 1 lists some of the types of front-end support activities, elicited in Kajko-Mattsson (2003b). Most of them are more or less integrated or related to the evolution and maintenance work, as briefly described in the following texts.

- *Software problem management:* As described earlier, front-end support organisations constitute a communication bridge between the customer and back-end support organisations. They receive problem reports from the customers, transfer them to the *back-end* support level, and deliver solutions to the customers.
- *Testing:* Front-end support engineers are a highly valuable resource within system testing. There are very few ones within the whole IT enterprise who have the complete "big picture" of the system, and knowledge of how the product is operated on by its users. This is because they are continuously exposed to different types of problems and difficulties encountered by the customers. They conduct two types of testing: pre-maintenance testing and post-evolution and post-maintenance testing. The first type of testing takes place when customers report on newly encountered software problems. While investigating them, the front-end support engineers conduct black box testing in order to confirm the presence of a software problem. Here, the testing is conducted before any changes are made to the product. Regarding the second type of testing, the front-end support engineers are involved in mainly system testing, during which extensions, adaptations, and corrections are being tested.
- *Participation in the change management process:* The front-end support often participates in the change management process. Most of the enterprises have an

enterprise-wide authority called a *Change Control Board (CCB),* mainly involved in the approval of suggestions for changes and plans for their realisation. Its members represent various roles within the enterprise who have interest in deciding upon changes. Some of its members come from the front-end support. Their role is to examine the appropriateness and correctness of the changes from the customer- and front-end support perspective.

- *Quality management:* The front-end support engineers do not only possess the best knowledge of the needs and requirements of their customers. They also have experience of how these systems are used by the end users. They gain feedback on the quality of the system as perceived by the customers. This knowledge and experience is extremely valuable when monitoring and improving product quality. Hence, the front-end support engineers are involved in different types of quality audits.
- *Consultation:* Customers need support in the daily operation of their applications. Many times, the front-end support organisations provide answers to different types of questions or give advice and simple suggestions for various types of operational hints, added values, and solutions. They may also provide specialised consultation requiring high technical expertise such as investigation of an IT design and architecture or design of security systems.
- *Technical support:* The front-end support organisations conduct various types of technical support activities such as assembly of hardware and software configurations, installations of different upgrades.
- *Education and training of customers:* Some front-end support organisations educate and train their customers. They continuously keep a watchful eye on the customers' competence, recommend education and training to the customers, if needed, prepare courses and educational material, give courses, and evaluate and improve these courses.
- *Self-education and training:* Due to the fact that the front-end support must work from the very first minute a system or its new release is delivered, the front-end support engineers must learn the new system features while they are being implemented (Pigoski, 1997). Otherwise, they cannot conduct efficient support. Lack of or insufficient self-education and training are a substantial productivity reducer at the front-end support level.
- *Preventive maintenance activities:* A subset of support activities concerns preventive maintenance, such as announcement of corrected releases to all customers (Adams, 1994), investigation and elimination of negative trends, building and maintaining user knowledge (Calow, 1991; Chapin, 1995), and the like.
- *Passive requirements elicitation:* Many times, the customers, together with the front-end support engineers, discover needs for new functionality or adaptations. The front-end support engineers should further report this discovery to the marketing and sales department/organisation (see our next type – *active requirements gathering*), whose task is to collect new requirements.
- *Active requirements elicitation:* Some front-end support organisations are active on gathering requirements for change. Usually, they are the marketing and sales departments/organisations placed at the *PSP* process level. They continuously keep in touch with their customers in order to gather new requirements. Many times, they also build visions of future requirements. In order to do this, they should not

only possess a thorough knowledge of the product but also of their customers, their businesses, and future needs.

- *Various monitoring activities:* The front-end support organisations continuously monitor the support process and provide feedback to all parties concerned. They monitor trends in order to identify deficiencies in the customers, and in their own and other support organisations' processes. This provides feedback important for modifying service level agreements and for improving the enterprise-wide support process. Front-end support organisations also supervise the problem management at the *back-end process* level in order to make the customers informed about the progress.
- *Management of customer profile:* The front-end support organisations keep records about their customers and their businesses in the so-called customer profiles. These data are important for delivering quality service to customers.
- *Measurement of customer satisfaction:* The front-end support organisations conduct different types of surveys in order to gather feedback on product and service quality.
- *Emergency corrective maintenance:* Usually, it is the front-end support that must first handle all types of emergency cases. If the problem is severe, then the front-end support acquires immediate help from the back-end service level. Emergency often means that customer operation is disrupted by some serious acute problem(s). The consequences may sometimes imply danger to human life, failure of a company, or substantial degradation in its operation. Hence, its resolution should have the highest urgency. The front-end support organisations should take part in identifying the problem, suggest and implement the immediate, often temporary solutions (usually called work-arounds in the industry), and recover the corrupted data and/or corrupted system parts, if possible.

Above, we have listed most of the support activity types conducted at the front-end support level. This does not mean that all the front-end support organisations conduct all of these types. They usually conduct a subset of them. The choice varies from enterprise to enterprise. Irrespective of this, we may draw a conclusion that the front-end support activities are greatly diversified.

The diversity of the front-end support types is reflected in the processes executed by the front-end support engineers. To be able to attend to the varying demands, the support process itself must be diversified, where each support type should follow its own specific sub-process. Many times, the front-end support engineers may conduct several different tasks simultaneously. For instance, the customer asks for advice on how to conduct a certain operation in order to leave a specific system state. When assisting the customer, the support engineer gives advice by demonstrating a work-around (temporary solution). When doing this, she may discover that the system does not behave as it should, even if the work-around has been implemented. What she should do is to analyse the system behaviour, check the global solution database in search of similar misbehaviours, find its underlying cause(s) either in the solution database or by executing the software herself, and if possible, eliminate it/them. She should update the global solution database with the incident and its temporary solution. This would provide feedback for updating the solution database with a new symptom for a probably not yet identified software problem. In cases when it is a software problem, she should identify it, confirm it, and escalate it to the next service level.

The above-mentioned example shows that several support activity types can be performed simultaneously. Here, we have identified four different types: (1) consultation, (2) problem management within corrective maintenance, (3) quality control, and (4) preventive maintenance. When expiating them, the front-end support engineer does not separately execute the organisational processes defined for each activity type. She rather integrates and tailors them "on the fly" in order to adapt to the customer demand and the service level agreement with the customer concerned. Still, however, she should not forget to separately record all these individual processes and their steps and relate them to the appropriate activity type.

PROBLEMS WITHIN FRONT-END SUPPORT

Front-end support organisations struggle with many problems today. In Kajko-Mattsson (2003c), we have identified four groups of problem categories within 37 front-end support organisations. Due to the fact that many problems are tightly interrelated to one another, it is difficult to categorise and divide them into exclusive partitions. Hence, our categories may somewhat overlap. The four identified categories are: *organisational problems, process problems, role problems*, and *product problems*.

Organisational Problems

The organisational problems concern the state and structure of the front-end support organisations. We have discerned three organisational problems: (1) size and complexity of front-end support organisations, (2) growing pains, and (3) continuous organisational restructuring.

Size and Complexity of Front-End Support Organisations

Many enterprises are large, highly decentralised and complex units consisting of many collaborating organisations, each having different cultural, language, political, time zone, and administrative barriers. These organisations often encounter many difficulties and problems when collaborating with one another. Some examples of them are: (1) communication difficulties with other support organisations at the same, higher, or lower service level, (2) difficulties in finding pertinent expertise, (3) ineffective decision-making, (4) co-operation difficulties due to time differences, (5) lack of global process visibility, and (6) difficulties in defining problem ownership (the responsibility for resolving a software problem).

Growing Pains

Some front-end support organisations are growing very fast. The number of customers and products to be supported is rapidly increasing. Their support processes have difficulties in catching up with this growth. This in turn results in personnel shortage, difficulties in learning new products and customers, and the inability to provide quality support.

Continuous Organisational Restructuring

Regarding the front-end support as a cost, not as a resource, one tries to optimise it as much as possible. Unfortunately, the optimisation is made too often and within too short periods of time. Support organisations are either merged or split into one or several organisations. This in turn results in changes in team structures, changes in product portfolios, dismissals, new employment, or rotation of personnel. All these changes lead to confusion with respect to who should support what, high personnel turnover, enormous costs to educate new hires in cases of new employment, additional workload for those who have stayed in cases of dismissals, loss of control of who to talk to, bad atmosphere within the front-end support organisations, and low motivation for conducting front-end support.

Process Problems

The process problems relate to the state and execution manner of the front-end support process. We have identified three groups of process problems: (1) process definition and adherence problems, (2) communication and relationship problems with other support organisations, and (3) problems in achieving customer satisfaction.

Process Definition and Adherence Problems

The organisations have difficulties in defining and establishing en effective front-end support process. Lack of an exhaustive process definition means that it is not always clear when and how to conduct certain process steps; for example, (1) when we should escalate the customer demand to the next support level, (2) when and how we should inform the customer about the progress, (3) how we should tackle unexpected events, and (4) how soon the support personnel should be available.

Even if the process is defined, it is not always certain whether it appropriately reflects the multitude and diversity of the front-end support activities. The process definition may be too general or too fixed and rigid, not covering important process nuances and situations. In some organisations, the process may be satisfactorily defined, however, not adhered to. Lack of process definition and adherence results in vague process visibility, non-uniform management of the front-end support tasks, and difficulties in tackling unexpected and unplanned events.

Communication and Relationship Problems with other Support Organisations

The front-end support organisations do not only communicate with customers, but also with other support organisations at any service level. Many times, these other organisations are situated in different countries. This substantially affects co-operation and common decision-making. The organisations have difficulties in communicating on solutions or work-arounds. They have problems concerning the escalation of the maintenance demands to the next service level; the lower support levels may escalate a problem report too early, without confirming the problem first (Kajko-Mattsson et al., 2000). Finally, the organisations have problems with getting/providing input from/to the engineers at the *MEL* (back-end support) level.

Customer Satisfaction Problems

Today, many support organisations have problems in meeting customer expectations and in providing timely feedback to their customers. All this strongly affects the relationship between the front-end support and customer organisations.

Many of the customer demands are unrealistic; for instance, the customers expect their demands to be fulfilled immediately. They do not understand their complexity and dimension. They do not realise that the demands may require substantial effort to be attended to.

Sometimes, the end-users of the customer organisations expect more support than they have the right to get. They simply do not possess the knowledge of the contents of the service level agreements. A lot of effort goes to explaining to the customers that they are not entitled to a certain service type.

Some service demands are time-consuming. It may take time to attend to them, especially in cases when several service levels are involved. Today, many front-end support organisations lack procedures and routines for continuously informing customers about the progress of attending to their service demands. They lack clear directives for who should inform who, when, and how. This strongly affects the customer satisfaction. Anxious to know, the customers contact the front-end support organisations demanding progress reports. This results in an unnecessary and time-consuming communication.

Role Problems

The role problems concern the ability to successfully fulfil a specific role within the enterprise. We have discerned two groups of role problems: maintainer and customer role problems.

Maintainer Role Problems

Many organisations suffer from personnel shortage. Often, the front-end support personnel works under stress and enormous workload. Lack of time and resources prevents them from providing quality service. Their work situation gets seriously aggravated by the unplanned absence such as sick leave, sudden emergency trips to the customer premises, quick company growth, or unexpected fire-fighting situations.

The personnel shortage often implies lack of competent personnel. The front-end support personnel should possess technical qualifications, knowledge of the application domain, and communication skills. Unfortunately, it is difficult to keep and recruit competent personnel today. In some organisations, the competence may be unevenly distributed, especially in organisations providing two types of front-end support: (1) agreement based support given to customer organisations, and (2) volume support given to private customers.

Concerning the first type of support, the organisations are very anxious to provide high quality support. They see to it that their engineers possess all types of necessary qualifications. Their work is often based on personal relations with the representatives coming from the customer organisations. The quality of support and customer satisfaction is under continuous monitoring and control.

Regarding the second type of support, the support engineers may sometimes lack competence in communication skills. Their work is not based on any personal relations at all. The customer turnover is very high and very little control of customer satisfaction is being made. All this makes the support work highly boring and non-motivating.

Personnel shortage and lack of competent personnel are often the main reasons for why the knowledge of the supported product(s) is not uniformly distributed within the organisation. A very typical scenario is that one or very few support engineers know the whole product, or its specific parts. This leads to severe security risks such as unplanned absence implying difficulties in finding quick substitutes, or loss of knowledge and competence when the personnel quit.

Customer Role Problem

Customers do not always possess the required knowledge of the products they are using. They may use the products incorrectly, get incorrect results, lose data, or think that the products are not working correctly. They may report on software problems, which later show to be operational mistakes. This, in turn, requires extra effort spent on explaining to the customers that the reported problems were due to their lack of product knowledge.

Product Problems

The product problems concern the state of the supported software products and difficulties in supporting them. We have identified two groups of product problems: (1) complexity of solutions (applications and their platforms), and (2) bad product quality.

Complexity of Solutions (Applications and Platforms)

The solutions being supported usually consist of applications and their platforms. Many organisations have difficulties in providing quality support due to the complexity of solutions, that is, the combination of a complex character of both/either the applications and/or their platforms.

Today, many applications are very complex. Often, they are integrated into even more complex applications, which are, in turn, implemented on very complex integrated hardware and software platforms. Due to their architectural design, they are not always easy to support at the front-end support level. Many front-end support engineers have expressed a wish that when designing a new application, one should consider its front-end support, just as one does when building cars and airplanes today. This would greatly facilitate the work of the engineers at the front-end support level.

Bad Product Quality

Due to their substantial age or other reasons, many applications are of bad quality. They may have been maintained and supported for many years. To keep or gain market shares, the organisations are always in a hurry to extend them with new functionality features without paying too much attention to the quality. This leads to quick product ageing and instability, which in turn strongly affects the work of the front-end support engineers. The engineers get overloaded with a great influx of problem reports, having little time for other types of front-end support activities.

CM³: UPFRONT MAINTENANCE

Presently, the author of this chapter develops a process model of corrective maintenance, called *Corrective Maintenance Maturity Model (CM³)*. Due to the fact that corrective maintenance is a complex activity, it is conducted by many different collaborating processes. Till now, CM³ consists of three process models. They are:

- *CM³: Problem Management:* Describing the problem management at the back-end process level (Kajko-Mattsson, 2001c, 2002a),
- *CM³: Upfront Maintenance:* Describing the problem management at the front-end support level (Kajko-Mattsson, 2003a, 2003b, 2003c; Kajko-Mattsson et al., 2001a), and
- *CM³: Maintainers' Education and Training:* Describing the process of educating and training the maintainers (Kajko-Mattsson et al., 2001b, 2002b).

In this section, we describe parts of *CM³: Upfront Maintenance*. We first present its upfront corrective maintenance process phases. We then provide explanations, rules, and recommendations important for achieving maximal efficiency at the front-end support level. Finally we present the three maturity levels inherent in *CM³: Upfront Maintenance* and their relation to the maturity levels inherent in *CM³: Problem Management*, the corrective maintenance process at the back-end support level. Please note that we are not describing *CM³: Problem Management.* Interested readers are most welcome to read our literature published in Kajko-Mattsson (2001c, 2002a).

Upfront Corrective Maintenance Process

Upfront corrective maintenance process is conducted both by the *HDP* and *PSP* levels. The process looks nearly the same at these two levels. The main difference between them lies in the competence of the support engineers and the complexity of the customer demands. As depicted in Figure 6, upfront corrective maintenance process consists of four main phases, which in turn consist of sub-phases and/or activities. The main phases are (1) *Problem Reporting* phase, (2) *Problem Analysis* phase, (3) *Supervision of Problem Management* phase, and (4) *Solution Delivery* phase. These phases are described next.

Figure 6: Process Phases within Upfront Corrective Maintenance.

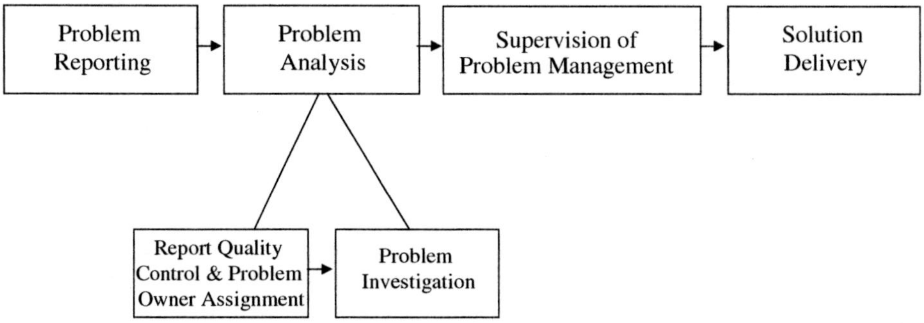

Table 2: CM³: Upfront Maintenance: Problem Reporting.

Problem Reporting

A-1.1:	Describe the problem
A-1.1.1:	Give a general textual description of the problem.
A-1.1.2:	Describe the problem effect(s) and consequence(s).
A-1.1.3:	Describe the symptoms of the problem.
A-1.1.4:	Describe the problem conditions.
A-1.1.5:	Indicate the reproducibility of the problem.
A-1.1.5.1:	Classify the problem as reproducible or non-reproducible.
A-1.1.5.2:	Indicate the repeatability of the problem.
A-1.1.5.3:	Describe how to reproduce the problem.
A-1.1.5.4:	Describe the alternative execution path(s) to the problem.
A-1.1.6:	Attach the relevant file(s).
A-1.2:	Write a short summary (title) of the problem **Comment**: For mnemonic identification and browsing purposes.
A-1.3:	Identify the support category.
A-1.4:	Identify type of a problem.
A-1.5:	Identify the product in which the problem was encountered.
A-1.6:	Identify the product release ID in which the problem was encountered.
A-1.7:	Identify the product component/function in which the problem was encountered.
A-1.8:	Identify the environment of the product.
A-1.9:	Identify the problem submitter.
A-1.10:	Classify the problem report as internal or external.
A-1.11:	Assign the submitter's judgement of the problem severity and priority.
A-1.12:	Identify the activity during which the software problem was encountered.
A-1.13:	Record the date and time when the problem was encountered, if relevant.
A-1.14:	Identify problems related to the reported problem, if any.
A-1.15:	Describe (a) work-around(s), if any.
A-1.16:	Suggest solutions to the reported problem, if any.
A-1.17:	Enter problem report data into the organisation-wide problem report database.
A-1.18:	Assign a unique identifier to the problem report.
A-1.19:	Record the date and time when the problem entered the problem report repository and tracking system.
A-1.20:	Record the additional activities/tasks performed during the activity "Problem Reporting".
A-1.21:	Record the effort and resources of the activity "Problem Reporting".
A-1.22:	Assign the status "Reported" to the problem report.
A-1.23:	Record the date and time when the problem report was assigned the status "Reported".

- *Problem Reporting Phase:* During this phase, problems get reported to the front-end support organisation by the problem submitter. Usually, the problem submitter is the customer filling out the problem report with relevant data about the problem. The problem submitter may also be a front-end support engineer. The engineer may either report the problem on some customer's account or she may report on a problem that she herself has encountered. The activities for this process phase are listed in Table 2. Not all of these activities apply to all problems. Some of them are specific to only internally reported problems, for instance, the activities such as *"A-1.20: Record the additional activities/tasks performed during the activity Problem Reporting"* and *"A-1.21 Record the effort and resources of the activity Problem Reporting."* These activities are required for future analysis and control of the front-end support process. At this phase, the problem report acquires the status value *"Reported"*.
- *Problem Analysis Phase:* During the second process phase, *Problem Analysis* phase, the front-end support engineers attempt to recreate the reported problems in order to confirm that the reported problem is in fact a problem. We divide this phase into two sub-phases: (1) *Report Quality Control and Problem Owner Assignment* phase, and (2) *Problem Investigation* phase. The activities relevant for this sub-phase are presented in Tables 3 and 4.

During the first phase, *Report Quality Control and Problem Owner Assignment*, the front-end support engineer controls the quality of the reported data. A problem report that is incorrect, incomplete and inconsistent may lead to inappropriate understanding of the software problem, thus obstructing the problem resolution process and decreasing support productivity (Arthur, 1988; Glass et al., 1981). Therefore, after a problem has been reported, the first task to be performed in this phase is to check the correctness and completeness of the reported data. If it is not satisfactory, then the problem submitter

Table 3: CM³: Upfront Maintenance: Report Quality Control and Problem Owner Assignment.

Report Quality Control and Problem Owner Assignment	
A-2.1.1:	Study the problem report.
A-2.1.2:	Check the correctness, consistency and completeness of the reported data.
A-2.1.3:	Confirm the problem. **Comment**: At this step, you just check whether the report communicates a problem.
A-2.1.4:	Check whether the problem is unique.
A-2.1.5:	Revise the maintenance category.
A-2.1.6:	Assign the maintainer's judgement of problem severity and priority.
A-2.1.7:	Assign the problem report to the relevant maintenance team.
A-2.1.8:	Record the additional activities/tasks performed during the activity *"Report Quality Control and Problem Owner Assignment"*.
A-2.1.9:	Record the effort and resources of the activity *"Report Quality Control and Problem Owner Assignment"*.
A-2.1.10:	Assign the status *"Assigned to Problem Owner"* to the problem report.
A-2.1.11:	Record the date and time when the problem report was assigned the status *"Assigned to Problem Owner"*.

should be contacted for clarification and supplementary additions (Arthur, 1988; Kajko-Mattsson, 2001c).

If the problem description is satisfactory, the front-end support engineer assigns the problem report to some front-end support engineer. The assigned engineer becomes a problem owner, the role responsible for resolving the software problem. She should keep this ownership until the management of the problem has been terminated, that is, until the tested release containing the problem solution has been delivered to the customer. The assignment of problem ownership is dependent on the expertise required for attending to the problem report. The expertise may be found within the same premises of the company, or it may be found within some other company, sometimes even belonging to a different time zone. At this sub-phase, the problem report acquires the status value *"Assigned to Problem Owner"*.

During the *Problem Investigation* phase, the problem report owner attempts to confirm the presence of a software problem. The key focus is to reproduce the problem mainly by executing software, or testing it using the black box testing approach. The

Table 4: CM³: Upfront Maintenance: Problem Investigation.

Problem Investigation	
A-2.2.1:	Study the problem report
A-2.2.2:	Check the correctness, consistency and completeness of the reported data.
A-2.2.3:	Confirm the problem.
A-2.2.3.1:	If the problem report owner suspects that the problem is unique, he conducts the steps relevant for confirming that the problem is new to the support organisation.
A-2.2.3.1.1:	Read the problem description.
A-2.2.3.1.2:	Study the software system.
A-2.2.3.1.3:	Designate/(Revise the designation of) an appropriate version(s) of the product in which the problem will be investigated.
A-2.2.3.1.4:	Create a pertinent execution environment for the version(s) of the product in which the problem will be investigated.
A-2.2.3.1.5:	Define a set of test cases required for problem investigation.
A-2.2.3.1.6:	Execute the software system until the problem is recreated.
A-2.2.3.1.7:	Revise and complement the description of the software problem, if necessary.
A-2.2.3.1.8:	Check and record whether the problem is unique or a duplicate.
A-2.2.3.1.8.1:	Use a list of known problems in order to determine the uniqueness of the software.
A-2.2.3.1.8.2:	Identify and classify the symptoms of the reported problem.
A-2.2.3.2:	If the report owner suspects (out of the problem description) that the problem report is a duplicate, then he conducts the steps relevant for managing duplicate problem reports
A-2.2.3.2.1:	Read the problem description.
A-2.2.3.2.2:	Identify the master report.
A-2.2.3.2.3:	Check and record whether the problem is unique or duplicate. If necessary, repeat the steps A-2.2.3.1.2 - A-2.2.3.1.7.
A-2.2.3.2.3.1:	Use a list of known problems in order to determine the uniqueness of the software.
A-2.2.3.2.3.2:	Identify and classify the symptoms of the reported problem.
A-2.2.3.2.4:	Revise and complement the description of the software problem in the master- and the duplicate problem report, if necessary.
A-2.2.3.2.5:	Check the progress of the problem resolution.
A-2.2.3.2.6:	Link the duplicate problem report to its unique correspondence (master report).
A-2.2.3.2.7:	Close the management of the duplicate software problem report.
A-2.2.3.4:	Report to the customer on the status of the problem investigation.
A-2.2.3.5:	Record the results of problem investigation.
A-2.2.3.6:	Suggest solutions to the reported problem, if any.
A-2.2.3.7:	Investigate whether there is a a work-around.
A-2.2.3.8:	Identify the support category.
A-2.2.3.9:	Revise the maintainer's judgement of the problem priority and severity.
A-2.2.3.10:	Submit additional problems encountered during the activity *"Problem Investigation"*.
A-2.2.3.11:	Record the additional activities/tasks performed during the activity *"Problem Investigation"*.
A-2.2.3.12:	Record the effort and resources of the activity *"Problem Investigation"*.
A-2.2.3.13:	Assign the status *"Problem Investigated"* to the problem report that has been identified as a unique report, and the status *"Cancelled"* to the duplicate problem report.
A-2.2.3.14:	Record the date and time when the problem report was assigned the status *" Problem Investigated "*.
A-2.2.3.15:	Deliver the results to the next service level This step is relevant in cases when the problem is unique or when a master report needs to be updated with additional data from the duplicate problem report.
A-2.2.3.16:	Report to the customer on the status of the problem resolution.

problem owner must determine whether the reported problem is unique or whether it is a duplicate. Hence, the exact steps taken during this stage may vary depending on the nature of the problem. If the problem is identified as a new problem, then the support engineer is obliged to report it to the next support level (the next front-end or back-end support level). If the problem shows to be an already known problem (a duplicate), then the engineer may close its resolution, and link the duplicate problem report to the master report (the report communicating the original unique problem). In some cases, however, she may complement the original master report with the extra information provided in the duplicate problem report, if she believes that this information would aid in better problem understanding and thereby in more efficient problem resolution. At this sub-phase, the problem report acquires the status value *"Problem Investigated"*.

- *Supervision of Problem Management Phase:* During the *Problem Management Supervision* phase, the problem report is being managed by the back-end support engineers. This fact, however, should not release the front-end support engineers from abandoning the problem report ownership.

During this phase, the front-end support engineers should continuously supervise the management of the problem at the back-end process level. They are either automatically notified about the progress via a process supporting tool or they do it on their own by regularly checking the contents in the global support database. They should also attend the *Change Control Board (CCB)* meetings during which the problems and problem solutions (modifications designs) are being discussed. Finally, the front-end support engineers should assist in system testing of the releases containing solutions to the reported software problems. At this phase, the problem report acquires the status value *"Under Resolution"*. The activities relevant for this sub-phase are presented in Table 5.

Table 5: CM³: Upfront Maintenance: Problem Supervision and Solution Delivery.

	Problem Supervision
A-3.1:	Continuously supervise the management of the problem at the back-end process level via the process supporting tool: **Comment**: The engineer is either automatically notified about the progress by the supporting tool or she does it actively on her own.
A-3.2:	Attend CCB meetings
A-3.2.1:	Study the problem description. **Comment**: The more the back-end support engineer works on a problem, the more understanding she gains. At the back-end process level, the problem descriptions are the closest possible interpretations of the true nature and complexity of a software problem. They may differ from the original problem descriptions as reported to the front-end support. Hence, it is important that the front-end support engineer reads the problem description anew. All the CCB-members should do so as well.
A-3.2.2:	Understand the underlying cause (defect).
A-3.2.3:	Study the modification design (problem solution). **Comment**: Usually, during the CCB meetings, the support engineers study the modification designs by listening to the oral presentations of the back-end support engineers.
A-3.2.4:	Analyse and comment on the modification design from the customer's perspective.
A-3.2.5:	Analyse and comment the modification design from the support perspective.
A-3.3:	Conduct system testing
A-3.3.1:	Conduct steps relevant for the system tests, defined in CM³: Testing. **Comment**: At this phase, the support engineer checks whether the reported software problem has been resolved.
A-3.4:	Record the additional activities/tasks performed during the activity "Problem Management Supervision".
A-3.5:	Record the effort and resources of the activity "Problem Management Supervision".
A-3.6:	Assign the status "Under Resolution" to the problem report.
A-3.7:	Record the date and time when the problem report was assigned the status "status name".
	Solution Delivery
A-4.1:	Deliver the release containing the problem solution to the customers affected by the problem.
A-4.2:	Announce to other customers that the release containing the problem solution is ready for delivery.

- *Solution Delivery Phase:* During the *Solution Delivery* phase, the front-end support delivers the release containing one or several solutions to all the customers affected by the resolved problems. It is also announces the release as available to all the other customers, who might encounter the resolved problems. The activities relevant for this phase are presented in Table 5.

Important Process Issues

When defining a process, it is not enough to only specify process phases and activities. To increase its objective understanding, the process must be further explained and motivated for. For this reason, *CM³: Upfront Maintenance* is supplemented with *Maintenance Elements* — the explanations, rules and recommendations necessary for preventing some of the problems as specified in the section titled *Problems within Front-End Support,* and for achieving an optimal process. Next, we list and describe some of the most important issues.

Scope of Support is Defined

It is important to define the amount and scope of support to be delivered to the customer. If the support organisations do not do it, they will then try to do everything and end up doing many things poorly (Czegel, 1998, p. 3). The customers may merely state any request and have the right to demand that it be expedited. Defining the scope of support may help the support engineers focus on providing only a specific set of services. CM³ suggests five levels of support scope:

1. *Support scope – level 1:* Meaning full maintenance support including perfective, adaptive, preventive, corrective maintenance, and a predetermined subset of the types of support activities as specified in Table 1. Within the framework of this scope, the organisations may negotiate whether education and training should be included (Pigoski, 1997).
2. *Support scope – level 2:* Implying full corrective maintenance, and a subset of the types of support activities as specified in Table 1. Management of all software problems is included in this scope (Pigoski, 1997). A predetermined subset of the types of support activities as specified in Table 1 is covered herein.
3. *Support scope – level 3:* Providing limited corrective maintenance, mainly the management of serious and business critical problems (Pigoski, 1997). A predetermined subset of the types of support activities as specified in Table 1 is included herein.
4. *Support scope – level 4:* Performing limited configuration and installation support (Pigoski, 1997), and a predetermined subset of the types of support activities as specified in Table 1.
5. *Support scope – level 5:* Performing any type of support within a certain predetermined or not predetermined (paid per hour) amount of time.

Scope of Supported Products is Carefully Defined and Agreed Upon

If the support organisations support too broad a range of products, they are setting themselves up for failure (Czegel, 1998, p. 27). They must keep a wide breadth of expertise by increasing staffing, expediting many diverse support demands and tackling many incompatibility problems. Limiting the scope of the supported products does not only imply less support effort, but also helps the support organisations tackle the prior-mentioned problems concerning personnel dependency, lack of competent personnel, and personnel shortage.

In reality, however, many support organisations must work in an environment that suits the customer. Setting standards or limitations of applications and environments may be next to impossible. Despite this, some limits should be set when making agreements on the scope of the product portfolio to be supported. This would help the support organisation control their staffing and competence development.

All Support Demands are Recorded

Just as in *CM³: Problem Management* at the back-end support level, we suggest that all service tasks be recorded at the front-end support level (Kajko-Mattsson, 2001c). This would help achieve insight into and control over the amount of support demands, help communicate the service requests in a formal, tractable and disciplined way, help assure that all the requests have been attended to, and enable the monitoring of the support process.

Recording of the support demands would be a starting point in tackling the intangibility, heterogeneity and perishability of the support processes (Zeithaml et al., 1996). If the support demands are not reported in writing but orally, they may be easily forgotten or misunderstood. The organisation cannot achieve control over the number of the demands and their types. Not recording the support demands, the organisations cannot define and estimate the scope of corrective and/or other non-corrective maintenance.

Recording may be time consuming, but it will pay back in the future. Inventories of the demanded and expedited support tasks would constitute a starting point towards understanding the support process, its workload, and the distribution of the support tasks per customer. It would help in pricing and articulating the support tasks, synchronising them, and reusing some of their results. Recording the support demands would provide a basis for historical data and service level agreements. Most importantly, it would help improve the support process and the quality of service.

Communication Pattern is Established between Customer and Support Organisations

A communication pattern must be established among the customer and support organisations. The goal is to avoid an ad hoc communication. As already mentioned, many collaborating support organisations are geographically dispersed all over the world. Creating a communication pattern would help make support more effective.

Customers should be offered a single point of contact at the *HDP* level. Only if the demands cannot be resolved at this level may they be passed on to the next service levels, first to the *PSP* level, and then, if required, to the *MEP* level (the back-end level). The customers should neither contact the *PSP* level nor *MEP* level themselves. The same applies when passing the solution or feedback on its progress to the customers from the *MEP* level. The *MEP* level should not deliver it directly to the customer. All information should be communicated through all the front-end support levels concerned.

Establishing a communication pattern is an important productivity issue. Lack of it would infuse too much chaos and disturbance into the maintenance work. A communication pattern ensures that all the organisations involved are informed about the problem and its progress.

Availability of Upfront Maintenance is Clearly Stated

Availability of the support organisations is one of the major factors of success (Bouman et al., 1999, p. 170). Usually, availability is too vaguely specified by a figure showing the availability percentage, such as 99%. It is not always clear what it means. It may then strongly affect customer relations.

CM³: Upfront Maintenance suggests that availability be clearly specified, preferably in measurable terms. Different levels of availability may be defined according to the scope of the support agreed upon. However, the following should be specified:

- *Availability of support via telephone:* Exact office and non-office hours should be stated, for instance, (1) ordinary office hours: 9-17 hours, and (2) non-office hours: 17-nine hours.
- *Availability of a pertinent specialist:* In cases when the customer encounters a problem, the support organisation should guarantee access to a specialist within, for instance, 30 minutes during the office hours. In cases of more serious problems encountered outside the office hours, the customers should be guaranteed to get in touch with a specialist within, for instance, one hour. In all other cases, the customer will have to wait until the next day.
- *Availability via a tool:* A guarantee is made that the tool is available 24 hours a day.

All Customer Demands are Acknowledged

All customer demands should be acknowledged within a pre-determined period of time. The goal is to increase customer satisfaction. Customers will often want rapid answers to their requests, or at least some kind of acknowledgement that their requests have been notified. Not acknowledging the requests in time may imply additional burden at the front-end support level and cause irritation of the customers. The simple measure is to determine a time unit for acknowledging customer requests, for instance, 12 hours.

Progress of Expiating Demands is Monitored and Reported

To expedite a demand may take time, especially when it concerns a software problem. Meanwhile, customers may require information on the progress of its resolution. To satisfy this, the front-end support should provide their customers with status information of the problem resolution and/or temporary work-arounds, if any. The reported status concerns the progress made at both the front-end and back-end support levels.

Monitoring the progress helps achieve control over the progress of attending to problems. It ensures that no problem gets overlooked. It helps in determining the problem age, and the workload of the support process and its individual engineers. It helps improve process discipline, and it facilitates the process of providing continuous feedback to the customers on the progress of problem resolution.

Service Level Agreement

Support processes are extremely vulnerable. The customer expects a quick solution. If it is not delivered within an agreed-upon period of time or not properly communicated, weak points within the organisation may quickly become obvious (Zuther, 1998, p. 2092). In many cases, there exists a gap between the customers' expectations for service and the maintainer's ability to supply service. Hence, some form of an agreement (contract) is recommended in order to avoid conflicts. Such an agreement/contract is usually called *Service Level Agreement (SLA)*.

The *SLA* specifies what the customer organisation has the right to expect from a support organisation (Radosevich, 1997; Steinke, 1997). Its contents are the specification of commitments, the result of a consensus building (two-way agreement) between the customer and support organisations (Niessink, 2000). The commitments should be based on the customers' needs and the support organisations' ability to satisfy these needs.

The SLA should be stipulated in writing. It should be clearly and simply verbalised so that it can be read by anybody involved within support. It should carefully consider all important promises and commitments in the greatest possible detail (Martin et al., 1983). Ideally, it should be closely tied to customers' business operation and its consequences (Steinke, 1997,). The SLA should contain the following elements (Czegel, 1998; Niessink, 2000; Passmore, 1996; Steinke, 1997):

- *Period:* Time interval covered by the agreement, which is usually six months or one year.
- *Objectives:* Motivation for why the support is needed.
- *Scope of support:* List of service types to be delivered. Is it only corrective maintenance support (Scope 2) or is it full support paid per hour (Scope 5)?
- *Product portfolio:* List of products to be supported.
- *Specification of critical components:* The specification of the components requiring additional attention. Usually, these components are critical for customers' business.
- *Support fee:* Cost of support to be paid by the customer organisation.
- *Availability of support organisations:* Dates and time when the support organisations are available.
- *Service access:* Specification of how the customers should contact the support organisations.
- *Warranty:* Written guarantee of the quality service and the specification of undertakings in cases when the quality is not satisfied.
- *Signatures of the parties involved:* Signatures of all the organisations providing and consuming support services.

Operation Level Agreement

It is not enough to have an agreement with the customer organisations only. Some kind of a formalised agreement must be made between the support organisations as well. In some organisations, such an agreement is called *Operation Level Agreement (OLA)*. If there is no formalised commitment amongst the service levels, then the support organisations cannot only deliver satisfactory service to their customers, but also, they cannot co-operate with one another in an optimal way. For instance, if there is no formalised commitment between the service levels, support demands may either be escalated too soon to the next service level, or bounced between many different support organisations. One weakly defined service level may undermine the whole enterprise.

Additional Issues in SLAs and OLAs

Both the *SLAs* and *OLAs* should be complemented with the following aspects:

- *Commitments and responsibilities of the parties involved in the SLA:* The list of commitments and responsibilities required from both the customer and support organisations. In order to avoid conflicts, one should specify where the responsibilities begin and end. The process of defining responsibilities has to be systematically repeated. As technology, organisations, and their product portfolios keep changing, lines of responsibility that were clear may become fuzzy (Czegel, 1998). Hence, they need to be modified.
- *Commitments and responsibilities of the parties involved in the OLA:* The organisations should define the vertical lines of commitments and responsibilities, that is, how the organisations on different support levels should co-operate, and what responsibilities they should have at each level. The organisations should also define the horizontal lines of responsibilities, that is, how the organisations belonging to the same service level should co-operate and what responsibilities they should have with respect to one another.
- *Agreement on how to assign ownership:* The organisations must define procedures for how to assign ownership to the software problems or other support demands, and how to shift this ownership.
- *Rules for problem escalation:* The organisations should define rules for how to escalate problems to higher service levels.
- *Reporting:* The organisations should agree upon the rules for providing service results. Rules for describing software problems should be stated as well.
- *Right to refusal to provide support:* Specification of cases when the support organisations have the right to refuse to provide support.
- *Conflict prevention measures:* Specification of situations leading to conflicts and specification of measures preventing these conflicts.
- *Rules, prerequisites and conditions to obey required for support realisation:* Specifications of rules to be obeyed when requiring or providing service.

By keeping detailed records of the support process, its process steps and experience, the support organisations should have sufficient data enabling them to evaluate their collaborating support organisations, their behaviour, and fulfilment of the assigned responsibilities. This, in turn, should help them state conditions for continued co-operation.

The support organisations together with their customer organisations should continuously ensure that support is delivered according to the common agreements specified in the *SLAs* and *OLAs*. The current support and maintenance needs of the customer should be compared to the needs specified in the contracts. As a result of this evaluation, the *SLAs* and *OLAs* may have to be adjusted and renegotiated to stay in line with possibly changing support and maintenance needs.

Customer Profiles

In business situations with many users, it may be difficult to determine and evaluate the needs and wishes of the customers. Hence, the knowledge of the customers and their business characteristics is an important prerequisite for defining and improving the support process. For this reason, all customers should be identified and recorded in the so-called customer profiles. Customer profiles should help in identifying the support needs per customer organisation. They should record general data describing the customer organisations, such as customer name, address, telephone numbers, and number of employees. They should also record information on customer business, its criticality, and the like. These data are important not only for delivering the support service results, but also for reaching the customers for other purposes such as, for instance, marketing. Knowing the number of customers would give an idea of the amount of potential support requesters. This, in turn, would help determine support dimension, service priorities and staffing requirements (Bouman et al., 1999; Czegel, 1998).

If properly recorded, the customer profiles would enable the support organisations to evaluate the customers, their behaviour, and fulfilment of the assigned responsibilities. This would in turn improve the communication between the support and customer organisations and facilitate the negotiations of future service level agreements. Customer profiles should record the following data:

- *Basic customer data:* Name, telephone number, address, and the like.
- *Inventory of customers' application and environment portfolios:* The support organisations must know what they are supporting. In this way, they may assess the size of the applications and their environments, the need for service, and the expertise and workload required to provide service. Access to this information also creates a platform for future business opportunities.
- *Customer business:* One and the same product may be used differently. To be able to determine the amount of support required for a certain customer, the support organisations should know the customers' business and application domain. This knowledge would help them determine priorities for customer demands and aid in working by these priorities.
- *Usage profile:* The information about the usage profile (or the support demand traffic) is very important for resource allocation reasons. Peak hours should be determined, not only during the days but also during the weeks, months, or years. This would help the support organisations get prepared to meet these peaks, by either increasing resources or by outsourcing some parts of support.
- *Technology literacy and friendliness:* Knowledge of the customers' literacy and friendliness of technology may be acquired by recording the types of service demands per customer organisation. This knowledge should be used to define the support load. It would help determine the measures required for improving the level of customer literacy. It would also help the support organisations plan for technology change and upgrades, and map out the difficulties to be expected.

Global Problem Solution Database

In a multiple support environment, there is always a danger that one organisation does not know when the other has detected a similar problem. This could result in a wasted effort of trying to resolve a problem that has already been recognised and addressed. Substantial amounts of resources may be saved if solutions for recurring problems (duplicates) are being globally recorded. By doing so, the previously encountered customer problems can be attended to more efficiently. This would lead to greater customer satisfaction, better up-front maintainers' productivity and lower up-front maintenance costs (Annick, 1993). This would also lead to a more coherent and consistent management of all customers (Allen et al., 1993).

Monitoring Trends

By having access to the detailed process information, detailed customer profiles and their product portfolios, the support organisations may study the customer demand records and identify positive and/or negative trends. Examples of such trends are: (1) an increase or decrease of demands in certain periods of time from a certain customer, (2) encounters of certain software problems in a specific environment and condition, and (3) the dominance of certain technical installation problems.

Trends may help the support organisations get an overview of the workload of their support tasks. This would in turn help them adapt to meet the new trends and plan for future work and resources. It would also help them take preventive measures in cases of recurring problems. Examples of preventive measures might be announcing a work-around for a certain problem or announcing a new release containing a permanent solution to the problem. In cases when it is an operational problem encountered due to the customers' poor competence, a preventive measure would mean to suggest education and training of the customer.

Maturity Levels

The problem management at the front-end support level is very complex. It may not always be easy for organisations to implement an optimal process from the very beginning. For this reason, we have divided our *CM^3: Upfront Maintenance* process model into three levels, where each level provides a different degree of process detail. Next, we briefly describe our levels and their collaboration with *CM^3: Problem Management,* the problem management process at the back-end support level (Kajko-Mattsson, 2001c, 2002a).

CM^3: Upfront Maintenance - Level 1 (Initial)

In organisations at the *Initial* level, the process of front-end support corresponds to a rather scattered picture of various types of defined and undefined activities. As a consequence, the process is difficult to manage in a formal and efficient way (Bouman et al., 1999; Czegel, 1998). The process is not defined, or if it is defined, it is not sufficiently documented and adhered to. Service demands may or may not be recorded. Communication channels between the customers and maintenance organisations are not defined. Availability of support is not or is vaguely specified. Service level agreements are specified in very general terms. Support organisations possess little knowledge of their customers and their businesses. There is little or no control over the types of demands, their amount, frequency, and progress of their expiation.

Both problem management processes at the front-end and back-end processes offer very little visibility, as visualised with the black boxes in Figure 7. Regarding the front-

Figure 7: Front-End and Back-End Support Process Visibility — Level "Initial".

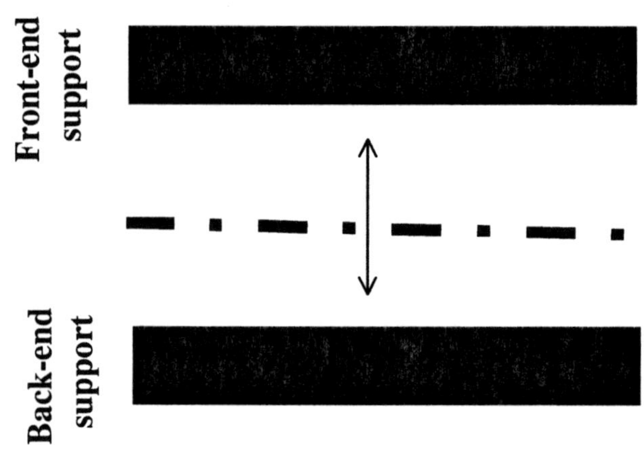

end support, at the very most, the organisations may have insight into the number of support demands (problems) that have been expedited. They cannot monitor the process and make reliable process analyses. The feedback provided by the process is not always meaningful. Success at this maturity level strongly depends on the competence and experience of individuals or groups of collaborating individuals.

CM³: Upfront Maintenance - Level 2 (Defined)

At the *Defined* level, a coarse-grained process for front-end support is defined, documented, and most importantly, adhered to. Types of services are identified, and process models for managing these service types are specified in terms of their constituent process phases. As depicted in Figure 8, the upfront corrective maintenance process follows a coarse-grained process by covering the most rudimentary process phases and activities. The problem management process at the back-end process level follows the same degree of detail. The phases/activities offer visible, however still coarse-grained, milestones for following the process, its progress and for making different kinds of intermediate decisions. All the support levels involved have established a process for managing emergency cases and disaster recovery.

Although simple, the process is consistently adhered to. Process compliance with its documentation is checked on a regular or event-driven basis. The most rudimentary data and measurements supplied at this level appropriately mirror the process. Hence, they are meaningful.

Because a proper problem description is the most important prerequisite for an efficient problem resolution at both the front-end and back-end levels, the organisations provide maximal support to problem submitters on how to describe and specify their requests (problem reports in our case) by institutionalising a template for problem description. Correctness, consistency, and completeness of the reported data are checked before starting to attend to the problem. Problems are first thoroughly investigated and confirmed as unique before being transferred to the next service levels.

Figure 8: Front-End and Back-End Support Process Visibility — Level "Defined".

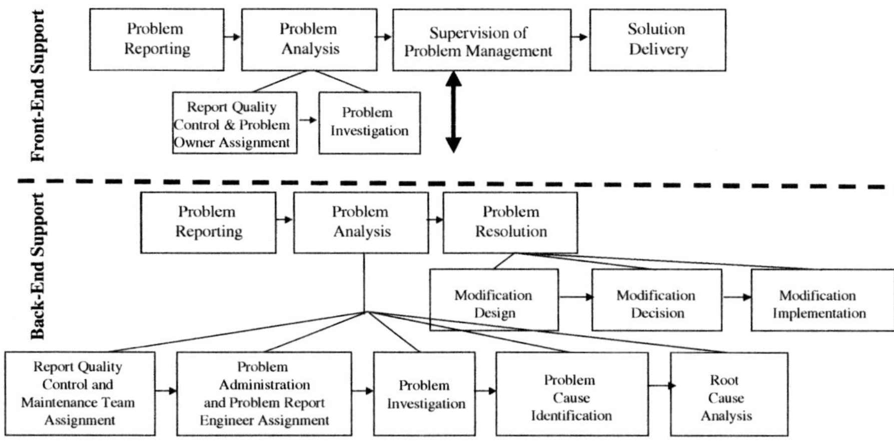

To optimise the front-end support process, the organisations control the scope of the systems to be supported. They define priorities for different support demands and follow these priorities. They specify a communication pattern to be followed by the customer and all the support organisations involved, and establish personal relationships with one another. They define the availability in quantitative terms. They measure progress of attending to the support demands. To provide better service and to better monitor the service provided, the support organisations have developed *SLAs, OLAs,* and customer profiles.

At this level, effort is mainly put on improving the processes to be executed locally within each individual support organisation. A global control and co-ordination of the collaborating support organisations has not yet been fully achieved.

CM³: Upfront Maintenance - Level 3 (Optimal)

At the *Optimal* level, the front-end and back-end support allow a fine-grained visibility into their status and progress (see Figure 9). The organisations have clear insight into every process step and its results. The process is uniformly defined, co-ordinated, and adhered to within all collaborating support organisations. This does not only lead to a more efficient process execution but also to a more coherent support of all customers worldwide.

The detailed process knowledge helps meaningfully analyse the front-end and back-end support processes and identify their weaknesses and strengths. For major common activities within the problem management process such as *Problem Investigation*, all the organisations involved define and follow detailed process models of how they should be conducted. This is a way of assuring that each process activity is conducted in as uniform a manner as possible, a way of assuring the quality of support and maintenance work, and a way of assuring that only unique problems are reported to the back-end support level.

Figure 9: Front-End and Back-End Support Process Visibility - Level "Optimal".

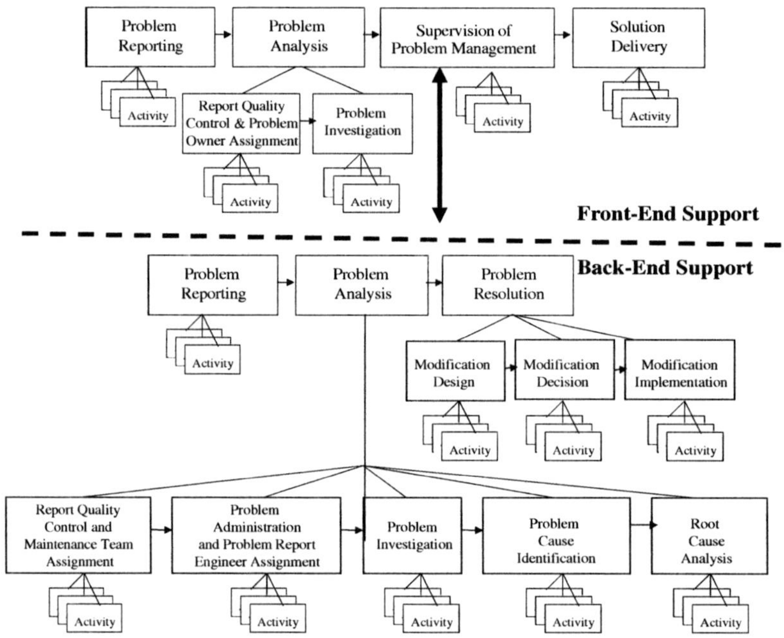

The organisations continuously evaluate the performance of their own, of their customers and of other collaborating support organisations. They efficiently manage unbalanced priorities and provide meaningful feedback to process improvement. This helps measure two-way performance against the *SLA*s and *OLAs* and determines whether the agreements are being met and whether there are any areas that need to be addressed.

Recording support demands due to customers' poor knowledge provides strong evidence for establishing the customers' needs for education and training. Keeping track of poor performance of other support organisations due to their lack of knowledge or lack of process effectiveness aids in stating conditions for continued co-operation or for choosing some other support organisation to co-operate with.

By recording all process steps, the support organisations have collected enough data allowing them to manage the complexity of their support tasks and the tight coupling of several strongly related but different support tasks, but still, however, allowing detailed visibility into each one of them. The support organisations also have good overview over the support volume, and its distribution over time not only at the vertical co-operational level but also at the horizontal co-operational level, if relevant and required. The support organisations also manage positive and negative trends. They either enforce or eliminate these trends. They are highly specialised in eliminating the reasons for some types of support demands.

The support process is highly automated. The common problem profiles are globally recorded so that the problem descriptions and their solutions may be easily accessed worldwide. In addition, a global register of all the support organisations is kept so that it may be easily accessed worldwide. Classification of symptoms enables an automatic identification of duplicate problems worldwide, thus substantially improving the upfront maintenance productivity.

Due to high automation, many support demands will have to be requested and attended to via a tool. The customers should primarily use the tool. They should be discouraged from contacting the support with just any demand, and they should know when they are entitled to contact support in person. In cases when they do contact support, the support organisations have the right to refuse to provide support and suggest where in the tool the customers might find the service required. The automation helps the customers perform certain tasks on their own, for instance, checking the progress of their problems or requests, and looking for similar support demands in the global database first, before contacting the support organisation. The automation also helps the support organisation eliminate the number of uninteresting and repetitive support tasks, thus making the support work more interesting and motivating.

SUMMARY

So far, the domain of upfront corrective maintenance has been strongly neglected. It is very immature in comparison with other software engineering disciplines. Today, we have very little knowledge and insight into the corrective maintenance at the front-end support level, despite the fact that it is the dominating cost within corrective maintenance.

To remedy this, we have described the domain of upfront corrective maintenance at the front-end support level in this chapter. We have placed it in the context of the whole IT enterprise and described its collaboration with the corrective maintenance process at the back-end support level. To increase the understanding of upfront corrective maintenance, we have placed it in the context of other support types, and identified problems currently encountered by the front-end support organisations. As a remedy for those problems, we have suggested *CM³: Upfront Maintenance*, a process model specialised to provide upfront corrective maintenance at the front-end support level. We have described its process phases, maturity levels, and collaboration with the *CM³: Problem Management* model, a problem management process model at the back-end support level. In the next chapter we investigate the differences between software maintenance and software development from a service point of view, and the consequences thereof for the maturity of software maintenance organizations.

ENDNOTES

1 B2B - Business-to-business (Kalakota, 2001; Nelson, 2002).

2 B2C - Business-to-customer (Kalakota, 2001; Nelson, 2002).

3 Software problems that have not been reported earlier by any customer are unknown. They are unique. They are not duplicates.

REFERENCES

Adams, E.N. (1994). Optimising preventive service of software products. *IBM Research and Development, 28*(1), 2-14.

Allen, P., & Marshall, J. (1993). Integrated services delivery multi-service delivery to major customer sites. *Proceedings of the X International Symposium on Subscriber Loops and Services (ISSLS)* (pp. 186-191). Los Alamitos, CA: IEEE Computer Society Press.

Annick, P.G. (1993). Integrating natural language processing and information retrieval in a troublshooting help desk. *IEEE Expert ISSN: 0885-9000, 8*(6), 9-17.

Arthur, L.J. (1988). *Software evolution: The software maintenance challenge.* John Wiley & Sons.

Bouman, J., Trienekens, J., & van der Zwan, M. (1999). Specification of Service Level Agreements, clarifying concepts on the basis of practical research. *Proceedings of software technology and engineering practice* (pp. 169-178). Los Alamitos, CA: IEEE Computer Society Press.

Calow, H. (1991). Maintenance productivity factors – A case study. *Proceedings of International Conference on Software Maintenance* (p. 250-253). Los Alamitos, CA: IEEE Computer Society Press.

Chapin, N. (1995). Interview with E. Burton Swanson. *Journal of Software Maintenance: Research and Practice, 7,* 303-315. Wiley & Sons.

Czegel, B. (1998). *Running an effective help desk.* John Wiley & Sons, Inc.

Glass, R.L., & Noiseux, R.A. (1981). *Software maintenance guidebook.* New York: Prentice-Hall.

Hart, S. (1993). Technical support: A valuable voice. *Proceedings of the International Professional Communication Conference* (pp. 57-59). Los Alamitos, CA: IEEE Computer Society Press.Kajko-Mattsson, M. (2001c). *Corrective Maintenance Maturity Model: Problem management.* PhD thesis, ISBN Nr 91-7265-311-6, ISSN 1101-8526, ISRN SU-KTH/DSV/R—01/15, Department of Computer and Systems Sciences (DSV), Forum 100, SE-164 40 Kista, Stockholm University and Royal Institute of Technology.

Kajko-Mattsson, M. (2002a). Problem management within corrective maintenance. In M. Polo, M. Piattini & F. Ruiz (Eds.), *Advances in software maintenance management: Technologies and solutions.* Hershey, PA: Idea Group Publishing.

Kajko-Mattsson, M. (2003a). Infrastructures of virtual IT enterprises. *Proceedings of International Conference on Software Maintenance.* Los Alamitos, CA: IEEE Computer Society Press.

Kajko-Mattsson, M. (2003b). Taxonomy of front-end support activities. *Proceedings of the Seventh International Conference on Integrated Design and Process Technology (IDPT).* Society for Design and Process Science.

Kajko-Mattsson, M. (2003c). Problems within support (upfront maintenance). *Proceedings of Conference on Software Maintenance and Reengineering* (pp. 331-340). Los Alamitos, CA: IEEE Computer Society Press.

Kajko-Mattsson, M., Forssander, S., & Andersson, G. (2000). Problem reporting and resolution process at ABB ROP: State of practice. *Journal of Software Evolution and Maintenance, , 12*(5), 255-285. John Wiley & Sons.

Kajko-Mattsson, M., Forssander, S., & Olsson, U. (2001b). Corrective Maintenance Maturity Model: Maintainer's education and training. *Proceedings of International Conference on Software Engineering* (pp. 610-619). Los Alamitos, CA: IEEE Computer Society Press.

Kajko-Mattsson, M., Forssander, S., Andersson, G., & Olsson, U. (2002b). Developing CM^3: Maintainers' education and training at ABB. *Journal of Computer Science Education, 12*(1-2), 57-89, Swets & Zeitlinger.

Kajko-Mattsson, M., Tjerngren, L.-O., & Andersson, A. (2001a). CM^3: Upfront maintenance. *Proceedings of Conference on Software Engineering and Knowledge Engineering* (pp. 371-378). U.S.: Knowledge Systems Institute.

Kalakota, R. (2002). *e-Business 2.0 roadmap for success.* Reading, MA: Addison-Wesley.

Kriegsman, M., & Barletta, R. (1993). Building a case-based help desk application. *IEEE Expert, ISSN: 0885-9000, 8*(6), 18-26.

Martin, J., & McClure, C. (1983). *Software maintenance, The problem and its solutions.* NJ: Prentice-Hall.

Nelson, W.H. (2002). *Building electronic commerce.* Reading, MA: Addison-Wesley.

Niessink, F. (2000). *Perspectives on improving software maintenance.* PhD thesis (No. 2000-1). SICS, Vrije University, Holland, Amsterdam.

Nihei, K., Tomizawa, N, Shibata, A., & Shimazu H. (1998). ExpertGuide for help desks–An intelligent information retrieval system for WWW pages. *Proceedings of 9th International Workshop on Database and Expert Systems Applications*, 937-942.

Passmore, D. (1996). Setting performance expectations. *Business communications review.* Canada: BCR Enterprises Incorporated.

Pigoski, T.M. (1997). *Practical software maintenance.* New York: John Wiley & Sons.

Radosevich, L. (1997). Service-Level Agreements gaining popularity. *Infoworld, 29,* 57-62. Available: http://www.infoworld.com

Steinke, S. (1997). Taking Charge of Service Levels, *Network.* http://www.network-mag.com, 77-80.

Zeithaml V. A, & Bitner M. (1996). *Services Marketing,* McGraw-Hill, 1996.

Zuther, M. (1998). Modular Based IT-Solutions for Efficient Worldwide Service Processes. *Proceedings of the 24th Annual Conference of the IEEE Industrial Electronics Society.* IEEE Computer Society Press: Los Alamitos, CA, 2089 -2093.

Chapter V

Evolving Legacy System Features into Fine-Grained Components

Alok Mehta, American Financial Systems, Inc., USA

George T. Heineman, WPI Computer Science Department, USA

ABSTRACT

There is a constant need for practical and cost-effective software evolution techniques. We have developed a novel evolution methodology that integrates the concepts of features, regression testing, and component-based software engineering (CBSE). Regression test cases are untapped resources, full of information about system features. By exercising each feature with its associated test cases using code profilers, code can be located and refactored to create components. These components are then inserted back into the legacy system, ensuring a working system structure. This methodology is divided into three parts. Part One identifies the source code associated with features that need evolution. Part Two deals with creating components and Part Three measures results. We have validated our approach on the evolution of a real-world legacy system. By applying this methodology, American Financial Systems, Inc. (AFS) has successfully restructured its enterprise legacy system and reduced the costs of future maintenance. In this chapter we show a simple example of this methodology in action.

INTRODUCTION

Execom (2003) estimates that legacy software systems capture and manage 75% of the world's data and that they consume at least 80% of available Information Technology resources. These legacy systems provide a competitive advantage to many organizations but are expensive to maintain. The constant pressure to evolve these systems is driven by escalating expectations of the customer for new enterprise standards, new products and system features, and improved performance. Thus, these organizations face a dilemma — they cannot afford to lose their competitive advantage by rewriting or redesigning the software system, nor can they continue to accept the high maintenance costs. To effectively evolve legacy systems in such a rapidly changing environment, organizations must answer two questions (Smith, Müller & Tilley, 1997): What are the critical success factors of system evolution? How can a system be evolved without adversely affecting operations and revenue? These pressing business concerns motivate this chapter.

Incremental Evolution of Legacy Systems

Of the many strategies for managing legacy software systems, such as doing nothing, rewriting, or replacing with other systems (Bergey, Northrop & Smith, 1997; Brodie & Stonebraker, 1995; Weiderman et al., 1997; Tilley & Smith, 1996), we recommend incremental evolution. Incremental evolution focuses on problems that are most visible to end-users. Rather than replacing or rewriting the entire legacy system, incremental evolution directly "fixes" end-user problems "one at a time". This is the only choice left to many organizations that must continue to receive revenue from software systems to stay competitive. However, many incremental evolution initiatives do not sufficiently incorporate the end user's point of reference (Dorda et al., 2000); such lack of consideration can leave end users unsatisfied because they may not see the benefit of the system evolution.

Problem and Solution Domains

Researchers have identified the two domains around which the entire field of software engineering revolves: the *problem domain* and the *solution domain* (Davis & Rauscher, 1979; Kaindl et al., 1998: Raccoon, 1995; Tsang & Magill, 1998). End users interact with the system through input files or a user interface. Because these users are directly concerned with system features, their perspective is always in the problem domain. Developers (and the software process team) are primarily concerned with creating and maintaining software development life cycle artifacts such as components; their perspective is therefore firmly rooted in the solution domain.

A major source of difficulty in developing, delivering, and evolving successful software is the *complexity gap*, as termed by Raccoon (1995), that exists between the problem and the solution domains, as shown in Figure 1. To view evolution from a single domain upsets the delicate balance between the two domains. Evolution focused solely on the problem domain may lead to changes that degrade the structure of the original code; similarly, evolution based solely on technical merits could create changes unacceptable to end users. *External evolutionary pressures* drive the implementation of new enhancements and functionality by causing developers to focus on implementing the

Figure 1: An Incremental Evolution Methodology is Needed.

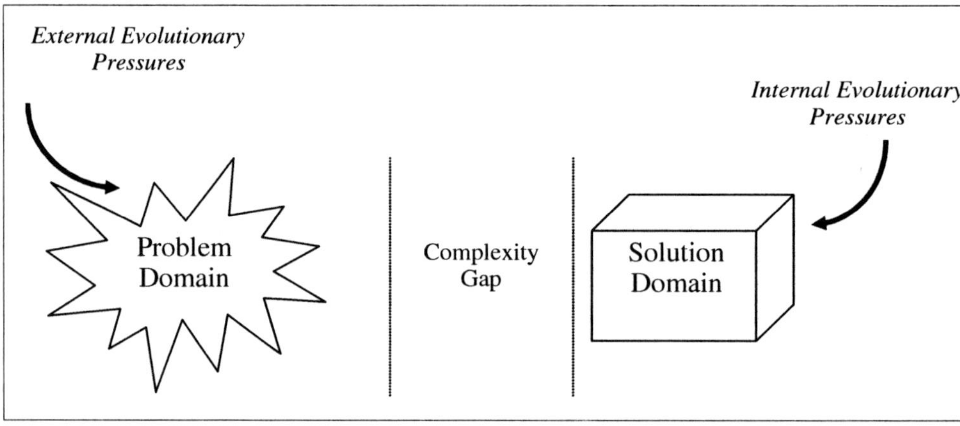

business logic that is *directly* visible to end users, such as a menu item that spell-checks a document in a word processing application. While responding to external pressures, developers often bypass standard processes to meet project deadlines; this results in inferior coding, such as adding a global variable when one is not required. *Internal evolutionary pressures* force developers to either restructure or refactor their code so the future enhancement or maintenance becomes manageable and cost-effective. During such evolution, code is refactored and standards are reestablished. End users are often unaware of these internal changes, except through possible performance improvements.

Motivation

Successful system evolution requires insights from software, managerial, and economic perspectives (Tilley & Smith, 1996). Endorsing evolution initiatives becomes easier if the end user perspective is kept as the primary focus. Additionally, when there is a product line, it is desirable to leverage evolution initiatives from one legacy system to another (Griss, 2000). The FOCAL (Features, Components, and Legacy systems) methodology can be summarized in one sentence: *By exercising each feature with its associated test cases using code profilers, feature implementations can be located and refactored to create reusable fine-grained components.* FOCAL reduces future maintenance costs without disrupting operations.

Reduce Future Maintenance Costs

One objective of FOCAL is to reduce the maintenance costs of features that are hard to maintain. We identify these system features with the help of end users, locate their implementation, and then evolve them into reusable units. In one of the first dissertations on Feature Engineering, Turner (1999) mentioned the possibility of using Feature Engineering for software evolution, but he was focused on using features for configuration management. We have developed techniques for identifying evolvable features with high maintenance costs to be refactored into reusable software components.

Reuse Components in a Product Line

The Internet makes it possible for an organization to attract potential customers from the global marketplace by breaking down communication barriers. The Internet also increases the need to evolve and refactor legacy systems to new hardware and software development platforms. Evolving a legacy software system to become Web-enabled is a challenging task for numerous reasons, including poor documentation and high maintenance costs. In addition, the legacy system must continue to operate (and thus bring in revenue) during the transition. Often organizations must support the two product versions (desktop and the Internet) longer than expected, so the evolution methodology must reduce maintenance costs during the migration period.

THE FOCAL METHODOLOGY

Various domain analysis and requirements engineering techniques push the end user perspective into the solution domain by either working toward design (Kop & Mayr, 1998; Krut, 1993) or through scenario and use cases (Booch et al., 1998; Kaindl et al., 1998; Fowler & Scott, 1997). These solutions help developers understand how a system is to be used, but they do not address the solution domain concerns of software evolution, configuration management, testing, and documentation. Similarly, many software evolution techniques exist (Bergey et al., 1997; Brownsword & Clements, 1996; Weiderman et al., 1997; Bracho, 1997; Dorda et al., 2000), but none consider Feature Engineering as a software evolution driver. This is an oversight because Feature Engineering is a promising discipline that can help to reduce the complexity gap between user expectations and software functionality. The techniques of software evolution and reengineering either focus on entire system rewrites (Woods, Carriere & Kazman, 1999) or using reverse reengineering for comprehension purposes (Letovsky & Soloway, 1986) rather than incrementally evolving the legacy system. Component-Based Software Engineering (CBSE) offers promising techniques to solve the problem of component construction (Brown, 1996), but CBSE has not yet been connected to the features that are present in a system; creating this connection explicitly is one of the contributions of FOCAL.

FOCAL has two important goals: **(G1)** Identify system features that have already exhibited disproportionate maintenance costs and are likely to change. **(G2)** Extract fine-grained components from these features within the legacy system to share between different applications within the product line.

Assumptions

FOCAL has three basic assumptions. First, we assume that the source code for the legacy system to be evolved is available and that it was developed using a modern programming language such as Visual Basic, C++, Java, or Fortran. The reason for this assumption is that we use off-the-shelf code profiling tools for tracing the source that implements a particular feature. Second, we assume that the legacy system has regression test suites. These regression test suites are untapped resources from the evolution point of view because they can be used to identify the features most important to the end users. Third, we assume that some domain knowledge and expertise is available, although this is not a binding constraint. FOCAL is not intended for all legacy systems; neither will all software evolution initiatives benefit from it. However, legacy software systems that have kept pace with compiler upgrades should greatly benefit.

Basic Approach

Using FOCAL, developers can trace functions within the source code that implement particular feature(s) by running regression test cases and profiling the behavior of the system. We use the results to evolve features into components using *refactoring* and CBSE techniques. We use Fowler's definition of refactoring code: "a change made to the internal structure of software to make it easier to understand and cheaper to modify without changing its observable behavior" (Fowler, 1999). FOCAL is novel because we leverage existing artifacts such as test cases and code profiling utilities. While we do not address the issue of architectural evolution, FOCAL does produce better-structured component-based code with reduced evolution and maintenance costs. Likewise, refactoring alone cannot be used to evolve a system. FOCAL promotes the systematic scheduling of evolution, and its results are measurable and can be validated.

A description of the input and output of each step is outlined in Appendix A. FOCAL uses currently available tools (code profilers such as cSuds (Telcordia Technologies, 1998) and NuMega's *TrueCoverage*™ (2003), and databases such as Microsoft Access) for immediate applicability.

Overview

The 10-step FOCAL methodology, as shown in Figure 2, consists of three phases. FOCAL demands that users examine the reasons that trigger evolution of a legacy system and **identify** the feature implementations within the legacy system. The system is then **evolved** to create fine-grained components. Finally, the effort is **verified** in three ways. First, we match the output of the regression tests after the insertion with original output. Second, we measure the costs of maintaining the feature after evolution and compare that to the prior costs (to show the cost-benefit). Third, we evaluate the reusability of the newly created components in other product line members.

Figure 2: FOCAL Evolution Methodology.

	Problem Domain	*Solution Domain*
Identify	1. Identify Evolution Reasons 2. Identify Problem Features 3. Map Test Cases to Features	4. Map Features to Functions 5. Identify Core & Feature Implementation
Evolve		6. Refactor & Create Components
Verify		7. Insert Component into Legacy System 8. Verify Results 9. Reuse Component in Product Line 10. Measure Savings Benefit

Identify

The end users work with testers and project managers to report the problems they are facing with a particular feature or a group of features. The developers then become involved to identify the underlying feature that is the source of the maintenance problem(s). Testers and end users work together to select test cases from the regression test suite for the feature(s) with problem(s). The execution trace of the selected test cases is compared with the regression test suite to ensure that no relevant test cases are missed.

Selected test cases are executed using code profilers to locate source code that implements features. Features are well known for being "cross-cutting" through software (Griss, 2000). Cross-cutting means that a function can implement many features and these features share the same code/data. The close relationship between features and functions means that features will interact with each other. This interaction is also defined as the feature-interaction problem in the literature (Griss, 2000; Tsang & Magill, 1998). Our **feature model** helps to identify where features are located within the legacy system, how features are related to other features, and how they interact with each other.

Finally, the data from the code profiler and the execution traces of the regression test cases are analyzed. Using heuristics, the developers decide if creating components will benefit other members of the product line as well as the existing legacy system. Table 1 briefly summarizes the properties a feature should possess to be a candidate for evolution; a detailed description of the feature model is provided elsewhere (Mehta, 2002).

Evolve

Once the location of a feature within the code is identified and it is decided to extract the feature implementation into a component, the component code must be refactored. Our **fine-grained component model** provides guidelines to extract feature-specific code and data that are then encapsulated by a fine-grained component. A detailed description of the feature model is provided elsewhere (Mehta, 2002).

Verify

The developers integrate these newly created components into the target legacy system and verify the stability of the newly integrated system using the regression suite.

Table 1: Properties of Evolvable Features.

Properties	***Description***
Visible to end user	End user must be able to execute the feature and see the problems
Testable	Testers must have test cases in the regression test suite to test the feature
Exhibit recurring problems	Fixing feature inadvertently affects other features
High maintenance costs	Due to recurring problems and unwanted side effects, the feature's maintenance cost is higher
Feature exists in other product line member	Reuse can be leveraged

The performance of the system is also compared. The project manager works with testers and the developers to use budget analysis to report maintenance savings to end-users and management. In addition, these feature-based fine-grained components can be reused across the product line for additional savings.

Validation

To validate the proposed benefits of FOCAL, we examine the evolution of a real-world legacy system, the American Financial Systems (AFS) Master System (AMS). Using interviews with testers, project managers, and end-users of the system, we developed a detailed model of the legacy system's features. Engineers at AFS prioritized the features to be extracted, and the regression test cases for these features were executed and code profile information was captured. Researchers used refactoring to isolate the code associated with extracted features to create components. These components were then inserted back into the legacy system to continue functioning to verify the results of this technique. In addition to verifying the integrity of the system, regression test suites can be used to guide refactoring efforts during software evolution to create reusable software assets (components) within the enterprise. Details of this case study can be found elsewhere (Mehta & Heineman, 2002).

MODELS

The FOCAL methodology depends on two important models. The **Feature Model** defines what a feature is, how it is implemented, how it interacts with other features, and how it is related to other features within the source code. The **Fine-Grained Component Model** describes the constituents of the refactored components using interfaces, properties, and methods. To support the results of our chapter we also rely on two additional models. The **Budget Analysis Model** lists and describes the elements that are necessary for performing the cost-benefit analysis of our evolution methodology. The **Formal Model** provides the theoretical foundation for our evolution methodology; this last model is outside the scope of this book, and details can be found in dissertation of Mehta (2002).

Feature Model

Intuitively, a feature is an identifiable unit of system functionality from the end user's perspective. Examples of features include the ability of a word processor to spell-check or the ability of an accounting system to generate a balance sheet statement for a given fiscal year. Software developers are expected to translate such feature-oriented requests into system design. **Feature Engineering** addresses the understanding of features in software systems and defines mechanisms for carrying a feature from the problem domain into the solution domain (Turner, 1999).

Feature Definition

We developed the following definition by extending an existing definition from (Raccoon, 1995):

*A **feature** is a group of individual requirements that describes a unit of functionality with respect to a specific point of view relative to a software development life cycle.*

This definition is rooted in the problem domain but shows how a feature can be used in software evolution. For example, a system might support a feature that performs complex calculations in batch mode without user interaction. To an end user, this feature is a time saver because input can be stored in a file or a database to be used at a later time. At the same time, testers might employ this feature to enable regression testing between two versions of the system; developers might design a specific set of modules to process user input without user interaction to analyze code coverage. A code-profiling tool executing regression test cases exercising that feature can locate the *feature implementation*, and evolution of that feature can commence.

Feature Implementation (FI)

End users comprehend a system through its features but are unaware of the specific way in which these features are implemented. Software developers view the same system in terms of data types, local and global control, reusable functions, and units of testing and maintenance. Table 2 outlines how a feature might be implemented within function(s). If the function and data implement only one feature, then the evolution is trivial. We are more interested in the remaining cases because it is more likely that a function is involved in the implementation of more than one feature. We define feature implementation as following:

*A **feature implementation (FI)** is the set of statements (including data) within all functions that execute when that feature is invoked.*

When a single feature implementation contains code from many functions, then the critical viewpoint regarding evolution is the solution domain because the feature "cross-cuts" the software (Griss, 2000). Such code is often highly coupled and deeply embedded within the legacy system. When many related features are implemented by a single function, then understanding the problem domain is critical for successful evolution.

Regression Testing

We propose a novel use of dynamic slicing (Korel & Laski, 1998) that uses regression test cases to identify where a feature is implemented in the legacy system and to incrementally refactor the code base to create fine-grained components. Not every feature is evolved during system evolution, nor should each feature be encapsulated in a fine-grained component. From a select candidate set, the organization must still

Table 2: Feature/Function Relationships.

Feature	*Functions*	*Critical Evolution Viewpoint*
1	Many	Solution domain
Many	1	Problem domain
1	1	None exists
Many	Many	N/A – Must be decomposed

prioritize specific features to evolve. These features must be associated with existing test cases to identify in which functions the features are implemented. Test cases can be associated with features as follows: (1) The regression test cases already identify the features being tested, or this information can be discovered through interviews with domain experts; (2) The regression test cases can be clustered to identify "like-minded" test cases that align with features.

Domain Knowledge and Documentation

With domain knowledge or suitable documentation, it is possible to identify test cases that represent a particular feature or to construct them from scratch. We found that testers know which test cases exercise specific features; our case study assumes this knowledge.

Clustering

Clustering analysis uses a measure of similarity to organize a collection of data points into clusters (Jain, Murty & Flynn, 1999). Our technique for grouping test cases by feature is based on the premise that related test cases exercise either a feature or closely related features. The dissertation of Mehta (2002) describes the details of a heuristic to cluster related test cases; here we sketch the main idea. Consider 10 test cases with five sets of input items that are considered the most important user inputs (Table 3). We analyze the user input and assign ordinal values to each valid user input for a given *item* (any field). We create a matrix of test cases and items and calculate the *regression* and *standard deviation.* For example, {T4, T6, T8, T2} are a group together because their regression values are similar and are higher than other test cases. Similarly, test cases {T1, T5, T3, T7, T9, T10} can be grouped together because they vary only by Item 1 and Item 5. Both regression and standard deviation should be used to ensure that only related test cases are mapped to the same cluster.

Table 3:Test Cases Versus Items.

Test Cases	Item 1	Item 2	Item 3	Item 4	Item 5	Regression	Std Dev
T4	1	1	1	9	9	2.4	4.38
T6	1	1	1	8	9	2.3	4.12
T8	1	1	1	9	8	2.2	4.12
T2	1	1	1	8	8	2.1	3.83
T1	1	3	3	3	4	0.6	1.1
T5	2	3	3	3	3	0.2	0.45
T3	2	3	3	3	1	-0.2	0.89
T7	3	3	3	3	2	-0.2	0.45
T9	3	3	3	3	1	-0.4	0.89
T10	4	3	3	3	1	-0.6	1.1

Figure 3: A Feature may be Invoked by Several Test Cases.

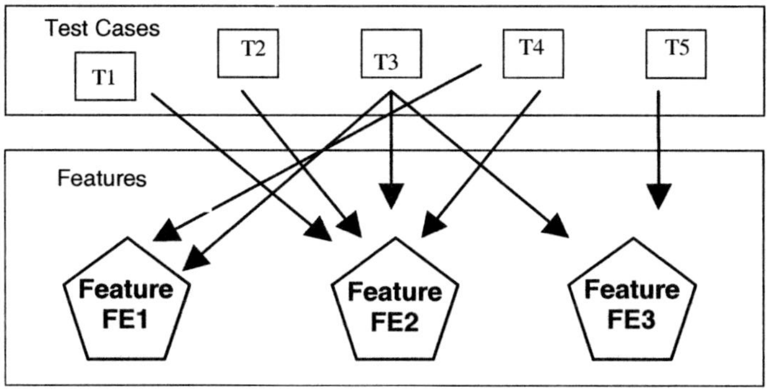

Features and Functions

We must identify the percentage of lines of code (LOC) coverage of a specific feature within a function to determine where a feature is implemented. To do so, we (1) identify test case(s) that represent that feature; (2) run the profiler to obtain execution traces in terms of LOC and features (see Figure 3); (3) determine the union of the LOC within all functions for all grouped test cases for a feature. We can then calculate the percentage coverage of each function. Often code profiles simply return a percentage of code covered, but this is not sufficiently fine-grained; we need individual line information.

The feature/function relationship via test cases is either one::one or one::many. When the feature/test case relationship is one::one, a code profiler can immediately identify the feature/function relationships. A one::many relationship is more realistic and complicated, requiring special attention.

Step 1: Map Test Case and Features

We start with the test case/feature mapping as discussed earlier. Table 4 provides a small example where shaded portions represent the exercising of a feature (in each row) by the test case (in the column).

Table 4: Test Case and Feature Mapping.

	Test Cases						
Features	**T1**	**T2**	**T3**	**T4**	**T5**	**T6**	**T7**
FE_1	■			■	■	■	
FE_2		■			■	■	
FE_3		■			■	■	■
FE_4	■		■		■	■	

Step 2: Run Test Case and Profiler

Test cases are run with the profiler and the results shown in Table 5. Each cell contains the LOC or each function as determined by the profiler. The next step is to merge the LOC within each function when exercising a feature (i.e., group columns together by cluster). Finally, we calculate the percentage coverage of each function (not shown here).

Step 3: Apply Heuristics

Table 6 provides information for how features and functions may be related. If a function is fully executed for all features then it is part of the CORE, and likely to be part of a shared library. These helper functions are typically stateless.

When the system is invoked in a batch mode all the test cases execute 100% of certain functions that are not part of any feature. These functions are typically part of system initialization, system shutdown and setting up global variables. While these functions are not part of CORE, they are part of the system architecture and its global control structure. Turner (1999) considers such functions as a baseline architecture. The

Table 5: Test Case and Function Relationship by Profiler.

	Test Cases						
Functions	**T1**	**T2**	**T3**	**T4**	**T5**	**T6**	**T7**
f_x	1,2,5,10					1—4	1—4
f_y	1—3,5,8,10	1—10		1—5		1—4	
f_z			1—5	1—3,5,8,10			
f_a		1—10					
f_b	1—10	1—10	1—10	1—10	1—10	1—10	1—10
f_c	1—6	1—6,10			1—6	1—10	1—10

Table 6: UNION of all LOC for a Feature Implementation.

Test Cases	**T1,T4,T5,T6**	**T2,T5,T6**	**T2,T5,T6,T7**	**T1,T5,T6**
Functions/Features	**FE$_1$**	**FE$_2$**	**FE$_3$**	**FE$_4$**
f_x	1,2,5,10	1—4	1—4	1—5,10
f_y	1—3,5,8,10	1—10	1—10	1—5,8,10
f_z		1—4	1—4	1—4
f_a		1—10	1—10	1—4
f_b	1—10	1—10	1—10	1—10
f_c	1—6	1—6,10	1—10	1—6

base-line architecture is product-specific and contains a specific caller/callee sequence, and is unlikely to be reusable in other components. We argue that such code does not change often and is not a candidate for evolution into a component.

Neighbouring Features (K)

Using Table 6, we see how features may interact within a function. Traversing through the matrix, one can identify the features that interact within a function. We start with a given feature and traverse down to each function where the coverage is greater than 0%. Once the feature implementation is identified, we traverse in the horizontal direction to identify the coverage of other features in that function (greater than 0%). Thus, traversing down, across and then up can identify neighbouring features; these neighbouring features form relationships.

Evolution Threshold (T)

FOCAL can be used to evolve any feature. However, we found that rewriting is preferable to features that cross-cut across many functions and interact with many features. We have developed heuristics concerning thresholds that can identify features that are good candidates for evolution. Using Table 6 to identify neighbouring features and the number of functions where the feature is implemented, we calculate the average coverage percentage within the function. This defines a threshold regarding evolution of the feature. In our experience, we found that FOCAL works best when K=3, NF=17 and C=80% (Mehta's dissertation (2002) contains a more detailed analysis). In general, if K is high, the feature being evolved cross-cuts through many other features. Conversely, if K is low, then the feature being evolved is trivial. Likewise, if a feature is implemented in many functions (i.e., high NF), then the feature is likely to be scattered in numerous functions. If NF is low (perhaps 1 or 2), then it is a trivial case, as the feature is totally contained in a low number of functions. If the average coverage of the feature within a function is low, then it certainly does not make sense to evolve that feature. Table 7 presents our decision matrix.

Feature Interactions

A legacy software system has many features. These features must interact with each other to provide wider system functionality. When features interact with each other, they

Table 7: Evolution Threshold (T) Decision Matrix.

Neighbouring feature (K)	Number of functions (NF)	Average Coverage (C)	Continue?
High	High	High	No
High	High	Low	No
High	Low	Low	No
High	Low	High	Possibly
Low	High	High	Possibly
Low	High	Low	No
Low	Low	High	Possibly
Low	Low	Low	No

Figure 4: Feature Interaction via Functions and Data.

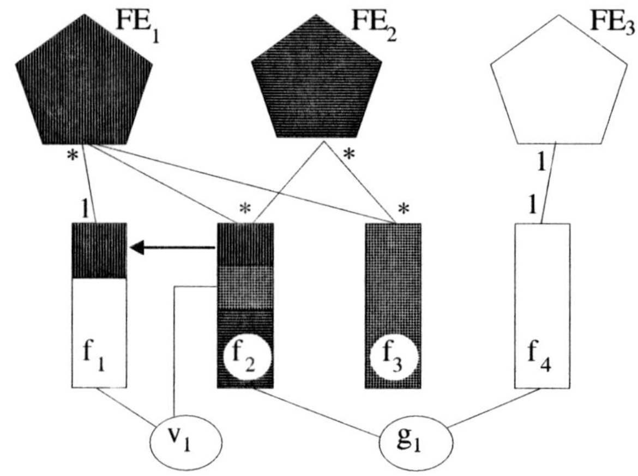

have an "effect" on the system. Depending upon the state of the legacy system, this effect can be either positive or negative (resulting in errors). We must distinguish between intended interactions between features, interactions between features that are not intentional but do not result in errors (or may even have positive side-effects), and unintended and undesirable feature interaction not known in advance and leading to faulty applications.

In Figure 4, functions are represented as rectangles, variables (both local and global) as circles, and features as pentagons. FIs are shaded using the same pattern as their corresponding feature (shown by the lines between pentagon and rectangle). A feature implementation is the set of shaded regions within the rectangle. When two or more feature implementations share common data or functions, there are four key interactions.

Shared Functions (SS & SSF)

A stateless function (Field, Ramalingam & Tip, 1995) can be shared between two FIs. For example, all statements in function f_3 are executed when both FE_1 and FE_2 are exercised and f_3 accesses no data. A statefull function (Field, Ramalingam & Tip, 1995) can be shared between two features. Refactoring may require complex variable and control analysis. Function f_2 accesses global variable g_1 and since f_2 is part of both FI_1 and FI_2, there is an implicit interaction between FE_1 and FE_2.

Dependent Data (DD) and Functions (DF)

An FI may be dependent on the data that is updated by another FI. For example, f_1 and f_2 access the local variable v_1, leading to an interaction between FE_1 and FE_2. An FI may be dependent on a function that is part of another FI. Function f_2 calls function f_1 (shown by the arrow in Figure 4) when FE_1 is exercised but not when FE_2 is exercised (note the consistent shading). The remaining statements in f_1 (shaded white) are associated with other features not shown and, FE_1 interacts with these features. As each feature is exercised, code profiling tools identify the code slices associated with each feature, providing the details necessary to identify interactions between features.

Feature Relationships

Turner identified several relationships among interacting features (Turner, 1999). We integrate and extend Turner's idea of feature relationships into our feature model. Understanding feature relationships allows us to better:

1. Interpret feature interactions, as feature relationships refine the concept of interaction by providing specification through calling sequence.
2. Refactor the existing FI into fine-grained component(s).
3. Define the communication among fine-grained component(s) that will compose the large reusable unit.

Categories

We expand this concept into direct and indirect relationships among interacting features and map relationships to FIs. We categorized the feature relationships into two broad categories, as shown in Table 8.

1. **Indirect relationships** are problem domain relationships and are abstract in nature. These relationships are important when talking to the end user and usually exist at the application level rather than at the function level. The end user comprehends the system to be composed of several features and has a perspective with respect to the software functionality.

Table 8: Feature Relationships.

Category	Relationship Type	Description	Example
Indirect	Generalization Specialization	Features can extend existing features like sub-classes extend parent classes.	Column breaks and page breaks are special instances of a generic "break" in text.
	Composed	Features can be composed of several sub-features.	Spell-check feature also has auto-correct sub-feature.
Direct	Compete Conflict	When multiple features cannot coexist at the same time (either at run time or when the system is configured and built).	See Mehta's dissertation (Mehta, 2002) for further discussion.
	Altered	When a feature's state (global data, object or implementation) is altered by another feature.	A text box might have its background turned to red when an error is identified (in its content).
	Shared	When a group of feature share resources (global data, objects or other implementation) with other features.	The Windows™ clipboard shares the text copied to it with other applications.
	Required	When a feature must be present for another feature to function.	Cross referencing and auto-numbering of figures

2. **Direct relationships** are solution domain entities. These relationships may be *visible* to the end users and typically consist of several *sub-features.* These relationships have concrete FIs associated with them. *Compete* and *conflict* are feature relationships that are implemented using multiple operating system threads (Mehta, 2002) and are not discussed further in this chapter.

Determining Feature Relationships

While indirect relationships are important, their purpose is mainly to communicate with end users. There is no FI associated with indirect relationships because these relationships are abstract in nature. Since we are interested in evolving the FIs into fine-grained components, our methodology is focused on direct relationships. The following three elements are important in understanding how features are related:

1. **Granularity** identifies neighbouring features associated with the feature that we are trying to evolve. There are two levels of granularity, inter-function and intra-function. In inter-function, the FI is exclusively in a function and that function does not implement any other FI. The neighbouring features communicate via global data. In intra-function, the function may have several Fis, and these FIs may interact via global and/or local data.
2. **Order of execution** identifies which neighbouring feature is executed first.
3. **Variable analysis** identifies which variables (local and global) are used among neighbouring features and how. Along with the order of execution, variable analysis identifies which global or local variables within the neighbouring features changed due to the execution.

We have developed techniques to identify feature relationships based upon order of execution, change in variable state, feature interaction, and feature implementation.

Figure 5: Fine-Grained Component Model.

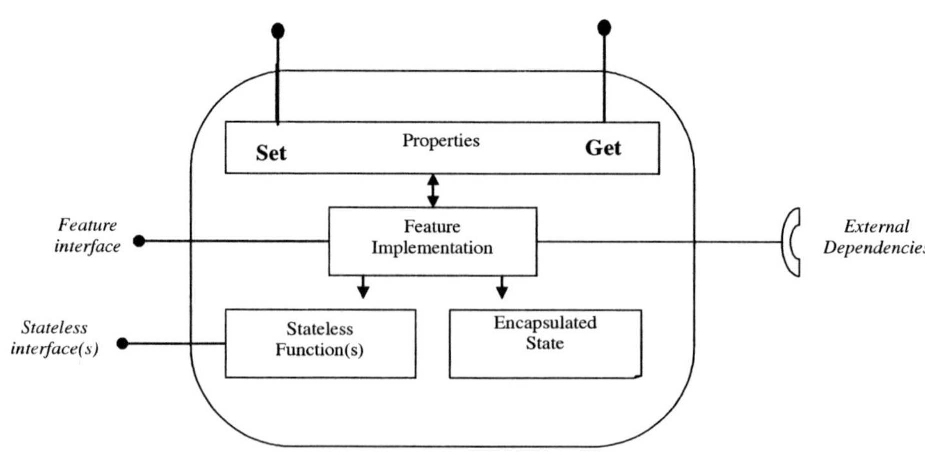

Fine-Grained Component Model

The fine-grained component (FGC) model sketched in Figure 5 is technology-independent and can be implemented using any contemporary component technology. While an FGC can maintain its own state, it may require data passed to it through its *properties*. The FGC model encapsulates a feature implementation that can be invoked by its public interface. An FGC can provide data via *property get*. An FGC can also implement any shared stateless functions and their interfaces. Finally, an FGC can access any external dependencies (such as CORE, public functions within the legacy system, or even other components) via specifying external dependencies.

We use the following definitions from Heineman and Councill (2001):

*A **component** is a software element that conforms to a **component model** and can be independently deployed and composed without modification according to a composition standard.*

A component model defines specific interaction and composition standards.

Our fine-grained component model has the following aspects: Properties, Feature Implementation, Stateless Functions, and Encapsulated State.

Property Set and Get

Our feature model explains the importance of global and local variables when evaluating feature relationships. When we refactor the FI code, we disable the old code within the legacy code that had previously depended upon accessing local or global variables. *Property set* is a way to pass these variables into the refactored component. Thus, *property set* must be called prior to invoking the FI component. Like *property set*, the FI can change the state of certain local or global variables that the legacy system may need to continue to function properly. Using *property get,* the legacy system retrieves the values of these local or global variables after invoking FI.

Feature Implementation

The FI from the legacy code is refactored and encapsulated here and may contain functions, classes, local data and other necessary data structures. The FI provides an interface invoked by the legacy system and other product line members. This FI can call other fine-grained components, CORE or any externally dependent functions.

Stateless Function(s)

The FI may need stateless functions (SS) that are not part of CORE (i.e., not every feature uses the function). An SS can be part of an FGC and its interface is exposed. The SS can call fine-grained components, CORE or externally dependent functions.

Encapsulated State

The FGC may maintain its own state, which is analogous to an EJB Session Bean. This state is maintained by variables local to the component. Maintaining state has its advantages and disadvantages. It allows for better performance, as the fine-grained component retains the values of its variables from one call to another. This saves the recalculation/resetting of variables. However, in a multiple-user environment, maintaining state can overload the server resources because state is stored in memory. State can also be serialized in a database, which usually provides a good compromise between performance and load issues discussed earlier. Our FGC model allows for maintaining the state but leaves the choice to the developer.

External Dependencies

The FGC can invoke SSF, CORE and other components using a well-defined interface for external access. This interface can be implemented using "events" to access any state set by an SSF. Typically, external dependencies are a list of declaration of functions and other components that the FI or the SS may need within the FGC.

Evolving Feature Implementation into Fine-Grained Components

Once we identify a FI using code profilers, we refactor that FI into a fine-grained component. The first step is to isolate each function that contains code belonging to the target FI. This analysis is often complex because local variables, global variables, and dependent functions can be shared between FIs. The FGC model shares the functions as well as the data that are scattered across various functions through explicit interfaces.

In the fine-grained components developed in this chapter, the interaction between components is clearly specified by the interfaces. Components can also access functionality using stateless interfaces. The FI is shielded from specific variable implementations by using the interface for external access; over time, the variable implementation will be replaced with explicit linkages to external interfaces.

The top part of Figure 6 shows a single function f_x whose code is shared between FI_1 and FI_2; similarly, function f_y is involved in $\mathbf{FE_3}$ and $\mathbf{FE_2}$. The purpose of the cascading functions is to show that $\mathbf{FE_2}$ is spread in many functions and interacts with other features. Common code and variables include: calls to SS f_1, global variable g_1, and local variables v_3 and v_4. Extracting FI_2 into $Comp_2$ involves several artifacts. Function f_1 can easily be extracted because it is stateless. Double arrowheads on the arrow to g_1 show that it is both read and updated by FI_2. Local variables v_3 and v_4 are used by both FIs but FI_2 only reads v_4 (as shown by arrowhead), while v_3 is both updated and read by FI_2; v_4 is set by FE_1 but v_4 is used by $FE_{2:1}$. FI_2 also accesses global variable g_2, SS function f_2, and SSF f_3. There are several important regions in Figure 6.

- $\mathbf{FE_1}$**:** The complete code in f_x that belongs to FE_1.
- $\mathbf{FE_2}$**:** The complete code in f_x that belongs to FE_2.
- $\mathbf{FE_{2:1}}$**:** $FE_{2:1}$ is the shared code between $\mathbf{FE_1}$ and $\mathbf{FE_2}$ that is responsible for the cross-cutting problem associated with features that makes evolution of legacy systems extremely difficult. The region $FE_{2:1}$ implicitly defines feature relationships because global or local variables are accessed.
- $\mathbf{FE_{1.Exclusive}}$**:** The complete code in f_x that belongs exclusively to FE_1 and is not shared with any other FIs including $FE_{2:1}$.
- $\mathbf{FE_{2.Exclusive}}$**:** The complete code in f_x that belongs exclusively to FE_2 and is not shared with any other FIs including $FE_{2:1}$.

Figure 6: Evolving FI into a Fine-Grained Component.

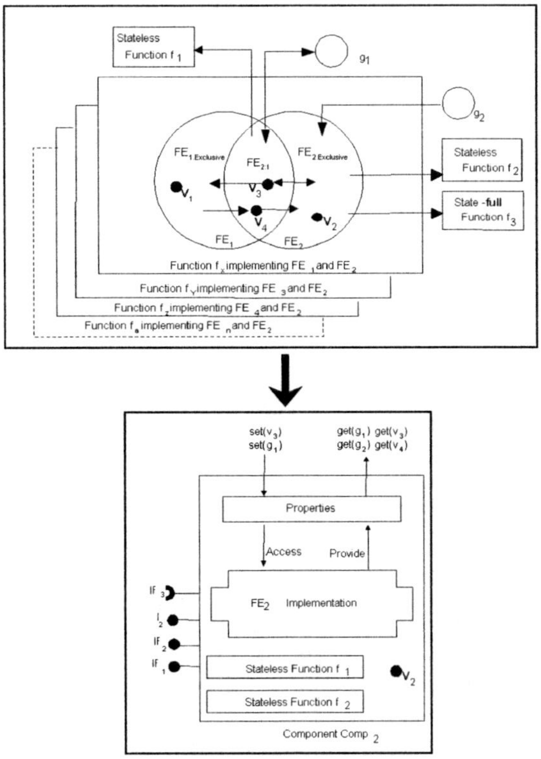

$Comp_2$ in Figure 6 encapsulates FI_2 and has several public interfaces (represented by circles attached by lines to $Comp_2$) to enable original code to access the moved artifacts. $Comp_2$ maintains data previously local to f_x, replaces global variable references with an interface that treats such data as properties, and contains stateless and statefull functions. Public interface I_2 is the primary interface for $Comp_2$. Stateless functions f_1 and f_2 are also encapsulated into $Comp_2$ and they can be accessed via the public interfaces IF_1 and IF_2. SSF f_3 is accessed with IF_3; through an outgoing interface, it is assumed that f_3 is not located inside $Comp_2$ but its state is accessed via IF_3. Local and global variables used by FI_2 can be accessed via *get/set* properties. Additionally, the *get* property provides a way to share local and global variables with other feature implementations. As related features are evolved, the interaction between fine-grained components will become increasingly specified and all implicit communication will vanish. Thus, we separate accessing variables from their implementation. When multiple features are extracted at the same time, many stateless functions will be common to several feature implementations; these will be encapsulated within a COREcomponent, rather than a fine-grained component, and will be treated as a shared library.

Table 9: Budget Analysis Model.

Cost of Mapping Features and Test Cases	Time taken by the software team to identify and map features and test cases.
Cost of identifying code using test cases and profiler	Time taken by the software team to run the code coverage tool to identify feature implementation.
Cost of Refactoring	Time taken to analyze heuristics and FIs.
Cost of Developing Components	Time taken to develop feature-based fine-grained components.
Cost of Developing CORE Component	Time taken to create the shared reusable library.
Cost of Configuration Management (CM)	Time taken to develop CM activities among the product line.
Cost of Testing	Time taken to test feature-based and CORE components.
Cost of Training and Documentation	Time taken to develop user's guide and train other members of the software process team.
Savings from Solving Feature Problems	Time saved from fixing the feature specific problems. It can be viewed as what it would cost in absence of the methodology.
Savings from improved architecture (explicit communication, reduced global variables, better understanding of features)	Time saved in training a new hire. This element is hard to measure because it is always implied. **We were unable to measure at AFS.**
Savings in reusing CORE	Time saved in re-development efforts in other product line members.
Savings in reusing feature-specific component	Time saved in re-development efforts in other product line members.
Net Cost (+)/Savings (-)	**Sum of all costs and savings. Negative number means a profit.**

Budget Model

We have developed a model that allows the project manager to quickly calculate the net gain or loss in applying FOCAL. While there are several cost models such as COCOMO and others (Boehm, 1981; Kitchenham & Taylor, 1985; Marwane & Mili, 1991; Miyazaki & Mori, 1985) that can be used, we developed a simple model, summarized in Table 9, to track costs relevant to FOCAL. Other cost savings are also possible, so this list is not exhaustive. The elements of our cost models are listed in Table 9 (full details can be found in Mehta's dissertation (2002)).

RELATED WORK

The novel combination of Feature Engineering and CBSE presented by this chapter greatly benefits software evolution by bridging the complexity gap between the problem domain and the solution domain. While a full and comprehensive analysis of related work is provided by Mehta in his dissertation (Mehta, 2002), we have chosen to provide just a snapshot of the related work by focusing on the two issues of (1) locating system features; and (2) approaches to legacy software system evolution.

Locating System Features

There are known techniques to locate system features using execution slices; however, they are predominantly used for system debugging rather than evolution. As far as identifying program features, there are four researchers whose work is directly related to ours. Wilde and Scully (1995) pioneered the use of execution trace to locate the implementation of features; Wong et al. (1999), Reps et al. (1997), and Deprez and Lakhotia (2000) developed techniques that operate on execution traces to collect information about features. A full comparison of FOCAL with each of these researchers' works can be found in Mehta's dissertation (2002). We present a tabular summary in Table 10.

Legacy System Evolution

Many software evolution techniques exist (Mehta & Heineman, 1999; Bergey et al., 1997; Weiderman et al., 1997; Bracho, 1997), but they focus on solution domain and do not consider Feature Engineering as a software evolution driver. System evolution is a broad term that covers a continuum from adding a field in a database to completely re-implementing a system.

Table 10: Comparison of Closely Related Work.

	Wilde & Scully (1995)	**Wong et al. (1999)**	**Reps et al. (1997)**
Motivation	Program Understanding	Program Understanding and Debugging	Year 2000 Solution
Key Elements	Features are entities that must be testable. Components are sub-routines.	Feature is the same as functionality represented in specification. Components are source file sub-routines.	No definition of feature or component provided.
Technique	Input sets developed by maintainers are used to identify program features using instrumentation tools.	Difference between execution traces (via input sets) that invoke a feature and those that do not is calculated.	Input sets are executed to generate program graph and path spectrum is analyzed. Input sets are varied incrementally.
Formalism	Set theory	Statistical and set theory	Graph theory
Applicability	Used in two large-scale C programs for research purposes but only as a prototype. Commercial application yet to be seen. Appears scalable.	Used in a medium sized C program. Appears to be scalable. Three metrics are developed to calculate disparity, dedication and concentration between features and program.	Used in solving Y2K problem. Cannot be used to identify specific end-user features as each graph requires several inputs and usually results in large number of permutations.
Tools	TraceView	χSuds/χVue	DYNADIFF
Feature Interaction Problem	Identify and solve by selecting proper test cases.	Identify and solve by selecting proper test cases.	Generally ignored but attempted to solve implicitly by analyzing graph via brute force.
Mapping Test Cases and Features	Left to developers. End user perspective is ignored.	Left to developers. End user perspective is ignored.	Brute Force. Enduser perspective is ignored.
Generate Reusable Components	No	No	No
Language Dependent	Yes	Yes	No. Use symbolic info from compiler.
Addresses Data	No	No	No
Identifies CORE	Yes, partially	No	No

Table 10: Comparison of Closely Related Work (continued)

	Deprez & Lakhotia (2000)	FOCAL
Motivation	Program Understanding and Testing	Evolution, bridging the complexity gap, and reuse.
Key Elements	A feature is the language used in feature syntax. Components are statements and procedures. Execution traces are defined.	Features, feature implementation, and components are well-defined. CORE and Execution traces are defined.
Technique	Features are mapped to input cases. Input set is classified into invoking and excluding sets. Execution traces of all input sets are collected to calculate differences.	Regression tests used by testers and end users that represent features are run using a code profiler to identify feature implementation for evolution.
Formalism	BNF grammar and formal automata	Relational models
Applicability	Theoretic in nature. No real practical application seen. It depends on large input data sets; thus identifying relevant code takes a long time. Generating BNF grammar is cumbersome.	Used in evolving features of large Visual Basic program into reusable components. Feature and component model provide theoretic foundation.
Tools	None	Any code profiler
Feature Interaction Problem	Identify and solve by selecting proper test cases.	Identify and provide explicit model for features that share code and data.
Mapping Test Cases and Features	Must use large test suite and end user perspective is ignored.	Regression test cases are used, as they represent end user features.
Generate Reusable Components	No	Yes
Language Dependent	No	No
Addresses Data	No	Yes
Identifies CORE	No	Yes

Regression Testing

Rothermel and Harrold (1996) group a variety of selective regression testing approaches into three categories. Safe approaches require the selection of every existing test case that exercises any program element that could possibly be affected by a given program change. Minimization approaches attempt to select the smallest set of test cases necessary to test affected program elements at least once. Coverage approaches attempt to assure that some structural coverage criterion is met by the test cases that are selected. All three categories have been extensively studied by researchers from a theoretical point of view to either minimize or prioritize test cases (Rothermel & Harrold, 1993; Rothermel et al., 1999; Agrawal et al., 1993; Harrold et al., 1993; Chen & Lau, 1996; Wong et al., 1998; Chen et al., 1994).

CONCLUSIONS

Methodology Applicability

Although our methodology is programming language-independent and does not depend on specific code profiler tools, several factors affect the applicability of our methodology.

- We applied FOCAL to a legacy system that was experiencing maintenance costs of certain key features visible to the end user. Furthermore, these features were evaluated to be useful across several applications. We expect that businesses will earn the most return on investment (ROI) under a scenario in which the refactored feature implementation can be reused.
- Organizations that seek to apply FOCAL must have a mature software process in place, as judged, perhaps, by CMM level, or ISO 9001 level; in particular, FOCAL requires regression test cases and the ability to track maintenance costs of making changes. Organizations that are at least CMM level II or ISO 9001 level I should be satisfactory.
- Our methodology has been applied and tested in a function-based system with numerous global variables, functions and sub-routines. The target legacy system application was coded using Visual Basic. While the overall approach is language-independent, we acknowledge that FOCAL will have to be customized to address object-oriented and real-time legacy systems.
- The primary refactoring technique we developed is the fine-grained component model within which the feature implementation will be contained. The developers used to refactor the code properly are based upon the information reported from FOCAL.

Sensitivity Relative to Average Coverage (C)

Not all features are ideal candidates for evolution. In Table 7, we showed whether to continue with the methodology or not based upon the *threshold* (T). Based upon data collected from AMS (see Table 11), we believe the average coverage (C) determines how sensitive a particular feature is for evolution. We found that the *inputprocessing* feature had values of {K=3, NF=17, C=80%}. Analyzing the feature/function matrix of *input processing* of AMS, we found the following: if we reduced C to 50%, K would increase to 8 and NF would increase to 19. If we reduced C to 25%, K would increase to 21 and NF would increase to 99. These findings indicate that we are dealing with less cohesive code, hinting that evolution would take longer (for a more detailed analysis see Mehta's dissertation (2002)). If, however, C were increased to be greater than 90%, K would decrease to 2 and NF would decrease to 1, indicating the trivial case. Note that {K=0, NF=0, and C=100%} represents the CORE.

The case study data is shown in Table 11 and plotted in Figure 7. Note that Figure 7 shows C on the x-axis (represents the first data point of 10%, 2 means 25%, 3 means 50% and so on) and a scale on the y-axis that is used to plot NF and K. We can see from Figure 7 that as C decreases, the distance between NF and K increases, indicating more time to evolve these features, and likewise as C increases, distance between NF and K decreases, indicating lesser time to evolve. We found that C for our case study was best suited

Table 11: Coverage Sensitivity Data in AMS.

Feature	Neighbouring Feature (K)	Number Functions (NF)	Average Coverage (C)
Log	125	35	10%
Constraints	99	21	25%
Callback	8	19	50%
Input Processing	3	17	80%
Import/Export	2	1	90%
CORE	0	0	100%

Figure 7: Coverage Sensitivity in AMS.

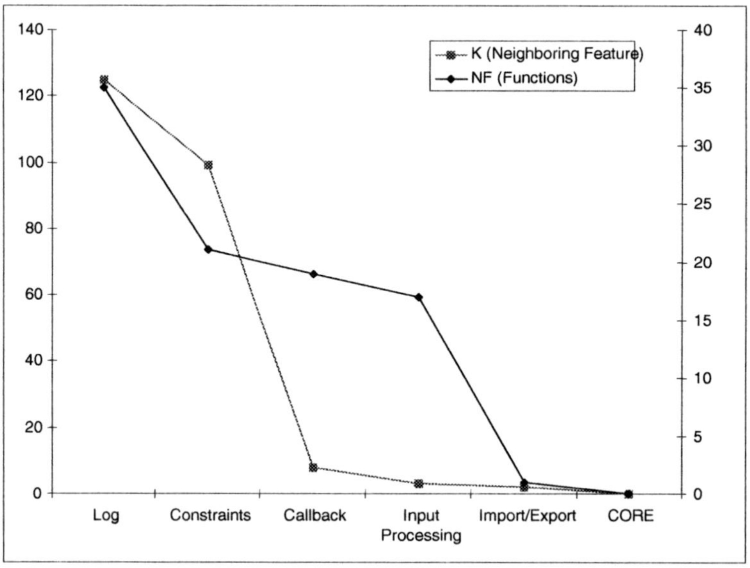

around 80%, which is the fourth data point in Figure 7 (suggesting an optimum for AMS's *input processing* feature). Note that different parts of the legacy system may be sensitive to C; we need more empirical studies to evaluate the sensitivity of these threshold values.

Selecting Evolvable Features

FOCAL provides several heuristics to avoid feature interaction issues by identifying closely related features. If two feature implementations are highly correlated, then it is certain that these features are intertwined, and a rewrite is probably warranted. In the case of AMS, if a feature is spread out across many functions, and if the code execution is below 80% using selected test cases within each of the functions, the feature is not a good candidate. Good candidates are those features that change often, are concentrated in fewer functions, depend on or share global variables as a means of communication and can be reused across product line members.

Heuristics on features that are evolvable can be further determined by analyzing Table 12. This table displays the results of running the profiler with regression test cases after the test cases have been mapped to the features. Each row represents a particular function; each function has been mapped to a pre-defined function type (SS, DF, DD, SSF), as indicated in the rightmost column. For example, f_1 is of the type Shared Stateless Function (SS). Each column represents a regression test case T_n (while FOCAL supports multiple test cases representing a single feature, we omit this detail for the purpose of this discussion); each test case is mapped to a feature (FE_n). For example, T_1 is mapped to FE_1. The numeric value in each cell is the percentage of coverage for the specific feature by that function. For example, f_1 has 100% coverage for FE_1 in T_1.

The concept of threshold is essential in this analysis of evolvability. For a given feature-function relationship, the threshold is based on the number of functions (NF), the number of neighbouring features (K), and the percentage of coverage (C) for the feature in each function. The coverage level must be significant; we have selected 80% as the minimum for evolvability based upon our experience with the AMS. There are two special cases: (1) The trivial case: K=1 and F=1; the feature and the function are coterminous; (2) C=0: zero coverage, hence there is no feature-function relationship. Optimum values for evolvability for a given legacy system (LS) might be K=3, NF=17, C=80%, with no cross-cutting and no trivial cases.

Table 12: Evolable Features.

Test Cases	T1	T2	T3	T4	T5	T6	T7	T8	T9	T10	T11	T12	
Function\Features	FE_1	FE_2	FE_3	FE_4	FE_5	FE_6	FE_7	FE_8	FE_9	FE_{10}	FE_{11}	FE_{12}	Type
f_1	100	100	100	0	0	0	0	0	0	0	0	0	SS
f_2	80	80	90	0	0	0	0	0	0	0	0	0	DF
f_3	100	100	100	0	0	0	0	0	0	0	0	0	SS
f_4	70	75	80	0	0	0	0	0	0	0	0	0	DD
f_5	100	100	100	0	0	0	0	0	0	0	0	0	SS
f_6	100	100	100	0	0	0	0	0	0	0	0	0	SS
f_7	100	100	100	0	0	0	0	0	0	0	0	0	SS
f_8	0	0	0	80	90	0	0	0	0	0	0	0	DF
f_9	0	0	0	100	100	0	0	0	0	0	0	0	DF
f_{10}	0	0	0	0	0	11	12	0	0	0	0	0	SSF
f_{11}	0	0	0	0	0	33	44	0	0	0	0	0	SSF
f_{12}	0	0	0	0	0	12	15	0	0	0	0	0	SSF
f_{13}	0	0	0	0	0	15	15	0	0	0	0	0	SS
f_{14}	0	0	0	0	0	22	22	0	0	0	0	0	SS
f_{15}	0	0	0	0	0	32	38	0	0	0	0	0	SS
f_{16}	0	0	0	0	0	15	15	15	15	15	15	15	SS
f_{17}	0	0	0	0	0	22	22	22	22	22	22	22	SS
f_{18}	100	100	100	100	100	100	100	100	100	100	100	100	SS
f_{19}	100	100	100	100	100	100	100	100	100	100	100	100	SS
f_{20}	100	100	100	100	100	100	100	100	100	100	100	100	SS
f_{21}	0	0	0	0	0	32	38	12	56	89	66	63	DD
f_{22}	0	0	0	0	0	22	22	34	52	23	43	34	DD
f_{23}	0	0	0	0	0	32	38	22	44	33	45	32	DD

Another important concept in this analysis is traceability. This is the ability, using a code-profiling tool, to traverse the implementation code path in order to identify feature-function relationships. Traceability can be used to examine three types of relationships: function-to-feature, feature-to-function, and feature-to-feature. The following discussion describes feature or function categories in terms of evolvability. Each category corresponds to a shaded region of Table 12.

- **Core:** Functions that are shared stateless (SS) and have 100% coverage for all test cases can be shared in a common library as CORE (i.e., functions 18-20 in Table 12).
- **Evolvable:** If a feature is contained within a few functions, and if the code execution is above 80% using selected test cases within each of the functions (above threshold), this feature is a good candidate to be evolvable — Features 1-3 (implemented in Functions 1-7) and Features 4-5 (implemented in Functions 8-12) meet these requirements.
- **Cross-cut:** These features are dispersed in too many functions and the coverage values are below threshold. Features 6-7 illustrate this category. A cross-cut feature is not recommended for evolution because the impact of change can create several unforeseen errors and the cost will exceed the benefits.
- **Non-evolvable:** If features are implemented in a small number of functions, but there are a large number of features and coverage values are below threshold, these features are not good candidates. The shaded area (Feature 8 through Feature 12, and function f_{16} through f_{23}) illustrates this category.
- **Zero coverage:** Represents all cells that have no coverage.

Our experience with AMS features is shown in Table 13 (partial listing). The *input processing* feature that was evolved had a K=3, NF=17 and C=80%. We also found that there were features within AMS that were implemented within one function only and no other feature was implemented in that function. An example of such a feature is importing data from another database. Cash value calculation is an example of non-evolvable feature because its FI is shared by nine other features in a single function, which means the impact of change will be unfavorable. Likewise, a cross-cutting feature, like a constraint to a non-linear equation solve, is also not a favorable candidate for evolution because it is dispersed in so many different features. Finally, we discovered a CORE of 42 functions, as shown in Table 13.

Table 13: Heuristics (Partial Listing).

Neighboring Feature (K)	Number Functions (NF)	Average Coverage (C)	Feature	Decision
3	17	80%	Input Processing	Evolvable
1	1	100%	Import	Trivial
10	1	100%	Cash Value	Non-Evolvable
1	54	35%	Constraint	Cross-cut
-	42	100%		CORE

Contributions

In this chapter, we have made the following contributions: First, FOCAL is an incremental methodology to evolve legacy code that improves the maintainability of legacy systems. Second, the technique describes a clear understanding between features and functionality, and relationships among features using our feature model. Third, FOCAL provides guidelines to construct feature-based reusable components using our fine-grained component model. Fourth, we bridge the complexity gap by identifying feature-based test cases and developing feature-based reusable components.

Incremental Evolution Methodology

Our ten-step methodology is incremental in nature and can provide rapid results. FOCAL provides "exit-points" in case the developers/testers are not satisfied with any of the results. For example, heuristics discussed in this chapter identify which features are good candidates for evolution and which ones are not. We have identified input and output criteria for each step of our methodology, and at any step if a parameter is missing the developer can stop the whole process without any side effects. Although we have not done so, this methodology can also be used to evolve multiple features at the same time.

Feature Model

Our feature model defines features in a way that considers evolution and provides a guide to identify the feature implementation within the source code. We have identified and provided solutions to various cases when features interact with each other. We provide a simple clustering technique to group test cases that represent indirect features. In addition, our feature model provides an intuitive way of addressing the feature interaction issue by considering feature relationships. Finally, our feature model forms the basis for heuristics for neighboring features and evolution threshold.

Fine-Grained Component Model

Feature Implementations (FIs) can be refactored into fine-grained components, which can then be reused across multiple product lines. Our fine-grained component model is simple to use and has minimum requirements in the sense that it allows the developers to provide better definition to the FI and the variables involved in invoking that FI. We provide guidelines for evolving a FI into a fine-grained component: A component's properties can simplify complicated scenarios such as when a code profiler results in same code for more than one feature in a function. Finally, our fine-grained component model reduces global variables if feature relationships are shared or required.

Bridging the Complexity Gap

We bridge the complexity gap in two ways. First, we map the regression test cases to the features and create a feature/function matrix. This matrix is used to select evolvable features. Regression test cases reflect the end user feature; they are already focused, so it is not necessary to collect execution traces on all inputs or to divide the input sets into *invoking* or *non-invoking* categories as proposed by other researchers. We suggest that regression test cases are the best choice for the input cases because regression test cases contain information regarding features. They can be used as a common entity between the end user and the software team. Second, the fine-grained components are feature-based components, as they implement a specific feature or a group of related features. Since these components are focused on specific features, we believe that they can represent end user requirements in a much more explicit way, thereby bridging the gap between user expectations and what the software can provide.

ACKNOWLEDGMENTS

This material is based upon work supported by the National Science Foundation under Grant No. 0220166. Mehta is supported by AFS.

REFERENCES

Agrawal, H., Horgan, J., Krauser, E., & London, S. (1993). Incremental regression testing. *Proceedings, IEEE Software Maintenance Conference,* Montreal, Quebec, 348—357.

Bergey, J., Northrop, L., & Smith, D. (1997). Enterprise framework for the disciplined evolution of legacy systems. *CMU/SEI-97-TR-007, ADA 330880*, Software Engineering Institute, CMU, Pittsburgh, PA, 12-14.

Boehm, B. (1981). *Software engineering economics* (pp. 182-194). Prentice Hall.

Booch, G., Rumbaugh, J., & Jacobson. (1998). *The Unified Modeling Language user guide* (2nd ed., pp. 160-165). Reading, MA: Addison-Wesley.

Bracho, R. (1997). Integrating the corporate computing environment with ActiveWeb. Santa Clara, CA: Active Software, Inc. Available: *http://www.activesw.com*

Brodie, M., & Stonebraker, M. (1995). Migrating legacy systems: Gateways, interfaces and the incremental approach (pp. 171-185). Morgan Kaufmann.

Brown, A. (1996). *Component based software engineering* (pp. 175-186). IEEE Computer Society.

Brownsword, L., & Clements, P. (1996). A case study in successful product line development. *CMU/SEI-96-TR-016, ADA 315802*, Software Engineering Institute, Carnegie Mellon University, Pittsburgh, PA.

Chen, T., & Lau, M. (1996). Dividing strategies for the optimization of a test suite. Information Processing Letters, *60*(3), 135-141.

Chen, Y., Rosenblum, D., & Vo, K. (1994). TestTube: A system for selective regression testing. *Proceedings, 16th International Conference on Software Engineering*, Sorento, Italy, 211-220.

Davis, A., & Rauscher, R. (1979). Formal techniques and automatic processing to ensure correctness in requirements specifications. *Proceedings, 1st Conference on Specifications of Reliable Software*, IEEE Computer Society, Cambridge, MA, 15-35.

Deprez, J., & Lakhotia, A. (2000). A formalism to automate mapping from program features to code. *Proceedings, 8th International Workshop on Program Comprehension,* International Conference on Software Engineering, Limerick, Ireland, 72-83.

Dorda, S., Wallnau, K., Seacord, R., & Robert, J. (2000). A survey of legacy system modernization approaches. *Technical Note CMU/SEI-00-TN-003*, Software Engineering Institute, CMU, Pittsburgh, PA, 37-46.

Execom Software: Legacy challenge. (n.d.). Available: *http://www.execom.com.au/legacy_challenge.html*

Field, J., Ramalingam, G., & Tip, F. (1995). Parametric program slicing. 22nd ACM SIGPLAN-SIGACT Symposium on Principles of Programming Languages, San Francisco, CA, 379-392.

Fowler, M. (1999). *Refactoring: Improving the design of existing code.* Addison-Wesley.

Fowler, M., & Scott, K. (1997). *UML distilled - Applying the standard Object Modeling Language* (pp. 150-172). Addison-Wesley.

Griss, M. (2000). Implementing product-line features with component reuse. *Proceedings, 6th International Conference on Software Reuse*, Springer-Verlag, Vienna, Austria, 134-152.

Harrold, M., Gupta, R., & Soffa, M. (1993). A methodology for controlling the size of a test suite. ACM Transactions Software Engineering and Methodology, *2*(3), 270-285.

Heineman, G., & Councill, W. (2001). *Component-based software engineering: Putting the pieces together.* Addison-Wesley.

Jain, M., Murty, M., & Flynn, P. (1999). Data clustering: A review. ACM Computing Surveys, *31*(3), 264-323.

Kaindl, H., Kramer, S., & Kacsich, R. (1998). A case study of decomposing functional requirements using scenarios. *Proceedings, 3rd International Conference on Requirements Engineering*, IEEE Computer Society, Vienna, Austria, 82-89.

Kitchenham, B., & Taylor, N. (1985). Software project development cost estimation. *The Journal of Systems and Software, 5*(4), 267-278.

Kop, C., & Mayr, H. (1998). Conceptual pre-design: Bridging the gap between requirements and conceptual design. *Proceedings, 3rd International Conference on Requirements Engineering*, IEEE Computer Society, Tucson, AZ, 90-98.

Korel, B., & Laski, J. (1998). Dynamic program slicing. *Information Processing Letters, 29*(3), 155-163.

Krut, R. (1993). Integrating 001 tool support into the feature-oriented domain analysis methodology. *Technical Report CMU/SEI 93 TR 01*, Software Engineering Institute, Pittsburgh, PA, 12-20.

Letovsky, S., & Soloway, E. (1986). Delocalized plans and program comprehension. IEEE Software, *3*(3), 41-49.

Marwane, R., & Mili, A. (1991). Building tailor-made software cost model: Intermediate TUCOMO. *Information and Software Technology*, 232-238.

Mehta, A. (2002). *Evolving legacy system features into fine-grained components.* Ph.D. Dissertation, WPI Computer Science Department.

Mehta, A., & Heineman, G. (1999). Architectural evolution of legacy system. *Proceedings, 23rd Annual International Computer Software and Applications Conference*, Phoenix, AZ, 110-119.

Mehta, A., & Heineman, G. (2002). Evolving legacy system features into fine-grained components. *Proceedings, 24th International Conference on Software Engineering*, Orlando, FL, 417-427.

Miyazaki, Y., & Mori, K. (1985). Constructive Cost Model (COCOMO) evaluation and tailoring. *Proceedings, 8th Conference on Software Engineering*, London, England, 292-299.

NuMega TrueCoverage for Visual Basic. (n.d.). Available: *http://www.microway.com.au/compuware/truecoverage_visualbasic.stm*

Raccoon, L. (1995). The complexity gap. *SIGSOFT Software Engineering Notes, 20*(3), 37-44.

Reps, T., Ball, T., Das, T., & Larus J. (1997). The use of program profiling for software maintenance with application to the year 2000 Problem. *Proceedings, 6th European Software Engineering Conference (ESEC) and 5th ACM SIGSOFT Foundation of Software Engineering (FSE),* Zurich, Switzerland, 432-449.

Rothermel, G., & Harrold, M. (1993). A safe, efficient algorithm for regression test selection. *Proceedings, IEEE Software Maintenance Conference*, Montreal, Canada, 358-367.

Rothermel, G., & Harrold, M. (1996). Analyzing regression test selection techniques. IEEE Transactions Software Engineering, *22*(8), 529-551.

Rothermel, G., Untch, R., Chu, C., & Harrold, M. (1999). Test case prioritization: An empirical study. Proceedings, International Conference on Software Maintenance, Oxford, UK, 179-188.

Smith, D., Müller, H., & Tilley, S. (1997). The Year 2000 problem: Issues and implications. *Technical Report CMU/SEI-97-TR-002*, Software Engineering Institute, Pittsburgh, PA.

Telecordia Technologies. (1998). *cSuds User's Manual.*

Tilley, S., & Smith, D. (1996). Legacy system reengineering. *International Conference on Software Maintenance*, Software Engineering Institute, Carnegie Mellon University, Pittsburgh, PA, 70-81.

Tsang, S., & Magill, E. (1998). Learning to detect and avoid run-time feature interactions in intelligent networks. *IEEE Transactions on Software Engineering, 24*(10), 818-830.

Turner, C. (1999). *Feature engineering of software systems.* Ph.D. Dissertation, University of Colorado, Boulder.

Weiderman, N., Bergey, J., Smith, D., Dennis, B., & Tilley, S. (1997). Approaches to legacy system evolution. *Technical Report CMU/SEI-97-TR-014*, Software Engineering Institute, CMU, Pittsburgh, PA.

Weiderman, N., Northrop, L., Smith, D., Tilley, S., & Wallnau, K. (1997). Implications of distributed object technology for reengineering. *CMU/SEI-97-TR-005 ADA326945,* Software Engineering Institute, CMU, Pittsburgh, PA.

Wilde, N., & Scully, M. (1995). Software reconnaissance: Mapping program features to code. *Journal of Software Maintenance: Research & Practice*, *7*(5), 49-62.

Wong, W., Gokahle, S., Horgan, J., & Trivedi, K. (1999). Locating program features using execution slices. *Proceedings, 2nd IEEE Symposium on Application-Specific Systems and Software Engineering Technology*, Richardson, TX, 68-79.

Wong, W., Horgan, J., London, S., & Mathur, A. (1998). Effect of test set minimization on fault detection effectiveness. Software Practice and Experience, *28*(4), 347-369.

Woods, S., Carriere, S., & Kazman, R. (1999). A semantic foundation for architectural reengineering. *Proceedings, International Conference on Software Maintenance (ICSM),* Oxford, UK, 391-398.

APPENDIX A
METHODOLOGY STEPS

Sequential methodology steps	**Input**		**Output**	
	Requirement	**Responsibility**	**Deliverables**	**Responsibility**
1. Evolution reasons and problem report.	Detailed textual description	End user, tester and project manager	List of product lines where the feature is used	Tester, project manager and developer
2. Identify feature(s) with problems.	Textual description and list of product lines	Tester and project manager	Map problem to feature(s).	Tester and project manager
3. Map feature(s) and test case(s).	Map problems to feature(s)	Tester and enduser	Select test cases from regression suite for the feature. Analyze and verify test cases. Regression test suite cluster compared with selected test cases cluster. Add missing test cases to selected list	Tester
4. Map features to functions.	Selected test cases, code coverage tool and legacy system	Developer	Feature-function cluster, feature-variable cluster and CORE functions report	Developer
5. Identify feature implementation and CORE using Feature Model.	Feature-function, feature-variable cluster and CORE functions report	Developers, tester, end-users and project manager	Impact analysis, evolvable feature, and refactoring decision	Developer
6. Refactor and create components using the fine-grained component model.	Feature implementation, legacy system and CORE	Developer	Fine-grained components and CORE library	Developer
7. Plug the component in the legacy system.	Fine-grained components and CORE library	Developer	Integrated legacy system	Developer
8. Verify results by running regression.	Integrated legacy system	Developer	Regression testing results. Report problem fix.	Tester
9. Reuse fine-grained components in other product lines.	Fine-grained components, usage guide and other product lines	Developers	Run regression after integration on all integrated product lines.	Tester
10. Measure results in terms of cost and report fix to end-users.	Past and current feature maintenance cost, cost to apply the methodology	Project manager	Budget analysis report showing the result of applying the methodology	Project manager

Chapter VI

Reengineering Legacy Systems Towards Web Environments

Ying Zou, Queen's University, Canada

Kostas Kontogiannis, University of Waterloo, Canada

ABSTRACT

With the widespread use of the Web, distributed object technologies have been widely adopted to construct network-centric architectures, using XML, Web Services, CORBA, and DCOM. Organizations would like to take advantage of the Web in its various forms of Internet, Intranet and Extranets. This requires organizations to port and integrate their legacy assets to distributed Web-enabled environments, so that the functionality of existing legacy systems can be leveraged without having to rebuild these systems. In this chapter, we provide techniques to re-engineer standalone legacy systems into Web-enabled environments. Specifically, we aim for a framework that allows for the identification of reusable business logic entities in large legacy systems in the form of major legacy components, the migration of these procedural components to an object-oriented design, the specification of interfaces of these identified components, the automatic generation of CORBA wrappers to enable remote access, and finally, the seamless interoperation with Web services via HTTP based on the SOAP messaging mechanism.

INTRODUCTION

With the widespread use of the Internet and pervasive computing technologies, distributed object technologies have been widely adopted to construct network-centric architectures, using Web services, CORBA, and DCOM. Organizations would like to take advantage of the Web in its various forms of Internet, Intranet and Extranets. This requires organizations to migrate and integrate their legacy assets within distributed Web-enabled environments. In this way, the functionality of existing legacy systems can be leveraged without having to rebuild these systems.

However, legacy systems are not designed as Web applications. Generally, a Web application is a loosely coupled, component-based program, which consists of three tiers including user interface, business logic and related databases with a clear distinction. The front-end user interface is accessed through Web browsers. The business logic runs in a Web server and application server. The databases reside on back-end severs. Each component communicates with others through standard protocols such as HTTP and XML. In contrast, legacy systems are usually standalone systems with complicated structures with all three tires intermixed and tightly coupled. According to the decomposability of a legacy system, the architecture of a system can be decomposable, semi-decomposable, or non-decomposable (Brodie & Stonebaker, 1995). In a decomposable system, the user interface, business logic and the related databases can be considered as distinct components with well-defined interfaces. Such systems are the best candidates for the migration. In a semi-decomposable system, only interface and business logic are separate modules. The business logic and databases are not separable, due to their complex structure. Such systems are more difficult to migrate, as the interaction of the business logic and the databases is not easy to understand. In a non-decomposable system, the system appears as a single unstructured and monolithic module. Such systems are the most difficult to migrate, as they are treated as black boxes, and their functionality and design cannot be recovered.

Problem Definition

To modernize legacy systems with Web technologies, there are three major issues to be addressed, namely, Web accessibility, componentization, and platform transformation.

- Web accessibility is a crucial requirement for a Web application. In this respect, the legacy interface should be replaced with a Web-enabled interface by placing a wrapper on top of the legacy system, or by re-generating a new interface in HTML form.
- Componentization focuses on the extraction of reusable components from the legacy systems. These components contain the evolving business logic and functionality of the legacy system. Once the components are identified, they can be easily maintained, and their interface can be described using standards such as WSDL (Web Service Description Language) (WSDL). Furthermore, components can be integrated with other components to produce new business functional units.
- Platform transformation involves migrating monolithic legacy systems into modern platforms such as the Web. In this context, there are two major types of strategies to be taken in order to leverage legacy assets into Web-enabled environments, namely:
  - Migration of legacy system into Web-enabled environments, and
  - Integration of the legacy system with new applications.

The migration strategies involve the activities to transform the legacy systems into Web-enabled platforms, such as client/sever, three-tier (multi-tier) architecture, along with changes to legacy systems. The integration strategies focus on the coordination and interoperation between legacy systems and Web applications. Legacy application integration aims to resolve the incompatibilities between legacy systems and Web applications, and allows them to seamlessly interoperate. In such a way, the lifecycle of legacy systems is greatly extended. Object wrapping is commonly used to adapt legacy systems to Web environments.

To minimize the risk involved in the reengineering process, the legacy system should be thoroughly analyzed to determine an appropriate strategy. The reengineering process should be exercised under a rigorous discipline because of the magnitude of the investment in the legacy systems, and the technical complexity inherent in such projects. As a result, software migration should be a well-planned, highly motivated and well-justified process.

Proposed Migration Framework

To address the aforementioned issues, we propose a framework that allows the migration and integration of existing stand-alone legacy services into a network centric Web-enabled environment, where they are considered as distributed Web Services. The framework consists of four major steps:

- *Identification of Legacy Components:* We aim to identify software components from monolithic legacy systems. The recovered components should conform to specific user requirements (i.e., relate to specific functionality, access and manipulate specific data, be free of side effects, and comply with specific pre- and post-conditions).
- *Migration of Identified Components to Object Oriented Platforms:* We migrate the recovered legacy system components to collections of object classes that encapsulate specific functionality of the legacy system. As an object encapsulates data and operations, flexible systems can be easily designed and implemented using the object-oriented paradigm. Furthermore, we analyze interfaces of the recovered components and define a specification to represent their interfaces. The service specification provides standard, enriched, and well-understood information about the interface and functionality of the offered services. The service specification language is defined in XML.
- *Migration to Distributed Environments:* We design a methodology to migrate the identified components into distributed environments by automatically generating CORBA/IDL and CORBA wrappers from the identified component interface specifications. Since the client processes only need to know the interface of their servers, the modification of the server implementation does not affect the client code as long as the server interface is kept unchanged.
- *Migration to the Web:* To enable CORBA components to be accessible by Web clients, and to be integrated with other Web services, we present a process based on the SOAP protocol to deploy these newly migrated components in Web Service environments.

Chapter Organization

This chapter is organized as follows. First, the chapter surveys existing techniques for migrating legacy systems into Web environments. Then, the chapter presents several approaches that recover reusable components from legacy systems. The next section discusses our migration techniques, which focus on the transformation of identified procedural components into object-oriented platforms. The chapter then describes a process that enables the migrated components to be integrated within a distributed environment using standards such as CORBA. We then present an approach to enable the migrated distributed components to interact in a Web service environment using standards such as SOAP to extend the CORBA standard for the Web. Finally, the chapter concludes and provides some insights and directions for future trends in software reengineering and the evolution of legacy systems.

EXISTING TECHNIQUES FOR MIGRATING LEGACY SYSTEMS INTO WEB ENVIRONMENTS

Initially, the Web was presented as a global URL-based file server for publishing static information in a hypertext electronic form. With the use of Java, and scripting language such as

CGI (Common Gateway Interface) scripts, the Web evolved into an interactive medium that provides dynamic information services in a client/server architecture. With the rapid growth of e-commence activities, the emphasis has shifted from the client-side browser and server-side applications to multi-tier architecture based on standards such as J2EE and .NET.

A multi-tier architecture emphasizes the separation of presentation logic, business logic and back-end services. A three-tier architecture is an example of a multi-tier architecture, as illustrated in Figure 1. A three-tier architecture is instrumental for the implementation of large Web-enabled systems. From an implementation point of view, the standard three-tier architecture can be seen as a composition of four layers (Dreyfus, 1998), namely: a) presentation layer (Web client); b) content layer (Web server); c) application layer (application server); and d) back-end data and services layer. The Web server is responsible for accepting HTTP requests from Web clients, and delivering them to the application server, while the application server is in charge of locating the services and returning responses back to the Web server. On the other hand, a thin client in the presentation layer has little or no application logic. It sends the request via HTTP to the Web server for an interactive view of the static and dynamic information (see Figure 1).

To provide static information, the Web server maintains a static content repository, such as a file system, where the information-based resources are stored and served as static HTML pages. Upon receiving a request from the client, the Web server retrieves the requested document from the content repository and sends it to the client. In this case, the client relies entirely on the Web server to fulfill its request. Programming languages, such as Java, and scripting standards, like CGI, can be used to enable Web clients to access databases on the server side.

Figure 1: Control Flows in Three-Tier Architecture.

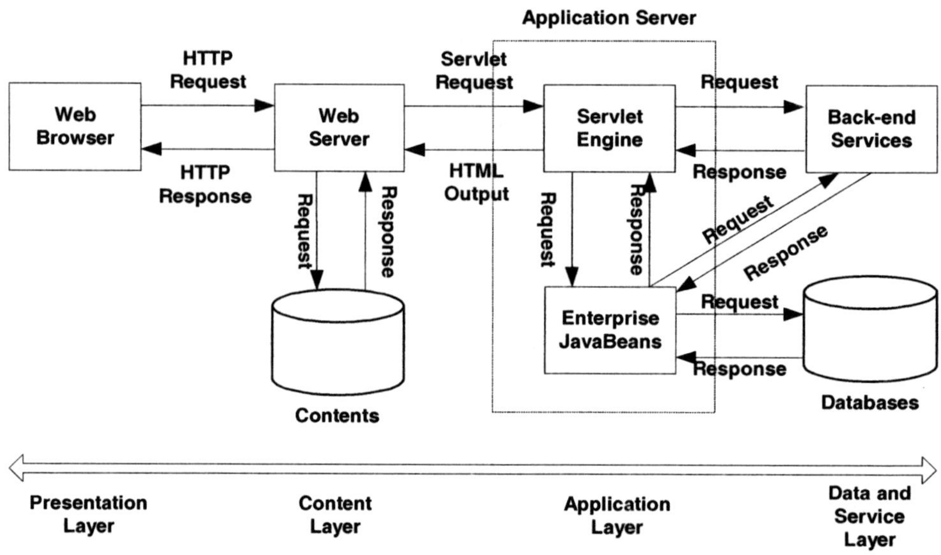

To provide dynamic information generated by software services, the Web server needs to constantly interact with the application server. A servlet or Java Server Pages (JSP) provides the dynamic HTML content to clients. When the Web server receives a request for a servlet, it re-directs the client's request along with the parameters to the application server, which loads the appropriate servlet and runs it. Servlets have all the features of the Java program. They also have automatic memory management, advanced networking, multithreading, and so forth. Moreover, they have enterprise connectivity through protocols such as JNI (Java Native Interface), JDBC, RMI, and CORBA. Servlets can initiate invocations to back-end services, other servlets, or to Enterprise JavaBeans (EJBs).

Back-end software components can be considered as software services. In this context, the Web has evolved from an *"information-based"* Web into a *"services-based"* Web. Such Web services offer specific business related functionality, reside in the application servers, can be programmatically integrated with other systems, and perform interactive tasks involving multiple steps on the user's behalf.

To allow for Web services to interoperate, common industry standards, such as SOAP (Simple Object Access Protocol), WSDL (Web Service Description Language), and UDDI (Universal Description, Discovery, Integration) have been proposed. In a nutshell, SOAP, encoded in XML and HTTP, is a message passing mechanism and serves as a uniform invocation mechanism between Web services. The WSDL describes the interface for a Web service. These interfaces are indexed in searchable UDDI repositories.

Migrating Monolithic Legacy Systems to Client/Server Architecture

To achieve a client/server architecture, migration activities are mostly concerned with the separation of user interface, the business logic and the backend data of a legacy application. Consequently, the user interface is replaced with a Web-based interface, written in XML or HTML. The application logic of the legacy system is wrapped as a server, and can be executed in its native environment. This approach can be applied for a transaction-oriented legacy system, which involves a lot of interactions between users, such as information entry, query and retrieval. In particular, it is the best choice for semi-decomposable and non-decomposable systems. Finally, backend data can be analyzed using data reengineering techniques, which have been investigated thoroughly in Blaha et al.(1995).

In general, a legacy user interface is often character-oriented, and system pre-emptive, meaning that the application initiates an interaction, and users only response upon the application's request. However, a Web-based interface is event driven and user pre-emptive, meaning that a Web user initiates a dialogue without the system's prompts. Events include keystrokes and cursor movements. For such an interface, a Web browser incorporates loop and call back mechanisms in order to constantly listen to user triggered events and respond promptly with the call back routines residing on a server. Therefore, shifting a system pre-emptive interface to a user pre-emptive interface focuses on the identification of events in the original system, and the associated call back routines.

The key step in this migration approach is to identify the user interface of the legacy system. In literature, several approaches are proposed based on the availability of the original source code. In the case in which the source code is not too complicated to tackle, Moore and Moshkina present an approach to perform the user interface re-engineering (2000). This approach is composed of three steps. Firstly, the input/output logic is detected by the analysis of control flow and data flow in the original code. The result of the flow analysis is applied to identify user components that are functionally equivalent to GUI toolkits. Secondly, such components are transformed to HTML forms. In the end, the legacy system is restructured to associate functions or routines with the user components. In this case, the legacy code is examined and modified to cope with the migration. Alternately, without modifying the source code of the legacy application, the legacy user interface is detected by tracking the user interaction with the system. Stroulia et al. present another re-engineering approach (1999). Firstly, an interface-mapping task identifies all individual screens and the possible states occurring due to screen transitions. The screen transitions are triggered by user actions, such as keystrokes and cursor movements. A graph of the system interface transitions is incrementally constructed to include screens and transitions. Such a graph supports the navigation of text-based user interface, and facilities the reorganization of the user's navigation plan. Secondly, a domain model is abstracted to specify the screen transitions, information flows, and exchanged information. Finally, based on the abstract domain model, the graphical user interface is specified and generated. The new interface consists of the bridge between the original interface and the Web-enabled interface.

These two approaches make an entire legacy system into a single reusable service by wrapping it as a black box. However, the larger the software component, the less flexible for reuse in different contexts it will be. In our migration framework, we aim to produce a new migrant system that is composed of several reusable components. These components can be flexibly integrated to accommodate changing business requirements over the lifetime of the software system. We migrate the system into an object-oriented design, which is consequently migrated into the Web. Since object-oriented design provides information hiding and encapsulation properties in classes, the identified software components are fine-grained classes that provide maximal reusability and flexibility.

Migrating Legacy Web Applications

A multi-tier application requires a clear separation of the user interface, business logic and databases. It is a complex and challenging process to migrate semi-decomposable and non-decomposable legacy systems into multi-tier architecture. As technology evolves, there is a practical demand to convert traditional Web applications, using CGI and Net.Data, into a multi-tier architecture using JSP, Servlets and EJBs technologies. In this case, such legacy Web applications are designed with a clear separation of client and server components. The migration task is mitigated. In this section, we present research projects in literature for this subject.

In Lau et al. (2003) an approach that deals with the separation of business logic and database in the migration of legacy e-commerce applications into EJB architecture is presented. Obsolete e-commerce applications intertwine business logic and database access code that uses SQL statements. In contrast, the target EJB architecture separates the business logic and database queries. Specifically, EJB contains two types of enterprise beans including session beans and entity beans. The session beans are used to implement activities, while the entity beans are utilized to represent persistent data in database. For example, one entity bean corresponds to one row in a table. Instead of using SQL statements to query a database, an entity bean provides methods to manipulate tables in a database. The paper presents a migration process that follows these steps:

- Build a relational database schema mapping from the source databases to the target databases,
- Convert control blocks in the original application to session beans in EJB architecture,
- Establish relations among the new entity bean objects with the conformance to the table relations in the databases,
- Generate plumbing code needed to integrate the new session beans and entity beans.

Using this approach, a prototype tool was developed to transform IBM Net.Data applications into JSP and EJB applications.

Similarly, in Hassan and Holt (2003), a Web application migration approach is presented. The approach deals with the migration of active pages, the building blocks of a Web application. Active pages from one vendor-centric development framework, such as ASP from Microsoft, are converted into active pages under a standardized Web development framework. Essentially, an active page consists of HTML tags for presentation, control code that makes use of the underlying object model and programming language to provide business logic. Such an object model provides comprehensive functionality needed by Web developers. For example, the object model contains request and response objects to allow the interaction between client and server. It also provides objects to maintain the states of sessions due to stateless nature of HTTP protocol. Furthermore, this paper abstracts the commonality between the object models provided by the various frameworks into a common object model. The paper summarized the migration process in four stages (Hassan & Holt, 2003):

- The preprocessing stage removes the HTML code and comments from the active page.
- The language transformation stage translates the active code from the initial programming language to the target programming language.
- The object model mapping stage transforms access to objects in the original application framework to the corresponding framework.

The post-processing stage reinserts the HTML code and comments that were removed in the preprocessing stage.

These two approaches focus on the migration of legacy Web applications into modern multi-tier architectures. Our proposed framework aims to migrate standalone procedural non-Web based systems into Web services residing in the back-end layer of a multi-tier architecture. Consequently, these back-end services can be composed to produce business logic. In the following section, we discuss our approach in more detail.

EXTRACTING LEGACY COMPONENTS

A software component can be considered as "an independently-deliverable software package that offers services through public interfaces" (Brown & Barn, 1999). A component offers specific functionality and can be easily integrated with other COTS (Commercial Off-The-Shelf) or custom-made software components. By the use of component-based technology in multi-tier architecture, the business logic can be easily composed from various back-end services as distributed software components. In such a way, a legacy system can be treated as a single back-end service. To extend the reusability of such legacy systems, finer grained components need to be identified to serve as building blocks in new distributed systems. In particular, the identified legacy components can be gradually migrated into Java to enable the seamless integration of legacy functionality with new applications. In addition, the data accessed by the legacy applications may need to be migrated from its present form, such as flat files, obsolete format, and legacy databases, to distributed relational databases, or to be represented in the Enterprise Java Beans framework.

So far in the field of reverse engineering, most software analysis techniques for the identification of components in monolithic systems focus on clustering and decomposition techniques that are based on cohesion and coupling properties. It is safe to say that in most cases, legacy system decomposition has become a clustering problem. Clustering is a successful technique for decomposing a legacy system into sub-systems. Nevertheless, these identified sub-systems are not guaranteed to be good candidates for becoming distributed software components. The reason is that clustering depends heavily on static code features (coupling, cohesion) as opposed to dynamic requirements that are imposed by the architecture of the new migrant target distributed application. Furthermore, it is especially difficult to recover via clustering alone components that would have clear interfaces and minimal dependencies with the rest of the system, due to side effects and extended modifications incurred by the prolonged maintenance of the legacy code being analyzed. A possible solution would be to make the whole legacy system a reusable unit by wrapping it as a black box to provide the signature of its input/output points as an API, such as presented in the previous section. However, the larger the software component wrapped, the less cohesive, flexible, and customizable it will be.

An alternative approach to address the component recovery problem is to transform the procedural code into a new object-oriented architecture, whereby components stem from collections of highly cohesive identified classes. The motivation to migrate procedural legacy systems to a new object-oriented architecture and to subsequently provide an infrastructure to make the new migrant systems available in a Web-enabled environment is twofold. Firstly, object-oriented languages provide mechanisms for information hiding and encapsulation and therefore it is easier to identify the loosely coupled, small-scale, reusable software components. Secondly, the objectification process provides means to define clear interfaces between the identified components, establish inheritance relations between the components, and minimize component interconnection. Collections of such classes that correspond to abstract data types can be used to associate parts of the original system to new components that are highly cohesive, and have minimal control and data flow dependencies with the rest of the system. In the following section, techniques for migrating procedural code into object-oriented platforms are presented.

MIGRATING TO OBJECT-ORIENTED PLATFORMS

Over the past years, it has become evident that the benefits of object orientation warrant the design and development of reengineering methods that aim to migrate legacy procedural systems to modern object-oriented platforms. With properties such as information hiding, inheritance and polymorphism inherent in object-oriented designs, essential parts of such a reengineered system can be reused or integrated with other applications using network-centric Web technologies or enterprise integration solutions.

In this context, the software reengineering community has already proposed a number of different methods to migrate procedural code into object-oriented platforms. In a nutshell, the existing migration methods aim to identify abstract data types (ADT) and extract candidate classes and methods from the procedural code. These methods include concept analysis (Lindig & Snelting, 1997; Sahraoui et al., 1997), cluster analysis (Mancoridis et al., 1998; Muller et al., 1992), slicing (Lanubile & Visaggio, 1997), data flow and control flow analysis (Lucia et al., 1997), source code features (Kontogiannis & Patil, 1999; Zou & Kontogiannis, 2001), and informal information analysis (Etzkorn & Davis, 1997). Moreover, it is important for the object-oriented reengineering process to address specific nonfunctional requirements, such as reusability, performance, and maintainability, so that the resulting migrant system conforms to specific constraints and properties.

There is a significant amount of related research for the migration of COBOL systems to object-oriented COBOL (Sneed, 1996), assembly to C (Ward, 1999), C to C++ (Kontogiannis & Patil, 1999; Zou & Kontogiannis, 2001), C to Java (Martin), and RPG to C++ (Lucia et al., 1997). In Lucia et al. (1997), the identification of an object model from RPG programs is presented. Objects are identified from persistent data stores, while related segments of source code in the legacy system become candidate methods in the new object-oriented system. In Kontogiannis and Patil (1999) and Zou and Kontogiannis (2001), an object model is discovered directly from procedural code written in C. Candidate objects are selected by analyzing global data types and function formal parameters. In Lindig and Snelting (1997) and Sahraoui et al. (1997), a transformation system that is based on concept analysis is proposed to identify modules from C code. It is based on lattices that are used to reveal similarities among a set of objects and their related attributes. Finally, a domain-based objectification method is presented in Etzkorn and Davis (1997). The method is based on documentation and informal information, such as user manuals, requirement and design specifications, and naming conventions. However, for legacy systems, the external information is not always available, and this technique may not always be applicable. In the following sub-sections, we propose a representative object-oriented reengineering framework, in which components of a procedural legacy system can be migrated to an object-oriented platform. Specifically, in addition to identifying objects based on abstract data types, the framework aims to discover an object model that incorporates the object-oriented characteristics of a well-designed system, namely, the characteristics of class inheritance, polymorphism and overloading. Furthermore, we discuss an approach that enables the migrant system to posses certain non-functional quality characteristics, such as high maintainability.

Framework for Migrating to Object-Oriented Platforms

The migration framework aims at the extraction of an object-oriented model by a series of iterative analysis steps applied at the abstract representation of the source code (i.e., the abstract syntax tree level). The overview of framework is illustrated in Figure 2. By the analysis of the abstract syntax tree (AST) annotation, class candidates are identified from procedural source code. Each class encapsulates a procedural global data structure and functions that use or update this data structure. In this case, the data fields in a procedural global data structure are converted into data members in the corresponding class. The functions are transformed into methods in the class. Consequently, class

Figure 2: Object-Oriented Reengineering Framework.

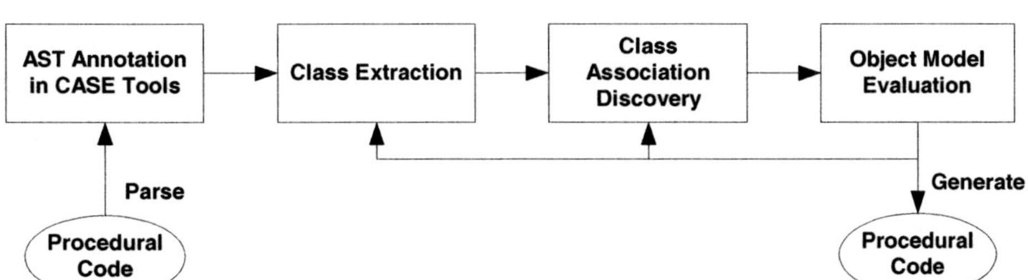

associations such as inheritance and polymorphism can be further recovered from specific procedural source code features. Once object model is produced, developers can evaluate the generated object model by introducing domain knowledge to refine the identified class candidates and class associations. In the end, a target object-oriented code is generated.

The key step in this migration is the extraction of classes and the identification of methods that can be attached to these classes. To facilitate this class creation phase, the framework focuses on the analysis of global aggregate data types, and formal parameter lists. Global data types and data types in formal parameter lists, found in the original legacy source code, become primary candidates for classes in the new object-oriented system. Similarly, functions and procedures in the original system become primary candidates for methods and are attached to the identified classes. This migration framework can be automated to a large extent using a number of different software analysis techniques. However, no matter how sophisticated the analysis techniques are, user assistance and domain knowledge play an important role in obtaining a viable, efficient object model. Therefore, the application domain of the code and the domain knowledge assist in evaluating the extracted object model. The migration process can iterate back to the class extraction phase or class association discovery phase to refine the identified object-oriented model. Finally, the target object-oriented code is generated.

Object-Oriented Model Discovery and Refinement

In the process of extracting an object-oriented model from procedural source code, it is important to identify the transformation steps and extraction rules that allow for the generation of a high quality target migrant system. In the following sections, we present a catalog of analysis and discovery rules that can be used for extracting a quality object model from procedural systems. The rules are divided into two categories: Class Creation and Object Model Extension. The rules for the class creation category define the criteria for the creation of class to form an object model from the procedural code. The rules on the object model extension provide heuristics to establish association between class candidates.

Class Creation

In the search for an object model that can be extracted from procedural source code, we aim at achieving high encapsulation, high cohesion within a class, and low coupling between classes. In an object-oriented system, software is structured around data rather than around services of systems. Therefore, an object model should be built around data that serve as seeds to gather the related data members and methods. Such data and method clusters are consequently considered as class candidates. In this respect, a class creation process is divided into three major steps: class identification, private data member identification and method attachment.

The first step is the selection of possible object classes. The object identification techniques focus on two areas: 1) the analysis of global variables and their data types, and 2) the analysis of complex data types in formal parameter lists. Analysis of global variables and their corresponding data types is focusing on the identification of variables that are globally visible within a module. A module is considered as a sequence of statements with an identifier, such as a file and a program. For each variable, its corresponding type is extracted from the abstract syntax tree, and a candidate object class is generated. Data type analysis focuses on type definitions that are accessible via libraries. Examples include *typedef* C constructs. Data types that are used in formal parameter lists become also primary class candidates. The union of data types that are identified by the global variable analysis and data type analysis forms the initial pool of candidate classes. Furthermore, based on the usage of a set of data types in formal parameter lists, groups of data types can be collected into one aggregated class to minimize the interface of the methods, which take the aggregate class as parameter instead.

In the second step, data fields in the user defined aggregated types and the global variables are converted into data attributes in the corresponding class candidates.

Finally, the procedural functions are assigned into class candidates. To achieve higher encapsulation, the data members in class candidates can only be directly used or modified by methods in the same class candidate, instead of by the methods in other class candidates. Therefore, procedural functions are attached to class candidates based on the usage of data types in the formal parameter lists, return types, and variable usage in the function body. For this task, only aggregate data types in the parameter list and return value are considered, and simple ones such as int, char, and float are ignored.

Private Data Member Identification

- *Data type analysis:* A structure is a collection of variables that can be of diverse types. Similar to C++ classes, the structure of a record groups related data items. In procedural code, for example, C struct and union are constructs that can be used to generate aggregate data structures, indicating a degree of functional and logical coupling among a group of data and functions that are using it. For migration purposes, each data member of a structure can be converted into a data field in the corresponding class.
- *Variable analysis:* Typically, there are three main scopes to access variables in a program, namely, local scope, file scope and global scope. According to their different scopes, variables can be transformed to private data members in the identified classes. In this context, variables that can only be referenced within a function can be declared as private data members of the class that encapsulates the method that corresponds to the referencing function.

Although C++ allows for global constant definitions to be accessible from within classes, in order to obtain a better object-oriented design for the migrant code, one should aim to eliminate file and global scoped variables that can be referenced from within a file or the whole program. File scope and global scope variables are similar in that they are used or updated by any function. Keeping the scope of these variables in the new object-oriented system would violate the principles of encapsulation and information hiding. A possible solution is that each of these variables can become a data field of a class that relates to these variables. Or, the class encapsulates the functions or part of functions that most often refer or update such variables. Finally, orphan variables that cannot be assigned to any class can be encapsulated in a container class.

Method Attachment

The method identification process focuses on the discovery of functions from a procedural code that can be transformed into methods in the appropriate classes.

- *Parameter type analysis:* A formal parameter of a function indicates that the function references a data item of a particular type. In the process of extracting an object model from procedural code, one key analysis is to consider functions of the procedural system as primary candidates for methods in the new object-oriented system. These methods can be attached to a class that corresponds to the data type appearing in the formal parameter list. In this context, a function or a procedure may be able to be attached to many different classes when more than one data type exists in the formal parameter list. We then say that this method produces an assignment conflict. The conflicts can be resolved by evaluating the alternative designs to achieve high cohesion and low coupling of the target system. Parameter type analysis is one of the alternative ways to consider when we would like to decide whether a function should be transformed to a method, or to which a class should be attached. The following points discuss such alternative types of analysis.
- *Return type analysis:* The return type of a function indicates that the function updates variables of a specific type that appears in the return statement. If this return type is also in the formal parameter list, then this provides stronger evidence that the function should be a method attached to the class stemming from this data type. The reasoning behind this analysis is that classes should encapsulate methods that update the state of objects that belong to this class. Moreover, this type of analysis provides valuable insights as to which class the method should be attached to, when no other information can be extracted from the formal parameter list.
- *Variable usage analysis:* Variable usage analysis allows for examining whether a function or a procedure references a particular data type. Based on the concept of information hiding, we are interested in attaching methods to classes in a way that a given method references, as much as possible, variables of the same type as the class it is attached to. Variable usage analysis provides such insights and counts as to how many times a variable of a particular class is referenced within a candidate method. This type of analysis is also of particular importance when no information from formal parameter list and return type analyses could be obtained to decide which class to attach a conflicting method.
- *Function splitting:* One of the features in legacy procedural code is the size of functions or procedures, which tends to increase with prolonged maintenance activities (i.e., when adding new functionality, or when correcting errors). This situation leads to complex code that is difficult to understand, maintain, and migrate. For the class creation process, such long function or procedure should be sliced into smaller chunks of code. The slicing criteria may vary, but the safest way is to consider slicing according to the first use of a data type that corresponds to a class that the specific function is a candidate to be attached to as a method. Function point analysis can also be used to confirm that a particular slice provides a highly cohesive piece of code. Finally, source code informal information such as comments and variable names also provide good cues for splitting a function or a procedure into more than one component (Fowler, 2000).

Object Model Extension

Inheritance, polymorphism, and overloading are some of the most important features of an object-oriented design. To achieve a good object-oriented design from a procedural legacy system, we have identified a number of heuristic analysis rules that can be used to establish associations between abstract data types. Next, we discuss several heuristics used to identify inheritance, polymorphism, and overloading opportunities in the extracted object model of the target migrant system.

Inheritance Identification

- *Data field cloning:* A typical indicator for identifying inheritance opportunities during the object model extraction process is data field cloning. In this respect, if two or more structures differ only with respect to a few fields, these can be the candidate sub-classes of a more general class. The common fields from those structures are extracted and form a super class. Sub-classes can inherit from it and add their own fields.
- *Data field mapping:* Certain functions copy values from fields in one data structure to fields in another data structure. These two data structures may not be of the same type, but they share common values. The relation of these data structures can be identified as inheritance by extracting the common fields into a super class.
- Function code cloning: Code clone analysis can identify inheritance in which two functions are identical, with the only difference that they operate on different data types. In this case, these data types may become sub-classes of a more general type, and methods can be attached to the sub-classes that inherit from the more general class.
- *Data type casting:* In cast operations, the compiler will automatically change one type of data into another where appropriate. For instance, when an integral value is assigned to a floating-point variable, the compiler will automatically convert the int to a float. Casting allows to make this type conversion explicit, or to force it when it would not normally happen. An implicit cast operation between two data types suggests that these data types share common data fields or are interchangeable. The inheritance between these two abstract data types can be deduced, in that the casted type becomes the sub-class of the type that it is casted to.
- *Anonymous union type:* Anonymous union types denote that their data members share the same memory space. This feature provides a subtle difference from the semantics of a C structure in which all members are referenced as a single distinct group. By contrast, only one union data member can be referenced at a time, and different data members cannot co-exist at the same time. In this context, the common structure of the union data member can be extracted as a superclass, while each of the union data members can be transformed into a sub-class. For example, *Personnel*, a C structure as illustrated in Program 1, contains an anonymous union type data field. The superclass *Personnel* is created and contains the field *age* without the union type data member, as illustrated in Program 2. Each of the union data fields becomes a sub-class.

```
typedef struct{
    union {
        int student;
        int teacher;
    }
    int age;
} Personnel
```

Program 1: structure definition.

```
class Personnel {
    int age;
};
class Student : public Personnel{
    int student;
};
class Teacher: public Personnel{
    int teacher;
};
```

Program 2: refactoring ADT into Class inheritance in C++.

Polymorphism Identification

- *Switch statement replacement:* One of the important characteristics of object-oriented design is the limited use of switch (or case) statements. Polymorphism provides an elegant way to limit the use of long, complex and cumbersome switch and case statements (Fowler, 2000). A switch statement in the procedural code that uses in its evaluation condition a type check variable can be replaced by polymorphic methods. Specifically, each of the case statement bodies may become a polymorphic method, while the data type codes that are used by the condition of the switch can be considered as candidate classes in the new migrant system.
- *Conditional statement replacement:* The branch of a conditional statement is executed according to the return value of the evaluating condition. When the type code is used in the conditional expression, then each branch of the conditional statement can be transformed to a polymorphic method, while the type code used by the conditional expression can be considered as a candidate class in the new design.

```
void printIt(void *itToPrint, int type)
{
        employee *thisEmp;
        market *thisMarket;

        if (type == EMPLOYEE){
                thisEmp = itemToPrint;
                // ......
        }
        if (type == MARKET){
                thisMarket = itemToPrint;
                // ......
}
```

Program 3: Conditional Statement Replacement.

- *Function pointer replacement:* There are two ways functions can be invoked in C: by name and by address. Invocation by name is by far the most common one, in which the functions to be called are decided at the compile time. Invocation by address is used to determine at run time the concrete functions to be executed. In this context, each possible function pointer reference can become a class and its corresponding source code can become a polymorphic method.
- *Generic pointer parameters replacement:* The generic C pointer is denoted by "void *". A "void *" variable can contain the address of any data type. Often, this technique is used to write highly generic functions that need to deliver some small piece of non-generic functionality. An example is illustrated in Program 3, in which the address of struct data type in C along with a type code is passed into the generic function as a parameter at the printIt() function. At run time, the appropriate struct is accessed by address. In this case, the generic function can be converted into a polymorphic method, whereas its behavior is determined according to the type of the object that is applied upon. Moreover, type codes that can be referenced by the generic pointer parameter can be transformed into classes in the new migrant system.
- *Source code cloning:* When two or more functions are identified as clones with minor differences in their structure and the data types they use, these functions can be overloaded on the data types in which they differ. The constraint is that these functions should return the same data type.
- *Functions with common prefix or suffix name:* Similar prefix and suffix names in functions or procedures provide important cues for overloading. For example, execl(), execv(), execlp(), execp() are functions to execute unix processes in various ways and all can be overloaded according to the type they operate upon.
- *Functions with union type parameter:* Functions with a union type parameter may become candidates for overloaded methods. The reason is that these functions usually have different behavior according to the type of the union parameter they are applied upon. These functions can be transformed into several overloaded methods with different parameter types that are obtained from the original union structure definition. Each overloaded method can operate on the specific case of the original union structure.

Object-Oriented Code Generation

Once the classes have been discovered and associations between them are established using operations and heuristics on the AST, the code of the final object-oriented system must be generated. The main objective of this task is to automatically generate Java or C++ source code from the identified object model. The new code should encapsulate functionality from the original legacy system being reengineered, and should be compiled with the fewest possible corrections by the user. The code generation process traverses the ASTs for each class and generates syntactically correct C++ (or Java) code placed in .h and .cpp files. In some cases, human intervention could be required for obtaining a better quality of even fully compilable code. However, this intervention should involve only minor changes and should not increase the complexity of the migration process.

The source code generation process is based on three steps. In the first step, from the obtained class list and method resolution results, the source code for the header files can be created. Once the header files are created, the second step allows the users to make manual modifications by utilizing UML visualization editing and authoring tools. In this respect, additional classes can be added in order to increase the design quality of the migrant system. The results from the method resolution process are examined and necessary changes can be made here. Finally, in the third step, any changes and relationships are incorporated in the source code and errors are removed and new skeleton code that conforms to a highly cohesive object model that is endorsed by the user is generated. The following two sections discuss this process in more detail.

Generating Class Header Files

For each class in the identified object model, C++ or Java source code can be automatically generated. Fields in the records or structures of the original code can become private member variables for newly generated classes. The bodies of functions in the original system can be transformed into bodies of public methods of the class they are assigned to. Moreover, if a class type appears in a function's formal parameter list, and if that function is attached as a method to that class, then the corresponding parameter is removed from the formal parameters. The functions with class type as a parameter can be kept as non-static. Static keyword from C functions is removed. Conversely, the functions returning assigned class type become static members. Also, the assigned class type is removed from the formal parameter list of mapped function. In order to access member variables, accessors and mutators are created.

As an example, consider the following data type and function prototype.

```
typedef struct ubi_btNodeStruct {
        struct ubi_btNodeStruct *Link[ 3 ];
        char                gender;
        char                balance;
          } ubi_btNode;
typedef ubi_btNode *ubi_btNodePtr;
ubi_btNodePtr ubi_RemoveTree (ubi_btRoot *RootPtr, ubi_btNode *Node)
```

These can be transformed into a class and method, respectively, as shown.

```
class  ubi_btNode {
private:
   ubi_btNode *Link[ 3 ];
    char   gender;
    char   balance;
public:
   void putLink(int index, ubi_btNode *value) { };
          ubi_btNode  * getLink(int index) {}
           void putGender(char value){};
           char getgender(){};
           void putBalance(char value){};
           char getBalance(){};
}
ubi_btNode* ubi_btNode:: ubi_btRemoveTree(ubi_btRoot *RootPtr);
```

Generation of Method Code

In this step, object-oriented source code is generated by utilizing the source code from the procedures or functions of the original legacy system. A source code generation module applies source code transformation rules as it traverses the abstract syntax tree (AST) nodes that correspond to the original procedures or function bodies. For each identified class, public methods are traced from their corresponding AST function nodes and transformation routines are called to generate the corresponding method body in C++ syntax or Java. As an example, consider the following code fragment.

```
ubi_btNodePtr ubi_avlRemove ( ubi_btRootPtr RootPtr, ubi_btNodePtr
      DeadNode)
{
      if ( ubi_btRemove(RootPtr,DeadNode))
            RootPtr->root = Debalance(RootPtr->root,
                        DeadNode->Link[01],
                        DeadNode->gender);
      return (DeadNode);
}
```

If ubi_avlRemove is attached to ubi_btNode in the object model identified in the earlier steps, then following piece of C++ code is generated.

```
ubi_btNodePtr ubi_btNode::ubi_avlRemove (ubi_btRootPtr RootPtr )
{
            if ( ubi_btRemove(RootPtr))
       RootPtr->putRoot(Debalance(getLink(0x01),getGender()));
      return this;
}
```

In the method body, to access member variables of other classes, accessors and mutators are used. Accessors and mutators for a class are automatically generated by the object model specification. However, no matter how complete the analysis is, it may be the case that the generated object-oriented code does not meet the requirement set by the user. For example, some methods cannot be assigned automatically to just one class. Such methods have to be split into smaller methods and assigned to the most appropriate classes. This process has to be done by applying slicing techniques and manual user intervention. In order to assist the user in evaluating the new generated code, the header files are further exported to object modeling and authoring tools (such as *Together/C++* (Together), *Rational Rose* (Rational)) as well as to metrics tools (such as *Datrix* (Datrix)).

Quality Evaluation

As mentioned above, object-oriented methodologies aim to facilitate the reuse and maintenance of a system. Reusability and maintainability can be quantified by internal quality attributes, such as abstraction and encapsulation. Specifically, the encapsulation is judged by the high cohesion in a class and low coupling between classes. The abstraction is reflected by object identification, inheritance and polymorphism. The satisfaction of such quality attributes is a major indicator of the success of the project. Therefore, it is critical to incorporate these target qualities into the migration process.

We propose a quality driven migration framework (Zou & Kontogiannis, 2002). Such a framework aims to monitor and evaluate software qualities at each step of the re-engineering process. The re-engineering process is considered as a sequence of transformations that alter the system's state. The initial state corresponds to the original system and the final state corresponds to the target migrant system. To incorporate quality control in the migration process, each state can be specified by a set of properties related to one or more target qualities (i.e., performance, maintainability, reusability) and denoted by feature vectors. The association of source code features with software quality requirements is achieved by the use of soft-goal interdependency graphs (Mylopoulos, 1992). In this context, each transformation is denoted by a likelihood that contributes towards the desired quality goals. Thus, a consecutive transformation is selected based on the likelihood that it will improve the final quality of the system. A full transformation path can be formed by the composition of transformations from original state to the final state. The research addresses three major issues, namely, the identification of a comprehensive set of possible transformation rules, the association of source code features with target qualities, and the design of an algorithmic process that can identify an optimal sequence of transformations to yield a target system with the desired qualities. To achieve the first research objective, the use of soft-goal graphs is proposed within the context of non-functional requirements. Such graphs allow for modeling the impact of specific design decisions towards a specific target requirement. The leaves of such graphs correspond to concrete system attributes that impact all the other nodes to which they are connected. In such graphs, nodes represent design decisions, and edges denote positive or negative dependencies towards a specific requirement. The second research objective is addressed by devising a comprehensive, yet extensible list of transformation rules that can be used to migrate a procedural system to an object-oriented one. A list of possible transformation rules is discussed in the previous sub-sections. Each transformation rule is formally specified in terms of pre/post conditions by the use of UML and OCL. Finally, the third research objective can be achieved by the utilization of Markov models and the Viterbi algorithm (Zou & Kontogiannis 2002), whereby the optimal sequence of transformations towards achieving the desired qualities is identified. The selection of the transformations is based on quantitative methods and a probabilistic model that aims to quantify the magnitude by which deltas in specific source attributes after applying a transformation may contribute towards achieving a desired system property.

REPRESENTATION OF MIGRATED COMPONENTS

Within the context of re-engineering legacy systems into a new platform, such as distributed environments, it is important to analyze the legacy software to recover its major functional components that relate to an application domain and specific business logic. In the previous sections, we have discussed the techniques to identify reusable components and transform them into object-oriented design. Once specific legacy components have been migrated into objects, their behaviors can be specified in terms of well-defined object-oriented interfaces and provide the required description for the middleware wrapping.

In general, the interface of a software component may contain information related to data types, references to external specifications that point to related components, descriptions of public attributes and methods, and return types and parameters that specify input and output. The representation of a component interface can be independent of a specific programming language, thus making it possible for wrapping technology to integrate software components into heterogeneous operating platforms and environments.

OMG IDL provides such a language-independent interface description for distributed CORBA components. It supports the basic specification for distributed components, such as the operations and attributes provided by the component. However, IDL cannot describe all of the information, such as the pre/post-conditions and semantic descriptions of functionality of the distributed component. For example, the server component may match perfectly to the client request by the signatures in the IDL interface, but the functionality of the offered service may not be the best one sought by the client process. Moreover, IDLs do not provide any additional information about the server's external dependencies such as the call-back invocation of a client's method. Although IDL is human-readable in terms of its syntax, it is a programmable specification language that can be compiled into executable code. The description for the functionality of the interface can be indicated in comments, but it is not easy for an algorithmic process to derive such information from the IDL syntax or free-style IDL comments alone.

XML is another key technology that is widely used as distributed standard format for data representation, data integration, data storage, and message exchanging. XML files can be transferred via HTTP on the Web, and provide a machine understandable and human readable syntax, which allows developers to define their own tags in different domains (Elenko & Reinertsen, 1999). In this context, XML tags can be used to define the configuration information and provide the semantic specification for distributed software components. As a result, the combination of XML and CORBA IDL can facilitate the specification and localization of distributed services in Web-based environments.

The XML interface representation of a software component consists of several aggregated elements, such as data type definitions, interface operation definitions, and interface data member definitions. The data type definition publishes the types other than the defined interface for the purpose of invoking interface methods. The interface data member definition declares the accessor and mutator methods associated with a data member. Such an example specification for a component extracted from the AVL GNU tree libraries is illustrated in Figure 3. The AVL tree library was written in C. By the use of the object identification techniques discussed in previous sections, C++ classes are extracted from the procedural code. The new migrant AVL tree libraries (Kontogiannis & Patil, 1999; Zou & Kontogiannis, 2001) can be considered as a collection of distributed components that consist of several classes. Therefore, the interface for the AVL tree component consists of several sub-interfaces that correspond to wrapper classes. Furthermore, with the XML specification, additional information can be easily encoded, such as the self-description information, URL address, pre- and post-conditions, and performance characteristics for the component. Such information introduces new functionality to wrappers, and can be used at the run time by a binder to efficiently locate a service in a transparent fashion to the client.

Figure 3: XML Representation of Component Interface.

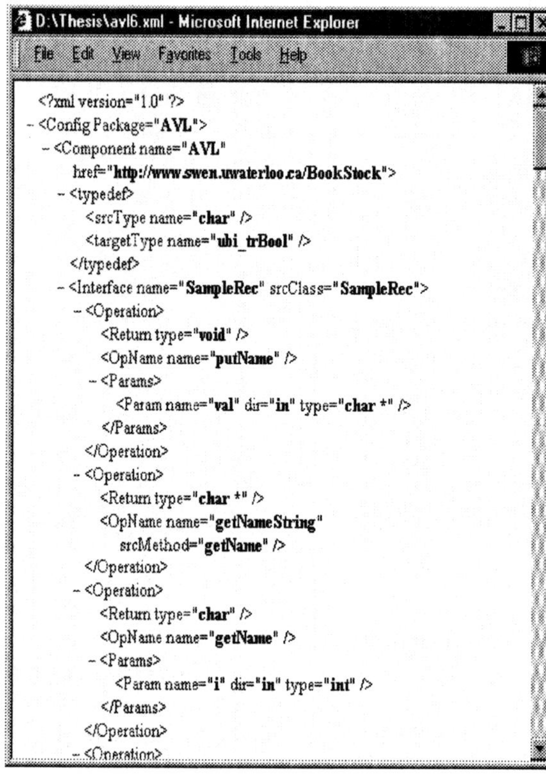

GENERATION OF OMG IDL AND CORBA WRAPER

Essentially, the wrapper acts as a facade: it offers clients a single, simple interface to the underlying objects. It glues together the CORBA distributed capabilities and the standalone

The wrappers implement message passing between the calling and the called objects, and redirect method invocations to the actual component services. The operations in the interface are the public operations in the CORBA wrapper. The concrete process to accomplish wrapping is accomplished in terms of three major steps.

The first step focuses on the specification of components in CORBA IDL as shown in Figure 4. In the second step, a CORBA IDL compiler translates the given IDL specification into language specific (e.g., C++), client-side stub classes and server-side skeleton classes. Client stub classes and server skeleton classes are generated automatically from the corresponding IDL specification. The client stub classes are proxies that allow a request invocation to be made via a normal local method call. Server-side skeleton

Figure 4: AVL Component Interface Definition Components.

```
module AVL{

interface corba_ubi_btRoot;
interface corba_ubi_btNode;
interface corba_SampleRec;

typedef char corba_ubi_trBool;

interface corba_SampleRec{
        void putName(in string val);
        string getName();
        void putNode(in corba_ubi_btNode val);
        corba_ubi_btNode getNode();
        long getDataCount();
        void putDataCount(in long aval);
};

interface corba_ubi_btNode {
        void putBalance(in char val);
        char getBalance();
        long Validate();
        //......
};

interface corba_ubi_btRoot{
        corba_ubi_trBool ubi_avlInsert(
              in corba_ubi_btNode NewNode,
              in corba_SampleRec ItemPtr,
              in corba_ubi_btNode OldNode );
        // ......
};
};
```

classes allow a request invocation received by the server to be dispatched to the appropriate server-side object. The operations registered in the interface become pure virtual functions in the skeleton class.

The third step focuses on wrapper classes that are generated and implemented as CORBA objects, directly inheriting from the skeleton classes. The wrapper classes encapsulate the standalone C++ object by reference, and incarnate the virtual functions by redirecting them to the encapsulated C++ class methods. The runtime structure of the wrapping process is illustrated in Figure 5. The new functionality of the legacy object can be added to the wrapper class as long as the method name is registered in the interface. The wrapper class can be generated automatically, using a high- level XML-based interface specification such as the one presented in Figure 3 and Figure 4. For example, the ubi_btRoot class is one of the classes identified within the AVL tree component. The wrapper_ubi_btRoot inherits from the skeleton class sk_AVL::_sk_corba_ubi_btRoot, which is generated from the CORBA IDL to C++ compiler (Figure 6). The wrapper class, wrapper_ubi_btRoot, encapsulates a reference of ubi_btRoot class as shown in Figure 7. When a client invokes a method through CORBA, it passes the parameters with data types registered in the IDL interface to the server side object. The wrapper classes translate the CORBA IDL specific data types from the client calls to the data types used by the encapsulated C++ classes. Figure 7 illustrates the transformation from the CORBA specific type such as corba_ubi_btRoot_ptr to the ubi_btRoot used in the corresponding C++ method. In the same way, the wrapper classes

Figure 5: Wrapping a Component.

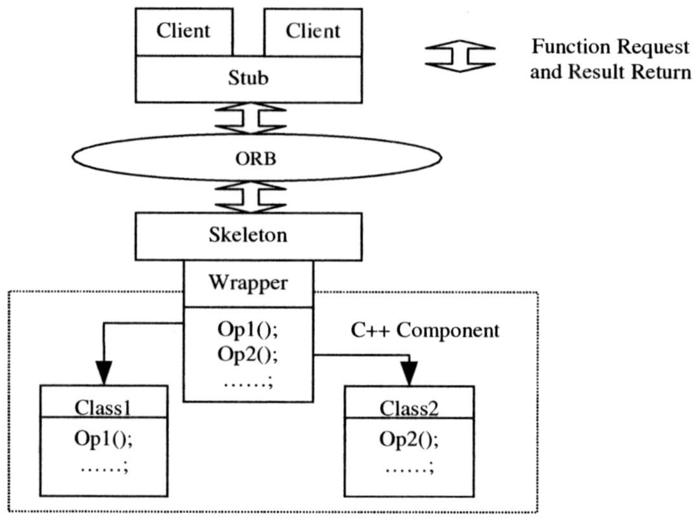

Figure 6: An Example Wrapper Class.

```
class wrapper_ubi_btRoot :
        public _sk_AVL :: _sk_corba_ubi_btRoot
{
private:
        ubi_btRoot& _ref;
        CORBA::Boolean _rel_flag;
        char *_obj_name;
public:
wrapper_ubi_btRoot(
        ubi_btRoot& _t,
        const char *obj_name=(char*)NULL,
        CORBA::Boolean _r_f=0):_ref(_t);
~wrapper_ubi_btRoot();
ubi_btRoot* translDLToObj(AVL::corba_ubi_btRoot_ptr obj);
void putRoot(AVL::corba_ubi_btNode_ptr val);
AVL::corba_ubi_btNode_ptr getRoot();
AVL::corba_ubi_trBool ubi_avlInsert(
        AVL::corba_ubi_btNode_ptr NewNode,
        AVL::corba_SampleRec_ptr ItemPtr,
        AVL::corba_ubi_btNode_ptr OldNode);
void Prune();
//Other methods are eliminated.
};
```

Figure 7: Example for Object Type Translation.

```
ubi_btRoot* wrapper_ubi_btRoot :: transIDLToObj(
          AVL::corba_ubi_btRoot_ptr obj)
{
 if (CORBA::is_nil(obj)) return NULL;

// set up the data members of _ref object.
// these data members are primary data types.
_ref.putCount(obj->getCount());
_ref.putFlags(obj->getFlags());

//translate the ubi_btNode to corba_ubi_btNode_ptr
//by wrapper class rootWrap
ubi_btNode *rootImpl= new ubi_btNode();
if (rootImpl==NULL)return NULL;
wrapper_ubi_btNode rootWrap(*rootImpl,
                    _obj_name);

//translate corba_ubi_btNode_ptr type returned from
//obj->getNode() to ubi_btNode * by transIDLToObj()
// in wrapper object rootWrap.
_ref.putRoot(rootWrap.transIDLToObj(
                    obj->getRoot()));

//......
 return &_ref;
}
```

convert the returned values from the C++ server class to the CORBA IDL specific data type, which is the wrapper class. In such a way, the wrapper object not only allows clients to send requests to the legacy object, but also allows the legacy object to return its result back to the clients. Since IDL does not support overloading and polymorphism, each method and data field within the interface should have a unique identifier.

If the polymorphic and overloaded methods occur in one class, it is necessary to rename these methods by adding a prefix or suffix to the original name when they are registered in the interface, avoiding changing the identified objects. This "naming" technique allows unique naming conventions throughout the system, without violating code style standards. The wrapper classes are responsible to direct the renamed overloaded and polymorphic methods to the corresponding client code.

If polymorphic and overloaded methods occur in the inheritance relationship, one can take advantage of C++ upcast feature; that is, to only register the sub-class in the component interface, and upcast the sub-class to its superclass when the polymorphic or overloading methods in a superclass are invoked.

AUTOMATIC GENERATION OF IDL AND CORBA WRAPPING

Once the interface is defined, the process of generating CORBA wrappers is similar to each identified component. Therefore, automatic generation of wrappers and IDL specifications is feasible by providing the information about each interface, such as signatures and renamed operation name for overloaded methods. A tool can be built to facilitate the automatic generation. Specially, such a tool implements three tasks, namely, the mapping between C++ to IDL Data Type, the mapping between CORBA C++ to Native C++ Data Mapping, and the generation of IDL and wrapper code. We discuss the details for each task in the following sub-sections.

C++ to IDL Data Type Mapping

In the XML interface specification, the signatures are indicated in terms of C++ types. Specifically, an IDL generator tool reads the XML interface description and converts the interface descriptions to IDL types, conforming to the mapping rules of the OMG IDL specification, and writes an IDL style interface to a new file.

The complete mapping of basic data types is given in Henning and Vinoski (1999). For example, C++ "long" is mapped into IDL "long", C++ "char *" to IDL "string". Due to the platform independence of OMG IDL, some basic C++ data types are not specified, such as "int", which is 16 bits in MS-DOS and Win3.1, but is 32 bits in Win32. For the identified component, we assume it works under a 32-bit operating system.

CORBA C++ to Native C++ Data Type Mapping

CORBA C++ stubs are generated from IDL compilers. Usually the CORBA C++ stubs are prefixed with the CORBA namespace. To invoke methods in the C++ code, parameters are passed from CORBA C++ wrapper objects to native C++ classes. Since the primary data types are passed by value, the parameters can be directly passed into native C++ methods, according to the same mapping rules from C++ to IDL. For complex data types, such as class, string, and array, parameters are passed by reference. Signatures of such types in wrapper classes are defined by pointers. In this case, the IDLToObj() method is added to CORBA wrapper object. The IDLToObj() method translates from a CORBA C++ wrapper pointer to a native C++ class pointer.

IDL and Wrapper Code Generation

According to the XML component interface representation, the wrapper IDL interface is generated. The <Interface> tag in the XML specification (Figure 3) denotes the interface to be generated. Externally visible operation identifiers are extracted from the children elements under the <Operation> elements. Operation name, return type and parameters' names and their corresponding types are some of the children elements. Meanwhile, C++ to IDL type conversion is automatically performed. In addition, the type definition information indicated under the <typedef> element is added to the top of the generated IDL file. Other global variables are defined as well. The generated IDL interface is shown in Figure 4. The CORBA wrapper header file, which declares a wrapper class in CORBA C++, is created using the same technique.

The wrapper function bodies are generated in a separated file, which provides the implementation of each method. According to the "srcClass" attribute (Figure 3) value in the <Operation> tag and "srcMethod" attribute value in <OpName> tag, the wrapper re-directs the invocation of its public operations to the corresponding source methods in the encapsulated source C++ object. At the same time, the wrapper generator provides the "glue" code, which is responsible for translating the CORBA IDL specific data typed to the native C++ data typed, and vice versa.

Although most of CORBA IDL compilers provide the generation of a "tie" class from the IDL specification, such a tie class is not sufficient for legacy code wrapping. Tie classes simply call the corresponding methods in the encapsulated class. However, they do not provide any functionality to translate CORBA IDL specific data types into native C++ data types. The code only works when the parameters are basic data types. For a complex data type, they cannot convert it to a native C++ pointer that can be recognized by the legacy code. In this context, the tie class is too simple to address the requirements for legacy code wrapping. The XML-based interface description of the software components and the CORBA IDL wrapper generation process overcome this limitation.

DEPLOYING MIGRATED COMPONENTS IN WEB SERVICE ENVIRONMENTS

Web service environments are Java based platforms. However, legacy systems are mostly written in procedural code. As aforementioned, CORBA provides a language-neutral solution to integrate legacy code in a distributed environment. Although CORBA provides the IIOP protocol to enable Web clients to access CORBA objects, IIOP messages cannot pass through firewall. Therefore, to enable the universal access to legacy components in the Web, the best way is to combine the CORBA and Web services, and implement CORBA objects as Web services. In previous section, we provided techniques to automatically generate CORBA wrappers that encapsulate the identified software components as distributed objects. The wrappers implement message passing between the calling and the called objects, and redirect method invocations to the actual component services. Furthermore, CORBA objects can be integrated into Web services environments. In this context, the SOAP protocol is adapted as a uniform messenger between CORBA objects and the rest of Web services. The layered structure is illustrated in Figure 8. A Web client sends a request, in conformance to SOAP, through HTTP to a Web server. The Web server redirects the request to the servlet engine, which is

Figure 8: SOAP Wrapping Structure.

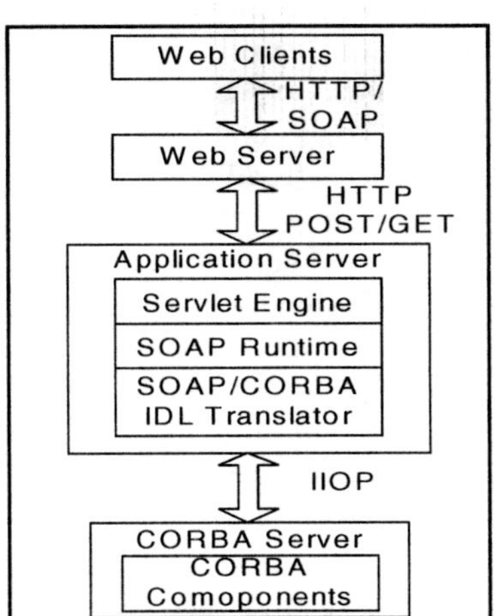

responsible for processing the HTTP/POST and HTTP/GET requests. The SOAP run time engine handles the interpretation and dispatching of SOAP message. At the heart of the structure, a SOAP/CORBA IDL translator is implemented as a collection of Java Beans to process inbound SOAP requests, which represent invocations to back-end CORBA objects. Internally it encapsulates all the services like SOAP serialization and deserialization, bridges the gap between the SOAP RPC and CORBA IDL, and finally, generates the stub to dispatch the requests to the back-end services on the client's behalf. A fully functional two-way SOAP to CORBA converter is provided by [Sopa2Corba]. Meanwhile, the WSDL (Web Service Description Language) is used to describe the services of back-end CORBA objects and to register them in a UDDI central repository. Thus the services can be located easily during runtime by querying the UDDI repository.

CONCLUSIONS AND FUTURE WORK

Ongoing technological advances in object-oriented programming, multi-tier architectures, and Web services pose great challenges in the modernization and evolution of legacy systems. In this chapter, we presented a comprehensive migration framework that leverages legacy software assets into Web environments. Instead of wrapping a legacy system as a black box, we focus on the techniques to decompose legacy systems into finer grain components, transform the identified components into object-oriented designs, wrap migrated components as distributed objects, and facilitate the universal Web enabled service invocation and integration of these components. In this context, these components can be easily reused and programmably composed to produce new business logic within Web service-oriented architecture. As a core of this framework, we adopt several software engineering design heuristics and rules as a guideline to identify object models from procedural code and establish inheritance and polymorphism relations among identified class candidates. We aim to achieve good qualities, such as high encapsulation, high cohesion, low coupling and high abstraction in the identified components. In this respect, these components have minimum dependencies on external resources and offer clear interfaces for later wrapping and integration. Moreover, it is important to specify the properties of distributed components in terms of functional and non-functional requirements, such as reliability, security, and performance. Therefore, the components can be selected to meet exact users' requirements. In this context, we utilized XML and CORBA IDL to specify component interfaces. Such an XML-based interface specification allows the automatic CORBA wrapper generation. Moreover, we can incorporate QoS requirements in the component identification and wrapping process. The capabilities of the identified components can be enhanced to conform to specific quality criteria and requirements which the user considers to be essential for the success of the migration into a distributed environment.

We believe that future research on the evolution of legacy systems in Web environments is very critical and needed due to the pervasive adoption of distributed architecture. Extensive research on the migration, description, composition, and localization of existing legacy systems to the Web service infrastructure is needed to adapt valuable legacy assets to continuously evolving requirements and environments. Furthermore, existing Web applications are the legacy systems of tomorrow. Reengineering techniques would be needed to restructure such applications in order to improve the qualities of today's Web applications.

REFERENCES

Aversano, L., Canfora, G., Cimitile, A., & Lucia, A.D. (2001). Migrating legacy systems to the Web: An experience report. *Proceedings of the Fifth IEEE Conference on Software Maintenance and Reengineering (CSMR).*

Blaha, M.R., & Premerlani, W.J. (1995). Observed idiosyncracies of relational database designs. *Proceedings of the Second IEEE Working Conference on Reverse Engineering*, Toronto, Ontario, July 14-16.

Bodhuin, T., Guardabascio, E., & Tortorella, M. (2002). Migrating COBOL systems to the WEB by using the MVC design pattern. Proceedings of the Ninth IEEE Working Conference on Reverse Engineering.

Brodie, M.J., & Stonebaker, M. (1995). *Migrating legacy systems – Gateways, interfaces & incremental approach.* San Francisco: Morgan Kaufmann Publishers, Inc.

Brown, A., & Barn, B. (1999). Enterprise-scale CBD: Building complex computer systems from components. *Proceedings of Software Technology Education & Practice.*

Datrix. Available: http://www.iro.umontreal.ca/labs/gelo/datrix/

Dreyfus, P. (1998). The second wave: Netscape on usability in the services-based Internet. *IEEE Internet Computing*, March/April.

Elenko, M., & Reinertsen, M. (1999). XML & CORBA. Available: *http://www.omg.org*

Etzkorn, L.H., & Davis, C.G. (1997). Automatically identifying reusable OO legacy code. *IEEE Computer,* October.

Fowler, M. (2000). *Refactoring: Improving the design of existing code*. Reading, MA: Addison-Wesley.

Henning, M., & Vinoski, S. (1999). *Advanced CORBA programming with C++*. Reading, MA: Addison-Wesley.

Kontogiannis, K. (1998). *Code migration through transformations: An experience report.* IBM Centers for Advanced Studies Conference.

Kontogiannis, K., & Patil, P. (1999). Evidence driven object identification in procedural code. *Software technology education & practice*. Pittsburgh, PA.

Lanubile, F., & Visaggio, G. (1997). Extracting reusable functions by flow graph-based program slicing. *IEEE Transactions on Software Engineering, SE-23*(4).

Lau, T., Lu, J., Mylopoulos, J., & Kontogiannis, K. (2003). The migration of multi-tier e-commerce applications to an Enterprise Java environment. *Information Systems Frontier, 5*(2), 149-160.

Lindig, C., & Snelting, G. (1997). Assessing modular structure of legacy code based mathematical concept analysis. *Proceedings of the 19th ACM International Conference on Software Engineering.*

Lucia, D., Di Lucca, G.A., Fasolino, A.R., Guerra, P., & Petruzzelli, S. (1997). Migrating legacy systems toward object oriented platforms. *Proceedings of IEEE International Conference of Software Maintenance (ICSM97).*

Mancoridis, S., Mitchell, B.S., Chen, Y., & Gansner, E.R. (1998). Using automatic clustering to produce high-level System organizations of source code. *IEEE Proceedings of the 1998 Int. Workshop on Program Understanding (IWPC'98).*

Martin, J. Ephedra – A C to Java migration environment. Available: *http://ovid.tigris.org/Ephedra/*

Moore, M., & Moshkina, L. (2000). Migrating legacy user interfaces to the Internet: Shifting dialogue initiative. *Proceedings of Working Conference on Reverse Engineering*, Brisbane, Australia, December.

Muller, H., Orgun, M., Tilley, S., & Uhl, J. (1992, August). *Discovering and reconstructing subsystem structures through reverse engineering* (Technical Report DCS-201-IR). University of Victoria: Department of Computer Science..

Mylopoulos, J., Chung, L., & Nixon, B. (1992). Representing and using nonfunctional requirement: A process-oriented approach. *IEEE Transactions on Software Engineering, SE-18*(6).

Rational Rose. Available: *http://www.rational.com/products/rose/index.jsp?SM SESSION=NO*

Sahraoui, H.A., Melo, W., Lounis, H., & Dumont, F. (1997). Applying concept formation methods to object identification in procedural code. Proceedings of the Twelfth IEEE Conference on Automated Software Engineering.

Sneed, H. (1996). Object oriented COBOL recycling. *Proceedings of the Third Working Conference of Reverse Engineering.*

SOAP. *SOAP: Simple Object Access Protocol*. Available: *http://www-4.ibm.com/software/developer/library/soapv11.html*

Soap2Corba and Corba2Soap. Available: *http://soap2corba.sourceforge.net/*

Stroulia, E. et al. (1999). Reverse engineering legacy interface: An interaction-driven approach. *Proceedings of the 6th IEEE Working Conference on Reverse Engineering*, 6-8 October, Atlanta, Georgia.

Together. *http://www.borland.com/together/controlcenter/index.html*

UDDI. *Universal Description, Discovery and Integration:* UDDI Technical White Paper. Available: *http://www.uddi.org*

Umar, A. (1997). *Application (re)engineering: Building Web-based applications and dealing with legacies.* Prentice Hall PTR.

Ward, M.P. (1999). Assembler to C migration using the FermaT transformation system. *IEEE International Conference on Software Maintenance.*

WSDL. *Web Services Description Language (WSDL) 1.0.* Available: *http://www-4.ibm.com/software/devleoper/library/w-wsdl.html*

Zou, Y., & Kontogiannis, K. (2000). Migration and Web-based integration of legacy services. *10th Centre for Advanced Studies Conference (CASCON),* Toronto, Ontario, Canada, November, 262-277.

Zou, Y., & Kontogiannis, K. (2001). A framework for migrating procedural code to object-oriented platforms. *Proceedings of the Eighth IEEE Asia-Pacific Software Engineering Conference (APSEC),* Macau SAR, China, December, 408-418.

Zou, Y., & Kontogiannis, K. (2002). Migration to object oriented platforms: A state transformation approach. *Proceedings of IEEE International Conference on Software Maintenance (ICSM),* Montreal, Quebec, Canada, October, 530-539.

Chapter VII

Applying Patterns for Reengineering to the Web

Uwe Zdun, Vienna University of Economics, Austria

ABSTRACT

This chapter examines the use of patterns for reengineering legacy systems to the Web. Today reengineering existing (legacy) systems to the Web is a typical software maintenance task. In such projects developers integrate a Web representation with the legacy system's application programming interface (API) and its responses. Often, the same information is provided to other channels than HTTP and in other formats than HTML as well, and the old (legacy) interfaces are still supported. Add-on services such as security or logging are required. Performance and scalability of the Web application might be crucial. To resolve these issues, many different concepts and frameworks have to be well understood, especially legacy system wrapping, connection handling, remoting, service abstraction, adaptation techniques, dynamic content generation, and others. In this chapter, we present patterns from different sources that resolve these issues. We integrate them to a pattern language operating in the context of reengineering to the Web, and present pattern variants and examples in this context.

INTRODUCTION

Many existing software systems have to be migrated to the Web. That means that the legacy system gets an interactive Web interface, typically in addition to its existing interfaces. This Web interface forwards Web requests to the legacy system, decorates the responses of the system with HTML markup, and sends the results to the Web client. Inputs are handled via the Web browser, say, using HTML links and forms. For small applications, building a Web interface is quite simple; however, for larger, existing systems there are some typical issues, including:

- high flexibility and adaptability of the Web interface,
- reuse of the presentation logic,
- high performance,
- preserving states and sessions,
- user management, and
- serving multiple channels.

That means that implementing a Web interface for a larger, existing legacy system is a non-trivial task that is likely to be underestimated. This underestimation, in turn, results in unexpected maintenance costs and development times. However, there are many successful projects that have avoided the common pitfalls.

Software patterns are a way to convey knowledge from successful solutions. To tackle the issues named above, we present patterns from various pattern languages and pattern catalogs that can be applied in the context of reengineering to the Web. In particular, we discuss connection and invocation handling, legacy system wrapping and adaptation, dealing with asynchronous invocations, concurrency handling, service and channel abstraction, session management, and dynamic content generation and conversion. The patterns are originally presented in different contexts; in this chapter we present them in variants specific for reengineering to the Web. This way we build up a pattern language for reengineering to the Web, consisting of patterns already documented elsewhere in related, yet different, contexts.

The remainder of this chapter is structured as follows. In the next section we give a brief problem outline, and then we briefly explain the concepts "pattern" and "pattern language". Next, we discuss connection and invocation handling in Web applications that connect a legacy system to the Web. Then we introduce solutions for legacy system wrapping, adaptation, and decoration. In the following section we discuss how to provide the services of a legacy system to more than one channel. Also we illustrate how to provide sessions and state in Web applications despite the HTTP protocol being stateless. Next we discuss content generation, representation, and conversion for the Web. The following section deals with the integration of typical add-on services, such as security or logging. Finally, we give an overview and discussion of the pattern language that we have explained incrementally in the preceding sections, provide a case study, and conclude.

PROBLEM OUTLINE

In the context of reengineering to the Web, a legacy application gets an (additional) interactive Web interface that decorates the outputs of the system with HTML markup and translates the (e.g., form-based) inputs via the Web browser into the (legacy) system's APIs. At first glance, this seems to be a conceptually straightforward effort, though it might turn out to be a lot of work for larger systems.

In Figure 1 we can see a simplistic three-tier architecture for interactive, Web-based applications. A Web user agent, such as a browser, communicates with a Web server. The Web server "understands" that certain requests have to be handled interactively. Thus, it forwards the request and all its information to another module, thread, or process that translates the HTTP request to the legacy system's APIs. An HTML decorator

Figure 1: Simplistic Three-Tier Architecture for (Re-) Engineering to the Web.

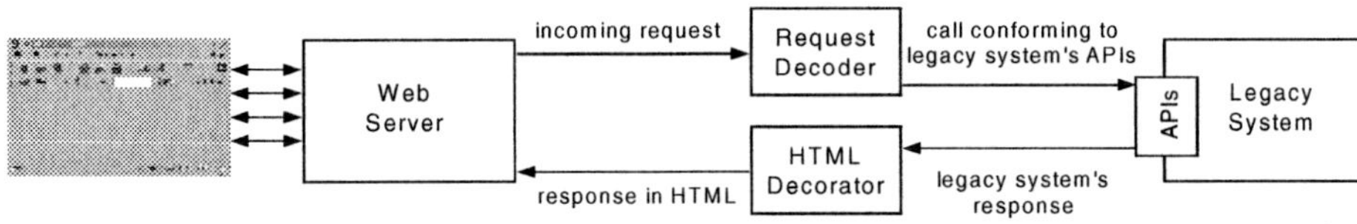

builds the appropriate HTML page out of the system's response and triggers the Web server to send the page to the Web client.

Using this simple architecture for a given legacy system, we can use a simple process model for migrating to the Web. In particular, the following steps have to be performed in general. Of course, there are feedback loops during these steps, and they are not in any particular order:

- *Providing an Interface API to the Web:* To invoke a system's functions/methods and decorate them with HTML markup, we first have to identify the relevant components and provide them with distinct interfaces (which may, in the ideal case, exist already). These interface have to satisfy the Web engineering project's requirements. To find such interfaces, in general, for each component there are two possibilities:
  - *Wrapper:* The developer can wrap the component with a shallow wrapper object that just translates the URL into a call to the legacy system's API. The wrapper forwards the response to an HTML decorator or returns HTML fragments.
  - *Reengineered or Redeveloped Solution:* Sometimes it is suitable to reengineer or redevelop a given component completely, so that it becomes a purely Web-enabled solution. For instance, this makes sense when the legacy user interface does not need to be supported anymore.
- *Implementing a Request Decoder:* A component has to map the contents of the URL (and other HTTP request information) to the legacy system's API or the wrapper's interface, respectively.
- *Implementing an HTML Decorator Component:* A component has to decorate the legacy system's or wrapper's response with HTML markup.
- *Integrating with a Web Server:* The components have to be integrated with a Web server solution. For instance, these components can be CGI programs, run in different threads or processes, may be part of a custom Web server, and so forth.

In our experience, this architecture is in principal applying for most reengineering to the Web efforts and for many newly developed Web-enabled systems (that have to serve other channels than HTTP as well). However, this architecture and process model does not depict the major strategic decisions and the design/implementation efforts involved in a large-scale Web development project well. There are many issues, critical for success, that are not tackled by this simplistic architecture, including: technology choices, conceptual choices, representation flexibility and reuse, performance, concurrency handling, dealing with asynchronous invocations, preserving states and sessions, user management, and service abstraction.

In this chapter, we will survey and categorize critical technical aspects for reengineering to the Web using the patterns of successful solutions. Thus, we will step-by-step enrich the simple architecture presented previously to gather a conceptual understanding of which elements are required for reengineering a larger system to the Web. Moreover, this way we will build up a framework to categorize Web development environments and packages. An important goal is to assemble a feature list and terminology for mapping requirements to concrete technological and conceptual choices so that new projects can more easily decide upon used frameworks.

PATTERNS AND PATTERN LANGUAGES

In this chapter, we present a pattern language for reengineering to the Web. In short, a *pattern* is a proven solution to a problem in a context that resolves a set of forces. Each pattern is a three-part rule, which expresses a relation between a certain context, a problem, and a solution (Alexander, 1979). In more detail, the context refers to a recurring set of situations in which the pattern applies. The problem refers to a set of goals and constraints that typically occur in this context, called the forces of the pattern. The forces are a set of factors that influence the particular solution to the pattern's problem. A *pattern language* is a collection of patterns that solve the prevalent problems in a particular domain and context, and, as a language of patterns, it specifically focuses on the pattern relationships in this domain and context. As an element of language, a pattern is an instruction that can be used over and over again to resolve the given system of forces, wherever the context makes it relevant (Alexander, 1979).

Our pattern language uses patterns that have been documented in the literature before, either as "isolated" patterns or in other pattern languages. In the pattern language presented, we specifically use these patterns in the context of reengineering to the Web. That means that we describe the patterns in this particular context. Note that there is a difference to the general-purpose use of these patterns.

We present the patterns within the explanations of the reengineering solutions, in which the patterns occur the first time. Each pattern is presented with a problem section, followed by a solution that starts with the word "therefore". We always cite the original pattern descriptions; refer to them for more details on the particular patterns.

CONNECTION AND INVOCATION HANDLING

There are many different kinds of frameworks that can be used to access objects running in a remote server, such as distributed object frameworks (like CORBA, DCOM, RMI), Web application frameworks, or object-oriented messaging protocols. In this chapter, we commonly refer to these kinds of frameworks as *remoting* frameworks.

Web application frameworks, such as Java Servlets and JSP, Apache and Apache Modules (Thau, 1996), AOL Server (Davidson, 2000), TclHttpd (Welch, 2000), WebShell (Vckovski, 2001), Zope (Latteier, 1999), or ActiWeb (Neumann & Zdun, 2001), provide a pure server-side remoting framework based on Web servers. That means that invocations sent with Web requests are interactively handled by code running in the Web server. Often, for reengineering to the Web an existing Web application framework can be reused. In some cases it makes sense to implement a custom invocation framework on top of a Web server; for instance, if the performance of existing Web application frameworks causes problems or if it is not possible to access or control required parameters in the HTTP header fields.

On the client side, in most cases, the Web browser is used as the primary client. If other programs are used as clients (or if a Web browser should be implemented), an HTTP client suite has to be chosen (or built) as well. A fundamental difference of Web application frameworks in comparison to other kinds of remoting frameworks, such as distributed object frameworks, is that the client (e.g., the Web browser) is a generic program handling all possible applications. Distributed object frameworks use an application-specific client implementation that is realized with the client components of the distributed object frameworks.

Many Web applications wrapping a legacy system have to support other remoting frameworks as well. For instance, distributed object frameworks that are also based on HTTP (such as Web services) can be supported, or frameworks that are based on other protocols (such as CORBA). Combining different protocols and remoting frameworks can be handled by a SERVICE ABSTRACTION LAYER (Vogel, 2001).

The named remoting frameworks use a similar basic remoting architecture, but there are many differences. The developer, who wants to use one or more of these remoting frameworks, has to understand the basic remoting architecture of the used frameworks well. Of course, in the Web reengineering context this especially means to understand the Web application framework used. This is important because it may be necessary to tune or configure the remoting frameworks, for instance, to optimize Quality of Service (QoS), tune the performance, use threading, use POOLING (Kircher & Jain, 2002), or extend the invocation process. Also, for integrating different frameworks it is important to understand their basic architecture well.

Layers of a Web Application Framework

In this section, we explain the remoting architecture of Web application framework using different LAYERS (Buschmann et al., 1996) (see Figure 2):

Pattern 1 - LAYERS:

> Consider a system in which high-level functionalities are depending on low-level functionalities. Such systems often require some horizontal structuring that is orthogonal to their vertical subdivision. Local changeability, exchangeability, and reuse of system parts should be supported.
> *Therefore,* structure the system into LAYERS and place them on top of each other. Within each LAYER all constituent components work on the same level of abstraction.

In a Web application framework, the lowest layer is an adaptation layer to the operating system and network communication APIs. The advantage of using an adaptation layer is that higher layers can abstract from platform details and therefore use a platform-independent interface. The operating system APIs are (often) written in the procedural C language; thus, if the communication framework is written in an object-oriented language, WRAPPER FACADES (Schmidt et al., 2000) are used for encapsulating the operating system's APIs.

Pattern 2 - *WRAPPER FACADE:*

> Consider an object-oriented system that should use non-object-oriented APIs (such as operating system APIs, system libraries, or legacy systems). Programming non-object-oriented APIs directly should be avoided.
> *Therefore,* for each set of related functions and data in a non-object-oriented API, create one or more WRAPPER FACADE classes that encapsulate these functions and data with a more concise, robust, portable, and maintainable interface.

The higher layers only access the operating system's APIs via the WRAPPER FACADES. Each WRAPPER FACADE consists of one or more classes that contain forwarder operations. These forwarder operations encapsulate the C-based functions and data within an object-oriented interface. Typical WRAPPER FACADES within the operating system adaptation layer provide access to threading, socket communication, I/O events, dynamic linking, and so forth.

On top of the adaptation layer the communication framework is defined. It handles the basics of connection handling and asynchronous invocation. The layer containing the HTTP client (e.g., the Web browser) and the HTTP server components, including the Web application framework, is defined on top of the communication framework layer.

The server application, finally, contains the wrappers for the legacy system. If the legacy system provides a procedural API, the pattern WRAPPER FACADE can be used to access it. Or, the legacy system might run in a different process or different machine (e.g., as a server process or a batch process). Then some kind of connection is required, such as inter-process communication or another communication framework.

Note that even though only the highest LAYER of the Web application framework is concerned with the reengineering to the Web task, the wrappers in it may have to access details in lower LAYERS. In general, low-level functionalities are hidden by higher-level LAYERS. But sometimes it is necessary to deal with the low-level functionalities directly, say, for configuration, performance tuning, or Quality of Service tuning. Thus the

Figure 2: Web Application Layers.

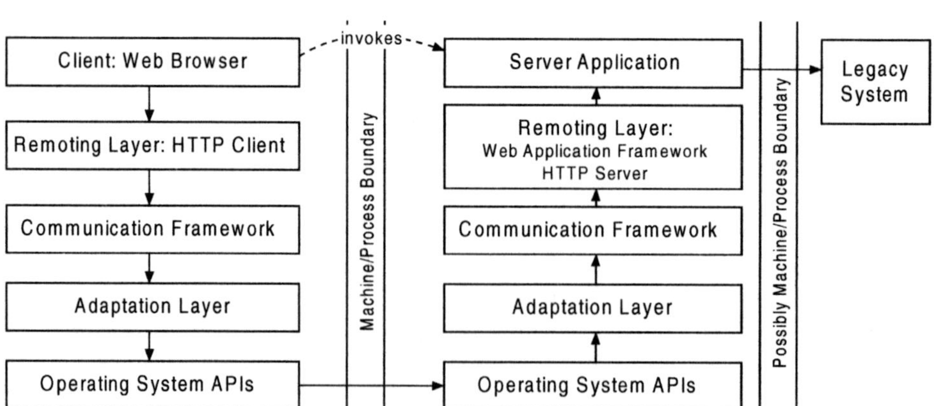

developer of a reengineering to the Web solution has to understand the lower LAYERS (APIs), even though it is usually possible to reuse existing lower LAYER implementations.

Web Connection vs. Connection to the Legacy System

As illustrated in Figure 2, there are possibly two connections between different systems. Besides the Web connection between Web client and Web server, there may be a second connection from the Web application framework to the legacy system. We might have to cope with characteristics of the Web connection when connecting to the legacy system as well. Typical problem fields are asynchronous invocations, concurrency, the statelessness of the HTTP protocol, missing support for sessions, and potential performance overheads. If a particular problem is not already resolved by the Web application framework, it has to be resolved within the connection to the legacy system. Out of these reasons, even if an existing Web application framework can be reused, a reengineer has to understand the solution to these problems in the Web application framework well. The connection to the legacy system has to use the invocation model of the Web application framework and/or customize it to its requirements.

As a typical example, consider a legacy system that allows for synchronous processing (e.g., batch processing) only. Web clients send asynchronous and concurrent requests. Thus, somewhere these requests have to be demultiplexed and synchronized. Potentially, the Web application framework can demultiplex and synchronize the requests already. But often for performance reasons, such requests are handled by multiple threads in the Web server. These threads again can concurrently access the legacy system. Then the connection to the legacy system has to handle demultiplexing and synchronization for the access to the legacy system.

That means that the patterns of connection handling and invocation handling discussed in the next sections either can be implemented within the Web application framework or as part of the connection to the legacy system.

Communication Framework: Connection Handling and Concurrency

For remote communication, connection establishment is typically handled by the ACCEPTOR/CONNECTOR pattern (Schmidt et al., 2000):

Pattern 3 - ACCEPTOR/CONNECTOR

Protocols like HTTP are based on connections (e.g., socket connections). Coupling of connection management and configuration code with the processing code should be avoided.

Therefore, separate the connection initialization from the use of established connections. A connection is created when the connector on the client side connects to the acceptor on the server side. Once a connection is established, further communication is done using a connection handle.

An HTTP server listens to a network port to accept connections sent by the client; in turn, the client (i.e., the Web browser) uses a connector to start an HTTP request. A connector and acceptor pair is also used for response handling. The server response connects to the client that awaits the server's responses with a response acceptor.

An HTTP server has to support asynchronous invocations to enable multiple simultaneous requests. Non-trivial clients (like most Web browsers) should not block during request and response, and thus, are also asynchronous. Therefore, the programming model of most Web applications is event-based both on the client side and the server side, meaning that an event loop and/or multi-threading is supported and connection handling is done using callbacks for the network events. A REACTOR (Schmidt et al., 2000) reacts on the network events and efficiently demultiplexes the events. It dispatches all requests to handler objects:

Pattern 4 - *REACTOR*

Event-based, distributed systems (may) have to handle multiple requests (and responses) simultaneously.

Therefore, synchronously wait for (connection) events in the REACTOR. The system registers event handlers for certain types of events with the REACTOR. When an event occurs, the REACTOR dispatches the event handler associated with the event.

In Web applications, a REACTOR is typically used on the client side and the server side.

Server side concurrency can simply be handled by the REACTOR and an event loop. That means the REACTOR queues up all network events in the order of demultiplexing. This is a very simple concurrency handling architecture that yields a good performance for relatively small, remote operations. Computation-intensive or blocking operations may cause problems, as queued requests have to wait for these operations.

If computation-intensive or blocking operations can be expected (which may be the case for a legacy system), the Web server should proceed with other work while waiting for the legacy system's response. Thus, in such cases, typically a multi-threaded server is used. Then only one thread of control has to wait for a computation-intensive or blocking operation, while other threads can resume with their work.

If we access a legacy system that requires synchronous access from multiple threads, we have to synchronize and schedule the accesses. This can done by using objects in the Web application server for scheduling access to the legacy system; there are two alternative patterns for synchronizing and scheduling concurrently invoked remote operations (Schmidt et al., 2000):

Pattern 5 - *ACTIVE OBJECT*

Consider that multiple clients access the same object concurrently. Processing-intensive operations should not block the entire process. Synchronized access to shared concurrent objects should be provided in a straightforward manner.

Therefore, decouple the executing from the invoking thread. A queue is used between those threads to exchange requests and responses.

Pattern 6 - *MONITOR OBJECT*

Consider that multiple client requests access the same thread of control concurrently. An object should be protected from uncontrolled concurrent changes and deadlocks.

Therefore, let a MONITOR OBJECT ensure that only one operation runs within an object at a time by queuing operation executions. It applies one lock per object to synchronize access to all operations.

Often threading is used for connection handling and execution. For each particular connection, a connection handle has to be instantiated. To optimize resource allocation for connections, the connections can be shared in a pool using the pattern POOLING (Kircher & Jain, 2002). This reduces the overhead of instantiating the connection handle objects.

Pattern 7 - *POOLING*

Consider a system that provides access to multiple resources of the same kind, such as network connections, objects, threads, or memory. Fast and predictable access to these resources and scalability are required.

Therefore, manage multiple instances of a resource type in a pool. Clients can acquire the resources from the pool, and release them back into the pool when they are no longer needed. To increase efficiency, the pool eagerly acquires a static number of resources after creation. If the demand exceeds the available resources in the pool, it lazily acquires more resources.

When the legacy system can be accessed concurrently, we can also pool the instances that connect to the legacy system to avoid the overhead of establishing a connection to the legacy system.

In the context of reengineering to the Web, it is especially important to select for a proper concurrency model. Also, connection and/or thread POOLING have to be adjusted to the requirements of the legacy application. Usually, these issues do not have to be implemented from scratch, but only the models of used remoting frameworks have to be well understood and integrated with the model of the legacy application. In contrast, the connection to the legacy system is most often hand-built.

Remoting Layer

On top of the connection handling and concurrency layer (the communication framework), there are a few basic remoting patterns (from Voelter et al., 2002) that are used for building the remoting layer.

In a remoting framework, clients communicate with objects on a remote server. On the server side the invoked functionality is implemented as a REMOTE OBJECT (Voelter et al., 2002):

Pattern 8 - *REMOTE OBJECT*

Accessing an object over a network is different from accessing a local object because of machine boundaries, network latency, network unreliability, and other properties of network environments.

Therefore, let a distributed object framework transfer local invocations from the client side to a REMOTE OBJECT within the server. Each REMOTE OBJECT provides a well-defined interface to be accessed remotely.

In Web application frameworks, the REMOTE OBJECT is responsible for building up the delivered Web pages dynamically. In the legacy reengineering context that means it has to invoke the legacy system and decorate it with HTML. That means that if a connection to the legacy system has to be established, the REMOTE OBJECT is responsible for building it up. As explained in the previous section the concurrency patterns and POOLING might also be applied within the REMOTE OBJECT.

The client invokes an operation of a local object and expects it to be executed by the REMOTE OBJECT. To make this happen, the invocation crosses the machine boundary, the correct operation of the correct REMOTE OBJECT is obtained and executed, and the result of this operation invocation is passed back across the network. In a distributed object framework a CLIENT PROXY (Voelter et al., 2002) is used by a client to access the REMOTE OBJECT:

Pattern 9 - CLIENT PROXY

The programming model on the client side should not expose the networking details to clients.
Therefore, provide a CLIENT PROXY as a local object within the client process that offers the REMOTE OBJECT's interface and hides networking details.

In Web applications, the CLIENT PROXY usually is a generic invocation handler that sends network requests for Web pages using an URL. In the URL or in the HTTP request, the details of the invocation (object ID, operation name, parameters) are encoded. These details are used by the server to find the correct object to be invoked. These tasks are performed by an INVOKER (Voelter et al., 2002) on the server side:

Pattern 10 - INVOKER

When a CLIENT PROXY sends invocations to the server side, somehow the targeted REMOTE OBJECT has to be reached.
Therefore, provide an INVOKER that is remotely accessed by the CLIENT PROXY with the invocation data. The INVOKER de-marshals the invocation data and uses them to dispatch the correct operation of the target REMOTE OBJECT.

Note that in distributed object frameworks that are primarily designed for program-to-program communication, such as CORBA or Web services, often CLIENT PROXIES and INVOKERS are specific for a REMOTE OBJECT type. They can be generated from an INTERFACE DESCRIPTION (Voelter et al., 2002). In contrast, in a Web application the interfaces are solely defined by the server and the correct access interfaces (and parameters) have to be delivered to the client using Web pages. For integrating Web application with distributed object frameworks it is necessary to integrate these differences of the remoting models. When the legacy system contains full INTERFACE DESCRIPTIONS, such as C header files for instance, these can potentially be used to generate the INVOKERS automatically.

Usually, there is more than one INVOKER in a Web application framework; for instance, one for delivering static Web pages from the file system and one for handling

Figure 3: Web Remoting Layer.

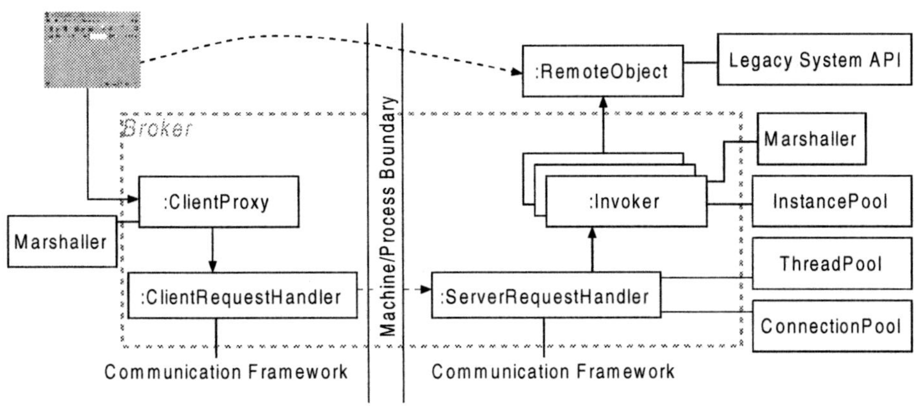

remote invocations of REMOTE OBJECTS. Thus, in some instances it is required to pick out the responsible INVOKER for an incoming request. On the client and server sides, a REQUEST HANDLER (Voelter et al., 2002) is used to abstract the communication framework for CLIENT PROXY and INVOKER:

Pattern 11 - REQUEST HANDLER

On the client and server sides the details of connection handling have to be handled. In particular, communication setup, resource management, threading, and concurrency have to be handled and configured in a central fashion. *Therefore,* provide a SERVER REQUEST HANDLER, responsible for dealing with the network communication on the server side, together with a respective CLIENT REQUEST HANDLER, responsible for the client side communication. These REQUEST HANDLERS interact with CLIENT PROXIES and INVOKERS respectively.

Usually, the same communication framework implementations can be used on client and server sides, but the REQUEST HANDLERS are different: the CLIENT REQUEST HANDLER connects to the server side and uses the REACTOR to wait for the reply, whereas the SERVER REQUEST HANDLER waits for incoming invocations and sends the reply back after it is processed. CLIENT PROXY, REQUEST HANDLER, and INVOKER together build a BROKER (Buschmann et al., 1996) (see Figure 3).

Marshalling of request and response has to happen on the client and server sides according to the HTTP protocol. This especially means adding HTTP headers, encoding URLs and form data, and converting binary data (e.g., using Base64 encoding). This is done by a MARSHALLER (Voelter et al., 2002):

Pattern 12 - MARSHALLER

The data to describe operation invocations of REMOTE OBJECTS consist of the target object's object ID, the operation identifier, the arguments, and possibly other context information. All this information has to be transported over the network connection.

Therefore, require each REMOTE OBJECT type to provide a way to serialize itself into a transport format that can be transported over a network as a byte stream. The distributed object framework provides a MARSHALLER (on the client and server sides) that uses this mechanism whenever a remote invocation needs to be transported across the network.

A MARSHALLER for Web applications also has to convert remote invocations into parts of Web pages. Usually, remote invocations are either modeled as HTML links or actions of HTML forms. In contrast to distributed object frameworks, in a Web application marshalling of invocations is only performed on the server side: the client side invocations are encoded into the delivered Web pages. For instance, the following invocation to the REMOTE OBJECT objectName and the method methodName can be embedded in an HTML document as a link:

http://www.myhost.org/objectName+methodName?arg=xyz

On the server side such invocations have to be de-marshalled when a request arrives (for instance, the URL string has to be split and/or the HTML form data have to be evaluated). Marshalling can be triggered by the INVOKER. If more than one INVOKER is used in the system, the REQUEST HANDLER can de-marshal the invocation partially to find the correct INVOKER to handle the invocation.

Note that the connection to the legacy system might need more context information, such as, for instance, a session identifier. Such context information also needs to be marshalled and embedded in HTML or HTTP (that is, either in the URLs of HTML links, in the HTML text with HIDDEN form fields, or as cookies).

Additionally, sensitive information, such as user authentications, can be encrypted during marshalling.

LEGACY SYSTEM WRAPPING, ADAPTATION, AND DECORATION

An important aspect of migrating a legacy system to the Web is *wrapping*. Wrappers are mechanisms for introducing new behavior to be executed before, after, in, and/or around an existing method or component. Wrapping is especially used as a technique for encapsulating legacy components. Common techniques of reusing legacy components by wrapping are discussed in Sneed (2000) and Brant et al. (1998).

On the server side of a Web application framework, we have to map incoming invocations into the legacy system. The invoker provides the invocation data that it has obtained by de-marshalling the URL and the HTTP request header. The invocation data reference a wrapper object. This wrapper is responsible for forwarding the invocation into the legacy system and obtaining the result.

The COMPONENT WRAPPER pattern (Zdun, 2002a) generalizes this form of (legacy) wrapping:

Pattern 13 - COMPONENT WRAPPER

A component should be used with its external interface only, but still we often require some way to customize and adapt a component to a degree that goes beyond pure parameterization.

Therefore, let the access point to a component be a COMPONENT WRAPPER, a first-class object of the programming language. Within this object the component access can be customized without interfering with the client or the component implementation.

The COMPONENT WRAPPER is a white-box for the component's client and enables us to bring in changes and customizations, for example, with DECORATORS (Gamma et al., 1994) and ADAPTERS (Gamma et al., 1994). Note that the legacy system can run in the same process as the COMPONENT WRAPPER, or it can run in a different process. When reengineering to the Web, a typical COMPONENT WRAPPER is also a REMOTE OBJECT running in the Web application framework. It exports (some of its) operations as URLs to the Web.

The COMPONENT WRAPPER methods can be simple forwarder operations. When a procedural API is supported by the legacy system, they are usually implemented as WRAPPER FACADES. Or, alternatively, the COMPONENT WRAPPER might build up a connection to the legacy system either with inter-process communication (e.g., for batch processing applications) or with a communication protocol (e.g., for server applications).

As an indirection mechanism, wrappers can also be used as a place for applying adaptations and decorations (Gamma et al., 1994):

Pattern 14 - ADAPTER

A client requires a different interface than that provided by a class, yet the class cannot be changed.

Therefore, use an ADAPTER to convert the interface of a class into another interface that clients expect. It can be realized as a class adapter using multiple inheritances or as an object adapter that forwards messages to the adapted object.

Pattern 15 - DECORATOR

An object should expose some additional behavior, yet the class of the object should not be changed.

Therefore, use a DECORATOR to dynamically attach additional responsibility to an object using a DECORATOR object that forwards invocations to the decorated object, after the decoration has taken place.

In the context of reengineering to the Web, ADAPTERS are especially used for adaptations of interfaces, if the legacy system does not support a required interface that should be exposed to the Web (or other remote clients). There are many tasks for DECORATORS in the context of reengineering to the Web, including logging, access control, encryption, and so forth. Besides DECORATORS of the COMPONENT WRAPPER, DECORATORS can also be applied for the INVOKER, if the whole invocation process should be decorated.

Both tasks, adaptation and decoration, can also be further supported by the pattern MESSAGE INTERCEPTOR (Zdun, 2002a):

Pattern 16 - *MESSAGE INTERCEPTOR*

Consider that decorations and adaptations take place for certain objects over and over again. Then it would make sense to support these tasks as a first-class mechanism, instead of programming them from scratch for each use.
Therefore, build a callback mechanism into the INVOKER working for all messages that pass it. These callbacks invoke MESSAGE INTERCEPTORS for standardized events, such as "before" a remote method invocation, "after" a remote method invocation, or "instead-of" invoking a remote method.

A MESSAGE INTERCEPTOR intercepts messages sent between different entities, and can add arbitrary behavior to the invocation and/or the response. Support for MESSAGE INTERCEPTORS can be provided on different levels. A MESSAGE INTERCEPTOR can be supported by the programming language used for building the COMPONENT WRAPPER (or a language extension). Also, interceptors can be provided in distributed systems by a middleware, as implemented in TAO or Orbix (see the pattern INTERCEPTOR [Schmidt et al., 2000] that describes this variant). The distributed variant of MESSAGE INTERCEPTORS can be implemented in a Web application framework on top of the INVOKER. This is specifically suitable for tasks that have to be handled per invocation, such as user rights management, marshalling, access control, logging, and so forth.

In Figure 4 an INVOKER that supports MESSAGE INTERCEPTORS is depicted. In this example, a request for a COMPONENT WRAPPER arrives. This COMPONENT WRAPPER has two "before" interceptors. These are dispatched before the actual invocation takes place. When these interceptors have returned, the COMPONENT WRAPPER is invoked and it forwards the invocation to the legacy system. The COMPONENT WRAPPER also has one "after" interceptor. It is dispatched by the INVOKER after the COMPONENT WRAPPER returns and before the result is sent back across the network. Using such a chained MESSAGE INTERCEPTOR architecture, developers can flexibly register add-on services as MESSAGE INTERCEPTORS at run time for specific COMPONENT WRAPPERS, as required.

Figure 4: Invoker Applying Message Interceptors for a Component Wrapper.

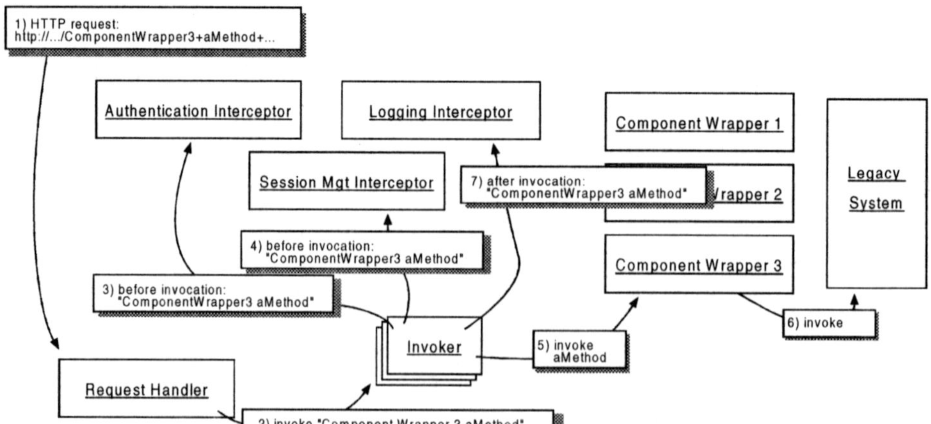

REMOTE OBJECTS can be pooled using POOLING (Kircher & Jain, 2002). In the case of COMPONENT WRAPPERS for legacy systems that means a COMPONENT WRAPPER pool is used to access the legacy system (one pool for each used COMPONENT WRAPPER type). For each invocation a COMPONENT WRAPPER is taken from the pool, handles the invocation, is cleaned up, and is put back into the pool. This way we can avoid the overhead of instantiating the COMPONENT WRAPPER and establishing a connection to the legacy system for each incoming invocation. This, of course, requires the legacy system to support multiple concurrent invocations (or synchronization).

SERVICE AND CHANNEL ABSTRACTION

Often a legacy system provides multiple services. Each COMPONENT WRAPPER type can be seen as one service of the legacy application, and all these services should be offered via the same Web application interface. Also, different requests coming from different clients, communicating over different channels, have to be supported by many Web application frameworks. It should not be required to change the application logic every time a new channel has to be supported or a new service is added to the application.

When reengineering large-scale systems to the Web, it can be expected that the problems of multiple channels and service abstraction are occurring together. These forces are often resolved by a SERVICE ABSTRACTION LAYER architecture (Vogel, 2001):

Pattern 17 - *SERVICE ABSTRACTION LAYER*

Consider a system that serves multiple services to multiple channels. If possible, services should be implemented independently from channel handling, and implementations should be reused.

Therefore, provide a SERVICE ABSTRACTION LAYER as an extra layer to the application logic tier containing the logic to receive and delegate requests. For each supported channel there is a channel adapter. The INVOKER does not directly

Figure 5: Service Abstraction Layer.

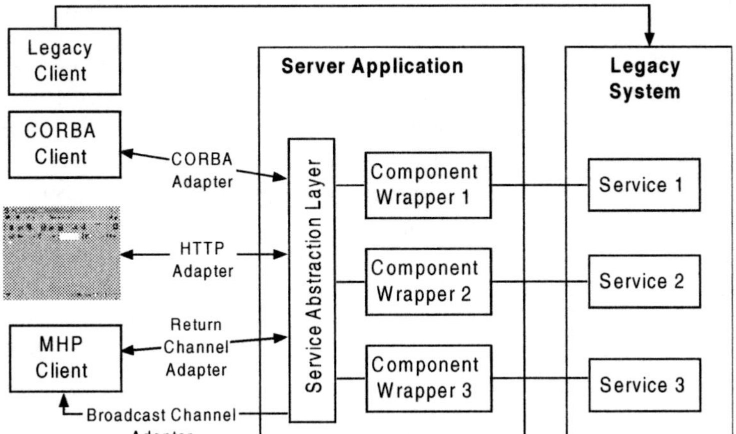

access the COMPONENT WRAPPER, but it sends invocations to the SERVICE ABSTRACTION LAYER first, which then selects the correct COMPONENT WRAPPER.

The SERVICE ABSTRACTION LAYER also converts the invocation data to a format understood by the COMPONENT WRAPPER, and converts the response back to the client format. This is done using CONTENT CONVERTERS (Vogel & Zdun, 2002).

SESSION MANAGEMENT AND STATE PRESERVATION

A client can be expected to make several subsequent requests over a time span, and often some state has to be preserved between these requests. For instance, especially in multi-user systems, users might have to log in and out. Most legacy applications are requiring states to be maintained for continued interaction with a client. The HTTP protocol is stateless and cannot be used for maintaining the state of an interaction.

The SESSIONS pattern (Sorensen, 2002) provides a solution to this problem:

Pattern 18 - *SESSIONS*

A system requires a state for an interaction with a client, but the communication protocol is stateless.
Therefore, state is tied to a session so that a request can access data accumulated earlier during an interaction. Such data are referred to as session-specific data. There is a session identifier to let REMOTE OBJECTS be able to refer to a session.

In Web applications, there are two variants of the SESSIONS pattern: sessions can be kept in the server or in the client. If the session is kept in the server, the session identifier is sent with each response to the client, and the client refers to it in the next invocation; if it is kept in the client, the client has to send it to the server, which refers to it in its responses.

To map a stateless client request properly to the correct session, we have different options in Web applications:

- *URL Encoding:* We can encode information, such as user name and password, in the URL by attaching them as standard URL parameters to the base URL. This works in almost any setting, but we have to be aware that some browsers have limitations regarding the length of the URL. Moreover, the information is readable on the user's screen (if URL contents are not encrypted form). For sensitive applications we can encrypt the contents of the URL.
- *HIDDEN Form Fields:* We can embed information in an HTML form that is hidden from display by using HIDDEN form fields. However, of course, they are readable as plain text in the HTML page's source. Again, we can use encryption for sensitive data.
- *Cookies:* Cookies are a way to store and retrieve information on the client side of a connection by adding a simple, persistent, client-side state settable by the server. However, the client can deactivate cookies in the user agent; thus, cookies do not always work. Cookies can optionally be sent via a secure connection (e.g., SSL).

In any case, when reengineering to the Web, it is necessary to integrate these SESSIONS with the session and user model of the legacy application (if there is any). For instance, one solution is that COMPONENT WRAPPERS log the user in and out for each invocation. Or, alternatively, the COMPONENT WRAPPERS can hold the session open until the next invocation. In case of many client sessions, it may be necessary to introduce LEASES (Jain & Kircher, 2002):

Pattern 19 - LEASES

A (Web) client can abort a stateful interaction without the server realizing it. Then existing SESSIONS are never stopped and opened connections are never closed.

Therefore, provide LEASES for each session (or connection) that expire after a certain amount of time. Let the COMPONENT WRAPPER close a session (or connection) that is held open, when its LEASE expires. When a client sends the next invocation in time, the LEASE is renewed so that the session is held open again for the full lease duration.

DYNAMIC CONTENT GENERATION AND CONVERSION

In Vogel and Zdun (2002), we present a pattern language for content generation, representation, and conversion for the Web. Here, we use a sub-set of this pattern language in the context of reengineering systems to the Web.

Dynamic content generation and conversion are usually central tasks of a project dealing with migration to the Web. In particular, the Web requests received by the INVOKER have to be translated into the API of the legacy system, and the response of the system has to be decorated with HTML markup. What seems to be a relatively simple effort at first glance may lead to severe problems when the resulting system has to be further evolved later on. Often we find systems in which the HTML pages are simply generated by string concatenation, such as the following code excerpt:

```
StringBuffer htmlText = new StringBuffer();
String name = legacyObject.getName();
...
htmlText.append("<BR> <B> Name: </B>");
htmlText.append(name);
```

Hard-coding of HTML markup in the program code may lead to severe problems regarding extensibility and flexibility of content creation. Content, representation style, and application behavior should be changeable ad hoc. In this section, we will discuss two conceptually different approaches for decorating with HTML markup: template-based approaches and constructive approaches.

Template-Based Approaches

A CONTENT FORMAT TEMPLATE (Vogel & Zdun, 2002) provides a typical template-based approach for building up Web content:

Pattern 20 - *CONTENT FORMAT TEMPLATE:*

A system requires content to be built up in a target content format. Content editors should be able to add dynamic content parts and invocations to legacy systems in a simple way. A high performance for building up Web pages is required.

Therefore, provide a template language that is embedded into the target content format (e.g., HTML). The templates contain special template language code, which is substituted by a template engine before the page is delivered to the client.

Known uses of template-based approaches are PHP (Bakken & Schmid, 2001), ASP, JSP, or ColdFusion. These let developers write HTML text with special markup. The special markup is substituted by the server, and a new page is generated. For instance, in PHP the PHP code is embedded by escaping HTML with a special comment:

```
<body>
    <h1> <?php echo("My PHP Heading\n"); ?> </h1>
</body>
```

In the same way, invocations to COMPONENT WRAPPERS can be embedded in template languages to connect to a legacy system.

On the first glance, the approach is simple and even well suited for end-users (such as content editors), say, by using special editors. The HTML design can be separated from the software development process and can be fully integrated with content management systems. However, some Web-based applications require more complex interactions than are simply expressible with templates. Sometimes, the same actions of the user should lead to different results in different situations. Most approaches do not offer high-level programmability in the template or conceptual integration across the template fragments. Application parts and design are not clearly separated. Thus template fragments cannot be cleanly reused. Complex templates may quickly become hard to understand and maintain.

Sometimes integration of different scripts can be handled via a shared dataspace, such as a persistent database connection. Sometimes, we require server-side components for integrating the scripts on the server side. In such cases a constructive approach can be chosen as an alternative.

Constructive Approaches

Constructive approaches generate a Web page on the fly using a distinct API for constructing Web pages. They are not necessarily well suited for end-users, as they require knowledge of a full programming language. However, they allow for implementing a more complex Web application logic than easily achievable with most template-based approaches.

The simplest constructive approach is the CGI interface (Coar, 1999). It is a standardized interface that allows Web servers to call external applications with a set of parameters. The primary advantages of CGI programming are that it is simple, robust, and portable. However, one process has to be spawned per request; therefore, on some operating systems (but, for instance, not on many modern UNIX variants) it may be significantly slower than using threads. Usually, different small programs are combined to one Web application. Thus conceptual integrity of the architecture, rapid changeability, and understandability may be reduced significantly compared to more integrated application development approaches. Since every request is handled by a new process and HTTP is stateless, the application cannot handle session states in the program, but has to use external resources, such as databases or central files/processes.

A variant of CGI is FastCGI (Open Market, Inc., 1996), which allows a single process to handle multiple requests. The targeted advantage is mainly performance. However, the approach is not standardized and implementations may potentially be less robust.

A similar approach integrated with the Java language is servlets. They are basically Java classes running in a Java-based Web server's run time environment. They are a rather low-level approach for constructing Web content. In general, HTML content is created by programming the string-based page construction by hand. The approach offers a potentially high performance. As different servlets can run in one server application (servlet container), servlets provide a more integrated architecture than CGI, for instance.

Most Web servers offer an extension architecture. Modules are running in the server's run time environment. Thus a high performance can be reached and the server's feature (e.g., for scalability) can be fully supported. Examples are Apache Modules (Thau, 1996), Netscape NSAPI, and Microsoft ISAPI. However, the approach is usually a low-level approach of coding Web pages in C, C++, or Java. Moreover, most APIs are quite complex, and applications tend to be monolithic and hard to understand.

Custom Web servers, such as AOL Server (Davidson, 2000), TclHttpd (Welch, 2000), WebShell (Vckovski, 2001), Zope (Latteier, 1999), or ActiWeb (Neumann & Zdun, 2001), provide more high-level environments on top of ordinary Web servers. Often they provide integration with high-level languages, such as scripting languages, for rapid customizability. A set of components is provided that implement the most common tasks in Webapplication development, such as: HTTP support, session management, content generation, database access/persistence services, legacy integration, security/authentication, debugging, and dynamic component loading. Some approaches offer modules for popular Web servers as well, as for instance the Apache Module of WebShell.

In these constructive approaches HTML markup can either be built by hard-coding, perhaps together with FRAGMENTS (see next section), or using a CONTENT CREATOR (Vogel & Zdun, 2002):

Pattern 21 - CONTENT CREATOR

Content in different content formats has to be built up dynamically with a constructive approach. But HTML text should not be hard-coded into the program text.

Therefore, provide an abstract CONTENT CREATOR class that contains the common denominator of the used interfaces. For each supported content format there are concrete classes that implement the common denominator interface for the specific content format. The concrete classes might also contain methods for required specialties.

For instance, WebShell (Vckovski, 2001) uses global procedures to define the elements of its CONTENT CREATOR:

```
proc dl {code} {
     web::put "<dl>"
     uplevel $code
      web::put "</dl>"
}
```

To code these procedures we have to interfere with HTML markup. However, we can avoid it later on when we combine such procedures to HTML FRAGMENTS:

```
dl {
     b {My first page}
     em {in Web Shell}
}
```

Here we have created a <dl> list entry with a bold and an emphasized text in it. Potentially, the procedure dl can be exchanged with another implementation for building a different content format.

In Actiweb (Neumann & Zdun, 2001) CONTENT CREATORS are used to build up pages. Thus we can use the same code to build up pages for different user interface types. A simple example just builds up a Web page:

```
HtmlBuilder htmlDoc
htmlDoc startDocument \
     -title "My ActiWeb App" \
     -bgcolor FFFFFF
htmlDoc addString "My ActiWeb App"
htmlDoc endDocument
```

We instantiate an object htmlDoc, then start a document, add a string, and end the document. The developer does not see any HTML markup at all. The page is automatically created by the CONTENT CREATOR class.

Many approaches combine the template-based and the constructive approach. However, often the two models used are not well integrated; that is, the developer has to manually care for the balance between static and dynamic parts.

Caching

When the Web client sends a request to the Web server, the requested page may be available on the file system of the server or it may be dynamically created. The template-based and constructive approaches introduced so far require dynamic page creation. Compared to static pages, dynamic creation has the problem of memory and performance overheads. A CONTENT CACHE (Vogel & Zdun, 2002) provides a solution:

Pattern 22 - CONTENT CACHE

The overhead of dynamic page creation causes performance or memory problems.

Therefore, increase the performance of Web page delivery by caching already created dynamic content.

In the context of reengineering to the Web, caching has to work in concert with the legacy application. Usually, we cannot change the legacy application to invalidate cached elements that are not valid anymore. We can therefore only cache those operations of the legacy system for which the COMPONENT WRAPPER can determine whether the cache is still valid or not.

Caching whole pages is only a good idea for simplistic pages. For larger Web applications, the dynamic Web pages should be designed in such a way that parts of pages can be cached. The pattern FRAGMENTS (Vogel & Zdun, 2002) solves this problem:

Pattern 23 - FRAGMENTS

Web pages should be designed to allow the generation of Web pages dynamically by assuring the consistency of its content. Moreover, these dynamic Web pages should be provided in a highly efficient way.
Therefore, provide an information architecture that represents Web pages from smaller building blocks, called FRAGMENTS. Connect these FRAGMENTS so that updates and changes can be propagated along a FRAGMENTS chain.

Thus FRAGMENTS can be cached instead of whole pages. Only parts of Web pages that have (or might have) changed since a previous creation of the FRAGMENT are dynamically created. Static FRAGMENTS of Web pages and dynamic FRAGMENTS that are still valid are obtained from the CONTENT CACHE.

Web Content Management

The full pattern language in Vogel and Zdun (2002) contains some additional patterns not described here (GENERIC CONTENT FORMAT, CONTENT CONVERTER, and PUBLISHER AND GATHERER). These are mainly used for content gathering, storing, and publishing. These content management tasks are usually not required for reengineering to the Web, as the content itself is managed by the wrapped legacy applications. Note that, in the content management context, the pattern CONTENT CONVERTER is mostly used to convert to and from a GENERIC CONTENT FORMAT, whereas in the Web reengineering context it can be used for converting to/from the content formats of the legacy system.

Note that there are also applications that contain content from multiple sources, and a wrapped legacy application is only one of these sources. For integrating and managing this content, the pattern language from Vogel and Zdun (2002) can be used in its original Web content management focus.

ADD-ON SERVICES

In a Web application that wraps a legacy system, many add-on services may be required per invocation. Typical examples are authorization, encryption, and logging. When a request arrives or when the response is sent, the add-on service has to be executed. That means that we can potentially apply those add-on services either within:

- the REQUEST HANDLER for request-specific services,
- the INVOKER for invocation-specific services, or
- the COMPONENT WRAPPER for services that are specific per REMOTE OBJECT or REMOTE OBJECT type.

As discussed before, the patterns DECORATOR and ADAPTER provide a simple, object-oriented solution for providing additional services. MESSAGE INTERCEPTORS can be used for providing a first-class solution for add-on services. Usually, higher-level LAYERS can configure MESSAGE INTERCEPTORS for lower levels.

Security issues are relevant for many Web applications that wrap a legacy system. These are often provided as add-on services. For instance, a login with user name and password may be required. Moreover, secure communication or securing transferred data is required. These issues have to be tightly integrated with session management. In general, we require user authentications and encryption as typical means to secure an interactive Web application, for instance:

- *HTTP Basic Authentication:* The definition of HTTP/1.1 (Fielding et al., 1999) contains some means for user authentication of Web pages, called basic authentication scheme. This simple challenge-response authentication mechanism lets the server challenge a client request and clients can provide authentication information. The basic authentication scheme is not considered to be a secure method of user authentication, since the user name and password are passed over the network in an unencrypted form.
- *HTTP Digest Authentication:* Digest Access Authentication, defined in RFC 2617 (Franks et al., 1999), provides another challenge-response scheme that never sends the password in unencrypted form.
- *Encrypted Connection (using SSL):* Using a secure network connection, supported by most servers, we can secure the transaction during a session.
- *URL Encryption:* To avoid readability of encoded URLs we can encrypt the attached part of the URLs.

HTTP authentication is usually handled on the REQUEST HANDLER level. The authentication information is obtained from the COMPONENT WRAPPER that connects to the legacy system. URL encryption is usually handled per invocation within the MARSHALLER.

An important aspect of most Web applications is the required high availability. Usually a Web site should run without any interruptions. This has several implications that have to be considered when choosing frameworks, concepts, implementations, and so forth. At least the following functionalities are usually provided as add-on services:

- *Permanent and Selective Logging:* All relevant actions have to be logged so that problems can be traced. Some selection criteria should be supported; otherwise it may be hard to find the required information out of the possibly large number of log entries. Sometimes, for legal reasons, even more information has to be logged, such as user transaction traces for e-commerce stores. Thus logging needs to be highly configurable. For instance, WebShell (Vckovski, 2001) supports log filters that distinguish different log levels and redirect log entries to different destinations, like files, stdout, or SMS.

- *Notification of Events:* In cases when certain events happen, such as certain error states, a person or application should be notified. For instance, when an error message is recurring, an email or SMS may be sent to the system's administrator.
- *Testing:* Load generators and extensive regression test suites are required for testing under realistic conditions.
- *Incremental Deployment:* Dynamically loadable components enable incremental deployment so that the application does not need to be stopped to deploy new functionality.

If multiple add-on services are required, as well as dynamic configuration of these, typically a chained MESSAGE INTERCEPTOR architecture is provided. This architecture can also be used for standard services, such as URL decoding, marshalling, and so forth.

PATTERN LANGUAGE OVERVIEW AND DISCUSSION

The pattern language presented in this chapter mainly can be used to explain different successful technical solutions in the realm of reengineering to the Web. There are the following main goals:

- *Design Guideline:* The patterns provide a design guideline for reengineering to the Web that can even be used in early project phases, when there is no decision for concrete technologies yet.
- *Project Estimation and Technology/Framework Selection:* The pattern language can help to estimate the effort for a reengineering to the Web project in general, and make import project-specific decisions, such as selecting a Web application framework. The project team has to compare the features of particular frameworks with the project requirements. These, in turn, can be obtained by selecting the required pattern variants. Even though this method cannot ensure the avoidance of all possible technical problems, it provides a good means to get a concrete estimation or basis for framework selection in early project phases. The aspects discussed in this chapter can also be used as a checklist for a project estimation.
- *Means for Communication:* Patterns provide a means for communication; for instance, between technical and non-technical stakeholders of a system that allows for accurate discussion, but without delving too deep into the technical details (as, for instance, when a discussion is based on the concrete technical design or implementation).

In Figure 6 an integrated overview of the pattern language is presented. The arrows indicate important dependencies of the patterns in the context of reengineering to the Web. Only the pattern LAYERS is not depicted here because it structures the other patterns (and thus has relationships to all other patterns).

As can be seen, the LAYERS and functionalities discussed in the previous sections can cleanly be separated from each other. That means individual parts of a solution can be developed in separate teams, except for common (i.e., reused) code and integration points.

Figure 6: Overview — Pattern Language for Reengineering to the Web.

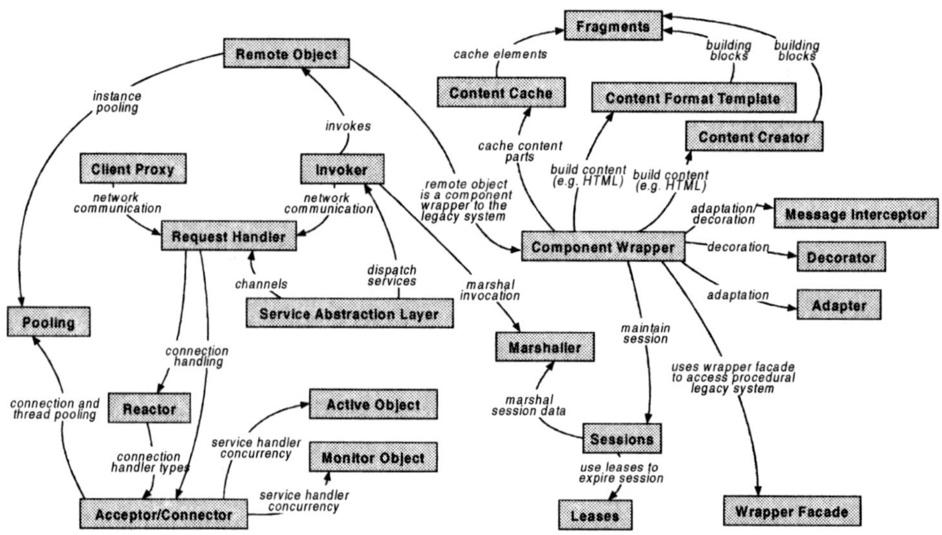

The main integration points are the two connections client/server and server/legacy system. We have to deal with asynchronous invocations, concurrency, state preservation, and performance issues at these integration points. When reengineering to the Web, we usually cannot change the legacy system or the CLIENT PROXY (as it is part of the Web browser). Thus we have to deal with these issues somewhere in the server's processing chain of REQUEST HANDLER, INVOKER, and COMPONENT WRAPPER. Therefore these three patterns can be seen as the central patterns of the pattern language.

When more than one service is provided to more than one channel, we can use a SERVICE ABSTRACTION LAYER. This situation is quite typical when reengineering to the Web, as possibly old interfaces still have to be supported and/or other channels than the Web should be supported (in the future). Thus, as far as possible, decoration and adaptation of the server's processing chain should happen at the end of the chain, so that they are reusable for different channels. Only those parts that are specific for the Web (i.e., for the HTTP protocol) should be handled at the REQUEST HANDLER. Thus it often useful to implement a generic MESSAGE INTERCEPTOR chain, in which add-on services (like SESSIONS, user control, LEASES, application-level marshalling, security, testing, etc.) can be defined for each COMPONENT WRAPPER object.

From a managerial point of view many important issues are only indirectly addressed by the software design and architecture patterns discussed in this chapter. Examples are multi-user concerns, detailed technology selection, security and security audits, or data access related to converting a legacy system. Some of these issues are directly related to the pattern language, such as multi-user concerns, which have to be considered when deciding on a SESSIONS model. As discussed above, technology choices only include those technology areas in focus of the patterns, and many important business aspects of a technology (such as costs, maintenance models, or credibility of business partners) are not in focus of the patterns. Other concerns go beyond the scope of this chapter and should be handled using the respective patterns in these areas. A good start for security pattern is Schumacher (2003). A good source for the broad area of data access to legacy systems and (relational) database management systems is Keller (2003).

USING THE PATTERN LANGUAGE IN PRACTICE: A CASE STUDY

As pointed out in the previous section, a main use of the pattern language (from a managerial point of view) is to provide a basis for communication both in early project phases and with non-technical stakeholders. It can also be used to discuss about technology decisions in case the patterns are already implemented by some technologies/frameworks potentially used within a project.

We have used the patterns as a basis for communication between technical and non-technical stakeholders in various projects (see for instance, Goedicke & Zdun, 2002; Zdun, 2002b for more details). In this section, we want to consider a few typical design decisions based on the patterns to illustrate these benefits of patterns for the communication compared to technical solutions. For space reasons, we cannot consider a whole project's design decisions here, but will only outline a few central ones. For each design decision we will describe the requirements within the project, explain the alternatives based on the pattern language and considered technologies/frameworks, and finally, explain the solution.

Consider a project in which a large legacy system stores, delivers, and manages documents on different kinds of storage devices. The system should get an additional Web interface; however, the old interfaces are still required. The code base is written entirely in C and has already distinct APIs for access by custom GUI clients. There are a few crucial requirements for the Web interface, including load balancing, performance, and simple adaptation to the customer's IT infrastructure (i.e., simple adaptations of branding and layout of forms). For all other features the Web system should be as simple as possible and only add minimal additional costs to the overall system. A management requirement is that a Java-based solution should be used, if possible.

The technology pre-selection for a Java-based solution limits the possible implementation alternatives. We could use a non-Java Web server and let a Web server module access the Java-based solution (e.g., via JNI). But this solution would require us to implement many parts of the pattern language by hand that are already somehow available in Java. A more Java-like solution is the use of a J2EE application server. Internally we can use different Java frameworks, including servlets, EJBs, JSP, and others.

As the potential customers for the system are quite diverse, the Web application system has high demands for load balancing and failover for some customers, but not for others. Here a simple solution with the whole Web application running in only one application server is not enough for all customer sites, but it may be enough for some customers. That means a solution should be scalable for customers with high hit rates, yet impose no extra costs for customers with low hit rates.

Figure 7: Scalable Architecture for the Web Application. (Mandatory elements have plain lines, and optional elements are presented with dotted lines. The optional elements are only present in up-scaled installations.)

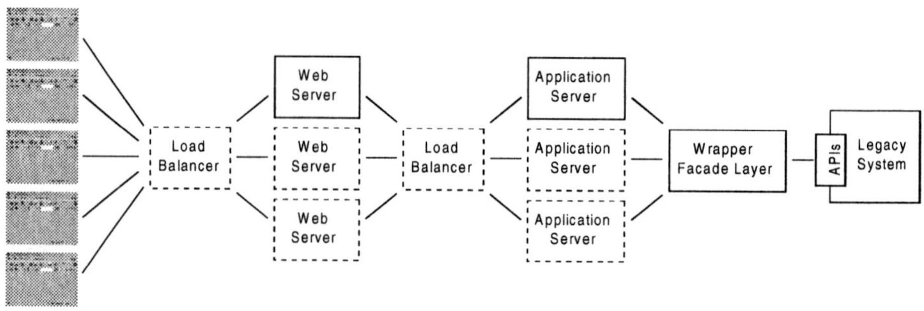

These requirements suggest a scalable LAYERS architecture with REACTORS for each LAYER. INVOKERS are used for interconnecting the LAYERS. There is one primary ACCEPTOR/CONNECTOR that accepts Web requests running in a front-end Web server. This front-end Web server also delivers static Web pages and static page FRAGMENTS, and it invokes dynamic page creation in a separate application server. The application server contains its own REACTOR waiting for requests for dynamic content. Within the application server the INVOKER is situated. It is actually responsible for invoking the REMOTE OBJECTS that connect to the legacy system. There are also other REMOTE OBJECTS that perform other tasks than legacy integration. Note that there is also a simple variant of the pattern INVOKER in the front-end Web server that is responsible for redirecting the invocations.

Each server has its own REACTOR, and INVOKERS are used to access the next LAYER. That means that the system uses an event-based form of communication between these LAYERS. As a positive consequence, there are no cyclic dependencies (back from lower LAYERS into higher LAYERS), which would make it hard to debug and maintain the Web application.

Another consequence of this architecture is that the Web application is highly down- and up-scalable. The extreme of down-scaling is that the whole Web application runs within a single server that serves as front-end Web server and application server. The extreme of up-scaling is that the primary ACCEPTOR/CONNECTOR is situated in a simple server that is just there for load balancing, then there is LAYER of multiple, redundant Web servers delivering static Web pages, then there is another load balancer, and finally there are multiple, redundant application servers. Figure 7 shows this scalable server architecture.

The REMOTE OBJECTS in the application server provide access to the legacy system. Here, we actually have two choices: In some cases it would be possible to let the Web system access the database directly (i.e., when data are only read from the database). In other cases we need WRAPPER FACADES to access the routines of the C-based legacy system to ensure consistency of data, especially when data are changed (i.e., the C-based interface accesses the internal database exclusively).

Because a distinct C-based interface already exists for separate clients within the legacy system, writing WRAPPER FACADES is quite straightforward. A WRAPPER FACADE LAYER should only be bypassed if really necessary; here, the C-based wrappers are quite lightweight and bypassing them for performance reasons is not necessary.

Note that in this architecture the legacy system is the bottleneck that cannot as easily be replicated as Web servers and application servers. It is necessary to synchronize access from concurrent application servers to the legacy system. This can be done using MONITOR OBJECTS that queue the access to the WRAPPER FACADES (here MONITOR OBJECT is chosen instead of ACTIVE OBJECT because it is already supported by Java's synchronized primitive). If this is too much a performance penalty, direct access to the database and replication of the database might be an option.

There are two kinds of REMOTE OBJECTS: COMPONENT WRAPPERS to the legacy system and helper objects that contain application logic solely used for the Web application. The REMOTE OBJECTS are realized as Enterprise Java Beans (EJB). Here, we have two main choices: We can use so-called entity beans that represent a long-living application logic object with container-managed persistence. Alternatively, we can use session beans. A session bean represents a single client inside the application server with a SESSIONS abstraction. Session beans can either be stateful or stateless.

The main task of the COMPONENT WRAPPERS in this architecture is to compose invocations to the operations of the WRAPPER FACADES as needed by the Web application. A central problem here is that legacy functionalities are required to be called in some order, within the same transaction, or with other invocation constraints. The same problem also arises for entity beans of the Web application (that do not access the legacy system).

As a solution to these problems, all REMOTE OBJECTS should be stateless and just used for composition of invocations to the stateful entities (COMPONENT WRAPPERS and entity beans). From the Web, we do not access the stateful entities directly, but use the dedicated REMOTE OBJECTS.

This solution is also chosen because entity beans provide many features (such as synchronization, pooling, and lifecycle management) that impose a performance penalty. If synchronization is already done in the WRAPPER FACADE LAYER for access to a legacy system and/or if only concurrent read access to data is required, these features are not necessarily required, and thus entity beans do not provide an optimal performance.

A more high-level and more complex alternative to the architecture described above is the Java Connector Architecture (JCA). JCA is especially applicable for connecting to heterogeneous information systems such ERP, mainframe transaction processing, database systems, and legacy applications not written in the Java programming language. A COMPONENT WRAPPER (called resource adapter in JCA) defines a standard set of contracts between an application server and the information system: a connection management contract to let an application server pool connections to an underlying legacy system, a transaction management contract between the transaction manager and the legacy system, and a security contract to provide secure access to the legacy system. As most of these features are not required or only in a simple fashion, JCA is not chosen here. This design decision also avoids the performance overheads of connection, transaction, and security management.

Invocations from front-end Web server to application server are typically realized by embed-ding URLs pointing to the pages or FRAGMENTS that are dynamically created in the application server. Somehow the application server has to embed these links as well as session identifiers and other context information in the Web pages. This is typically done by multiple levels of MARSHALLERS. First, there is the HTTP MARSHALLER of the Web server. It marshalls and de-marshalls all elements in the HTTP header fields. URL marshalling and de-marshalling is used to access the correct REMOTE OBJECT. Other context information can either be transported in the header fields, by means of cookies, or within the URL.

The overall system architecture already implements a simple form of CONTENT CACHE and FRAGMENTS because static FRAGMENTS are "cached" in dedicated servers. If additional performance is required, dynamic parts might be additionally cached by storing the FRAGMENTS in a database. There is also a CONTENT CACHE for the documents retrieved from storage devices within the legacy system. Thus a CONTENT CACHE in addition to these caching measures rather seems to be an overhead.

There are some customization requirements for the system, but the system functionality is similar in most installations of the Web application. To ensure rapid deployment at the customer, a programmatic description of the Web interface, as in CONTENT CREATOR pattern, is not the best solution. Thus the CONTENT FORMAT TEMPLATE language Java Server Pages (JSP) is used. Java servlets are used where programmatic, dynamic pages are required. JSP provides for simple changeability at the customer, because only the templates need to be adapted to the customer's requirements. The downside is that the rapid changeability is limited to those changes envisioned during design of the CONTENT FORMAT TEMPLATES.

Note that the architecture already implements a SERVICE ABSTRACTION LAYER, even if not used as such. That means that future channels can be integrated easily. For instance, one possible addition would be to offer a Web service interface in the future.

Programmatic adaptations of COMPONENT WRAPPERS can be expected to be occurring in rare cases because the legacy system already has a mature interface API that is in long use. Thus changes can be simply introduced with ADAPTERS and DECORATORS. It is sensible to avoid the implementation effort and performance penalty of a custom MESSAGE INTERCEPTOR architecture.

There are already different ways of POOLING supported in this architecture, including connection pooling by the Web server or component pooling by the EJB server. Thus it does not seem necessary to add additional pools.

CONCLUSIONS

In this chapter, we have presented a pattern language for reengineering to the Web. It is built from patterns already published in other contexts. The main contribution of the pattern language is that it provides clear alternatives and sequences for applying a project for reengineering to the Web. The patterns allow for important technical considerations in a mostly framework-neutral way (like estimations and technology/framework selection), as well as a means for communication. Also they provide design guidelines for system parts that have to be developed from scratch, such as the wrappers and connections to the legacy system. Patterns, however, do not provide an out-of-the-box solution, but a design effort is required for each project. As different systems in focus of reengineering to the Web projects can have quite different characteristics, this variability of the pattern approach is a strength for finding a suitable solution in such a project.

Note that some parts of the pattern language are concerned with forward engineering of Web applications. That means they can also be applied without a connected legacy system; yet, in this chapter we have focused on the more complex reengineering of the Web case.

REFERENCES

Alexander, C. (1979). *The timeless way of building*. Oxford University Press.

Bakken, S.S., & Schmid, E. (1997-2001). *PHP manual*. Available: *http://www.php.net/manual/en/*

Brant, J., Johnson, R.E., Roberts, D., & Foote, B. (1998). Evolution, architecture, and metamorphosis. *Proc. of 12th European Conference on Object-Oriented Programming (ECOOP'98)*, Brussels, Belgium.

Buschmann, F., Meunier, R., Rohnert, H., Sommerlad, P., & Stal, M. (1996). *Pattern-oriented software architecture - A system of patterns*. J. Wiley & Sons Ltd.

Coar, K.A.L. (1999). *The WWW common gateway interface* – version 1.1. Available: *http://cgi-spec.golux.com/draft-coar-cgi-v11-03-clean.html*

Davidson, J. (2000). *Tcl in AOL digital city the architecture of a multi-threaded high-performance Web site*. In Keynote at Tcl2k: The 7th USENIX Tcl/Tk Conference, Austin, Texas.

Fielding, R., Gettys, J., Mogul, J., Frysyk, H., Masinter, L., Leach, P., & Berners-Lee, T. (1999). *Hypertext transfer protocol* – HTTP/1.1. RFC 2616.

Franks, J., Hallam-Baker, P., Hostetler, J., Lawrence, S., Leach, P., Luoto-nen, A., & Stewart, L. (1999). *HTTP authentication: Basic and digest access authentication*. RFC2617.

Gamma, E., Helm, R., Johnson, R., & Vlissides, J. (1994). *Design patterns: Elements of reusable object-oriented software*. Reading, MA: Addison-Wesley.

Goedicke, M., & Zdun, U. (2002). Piecemeal legacy migrating with an architectural pattern language: A case study. *Journal of Software Maintenance and Evolution: Research and Practice, 14*(1), 1–30.

Jain, P., & Kircher, M. (2002). Leasing pattern. *Proceedings of the Conference on Pattern Languages of Programs* (PLoP), Illinois, USA.

Keller, W. (2003). *Patterns for object/relational access layers*. Available: *http://www.objectarchitects.de/ObjectArchitects/orpatterns/*

Kircher, M., & Jain, P. (2002). *Proceedings of the 7th European Conference on Pattern Languages of Programs (EuroPLoP)*, Irsee, Germany.

Latteier, A. (1999). The insider's guide to Zope: An open source, object-based Web application platform. *Web Review, 3*(5).

Neumann, G., & Zdun, U. (2001). Distributed Web application development with active Web objects. *Proceedings of The 2nd International Conference on Internet Computing (IC'2001)*, Las Vegas, Nevada, USA.

Open Market, Inc. (1996). *FastCGI: A high-performance Web server interface*. Available: *http://www.fastcgi.com/devkit/doc/fastcgi-whitepaper/fastcgi.htm*

Schmidt, D.C., Stal, M., Rohnert, H., & Buschmann, F. (2000). *Patterns for concurrent and distributed objects. Pattern-oriented software architecture.* John Wiley & Sons Ltd.

Schuhmacher, M. (2003). Security patterns. Available: *http://www.securitypatterns.org*

Sneed, H.M. (2000). Encapsulation of legacy software: A technique for reusing legacy software components. *Annals of Software Engineering, 9.*

Sorensen, K.E. (2002). Sessions. *Proceedings of the 7th European Conference on Pattern Languages of Programs (EuroPLoP),* Irsee, Germany.

Thau, R. (1996). Design considerations for the Apache server API. *Proceedings of Fifth International World Wide Web Conference*, Paris, France.

Vckovski, A. (2001). Tcl Web. *Proceedings of 2nd European Tcl User Meeting*, Hamburg, Germany.

Voelter, M., Kircher, M., & Zdun, U. (2002). Object-oriented remoting: A pattern language. *Proceedings of The First Nordic Conference on Pattern Languages of Programs (VikingPLoP),* Denmark.

Vogel, O. (2001). Service abstraction layer. *Proceedings of the 6th European Conference on Pattern Languages of Programs (EuroPLoP)*, Irsee, Germany.

Vogel, O., & Zdun, U. (2002). Content conversion and generation on the Web: A pattern language. *Proceedings of the 7th European Conference on Pattern Languages of Programs (EuroPLoP),* 2002, Irsee, Germany.

Welch, B. (2000). The TclHttpd Web server. *Proceedings of Tcl2k: The 7th USENIX Tcl/Tk Conference*, Austin, Texas, USA.

Zdun, U. (2002a). *Language support for dynamic and evolving software architectures.* PhD thesis, University of Essen, Germany.

Zdun, U. (2002b). Xml-based dynamic content generation and conversion for the multimedia home platform. *Proceedings of the Sixth International Conference on Integrated Design and Process Technology (IDPT*), Pasadena, USA.

Chapter VIII

Architectural Slicing to Support System Evolution

Jianjun Zhao, Fukuoka Institute of Technology, Japan

Limin Xiang, Kyushu Sangyo University, Japan

ABSTRACT

Change impact analysis is a useful technique in software maintenance and evolution. Many techniques have been proposed to support change impact analysis at the code level of software systems, but little effort has been made for change impact analysis at the architectural level. In this chapter, we present an approach to supporting change impact analysis at the architectural level of software systems based on the architectural slicing and chopping technique. The main feature of our approach is to assess the effect of changes in a software architecture by analyzing its formal architectural specification, and therefore, the process of change impact analysis can be automated completely.

INTRODUCTION

Software change is an essential operation for software evolution. The change is a process that introduces new requirements into an existing system, modifies the system if the requirements were not correctly implemented, or moves the system into a new operational environment. The mini-cycle of change during software evolution (Yau et al., 1978) is composed of several phases: *request for change; planning phase,* consisting of program comprehension and change impact analysis; *change implementation,* including restructuring for change and change propagation; *verification and validation;* and *re-documentation.*

Change impact analysis (Bohner & Arnold, 1996; Lindvall & Sandahl, 1998), one of the system analysis methods, is the task through which the programmers can assess the extent of the change, that is, the software component that will impact the change, or be impacted by the change. Change impact analysis provides techniques to address the problem by identifying the likely ripple effect of software changes and using this information to re-engineer the software system design.

Change impact analysis may have different dimensions (regarding the levels of abstraction of a system) according to which the separation of concerns (Parnas, 1972) can be made. For example, change impact analysis can be performed at the code level to obtain the detailed information regarding the effect of changes at the code level of the system. And also, change impact analysis can be performed at the architectural level of a system to reduce the complexity of code-level change impact analysis and to allow a programmer of software maintenance to assess the effect of changes of the system structure at the architectural level so that software evolution actions can be made earlier (Rombach, 1990). The separation of change impact analysis into different levels is therefore a necessary step to reduce the cost of change impact analysis during software evolution.

In order to develop change impact analysis techniques at the architectural level of software systems to support architectural evolution during software design, formal modeling of software architectures is required. The software architecture of a system defines its high-level structure, exposing its gross organization as a collection of interacting components. A well-defined architecture allows an engineer to reason about system properties at a high level of abstraction (Shaw & Garlan, 1996). Architecture description languages (ADLs) are formal languages that can be used to represent the architecture of a software system. They focus on the high-level structure of the overall application rather than the implementation details of any specific source module. In order to support formal representation and reasoning of software architecture, a number of ADLs such as W_{RIGHT} (Allen, 1997), Rapide (Luckham et al., 1995), and UniCon (Shaw et al., 1995) have been proposed. By using an ADL, a systems architect can formally represent various general attributes of a software system's architecture. This provides a promising solution to developing techniques to support change impact analysis at the architectural level because formal language support for software architecture provides a useful platform on which automated support tools for architectural level impact analysis can be developed.

In this chapter, we focus our attention on the issue of the planning phase of the mini-cycle for software change during software evolution, in particular, the *change impact analysis,* to support architectural level evolution of software systems. We introduce an approach to supporting change impact analysis at the architectural level of software systems based on *architectural slicing* techniques (Zhao, 1997, 1998). The main feature of our approach is to assess the effect of changes in a software architecture by analyzing its formal architectural specification, and therefore, the process of change impact analysis can be automated completely.

Traditional program slicing, originally introduced by Weiser (1979), is a decomposition technique that extracts program elements related to a particular computation. A *program slice* consists of those parts of a program that may directly or indirectly affect the values computed at some program point of interest, referred to as a *slicing criterion.* The task of computing program slices is called *program slicing.* As shown in Bohner and Arnold (1996), program slicing is an essential technique to support change impact analysis of software systems at the source code level. In contrast to traditional program slicing, architectural slicing is designed to operate on a formal architectural specification of a software system, rather than the source code of a conventional program. Architectural slicing provides knowledge about the high-level structure of a software system, rather than the low-level implementation details of a conventional program.

Using architectural slicing to support change impact analysis of software architectures promises benefits for architectural evolution. When a maintenance programmer wants to modify a component in a software architecture in order to satisfy new requirements, the programmer must first investigate which components will affect the modified component and which components will be affected by the modified component. By using a slicing tool, the programmer can extract the parts of a software architecture containing those components that might affect, or be affected by, the modified component. A tool that provides such change impact information can assist the programmer greatly.

The rest of the chapter is organized as follows. We briefly introduce how to represent a software architecture using W_{RIGHT}. Next, we introduce some notions about architectural slicing. This is follwed by direction on how to perform change impact analysis of software architectures. Conclusions are given at the end of the chapter.

SOFTWARE ARCHITECTURAL SPECIFICATIONS IN WRIGHT

We choose the W_{RIGHT} architectural description language (Allen, 1997) as our target language to formally specify software architectures. This selection is based on the fact that components, connectors, and configurations in W_{RIGHT} are clearly specified and W_{RIGHT} has already been well studied.

Figure 1: Architecture of the Gas Station System.

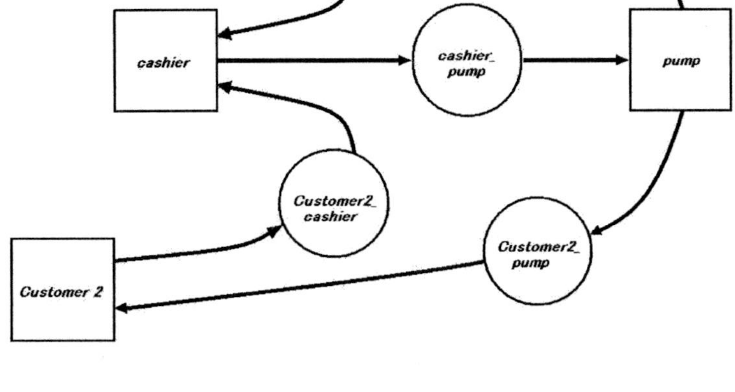

Figure 2: (a) Architectural Specification in W_{RIGHT} and (b) Backward Slice of It.

(a)

Configuration GasStation
Component Customer
Port Pay = $\overline{pay\,!x} \rightarrow$ Pay
Port Gas = $\overline{take} \rightarrow$ pump?x $\rightarrow$ Gas
Computation = $\overline{Pay\,.pay\,!x} \rightarrow \overline{Gas\,.take} \rightarrow$ Gas.pump?x $\rightarrow$ Computation
Component Cashier
Port Customer1 = Pay?x $\rightarrow$ Customer1
Port Customer2 = Pay?x $\rightarrow$ Customer2
Port Topump = $\overline{pump\;\;!x} \rightarrow$ Topump
Computation = Customer1.pay?x $\rightarrow$ $\overline{Topump.pump!x} \rightarrow$ Computation []
Customer2.pay?x $\rightarrow \overline{Topump\,.pump!x} \rightarrow$ Computation
Component Pump
Port Oil1 = take $\rightarrow \overline{pump!x} \rightarrow$ oil1
Port Oil2 = take $\rightarrow \overline{pump!x} \rightarrow$ oil2
Port Fromcashier = pump?x $\rightarrow$ Fromcashier
Computation = Fromcashier.pump?x $\rightarrow$
(Oil1.take $\rightarrow \overline{Oil1.pump\,!x} \rightarrow$ Computation)
[] (Oil2.take $\rightarrow \overline{Oil\,2.pump\,!x} \rightarrow$ Computation)
Connector Customer_Cashier
Role Givemoney = $\overline{pay!x} \rightarrow$ Givemoney
Role Getmoney = pay?x $\rightarrow$ Getmoney
Glue = Givemoney.pay?x $\rightarrow \overline{Getmoney\;\,.pay\,!x} \rightarrow$ Glue
Connector Customer_pump
Role Getoil = $\overline{take} \rightarrow$ pump?x $\rightarrow$ Getoil
Role Giveoil = take $\rightarrow \overline{pump!x} \rightarrow$ Giveoil
Glue = Getoil.take $\rightarrow \overline{Giveoil\;.take} \rightarrow$ Giveoil.pump?x $\rightarrow \overline{Getoil\;.pump\;!x} \rightarrow$ Glue
Connector Cashier_pump
Role Tell = $\overline{pump!x} \rightarrow$ Tell
Role Know = pump?x $\rightarrow$ Know
Glue = Tell.pump?x $\rightarrow \overline{Know\,.pump\,!x} \rightarrow$ Glue
Instances
Customer1: Customer
Customer2: Customer
cashier: Cashier
pump: Pump
Customer1_cashier: Customer_Cashier
Customer2_cashier: Customer_Cashier
Customer1_pump: Customer_Pump
Customer2_pump: Customer_Pump
Attachments
Customer1.Pay as Customer1_cashier.Givemoney
Customer1.Gas as Customer1_pump.Getoil
Customer2.Pay as Customer2_cashier.Givemoney
Customer2.Gas as Customer2_pump.Getoil
cashier.Customer1 as Customer1_cashier.Getmoney
cashier.Customer2 as Customer2_cashier.Getmoney
cashier.Topump as cashier_pump.Tell
pump.Fromcashier as cashier_pump.Know
pump.Oil1 as Customer1_pump.Giveoil
pump.Oil2 as Customer2_pump.Giveoil

(b)

Configuration GasStation
Component Customer
Port Pay = $\overline{pay\,!x} \rightarrow$ Pay
Computation = $\overline{Pay\,.pay\,!x} \rightarrow \overline{Gas\,.take} \rightarrow$ Gas.pump?x $\rightarrow$ Computation
Component Cashier
Port Customer1 = Pay?x $\rightarrow$ Customer1
Port Customer2 = Pay?x $\rightarrow$ Customer2
Port Topump = $\overline{pump\;\;!x} \rightarrow$ Topump
Computation = Customer1.pay?x $\rightarrow$ $\overline{Topump.pump!x} \rightarrow$ Computation []
Customer2.pay?x $\rightarrow \overline{Topump\,.pump!x} \rightarrow$ Computation
Connector Customer_Cashier
Role Givemoney = $\overline{pay!x} \rightarrow$ Givemoney
Role Getmoney = pay?x $\rightarrow$ Getmoney
Glue = Givemoney.pay?x $\rightarrow \overline{Getmoney\;\,.pay\,!x} \rightarrow$ Glue
Instances
Customer1: Customer
Customer2: Customer
cashier: Cashier
Customer1_cashier: Customer_Cashier
Customer2_cashier: Customer_Cashier
Instances
Customer1.Pay as Customer1_cashier.Givemoney
Customer2.Pay as Customer2_cashier.Givemoney
Customer2.Gas as Customer2_pump.Getoil
cashier.Customer1 as Customer1_cashier.Getmoney

In the rest of the section, we use a W_{RIGHT} architectural specification taken from Naumovich et al. (1997) as a sample to briefly introduce how to use W_{RIGHT} to specify a software architecture. The specification shown in Figure 2 models the system architecture of a Gas Station system (Helmbold & Luckham, 1985) shown in Figure 1.

Specifying Architectural Structure

W_{RIGHT} uses a *configuration* to describe the architectural structure as a graph of components and connectors. *Components* are computation units in the system. In W_{RIGHT}, each component has an *interface* defined by a set of *ports*. Each port identifies a point of interaction between the component and its environment. *Connectors* are patterns of interaction between components. In W_{RIGHT}, each connector has an *interface* defined by a set of *roles*. Each role defines a participant of the interaction represented by the connector. A W_{RIGHT} architectural specification of a system is defined by a set of component and connector type definitions, a set of instantiations of specific objects of these types, and a set of *attachments*. Attachments specify which components are linked to which connectors.

For example, in Figure 2 there are three component type definitions, *Customer, Cashier* and *Pump,* and three connector type definitions, *Customer_Cashier, Customer_Pump* and *Cashier_Pump.* The configuration is composed of a set of instances and a set of attachments to specify the architectural structure of the system.

Specifying Architectural Behavior

W_{RIGHT} models architectural behavior according to the significant events that take place in the computation of components, and the interactions between components as described by the connectors. The notation for specifying event-based behavior is adapted from CSP (Hoare, 1985). Each CSP process defines an alphabet of events and the permitted patterns of events that the process may exhibit. These processes synchronize on common events (i.e., interact) when composed in parallel. W_{RIGHT} uses such process descriptions to describe the behavior of ports, roles, computations and glues.

A *computation* specification specifies a component's behavior: the way in which it accepts certain events on certain *ports* and produces new events on those or other ports. Moreover, W_{RIGHT} uses an over-bar to distinguish initiated events from observed events. For example, the *Customer* initiates *Pay* action (i.e., $\overline{pay!x}$) while the *Cashier* observes it (i.e., $pay?x$). A *port* specification specifies the local protocol with which the component interacts with its environment through that port. A *role* specification specifies the protocol that must be satisfied by any port that is attached to that role. Generally, a port need not have the same behavior as the role that it fills, but may choose to use only a subset of the connector capabilities. For example, the *Customer* port *Gas* and the *Customer_Pump* role *Getoil* are identical. A *glue* specification specifies how the roles of a connector interact with each other. For example, a *Cashier_Pump* tell ($Tell.pump?x$) must be transmitted to the *Cashier Pump* know ($\overline{Know.pump!x}$).

Based on the formal W_{RIGHT} architectural specification of a software architecture, we can infer the information flows within a component/connector by analyzing its computation/glue specification, and the information flows between a component and a connector by analyzing both port and role specifications belonging to the component and connector. Such kinds of information can be used to construct the architectural dependence graph of a software architecture for computing an architectural slice.

In the rest of the chapter, we assume that a software architecture be represented by a formal architectural specification that contains three basic types of design entities, namely, *components* whose interfaces are defined by a set of elements called *ports, connectors* whose interfaces are defined by a set of elements called *roles* and the *configuration* whose topology is declared by a set of elements called *instances* and *attachments.* Moreover, each component has a special element called *computation* and each connector has a special element called *glue* as we described above. In the rest of the chapter, we assume that an architectural specification P be denoted by (C_m, C_n, C_g) where C_m is the set of components in P, C_n is the set of connectors in P, and C_g is the configuration of P.

ARCHITECTURAL SLICING

We introduce some notions for architectural slicing and show how an architectural slice can contribute to a change impact analysis problem.

Before we define some notions for architectural slicing, we first introduce the concepts of a reduced component, connector and configuration that are useful for defining architectural slice. Let $P = (C_m, C_n, C_g)$ be an architectural specification and $c_m \in C_m$, $c_n \in C_n$, and C_g be a component, connector, and configuration of P respectively.

- A *reduced component* of c_m is a component c_m' that is derived from c_m by removing zero or more elements from c_m.
- A *reduced connector* of c_n is a connector c_n' that is derived from c_n by removing zero or more elements from c_n.
- A *reduced configuration* of C_g is a configuration C_g' that is derived from C_g by removing zero or more elements from C_g.

The above definition showed that a reduced component, connector, or configuration of a component, connector, or configuration may equal itself in the case that none of its elements has been removed, or an *empty* component, connector, or configuration in the case that all its elements have been removed.

Architectural Slices

In a WRIGHT architectural specification, for example, a component's interface is defined to be a set of ports that identify the form of the component interacting with its environment, and a connector's interface is defined to be a set of roles that identify the form of the connector interacting with its environment. To understand how a component interacts with other components and connectors for making changes, a maintainer must examine each port of the component of interest. Moreover, it has been frequently emphasized that connectors are as important as components for architectural design, and a maintainer may also want to modify a connector during the maintenance. To satisfy these requirements, for example, we can define a slicing criterion for a WRIGHT architectural specification as a set of ports of a component or a set of roles of a connector of interest. Let $P = (C_m, C_n, C_g)$ be an architectural specification.

- A *slicing criterion* for P is a pair (c, E) such that (1) $c \in C_m$ is a component and E is a set of ports of c, or (2) $c \in C_n$ is a connector and E is a set of roles of c.

Note that the selection of a slicing criterion depends on users interests on what they want to examine. If they are interested in examining a component in an architectural specification, they may use slicing criterion 1, and E may be the set of ports or just a subset of ports of the component. If the users are interested in examining a connector, they may use slicing criterion 2, and E may be the set of roles or just a subset of roles of the connector. Let $P = (C_m, C_n, C_g)$ be an architectural specification.

- A *backward architectural slice* S_{bp} of P on a given slicing criterion (c, E) consists of all reduced components, connectors, and configuration in P that might directly or indirectly affect the behavior of c through elements in E.
- A *forward architectural slice* S_{fp} of P on a given slicing criterion (c, E) consists of all reduced components, connectors, and configuration that might be directly or indirectly affected by the behavior of c through elements in E.
- A *unified architectural slice* S_{up} of P on a given slicing criterion (c, E) consists of all reduced components, connectors, and configuration that might affect or be affected by, directly or indirectly, the behavior of c through elements in E.

Intuitively, an architectural slice may be viewed as a subset of the behavior of a software architecture, similar to the original notion of the traditional static slice. However, while a traditional slice intends to isolate the behavior of a specified set of program variables, an architectural slice intends to isolate the behavior of a specified set of a component or connector's elements.

Architectural Slices and Change Impact Analysis

The architectural slices defined previously form the basis for performing change impact analysis at the architectural level of software systems. For architectural-level change impact analysis, we are interested in questions such as:

(1) If a change is made to a component c, what other components might be affected by c?
(2) What components might potentially affect a component c?
(3) If a component c is dynamically replaced, what are the potential effects of the replacement related to c?

In terms of our architectural slice definitions, a backward architectural slice would contribute to answer the first question, a forward architectural slice would contribute to answer the second question, and a unified architectural slice would contribute to answer the third question.

PERFORMING CHANGE IMPACT ANALYSIS

Roughly speaking, the process of change impact analysis for a software architecture is how to find some backward, forward, and unified architectural slices of its formal architectural specification by starting from a component and/or a connector of interest.

In the following we demonstrate the process of performing change impact analysis at the architectural level. The process consists of three phases, which include constructing the architectural dependence graph, finding slices over the graph, and mapping the slices to the actual code of an architectural specification.

A Scenario for Change Impact Analysis

We first examine a scenario of our slicing-based approach in performing architectural-level change impact analysis of a software system.

Consider the Gas Station system whose W_{RIGHT} specification is shown in Figure 2. Suppose a maintenance programmer wants to make a change on the component *cashier,* or more particularly, the port *Topump* of *cashier* in the architectural specification in order to satisfy some new design requirements. The first thing the programmer has to do is to investigate which components and connectors directly or indirectly interact with component *cashier* through its port *Topump.* Without a change impact analysis tool, the programmer has to manually check the actual code of the specification to find such information. However, it is time-consuming and error-prone even for a small size specification because there may exist complex dependence relations between components and connectors in the specification. If the programmer has a change impact analysis tool at hand, the work may probably be simplified and automated without the disadvantages mentioned above. In such a scenario, the impact analysis tool is invoked, which takes as input: (1) a complete architectural specification of the system, and (2) a port of the component *cashier,* that is, *Topump* (this is actually an *architectural slicing criterion*). The tool then computes a backward, forward, or unified architectural slice with respect to the criterion to answer questions such as which components and connectors might affect, or be affected by, directly or indirectly, component *cashier* through port *Topump,* and outputs such information to the programmer for change management. The other parts of the specification that might not affect or be affected by the component *cashier* will be removed, that is, sliced away from the original specification. The programmer can thus examine only the contents included in these slices to assess the effect of changes. In the rest of the section, we explain the process of change impact analysis in more detail.

Constructing Architectural Dependence Graphs

The first phase of our change impact analysis is to build a dependence graph model, called the architectural dependence graph for software architectures, on which architectural slices can be computed efficiently.

The *architectural dependence graph* (ADG) of an architectural specification p is an arc-classified digraph (V_{com}, V_{con}, *Com, Con, Int*), where:

- V_{com} is the set of port vertices of *P*;
- V_{con} is the set of role vertices of *P*;
- *Com* is the set of component-connector dependence arcs;
- *Con* is the set of connector-component dependence arcs;
- *Int* is the set of internal dependence arcs.

In an ADG, vertices represent the ports of components and the roles of the connectors in an architectural specification, and arcs represent possible dependences between ports of components and/or roles of connectors in the specification. There are three types of dependence arcs in the ADG. *Component-connector dependence arcs* represent dependence relationships between a port of a component and a role of a connector in an architectural specification. Informally, if there is an information flow from a port of a component to a role of a connector in the specification, then there is a component-connector dependence arc in the ADG that connects the corresponding port vertex to the corresponding role vertex. *Connector-component dependence arcs* represent dependence relationships between a role of a connector and a port of a component in an architectural specification. Informally, if there is an information flow from a role of a connector to a port of a component in the specification, then there is a connector-component dependence arc in the ADG that connects the corresponding role vertex to the corresponding port vertex. *Internal dependence arcs* represent internal dependence relationships within a component or connector in an architectural specification. Informally, for a component, there is an internal dependence from an input port to an output port, and for a connector, there is an internal dependence from an input role to an output role.

Since the information flow in a W_{RIGHT} specification can be inferred statically, we can construct the ADG of a W_{RIGHT} architectural specification automatically by using a static analysis tool that takes an architectural specification as its input.

Figure 3 shows the ADG of the architectural specification in Figure 2. In the ADG, large squares represent components in the specification, and small squares represent the ports of each component. Each port vertex has a name described by *component_name.port_name*. For example, *pv*5 *(cashier.Customer1)* is a port vertex

Figure 3: ADG for the Architectural Specification in Figure 2.

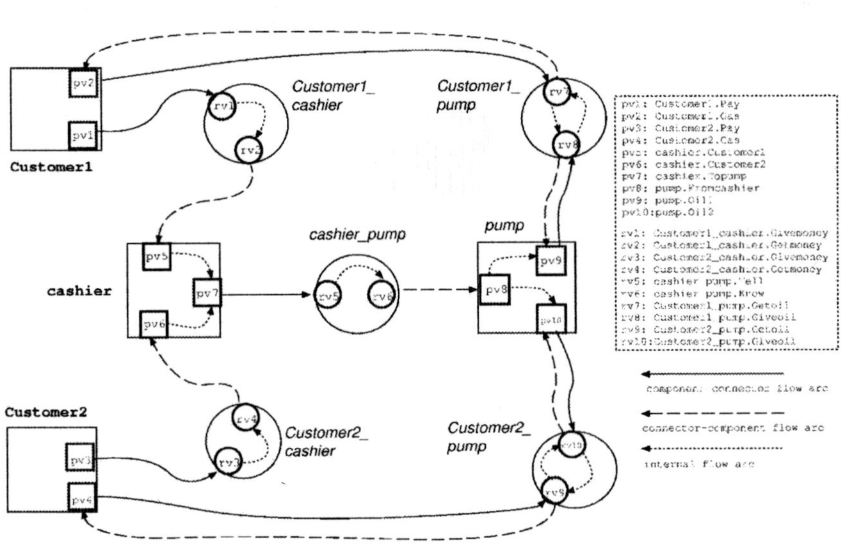

that represents the port *Customer1* of the component *cashier.* Large circles represent connectors in the specification, and small circles represent the roles of each connector. Each role vertex has a name described by *connector_name.role_name*. For example, *rv5(cashier_pump.Tell)* is a role vertex that represents the role *Tell* of the connector *cashier_pump*. The complete specification of each vertex is shown on the right side of the figure.

Computing Architectural Slices

The second and third phases of our change impact analysis are to compute some architectural slices for recording change impact information. However, the slicing notions defined in Section 3 give us only a general view of an architectural slice, and do not tell us how to compute it. In this section we present a two-phase algorithm to find an architectural slice of an architectural specification based on its architectural dependence graph. Our algorithm contains two phases: (1) computing a slice S_g over the architectural dependence graph of an architectural specification, and (2) constructing an architectural slice S_p from S_g.

Finding Slices over the ADG

To compute a slice over the graph G, we refine the slicing notions defined in Section 3. Let $P = (C_m, C_n, C_g)$ be an architectural specification and $G = (V_{com}, V_{con}, Com, Con, Int)$ be the ADG of *P*. We first refine some slicing notions over the ADG.

- A *slicing criterion* for *G* is a pair (c, V_c) such that $c \in C_m$ and V_c is a set of port vertices corresponding to the ports of *c*, or $c \in C_n$ and V_c is a set of role vertices corresponding to the roles of *c*.
- A *backward slice* S_{bg} of *G* on a given slicing criterion (c, V_c) is a subset of vertices of *G* such that for any vertex *v* of *G*, $v \in S_{bg}(c, V_c)$ if there exists a path from *v* to $v' \in V_c$ in the ADG.
- A *forward slice* S_{fg} of *G* on a given slicing criterion (c, V_c) is a subset of vertices of *G* such that for any vertex *v* of *G*, $v \in S_{fg}(c, V_c)$ if there exists a path from $v' \in V_c$ to *v* in the ADG.
- A *unified slice* S_{ug} of *G* on a given slicing criterion (c, V_c) is a subset of vertices of *G* such that for any vertex *v* of *G*, $v \in S_{ug}(c, V_c)$ if there exists a path from *v* to $v' \in V_c$ or $v' \in V_c$ to *v* in the ADG.

According to the above descriptions, the computation of a slice over the ADG can be solved by using a usual depth-first or breadth-first graph traversal algorithm to traverse the graph by taking some port or role vertices of interest as the starting point of interest. Figure 4 shows a backward slice over the ADG with respect to the slicing criterion *(cashier, V_c)* where $V_c = \{pv7\}$. The slice can be computed by finding all vertices on the ADG that can reach to *pv7* through a path. Therefore, we can obtain the slice as $\{pv1, pv3, pv5, pv6, pv7, rv1, rv2, rv3, rv4\}$ from two paths ($pv3 \rightarrow rv3 \rightarrow rv4 \rightarrow pv6 \rightarrow pv7$) and ($pv1 \rightarrow rv1 \rightarrow rv2 \rightarrow pv5 \rightarrow pv7$).

Figure 4: A Backward Slice over the ADG of the Specification in Figure 2.

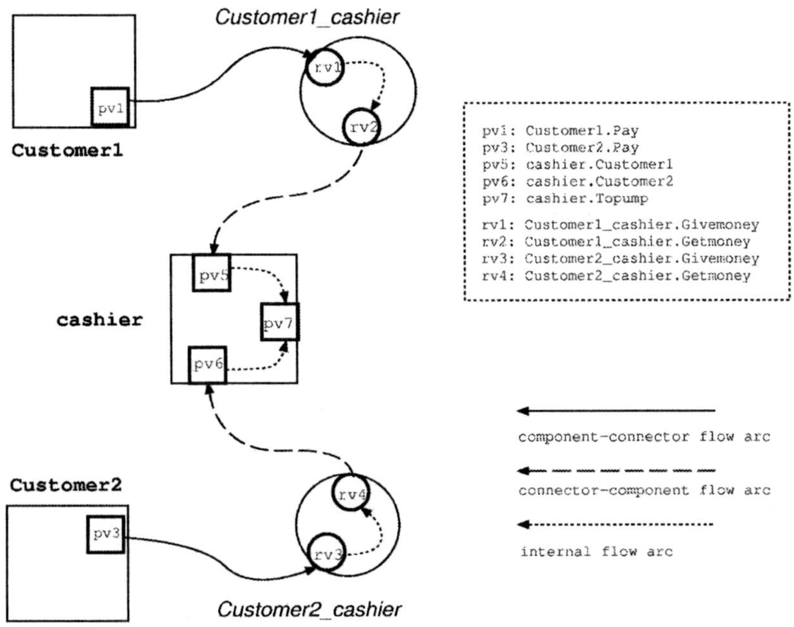

Deriving Architectural Slices

A slice computed above is only a slice over the ADG of an architectural specification, which is a set of vertices of the ADG. Therefore we should map each element in the slice to the actual code of the specification. Let $P = (C_m, C_n, C_g)$ be an architectural specification, $G = (V_{com}, V_{con}, Com, Con, Int)$ be the ADG of P, and $S_g \in \{S_{bg}, S_{fg}, S_{ug}\}$. By using the concepts of a reduced component, connector, and configuration introduced in Section 3, a slice of an architectural specification p can be constructed as follows.

1. Constructing a reduced component $c_m{}'$ from a component c_m by removing all ports such that their corresponding port vertices in G have not been included in S_g and unnecessary elements in the computation from c_m. For example, the following shows component *Customer* and its reduced component (with * mark) in which the port *Gas* has been removed.

Component Customer

Port Pay = $\overline{pay!x} \rightarrow$ Pay

Port Gas = $\overline{take} \rightarrow$ pump?x $\rightarrow$ Gas

Computation = $\overline{Pay.pay!x} \rightarrow \overline{Gas.take}$
$\rightarrow$ Gas.pump?x $\rightarrow$ **Computation**

* **Component** Customer

Port Pay = $\overline{pay!x} \rightarrow$ Pay

Computation = $\overline{Pay.pay!x} \rightarrow \overline{Gas.take}$
$\rightarrow$ Gas.pump?x $\rightarrow$ **Computation**

2. Constructing a reduced connector c_n' from a connector c_n by removing all roles such that their corresponding role vertices in G have not been included in S_g and unnecessary elements in the glue from c_n. For example, the following shows connector *Customer_Cashier* and its reduced connector (with * mark) in which role *Givemoney* has been removed.

Component Customer_Cashier
  Role Givemoney = $\overline{pay!x} \rightarrow$ Givemoney
  Role Getmoney =pay?x $\rightarrow$ Getmoney
  Glue =Givemoney.pay?x $\rightarrow \overline{Getmoney.pay!x}$
    $\rightarrow$ **Glue**

* **Component** Customer_cashier
  Role Getmoney = pay?x $\rightarrow$ Getmoney
  Glue =Givemoney.pay?x $\rightarrow \overline{Getmoney.pay!x}$
    $\rightarrow$ **Glue**

3. Constructing the reduced configuration C_g' from the configuration C_g by the following steps: (1) removing all component and connector instances from C_g that are not included in C_m' and C_n', and (2) removing all attachments from C_g such that there exists no two vertices v_1 and v_2 where $v_1, v_2 \in S_g$ and **v1 as v2** represents an attachment. For example, the following shows the configuration and its reduced configuration (with * mark) in which some instances and attachments have been removed.

Instances
  Customer1: Customer
  Customer2: Customer
  Cashier: Cashier
  pump: Pump
  Customer1_cashier: Customer_Cashier
  Customer2_cashier: Customer_Cashier
  Customer1_pump: Customer_Pump
  Customer2_pump: Customer_Pump
  Cashier_pump: Cashier_Pump
Attachments
  Customer1.Pay as Customer1_cashier.Givemoney
  Customer1.Gas as Customer1_pump.Getoil
  Customer2.Pay as Customer2_cashier.Givemoney
  Customer2.Gas as Customer2_pump.Getoil
  cashier.Customer1 as Customer1_cashier.Getmoney
  cashier.Customer2 as Customer2_cashier.Getmoney
  cashier.Topump as cashier_pump.Tell
  pump.Fromcashier as cashier_pump.Know
  pump.Oil1 as Customer1_pump.Giveoil
  pump.Oil2 as Customer2_pump.Giveoil

* **Instances**
  Customer1: Customer
  Customer2: Customer
  Cashier: Cashier

  Customer1_cashier: Customer_Cashier
  Customer2_cashier: Customer_Cashier

* **Attachments**
  Customer1.Pay as Customer1_cashier.Givemoney

  Customer2.Pay as Customer2_cashier.Givemoney

  cashier.Customer1 as Customer1_cashier.Getmoney
  cashier.Customer2 as Customer2_cashier.Getmoney

Figure 2 shows a backward architectural slice of the W_{RIGHT} specification with respect to the slicing criterion *(cashier, E)* where *E={Topump}* is a port of component *cashier*. The slice is obtained from a slice over the ADG in Figure 4 according to the mapping process described above and consists of some reduced components and connectors as well as the reduced configuration of the original specification.

CONCLUSIONS

In this chapter, we introduced an approach to supporting change impact analysis at the architectural level of software systems based on the *architectural slicing* technique. The main feature of our approach is to assess the effect of changes of a software architecture by analyzing its formal architectural specification, and therefore, the process of change impact analysis can be automated completely.

Our approach showed that separation of change impact analysis of a system from code level to architectural level is an efficient step to reduce the cost of change impact analysis during software evolution, because this allows a maintenance programmer to assess the effect of changes of the system at the architectural level so that many implementation details of the system need not to be considered. This is especially useful for large-scale software systems that consist of numerous components and connectors.

In architectural description languages, in addition to providing both a conceptual framework and a concrete syntax for characterizing software architectures, they also provide tools for parsing, displaying, compiling, analyzing, or simulating architectural specifications written in their associated language. However, existing language environments provide no tools to support architectural-level change impact analysis from an engineering viewpoint. We believe that such a tool should be provided by any ADL environment as an essential means to support software architecture development and evolution.

REFERENCES

Allen, R. (1997). *A formal approach to software architecture.* PhD thesis, Department of Computer Science, Carnegie Mellon University.

Bohner, S.A., & Arnold, R.S. (1996). *Software change impact analysis.* IEEE Computer Society Press.

Helmbold, D., & Luckham, D. (1985). Debugging Ada tasking programs. *IEEE Software*, *2*(2), 47-57.

Hoare, C.A.R. (1985). *Communicating sequential processes.* Prentice Hall.

Lindvall, M., & Sandahl, K. (1998). How well do experienced software developers predict software changes? *Journal of Systems and Software*, *43*(1), 19-27.

Luckham, D.C., Augustin, L.M., Kenney, J.J., Veera, J., Bryan, D., & Mann, W. (1995). Specification analysis of system architecture using Rapide. *IEEE Transaction on Software Engineering*, *21*(4), 336-355.

Naumovich, G., Avrunin, G.S., Clarke, L.A., & Osterweil, L.J. (1997). Applying static analysis to software architectures. *IEEE Proceedings of the Sixth European Software Engineering Conference,* 77-93.

Parnas, D. (1972). On the criteria to be used in decomposing systems into modules. *Communication of the ACM*, *15*(12), 1053-1058.

Rombach, H.D. (1990). Design measurement: Some lessons learned. *IEEE Software*, 17-25.

Shaw, M., & Garlan, D. (1996). *Software architecture: Perspective on an emerging discipline.* Prentice Hall.

Shaw, M., DeLine, R., Klein, D.V., Ross, T.L., Young, D.M., & Zelesnik, G. (1995). Abstractions for software architecture and tools to support them. *IEEE Transaction on Software Engineering*, *21*(4), 314-335.

Weiser, M. (1979). *Program slices: Formal, psychological, and practical investigations of an automatic program abstraction method.* PhD thesis, University of Michigan.

Yau, S.S., Collofello, J.S., & MacGregor, T. (1978). Ripple effect analysis of software maintenance. *Proc. of the COMPSAC'78*, 60-65. IEEE Computer Society Press.

Zhao, J. (1997). Using dependence analysis to support software architecture understanding. In M. Li (Ed.), *New technologies on computer software* (pp. 135-142). Beijing: International Academic Publishers.

Zhao, J. (1998). Applying slicing technique to software architectures. *Proceeding of the 4th IEEE International Conference on Engineering of Complex Computer Systems*, 87-98.

Chapter IX

An Open Architecture for Visual Reverse Engineering

Alexandru C. Telea, Eindhoven University of Technology, The Netherlands

ABSTRACT

Tool support for program understanding becomes increasingly important in the software evolution cycle, and it has become an integral part of managing systems evolution and maintenance. Using interactive visual tools for getting insight into large evolving legacy information systems has gained popularity. Although several such tools exist, few of them have the flexibility and retargetability needed for easy deployment outside the contexts they were initially built for. The lack of flexibility and limitations for customizability is a management as well as a technical problem in software evolution and maintenance. This chapter discusses the requirements of an open architecture for software visualization tools, implementation details of such an architecture, and examples using some specific software system analysis cases. The focus is primarily on reverse engineering, although the proposed tool architecture is equally applicable to forward engineering activities. This material serves the software architects and system managers as well as the tool designers.

INTRODUCTION

Businesses of many organizations heavily depend on effective maintenance of increasingly aging software. As software ages, the task of managing to maintain it becomes more complex and more expensive. Poor design, unstructured programming methods, and crisis-driven maintenance can contribute to poor code quality, which in turn affects understanding of the system properties. Program understanding (Tilley,

1998; Muller et al., 1993; Tilley et al., 1998) is a relatively young and evolving field concerned with identifying artifacts and their relationships and understanding their structure and semantics. The essence of this process is essentially pattern matching at different abstraction levels. These levels induce in turn different representations of the candidate system. Overall, the aim is to aggregate these artifacts in a hierarchical representation in order to achieve a more refined and abstract understanding of the original system. Low-level representations, such as call or module dependency graphs, help the developers to grasp the system properties. More abstract and higher-level representations, such as simplified functional, task, or architectural diagrams may be used by the management to succinctly overview the status and evolution of a given software project.

Program understanding uses several information sources, such as direct source code examination, leveraging corporate knowledge, and computer-assisted methods. In this chapter, we focus on reverse engineering (RE) methods that address the process of understanding existing (large) software systems. However, note that the analysis and results presented in this work are also useful for the forward engineering activity.

Furthermore, we shall focus on computer-assisted RE methods, which have a number of important advantages. Firstly, they represent a deterministic representation of a software system, as compared to subjective interpretations. Secondly, they are used to analyze large systems, whereas direct source code examination fails for systems larger than approximately 50,000 lines of code (Stasko et al., 1998). Thirdly, they require, in virtually all cases, less time to learn and apply. Finally, automated methods are the only ones applicable in the vast majority of the cases, given the size of the systems at hand. Managing the evolution of large software systems thus requires automated support for their understanding, which implies, at some point, the need for flexible RE tools.

Reverse engineering provides a conceptual framework for describing the process of software understanding and conceptual abstraction. This framework is supported by several RE tools. In the recent past, an impressive number of such RE tools has emerged. However, finding the "right" tool for a given application domain remains a challenging problem. This is mainly due to the fact that application systems vary from systems to systems, and thus may spawn different, often divergent requirements.

Given the above, practitioners in the RE field are left with two main choices: either pick one of the available RE tools and adapt it to one's specific data and requirements or create a new RE tool from scratch. In most cases, the solution of choice falls somewhere between the above two scenarios. If tool adaptation or design is required, it is thus of great importance for the RE practitioner to:

- understand the often subtle trade-offs the existing tools make in their implementation,
- be able to predict the limitations before adopting a given tool,
- avail a framework for designing a customized RE tool, in case adapting an existing one is too difficult for a particular application.

Overall, these often require a detailed analysis of the *architecture* of the RE tools. Based on such an analysis, the RE practitioner can compare different tools to a set of requirements, estimate the customizability of a tool of choice, or estimate the effort and way to design a custom RE tool. In absence of this analysis, tool evaluation is a time-consuming trial-and-error procedure that is not often feasible in most situations due to various constraints.

We continue our analysis by first noting that most RE tools provide two main features:

- *construction* of a layered program representation by automatic and user-driven (interactive) operations,
- *visualization* of this representation in various ways, such as navigable graphical views at different levels of detail.

As mentioned, most RE tools differ in the way and extent they address the above two requirements. Some tools focus on program analysis and domain modelling, and thus on the program representation construction, but provide little for the visual examination and editing of the constructed representation. Other tools focus on data visualization but do not perform program analysis and are hard to integrate with tools that support this task. Overall, one may conclude that most existing RE tools are based on internal architectures that seriously limit the options for customization of several RE tasks such

Several attempts have been made to design generic RE tools in the form of software frameworks allowing users to define and customize operations for their specific tasks. Ideally, such frameworks would minimize the time needed by the software engineer to adapt them to specific application requirements. However, the RE framework tools we are aware of are still too rigid to be easily reusable out of the context for which they were initially designed.

We propose here a software architecture for reverse engineering tools that tries to capture most of the concepts presented in the abstract RE framework. We next propose in detail how such an architecture can be implemented. Special attention is paid to the visual aspect of the reverse engineering process. Our first objective is to build a simple prototype of the RE data exploration scenarios by combining and customizing existing software components. We compare various aspects of our proposed architecture with existing RE tools and outline the differences. Finally, we present a number of RE applications in which we used the proposed architecture.

BACKGROUND

Several studies (Tilley, 1998; Telea et al., 2002; Riva et al., 2002) in the past have identified five major tasks that an RE tool should support. These tasks are defined at various abstraction levels of the hierarchy: *program analysis*, *plan recognition*, *concept assignment*, *redocumentation*, and *architecture recovery*. *Program analysis* is the basic task that any RE tool should support and consists of two services: *construction* of a layered program model and *presentation* of this model to the user, that is, via graphical navigable views at different levels (Eick & Wills, 1999; Stasko et al., 1998). *Plan recognition* aims at finding certain *design patterns* in the software (Gamma et al., 1995; Mendelzon & Sametinger, 1997). These design patterns form the so-called *domain model*, that is, the concept group describing a particular application field. A first attempt for plan recognition would be an editor for manual assignment of design patterns to elements obtained from program analysis and the visualization thereof, for example, UML

Figure 1: (a) Reverse Engineering Pipeline, and (b) Toolkit Architecture Overview.

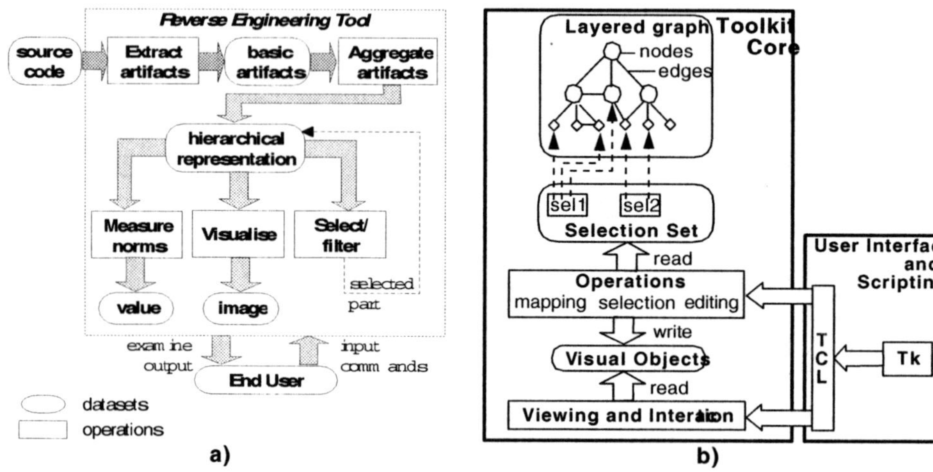

diagrams. *Concept assignment* (Biggerstaff et al., 1994) is the task of discovering concepts and assigning them to their implementation counterparts. RE tools might support concept assignment by annotating the software artifacts with *concepts* retrieved from a domain-specific concept database and visualising this annotation. *Redocumentation* (Tilley et al., 1998) is the task of retroactively providing documentation for existing software systems. Since redocumentation spans three tasks discussed so far, an RE tool could support it by the mechanisms outlined so far. *Architecture recovery* (Wong et al., 1995) focuses on the recovery of architectural aspects of large systems.

The five mentioned RE tasks concur, and not compete, to the overall RE goal, that is, *extracting low-level code information* and *enriching it with information from other sources*. Since we are interested in RE tool support, we shall refine the above RE tasks into the following generic steps that an RE tool should implement (see Figure 1a) (Wong et al., 1995; Young, 1997; Wong, 1999):

1. *Extract* the low-level artifacts from the source code.
2. *Aggregate* the extracted artifacts into a hierarchical model.
3. *Measure* the model's quality using computed norms; if needed, re-execute the aggregation differently.
4. *Select* a sub-hierarchy to examine, if the whole is too large, complex, or unclear to display.
5. *Visualize* the data, for example by producing a graph layout, followed by drawing the selected data (Telea et al., 2002).

In other words, for an RE tool to address the tasks mentioned previously, it has to implement the above five operations. Steps 2 to 5 can occur in any order — one may, for example, first visualize the whole model produced by Step 1, then apply some user- or system-driven aggregation (Step 2), measure the result's quality (Step 3), select a feature to look at (Step 4), and then repeat from Step 2. This matches the program understanding cognitive model (Young, 1997) that consists of alternate top-down and bottom-up passes. Step 5 may provide different visualizations besides graph drawing. However, in most cases we are aware of, RE users desire to focus on the specific relations between (groups of) software components, and so graph visualization is their first choice.

THE NEED FOR INTEGRATION AND GENERICITY

Numerous papers address the conceptual problems of reverse engineering sketched in the previous sections. Ample material has been written over various RE tool implementations. However, it seems in practice that every attempt to reverse engineer a large system reaches some functional limitation of the existing RE tools. Concretely, such tools may fail at providing, or allowing customization of one (or several) of the RE pipeline steps described in the section titled *Background*. For example, many tools emerging from the program analysis and formal method community fail at providing interactive means for visual program inspection. At the other extreme, there exist many tools providing extensive, sometimes exotic visualization metaphors for program data, but little in program analysis (Stasko et al., 1998). One reason for this situation is that building a good RE tool spans two traditionally different fields: software engineering and information visualization. Another reason is that information visualization, the discipline that analyzes how detail program information could be conveyed in abstract relational data via images, is a relatively new field. We believe that a successful RE tool should provide a flexible architecture encompassing all the five pipeline steps discussed previously, as well as a generic way to customize and extend these for particular domain models.

ARCHITECTURE PROPOSAL

We propose here a novel architecture for an RE tool that is consistent with the genericity and flexibility requirements detailed in the previous section. This architecture borrows some ideas from the scientific visualization systems community (Upson et al., 1989; Schroeder et al., 1995). In this sense, the proposed architecture consists of a number of *operations* performed on a number of *datasets*. To this model, we add specific operations and structure of the RE pipeline as outlined in the section titled *Background*. Given the increasing importance of providing effective RE tools and the lack of detailed RE tool architecture presentation in the literature, we believe that this will help practitioners in the field needing to assess, develop, adapt, or extend RE tools.

The proposed architecture comes as a layered system consisting of a compiled core and an interpreted based user interface (UI) and scripting front-end, as shown in Figure 1b. Our implementation used C++ for the core and Tcl/Tk (Harrison & McLennan, 1997) for the UI and scripting. However, as detailed later, other implementations of the same architecture could be easily achieved. The core is responsible for the RE data and operation implementation, whereas the front-end provides customization and interaction mechanisms. Virtually all RE tools we are aware of follow this pattern. We describe the data and operation model implemented by the core in the next section.

Data Model

Our data model consists of two main elements: *a layered graph* and *selections,* as depicted in Figure 1b. The layered graph consists of structure and attributes.

Structure

Although many work on RE tools use different terminologies (Wong, 1999; Card et al., 1999; Stasko et al., 1998), virtually all models represent the basic RE data as a *hierarchical* (layered) *attributed graph*. In the graph's nodes model, software artifacts are created from program analysis, for example, source code parsing. In the graph's layers model, node aggregations (clusterings) are done during plan assignment throughout architecture recovery. In the edges model, both relational and containment information is used. In contrast to research work reported by others, we do not impose any restrictions on the graph topology, but rather it is determined by the user-driven RE aggregation process. In other words, we model all data as a graph whose nodes represent software artifacts (e.g., classes, files, methods, packages, tasks) and edges represent relationships (e.g., containment, calls, dependencies).

Attributes

Both nodes and edges may have key-value pair attributes. These represent both the acquired data, for example, number of lines of code of a module or number of bugs, or data derived during the RE process itself, for example, via software metrics. The keys are used as data identifiers. We implement keys as string literals and values as primitive types (integer, floating-point, pointer, or string). In particular, each node and edge has a set of attributes with distinct keys, managed in a hash-table-like fashion. Attributes automatically change type if written with a value of another type. Several *attribute plans* can thus coexist in the graph. An attribute plan is defined implicitly as all attributes of a given set of nodes/edges for a given key, for example, all values of the "number of bugs" key. Our attribute model differs from the one used by most RE applications (Eick & Wills, 1999; Wong, 1999; Kazman & Carriere, 1996) which choose a fixed set of attributes of fixed types for all nodes/edges. Our choice is more flexible, since: a) certain attributes may not be defined for all nodes; and b) attribute plans are frequently added and removed in a typical RE session. See section "Attribute Editing" for more details. Moreover, both memory and access time for attributes are kept low in this way, which is essential for coping with the graphs of tens of thousands of elements. In this sense, our model resembles the one used by the GVF (Marshall et al., 2001) and Visage (Kolojechich & Roth, 1997) tools.

Selections

Selections, defined as sets of nodes and edges, allow executing toolkit operations on a *specific subset* of the whole graph. To make the toolkit flexible, we decouple the subset specification (*which* are the nodes and edges to work on) from the operations' definitions (*what* to do with the selected data), similarly to the dataset-algorithm decoupling in scientific visualization. Selections are named, and play the role of variables in a usual program. Our graphs are *structurally* equivalent to the node-and-cell dataset model in scientific visualization (SciViz) frameworks, whereas our selections do not have a direct structural equivalent. Selections are *functionally* equivalent to SciViz datasets, since they are the operations' inputs and outputs. This is one of the main differences between SciViz and software visualization tools, which leads to different architectures for the two. In other words, our architecture is more data-centric than classical SciViz frameworks, as data elements are explicitly addressable via selections. However, our architecture is also operation-centric. More is available from Kolojechich and Roth (1997) for a comparison of the data and operation-centric models, since operations can be explicitly specified, as described in the following texts.

Selections have functional equivalents in some software visualization tools. In GVF (Marshall et al., 2001), they are represented by group nodes. In Rigi (Wong, 1999), they are implicitly represented by the slicing or filtering of operation output. See the section "Selection Operations" for more details. However, neither GVF nor Rigi has an explicit structure similar to selections. Visage's collections (Kolojechich & Roth, 1997) come closest to our selection concept, both structurally and functionally.

OPERATION MODEL

Operations have three types of inputs and outputs: *selections* that specify on which nodes and edges to operate; *attribute keys* that specify on which attribute plan(s) of the selection to work; and operation-specific *parameters*, such as thresholds or factors. We distinguish four operation types, based on their read/write data access:

- Selection operations create selection objects.
- Structure editing modifies the graph topology.
- Attribute editing modifies the graph attributes.
- Mapping maps the graph data to visual objects.

The above data-operation interface allows the core to automatically update all components that depend on the modified data after an operation's execution, using a simple Observer design pattern (Gamma et al., 1995). For example, the selections are automatically updated after a structure editing operation that deletes selected nodes or edges. Similarly, the data viewers (see the section "Visualization") are updated when the monitored selections change. This operation model based on observers monitoring a fixed number of operation types is a simplification of the more general idea of dataflow pipelines widely used by SciViz tools (Upson et al., 1989; Schroeder et al., 1995). The dataflow pipeline advantage is that it allows automatic update of more complex data dependencies. However, the practical experience suggests that constructing and maintaining an explicit dataflow pipeline is not a simple task for average non-programmer users. The simple structure of the RE pipeline as depicted in Figure 1a suggests our operation model serves the purpose.

Selection Operations

Selection operations add nodes and edges to selection objects. Several such operations can be implemented as follows. *Level selections* (called "horizontal slices" in the RE literature (Wong, 1999)) gather all nodes and association edges on a certain aggregation level in the layered graph, and are useful for visualizing the software at a given level of detail. *Tree selections* (called "vertical slices" in Wong, 1999) gather all nodes and containment edges reachable from nodes in an input selection, and are useful in for example, visualizing sub-system structures or change propagation (Marshall et al., 2001). *Conditional selections* (called "filters" in most RE papers) gather all elements in an input selection that obey some attribute-based condition, and are useful in queries such as "show all nodes where the cost attribute is higher than some threshold". Finally, *boolean selections* allow combining existing selections via intersection, union, and so forth, and are useful as part of more complex activities. As compared to many software visualization tools (e.g., Wong, 1999; Marshall et al., 2001), performing a horizontal or vertical slice or a filtering, in our case, does not alter the graph data — it just creates some new selection objects.

Structure Editing

Structure editing operations construct and modify the graph. Such operations include the standard node and edge addition and removal, as well as reading several graph formats such as file formats like RSF (Wong, 1999), GraphEd, DOT (Koutsoufios & North, 1996), and GXL (Marshall et al., 2001). Aggregation operations usually take the nodes in an input selection and produce a unique parent node. The input selection can either be programmatically constructed, such as automatic clustering methods, or can be the output of user interaction (section titled *Visualization*).

Attribute Editing

Attribute editing operations take a selection as input and compute one or several attributes on the selection's nodes and/or edges (see the section "Attributes"). We found this system much more flexible than, for example, strong-typed designs, which associate a fixed set of typed attributes with a node or edge. Attribute editing operations can be further classified on their function, from a user perspective. In most software analysis scenarios, we have encountered two types of attribute editing: *metric computation* and *layout computation*. These are discussed later. However, note that this classification is one of the many possibilities — other attribute editing operation classes may be created, depending on the specific application domain at hand.

Metrics Computation

We treat RE metrics as attribute editing operations. Examples of RE metrics are component coupling strength, the number of provisions, requirements, and internalizations (Wong, 1999; Tilley, 1998). Metrics may produce new attribute-plans, as the above metrics do, or single values, for example, a sub-graph's cyclomatic number or size. Decoupling the metric's selection input from the selection operation allows applying *any* metric on *any* sub-graph, which is not the case in other RE tools (Wong, 1999; Kazman & Carriere, 1996). Moreover, explicitly specifying the input and output attribute-plan names allows easy run-time prototyping of various combinations of metrics, similarly to the way one works with function or matrix objects in systems such as Matlab of Mathematica. Finally, the above decoupling allows the metrics, attributes, and selections to be coded independently in our architecture.

Figure 2: (a) Custom Layouts: 3D Stacked Layout, and (b) 2D Nested Layout.

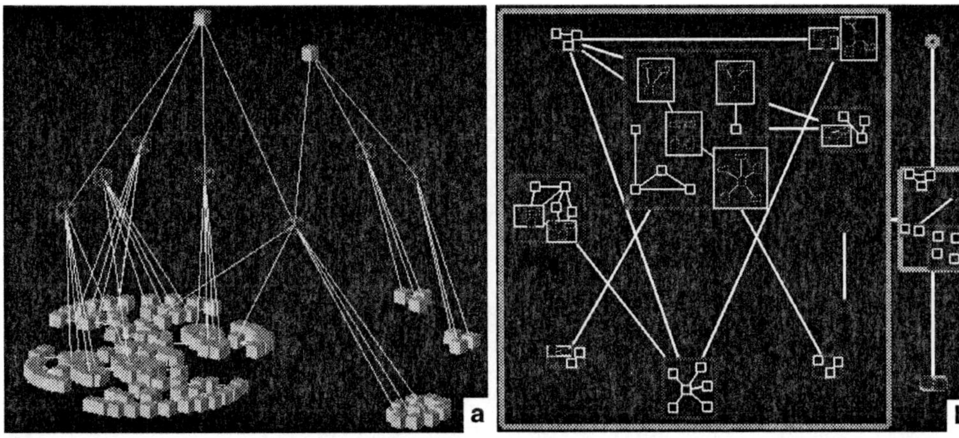

Layouts Computation

In contrast to most RE systems (e.g., Wong, 1999; Kazman & Carriere, 1996; Marshall et al., 2001), we treat graph layouts simply as attribute editing operations and thus decouple them *completely* from mapping and visualization (see the section "Visualization"). This has several benefits. Firstly, we can layout different sub-graphs separately; for example, using spring embedders for call graphs and tree layouts for containment hierarchies (see Figure 2). Secondly, we can precompute several layouts, for example, to quickly switch between them. Finally, we can cascade different layouts on the same position attributes, for example, to apply a fish-eye distortion or refine an existing layout. We have implemented several custom layouts by cascading simpler ones, as follows. *Stacked layouts* (see Figure 2a) provide a selection spanning several layers of a graph by applying a given 2D layout (e.g., spring embedder) per layer and then stacking the layers in 3D. The layers are computed as horizontal slices (see the section "Selection Operations"). Stacked layouts visualize effectively both containment (vertical) and association (horizontal) relations in a software system. *Nested layouts* (see Figure 2b) provide a similar selection as above, by recursively laying out the contents of every node separately and then laying out the bounding boxes of the containing nodes. Nested layouts produce images similar to package UML diagrams and have proven to be very helpful in RE applications, as they are quite familiar to software engineers. Users can easily combine any 2D layouts as the building bricks for the stacked and nested layouts. In the example cited in Figure 2a, we use a tree layout, whereas in Figure 2b we use a spring embedder as basic layout. Adding new layouts to the toolkit is reasonably simple. The implementation of the generic spring embedder and tree layout we added to the framework of Koutsoufios and North (1996) exceeds 50,000 lines in C programming language. Adding them in a black-box fashion required less than 100 C++ lines each, whereas our custom layouts have each under 200 C++ lines. In this respect, our layout composition is very similar to the "power tool" design in Visage (Kolojechich & Roth, 1997).

Figure 3: Software Components of the Mapping Operation.

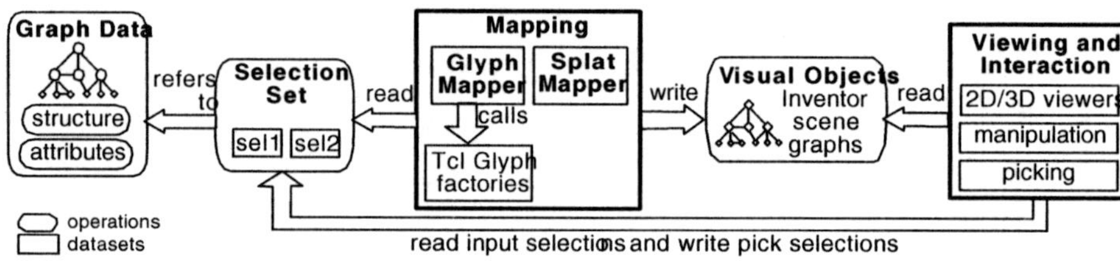

VISUALIZATION

Mapping and visualization operations enable users to see and interact with the RE data. These operations have four sub-components: *mappers, viewers, glyph factories*, and *glyphs* (see Figure 3).

These operations are implemented using the Open Inventor C++ toolkit (Wernecke, 1993), which offers sophisticated mechanisms for object direct manipulation, picking, and rendering. If deemed necessary, the architecture allows using other similar toolkits, for example, Java 3D.

The central visualization component is the mapper, which creates 2D and 3D drawable representations out of the core graph data. We have implemented several mappers, as follows. The *glyph mapper* creates a glyph, that is, an iconic symbol, for each node and edge in the input selection, and positions these glyphs at the 2D or 3D coordinates provided by a node/edge attribute plane, computed by a layout operation (see the section "Layout Operations").

The *splat mapper* produces a height map, coloured by mapping the height attribute via a red-to-blue colormap. The height map shows the variation of node density per unit area, weighted by a given attribute, but does not draw the edges explicitly. This effectively visualizes large software structures exhibiting local node agglomerations, for example, corresponding to highly coupled clusters (see van Liere & de Leeuw, 2003 for details). For example, Figure 4c shows a height field weighted by the package provision metric. The String and ListIter implementation classes show up clearly, as they are used by most other system components. In the previous example, one sees that the system heavily depends on String and ListIter, so changes to these two components potentially have a strong impact on the system stability.

A *glyph* is a 2D or 3D graphical object that visualizes a node or edge. The glyph mapper calls, for every node and edge it maps, a Tcl script, called a *glyph factory*, which builds the desired glyph as an Inventor node. The script sets the glyph's graphical properties (color, shape, size, annotation, and so on) from the attributes of the input node or edge. Users may edit these scripts at run-time, so it is very easy to customize the visualization. Figure 4 shows a glyph-based visualization of the software of a program analysis system developed at Nokia. Figure 4a shows all 1,200 software artifacts (methods, classes, packages, and files) extracted from the code. Figure 4b shows a simplified view of the system's core, after several graph-editing operations have been

Figure 4: (a) Visualization of Program Analysis Tool, (b) Glyphs Showing Clustered Core Detail, and (c) Splat Mapper Visualizing Class Provisions.

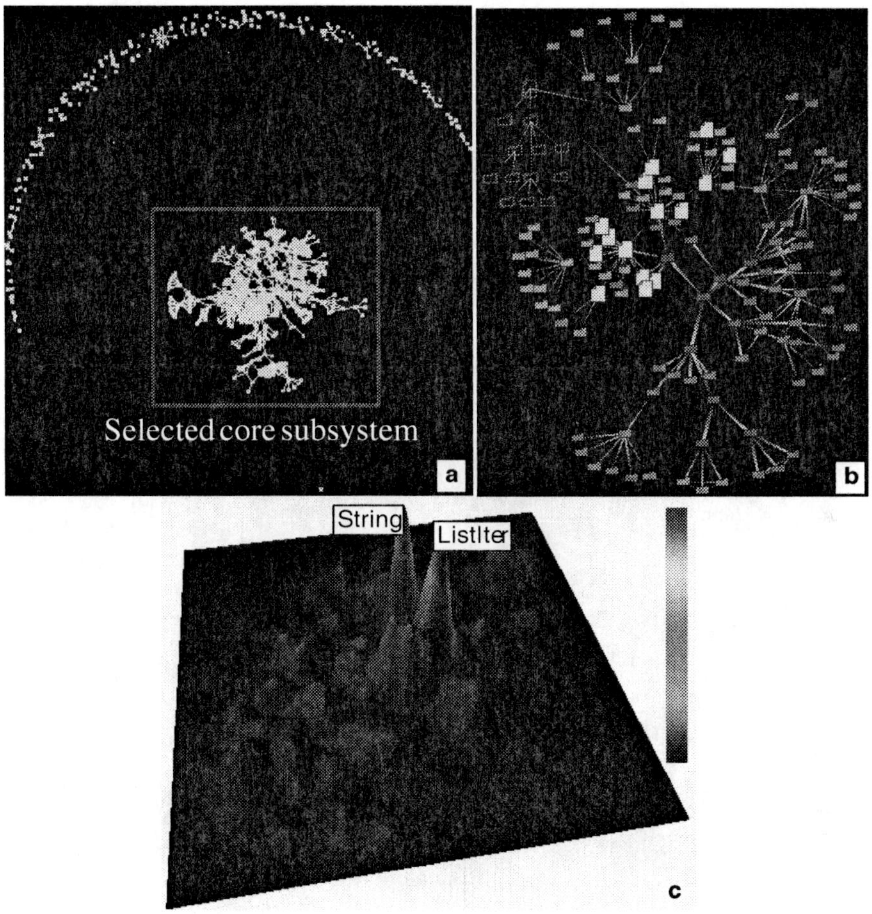

applied to filter the less important artifacts and cluster the remaining ones into higher-level units. Different glyphs have been used to show the different unit types, whereas the sub-system coupling strength (Tilley, 1998) is visualized by edge glyphs of different thicknesses. The separation of the glyph placement done in the layout phase, and the glyph construction done in the mapping phase, is a simple but powerful way of specifying the visualization. New glyph factories can be developed without being concerned by the layout, whereas new layout tools can be added to operate on existing glyphs.

We show next a second example that illustrates the comparison of related software product families shown in Figure 5. For a detailed treatment on this (Telea et al., 2003). Here, we show the RDF schema instances describing the UAProf notation (WAP Forum, 2000), a language for modeling device capabilities and user preferences for mobile phones. We used the glyph shapes to indicate various types of the UAProf language

Figure 5: Visual Comparison of Four Mobile Phone Specifications (RDF Schema Instances).

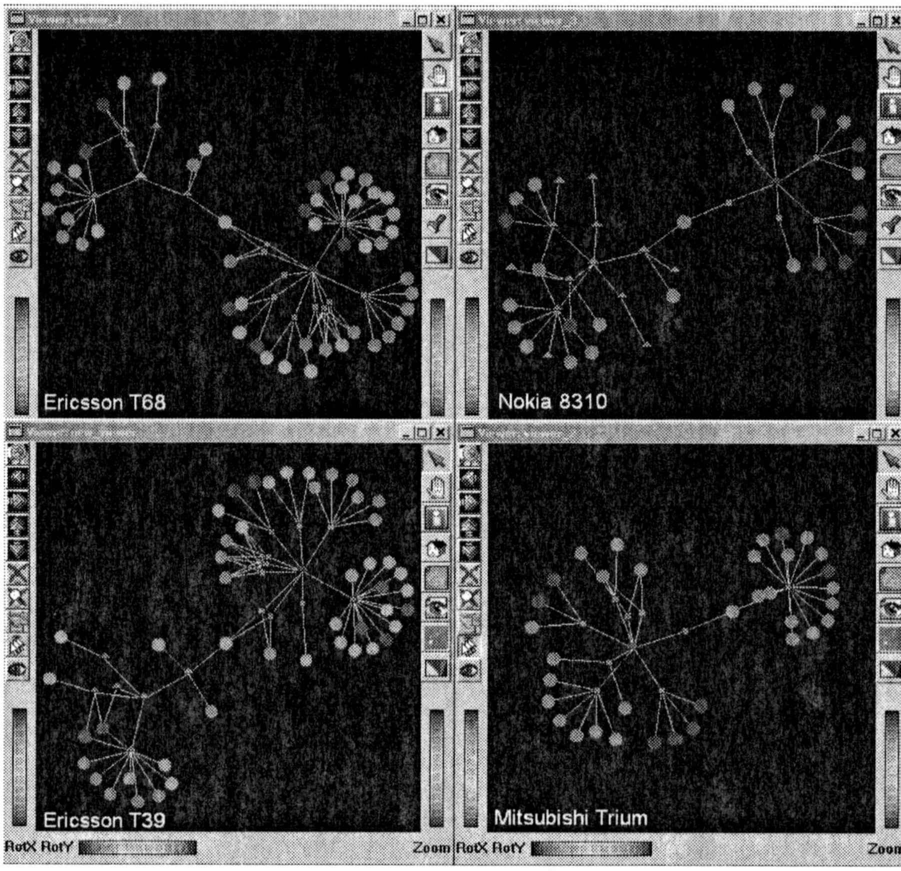

elements: Triangles are named resources, literals are circles, and rectangles are anonymous resources. The coloring scheme allows comparing different software products: nodes specific to a single instance are the light gray; nodes shared by the two Ericsson products are the lightest shade of gray; and nodes common to all instances are the darkest shade of gray. This simple visualization already allows one to see that all four products have roughly the same structure and identify the potentially important components shared by two, all, or just one product.

In a final example, we show a component-based architecture of a Nokia mobile phone software system, as shown in Figure 6. The top image shows the system containment tree, in which the user has selected two sub-system sub-trees, denoted by Sub-system 1 and Sub-system 2 (drawn in dark gray). The bottom image shows, using a nested layout (see the section "Layout Operations"), the function call relations between the components contained in the two selected sub-systems. By interactively selecting different sub-system tree via clicking the tree root icons in the first view,

Figure 6: (top) Mobile Phone Layered Architecture and (bottom) Sub-System Call Dependencies for User-Selected Components.

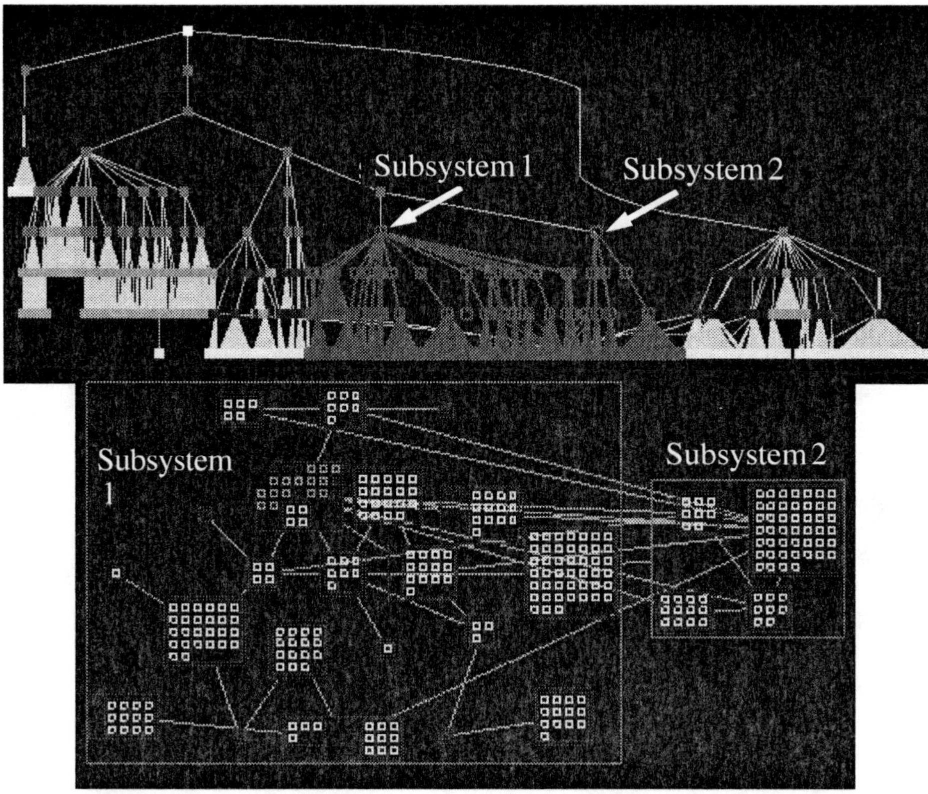

architects get, in the second view, insight into the sub-system call interdependencies on each architectural layer. In the previous example, we immediately see which are the "interface" components, that is, the components through which Sub-systems 1 and 2 communicate. Secondly, we see that lower level components (the small, light colored boxes on the lowest containment level) do not make cross-system calls, a desired property of many architectures.

Concluding this section on operations, the properties of the selection, structure and attribute editing, and mapping operations discussed here make our operation concept quite similar to Visage's "primitive tools" (Kolojechich & Roth, 1997). The main difference between the two concepts is the way of classifying operations. We group operations *structurally*, depending on what data are read and/or written. Visage (and several other tools) groups operations *functionally* into primitive tools, power tools, and appliances. Both classification models have their own merits. Our proposed framework helps the tool designer implement related operations easily by sharing code and behavior. Visage's model helps the user find related operations in the same class.

EVALUATION

We have used the RE tool presented so far for reverse engineering and exploring several software systems. In all cases, parsing the data (source code or RDF schemas) to produce the attributed graph input data has been done by external parser tools that the users already had. The input source code ranged between a few hundred lines up to 600,000 lines of code. Depending on the concrete application, RDF, C, C++, or Java code was parsed. Specific user interfaces (GUIs) were constructed in Tcl and added to the RE tool core described in this chapter in order to provide application-specific functionality atop the generic core. Such functionality included specific queries and filtering; for example, "show all system components programmed after a given date", or "eliminate all system components having less than 200 lines of code". Custom user interaction, such as constructing a nested layout of an interactively selected sub-graph shown in Figure 6, is also programmed via small Tcl scripts.

An important question is what the costs associated with adding visual reverse engineering support to an existing software workflow are. The above cost has three components:

1. *learning* to use the visual RE tool,
2. *adapting* the tool by writing custom Tcl scripts, and
3. *abstracting* the domain-specific questions into RE operations.

All three cost components are essentially determined by the *abstraction level* required by the end users. Low-level visual RE, for example, getting insight into the call or structure relationships of a software system, is the easiest to add. The main reason is that the end users, software developers in this case, are quite familiar with call graphs and thus they can easily adapt to the visual metaphors we use. Secondly, writing small Tcl scripts to customize the tool's operation, usually done by adapting existing examples, was quickly learned by end users different from the tool developers. So far, most Tcl-based custom operations we have seen written range from 20 to 150 Tcl script lines. Learning to use the tool took one to two hours. Adding custom operations, starting from the existing examples, took another one to two hours for programmers familiar with Tcl or similar scripting languages but not with our tool. All examples presented in this chapter fall into this category. When users were not familiar with RE and/or tool scripting, we took the path of first programming a "visualization scenario" (consisting of a custom Tcl scripting of queries, filtering, visual mapping, and interaction), and then letting the users use and/or modify this scenario. In all cases, users were able to reuse and modify these scenarios after a number of hours. Once this one-time cost was paid, users reported being able to apply a given visualization scenario to new datasets in a matter of minutes, more or less as reusing document templates in word processors.

The last cost component, abstracting domain-specific questions into (tool supported) RE operations, is in our experience the largest and most unpredictable cost component. Again, this heavily depends on the abstraction level of the application at hand. Low-level (code level) RE tasks easily map to the often one-to-one operations supported by our framework, as explained in the previous sections. Higher level questions, such as, "what is the impact on the system of removing a certain component?" or, "how do two architecture instances of the same system at different time instants or of two (similar) systems compare?", are much more difficult to support by an automatic tool. However, these were the typical questions we encountered when advocating the use of our tool to different end users from both academia and industry. Two statements should be made here. First, these questions can be supported by our (or a similar) RE visual framework, if one invests the effort to *translate* the questions into a number of: a) familiar visual representations, and b) queries and filters that analyze the data at hand to produce a quantitative to answer the qualitative questions. As stated already, the visual representations we advocate here are easily learnt and understood even by people unexposed to information visualization metaphors. Designing *appropriate queries and filters for domain-specific questions* is, in our view, by far the costliest component of adopting (visual) reverse engineering. However, this is a generic, and so far unanswered, problem of automated program analysis.

Overall, the resulting end-user applications are functionally very similar to other RE tools such as Rigi (Wong, 1999), VANISH (Kazman & Carriere, 1996), Visage (Kolojechich & Roth, 1997) or relational data exploration tools such as Royere (Marshall et al., 2001). However, several differences must be mentioned. The main difference is our toolkit's core architecture, which is based on a few loosely coupled, orthogonal concepts: graph and selection data objects, operations, mappers, glyphs, and viewers. The data-operation with loose coupling via selections encourages developers to write small, independent operations. As stated, all our operations range from 20 to 150 C++ or Tcl lines. In contrast, Rigi (Wong, 1999) uses a monolithic core architecture. Although somewhat adaptable via Tcl scripts, this architecture offers no sub-classing or composition mechanisms *for the core itself*. It is not possible, for example, to change the graphic glyphs, the interactive selection policy, or to add a new mapper without recoding the core. Similarly, adding a new layout, selection operation, or metric involves a low level API to access nodes and edges, as Rigi has no notion of manipulating these as selections. VANISH (Kazman & Carriere, 1996) provides a way to build custom glyphs very similar to our glyph factories. However, VANISH uses node and edge attributes based on compiled C++ classes, which prove inflexible for our targeted RE scenarios. Visage (Kolojechich & Roth, 1997), used in a larger context than software visualization, is the system that shares the most architectural traits with our framework. The main limitation we could name for Visage is its limited customizability of the rendering (layouts and glyphs) it offers.

Finally, we briefly discuss the large class of library-level toolkits, such as GVF (Marshall et al., 2001), GTL, or Graphlet (Himsolt, 2000). These toolkits provide basic graph data manipulation and usually do not address visualization, interaction, and RE-specific operations together. From these, our toolkit resembles GVF the most. However, we found GVF's Java-based API rather complex to understand and use, especially for non object-oriented expert end users, which led us to our choice for a light Tcl customization layer to a C++ core.

CONCLUSIONS

The work reported in this chapter suggests that getting insight into large relational datasets is an intrinsic part of managing the evolution of complex software systems. Interactive, user-driven visualization tools come here as an indispensable aid. In this chapter, we have provided a top-down view of the path leading from the software comprehension goal and its requirements to the design of an open, flexible architecture for a software visualization tool and its applications. Reverse engineering was our main and most challenging application area, due to the size of the involved software systems, although we show examples from different fields engineering (RE) activity. Analyzing the tasks that RE provides, we distilled them into a set of operations and requirements that any RE tool should provide, from program analysis to the final data visualization phase. Since an essential problem in applying RE to industrial software systems is the lack of flexible, generic RE tools, we have presented the architecture of such a tool implemented by ourselves and outlined the various aspects in which it performs better than other similar RE tools. We did not focus on the concrete implementation of an RE visual tool here for two main reasons. First, several such tools are already available. Second, what is obviously less treated in the literature is the description of what such tools are built upon and how to build or adapt them to the new, changing requirements imposed by system evolution.

The RE tool architecture presented here can be used in various ways. Firstly, it conveys insight into the various features and *flexibility* such tools should offer. This should help practitioners in the field judge whether existing tools present potential inflexibilities for a given task. Secondly, it discusses the *mechanisms* needed to obtain a certain degree of flexibility of a software visualization tool. This should help one judge whether an existing tool can be easily adapted to new requirements. Finally, given the novelty of the software visualization field, this can serve as a blueprint or starting point for implementing new tools that help in examining, understanding, and maintaining concrete software systems.

REFERENCES

Biggerstaff, T., Mittbrander, B., & Webster, D. (1994). The concept assignment in program understanding. *Communications of the ACM, 37*(5), 72-83.

Card, S., Mackinlay, J., & Shneiderman, B. (1999). *Readings in information visualization: Using vision to think.* Morgan Kaufmann Inc.

Eick, S., & Wills, G. (1999). *Navigating large networks with hierarchies.* In S. Card, J. Mackinlay & B. Shneiderman, (Eds.), *Readings in information visualization.* Morgan Kaufmann Inc.

Gamma, E., Helm, R., Johnson, R., & Vlissides, J. (1995). *Design patterns: Elements of reusable object-oriented software.* Reading, MA: Addison-Wesley.

Harrison, M., & McLennan, M. (1997). *Effective Tcl/Tk programming: Writing better programs with Tcl and Tk.* Reading, MA: Addison-Wesley.

Himsolt, M. (2000). Graphlet: Design and implementation of a graph editor. *Software: Practice and Experience, 30*(4), 1303-1324.

Kazman, R., & Carriere, J. (1995). Rapid prototyping of information visualizations using VANISH. *Proceedings of 1996 Symposium on Information Visualization (InfoVis '96)*, pp. 21-28. IEEE CS Press.

Kolojechich, J., & Roth, S.F. (1997). Information appliances and tools: Simplicity and power tradeoffs in the Visage exploration environment. *IEEE Compute Graphics & Applications, 17*(4), 32-41.

Koutsoufios, E., & North, S. (1996) *GraphViz, DOT and NEATO documentation* (technical report). AT&T Research Center. Available: *http://www.research.att.com*

Marshall, M.S., Herman, I., & Melançon, G. (2001). An object-oriented design for graph visualization. *Software: Practice and Experience, 31*(8), 739-756.

Mendelzon, A., & Sametinger, J. (1997). Reverse engineering by visualizing and querying. *Software – Concepts and Tools, 16*(4), 170-182.

Muller, H., Orgun, M., Tilley, S., & Uhl, J. (1993). A reverse engineering approach to subsystem structure identification. *Software Maintenance: Research and Practice, 5*(4), 181-204.

Riva, C., Maccari, A., & Telea, A. (2002). An open visualisation tool for reverse architecting. *International Workshop of Program Comprehension (IWPC 2002),* 3-10. IEEE CS Press.

Schroeder, W., Martin, K., & Lorensen, B. (1995). *The visualization toolkit: An object-oriented approach to 3D graphics.* PrenticeHall.

Stasko, J., Domongue, J., Brown, M.H., & Price, B.A. (1998). *Software visualization: Programming as a multimedia experience.* MIT Press.

Telea, A., Frasincar, F., & Houben, G.J. (2003). Visualizing RDF(S)-based information. *7th International Conference on Information Visualization (IV'03),* 294-299. IEEE CS Press.

Telea, A., Maccari, A., & Riva, C. (2002). An open toolkit for prototyping reverse engineering visualizations. *Data visualisation 2002*, Eurographics / IEEE TVCG Symposium Proceedings, The Eurographics Association, Aire-la-Ville, Switzerland, 241-250.

WAP Forum. (2000). *Wireless Application Group (WAP) forum: User agent profile.* Available: *http://www.wapforum.org*

Chapter X

Software Architecture Analysis and Reconstruction

Kamran Sartipi, McMaster University, Canada

Kostas Kontogiannis, University of Waterloo, Canada

ABSTRACT

This chapter addresses the research challenges in the area of software architecture reconstruction and discusses the state-of-the-art and practice solutions to these challenges. Software architecture analysis and reconstruction is an area within the software architecture domain that refers to the techniques and tools for processing and recovering high-level information from a low-level software system representation such as the source code. The importance of architecture analysis and reconstruction of a large and complex software system stems from the need to perform continuous maintenance activities to keep a mission critical system operational. Such activities include adopting a new implementation technology, error correction, feature enhancement, and migration to a new platform, in which the architectural reconstruction constitutes the major part of these activities. The authors believe that the discussions of this chapter expose the reader to a systematic approach to the important issues, alternative solutions, and future research in the field of software architecture analysis and reconstruction.

INTRODUCTION

For several decades, we have been witnessing the importance and influence of large and complex software systems into various aspects of our lives. Managers as well as engineers have been confronted with the problem of *legacy systems,* which are large, mission critical, and complex software systems that have been operational and modified over a number of years. The average lifetime of legacy software systems is between 10 to 15 years (Wallmuller, 1994) and the replacement of these systems is very expensive; therefore these systems are subject to re-designing and re-engineering. *Software architecture analysis and reconstruction* encompasses various methods and supporting tools for extracting high-level information from some lower level representation of a software system such as the source code. Migrating a legacy system to a new platform such as Windows or Unix operating system requires functional and behavior description of the system's components, which necessitates understanding the component's functionality and behavior. The discussions in this chapter are geared towards two main objectives.

The first objective is to address the definitions and the major issues in the field of software architecture reconstruction and the challenges that researchers in this field encounter. These issues include: specific views of the system to extract; representation models for the software system entities and relations; architecture reconstruction techniques; tractability of the reconstruction process; and evaluation methods for the result of the reconstruction process. The second objective is to address the possible solutions to these issues as they are presented by the state-of-the-art techniques in this field. These techniques include: clustering techniques, concept-lattice analysis, query-based techniques, and system composition and visualization. Finally, the proposed future trends in this chapter will serve as a starting point for further research in this field.

SOFTWARE ARCHITECTURE RECONSTRUCTION

The following observations form the basis for a definition for software architecture reconstruction. Despite several attempts for automating the architectural reconstruction process it is generally accepted that a fully automated technique is not feasible. It is rather impossible to define the architecture of a large system at once; hence, the architectural reconstruction should be an incremental process. Software systems usually consist of architectural patterns in their design, which are the basis for the reconstruction process. Most reconstruction processes focus on the structural properties of a system, ignoring the high-level behavior of the system. Finally, the role of the user is increasingly important in incorporating the domain knowledge and system documents into the reconstruction process. Based on the above discussion, in Sartipi (2003) the software architecture reconstruction is defined as:

Devising a tractable process, required techniques, and supporting tools for interactively and incrementally extracting a system's high-level structure or behavior using domain and system knowledge.

The entire software reconstruction process is divided into two phases. In the first phase, namely the *extraction* phase, a tool automatically builds a more abstract system representation, that is, the *source model*, out of the program representation. In the second phase, namely the *analysis* phase, a user-assisted process constructs a high-level view of the system from the source model. For the discussions in this chapter, the software architecture, component, connector, and architectural pattern are defined as follows:

- *Software architecture:* a partition of the software system entities into components that reflects the system characteristics and domain knowledge, and meets the structural constraints defined by a given architectural pattern.
- *Component:* a named grouping of system entities (e.g., files, functions, datatypes, and variables) according to some architectural properties, which interacts with other groups through using or providing the system services.
- *Connector:* a relation abstraction between two components using a group of system entities (e.g., files, functions, datatypes, and variables) that allows the interaction between two components.
- *Architectural pattern:* a set of fully or partially specified components and a number of (size and type) constrained connectors among the components that collectively represent the core functionalities and interactions within the software system.

Issues in Software Architecture Reconstruction

This section provides a brief overview on various issues that an approach to software architecture reconstruction must address. A detailed discussion on each issue will be presented in a corresponding section.

What Views of the System to Recover

The views of a software system are the result of applying *separation of concerns* on a development or reverse-engineering process of the software in order to classify the related knowledge about that process into more understandable and manageable forms. Recovering the functionality of a large and poorly documented legacy system is a non-trivial, if not impossible, task. The section "Architectural views" introduces a set of views of a software that is suitable for reconstruction process.

How to Represent the Software System

In software architecture reconstruction an appropriate representation of the software system is important in both extracting the desired properties from the software, and providing support for programming language independent analysis. In general, the preserved information and the level of abstraction for analysis are trade-offs that need to be considered at this stage. In the section "Software system representation" the methods for representing low-level software systems using the notion of domain model are discussed.

What Reconstruction Technique to Use

In a nutshell, approaches to architectural reconstruction can be classified as clustering-based techniques and pattern-based techniques. The clustering-based techniques generate architectural components by gradually grouping the related system entities using a similarity measure. The pattern-based approaches first compose a high-level mental model of the system architecture (i.e., the conceptual architecture or architectural pattern) using a modeling means, and a search engine identifies the pattern in the software representation. The clustering category and pattern-based category are further divided into several techniques, each with particular advantages and disadvantages that make the basis for the user to adopt a technique. In the section "Techniques for architectural reconstruction" different techniques will be presented.

How to Make the Reconstruction Process Tractable

Searching for a particular property or groups of related properties in a large database is a computationally intensive process. In some cases, the search algorithms are intractable for a large number of inputs; for example, finding a subgraph pattern in a graph representation of a large system. Efficient techniques and heuristics are essential in managing the inherent complexity of architectural reconstruction tasks. In the section "Scalability of the reconstruction process" several heuristics to deal with scalability will be discussed.

How to Involve the User in Reconstruction

The role of the user, as an integral part of an architectural reconstruction process, is important for directing the reconstruction process. In fact, the ambitious goal of fully automating the reconstruction process is no longer supported by the research community. Instead, a cooperative environment of human and tool is the most promising solution for relaxing the reconstruction complexity. This trend necessitates that the domain knowledge and system documents be incorporated in the reconstruction process by the user inspection. The section "User involvement in the reconstruction process" addresses the importance of the user in this process.

How to Validate the Recovered Architecture

Similar to validation testing in forward engineering, a reverse engineering process is also expected to generate results that can be validated against the actual or intended architecture of the software system. However, the validation of a recovered architecture is still in its early stages and requires more attention from the research community. In the section "Architectural evaluation techniques" the current techniques for assessing the result of the reconstruction process are discussed.

In the rest of this chapter, the detailed discussions on the above issues along with the proposed solutions by the different techniques are presented.

ARCHITECTURAL VIEWS

The significance of software architecture *views* has been widely addressed in the literature (Zachman, 1987; Kruchten, 1995; Soni et al., 1995; Poulin, 1996). In a broad sense, views are the result of applying *separation of concerns* on a development or reverse engineering process in order to classify the related knowledge about that process into more understandable and manageable forms. The proposed sets of views for developing or specifying a system consists of: data, function, and network (Zachman, 1987); function, process, development, and physical (Kruchten, 1995); conceptual, module-interconnection, execution, and code (Soni et al., 1995).

Figure 1 illustrates a categorization of essential features used for describing software architecture and a set of three architectural views, namely *structure, behavior* and *environment,* which are suitable for reconstruction. The scope of the architecture

Figure 1: Classification of a Software System Features into Three Views.

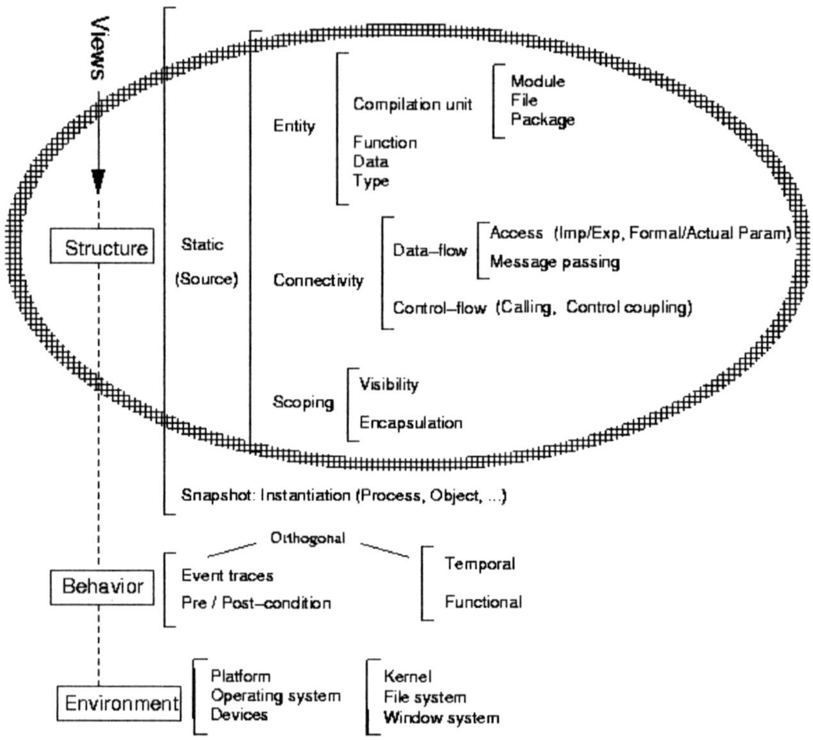

reconstruction techniques discussed in this chapter has been shown inside an oval in Figure 1.

The chosen views are orthogonal and carry most of the important information that encompass the systems in different domains such as information, concurrent, reactive, distributed, and command and control. A brief description of the different views follows.

Structure View

- *The structural view covers all building blocks and interconnections (glues) that statically describe the architecture of a software system.*

The structural view is the most appropriate architectural view to be recovered and a number of approaches and tools already exist (Finnigan et al., 1997; Rigi, URL). The structural view consists of two parts:

a) The *static* features are the property of the source code; hence, they can be extracted by static analyzing of the source program. An *entity* refers to a basic block of code that constitutes in building a software's structure. A *connectivity* refers to an interconnection between two entities. A *scope* refers to the maximum range that a definition is effective. Scope is further divided into *visibility,* such as local and global; and *encapsulation,* such as public and private access privileges.

b) The *snapshot* features change over time; hence, it represents dynamic aspects of a program. These features can be detected statically by interrupting a running program and registering the program's context and state. Spawned concurrent processes, class instances (objects), and so forth are typical information to be discovered.

Behavioral View

- *The behavioral view of a system refers to the services that a system provides to its environment through its interactions with the environment.*

The behavioral view can be expressed from two orthogonal aspects of the program properties such as: i) event traces (sequences of function invocations using the profiling techniques) (Bojic & Velasevic, 2000; El-Ramly, Stroulia & Sorenson, 2002; Eisenbarth, Koschke & Simon, 2001) and Pre/Post-conditions (input/output constraints of a function or module) (Zaremski & Wing, 1995); ii) temporal properties (concurrency issues) and functional properties (data transformation characteristics), which are difficult to be analyzed and recovered.

Environment View

- *The environment view of a software system (application) refers to all supporting facilities, including hardware and software that encompass the system and enable it to operate and provide its services to the environment.*

The environment view consists of: platform, operating system, and devices, where the operating system can be further subdivided.

Specifically, the features inside the oval in Figure 1 highlight the scope of the architecture reconstruction techniques discussed in this chapter. The techniques pertinent to the recovery of different views of a system are significantly different in both the system representation and the adopted reconstruction technique. Therefore, as an important design decision to make, the engineer should restrict the scope of the reconstruction to a subset of the features in a view of the system. For example, the highlighted area in Figure 1, except the features "Scoping, Message passing, and Control coupling", indicates the scope of a pattern-based architectural reconstruction approach presented in Sartipi (2003).

SOFTWARE SYSTEM REPRESENTATION

In software architecture reconstruction, an appropriate choice of a source model is central in: recovering desired properties from a program; matching algorithm efficiency; and programming language independence. In this section, the alternative models for representing the parsed software system are introduced. Because of its expressiveness, the graph representation of a software system has been adopted by most of the current approaches; however, different graph modeling techniques can be used.

Domain Model

In a software system, entities and their interactions both at design level and source-code level can be represented by various formalisms, including: entity relation diagrams, module interconnection diagrams, structure charts, program dependency graphs, and abstract syntax graphs. A domain model provides a schema for such a representation formalism and can be represented as a class diagram. For example, the entity relation diagram of a system at the source-code level can be extracted from the domain model of the corresponding programming language, by considering: i) source code constructs as instantiations of domain model classes (i.e., file, function, statement, expression, type-specifier, and variable); and ii) relationships between source code entities as instantiations of associations between domain model classes. The instantiation of the classes and associations into objects and relationships is the result of parsing a software system according to the corresponding grammar in which an abstract syntax tree of the class objects and their links is generated. Figure 2 illustrates a simplified class diagram of the domain model for a typical procedural language. This model has been derived from a

Figure 2: The Class Diagram of a Simplified Domain Model.

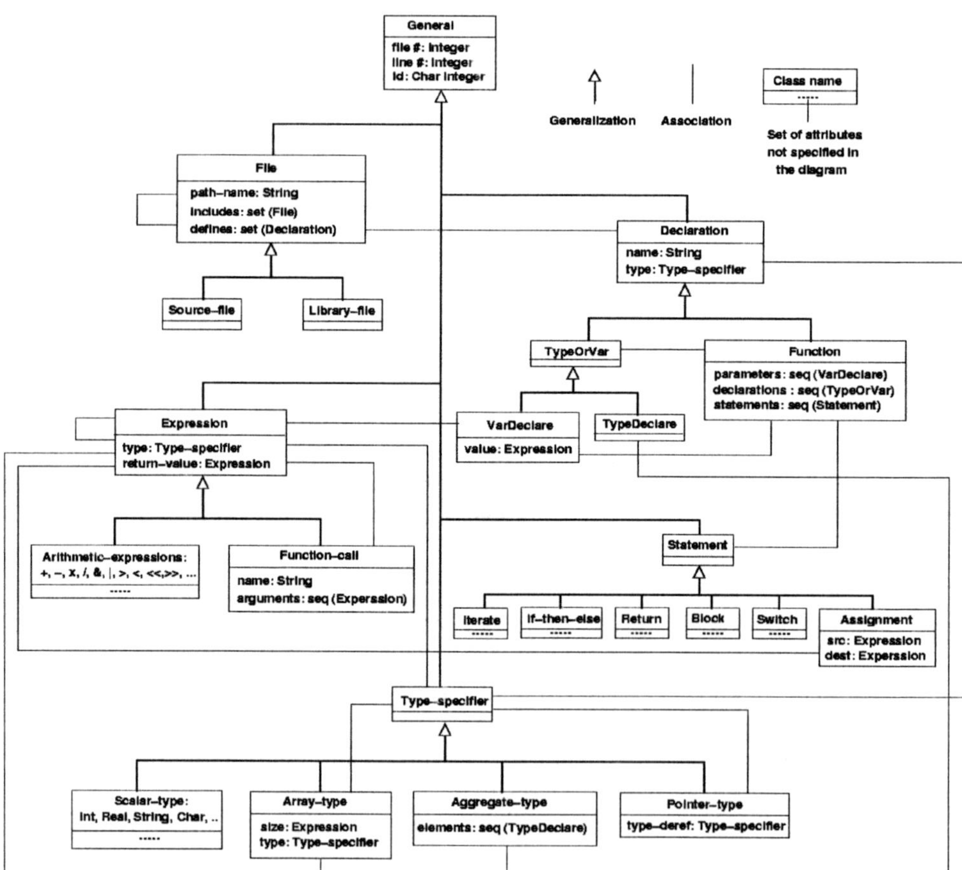

complete domain model for the C language (RefineC98, 1998), and can be used as the basis to define a source model for the software system.

Source Model Definition

The source model for an architecture reconstruction process is a database of entities and relationships that is used by the analysis process in order to build a high-level view of the system, that is, software architecture. The source model is defined via a domain model that is derived from the source-level domain model and defines the types of entities and relationships that are suitable for a specific architecture-level analysis. The resulting domain model deletes the unnecessary details of entities and relationships and hence it is sometimes called *abstract domain model* (Sartipi & Kontogiannis, 2003), *concept model* (Chen, Nishimoto & Ramamoorthy, 1990), or *schema* (Finnigan et al., 1997). In such a domain model, the set of entity-types is a sub-set of entity-types in the source-level domain model and each relation-type is an aggregation of one or more relation types in the source-level domain model. The source models of four reconstruction environments are discussed below.

The Alborz environment (Sartipi, 2001a) defines an "abstract domain model" in which the types of entities are: source file, function, datatype (including aggregate and

Figure 3: Relationships between the Types of Entities and Relations.

Source code entities	***Architectural entities***
source-file "*main.c*"	abstract-file L_i
function "*foo*"	abstract-function F_j
aggregate-type "*bar*" or array-type "*bar*"	abstract-type T_k
global-variable "*kam*"	abstract-variable V_m

Source code relations	***Architectural relations***
function "*foo*" calls function "*foobar*"	F_j use-F F_x
function "*foo*" passes, receives, or uses aggregate-type / array-type "*bar*"	F_j use-T T_k
function "*foo*" references or updates global-variable "*kam*"	F_j use-V V_m
source-file "*main.c*" defines function "*foo*", defines aggregate-type / array-type "*bar*", defines global-variable "*kam*"	L_i cont-R F_j L_i cont-R T_k L_i cont-R V_m
one or more functions defined in source-file "*main.c*" call function "*foo*", or use aggregate-type / array-type "*bar*", or reference / update global-variable "*kam*"	L_i use-R F_j L_i use-R T_k L_i use-R V_m

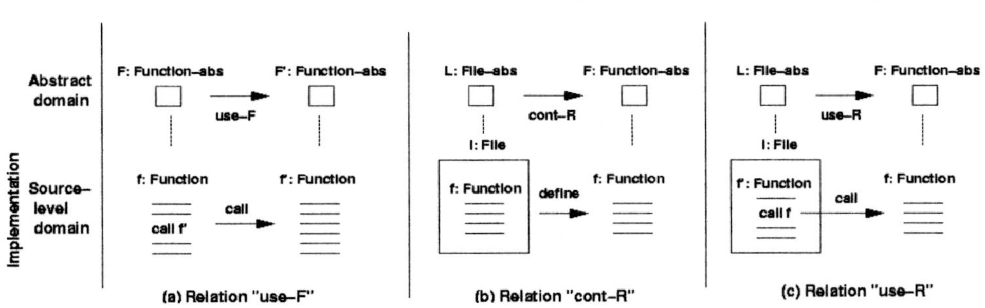

array types), and global variables. Also, the types of relations are: *use-F, use-T, use-V, cont-R, use-R, imp-R*, and *exp-R*. Figure 3 illustrates the correspondence between the types of entities and relations in the source code (defined by the source-level domain model) and the types of entities and relationships at the architectural level (defined by the abstract domain model in Sartipi & Kontogiannis, 2003). This source model allows maintainers to analyze a software system at two levels of entity granularity, that is, at module-level the lower grained entities such as functions, datatypes and variable are analyzed, and at subsystem-level the higher grained entities such as files are analyzed.

Now, we discuss how the source-level domain model in Figure 2 can be used to specify the steps for extracting the entities that are related according to the aggregated relations in the abstract domain model we defined previously. As a simple example, we extract all the functions that are related with function "foo" with the relation *use-F,* which is in fact the simple relation *call function*. The steps are as follows:

1. Get the sequence *S* of statements in function "foo".
2. For each statement *s* in *S* that is either: *iteration, if-then-else, return, block, switch, assignment*, get all the expressions *E* in *s*.
3. Check each expression *e* in *E* and keep only those that are of type *Function-call.* The name of the called function can be obtained from the "name" attribute of the function-call expression.

In the case of an aggregate abstract relation such as *use-V*, each simple relation such as reading from the global variable and writing to the global variable must be extracted separately, and consequently their relations be aggregated.

The CIA (C Information Abstraction System) proposed by Chen et al. (1990) defines a *concept model* using an attributed entity relation diagram in which the entities represent "file, function, type, global variable, and macro" and the relations represent the "reference" relation. The attributes for an entity define the name and location properties of the entity. In this model a "reference" relation is defined between two entities A and B if the definition of A refers to B such that A can not be compiled and executed without the definition of B. Therefore, in this model the relation "reference" denotes to either of the relations in the above abstract domain model.

The PBS (Portable BookShelf) (Finnigan et al., 1997) uses a complex and general *schema* for modeling information in the repository using generalization and aggregation in an object class diagram. This general schema has been derived from a conceptual modeling language originally defined in Telos (Mylopoulos, Borgida, Jarke & Koubarakis, 1990). The general schema allows defining a customized schema to model the information for different analysis purposes.

Due to their expressiveness and mathematical foundation, graphs are commonly used as the representation model for the software systems. All the above schemas or domain models define the types for system entities and their relationships, which allow representing the software system as a typed, attributed, directed graph. In this connection, the research on GXL (Graph eXchange Language) (Holt et al., 2000) is aimed at providing a standard exchange format for graph-based tools. The design of GXL is based on XML (Extensible Mark-up Language) (URL, XML), which is a simple and flexible text format that was originally designed to meet the challenges of large-scale electronic publishing. The domain model for the GXL is defined using the DTD (Document Type Definition) of XML.

TECHNIQUES FOR ARCHITECTURAL RECONSTRUCTION

In the following sections, two broad categories of the software architecture reconstruction techniques are discussed. In the first category, namely, *clustering*, a technique generates architectural components by gradual grouping of the related system entities. The clustering category is comprised of: *automatic/semiautomatic clustering* techniques that collect the related parts of a software system into cohesive components using a proximity metric (Wiggerts, 1997; Lakhotia, 1997; Tzerpos & Holt, 1998); *concept lattice* techniques that aggregate the groups of maximally related entities, arranged in the neighboring nodes of a concept lattice (Siff & Reps, 1999; Lindig & Snelting, 1997; Deursen & Kuipers, 1999); *composition and visualization* techniques that recover the containment-hierarchy of the system components using visualization and graph manipulation methods (Muller et al., 1993; Finnigan et al., 1997); and *data mining* techniques that discover the groups of entities that are related by association relation (Sartipi, Kontogiannis & Mavaddat, 2000a; Miller & Gujarathi, 1999).

In the second category, namely, *pattern-based*, a technique initiates by composing a high-level view of the system architecture (also known as the conceptual architecture or architectural pattern) using a modeling means, and then a search engine identifies the pattern in the software representation. The pattern-based techniques are comprised of: *pattern matching* techniques that model the high-level view of the system using a pattern modeling means and use approximate matching techniques to recover the pattern; *compliance checking* techniques that check the degree of conformance between a pattern and source-code; and *constraint checking* techniques that identify groups of entities that satisfy the constraints defined among them.

Clustering Techniques

The cluster analysis is defined as the process of classifying entities into subsets that have meaning in the context of a particular problem (Jain, 1988). The clustering techniques are designed to extract groups of related entities. The choice of a technique affects the detected clusters, which may or may not relate to the actual or intended structure of the system. These techniques provide tractable means to identify cohesive system components.

Requirements for a Clustering Technique

The requirements of clustering techniques include: i) type of entities to be grouped; ii) similarity measure between two entities; and iii) clustering algorithm. Wiggerts (1997), Anquetil (1999), and Tzerpos (1998) have surveyed different aspects of clustering algorithms for software systems.

- *Entities to be clustered:* In clustering analysis, the granularity level of the selected source code entities depends on the purpose of the analysis. For example, function, datatype, and variable (lower-level of granularity) are usually used for clustering at the module level, and file (higher-level of granularity) is used for clustering at the subsystem level. The application of domain model in extracting a suitable source model for the architectural reconstruction purpose was discussed earlier.

- *Similarity measure:* A similarity measure is defined so that two entities that are alike would possess a higher similarity value than two entities that are not alike. Different methods for similarity measure fall into two general categories. The first category is based on *relationships* between the entities (e.g., function call, or data use) in which the similarity is measured as a function of the number of static occurrences of such relationships. The second category is based on *shared properties* (namely *features*) between two entities, in which the similarity is measured based on the number of shared features. Patel (1992) provides an interesting social relation analogy between "finding similar entities to an entity" and "finding the friends of a person in a party". Wiggerts provides a summary of different categories, namely *association coefficients, correlation coefficients*, and *probabilistic measures* (Wiggerts, 1997). An evaluation of these similarity metrics can be found in Davey and Burd, 2000. Based on the size ratio of different unions and weights of the sets of shared features, a variety of association-based similarity metrics have been suggested (Everitt, 1993) such as *Jaccard* and *matching coefficient*.
- *Clustering algorithms:* Important clustering algorithms that apply to the field of software reverse engineering can be categorized as: i) *hierarchical algorithms*, in which each entity is first placed in a separate cluster and then gradually the clusters are merged into larger and larger clusters until all entities belong to a single cluster; ii) *optimization algorithms*, in which a partitioning of the whole system into clusters is considered and with iterative entity relocation among the clusters the partition is improved towards an optimal partition; and iii) *graph-theoretic algorithms*, in which an entity relationship graph of the system is considered and the algorithm searches to find subgraphs with special properties such as maximal connected subgraphs or minimal spanning trees. A *supervised* clustering technique requires guides from the user in different stages to perform the clustering, whereas an *un-supervised* clustering only relies on the similarity matrix, consisting of the similarity of every pair of entities (Jain, 1988). Figure 4 illustrates examples of hierarchical clustering and optimization clustering (also called partitioning). In hierarchical clustering, the entities in an initial partition are relocated among clusters based on some criteria until the partition is stable and no relocation is performed any more.

Automatic and Semi-Automatic Clustering Techniques

A technique in this group (Sartipi & Kontogiannis, 2001; Koschke, 1999; Anquetil & Lethbridge, 1999; Canfora, Czeranski & Koschke, 2000; Davey & Burd, 2000; Mancoridis et al., 1998; Hutchens & Basili, 1985; Kunz & Black, 1995) uses a similarity metric (e.g., association coefficient, correlation coefficient, or probabilistic measures), which reflects a particular property among the system entities, and a clustering algorithm (e.g., agglomerative, optimization, graph-based, or construction) to partition the system into groups of related entities (Wiggerts, 1997). Lakhotia (1997) provides a unified framework

Figure 4: (a) Hierarchical Clustering and (b) Optimization Clustering (Partitioning).

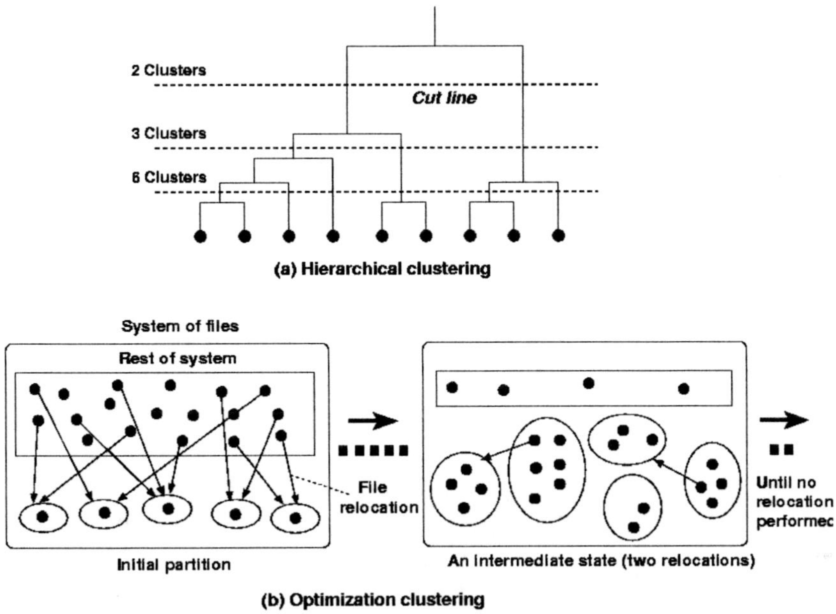

that categorizes and compares the different software clustering techniques. In Mancoridis et al. (1998), a partitioning method is used to partition a group of system files into a number of clusters. The method uses a hill-climbing search to consider different alternatives based on neighboring partitions, in which the initial partition is randomly selected. In Tzerpos and Holt (2000), a number of system structural properties are used to cluster the system files into a hierarchy of clusters. The method uses subgraph dominator nodes to find subsystems of almost 20 members, and builds up the hierarchy of subsystems accordingly. To simplify the computation, the interactions of more than a specific number (e.g., 20 links) to/from a file are disregarded.

Concept Lattice Analysis

The *mathematical concept analysis* was first introduced by Birkhoff in 1940. In this formalism, a binary relation between a set of "objects" and a set of "attribute-values" is represented as a lattice. Recently, the application of concept analysis in reverse engineering has been investigated (Siff & Reps, 1999; Lindig & Snelting, 1997; Deursen & Kuipers, 1999). In such applications, a *formal concept* is a maximal collection of objects (i.e., system functions) sharing maximal common attribute-values (i.e., called/used functions, datatypes, variables). A *concept lattice* can be composed to provide significant insight into the structure of the relations between objects and attribute-values such that each node of the lattice represents a concept.

The steps of using concept lattice for the modularization of a software system have been presented in Siff and Reps (1999) as follows. First, a matrix of functions and their attribute-values is built, which is called a *context table*. Second, based on this matrix a

Figure 5: Application of Concept Lattice Analysis in Grouping the System Entities into Modules.

Functions, datatypes, variables that are called or used by the object functions

Object functions (Obj) \ Attr–Val	F2	F7	T3	T1	V2	V3	T2
F1	X	X	X	X	X	X	
F2							X
F3	X	X	X				
F4				X	X	X	
F5	X	X	X	X		X	

(a) Context table

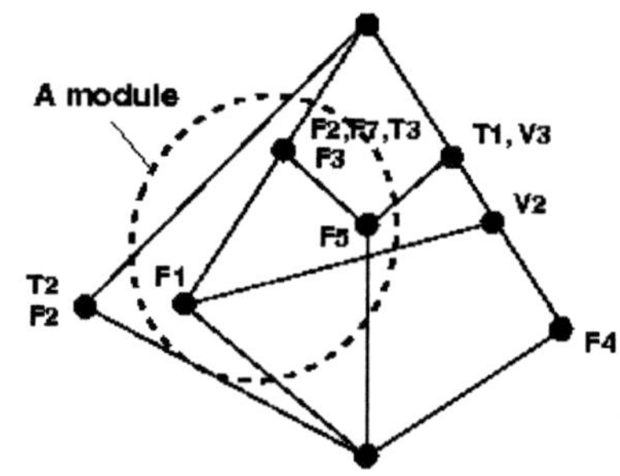

(b) Concept lattice

concept lattice is constructed, using a bottom-up iterative process. Finally, a collection of the *concept partitions* is identified, in which each partition is a group of disjoint sets of concepts, and the attribute-values in each set of concepts have significant overlap. In this context, each partition corresponds to a potential decomposition of the system into modules. Figure 5 illustrates the application of concept lattice analysis in collecting a group of system entities that exist in neighboring concepts in a lattice. This group of entities constitutes a high cohesive module. The dashed areas in Figure 5 are two representations of the same group of entities, that is, F1, F3, F5, F2, F7, T3.

However, even in medium software systems (+50 KLOC) the concept lattice may become so complex that the visual characteristic of the lattice is obscured. In such cases, the researchers seek automatic partitioning algorithms to assist the user in finding distinct clusters of highly related concepts. Anquetil (2000) addresses this problem and argues that concept lattice produces much more information, that is, concepts, than it was given as input (i.e., a set of entities describing the software system), and hence he proposes a technique that only extracts the most interesting concepts. Godin (1993) proposes a solution to the overwhelming number of concepts by pruning the concepts that do not introduce any attributes of their own, from the lattice of concepts. The pruned concepts are considered as non-important concepts. In the resulting lattice, each concept has at least one new attribute. Van Deursen (1999) proposes a technique to simplify the data set before extracting the concepts, for example, by eliminating the programs with a high number of fan-in or fan-out. This approach uses the concept lattice to extract components in the term of classes of objects in the Cobol programs.

Visualization Techniques

The approaches in this group (Finnigan et al., 1997; Muller et al., 1993; Storey, Best & Michaud, 2001) are based on tool usage, domain knowledge, and visualization means, to perform an iterative user-assisted clustering process. Such user-assisted techniques have been proven useful in handling large systems (Finnigan et al., 1997).

In the PBS approach (Finnigan et al., 1997), the user defines a containment structure for a hierarchy of subsystems, which is derived from: developers, documentation,

Figure 6: A Structural View of a Software Generated by the SHriMP Tool.

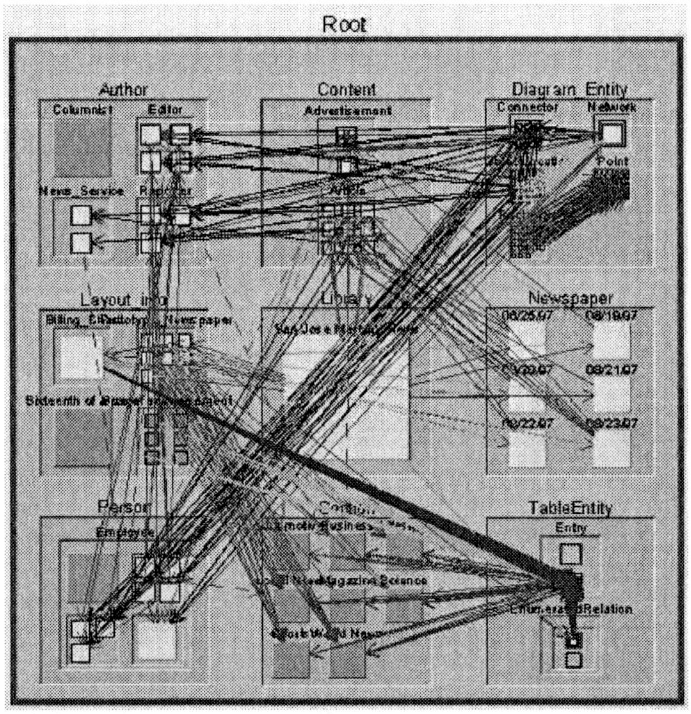

directory structure, and naming conventions. The tool consequently reveals the relations between subsystems and represents the system architecture as "landscapes" in HTML pages for the user's inspection and manipulation. In the Rigi tool (Muller et al., 1993), the extracted facts in the form of RSF tuples are represented as an entity-relation graph of attributed boxes and relationship links. Interactive facilities for graph filtering and clustering operations to build and explore subsystem hierarchies are also provided.

SHriMP (Storey et al., 2001) is an information visualization and navigation system that employs zooming features to provide insight into the structure of the system under analysis. The fish-eye zooming feature allows the user to zoom in on a particular piece of the software, while preserving the context of information. The tool uses search algorithms that allow the user to find and visualize the intended artifact in the system. The process is assisted by the user in order to construct high-level views of a system by grouping the elements in a graph. Figure 6 illustrates a view of the software system structure with links between different subsystems that has been generated by the SHriMP visualization tool.

Data Mining

Data mining, or Knowledge Discovery in Databases (KDD), refers to a collection of algorithms for discovering or verifying interesting and non-trivial relations among data in large databases (Fayyad, 1996). A substantial number of data mining approaches in the related literature are based on extensions of the *Apriori algorithm* by Agrawal (Agrawal & Srikant, 1994). These approaches are pertinent to the concept of *market baskets* (or *transactions*). A market basket (or simply basket) contains different kinds of items, in which the quantity of items of the same kind in the basket is not considered. The *association rules* (Agrawal & Srikant, 1994) express the frequency of pattern occurrences; such as, 40% of baskets that contain the set of items {A,B} also contain the set of items {C,D}. The association rules can be extracted by the iterative algorithm Apriori in two steps. The first step extracts all combinations of items in which the number of common container baskets for each combination exceeds step generates association rules using such frequent itemsets. The general idea is that if, for example, {A,B,C,D} and {A,B} are frequent itemsets, then the association rule {A,B} ⇒ {C,D} can be extracted by computing the ratio:

$$r = \frac{no.\_of\_common\_baskets(\{A,B,C,D\})}{no.\_of\_common\_baskets(\{A,B\})}$$

which is known as *confidence r*. The association rule holds only if $r >$ *minimum confidence*.

The reverse engineering approaches using data mining are very few. Montes de Oca and Carver (1998) use data mining association rules and a visual representation model to graphically present the subsystems that are identified from the database representation of the subject system. Miller and Gujarathi (1999) propose a knowledge discovery framework and work with association rules that essentially address the statistical information about relation between groups of entities in the database. Sartipi (2001) uses a by-product of association rules, by considering frequent itemsets along with their container baskets. This information allows encoding of the structural property of the groups of entities with maximum level of interaction as a similarity measure between system entities. Figure 7 illustrates the steps for representing the software system

Figure 7: Application of Data Mining Algorithms: (a) Representation of Functions as Baskets and Called Functions and used Datatypes/Variables as Items in the Baskets, (b) Representation of an Iterative Algorithm for Generating Frequent ItemSets, and (c) A Discovered Group of Highly Related Entities Constitute a Cohesive Module.

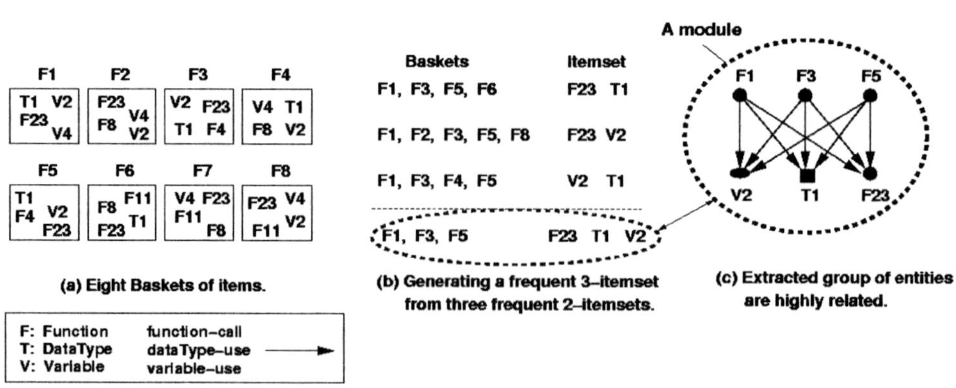

entities as data mining baskets and their items, as well as a discovered group of highly related entities as the collection of the baskets and the corresponding itemset. Figure 7(a) is the representation of functions as baskets and called functions and used datatypes/variables as items in the baskets. Figure 7(b) is the representation of an iterative algorithm for generating frequent itemsets. And Figure 7(c) shows that a discovered group of highly related entities constitute a cohesive module.

Pattern Based Techniques

The software architecture reconstruction techniques in this category are mostly designed as a top-down process in which the high-level view of the system is built as the user's mental model of the system architecture. The pattern matching process then searches the source model, which is either an abstract syntax tree, a repository of architectural elements, or a relational database to identify an exact or an approximate instance of the high-level view in the source model.

Modeling High-level System Specification

The high-level specification of a system, also called "architectural pattern" or "conceptual architecture" is an integral part of the pattern-based architectural reconstruction techniques. The specification should represent an abstraction of the components and their interactions as well as a mechanism to constrain the type of the involved system entities and data/control dependencies.

In most cases, the high-level specification is defined as a query that specifies the expected architectural structure or behavior in the target system. An architectural query is defined using architectural notations, that is, component, connector, module, and import/export. The notions such as *entity*, *connectivity*, and *scope* are used for structural view reconstruction, whereas the temporal operators are used to specify the expected behavioral view of the system. The notions of event, event pattern, and event tracing are intended for behavioral recovery. The query may use directives to lead the analysis algorithm to a specific architectural analysis task. In these techniques, the high-level view of the system is modeled either as a collection of architectural styles (Harris et al, 1995), a graph of architectural elements (Kazman & Burth, 1998), an ADL-based query (Sartipi, 2003), an SQL-based query (Kazman & Carriere, 1999), or an XML-based query (Pinzger & Gall, 2002).

Pattern Matching Techniques

Sartipi (2003) proposes a pattern-based architecture reconstruction approach that uses an architecture query language (AQL) to model the architectural pattern of the system as a constrained graph of components and connectors. The design of the AQL language has been inspired from the current architecture description languages (ADL). In this approach, a graph-matching engine incrementally expands the architectural pattern (defined in AQL language) into a pattern graph and matches it with the system graph. The search algorithm uses a graph distance measure computed using costs of node/edge deletion/insertion to find a sub-optimal match as the recovered architecture.

Kazman and Burth (1998) introduce an interactive architecture pattern recognition to recover user defined patterns of architectural elements in a system. The system is modeled as a graph of architectural elements, that is, components and connectors. Each component or connector is defined using common features, namely static and temporal features, causing the elements to be treated in the same way (Kazman, Clements, Abowd & Bass, 1997). The user defines an architectural pattern or style as a graph of elements. The tool then searches to identify instances of that graph in the source model. The tool uses the constraint satisfaction paradigm (Woods & Yang, 1995) to restrict the search space. The hard/soft features of the elements allow the relaxation of the exact matching in order to perform approximate matching. The approach provides statistics about the regularity of a system in terms of its coverage by a particular pattern.

Kazman and Carriere (1999) propose *Dali* as a workbench that allows different light-weight tools and techniques to integrate for an architectural reconstruction task. Dali extracts *elements* (function, files, variables, objects), a collection of *relations* (e.g., function calls), and a set of attributes of elements and relations (e.g., function calls function N times), and stores them in a relational database. In this context, a pattern consists of a collection of SQL queries that have been integrated via Perl expressions. The primitive SQL queries collect the architectural components and their derived relations by querying the relational database. The reconstruction process requires the involvement of the user who is familiar with the system's domain (domain expert) and has experience with composing SQL queries. In order to recover the architecture of a system the user composes two sets of pattern queries, namely "common application patterns", which are used for all systems, and "application-specific patterns" that require knowledge about the domain's reference architecture. In each set of queries the smaller entities are collapsed into larger components, and relations between components are derived.

Harris et al. (1995) identify architectural styles (about nine styles) in the source model. The method uses an annotated AST of the system as the search domain and an architectural query language, built on top of the Refine language, that codifies the desired architectural styles. A number of style recognition queries (around 60) constitute the base of the recognition process. A specialized query is composed to search for specific style-related properties in the source model. This query triggers a set of more specific style queries as subgoals, and then reports on the degree of success in recognizing that style and its code-coverage. In a similar approach, Fiutem et al. (Fiutem et al., 1996; Fiutem, Tonella, Antoniol, & Merlo, 1996) use "recognizers" and flow analysis techniques in architectural reconstruction.

Compliance Checking Techniques

In these techniques, the analyst first defines his/her assumed high-level model of the software in an appropriate form (e.g., modules and interconnection, inheritance hierarchy, design pattern, architectural style, or query). The tool then checks the degree of conformance between the proposed model and the source model. The following approaches are examples of compliance checking techniques.

Murphy and Notkin (1995) have proposed the software Reflexion model to assist the user in testing whether his/her mental model of the system conforms to the system. The user employs a textual declarative form to define a high-level model of the system, and link this model to the source model. The source model is a call graph or an inheritance hierarchy. A software Reflexion model is then computed to determine where the user's high-level model conforms to the source model and where it does not conform. The user interprets the Reflexion model and defines new relations based upon the results. Regular expressions are used in the forms to facilitate the link of a group of source model entities to a high-level entity.

Kontogiannis et al. (1995) propose a stochastic approach for structure compliance checking, which is based on the notion of concept-to-code mapping. In this approach, a concept language models abstract properties of a desired code fragment. The pattern matching process is based on the *Markov* model and a similarity measure between an abstract pattern and a piece of code is defined in terms of the probability that the abstract pattern can generate that piece of code. Dynamic programming has also been used to reduce the complexity of the required computations.

Constraint Checking Techniques

Software architecture reconstruction has also been considered as a *constraint satisfaction problem* (CSP). In CSP the values of a set of variables are restricted by the constraints that are defined between the variables. A solution to a CSP is an assignment of values to variables such that the constraints are satisfied. In the CSP problems the constraints are considered as "hard", meaning that they cannot be violated. Woods (1995) generalizes the problem of program understanding as an instance of the constraint satisfaction problem. Other variations of CSP may consider *soft* constraints that can be violated to a certain extent.

Sartipi et al. (2000b) propose an approach to software architecture reconstruction that uses an extension to the CSP problem known as *Valued Constraint Satisfaction Problem* framework (VCSP) (Schiex et al., 1995), which allows over-constraint problems to be dealt with. In the VCSP framework a cost function assigns a cost for violation of each constraint, and the cost for a certain value to variable assignment is the overall cost of constraints that are violated by such an assignment. The goal is to find a complete assignment of minimum cost.

SCALABILITY OF THE RECONSTRUCTION PROCESS

The large size and the complexity of relations among the system entities are the sources of problem in dealing with large systems. The main idea is to decrease the domain space in searching for architectural information without losing relevant information. In this connection, in Sartipi (2003), several heuristics have been proposed that are briefly discussed below.

Incremental Reconstruction

An effective heuristic in decreasing the time and space complexity of the search process is to divide the whole search space into sub-spaces and then perform an incremental reconstruction process in which the architectural components are recovered one at a time. The heuristic consists of two steps. In the first step, the search space is divided into many sub-spaces according to the particular property. For example: a sub-space can be a group of associated entities if the objective is to recover components that are highly associated; or a sub-space can be a group of functions that perform data read and write on specific files in order to recover "filter" components. Then at each iteration of the incremental reconstruction process, one sub-space is selected according to its eligibility, which is determined by a ranking mechanism to choose the best candidate sub-space.

Sub-Optimal Reconstruction Process

The search techniques play an important role in exploring non-trivial relationships in a software system as a part of a reverse engineering task. Because of the prohibitive size of the search space in dealing with large systems, it is imperative to make a trade-off between the quality of the recovered components and the search complexity. In this context, some researchers use non-complete and non-optimal but fast search techniques such as *hill climbing* (Mancoridis et al., 1998). In Sartipi and Kontogiannis (2001), a heuristic version of the optimal search algorithm A* is proposed that significantly reduces the time/space requirement of the A* search with the cost of having a sub-optimal reconstruction process. Also, approximate matching is another technique that uses a cost function and recovers the architectures that are close to an intended architecture within a boundary of a particular threshold (Kazman & Burth, 1998).

Hierarchical Reconstruction Process

The architectural reconstruction process of large systems with several hundred thousands of lines of code such as Linux operating system (Bowman et al., 1999) is usually limited to activities such as consulting with the existing system documents, relying on the exactness of the naming conventions (if they exist) for files and directories, and the directory structure. In such cases, the lowest granularity of the system entities is file and directory. However, a detailed analysis is not directly feasible where the lowest granularities are function, user-defined aggregate types, and global variables. The hierarchical reconstruction of large systems usually consists of three levels, as: i) decomposing the system into a few large subsystems; ii) decomposing each large sub-system into a number of smaller sub-systems of files and directories; and iii) decomposing each small sub-system into a number of modules of functions, aggregate/array types, and global variables.

USER INVOLVEMENT IN THE RECONSTRUCTION PROCESS

In the current approaches to architectural reconstruction the role of user is increasingly important in order to incorporate design-specific criteria in the process of structure reconstruction of a software system. Such design-specific criteria cannot be fully formulated in order to be automatically investigated by the analysis program. In such a cooperative environment, the mission of the tools has also been shifted from complex search and recovery strategies to semi-automatic, user-assisted based strategies allowing a variety of domain-specific information to be considered during the reconstruction process (Finnigan et al., 1997; Chin & Quilici, 1996). In this context, the new terms such as *librarian* and *patron* (Finnigan et al., 1997) refer to the system information accumulation for human usage.

In such cases, the analysis tool, as the user assistant, must process the raw information that represents the software system so that the user, as the high-level decision maker, can interpret and assess the processed information, in order to get insight into the system and also to make decisions for the next step of the reconstruction. Examples of such information include:

- *Statistical metrics:* Association relation among the system files; fan-in and fan-out; and architectural design views (Sartipi, 2001b).
- *Visualization means:* Simplifying the graph views (Sartipi & Kontogiannis, 2003b); Source code browsing mechanism through HTML pages (Finnigan et al., 1997; Storey et al., 2001; Sartipi & Kontogiannis, 2003b).
- *Pattern generation:* Analyzing the system representation database in order to identify the locus of interactions among system entities; this would allow the user to select the cores of functionality of the system via a ranked list (Sartipi, 2003).

ARCHITECTURAL EVALUATION TECHNIQUES

Evaluating the result of the reconstruction process is a debated issue with no generally accepted evaluation criteria. Different characteristics of the recovered architecture may be tested, including modularity quality of the architecture through coupling and cohesion metrics, and the non-functional qualities. One important characteristic of the recovered architecture to evaluate is the accuracy of the reconstruction technique that can be assessed using the information retrieval metrics Precision and Recall (Grossman & Frieder, 1998). These metrics assess the compatibility of the recovered architecture with the documented system architecture. In this evaluation, the software system must possess an updated architectural document as the reference architecture.

Figure 8 illustrates the accuracy assessment of the recovered subsystems for the Clips system. Clips is an expert system builder with 40 Kilo lines of code that is supported by a complete architectural manual (Clips, 1989). The evaluation steps are discussed as follows. First, the sub-systems of the reference architecture must be identified. Second, the recovered sub-systems must be matched against the sub-systems from the reference architecture. It is common that the reference and recovered sub-systems overlap to some

Figure 8: Architectural Reconstruction and Evaluation of the Clips System.

No. of files in recovered subsystems	Subsystems specified in CLIPS reference architecture	No. of files in reference subsystems	No. of shared files among recovered & reference subsystems	Precision	Recall
S1: 11	– Defrule structures – Inference engine	13	9	82%	70%
S2: 10	– Rule manipulation	6	5	50%	83%
S3: 4	– Object	3	3	75%	100%
S4: 4	– Expression evaluation	4	3	75%	75%
S5: 10	– System function – User interface	7	4	40%	57%

extent, or one or more recovered sub-systems may partially fit in one reference sub-system (or vice versa). In such cases we implicitly merge the sub-systems into one to allow almost one-to-one comparison between sub-systems. Third, the precision and recall metrics are computed for each recovered sub-system. Precision is defined as the percentage of the number of the "shared files" in the corresponding recovered and reference sub-system, to the number of "recovered files" for that sub-system. Whereas, recall is defined as the percentage of the number of "shared files" to the number of "reference" files for that sub-system.

Figure 8 presents the evaluation of the reconstruction of the Clips system. Overall, such values of precision and recall indicate a promising reconstruction result.

Validation of the Reconstruction Approach

In this section, three evaluation techniques are discussed, which are based on the level of conformance between the elements of the recovered components (i.e., sub-systems of files or modules of functions, types, variables), namely *candidate* components, and the elements of the *reference* component. The evaluation computation in these techniques is extensions of the precision and recall measures that were discussed previously.

Lakhotia (1995) evaluates the level of agreements between individual pairs of components in candidate and reference components in a hierarchical subsystem clustering. The metric, called *congruence measure*, uses both: difference between component similarities, and overlap between component elements among the candidate and reference component.

Koschke (2000) proposes an evaluation metric for non-hierarchical clustering that is only based on the degree of overlap between the corresponding components in candidate and reference components. The technique is an extension to Lakhotia's method by measuring the overall *accuracy* and *recall* for the whole clustering result, as opposed to separately comparing different pairs in Lakhotia's method. The reference components are subjectively determined based on a set of guidelines to the software engineer. In Koschke and Eisenbarth (2000), different cases such as 1-to-n or n-to-1 relation between the matching of candidate and reference components are also considered. Koschke defines the overall *accuracy* of the reconstruction process as:

$$accuracy(M) = \frac{\sum_{(C,R)\in M} \frac{elements(C) \bigcap elements(R)}{elements(C) \bigcup elements(R)}}{|M|}$$

where C and R represent a pair of matching candidate and reference components and M is the set of matching pairs (C, R). Considering the reconstruction example of Figure 8, the accuracy of the reconstruction is computed as follows:

$$accuracy(M) = \frac{\frac{9}{15} + \frac{5}{11} + \frac{3}{4} + \frac{3}{5} + \frac{4}{13}}{5} = 0.586$$

Mitchell (2001) proposes an automated method and a tool to extract the reference components in the absence of a benchmark decomposition that is used by Koschke's method. A set of clustering techniques is used to produce different clustering results, which are separately stored in a database as pairs of "a component, an element of component". A further analysis of the tuples generates the reference components.

FUTURE TRENDS

The variety, size, and complexity of the modern software systems are continuously increasing to meet the new demands in different industrial applications such as telecommunications, automotive, banking, insurance, medical, and air-traffic control. As a result, the current maintenance techniques (in particular, reverse engineering and architecture reconstruction techniques) must be more sophisticated in order to tackle the new challenges that the software maintainers will face. In this respect, several research areas as the potential future trends in the field of software architecture reconstruction techniques are presented below.

- *Dynamic run-time analysis:* Research on dynamic aspects of a software system is more challenging than research on structural analysis. This may be due to the difficulty of defining proper task scenarios that generate execution traces, and the difficulty of finding actual patterns in the generated executions traces. Therefore, more research on how to extract and how to use dynamic information for behavioral recovery is required.
- *Distributed and heterogeneous systems:* With the rapid growth of distributed and network-centric systems, architecture reconstruction techniques and tools should tackle the non-monolithic and heterogeneous systems that are operating in platforms with different hardware and software requirements, programming languages, and architectural patterns. In this respect, more research is needed in analyzing distributed multi-language multi-platform systems.
- *Dealing with large-scale systems:* Currently, the architecture reconstruction of large systems mostly relies on non-formal facts such as naming convention and directory structure. More research on tractable heuristics for hierarchical architecture reconstruction would allow incorporation of structured information generated by extraction techniques at different levels; that is, at function-level, file-level, and directory level.
- *Consistency and traceability among views:* Most reconstruction techniques focus on only one view of the system to recover. New techniques based on multiple view reconstruction or multiple abstraction-level reconstruction techniques would provide much deeper understanding about the system. In such techniques, maintaining the consistency and traceability among the views or abstraction levels would be of importance.
- *Reconstruction techniques for the development process:* This research aims to assist the project managements to ensure that the design objectives and requirements are met during the implementation or the evolution of a system.
- *Information exchange:* Because of the expressiveness and mathematical foundation of graphs, most of the reconstruction approaches use a customized attributed

graph representation for the software system. The research activities for standardization of the software representation have been focused on using XML (extensible markup language) to provide a customizable typed attributed graph representation for different software artifacts. This standard graph can be exchanged among different tools for the purpose of information extraction, architectural reconstruction, and analysis of the software systems. This new trend has already attracted lots of attention among the researchers, and the project GXL (graph exchange language) has been launched to achieve this research goal (Holt et al., 2000).

CONCLUSIONS

The software technology is evolving and new methodologies, techniques, and tools are emerging on the quest for better design, implementation, and maintenance of large and mission critical software. However, when the software system is operational, its functionality constantly evolves and, if not maintained properly, in most cases its current structure drifts from its documented and intended structure. In such cases, any well-designed software system becomes a legacy system that costs a lot for the organization to operate reliably. As an alternative to the costly replacement of such systems, the organizations may choose to re-engineer or re-structure the systems. In these maintenance activities, reverse engineering or architecture reconstruction is performed first to allow the engineers to understand the structure or behavior of the software system. The scope of research in software architecture reconstruction techniques and tools spans several research areas, including: compilers, profilers, programming languages, clustering, concept lattice analysis, pattern recognition, data mining, graph theoretic, constraint programming, and graphical user interfaces.

The notion of software views allows the achievement of separation of concern in the reconstruction process by classifying the set of features that are relevant to the structure, behavior, or environment views. In this chapter, we attempted to cover the techniques for reconstruction of the structure view of a software system. The approaches to architectural reconstruction are expected to address the following issues: i) the view(s) of the system to be recovered, in which the structure view is the most common view to consider; ii) the software representation model, which specifies the intended granularity of the system entities and their relations, defined by a domain model or schema; iii) the adopted high-level model of the software system, which is particularly important in the pattern-based reconstruction approaches; iv) the employed architecture reconstruction technique, which is generally categorized as either a clustering-based technique which tends to be automated, or a pattern-based technique which extensively relies on user for pattern definition; v) the tractability of the reconstruction process, which is particularly important in dealing with large systems in which the heuristics may be used to trade the tractability of the process against the quality of the result; and vi) the method of evaluating the result of reconstruction, which is important for the research community to assess the variety of existing or emerging approaches.

Finally, in the discussions of this chapter it was attempted to expose the reader to a systematic approach to the important issues, alternative solutions, and future research in the field of software architecture analysis and reconstruction. We believe that this chapter will provide enough insight into this exciting area to be used as a starting point by the interested reader to perform further research in this area.

REFERENCES

Agrawal, R., & Srikant, R. (1994). Fast algorithms for mining association rules. *Proceedings of the International Conference on Very Large Databases (VLDB),* 487-499.

Anquetil, N. (2000). A comparison of graphs of concepts for reverse engineering. *Proceedings of the International Workshop on Program Comprehension (IWPC),* 231-240.

Anquetil, N., & Lethbridge, T.C. (1999). Experiments with clustering as a software remodularization. *Proceedings of the Working Conference on Reverse Engineering (WCRE),* 235-255.

Birkhoff, G. (1940). *Lattice theory.* American Mathematical Society.

Bojic, D., & Velasevic, D. (2000). A use-case driven method of architecture recovery for program understanding and reuse reengineering *Proceedings of the European Conference on Software Maintenance and Reengineering (CSMR),* 23-31.

Bowman, I.T., Holt, R., & Brewster, N. (1999). Linux as a case study: Its extracted software architecture. *Proceedings of the International Conference on Software Engineering (ICSE),* 555-563.

Canfora, G., Czeranski, J., & Koschke, R. (2000). Revisiting the delta IC approach to component recovery. *Proceedings of the Working Conference on Reverse Engineering (WCRE),* 140-149.

Chen, Y.F., Nishimoto, M.Y., & Ramamoorthy, C.V. (1990). The C information abstraction system. *IEEE Transactions on Software Engineering, 16*(3), 325-334.

Chin, D.N., & Quilici, A. (1996). Decode: A co-operative program understanding environment. *Software Maintenance: Research and Practice, 8*(1), 3-33.Davey, J., & Burd, E. (2000). Evaluating the suitability of data clustering for software remodularization. *Proceedings of the Working Conference on Reverse Engineering (WCRE),* 268-276.

De Oca, C.M., & Carver, D.L. (1998). A visual representation model for software subsystem decomposition. *Proceedings of the Working Conference on Reverse Engineering (WCRE),* 231-240.

Eisenbarth, T., Koschke, R., & Simon, D. (2001). Feature-driven program understanding using concept analysis of execution traces. *Proceedings of the International Workshop on Program Comprehension (IWPC),* 300-309.

El-Ramly, M., Stroulia, E., & Sorenson, P. (2002). Mining system-user interaction traces for use case models. *Proceedings of the International Workshop on Program Comprehension (IWPC),* 21-29.

Everitt, B.S. (1993). *Cluster analysis.* John Wiley.

Fayyad, U.M. (1996). *Advances in knowledge discovery and data mining.* MIT Press.

Finnigan, P., Holt, R., Kalas, I., Kerr, S. Kontogiannis, K. et al. (1997). The software bookshelf. *IBM Systems Journal, 36*(4), 564-593.

Fiutem, R., Merlo, E., Antoniol, G., & Tonella, P. (1996). Understanding the architecture of software systems. *Proceedings of the Workshop on Program Comprehension,* 187-196.

Fiutem, R., Tonella, P., Antoniol, G., & Merlo, E. (1996). A cliché-based environment to support architectural reverse engineering. *Proceedings of the International Conference on Software Maintenance (ICSM),* 319-328.

Godin, R., & Mili, H. (1996). Building and maintaining analysis-level class hierarchies using galois lattices. *ACM SIGPLAN Notices, ACM Press, 28*(10), 94-410.

Grossman, D.A., & Frieder, O. (1998). *Information retrieval: Algorithms and heuristics.* KluwerAcademic Publishers.

Harris, D.R., Reubenstein, H.B., & Yeh, A.S. (1995). Reverse engineering to the architectural level. *Proceedings of the International Conference on Software Engineering (ICSE),* 186-195.

Holt, R., Winter, A., & Schurr, A. (2000). GXL: Toward a standard exchange format. *Proceedings of the Working Conference on Reverse Engineering (WCRE),* 162-171.

Hutchens, D.H., & Basili, V.R. (1985). System structure analysis: Clustering with data binding. *IEEE Transactions on Software Engineering, SE-11*(8), 749-757.

Jain, A.K. (1988). *Algorithms for clustering data.* Prentice Hall.

Kazman, R., & Burth, M. (1998). Assessing architectural complexity. *Proceedings of the European Conference on Software Maintenance and Reengineering (CSMR),* 104-112.

Kazman, R., & Carriere, S.J. (1999). Playing detective: Reconstruction software architecture from available evidence. *Journal of Automated Software Engineering, 6*(2), 107-138.

Kazman, R., Clements, P., Abowd, G., & Bass, L. (1997). Classifying architectural elements as a foundation for mechanism matching. *Proceedings of the International Computer Software and Applications Conference (COMPSAC),* 14-17.

Kontogiannis, K., DeMori, R., Bernstein, M., Galler, M., & Merlo, E. (1995). Pattern matching for design concept localization. *Proceedings of the Working Conference on Reverse Engineering (WCRE),* 96-103.

Koschke, R. (1999). An incremental semi-automatic method for component recovery. *Proceedings of the Working Conference on Reverse Engineering (WCRE),* 256-267.

Koschke, R., & Eisenbarth, T. (2000). A framework for experimental evaluation of clustering techniques. *Proceedings of the International Workshop on Program Comprehension (IWPC),* 201-210.

Kruchten, P.B. (1995). The 4+1 view model of architecture. *IEEE Software, 12*(6), 42-50.

Kunz, T., & Black, J.P. (1995). Using automatic process clustering for design recover and distributed debugging. *IEEE Transactions on Software Engineering, 21*(6), 515-527.

Lakhotia, A. (1997). A unified framework for expressing software subsystem classification techniques. *Journal of Systems and Software, 36*(3), 211-231.

Lakhotia, A., & Gravley, J. (1995). Toward experimental evaluation of subsystem classification recovery techniques. *Proceedings of the Working Conference on Reverse Engineering (WCRE),* 262-269.

Lindig, C., & Snelting, G. (1997). Assessing modular structure of legacy code based on mathematical concept analysis. *Proceedings of the International Conference on Software Engineering (ICSE),* 349-359.

Lyndon B. Johnson Space Center, AI Section. (1989). *Clips architectural manual version 4.3.*

Mancoridis, S., Mitchell, B., Rorres, C., Chen, Y., & Gansner, E. (1998). Using automatic clustering to produce high-level system organizations of source code. *Proceedings of the International Workshop on Program Comprehension (IWPC)*, 45-53.

Miller, R.J., &Gujarathi, A. (1999). Mining for program structure. *International Journal on Software Engineering and Knowledge Engineering, 9*(5), 499-517.

Mitchell, B.S., & Mancoridis, S. (2001). Craft: A framework for evaluating software clustering in the absence of benchmark decompositions. *Proceedings of the Working Conference on Reverse Engineering (WCRE)*, 93-102.

Muller, H.A., Orgun, M. et al.(1993). A reverse-engineering approach to subsystem structure identification. *Software Maintenance: Research and Practice, 5,* 181-204.

Murphy, G., Notkin, D., & Sullivan, K. (1995). Software reflexion model: Bridging the gap between source and higher-level models. *Proceedings of the ACM SIGSOFT SFSE*, 18-28.

Mylopoulos, J., Borgida, A., Jarke, M., & Koubarakis, M. (1990). Telos: Representing knowledge about information systems. *ACM Transactions on Information Systems, 8*(4), 325-362.

Patel, S., Chu, W., & Baxter, R. (1992). A measure for composite module cohesion. *Proceedings of the International Conference on Software Engineering (ICSE)*, 38-48.

Pinzger, M., & Gall, H. (2002). Pattern-supported architecture recovery. *Proceedings of the International Workshop on Program Comprehension (IWPC)*, 53-61.

Poulin, J.S. (1996). Evolution of a Software Architecture for Management Information Systems. *Proceedings of the International Software Architecture Workshop (ISAW-2)*, 134-137.

Rigi. Reverse engineering toolkit. Available: *http://www.rigi.csc.uvic.ca/index.html*

Sartipi, K. (2001a). Alborz: A query-based tool for software architecture recovery. *Proceedings of the International Workshop on Program Comprehension (IWPC)*, 115-116.

Sartipi, K. (2001b). A software evaluation model using component association views. *Proceedings of the International Workshop on Program Comprehension (IWPC)*, 259-268.

Sartipi, K. (2003). *Software architecture recovery based on pattern matching.* Doctoral dissertation, School of Computer Science, University of Waterloo, Waterloo, ON, Canada.

Sartipi, K., & Kontogiannis, K. (2001). Component clustering based on maximal association. *Proceedings of the Working Conference on Reverse Engineering (WCRE)*, 103-114.

Sartipi, K., & Kontogiannis, K. (2003a). On modeling software architecture recovery as graph matching. *Proceedings of the International Conference on Software Maintenance (ICSM)*, 224-234.

Sartipi, K., & Kontogiannis, K. (2003b). A user-assisted approach to component clustering. *Journal of Software Maintenance: Research and Practice (JSM), 15*(4), 265-295.

Sartipi, K., Kontogiannis, K., & Mavaddat, F. (2000a). Architectural design recovery using data mining techniques. *Proceedings of the European Conference on Software Maintenance and Reengineering (CSMR)*, 129-139.

Sartipi, K., Kontogiannis, K., & Mavaddat, F. (2000b). A pattern matching framework for software architecture recovery and restructuring. *Proceedings of the International Workshop on Program Comprehension (IWPC)*, 37-47.

Schiex, T., Fargier, H., & Verfaillie, G. (1995). Valued constraint satisfaction problems: Hard and easy problems. *Proceedings of the International Joint Conference on Artificial Intelligence (IJCAI)*, 631-637.

Siff, M., & Reps, T. (1999). Identifying modules via concept analysis. *IEEE Transaction on Software Engineering, 25*(6), 749-768.

Software development kit: *Refine/C user's guide for version 1.2.* (1998). 700 E. El Camino Real, Mountain, CA 94040, USA.

Soni, D., Nord, R.L., & Hofmeister, C. (1995). Software architecture in industrial applications. *Proceedings of the International Conference on Software Engineering (ICSE)*, 196-207.

Storey, M.A., Best, C., & Michaud, J. (2001). Shrimp views, an interactive environment for exploring Java programs. *Proceedings of the International Workshop on Program Comprehension (IWPC)*, 111-112.

Tzerpos, V., & Holt, R.C. (1998). Software botryology: Automatic clustering of software systems. *Proceedings of the International Workshop on Large-Scale Software Composition*, 811-818.

Tzerpos, V., & Holt, R.C. (2000). ACDC: An algorithm for comprehension-driven clustering. *Proceedings of the Working Conference on Reverse Engineering (WCRE)*, 258-267.

Van Deursen, A., & Kuipers, T. (1999). Identifying objects using cluster and concept analysis. *Proceedings of the International Conference on Software Engineering (ICSE)*, 246-255.

Wallmuller, E. (1994). *Software quality assurance: A practical approach.* Prentice Hall.

Wiggerts, T.A. (1997). Using clustering algorithms in legacy systems modularization. *Proceedings of the Working Conference in Reverse Engineering (WCRE)*, 33-43.

Woods, S.G., & Yang, Q. (1995). Program understanding as constraint satisfaction. *Proceedings of the Working Conference on Reverse Engineering (WCRE)*, 314-323.

XML. Extensible Markup Language. Available: http://www.w3.org/XML/

Zachman, J.A. (1987). A framework for information systems architecture. *IBM Systems Journal, 26*(3), 276-292.

Zaremski, A.M., & Wing, J.M. (1995). Specification matching of software components. *Proceedings of the SIGSOFT 95 Software Engineering Notes, 20*(4), 6-17.

Chapter XI

Evolution and Maintenance of Web Sites: A Product Line Model

Rafael Capilla*, Universidad Rey Juan Carlos, Spain

Juan C. Dueñas**, Universidad Politécnica de Madrid, Spain

ABSTRACT

In this chapter we describe the product line models, and show how to apply them for developing and evolving Web products. A product line captures the common and variable aspects of software systems as key assets under a common architecture. Software companies are increasingly adopting this approach in order to accelerate the development of families of similar software products. In certain domains, such as the Web systems, development and maintenance operations are required more often. New techniques to engineer Web sites are needed in order to reduce the time to market for the Web products and to maintain the systems afterward. The authors believe that understanding the notion of lightweight product line and the role that the architecture plays will help software engineers in the construction of software products, and they will be able to manage the evolution effectively against future changes.

INTRODUCTION

For several years, software engineers have been taught to build software systems from a set of technical requirements. Requirements lead to a software design and finally to a software system. As far as we know from our experience, software systems must be continuously improved or fixed due to new requirements or problems not previously identified. The notion of software evolution (Lehman, 2001) aims at the improvement of existing systems in order to correct faults, to adapt them to new changes or to develop new versions, among others. Nevertheless, software evolution is not an isolated concept. In fact, the evolution of a system is closely related to the software maintenance process. Although some authors consider them as synonyms, we understand that the proper evolution of a system relies on specific software maintenance operations. *Software evolution* generally describes the changes a system suffers in the long term, regarding unexpected sources for change (Kniesel, Constanza & Dmitriev, 2002). In contrast, the term *software maintenance* is usually employed for describing a set of activities or tasks for correcting, adapting or improving a software system.

There is a general consensus that maintenance processes are time and cost consuming. In order to reduce this impact, we need to employ appropriate techniques to reduce the time spent in maintenance processes as well as the budget needed to support the evolution of a system. The maintenance activity is considered as an integrated phase under the development process, and the use of specific methods and models for maintenance operations is frequently forgotten. This situation usually arises in those applications with strong time to market requirements and short product delivery deadlines, so the time to perform changes or improvements in the code or even to plan and design changes is much less compared to the actual time required to do these effectively and properly. For example, Web-based applications allow very short development time, and maintenance operations for these systems are usually performed in days or weeks. In order to address these, both the development and the maintenance of Web systems (i.e., Web products) require agile methods in order to support the fast evolution of such systems. The main goal of this chapter is to study agile and efficient methods, such as lightweight product line architectural (PLA) models, and analyze the benefits expected in the development of software systems, employing successful techniques to improve the maintenance operations of Web products.

BACKGROUND OF PRODUCT LINE MODELS

A Product Line Architecture (PLA) defines a set of similar systems that share a common software architecture (Bass, Clements & Kazman, 2003), a group of features and satisfy the needs of a particular market segment. More formally, a software product line is *"a set of software-intensive systems sharing a common, managed set of features that satisfy the specific needs of a particular market segment or mission and that are developed from a common set of core assets in a prescribed way"* (Clements & Northrop, 2003). A key aspect in this definition is that a product line refers to a set of related systems as those ones belonging to a particular domain or market segment. In this way, product lines are strongly market-driven because they try to cover the needs of a market niche. Such products are usually similar and they share common elements. Other authors call them "product family"; in this chapter we use the terms "product family" and "product line" interchangeably.

Software architecture is very much related to the notion of product line model. A *software architecture* represents the design of a set of similar systems and is formed by components and connectors. The components in the architecture describe the functionality of parts of the system or sub-systems, whereas the connectors describe the way in which the components are integrated. Software architectures usually employ architectural styles (Shaw & Garlan, 1996) or design patterns (Buschmann et al., 1996) to impose restrictions to the architecture, specifying how the sub-systems and components are connected. Discovering the variable and common points of systems is usually known as commonality and variability analysis. The goal is to know which parts are commonly shared by most of the products and which are the differences that distinguish one product from another (Weiss & Lai, 1999). Such variations are usually defined under specific variation points (Bosch et al., 2002) that can be applied at several binding times (e.g., design time or runtime) during the overall design process (Bosch, 2000).

Nokia Mobile Phones is a successful example in the industry. Nokia handles a large variety of products whose lifetime must be kept under control. In this situation, there is a market driver for the introduction of a product line; but also issues such as the huge testing effort per new feature in the set of phones clearly pushed the company towards producing sets of products trying to maximize the common parts. The variable and common features in the product family are made explicit in the product line architecture, keeping the products evolution under control (Fey, Fajta & Boros, 2002).

In addition, there are other important aspects concerning the adoption of a product line. Part of these refers to organizational, business, process or evolution questions, such as we mention below:

- *Product Line Scoping:* The scope of the product line is closely related to the notion of domain (Clements, 2002). Before we set up the product line, we need to encompass the domain in which the products will be developed. These early step results are key for the success of the product line because they try to delimit which products will be engineered under the product line and which will not. Therefore, it would be easier to establish a feasibility study of the products and reusable components to be engineered as well as help to determine the expected costs and benefits.
- *Costs and Benefits of a PLA:* Once we know which products are inside the PLA, it would be useful to determine the costs and the benefits of initiating a product line model. This topic is a difficult question due to the lack of appropriate metrics or cost models. Also, companies do not provide the results of the experience gained of using product lines and therefore it seems complex to estimate how much a product lines costs and when the benefits will return to the organization. Some of these expected benefits are: decreased time-to-market, increased quality of products, software productivity or large-scale production, among others.
- *Organizational Issues:* The use of a product line model suggests changes in the organization compared to the traditional software development process. The nature of product lines implies that software engineers must assume several roles. In this way, a software architect is needed to be responsible for the design process. Additionally, the roles of the development team must be divided between those ones dedicated to create, maintain and evolve the reusable components engineered under the product line, while other parts of the team should be responsible to engineer the new software products employing the reusable components stored in the repository. Moreover, a coordination team formed by project leaders should establish appropriate relations and coordination tasks among all the members of the teams.

- *Evolution:* Due to new requirements, the products evolve over time and this should be properly controlled. Sometimes, these new requirements will be well supported by the architecture but in some other cases, due to technology or market changes, the architecture and the components need to reflect these variations. Anticipating future changes is a challenge when developing a product line architecture.

In this chapter we will focus on technological and process aspects related to the development of a product line model. One of the main reasons of using product line models is that software projects must not be developed in an isolated form. Instead, we need to view the development of software systems in a similar context in which similar products differ only on a reduced set of variances. Therefore we will be able to reuse not only experience but also software components that can be used in the development of similar related systems. To achieve this goal, first we will explore some existing product line approaches and then we will focus on lightweight approaches that seem to be more suitable in the construction and maintenance of Web products.

The Cards Product Line Approach

In the last two decades several product line initiatives have emerged. Several companies such as Nokia, Cummins, Celsius Tech (Bass, Clements & Kazman, 2003) and Philips Medical systems (Ommering, 2002; Linden, 2002), among others have introduced a product line model in their organizations. The U.S. Air Force (USAF) Comprehensive Approach to Reusable Defense Software (CARDS) Program describes one of the clearest product line models. The main goal of this model is to reduce the increasing costs of software development and maintenance. The point of view of CARDS is based on a tri-lifecycle software engineering model (Maymir-Ducharme, 1996) that provides support for three activities: Enterprise Engineering, Domain Engineering and Application Engineering. Figure 1 illustrates the CARDS Product Line Domain Engineering approach as a systematic model that puts emphasis on economic analysis focusing on specific markets.

This tri-lifecycle extends the DARPA Software Technology for Adaptable, Reliable Systems' (STARS) dual life cycle by adding an Information/Enterprise Engineering phase (Martin, 1989).

The *enterprise engineering* phase analyzes business processes to identify and scope candidate domains. Then, a *domain engineering* process (Arango, 1991; Schäfer et al., 1994; Simos et al., 1996; Mili & Yacoub, 2001) analyzes and identifies each candidate domain in order to produce reusable components valid to be used in the construction of new software systems. Domain analysis is a key activity in a domain engineering process, which tries to identify potential reusable structures to produce a domain model capable of supporting the construction of reusable candidates (e.g., a piece of code with enough functionality). The market analysis in conjunction with the domain analysis phase selects the optimal domain requirements to meet the business needs.

Once we count with a domain model able to represent the knowledge of a domain, we build an architecture to gather the functionality of a set of similar systems in the domain. Such architecture is composed of components (e.g., sub-systems) and connectors that show how the components are related (e.g., through appropriate interfaces). Finally, the infrastructure development process constructs a series of components (i.e.,

Figure 1: CARDS Tri-Lifecycle Product Line Domain Engineering Model (Maymir-Ducharme, 1996).

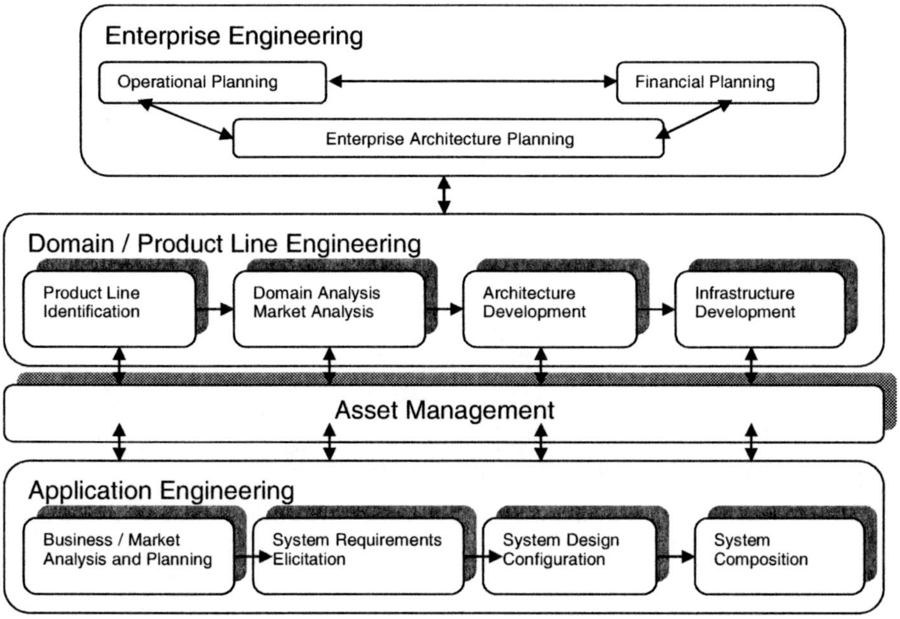

core components) that meet the functionality of the different parts of the architecture. Such components are stored for reusable purposes to be used by the application engineering phase.

Afterwards, an *application engineering* process constructs new software products using the reusable components developed in the domain engineering phase. When a new system is needed, we elicit the system requirements and we try to customize the software architecture developed by the domain engineering process and determine if the architecture satisfies the requirements. At last, the new system is built by composition, using the reusable components previously developed and building new components for the rest of the requirements not supported by the core components. In this way, similar software systems can use the same software architecture and customize it to support new requirements or changes demanded by the customer.

Café Reference Model for Product Family Engineering

The CAFÉ project (from Concepts to Applications in Family Engineering) is a large European research project in the context of Product Family Engineering, under the ITEA/ Eureka programme, that groups the main companies producing or using software in Europe (Philips, Nokia, Siemens, Thales, Telvent, among others). The main aim of this project is to implement the Product Family Engineering approach in the following aspects: the business area, the architecture, the process, and the organization (Linden, 2002). The CAFÉ project continues a mature work started in the European projects ARES

Figure 2: CAFÉ Reference Model for Product Family Engineering.

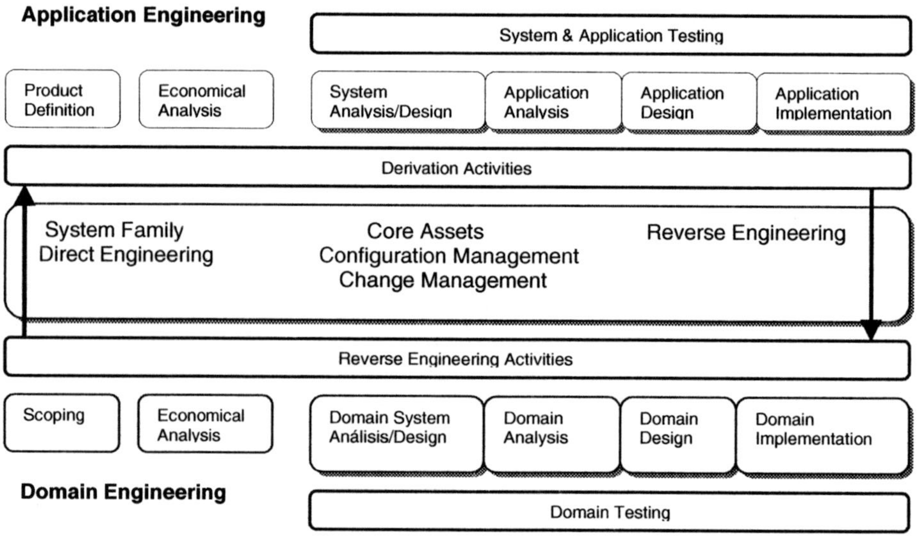

(Architectural Reasoning for Embedded Systems, IST) and ESAPS (Engineering Software Architectures, Processes and Platforms for System-Families).

The CAFÉ Reference Model (included in Figure 2) is partially based on the CARDS model, containing several required activities in order to perform a whole product family engineering process. There are two main tracks in the development, one for the creation of the domain or common elements (requirements, architecture, components), and the other one for the assembly of applications or products. With respect to the traditional waterfall lifecycle, a new dimension in development appears, shown in Figure 2 with the lines that cross forward and backward between domain and application engineering.

However, it is recognized that there are several requirements for the adoption of the approach, depending on the organizational context (the size of the company and its previous structure), the product portfolio, and the application domain. Among the key issues in the application of the approach, and common to all of them (including the Web domain), we outline the following:

- *Variability/commonality management*, as the capability to identify the common and variable assets in the family, and handle them differently. This capability appears mainly in the intermediate layer in the figure; while the domain engineering area contains the common assets, the application engineering area handles products composed of both the common parts and the variable ones.
- *Selection/generation/derivation*, as the activities that allow a company to create the actual products from the internally or externally available assets. In the figure, whenever the process moves from the domain engineering to the application engineering, any of these activities is performed.

- *Decision management* to perform a selection/generation/derivation process, decisions must be recorded, represented and assessed. The modeling, store and management of these decisions is usually out of the current practices in product family engineering, but this information reveals to be so important as to include it into the core assets.
- *Traceability*, as the general capability to make explicit the relationships between the assets in different stages of the development.

Although the CAFÉ project has shown the improvements in time-to-market and cost reduction for the development of product families, there is no universally accepted roadmap for adoption of the approach yet. In our research, we have found that, among the different adoption strategies, the lightweight approach suits better for domains in which the requirements change often or when there is a strong market pressure, such as is the case for the Web applications.

Lightweight Product Line Approaches

As we have seen before, some of the product line models mentioned above require complex processes such as domain analysis or domain engineering. Other PLA models such as PuLSE (Bayer et al., 1999) from the Fraunhofer IESE Institute also describe a complete methodology for enabling product lines across a variety of enterprise contexts.

However, no one can expect that all methods work equally effectively in all contexts. In this way, complex PLA models do not fit well because of the existence of critical requirements. Such requirements can refer to shortening product time-to-market, performing changes in short time periods, or employing several programming languages at the same time for a unique product. Examples of such kinds of systems are Web-based systems where time-to-market (Reifer, 2000) is a critical factor in the development process in opposite to other software products. The alternative to other PLA methods is to employ lightweight versions of existing practices. In this way we understand by lightweight product lines, *"an incremental approach to the adoption of product family engineering in which the number of product line specific practices introduced is kept small."*

Additionally, the difficulty for building several systems rather than one at a time relies on a proper customization process that gathers the variations of a set of similar systems in a suitable manner. In order to simplify the software customization, we can adopt several strategies (Krueger, 2002): a *proactive* approach (similar to the waterfall approach for single systems) is appropriate when the requirements are well defined and stable. This approach performs a domain analysis and a domain scoping process in order to identify those variations the product line must support. Then, the product line architecture is modeled for supporting all the products we want to engineer and then the common and variant parts can be implemented. Maintenance and evolution activities are performed on a single product line.

The *reactive* approach is an incremental model appropriate when we have unexpected requirements of new products. For instance, when unexpected requirements from new products appear, this approach is suitable to customize software systems. The reactive approach characterizes the requirements for a new product. If this product is under the scope of the product line, the reactive approach creates the product definition by selecting values for each feature of the product. If it is not in the scope, we must extend this to include the new requirements. This approach is less heavy than the proactive model and permits a quick customization process.

Finally, with the *extractive* approach, the organization can adopt a software mass customization process very quickly due to the high level of reuse employed. The extractive approach identifies commonality and variation in the existing systems and creates "feature declarations" that model the scope of variations among the systems. Finally, we create product definitions for product instances by selecting values for each feature. This approach is suitable when we can reuse an existing collection of customized systems that have a significant amount of commonality among them. After the production line has been populated, software mass customization enhances the single production line.

The controversy of which approach or model is better suited will depend on several factors such as: the domain of interest, the product requirements, the number of product families we need to set up, the time and cost restrictions, the particular organization or even the combination of several factors. Software architectures (SA) and product-lines architectures (PLA) are being adopted by companies to improve the development of software systems in several domains (e.g., telecommunications, multimedia devices, medical systems, military and others). Some of these well-known examples of success are the following.

Cummins is the largest manufacturer of commercial diesel engines. In 1993, the increasing number of ongoing software projects for delivering new models of engines led to an unmanageable number of features present in different products. Therefore, Cummins decided to start a product line for covering the business case. Cummins employed a combination of traditional requirements analysis and lightweight domain analysis to establish the product line requirements and common features implemented by the core asset group. Finally, the product line started running and the main benefits obtained were more than 20 product groups successfully launched, more than 75% of products from the core assets, a reduction in the product cycle time, an improvement on the software quality and, of course, a higher customer satisfaction, among others (Clements & Northrop, 2002).

Market Maker is a German company funded in 1989 whose main activity was the development of stock market tracking systems. They produced a successful system for personal tracking, based on the provision of data and its delivery by physical means (diskettes) to the customers using the personal tracking system. Soon they had to modify the application in order to cope with downloading the data from servers operated by the company, and to get the stock market data to these servers from different sources. After this, the system had to be customized to the different data packages the users could subscribe to and to the range of data analysis functions available (trend analysis, option strategies, etc.). In 1996, among the several products purchased by the company, MMLive! offered the capability to provide Web access to real-time data. All functionalities and products were combined into the MERGER product line in 1999, which was organized around a single three-tier (presentation, application, data access) Web technical architecture. This architecture provides solution to several degrees of customization of the products that can be derived from the product line, ranging from the support infrastructure (open source operating systems and commercial ones), the amount and kind of information handled, and the number, type and functional qualities of the networks used. The large number of variants to be handled forced them — and at the same time provided the opportunity — to adopt the product family approach in order to survive (Clements & Northrop, 2002). This product line is centered on an architecture able to accommodate all variation sources (the variations are solved for each product only at the configuration phase). The product line was introduced in an incremental way into the company, which could be understood as a lightweight product line, since not all the practices of product lines adoption have been put in practice at once (Schmid & Verlage, 2002).

A PRODUCT LINE APPROACH FOR WEB-BASED SYSTEMS

To this point, the models and experiences presented before show how product lines are a promising technique that works for engineering product families that share common characteristics. Several issues such as initiating the product line, cost and benefits expected, how the products and the architecture evolve, which kind of product line model we should apply, and more, are open issues to be treated. Today, Web engineering covers a great part of the systems being developed and from our point of view they constitute an excellent candidate to apply a product line model for developing, maintaining and evolving Web products. In this section we will study how product lines can be successfully employed in the development and maintenance of Web systems.

Web Development and Maintenance Issues

The development of Web systems is not done in the same way as classical software applications. One of the main problems is that time-to-market is frequently too short because the customers demand a rapid solution for their needs. A solution to satisfy time requirements is to increase the size of the development group, but this leads to an increment of the staff costs. Another problem occurs when the diversity of languages employed in Web developments (e.g., HTML, XML, JavaScript, ASP or PHP) means that most of the development team have to know several languages or even graphical design.

Moreover, when HTML code is completely embedded with other scripting languages, source code files are more difficult to maintain. Also, a low modularity of Web files increases both development and maintenance operations, turning these into time-consuming tasks.

If we want to reduce the time spent in the modifications or even to develop new Web products quickly, we need to change the way in which the products are engineered by reducing the complexity of the Web files. This challenge can be solved by employing product line models because they foster the following goals:

- The use of reusable components in the construction of new Web systems.
- The identification of product families that share common aspects among them.
- The identification of groups of core requirements that can be applied to a related set of systems.

- The maintenance and development of Web products in a systematic way under a PLA approach.
- The provision of facilities for controlling the evolution of the products and components.

A Lightweight Product Line Model for Web-Based Systems

To reinforce the idea of applying lightweight processes in product line architectures for developing Web systems (Bandinelli, 2001), we employ a product-line model for developing new Web products in a better and faster way fostering the reuse across the entire PLA. We analyzed the following Web sites:

- A university Web portal containing information for several categories of users: students, staff, professors and visitors. The most frequently changing information is stored in databases. Also, a library zone has special features different from the rest of the Web because it is based on a specific library management software called Unicorn. The Web site is built using HTML, JavaScript and PHP as main languages.
- The second Web site belongs to a research information point of a Spanish Regional Government. We analysed only the most frequently changing area, which is an electronic magazine formed by several sections such as editorial, news, and headlines, among others. The Web uses HTML, JavaScript, ASP and MS-Access databases.
- The last Web system on which we proved our lightweight product line is divided in three parts. The first part contains general information about environmental news. The second part is an e-learning system and the third one is an environmental observatory. The system is built using HTML, JavaScript, PHP, Flash and MS-Access databases.

Using this approach under a product line model we can discover commonality and variability issues of Web systems by analyzing the information extracted using simple reverse engineering processes. Other methods try to perform reverse architecting processes (Maccari & Riva, 2002) to recover the architectural descriptions or, like OAR (Options Analysis for Reengineering) (Bergey, O'Brien & Smith, 2001), perform a mining process of the existing assets for a product line or new software architecture.

Our process does something similar but in a more simple and straightforward manner. It uses a *factorization process* that extracts the commonalities and the differences of the assets. This factorization process uses the output of a visual version of the Unix *diff* command to extract differences among the assets and hence tries to derive groups of similar assets. Such groups are later factorized to extract the common and variable parts of the new assets for the product line. The steps of the process are shown in Figure 3.

In step 1, we have studied the different classes of code (e.g., PHP, HTML, JavaScript) and identified which assets would be candidate to be factorized. Then in step 2, we took into account the organization of Web sections and the types of source code inspected before and we compared pairs of files in order to get degrees of similarity between them. A simple metric for this is to measure the lines of code that are common between pairs of assets,

Figure 3: Factorization Process Example (Reverse Engineering Process).

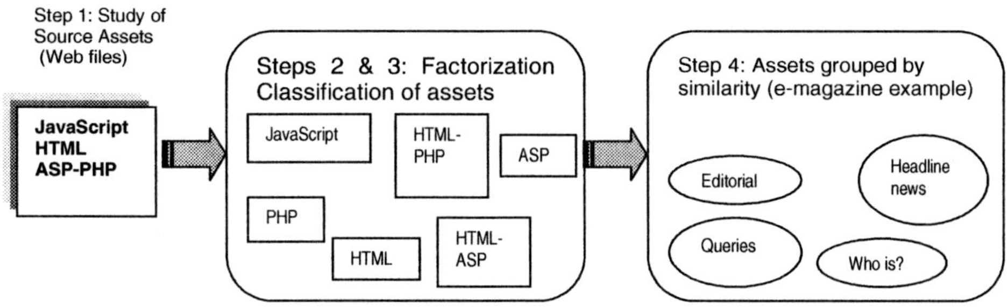

because browsers display Web pages in the same order as they are written. The *diff* UNIX command is an easy way to obtain valuable information in order to compute similarity between files, although there are other widely available tools that can be used for the same purposes.

Afterwards, in step 3, a factorization process separates different parts of code (HTML tables, PHP mail functions or HTML CSS templates, for example) in order to reduce the complexity of the source files. This factorization process is employed to distinguish different types of components that can be used as core in the product line.

Finally, in step 4, we grouped assets that share common structure, code and functionality (examples for the e-magazine Web are the editorial, headlines and queries components). These resulting assets will be engineered under the product line for reuse purposes.

The purpose of the factorization process is to reduce the complexity of the Web files and turn these into core assets of the product line focusing on reuse for the development of new Web products. This straightforward manner saves more time than if we employ other complex techniques such as domain analysis.

A Lightweight Product Line Process

The lightweight product line model for developing new Web products is given in Figure 4.

The first activity is devoted to the *asset analysis*. Instead of a domain analysis and a domain scoping process, we have performed an analysis of the existing assets using a simple and straightforward reverse engineering process by collecting and analyzing a number of representative assets. We have also looked for the functionality of the extracted Web modules.

Afterwards, we factorized the assets by grouping those sharing similar parts of code (*the core asset identification and architectural design*). Then, we identified common modules by its functionality as well as those parts of code able to be reused, looking for its modularity and independence from the rest of the code. For example, many JavaScript functions can be developed, grouped and reused in single files but part of the ASP or PHP code is inevitably part of the HTML source file. After, we have developed a layered architecture to support the development of the core assets needed for building the

Figure 4: Lightweight Product line Model for Developing and Evolving Web sites.

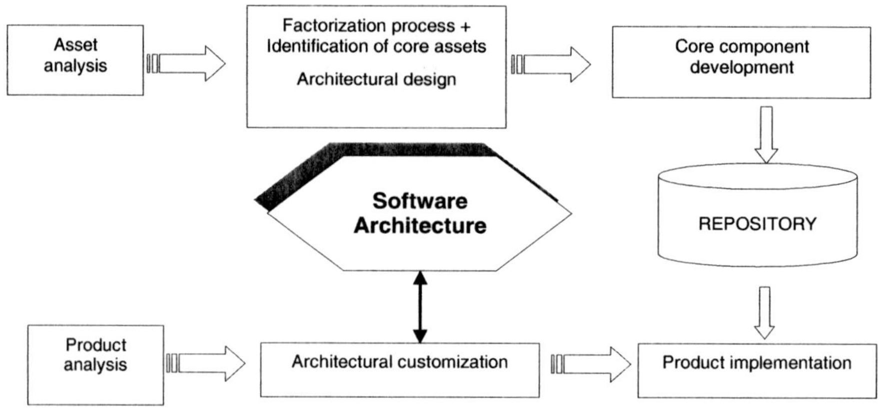

software products. The architecture facilitates the customization of the core components through specific variability mechanisms.

We have then classified and stored the assets identified earlier for reuse (*core component development*). This constitutes the baseline of the product line. Of course, core assets must be maintained to achieve a proper evolution of the product line over time. Core assets can be customized through specific variation points defined at the design level.

In a second phase, *product analysis* is performed: after the infrastructure needed for developing new products is available, we analyze the requirements of the product we want to build. Later, an *architectural customization* process is usually performed for supporting the new requirements specified in the product analysis phase. Sometimes, the architecture fits suitable to the new requirements while the rest of the time a customization process is needed. The depth of the customization changes will depend on the requirements specified in the product analysis.

Finally, in the *product implementation* activity, we have built the product using the customized design and the core assets developed during previous phases. Part of the new product is assembled using the core components and part is obtained developing assets specific for that product. The big picture of the architecture that supports all these processes is shown in Figure 5 (Capilla & Dueñas, 2003).

The lower layer of the architecture provides support for several operating systems and different transport protocols for communicating purposes. The middleware application tier groups some modules that behave as a link between the core components and the databases (e.g., ODBC drivers) or specific extensions to support several Web servers. Finally, and in order to span several Web products (which are shown in the left side of Figure 5 but are not part of the architecture; only represent similar products with variants that can be developed using the same design), the tier that groups the core modules of the product line represents several pieces of code with different functionality. Such code is used to develop the HTML files needed to build different Web products. The core components employed in the construction of these products are, for instance: database

Figure 5: Software Architecture for Supporting a Lightweight Product Line for Developing and Evolving Web-Based Systems.

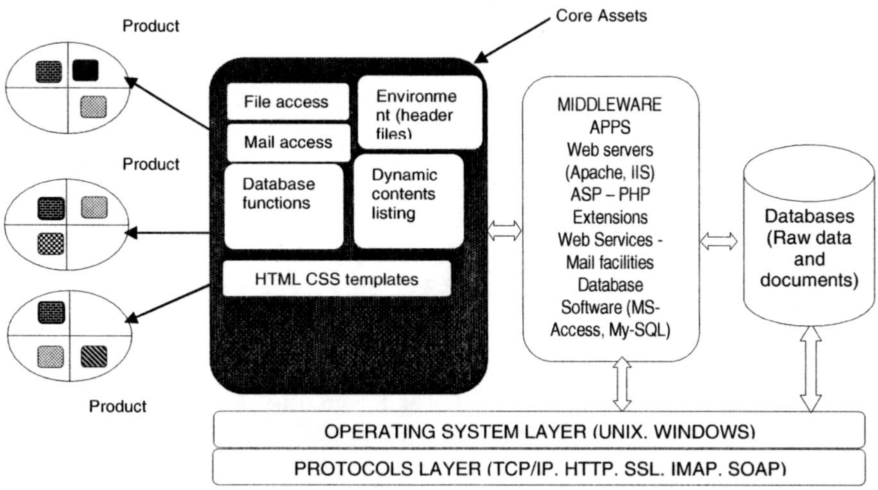

functions (e.g., different databases accessed through PHP code), mail facilities, animated menu options in JavaScript code and more.

The modularity of the architecture constitutes a strong aspect of the design because several products can be built using the same architecture. Even new modules (e.g., those based on XML) can be incorporated into the design with minor changes. Therefore, the software architecture has a strong impact on the system ability to support the development of new products and evolve the existing ones. A more detailed view of the architecture should include the modules and the connectors, but we have preferred to provide a big picture showing only the most relevant parts of the design.

An Experience in Developing Web Systems

The infrastructure explained in the previous sections was used to test the suitability of the model for developing and maintaining several Web site employing the core assets already developed. The commonality and variability analysis performed at the beginning of the product line served to identify several variation points that we classified in the following categories:

- *Markup language variation points:* these variation points refer to different parts of HTML code. An example of this can be the variations of the TABLE element (e.g., rows, columns, border) or those related to the FRAME element.
- *JavaScript functions:* several JS functions for providing dynamism to the HTML code were extracted and classified.
- *Different types of database code:* such as PHP and ASP functions, depending on the type of database selected (e.g., PHP code with My-SQL databases).
- New modules that can be included, such as XML or XSLT files.

Table 1: Code-Based Variation Points of the Examined Assets.

Type of Source Asset	Functionality	Core Asset	Other Assets
JavaScript functions	Menus, Animation	Yes	
ASP code	Dynamic HTML	Yes	
PHP code	Dynamic HTML	Yes	
HTML HEAD	Header definition	Yes	
HTML BODY	Body definition	Yes	
<TABLE>	Table definition	Yes	
<DIV>	Layer definition	Yes	
<TABLE> with ASP		No	
<DIV> with ASP		No	
Database functions	Database	Yes	
Mail functions	E-mail	Yes	
Documents			Word / PDF Documents

Such variation points were represented at design time but they can also be used at the implementation time for customizing both the core assets as well as the Web products before they are delivered. The variation points act as controls in the architecture to support the evolution of existing products or even in the development of new ones. An example of the variation points is shown in Table 1.

The analysis was performed only on a subset of the existing files (e.g., 77 files including header files and ASP files in the second Web site belonging to the e-magazine). From the results obtained, several code patterns were identified and catalogued as code components for building the new core assets as well as other assets for the product line. These assets were stored in a repository for reuse purposes.

Table 1 does not show the specific variants for each variation point. An example of this is shown in Figure 6, in which the PHP database component exhibits several variants and attributes for accessing different databases.

Finally, we provide some measures obtained from the effort used in the development of the third Web site. Figure 7 shows a comparison of the hours spent in the development of an environmental observatory (EO), which represents around the 30% of the third Web site.

First we have developed the 70% of Web product (i.e., the environmental observatory) from scratch and without using any product line approach. This took nearly 230 effort hours. Later we decided to engineer the same product using reusable components built in an informal way. These reusable components were obtained from the experience gained in the development of the e-learning platform, which has several similarities to the environmental observatory. The development of the reusable assets took over 140 effort hours. Afterwards, we have engineered again the environmental observatory, but with taking advantage of such reusable assets. We have spent 120 effort hours building the same product with reuse; thus the effort reduction is evident. Finally, we have built the product using our lightweight product line model. Establishing the PLA took around 130 effort hours and the construction of the core assets under the product line was done in 120 effort hours. At last, the product was engineered in only 66 effort hours. Therefore, we can see a significant reduction in the time employed to engineer the environmental observatory compared to the other two approaches. Of course we have to employ time for setting up the product line and for developing the core assets but as we build more products, the product line will be more profitable.

Figure 6: Example of Variation Points with their Particular Variants, Attributes and Values.

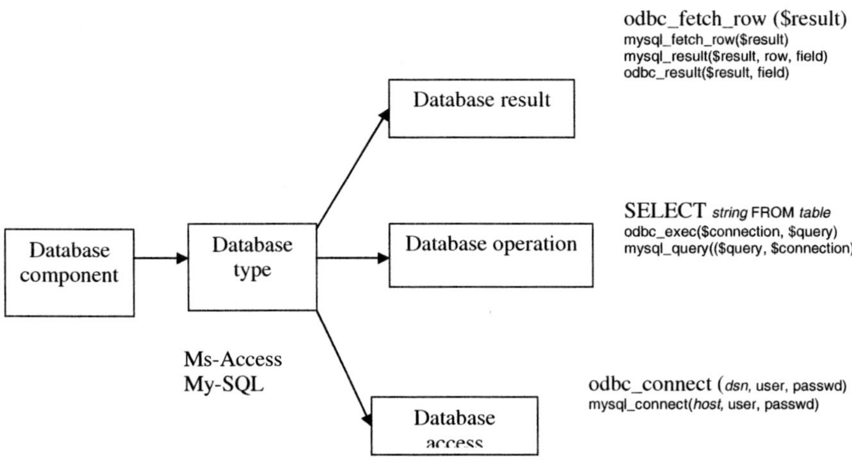

Figure 7: Results from the Development of the Environmental Observatory using the Lightweight Product Line (LW-PLA).

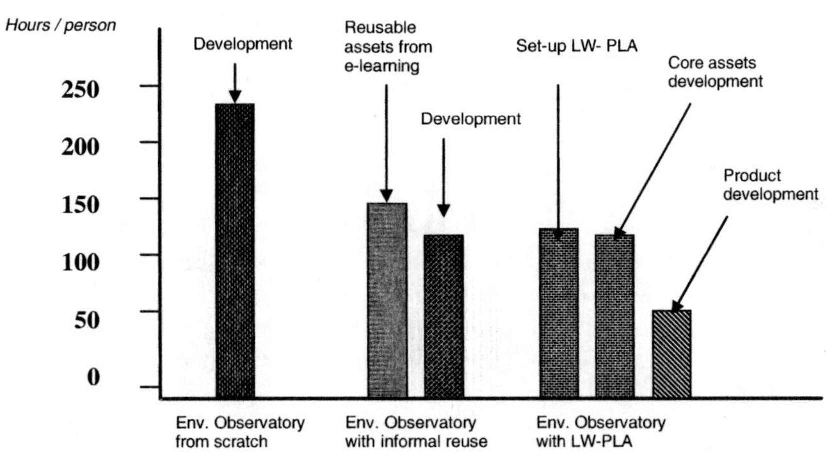

FUTURE TRENDS

Product line architectures constitute a sensible technique that has achieved successful results both in the industry and in the academic arena. Despite this, flexible methods and experience results are needed to expand this software engineering approach. In addition, variability is becoming an important topic in the development of product families rather than single systems. Therefore we need suitable and flexible mechanisms and tools to manage and represent the variability of systems for evolving and maintaining the products in an easy way.

CONCLUSIONS

One of the advantages of using product lines is the reduction of time in the construction of new products, but the goal for a rapid production must be carefully balanced with respect to the quality of the software products. The main idea of the proposed lightweight approach is to reduce the initial investment barrier when introducing system families.

Additionally, not only technical factors are important to success. Organizational and business factors are equally important (Clements, 1997). In this way we have to mention that many of the difficulties found were in convincing the managers to adopt a product line model, because this implies changes in the way in which developers perform their work. The main limitations of the usage of product lines for the evolution of Web products appear in those cases in which new technology needs to be incorporated to a large number of core components, in a way that the current architecture is not able to hold. In the rest of the cases we believe our approach works well even if we increase the complexity of new Web products, because the architecture allows the customization of the core components.

ENDNOTES

(*) The work done by Rafael Capilla has been performed in the Biodiversidad Project, partially funded by the Spanish Ministry of Environment.

(**) The work done by Juan C. Dueñas has been performed in the projects CAFÉ and FAMILIES (Eureka 2023, ITEA ip00004 and ip02009), partially supported by the Spanish company Telvent and by the Spanish Ministry of Science and Technology, under reference TIC2002-10373-E.

REFERENCES

Arango, G. (1991). *Domain analysis: From art to engineering discipline in domain analysis and software systems modeling*, 81-88. IEEE Computer Society Press.

Bandinelli, S. (2001). Light-weight product-family engineering. *4th International Workshop on Software Product-Family Engineering,* European Software Institute, Bilbao (Spain), 327-331.

Bass, L., Clements, P., & Kazman, R. (2003). *Software architecture in practice* (2nd ed.). Reading, MA: Addison-Wesley.

Bayer, J., Flege, O., Knauber, P., Laqua, R., Muthig, D., Schmidt, K., Widen, T., & DeBaud, J.M. (1999). PuLSE: A methodology to develop software product lines. *5th Symposium on Software Reusability*, 122-131. ACM Press.

Bergey, J., O'Brien, L., & Smith, D. (2001). *Option analysis for reengineering (OAR): A method for mining legacy assets* (CMU/SEI-2001-TN-013 Technical Report). Pittsburgh, PA: Carnegie Mellon University, Software Engineering Institute.

Bosch, J. (2000). *Design and use of software architectures.* Reading, MA: Addison-Wesley.

Bosch, J., et al. (2002). Variability issues in software product lines. Software Product-Family Engineering, *Lecture Notes in Computer Science 2290*, Springer-Verlag, 13-21.

Buschmann, F., Meunier, R., Rohnert, H., Sommerlad, P., & Stal, M. (1996). *Pattern-oriented software architecture*. John Wiley & Sons.

Capilla, R., & Dueñas, J.C. (2003). Light-weight product lines for evolution and maintenance of Web sites. *7th IEEE Conference on Software Maintenance and Reengineering,* Benevento, Italy, 53-61.

Clements, P. (1997). Successful product line engineering requires more than reuse. *8th Workshop on Institutionalizing Software Reuse*, Ohio, USA, 63-68.

Clements, P. (2002). On the importance of prduct line scope. Software product-family engineering. *Lecture Notes in Computer Science 2290*, Springer-Verlag, 70-78.

Clements, P., & Northrop, L. (2002). *Software product lines. Practices and patterns.* Reading, MA: Addison-Wesley.

Fey, D., Fajta, R., & Boros, A. (2002). Feature modeling: A meta-model to enhance usability and usefulness, in Second International Conference, SPLC 2, San Diego, CA, USA. *Lecture Notes in Computer Science 2379*, 19-22, Springer Verlag.

Kniesel, G., Constanza, P., & Dmitriev, M. (Eds). (2002). Online proceedings of USE 2002. *First International Workshop on Unanticipated Software Evolution.* Available: *http://joint.org/use/2002/sub*

Krueger, C.W. (2002). Easing the transition to software mass customization. Software product-family engineering. *Lecture Notes in Computer Science 2290*, 282-293. Springer-Verlag.

Lehman, M.M., & Ramil, J.F. (2001). Software evolution. *IWPSE 2001, 2nd Intl. Workshop on the Principles of Software Evolution.*

Linden, F. Van den (2002). Software product families in Europe: The ESAPS & Café Projects. *IEEE Software*, *19*(4), July/August, 41-49.

Maccari, A., & Riva, C. (2002). Architectural evolution of legacy product families. Software product-family engineering. *Lecture Notes in Computer Science 2290*, 64-69. Springer-Verlag.

Martin, J. (1989). *Information engineering: A trilogy*. Englewood Cliffs, NJ: Prentice Hall.

Maymir-Ducharme, F.A. (1996). Product lines, just one of many domain engineering approaches. *A NASA Focus on Software Reuse*.

Mili, A., & Yacoub, S.M. (2001). A comparative analysis of domain engineering methods: A controlled case study. *Proceedings of Software Product Lines, Economics, Architectures and Implications*. Fraunhofer IESE TR-070.00/E.

Ommering, R. (2002). Roadmapping a product population architecture, in software product-family engineering. *Lecture Notes in Computer Science* 2290. Springer-Verlag.

Reifer, D.J. (2000). Web development: Estimating quick-to-market software. *IEEE Software*, *17*(6), 57-64.

Schäfer, W., Prieto-Díaz, R., & Matsumoto, M. (1994). *Software reusability*. Ellis Horwood.

Schmid, K., & Verlage, M. (2002). The economic impact of product line adoption and evolution. *IEEE Software*, *19*(4), July/August, 50-57.

Shaw, M., & Garlan, D. (1996). *Software architecture*. Prentice Hall.

Simos, M., Creps, D., Klinger, C., Levine, L., & Allemang, D. (1996). Organization Domain Modeling (ODM) version 2.0. STARS-VC-A025/001/00.

Weiss, D.M., & Lai, C.T.R. (1999). *Software product-line engineering: A family-based software development process*. Reading, MA: Addison-Wesley.

Chapter XII

Software Maintenance Process Modeling and Analysis

Zeljka Car, University of Zagreb, Croatia

ABSTRACT

The chapter provides the insight into software maintenance process, its features, actors, activities and results, with the emphasis on the importance and complexity of systems maintenance. The issues related to maintenance modeling, maintenance process evaluation and improvement are addressed. The chapter proposes a method for system maintenance modeling and analysis. Software maintenance process is modeled in terms of queuing network with applied simulation. Method implementation is described by a case study of telecommunication maintenance with the field process data. The case study and the related maintenance activities with data are described in detail. The results of the method application show how the process bottlenecks are formally identified and how new proposals for the improved process design should be analyzed. The chapter emphasizes the importance of a well-defined and balanced process indispensable for efficient maintenance of the large telecommunication software.

INTRODUCTION

As information systems become more complex, software organizations are looking for the solutions that outline the improvement of the software process. Process efficiency is laborious to determine and improve. The analysis of any software process requires that it runs over some time. Since introduction of changes into the running process is very risky and expensive, it is essential to develop a valid process model and to perform competent model analysis. It is necessary to determine how the existing process responds to the proposed changes and whether the available infrastructure can fulfill the requirements set by the new process proposals.

Despite availability of the generic models for software maintenance, there is an obvious need for some specific modeling and analytical methods for particular software processes that have a certain level of maturity. These methods should be efficient in analyzing both the existing process in the organizational setting and a new or redesigned process in the same organizational setting (Car & Mikac, 2002). The risks and expenses related to the field experiment need to be reduced in any process improvement. The overall process has to be reviewed and the impact of the changed inputs on its outputs and performance must be measured.

As a possible solution to the mentioned problem of software process evaluation, this chapter introduces the method for modeling and analyzing the performances of the software maintenance process. The method is aimed at improving the maintenance process. It is based on the process model in the form of the queuing networks, and it applies discrete simulation to determine process performances. Simulation is an empowered analytical technique, capable of encompassing complex system interactions and time variant behaviors important to capture. This particular method is easy to implement, and uses the existing historical data about maintenance. It can be employed as a special technique within the given generic model, as a part of an organizational effort to upgrade the process maturity and efficiency. Its implementation allows efficient comparison of the alternative process designs without the risk associated with the experiments in the online process. A detailed description of the method can be found in Car (2001).

The method implementation is demonstrated on a case study of software maintenance in a telecommunication company. A graphical presentation of the maintenance case study is shown in Figure 1. The case study is based on the maintenance activities in a large ISO-certified manufacturing telecommunication company with CMM level 3. This particular domain is chosen since it offers great opportunity for practical employment of the method. The presented quantitative and qualitative process data as well as the results of the process analysis are presented to demonstrate the maintenance process in reality, expressing the process performances, and the relations between different process performances.

The objectives of this chapter are:

- Providing insight into a telecommunication software maintenance process, its features, actors, activities and results, with the emphasis on the importance and complexity of this kind of maintenance.
- Presenting how the process actors recognize in practice what the critical points are and how they adopt process definition to reach business goals.
- Showing how the need for process improvement is recognized.
- Revealing complexity and other problems associated with the maintenance process analysis and improvement.
- Providing a detailed description of the particular method for software maintenance process modeling and analysis based on the simulation, and describing the method implementation for the case study of telecommunication maintenance with the field process data.

Figure 1: Software Maintenance Process of the Telecommunication Case Study.

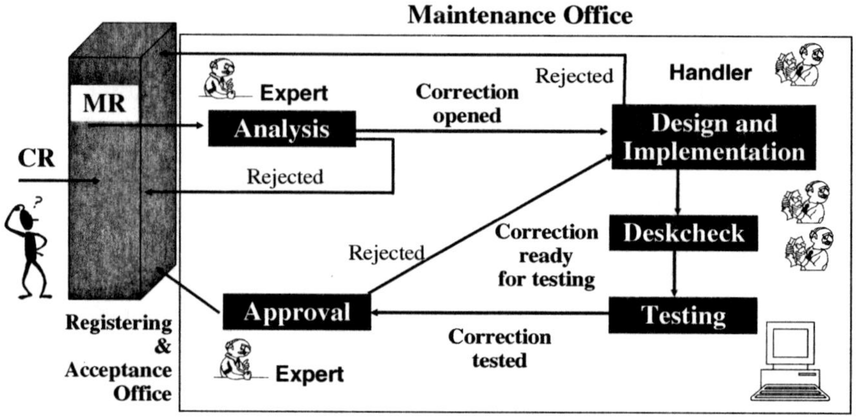

- Showing the results of the process modeling and analysis for the maintenance case study, and describing how the process bottlenecks are formally identified and how new proposals for the improved process design are also analyzed.
- The chapter concludes with a statement about the importance of a well-defined and balanced maintenance, proving that without it there can be no efficient maintenance of the large telecommunication software.

The author believes that the practitioners, researchers and students interested in the software maintenance will benefit from this work. The readers are given the opportunity to see the complexity of software maintenance in telecommunications and the structured technique of analyzing and improving this kind of software maintenance.

TELECOMMUNICATION SOFTWARE MAINTENANCE PROCESS

General Perspective

Maintenance is a complex, resource intensive and costly part of the software life cycle. The lack of control and systematic approach to software development generates problems in software maintenance. The maintenance process describes how to organize maintenance activities. Its focus is on the product correction and adaptation, rather than on mere transformation of requirements upon software functionality. Maintenance is characterized by quality, cost and time parameters.

Telecommunication is one of the most rapidly developing technologies. The evolving architectures impact the hardware, centralized computing, client/server and hybrid architectures. Qualitative improvements in mobility and transmission to long distances resulted in a highly complex communication medium. Telecommunication distributed networks in the heterogeneous environment contain the equipment of different capabilities and generations, operating by different standards. Additional services and service features are introduced, and their number and complexity are extraordinarily increased. Telecommunication systems and services consist of a vast number of very complex software systems. These also comprise many interactions between the people, hardware and software. Other important features of telecommunication systems are their outstanding volume, high complexity, the requirement for high efficiency and reliability, continuous servicing, customer- and market dependency, heterogeneous and distributed environment, longevity, and so forth. Maintenance of telecommunication systems is very complex. Since software in telecommunication is maintained on an ongoing manner, the company must keep providing its services to its end users.

The maintenance process presented in the chapter is a corrective customer-initiated software maintenance for a large telecommunication software product. It is a repetitive process, responsible for identifying and resolving reported software failures. The process runs according to its specification, and can be formally described. The maintainers identify the critical points of the system from its execution. The *critical points* or *bottlenecks* are referred to as the resource or service facilities that seriously limit performance of the entire process. They are created at some resource when the requested traffic to that resource approaches the resource capacity. To reach the defined business goals, the maintainers compile two separate process phases into a new specific process phase. The present research was performed to find out the answers to the following questions: How to evaluate the existing telecommunication software maintenance process, and the proposals for its improvement? Is the scarcity of resources a real problem in the process? How justified is the practice of the process actors to combine different process phases?

Case Study

Corrective maintenance is aimed at resolving customers' problems caused by the program faults that were unintentionally introduced into the code during the development or maintenance of the software product.

The maintenance team is organized in three groups based on their activities: (i) *Registering Office,* which is responsible for accepting *Trouble Reports* from the customers; (ii) *Maintenance Office,* which performs corrective maintenance process; and (iii) *Acceptance Office,* which approves the solutions proposed by *Maintenance Office*. Figure 1 graphically shows the connections between these offices as well as the activity sequence, process actors and correction states important for further analysis. It is a simplified presentation of the SW maintenance case study, explained in detail in the further text.

Maintenance process begins as soon as a customer sends the *Correction Request* (CR) to the *Registering Office* due to the system failure. The correction request can be received in different forms (by phone, e-mail, fax, etc.). The *Registering Office* team writes a *Modification Report* (MR). MR writing, registering and delivery procedures are precisely defined and documented. Each MR, as a minimum mandatory information, has a short description of the problem, defined priority, basic information about hardware version, information about the *application system*, information about the customer, site of the problem, and so forth. Even the suggestion as to how to solve the problem can be included, but this is not mandatory information. There is a specific tool called *Modification Handling System* for the maintenance and customer support functions. It is an administrative system that supports handling of *modification requests* and adequate responses to them (corrections of the faults with answers and explanation). Generally, the customer does not have any direct access to this tool. MR may exist for some time in the *Registering Office*. The *Registering Office* team tries to solve the customer's problem. Most correction requests are not specifically software related. The non-software problems can be solved by supplying the customer with documentation, customer's better training or helping with configuration parameters relevant to a specific problem. If the problem cannot be handled at this instance, MR becomes registered, that is, visible through the *Modification Handling System*. The *Registering Office* assigns the MR one of the three possible priorities: *A*, *B* or *C*, with *A* being the highest priority. Each priority is assigned a deadline to address the problem specified in the MR. The setting of the deadline is mutually agreed upon by the user and the company. After creating the MR, it is forwarded to the *Maintenance Office*.

Each *Maintenance Office* team has an expert and three handlers. In the *Maintenance Office*, MR is directly handled by the expert. The *expert* is a highly experienced maintainer. The expert performs preliminary analysis to find out whether his or her office is responsible for the maintenance of the product causing the reported problem and for proper prioritization. Then, the expert forwards the MR to the handler who also analyses it to find the solution based on the MR's history data. If the handler needs more information, he or she contacts the corresponding person accordingly (usually the MR author). Provided the solution of the problem is found in the database of all previous MRs, the *Modification Request Answer* (MRA) stating *"Already corrected"* is sent to the *Registering Office*. If the additional information is required but not received within the deadline, the MRA is sent back to the Registering Office signifying that the MR contains insufficient information. Should a handler need the team's assistance for a complex problem, the handler presents the problem at the maintenance team meeting or contacts the responsible staff from another department.

To analyze the problem and to find out the solution, it is necessary to reproduce the fault reported in the particular MR at the test-site. Therefore, the handler reserves a test-site for a complex MR. In this particular case study there are two test sites assigned to one maintenance team. If a fault cannot be reproduced at the test-site, the MRA is prepared and sent to the *Registering Office* with the corresponding information. This is the end of the MR life cycle. There are two possible process outcomes: (*i*) if the correction is not necessary, the answer "*No action*" is sent to the *Registering Office;* (*ii*) if some changes in the program code are required, the *Approved Correction* (AC) is prepared. The *Approved Correction* is a software patch that corrects the identified software fault. It is attached to the *Modification Handling System*. Following this, two other team members independently check the correction and add their comments at the phase called *deskcheck*. If possible, the correction is tested either at the maintenance test-site, or the customer's site. During the correction testing, all problems are either discussed with the responsible expert or presented at the meeting, depending on the complexity of the MR.

When the testing is completed the MR reappears on the expert's list in order to be approved. The expert writes down the MR's answer and releases the approved correction. The proposed solution is also approved by the *Acceptance Office,* which contacts the customer. If the customer agrees with the suggested correction, the *Acceptance Office* expert sends it back to the *Maintenance Office* where MR's life cycle closes in MR's database where the approved correction is released. If the customer rejects the proposed solution the MR is sent back again to the *Maintenance Offices* for further analysis, and the whole process is repeated.

METHOD FOR SOFTWARE MAINTENANCE PROCESS MODELING AND ANALYSIS

To improve a particular software process, it is necessary to list all elements potentially relevant for a model, to identify a set of critical parameters and to find the relations for the overall process performance and the parameters. Formal methods used in the analysis of the software process are based on mathematical techniques for modeling and analyzing software process performance. They have sound mathematical bases and can concisely describe the process outcomes. Although there are generic models for software maintenance, there is a practical need in some specific methods for modeling and analyzing current software processes with a certain level of maturity.

This section describes a method for modeling and evaluating the performance of the telecommunication software maintenance. The method is applied in the analysis of the described maintenance case study. The method defines the activities to be undertaken, all assumptions about the process and other conditions necessary for adequate modeling of a particular maintenance. The aim is to introduce the changes into the process design, analyze their impact, and find out optimal solutions for process improvement. The method is based on the modeling of software maintenance in the form of queuing networks. It employs simulation to determine process performance.

Since the majority of maintenance performance problems are related to queuing delays caused by contention for resources, the maintenance model within this approach is based on the queuing network. The queuing network model suggests different ways of software process reconfiguration, for example, change of the activity sequence, recruitment or additional resources. This provides a better survey of the potential process bottlenecks. The analysis is focused on the process performance that can be expressed as the queuing network parameters.

The main idea of the method is described in Figure 2. The existing software maintenance process that is to be analyzed and improved is studied by examining process documentation and historical quantitative data from the process database. These data should be automatically measured during the process operation. Thereafter particular quantitative and qualitative data are collected and the process is modeled as the queuing network. Simulation is applied to obtain process performance. After performance analysis, the structural changes are introduced into the model of the existing process, and a new process design is proposed. The method is iteratively applied to a new process design. The results can support a decision-making process for efficient relocation or change of the software maintenance resources. The method will be illustrated in the following text by explaining the implementation of its activities in the described maintenance case study.

The successful method implementation is assumed as:

- Software maintenance process runs according to its definition and can be formally described;

Figure 2: Idea of Method for Modeling and Analyzing Software Maintenance Process.

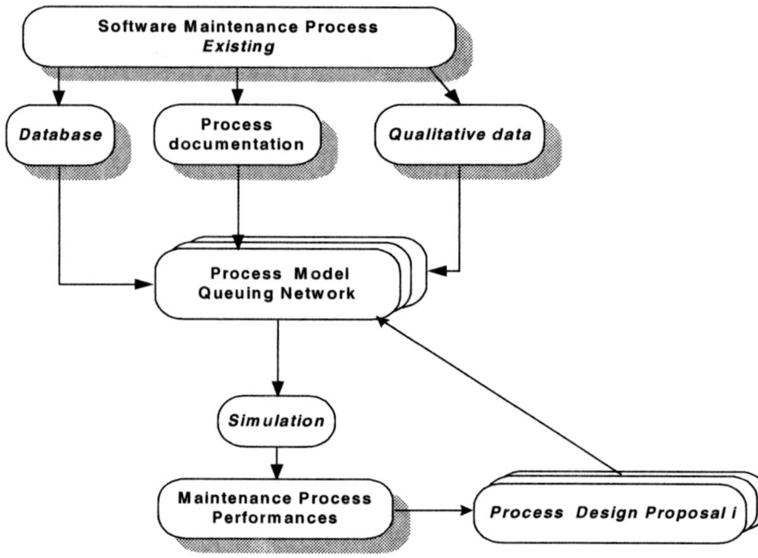

- There are historical quantitative data describing the times of activity at certain process phases automatically measured during the process;
- There is a database containing all user modification requests and data about their life cycle;
- Business goals for successful software maintenance performance and improvement are clearly defined and quantitatively expressed.

The following text describes the activities contained within the method for maintenance process modeling and analysis, classified into three general activity groups: (1) Maintenance Process Knowledge and Data Collection and Analysis; (2) Maintenance Process Modeling and Simulation, and (3) Analysis of Alternative Maintenance Process Designs. Each of these is explained in the following subsections.

Maintenance Process Knowledge, Data Collection and Analysis

The initial activity of a maintenance process is a project definition. A project is defined as an undertaking that requires concerted effort focused on describing, analyzing and improving the existing software maintenance process (Raffo, 1999).

This activity identifies the following issues:

- process phases;
- process actors;
- tools used in the process;
- process inputs and outputs; and
- interfaces to other processes.

The following tasks are included:

1. Acquiring knowledge about the process (studying process documentation, observing process actors, database and other references with relevant information about the process);
2. Defining project goals;
3. Identifying important process time parameters and resources; and
4. Studying the scope definition (the entire process or its particular phase).

Maintenance Process Modeling

The analysis of the maintenance process is made on the basis of the formal process description. *Mapping* is employed to translate real maintenance from the physical layer into the queuing model at the logical layer, as depicted in Figure 3. Mapping denotes finding the correspondence between the process entities and the model elements, and finding an adequate level of the model details. The queuing model is applied since the majority of maintenance problems are related to queuing delays due to scarcity of resources. The queuing theory provides a mathematical framework for formulating such problems.

The unit of the operational flow through the queuing system is called a *customer*. A sequence of customers arrives in a *server;* if the server is busy the customers join the server-associated *queue* and wait. After some time a customer is selected for the service; this rule is known as the *service discipline*. The server then performs the requested service for the customer, and when it is completed, the customer leaves the system. There are many assumptions that can be made about the queuing system elements. Therefore, it is important to point out the issue to be analyzed during modeling of the system after the queuing theory.

Figure 3: Mapping between the Implemented Maintenance Process and Its Queuing Network Model.

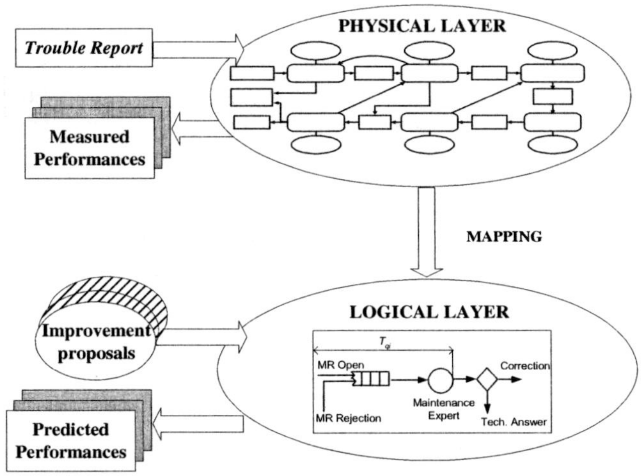

Maintenance modeling must take into account difficulty of performances prediction, since the nature of the interactions is highly nonlinear and non-deterministic. Another important type of interaction exists called *feedback loops* in the process. The increased turnaround time generates more service requests, which in turn causes further increase in the turnaround time. The resulting delays can range from minutes to years.

Modeling of the software maintenance process into the queuing network requires the following steps:

1. *Development of the introductory model:* The software maintenance process is graphically presented with its process phases. The queuing network node is assigned to each process phase. Basic process phases are further decomposed into lower-level activities. Each activity is presented by a separate queuing network node.
2. *Determining the level of detail:* The level of a model's detail is limited by the majority of data for the lowest level activity description.
3. *Final model development:*
   - *Clients* in the queuing network are *modification requests* (MR).
   - *Client source* is identified (Who creates the MR?).
   - *Client destination* is identified. It is one of the possible process outcomes, and answers the following questions: Is there any real action aimed at solving a particular problem? Is any document produced? Is there any answer to the modification request regarding the documentation, users, and so forth?
   - *Queuing network nodes* are the activities performed by a particular process actor at some modification request and at certain process phases.
   - *Servers* are the process actors performing their roles at different process phases.
   - *Queuing network links* are the connections between the nodes defining the flow of customers in the process. They define all possible routes of modification requests in the maintenance process.

The following issues are analyzed:

1. *Arrival process:* The *arrival process* of *maintenance request* is called *general independent arrival process,* since the inter-arrival times between two *request* arrivals are independent. In other words, even if an interval between two arrivals is extraordinarily long or short, distribution of the next inter-arrival time is still unaffected. Also, the inter-arrival times between the two *modification request* arrivals are identically distributed.
2. *Service process:* Despite some theoretical results related to the queuing process feasible through general service distribution, it is practically useful to assume that distribution is of a special type that can be characterized by few parameters.
3. *Service discipline:* Some servers have FIFO - *First In First Out* queuing discipline. Other servers have a priority scheduling procedure according to the assigned *modification request* priorities. Priority queues do not allow a pre-emption, so the service discipline is *non pre-emptive.*
4. *Number of servers*
5. *Server utilization* is a dimensionless quantity, which represents the time fraction of a busy server.

6. *Waiting time* is the average queuing time spent by a customer. *Response time* is the average time spent by a customer in the system. Response time is considered random variables; its distribution, expected value, variance and other similar values can be calculated. Response time can be calculated from the following equation.

The following *quantitative data* are needed (Car, Mikac & Sinkovic, 2002) and should be either extracted from the database or calculated:

- arrival times of the user modification requests at each process phase;
- service times for each process phase;
- modification request priorities;
- response types (determining possible outcomes of maintenance); and
- modification request states and times of state changes.

Qualitative data are presented as words and pictures, rather than numbers. They are collected when some quantitative data are missing and for better explanation of the results of statistical analysis based on the quantitative data. Three qualitative data collection methods are employed within the method: participant observations, interviewing and examining of the process documentation. *Coding* is applied to extract the values for quantitative variables from the qualitative ones (Law & Kelton, 2000). Statistical techniques used within the suggested method determine statistical relationships between the quantitative data: assessment of sample independence, hypothesizing of distribution families and determination of distribution parameters. The details (Law & Kelton, 2000) are left out, since they are beyond the scope of this chapter. Statistical hypothesis tests are applied to formally assess how well the assumed distributions represent a true underlying distribution of the collected data, and to suggest which of the assumed distribution differs the least. Given the lack of some key data, two heuristic approaches are used to select a distribution: triangular approach and beta distribution (Law & Kelton, 2000).

Example

The introductory model was developed by Mikac et al. (1999) for a described case study. It contained the nodes assigned to the Registration Office, expert, handler, test site and Acceptance Office. Basic process phases were decomposed further into the activities. The level of the model detail was limited by availability of the majority data for the highest-level activity description. The final queuing network model of the actual software maintenance is shown in Figure 4 and was obtained by Micro Saint general simulation software package GUI (Micro Saint, 1998). Composite node for modeling "Fault reproduction/Correction testing" is shown in Figure 5.

The customers in the queuing network are the modification requests (MR). The customer source is either the Registration Office or the Maintenance Office itself (a handler creates the MR). The customer destination is one of the possible process outcomes: Technical Answer, Correction, or MR Rejection. An expert has FIFO and handlers have a priority service discipline. A non-preemptive service is assumed. The situation in which the MR has an assigned false priority is modeled as the MR rejection.

Figure 4: Queuing Network Model for Maintenance Process Case Study.

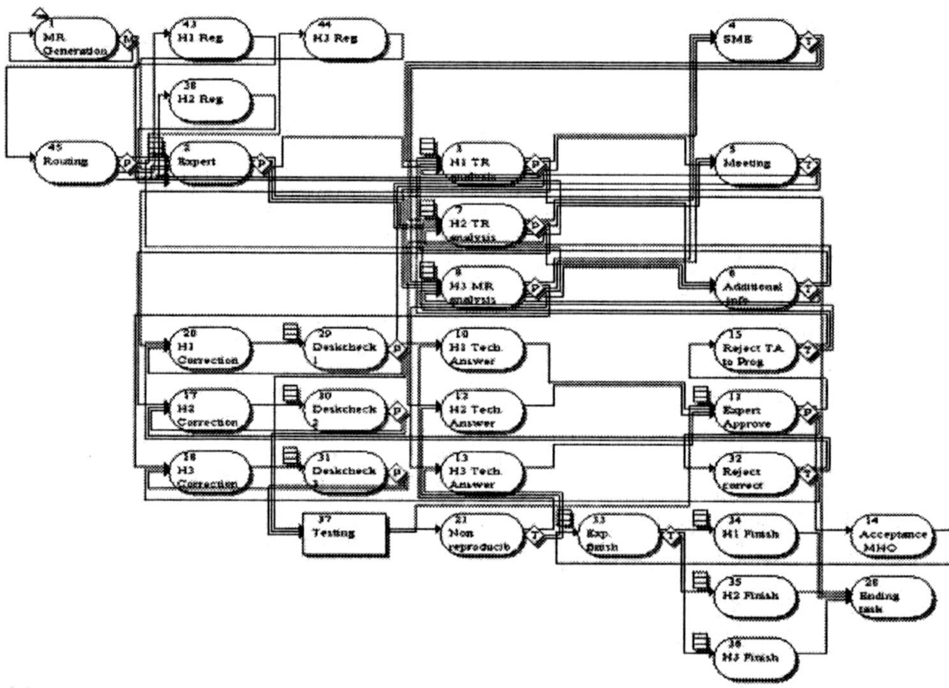

Figure 5: Composite Node Modeling Process Phase "Fault Reproduction/Correction Testing".

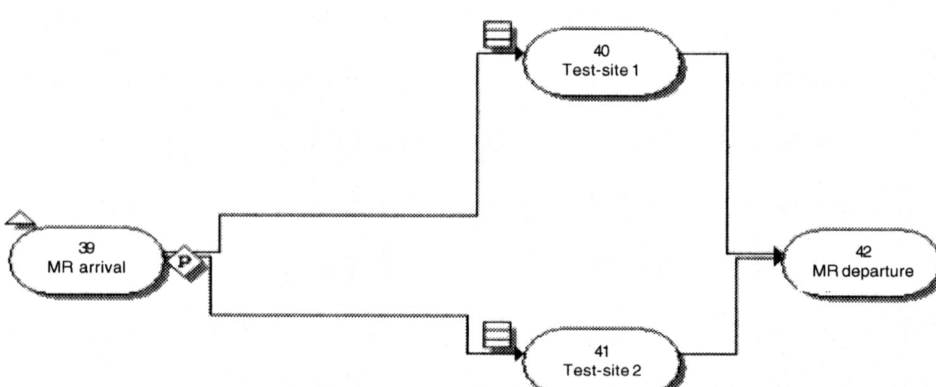

Data about all MRs were collected within 28 months, over which the structure of the Maintenance Office was fairly constant.

The following data were obtained by coding of the collected qualitative data:

1. *Service time in a particular process phase:* Service times were collected qualitatively by interviewing the process actors. The collected data were coded and adequate statistical analysis was performed to obtain quantitative data.
2. *Service times for the fault reproduction and correction testing:* Historical data about the test sites include total time during which a test site was occupied by a particular process actor. Consequently, actual service time needed for testing was obtained by interviewing the process actors and by examining the test site log files.
3. The response times in the activities not registered with the automated process tool (meetings, requesting additional information, etc.)

Queuing Model Simulation

A conceptual process model is now transformed into a *simulation model,* which is a computer model for simulation. Correlations between the maintenance process, queuing network and simulation model are shown in Figure 6.

There are many reasons for simulation of the software process models. Simulation of software maintenance attempts to identify structural relations and addresses the process issues indispensable to support process improvement and management. Discrete simulation is applied in determining process performances, since it is particularly suitable for capturing the well-specified process tasks, queuing and scheduling considerations.

All simulation aspects are presented with variables. Some variables represent process performances, and their values are automatically collected during simulation. The examples are mean response times of *modification requests* in the process or at a specific process phase, average number of *modification requests* in the process or at a specific process phase, and resource utilization (Car & Mikac, 2002). First, the precondition and simulation scenario has to be defined. Simulation scenario is defined by the

Figure 6: Correlation between the Process, Queuing Network and Simulation Model.

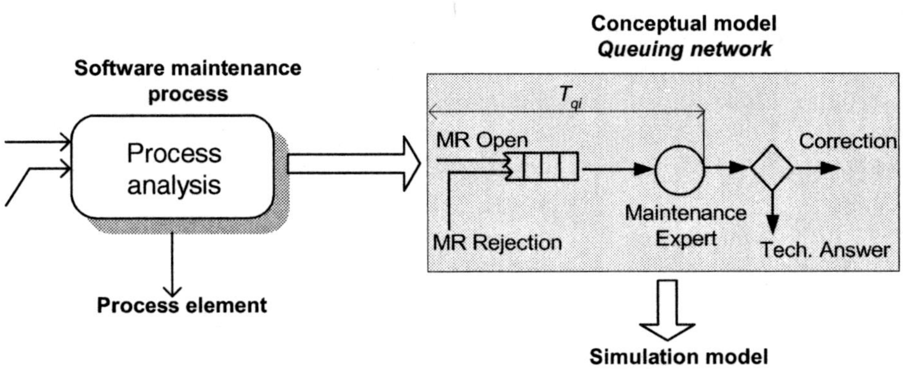

queuing network, input probability distributions and other stochastic parameters. The analysis is focused on the process performances that can be expressed as the queuing network parameters.

The predictable power of simulation depends on how well the simulation model is validated. To do it, simulation results must closely resemble the output data expected from the actual process (Law & Kelton, 2000). The measure of performance used to validate a model should include those that will actually be used for evaluating process designs. Simulation is effective only if the model and its driving data accurately reflect the real process. This assumption requires consistent collection of metric data and gives the guidelines as to what is essential. Since simulation results are merely particular realization of the random variables that may have large variances, they can differ greatly from the corresponding true process performances. Consequently, the conclusions about the process cannot be made on one simulation only. Replication of simulation is defined as a particular independent simulation run, in which each run uses separate sets of different random numbers, the same initial conditions and resets statistical counters (Law & Kelton, 2000). It is very important to apply sufficient number of applications. One way of calculating this number from the process performances is described in the following example.

Simulation parameters that are analyzed are:

- Response times of modification requests in the process;
- Server utilization for each process phase;
- Total utilization of each server;
- Mean waiting time in each queue; and
- Mean number of modification requests in each queue.

Server utilization for a specific process phase is defined as an expected proportion of time during simulation during which the server is busy performing that activity. *Total server utilization* is defined as an expected proportion of time during simulation during which the server is totally busy. It is important to point out that simulation time includes the calendar time within the given time period and non-working hours. For all parameters in each replication, current values are calculated and mean value and variance of all values for a certain parameter are statistically obtained (Car & Mikac, 2002).

In order to correctly interpret simulation results, the context of the existing software maintenance process should be considered. This means that the relation between the obtained process performances, rather than their values, should be analyzed.

One must have in mind that simulation produces stochastic outputs on the basis of stochastic inputs. For correct interpretation of simulation results, performance analysis must be placed in the context of the existing process. Therefore, the obtained parameters, rather than the absolute values, must be viewed from the point of their relation.

Example

Simulation is performed by Micro Saint (1998) simulation software package. Simulation terminates after 20,400 hours of simulation time, which corresponds to the time interval of the collected historical quantitative data. At the moment t = 0 of simulation time, the number of customers in the model is 0, and all servers are available (Car & Mikac, 2002).

For verification and validation of a simulation model the following parameters are used:

- Mean response time of the MR in the process (disregarding priority).
- Mean response time of the MR in the process for priorities A, B, C.
- Total number of the generated MRs during the simulation time.
- Total number of the generated MRs regarding priority.

The response time and actual number of modification requests arriving in the Maintenance Office, which are obtained by statistic analysis of historical data, are shown in Figures 7 and 8.

The technique for statistic analysis of the terminating simulation results suggested within the method is a fixed-sample-size procedure (Law & Kelton, 2000). This defines unbiased point estimator $\bar{X}(n)$ for the mean $\mu = E(X)$, where X is a random variable defined on a particular replication. The approximate number of replications to obtain relative error of γ is given by the following expression :

$$i \geq S^2(n)\left[z_{1-\alpha/2} /(\gamma' \bar{X}(n))\right]^2$$

where $\bar{X}(n)$ is a mean value of the random variable defined on a particular replication, $S^2(n)$ is sample variance of data chosen for the comparison of simulation results and actual process, $z_{1-\alpha/2}$ is a critical point for the standard normal random variable, and $\gamma' = \gamma/(1+\gamma)$ is a relative error. As a basic parameter for calculating the number of replications, mean response time of MRs in the process (disregarding their priority) $\bar{X}(n) = 387.04$ was used (Car & Mikac, 2002). This response time was calculated on the basis of the historical process data. Variance is $S^2(n) = 62.55 \cdot 10^4$, critical point for the standard normal random variable $z_{1-\alpha/2} = z_{0.95} = 1.645$, relative error $\gamma = 0.15$ and confidence level of 90%, $\alpha = 0.1$. The obtained minimal number of replications regarding the above parameters is n = 166. Response times of MRs, disregarding priorities and regarding priorities, obtained by simulation are shown in Figure 7. Total number of MRs in the maintenance process is shown in Figure 8.

Figure 7 shows that the response times obtained by simulation and from the historical data differ very slightly, the largest difference being 15%. Similar acceptable simulation results are obtained for the number of MRs in the process (for all MRs and for MRs with particular priority). Considering that from the total of eight simulation parameters for the comparison of the existing maintenance process with simulation outputs, only one parameter shows considerable deviation, it can be concluded that the described simulation model satisfactorily presents the existing process and is considered valid (Car & Mikac, 2002).

When the first and most important step of model validation is completed, other process performances of interest can be determined. The results of the particular telecommunication process analysis can be expressed qualitatively and quantitatively.

Figure 7: Mean Response Times of Modification Requests Obtained from Historical Data and by Simulation.

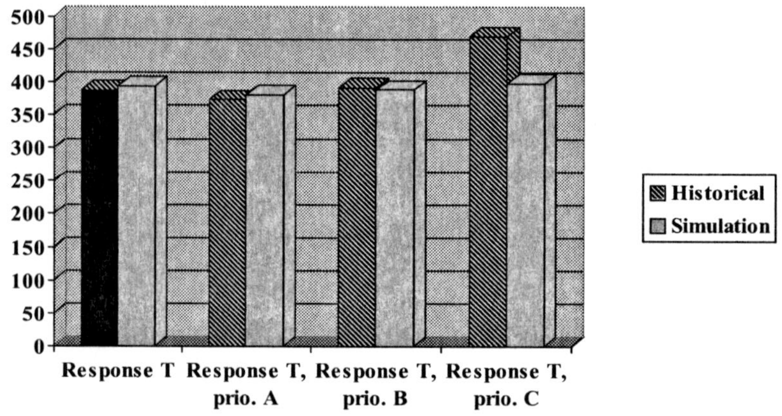

Figure 8. Total Number of MRs in the Maintenance Process Case Study.

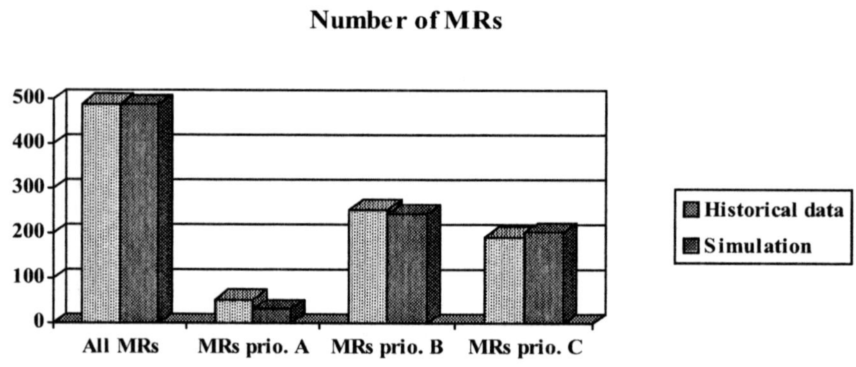

They are obtained by simulation and by the analysis of the collected quantitative and qualitative data.

Qualitative Results

The analysis shows that the company has a well-balanced performance in all process areas. Generally, the purpose of the process has been achieved. The origin of MR is twofold — outside the customer and developers of the company. All MRs are handled in the same way, except the original information is relevant. According to the process metrics, the MRs with priority B influence most MRs' distributions within the given goals. Most activities are performed sequentially, since they are dependent; for example, the successive action needs the information gathered during its preceding activity.

Basic driving factors of the process for the described maintenance are: maintenance quality, answering time and process costs. Maintenance quality is constantly monitored from the customer's point of view. The approved corrections quality is of supreme importance for the company. Goal value for the Approved Correction quality is set to the limit value, meaning that only a limited percent of all released corrections may be faulty. The emphasis is on the preventive actions, that is, expert inspection, team desk check, extensive use of Simulation Test Environment and employment of Test Configuration Management methods. Regression testing is applied to avoid the faulty interfaces. The described procedure can assure high quality of delivered corrections. However, deficiencies are still possible due to inadequate testing environments or complex interfaces. Answering performance is continuously monitored. When it degrades, preventive actions are taken. These are acquiring new maintenance staff or excessive training of the maintenance team.

During the research, some of the problems in the existing maintenance were recognized:

- Abundance of interfaces between different offices performing maintenances;
- Lack of overall responsibility for the whole MR life cycle;
- MR can exist for quite a while, both on someone's desk or registered in the maintenance administrative system before being taken into the procedure;
- Continuously growing product set, obtaining insufficient information from the customer; and
- MR can be routed to several different Maintenance Offices before being processed.

Quantitative Results

From the process organization point of view, the obtained results of quantitative analysis are important to resolve the relations between the process actors. For instance, the relationship between the expert and handler utilization factors suggests conceivable altering of the number of programmers under the expert responsibility within Maintenance Office. It is important to point out that simulation time includes the calendar time within the given period and non-working hours. Servers' utilization factors are shown in Table 1 and Figure 9.

Table 1: Utilizations Factors for Expert and Handlers in each Process Phase.

Process phase	Expert	Handler	Node index in the simulation model (Figure 4)	
MR analysis	0.89	0.23	(2)	(3, 7, 8)
Writing Technical Answer	-	0.08	-	(3, 7, 8)
Reproduction/Testing	-	0.45	-	(37)
Writing correction	-	0.13	-	(17, 18, 20)
Deskcheck	-	0.09	-	(29, 30, 31)
Approval	0.05	-	(11)	-
MR Finishing	0.05	0.01	(33)	(34, 35, 36)
Office Meetings	0.01	0.01	(5)	(5)

Figure 9: Total Utilization Factor for the Expert and Handler.

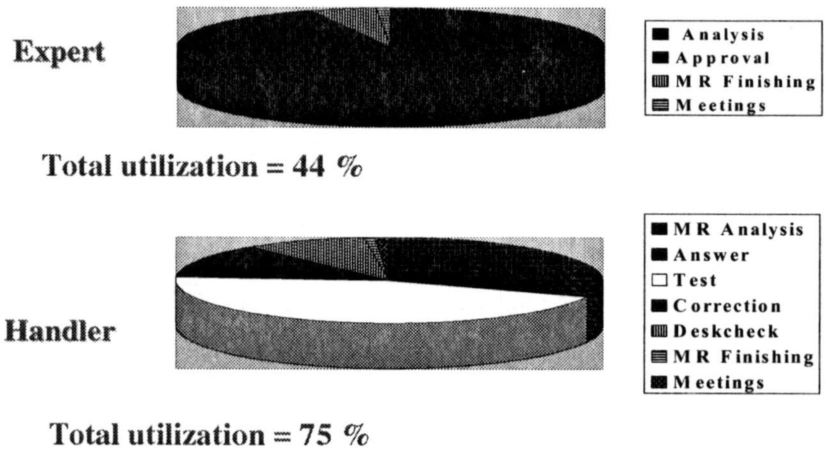

The software maintenance simulation model assumes that an expert performs only those activities defined within the maintenance process. In practice, an expert usually performs the activities that the handlers do (writing corrections, testing and desk checking), so that the actual utilization is well above the stated 44%. The time for completion of some process phases are very short, which explains low handler utilization in these activities. According to the simulation results, a handler spends most of the time reproducing the faults and testing the corrections (Car & Mikac, 2002).

This analysis is also capable of determining other process performances. Some of them are queue parameters that can be practically employed for efficient use of the process resources. Too short queues indicate low resource utilization, and long queues indicate congestion of a resource and process bottlenecks. Accordingly, queue parameters analysis can support organizational efforts in optimizing utilization of the software maintenance resources. The analysis confirms that the test sites, which are limited resources, are the process critical points of the process. Simulation results for queue parameters are shown in Table 2.

Table 2: Comparison of Queue Parameters in each Process Phase for Different Process Designs.

Parameter	**Queue length**			**Waiting time [h]**		
Process phase	**Existing**	**Design 2**	**Design 3**	**Existing**	**Design 2**	**Design 3**
[1] Expert analysis	0.34	13.89	0.33	0.34	13.89	12.83
Handler analysis	0.08	5.78	0.09	0.08	5.78	6.98
Deskcheck	0.23	18.4	0.29	0.23	18.4	22.59
Testing	0.99	53.33	0.65	0.99	53.33	31.67
Expert approval	0.68	11.60	0.73	0.68	11.60	8.68
Expert finishing	0.25	10.75	0.18	0.25	10.75	8.21
Handler finishing	0.06	7.40	0.06	0.06	7.40	8.00

Figure 10: Obtaining the Alternative Process Designs.

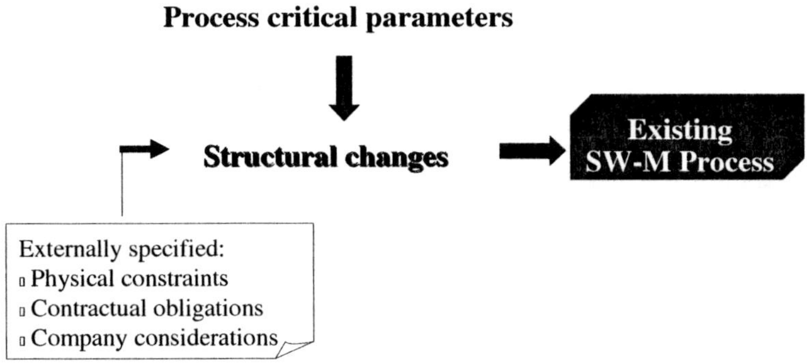

Analysis of the Alternative Maintenance Process Designs

New process designs require change of various model parameters and observing of the effect on the process parameters. *Given alternative process designs* are suggested by examining process critical parameters and by introducing some changes into the process that are externally specified and based on the physical constraints, contractual obligations or company considerations (see Figure 10). When the changes to a process are proposed, the experience is likely to be of major influence. Since the software maintenance process is a result of many interactions and includes complex human activity, there is no control over some parameters, such as the rate of service performed by the process actors. Other process issues, like the number of staff, amount of resources or activity sequence, can be changed if aimed at process improvement.

Different process design performances are compared using appropriate statistical techniques. *Welch approach* is used to form several confidence intervals, each interval referring to the difference between two values of the same performance. An individual level of each interval must be adjusted so that the overall confidence level resembles the desired one. Each interval must have the confidence level $1-\alpha/(k-1)$ and each interval is referred to as the difference between performance expectations $\mu_2-\mu_1, \mu_3-\mu_{1,\dots,}\mu_k-\mu_1$. With the confidence level of at least $1-\alpha$ particular process designs can significantly differ if the interval $\mu_i-\mu_1$ misses zero value (Law & Kelton, 2000).

Example

In order to reach business goals, and by recognizing from the process operation that the test sites needed for fault reproduction and correction testing are the critical points, the process actors in the software maintenance case study join the phases "Fault Reproduction" and "Correction Testing". This means that each handler adopts the process definition in the following way: if testing is needed to analyze the problem and reproduce the fault, the handler has to reserve one test site. Then, the handler partially solves the MR and keeps it idle in his or her list. While waiting for his or her turn for the test site, the handler takes a new MR and also partially solves it. By the time the test site is available for a particular handler, the handler performs fault reproduction and correction testing of several partially solved MRs. Actually, the handler adopts the process definition by combining process phases of fault reproduction and correction testing in

Figure 11: Introducing an Additional Test site into the Process Model.

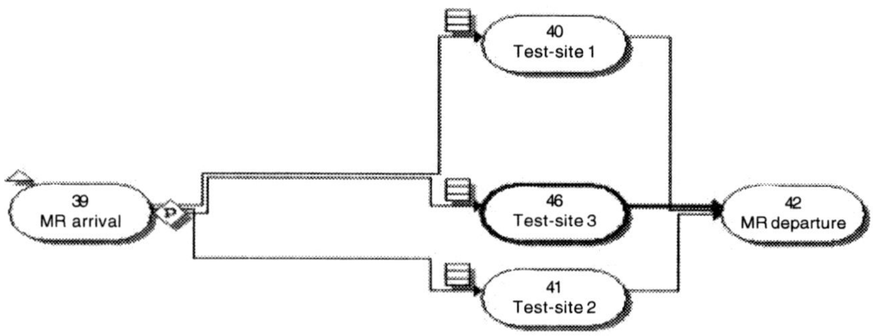

one process phase. The remaining process phases are performed as stated in the process definition.

The field maintenance process is a starting point for the analysis. Consequently, maintenance process design according to the definition, with clearly distinguished phases of the fault reproduction and correction testing, is considered as the alternative. Therefore, two alternative designs were evaluated for the software maintenance case study (Car & Mikac, 2002). Simulation was performed under the same conditions as the existing process and the number of replications was n = 166 for both new designs. It was assumed that the input probability distributions were equal to those in the existing process model. Some of the obtained simulation parameters are shown in Figures 14 and 15.

Alternative Design 1: Increasing the Number of Test Sites

An additional test site is introduced into the process model. Queuing network topology is preserved and the only difference is in the composite node for modeling of testing activity (Figure 11).

Introduction of an additional test site in the process reduced the response times of MRs by about 20%. Queue length for the process phase "Fault reproduction/Correction testing" was reduced by 70% and waiting time by 60% in comparison with the existing process. The activities preceding testing had insignificant changes in the parameters and some activities following testing had very moderate changes of queue parameters because of different distribution rate of MRs after testing (Car & Mikac, 2002).

Alternative Design 2: Separation of Reproduction and Testing Activities

The existing maintenance process has the same node for modeling fault reproduction and correction testing. For the analysis of the process modifications related to these activities, a new process design is assumed in which reproduction and testing are modeled as the separate nodes (see Figure 12). Composite node for fault reproduction and correction testing is shown in Figure 13.

Performances of this alternative process design do not differ significantly from those of the existing process. The response times are increased by 2-4% (see Figure 14). Queue lengths remain the same for most of the process phases. This process design introduces two new queues for testing (instead of one, as in the existing process) and

Figure 12: Process Design with Separated Phases of Testing and Reproduction.

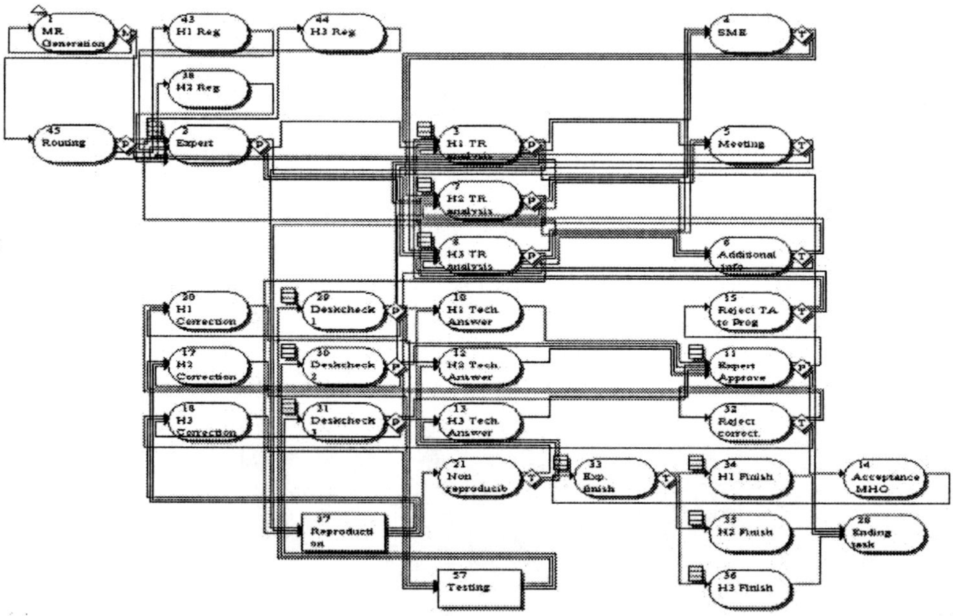

the queue for testing activities is long since this design requires that all handlers have twice as many test sites. Although mean waiting time obtained on the basis of the waiting times in both testing activities is approximately equivalent to the waiting time in the existing process, this alternative design introduces more feedback loops in the process, which prolongs response times (Car & Mikac, 2002).

In order to determine whether there is a significant difference in the process parameters between the existing and new process designs (or if the difference arises from the simulation's stochastic nature), a calculation technique for the Welch confidence

Figure 13: Composite Node for "Fault Reproduction" and "Correction Testing" Phases.

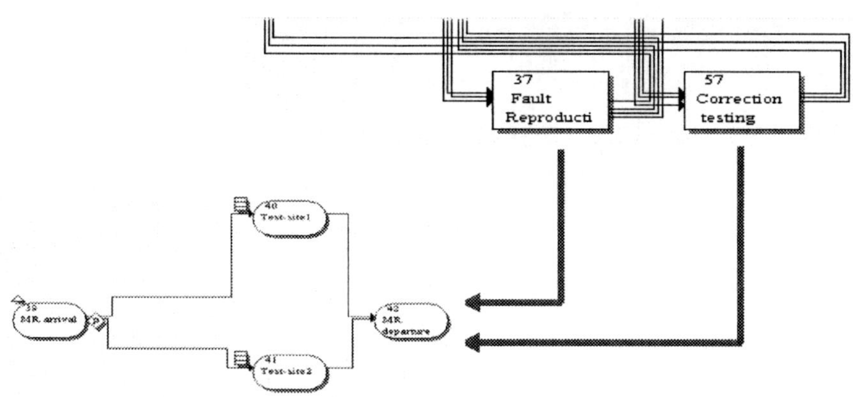

interval is applied. Each confidence interval is referred to as the difference of performances' queue lengths and waiting time for each process design. The results show that both alternative process designs significantly differ at testing phase, while the process performances for other process phases do not show significant differences (Car & Mikac, 2002).

Finally, the following can be concluded: introduction of an additional test site improves the overall process performances, especially those related to queue length and waiting time in the testing activity. The results for process design with separated testing and reproduction evidence deteriorating queue parameters. This justifies the process actor practice of joining activities "Fault reproduction" and "Correction testing".

Figure 14: Response Times for the Existing and Alternative Process Designs.

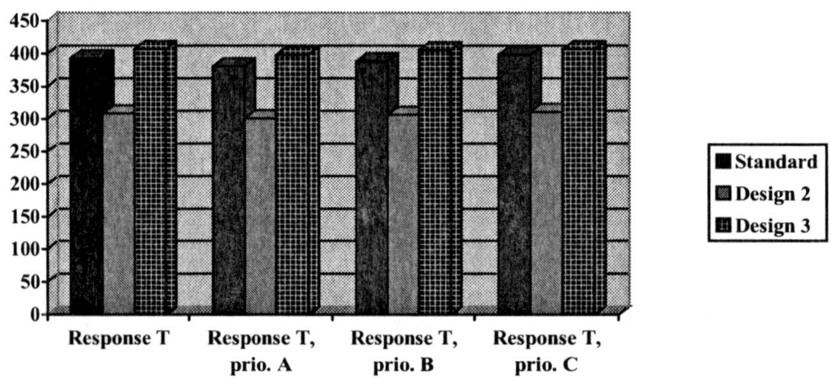

Figure 15: Waiting Times in Different Process Phases for the Existing and Alternative Process Designs.

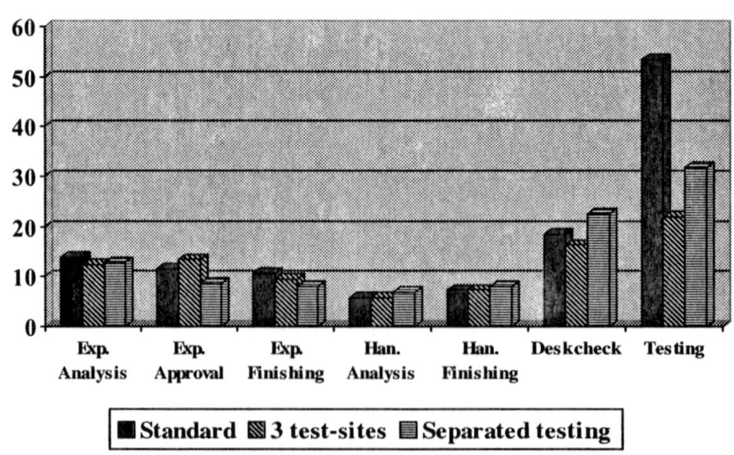

Other proposals for the process improvement that could be analyzed lead to the increase of maintenance staff and efficient rapid provision of test environment for small maintenance projects.

CONCLUSIONS

The analysis and improvement of software maintenance are complex tasks because of numerous interactions with other software processes and feedback loops within the actual maintenance process. In order to formally describe the process and determine its performances, it is necessary to observe its behavior over time and to perform the experiments. New proposals for the process design should be also analyzed.

Without a well-defined and balanced process, the efficient maintenance of the large telecommunication software is not possible. The importance of a successfully implemented process is in the complexity of the software system, and a large number of customers, developers and maintainers.

Formal description of software process is important for its better understanding and for its complete and consistent description. From the process organization point of view, simulation results are important in the sense that they resolve the relations between the process actors and support decision-making in the efficient reorganization of software process resources. This chapter presents a method for modeling and evaluating software maintenance performances. The method has been verified in the case study with software maintenance in the telecommunications company and through the examples in which the method was implemented in the maintenance case study. This provides a reader with the idea of systematic approach for maintenance analysis and improvement.

REFERENCES

Car, Z. (2001, October). *Modeling of telecommunication software maintenance process.* Ph.D. dissertation, University of Zagreb, Croatia.

Car, Z., & Mikac, B. (2002). A method for modeling and evaluating software maintenance process. *Proceedings of the 6th European Conference on Software Maintenance and Reengineering*, Budapest, Hungary, 15-24.

Car, Z., Mikac, B., & Sinkovic, V. (2000). Queuing model of the maintenance process case study. *Proceedings of the Asia Pacific Software Process Group and International Software Development and Management Conference,* Hong Kong, 302-311.

Car, Z., Mikac, B., & Sinkovic, V. (2002). A simulation method for telecommunication software maintenance process. *Proceedings of the 20th IASTED International Conference Applied Informatics AI 2002,* Innsbruck, Austria, 69-74.

Law, A.M., & Kelton, W.D. (2000). *Simulation modeling and analysis.* McGraw-Hill Inc.

Micro Saint. (1998). *User's manual.* UK: Micro Analysis & Design Simulation Software Inc., UK.

Mikac, B., Lovrek, I., Sinkovic, V., Car, Z., Pehar, H., Podnar, I., Caric, A., Burilovic, A., Naglic, H., & Viskic-Huljenic, T. (1999). Assessing the process of telecommunications software maintenance. *Proceedings of the Combined 10th European Soft-*

ware Control and Metrics Conference and 2nd SCOPE Conference, Herstmonceux, 267-275.

Raffo, D.M., Vandeville, J.V., & Martin, R.H. (1999). Software process simulation to achieve higher CMM levels. *Journal of Systems and Software*, *46*(2/3).

Chapter XIII

Evolving Legacy Systems Towards E-Business

Lerina Aversano, RCOST – University of Sannio, Italy

Raffaele Esposito, RCOST – University of Sannio, Italy

Teresa Mallardo, RCOST – University of Sannio, Italy

Maria Tortorella, RCOST – University of Sannio, Italy

ABSTRACT

In e-business, addressing the technical issues alone is not enough to drive the evolution of existing legacy applications, but it is necessary to consider problems concerning the strict relationship that exists between the evolution of the legacy system and the evolution of the e-business process. To fulfill this purpose, this chapter proposes a strategy for extracting the requirements for a legacy system evolution from the requirements of the e-business process evolution. The strategy includes a toolkit composed of a set of decision tables and a measurement framework, both referring to the organization, business processes, and legacy software systems. The decision tables allow the identification of the processes to be evolved, the actions to be performed on them and their activities, and the strategies to be adopted for evolving the information systems. The measurement framework aims at achieving a greater understanding of the processes and related problems, taking into account organizational and technological issues.

INTRODUCTION

In the past, development and maintenance of monolithic applications were carried out with relatively few tools, and integration problems were less relevant. Today, technology continuously changes with innovative development environments, new communication platforms, and new architectural solutions, and so an enterprise cannot ignore the need for renovation of its information systems (Sneed, 2000). The renovation process has to consider the existence of legacy applications that need to be integrated with new applications, and evolved toward innovative technologies (Berztiss, 2001; Steven et al., 2002).

Fast change of business requirements encourages enterprises to evolve their business processes and organizations by considering the future of the legacy systems. The evolution requirements for business processes and legacy systems reciprocally influence each other and, therefore, these have to be analyzed and considered together. When an enterprise addresses organizational issues, business processes, and supporting software applications, it then can successfully transform its legacy systems.

The joint usage of Business Process Reengineering (BPR) (Hammer & Champy, 1993; Jacobson et al., 1995), and legacy system evolution approaches should provide a comprehensive means for transformation by recovering the experience, expertise, and knowledge contained in the processes and legacy systems, and converting them into an effective evolution strategy. BPR approaches involve the business process evolution in terms of fundamental rethinking and radical redesign of an enterprise's business practices and processes to maximize value by creating activities (Hammer & Champy, 1993); while legacy system evolution approaches assess the enterprise's systems and develop a conversion strategy consistent with the enterprise's future business objectives and technology strategies. In this chapter, a strategy is proposed that combines needs and goals of organizational improvement, business processes and legacy system evolution activities.

The strategy specifically targets the evolution of legacy systems by considering business assets coming from the analysis and assessment of the organization and business processes. It can be used to identify suitable business and technological solutions and evolution strategies to meet emerging business needs. The final goal is to analyze an existing operational information system embedded in the organization and business processes to be evolved, and recommend the best combination of strategic alternatives for each legacy component. The strategy takes into account the following three aspects:

- *Business.* To analyze whether the technology is properly applied for accomplishing the business needs, redesigning the business processes to satisfy the new business goals, and identifying the legacy information systems that should be changed to accommodate new business functionalities. These aspects have an impact on business performance by introducing meaningful improvements in productivity, speed, and quality.
- *Technology.* To identify the innovative technology that needs to be considered in the evolution of business towards e-business and in the future environment of the legacy applications. The technological aspects together with the business process evolution allow for linking of the legacy system evolution activities to the business objectives.
- *Legacy Software System.* To assess the software system and identify the requirements for evolving the legacy software components in order to exploit the new technologies and meet the business process evolution requirements. The assess-

ment results are used for defining an adequate evolution strategy for evolving the legacy system.

To analyze these three aspects, the proposed strategy introduces a toolkit aimed at providing software engineers and assessors with useful guidelines to identify the processes to be reengineered, the objects to be analyzed and evaluated, the necessary measurements to be performed, and the manner in which the collected information can be synthesized to achieve the reengineering objectives. The toolkit is composed of a set of decision tables and a measurement framework, both referring to the organization, business processes, and legacy information systems. The decision tables allow the identification of the processes to be evolved, the actions to be performed on them and their activities, and the strategies to be adopted for evolving the information systems. The creation of such tables requires the assessment of the organization, business processes and supporting information systems. They guide the choice of the actions to be performed on the basis of the obtained assessment results. With this in mind, the toolkit contains a measurement framework to be used for both quantitative and qualitative assessment. The goal of the measurement framework is to achieve a greater understanding of the processes and related problems, taking into account organizational and technological issues.

A wide variety of metrics can be identified, and consequent approaches to collect them can be defined. Metrics can be used at all stages of the reengineering activities and can be formulated at various levels of abstraction. For example, high-level metrics can be useful to evaluate the enterprise and ensure that the goals of business processes are consistent with the enterprise mission. Low-level metrics are required to describe the efficiency of the processes and supporting software systems.

The measurement framework proposed in the toolkit is defined on the basis of the Goal-Question-Metrics, GQM, paradigm (Basili & Weiss, 1984), and refers to the three cited levels: Organization, Process and Software System. The next section describes some related work. The third section describes the proposed strategy and the interaction of the organization, process and system levels. It also includes two subsections presenting the toolkit tables and measurement framework used for transforming the organizational goals into terms of requirements and strategies for evolving business processes and information systems. A case study is used to demonstrate how the strategy can be applied. Concluding remarks are given in the final section.

RELATED WORK

Some research activities focus on the relationships that exist between business processes and information systems during their evolution. In Kelly et al. (1999), the authors underline the importance of information technology in moving towards a process-oriented view of management. They argue that in addition to other factors that influence the outcome of BPR projects, such as top management support and project management, legacy information systems have a critical impact on BPR projects. Moreover, they present a framework for understanding BPR, which is based on a study of twelve European organizations from a cross-section of industries dealing with BPR projects. From their experiment they found that the outcomes of BPR strategies are influenced by the state of the legacy information systems.

The paper (Bernd & Clifford, 1992) suggests an integral view of business process reengineering based on both strategic and technological needs at the operational level.

It is widely documented in literature (Sneed, 1995, 1999; Brodie & Stonebaker, 1995) that migrating a legacy system towards a new networked platform entails costs and risks

Table 1: Approaches for Evolving a Legacy System.

Reverse Engineering	It involves extracting the business rules from the source code and transitioning into the new application development environment. From this environment, the system can be regenerated and maintained at the specifications level. Reverse engineering may be done in conjunction with any of the reengineering activities. Reverse engineering consists of Data Reverse Engineering and Process Reverse Engineering (Rishe, 1992; Beck & Eichmann, 1993; Deng et al., 2001; Biggerstaff et al., 1994).
Data Reverse Engineering	The Data Reverse Engineering involves extracting high-level data relationships from existing data structures or program source code (Rishe, 1992).
Process Reverse Engineering	Process Reverse Engineering consists of extracting higher-level specifications, such as data flow diagrams, action diagrams, and structure charts, from program source code (Hammer & Champy, 1993; Jacobson et al., 1995).
Redocumentation.	It entails the understanding of the software and its recording in documents, and, therefore, simplifying the future program comprehension (Basili & Mills, 1982; Wong et al., 1995, January; Fletton & Munroe, 1988).
Design Recovery	It involves the examination of legacy code in order to reconstruct design decisions taken by the original implementers. Artefacts in both the source code and in executable images need to be examined and analyzed (Rugaber et al., 1990; Elliot et al., 1990).
Security Management	It entails the deploying of security management policy.
Reformatting	It involves indenting and aligning program key words, data element names, and data attributes following defined programming standards (Cowan et al., 1994; Oman & Cook, 1990).
Control Restructuring	It involves converting unstructured code into functionally equivalent structured code. This enhances code maintainability, creates logic flows that are easier to be followed, creates programs that are easily understood, and removes recursive code. All these results favour reduced maintenance and enhancement costs (Ammarguellat, 1992; Williams & Ossher, 1978; Ramshaw, 1988).
Data Restructuring	It transfers data from one form or structure to another. This involves designing or creating the new data structure, and then converting the data to the new data structure (Behm et al., 1997; Chiang et al., 1994, March; Hainaut, 1991; Rishe, 1992).
Modularization	It improves program reliability by breaking complex multifunction programs into simpler single-function programs. This decomposition reduces module complexity, making the logic flow easier to follow and reducing the likelihood of a negative impact by module modifications (Darwen & Yao, 1997; Yadav, 1990).
Data Migration	It entails the migration of data from one kind of database to another kind. This usually requires converting the data into some common format that can be output from the old database and input into the new one (Wu et al., 1997, October; Boehm et al., 1997).
User Interface Migration	It involves the re-engineering of user interfaces, the migration from PCs or mainframes to workstations, which requires a change to an industry standard graphical user interface (Claßen et al., 1997; Csaba, 1997; Merlo et al., 1993, May; Moore & Rugaber, 1993).
Language Migration	It translates a software program from one programming language into another programming language (Dershowitz & Jouannaud, 1990; Cifuentes et al., 1998).
Platform Migration	It entails the migration of the entire software system from one platform to another (Brodie & Stonebraker, 1995; Richardson et al., 1997).
Architecture Migration	It involves the transformation of the architecture of a software system. Typical examples include the migration of a procedural system toward an object-oriented architecture, or the migration from a monolithical system toward distributed client server architectures (Brodie & Stonebraker, 1995; Richardson et al., 1997).
Reengineering	It entails the analysis of the legacy systems to understand the current architecture and develop a strategy for mining and reusing existing assets. Mining involves rehabilitating parts of an old system for use in a new system (Rishe, 1992; Beck & Eichmann, 1993; Deng et al., 2001; Biggerstaff et al., 1994).
Redevelopment	It involves a rewrite of the system or parts of the system by using the new application development environment. Redevelopment may be done in conjunction with any of the other reengineering activities.
Encapsulation	It entails the definition and implementation of a software interface that allows the access to the system, and its subsystems, from other applications (Brodie & Stonebraker, 1995; Richardson et al., 1997).

that depend on the characteristics of both source system architecture and target platform. There are a number of options available in managing legacy systems. Typical solutions may include: discarding it and building a replacement system; freezing the system and using it as a component of a new larger system; and modifying the system in order to continue to use it. Modifications may range from a simplification of the system (reduction of size and complexity) to preventive maintenance (redocumentation, restructuring, and reengineering) or even to extraordinary processes of adaptive maintenance (interface modification, wrapping, and migration) (Canfora & Cimitile, 1997; Pigoski, 1997; De Lucia et al., 2001). Table 1 lists the main alternative approaches proposed in literature. These alternatives are not mutually exclusive and the decision on which approach or combination of approaches is the most suitable for any particular legacy systems must be made based on an assessment of its technical and business value.

Apart from identifying possible alternatives for dealing with legacy systems, several authors have proposed decision frameworks to select among the alternatives. Bennett et al. (1999) identify six strategies to deal with a legacy system: discard, wrap, outsource, freeze, carry on with maintenance and support, and reverse engineering. They stress the need to model the business strategy of an organization from a top-down perspective to make informed decisions regarding legacy systems. They introduce a two-phase model called SABA, Software As a Business Asset, which uses an organizational scenario tool to generate scenarios for the organization's future and a technology scenario tool to produce a prioritized set of solutions for the legacy system. Prioritization of solutions is achieved by comparing the current (legacy) system with the systems required by each generated scenario.

Sneed (1995) suggests that five steps should be considered when planning a re-engineering project: *project justification*, to determine the degree to which the business value of the system will be enhanced; *portfolio analysis*, to prioritize the applications to be re-engineered based on their technical quality and business value; *cost estimation*, to estimate the costs of the project; *cost-benefit analysis*, to compare costs and expected returns; and *contracting*, to identify tasks and distribution of effort.

In general, decision frameworks are required to assess a legacy system from two points of view: a business dimension and a technical dimension (Bennett et al., 1999; Vergugo, 1988; Sneed, 1995). A typical decision framework for the management of legacy systems based on four main alternatives is proposed in De Lucia et al. (2001). The ordinary maintenance decision is generally adopted in the case of a system with a good technical and business value; this alternative entails only ordinary interventions on the system aimed at adding new functionality or at resolving specific problems. On the other hand, the elimination of the system and its replacement with a new one, developed ad-hoc or acquired from the market, is generally needed when the technical and business value of the existing system is low. The evolution alternative aims at evolving the system by providing it with new functionalities or adapting the existing ones in order to improve its business value, while maintaining the high technical value. The last option is the reengineering/migration alternative. In this case, the goal is more complex and entails moving the legacy system towards a new and more flexible environment, while retaining the original system's data and functionalities. Typically, reverse engineering, restructuring, and architecture transformation interventions are suggested to improve software technical attributes in a system with high business value.

The relationships among the organizational and process aspects, and the software systems have already been considered with reference to the development of new software systems (Yu, 1993, 1995; Mylopoulos et al., 1999; van Lamsweerde, 2001; Dardenne et al., 1993; Antòn, 1996). In those studies, the focus is on how to capture the organizational requirements for defining the enterprise goals, why it is necessary, what the possible alternatives are, and so forth. The developed technique, such as I* (Yu, 1993,1995), represents these aspects. I* offers two models to represent organizational requirements: the Strategic Dependency Model and the Rationale Dependency Model. The Strategic Dependency Model focuses on the intentional relationships among organizational actors, while the Rationale Dependency Model allows for the modelling of the reasons associated with each actor and their dependencies.

A family of goal-oriented requirements analysis (GORA) methods such as I* (Yu, 1993, 1995; Mylopoulos et al., 1999), KAOS (van Lamsweerde, 2001; Dardenne et al., 1993) and GRL (Antòn, 1996) have been proposed as top-down approaches for refining and decomposing the customers' needs into more concrete goals to be achieved. However, all these methods regard the definition of requirements for the development of the information system.

THE PROPOSED STRATEGY

Figure 1 depicts a layered view of the proposed strategy. It highlights that the strategy considers activities that are distributed on three layers, referred to as Organization, Processes and Software Systems. The three layers interact in order to achieve the goals defined within the organization. The goals guide the evolution of processes and information systems.

The activities of the *Business Innovation* layer aim at assessing the organization and identifying the improvement opportunities for the organization moving towards *e-*

Figure 1: Layered View of the Proposed Strategy.

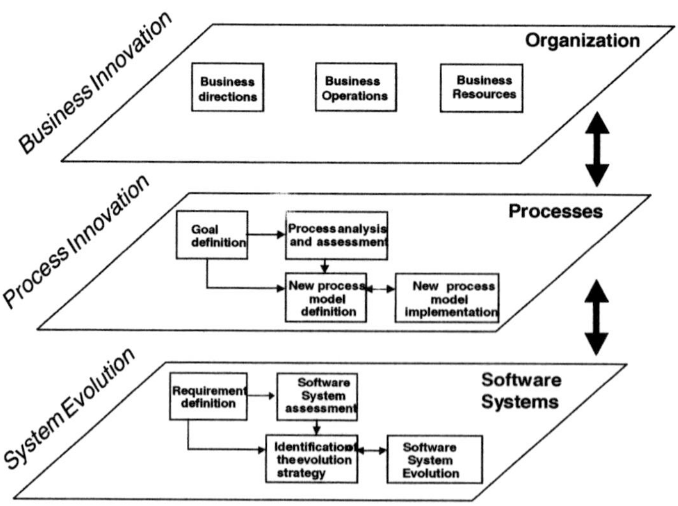

business. The activities of the *Process Innovation* layer aim at providing guidelines to drive the rethinking and redesigning of the enterprise core business processes. The activities of the *System Evolution* layer require a thorough examination of the characteristics of the legacy system and its business and technical values. The three layers will be described in greater detail in the following subsections.

Business Innovation

In this layer, it is important to perform a monitoring activity of the internal and external environments of the organization in order to identify all the aspects that could have an impact on it. This activity aims at indicating the opportunities for:

- Anticipating and accelerating the changes and, therefore, anticipating their benefits,
- Capturing the change in the internal and external environment of the organization.

The external aspects to be investigated during the monitoring activity mainly refer to Mega Trend, Market Areas and Competitors. The internal aspects, on the other hand, to be investigated are related to Processes, Measurement and Management System, Values and Behaviors, and Work and Structures. Indeed, by analyzing these aspects it is possible to obtain the following information:

- Possible change to be executed in the organization.
- Personnel responsible for the change.
- Type of impact on the organization (High/Medium/Low).
- Probability that the change occurs (High/Medium/Low).

Therefore, the assessment of the organization is used, together with an analysis of future trends in technological and organizational fields, for addressing the ideas of its possible evolution and projecting its future vision. In literature (Laubacher & Malone, n.d.; Sieber & Griese, 1999), there are several studies proposing methods that indicate how to use the assessment data. Two main directions are the following:

- The *external pushes the internal,* in which the internal changes are enacted after the analysis of the external opportunities.
- The *internal requires the external,* in which the internal requirements determine the need to find opportunities in the external environment.

In relation to these two approaches, different management strategies have been proposed. In particular, directions from the *Planning School*, using the first approach, and the *Competence-Based School*, using the second approach, are considered in the Business Innovation. In fact, the assessment proposed here includes, for example, the execution of the SWOT analysis (an analysis of the Strengths, Weaknesses, Opportunities, and Threats of the organization) typical of the Planning School, and at the same time, the analysis of the Strategic Intent and the Vision Statement typical of the Competence-Based School.

The main activities of the Business Innovation layer are the following three:

Business Direction

This is used to identify what are the current and future directions of the business and improvement opportunities. With this in mind, it is important to understand the roles and responsibilities of the managers, define the management strategy (considering the mission and vision of the organization), understand how to connect the vision with the daily procedures of the organization, and consider the relevance of the technologies.

Business Operations

This is used to define how the business works and how it should work in order to support the organization. It is useful to achieve a description of the executed processes. A selection of the technologies and methodologies to be used is also required, together with the identification of the interaction points with the external, and the modalities of this interaction.

Business Resources

This is used to identify and assess every resource the organization uses for creating its products and services, that is, everything is useful to react to the market opportunities. The resources can be physical, such as the structure, or intangible, such as the information.

The result of the analysis of the organization is the Improvement Plan that contains the following information: the diagnosis of the organization, with the specifications of the improvement opportunities; the indications for a more detailed analysis of some processes of the organization; and the assessment of the organization with the collection of all information required for establishing its business value.

Process Innovation

It consists of independent activities shown in the process layer of Figure 1. Each activity is iteratively performed and directly affects the others. A description of these activities follows.

Goal Definition

It selects one of the enterprise's core business processes as the candidate for reengineering and aims at identifying processes and technologies that can achieve more competitive advantages in the Internet-based Market Model. It is important to understand the enterprise's strategic direction, including the mission statement and strategic intent. This can be accomplished by interviewing the enterprise's executive leadership.

Process Analysis and Assessment

To understand the process to be reengineered, the analysis is conducted to develop a model of the process and collect data to further understand its performance and execution mode. All the data collected and assessed represent the primary output of the activity. Executing the activity, the team starts to assess the infrastructure in which the selected process is embedded. A high-level view of the process is needed in order to discover how the process works and what is going on, and to be able to spot opportunities to redesign. It is important to identify the customers of the process and their needs. Anyone who receives output from the process, either directly or indirectly, is a customer. A customer can be within the organization or outside it. The activities are to be documented at the level needed to provide a meaningful picture of the current process. Activities defined in too much detail may complicate the overall analysis without adding useful information. Activities defined too broadly will fail to reveal opportunities for improvement. It is also important to identify the software systems that support the activities and thus need to be evolved. Using the decision table of the toolkit, the results of this activity allow the definition of the actions to be performed on the process or on its activities. The execution of the selected actions permits the identification of the requirements for the process evolution. These requirements will impact on the identification of the requirements for the evolution of information systems.

New Process Model Definition

This is done to redesign the process, by taking into account the introduction of Internet-based innovations and e-business context and on the basis of the process evolution requirements. In the process redesign, the technical dimension of the new process is specified. For the new model, a clear description of the technologies, standards, procedures, systems, and controls employed by the reengineered process has to be developed. It is necessary to consider also the social dimension of the new process, regarding the organization, staffing, jobs, career paths, and employees' incentives.

New Process Model Implementation

This is done to execute the process innovation by connecting all the results together and institutionalising the reengineered process throughout the affected areas of the enterprise. Prior to implementing the new model, it is critical to ensure that the environment is ready to encompass the change. Before starting the implementation, it is also important to: assess whether the leadership is ready and willing to lead the effort; ensure that all the process stakeholders are aware of the forthcoming changes; and resolve all the implementation barriers.

System Evolution

It mainly consists of four activities shown in the System Evolution layer in Figure 1. A description for each of them follows.

Requirements Definition

The evolution of legacy systems is strictly related to the evolution of business processes. The challenge of this activity is the identification of the business knowledge captured in the legacy systems to establish their evolution requirements considering the requirements of the process evolution, which reflect the business indications regarding the enterprise mission and the technology to be introduced.

Software System Assessment

Assessment is used to determine the future of the legacy system. This activity collects an inventory of the current situation and includes an analysis of what could happen. The functional and technical quality of the systems is analyzed to determine the most appropriate maintenance and software performance engineering strategies. The legacy system assessment includes the following activities:

- *Business Assessment.* This is used to gain a business view of the system being assessed. In particular, this activity focuses on the customer's point of view.
- *Technical Assessment.* This is used to assess the technical quality of the software system. This is achieved through the collection and analysis of metrics and survey information. This activity gives an understanding of the technical condition of the system. The information is obtained from static analysis and interviews.
- *Data Assessment.* This is used to gain an understanding of the data usage and data characteristics of the system. Information of interest is the following: degree of conformance to data naming standards; degree of data name redundancies; potential data conversion; and impact of interfaces on external systems.
- *Gap Analysis.* This is done to analyze how system components are mapped to current and future business and data needs for identifying gaps in the system. One of the functions of the Conversion Strategy is to identify solutions for the identified gaps.
- *Maintenance Process Analysis.* This is done to look at maintenance processes and history to help the identification of system components that may require improvements.
- *Conversion Strategy.* This is to identify the course of action suggested by the legacy system assessment activity. It is the final output of a legacy system assessment activity.

Identification of the Evolution Strategy

The data and information collected during the previous assessment activity and the process evolution requirements are used to identify the evolution strategies to be applied for evolving the information system. To this purpose, some decision tables of the toolkit can be used. The evolution of the information system may involve activities necessary to reengineer the application in order to exploit new technologies and platforms, or may involve activities for reducing maintenance complexity of existing systems, or to perform data and resource modifications for addressing identified technical and business drivers. Depending on the circumstances, a system may go through a full or partial improvement, and may or may not go through transformation activities (Bennett et al., 1999). The alternative interventions that may be considered are those listed in Table 1.

Software System Evolution

This activity entails the implementation of the evolution strategy selected in the previous step on the legacy system. It permits the embedding of the information system into the business process evolved on the basis of the requirements that drove the identification of the requirements of the software systems evolution.

SUPPORTING TOOLKIT

As already stated, the strategy is supported by a toolkit composed of decision tables and a measurement framework. The measurement framework supports the assessment activities, while the decision tables can be used for interpreting the collected information and indicating the actions to be undertaken in the future evolution activities in the three layers of Figure 1. The following subsections discuss the decision tables used in the three layers, and the measurement framework defined for evaluating the parameters whose values are considered in the decision tables.

Decision Tables

At the Business Innovation layer, once the organizational mission and future vision are identified, the *strategic goals* can be defined in the Business Direction activity; while during the Business Operations activity, the processes of the enterprise can be analyzed in order to identify their relevance for reaching each strategic goal. Table 2 is used for collecting this information by including a weight in each cell, ranging from 1 to 3 on the basis of the relevance that the managers attribute to the related process for reaching the corresponding strategic goal.

The total of the weights helps to identify the *key processes*, that is, those processes that are considered important for the accomplishment of the strategic goals. Table 3 allows for the characterization of each strategic goal in terms of *critical success factors* related to all external and internal aspects that contribute to the successful completion of the goal. On the basis of this information and the identified key processes using Table 4, it is possible to select the candidate processes for the evolution activities. In fact, each cell of Table 4 can be used for indicating, with a weight ranging from 1 to 3, how relevant

Table 2: Cross-Reference Table of Processes and Strategic Goals of the Organization.

	Process 1	**Process 2**	**...**	**Process n**
Strategic goal 1				
Strategic goal 2				
...				
Strategic goal m				
Total				

Table 3: Cross-Reference Table of Strategic Goals and Critical Success Factors.

	Strategic goal 1	**Strategic goal 2**	**...**	**Strategic goal m**
Critical success factors 1				
Critical success factors 2				
...				
Critical success factors p				
Total				

Table 4: Cross-Reference Table of Critical Success Factors and Key Processes.

	Key process 1	Key process 2	...	Key process q
Critical success factors 1				
Critical success factors 2				
...				
Critical success factors p				
Total				

the related critical success factor is in the execution of the corresponding key process. The key processes that include more critical success factors are the ones that may be considered for reaching the strategic goals and for the execution of the following process innovation approach.

The process analysis and understanding in the process layer analyzes a business process to identify the actions to be executed for defining its evolution requirements and guiding its re-engineering. The analysis of a business process requires its assessment on the basis of a set of parameters. At this level, each identified parameter should be measurable on the analyzed process or its activities and used resources. Moreover, the type of values the parameter can assume characterizes it. Each enterprise should indicate a threshold value for each parameter. If the value assumed by that parameter is below/above the assigned threshold value, it is not considered valid and indicates eventual anomalies to be investigated in the component (process, activity or resource) to which the value refers. A sample set of parameters considered at a business process layer is listed as row headings of Table 5. In particular, the process *effectiveness* measures the achievement level of the process scope in terms of user and staff satisfaction and adequacy to the enterprise's required standards, operative procedures, choices and expected results. The *sequential execution degree of the process activities* parameter indicates the way the activities are executed in order to identify the possibility to make parallel some of them and reduce the execution time. Finally, the last parameter is the *online interaction level with the users*. It refers to the plan for the *e*Government of the European Union (Presidenza del Consiglio dei Ministri). The aim of this plan is to facilitate the service exploitation by the citizen. In particular, four interaction levels have been defined regarding the provided services: the first level is informative and entails the online availability of the required information to exploit the services; the second level entails a one-way interaction, in which it is only possible to download the required modules; the third level is the two-way interaction, in which it is possible to activate an online interaction with the process; the fourth level entails the execution online of the process, including transactions such as payment and delivery.

Each column of Table 5 refers to a possible action to be undertaken for evolving the process on the basis of the values of the parameters. An L/H in correspondence of a parameter and an action indicates that the related action can be undertaken when the parameter value that is lower/higher than the threshold is reached. For example, if the *staff satisfaction* is lower than the assigned threshold value, the actions to be undertaken

Table 5: Process Parameters and Actions.

			PA1	PA2	PA3	PA4	PA5	PA6	PA7	PA8	PA9	PA10	PA11	PA12	PA13	PA14	PA15	PA16	PA17	PA18
Effectiveness	Users Satisfaction	Tangibility											L			L				L
		Reliability				L	L	L												
		Responsiveness	L	L				L									L	L	L	L
		Assurance				L	L							L	L					
		Empathy			L									L	L					
	Staff satisfaction										L	L	L							
	Adequacy				L				L		L				L					
Sequential execution degree of the process activities																	H		H	
Online interaction level with the users					L					L						L				L

PA1. Identify the activities that do not add value to the process and its services
PA2. Identify the process activities that represent a bottleneck in the process execution
PA3. Evaluate the possibility to involve the users of the process services with an active role in the process
PA4. Analyze the information routing among the process activities to verify if each activity can achieve the needed information, preventing errors
PA5. Introduce knowledge management techniques and tools for increasing the employees' competences by using already existing solutions
PA6. Evaluate the technological infrastructure supporting the process
PA7. Introduce a process monitoring activity and define metrics and a measurement system
PA8. Reduce the usage of paper documents
PA9. Introduce a system for the evaluation of the human resources and benefits
PA10. Introduce formation courses for the employees
PA11. Improve the work environment, and, where necessary, use innovative solutions
PA12. Review the allocation of the human resources
PA13. Improve the relationship's quality with the customer
PA14. Provide the user with online documentation, and clearer guidelines and templates
PA15. Analyze the possibility to parallelize part of the process activities
PA16. Delete the redundant activities that do not correspond to security and/or control requirements
PA17. Evaluate the possibility of widening, combining and joining the fragmented activities
PA18. Extend the software system functionalities by using Web-based technologies

have to be oriented to increase it by introducing a system for evaluating the human resources and offering benefits (PA9), organizing courses for educating the employees (PA10) regarding the subjects treated in the process, or improving the work environment (PA11). The existence and level of attention paid to these aspects can be considered and related decisions can be taken.

Another example is the *online interaction level with the user*. In this case, if the parameter achieves a low value, the possibility to involve its users with an active role (PA3) in the process, or check for reducing the usage of paper documents (PA8) in favour of more innovative communication means such as online information (PA14), implying in this way the introduction of the Web-based technologies (PA18), can be taken into consideration.

Similarly to Table 5, a set of sample parameters to be considered at activity level are listed as row headings in Table 6. In particular, the process *efficiency* is evaluated as the ratio between the results of the process activities' output and the resources they require as input. The resources are measured in terms of time, costs, and productivity (Batini & Santucci, 1999). The *automation level* indicates the percentage of activity tasks that are executed automatically. The *interaction level with the external user* identifies if external actors participate in the activity. Even in this case, Table 6 indicates which actions should be undertaken at which activity level, if a parameter assumes a value below/above the established threshold. For example, if the activity *productivity* is low, some of the actions to be undertaken should be: the evaluation regarding the possible deletion of the activity

Table 6: Activities' Parameters and Actions.

		AA1	AA2	AA3	AA4	AA5	AA6	AA7	AA8	AA9	AA10	AA11	AA12	AA13	AA14
Efficiency	Allocation time of human resources	H	H		H	H	H		H	H	H	H			
	Allocation time of software resources				L	L	L		L	L					
	Allocation time of hardware resources				L	L	L		L	L					
	Cost of human resources	H				H	H		H	H	H	H			
	Cost of software resources												H	H	
	Cost of the hardware resources														H
	Other costs	H			H	H	H	H							
	Productivity	L	L		L	L	L	L	L	L	L	L			
	Number of output	H	H					H				H			
Automation level				L		L		L				L			
Interaction level with the users				H		H						H			

AA1. Consider the possibility to delete the activity if it does not add value to the process services
AA2. Verify if the activity represents a bottleneck in the process and consider its redesign
AA3. Evaluate the possibility of involving the users of the activity services in the activity with an active role
AA4. Analyze if the activity can include techniques and tools for increasing the employees' competence by using existing solutions for performing the activity
AA5. Evaluate the adequacy of the software system supporting the activity, considering the possibility of evolving it
AA6. Introduce the activity in the monitoring plan of the process, defining metrics and a measurement system
AA7. Reduce the production of paper documents in the activity
AA8. Introduce a system for the evaluation of the human resources and benefits
AA9. Review the allocation of the human resources
AA10. Evaluate the possibility of widening, combining and joining the activity with other process ones
AA11. Evolve the functionalities of the software system by introducing Web-based technologies
AA12. Analyze the software system used for supporting the activities to evaluate the possibility of substituting it with other, more convenient solutions
AA13. Evaluate the maintenance costs of the software system in order to candidate it for evolution
AA14. Evaluate the hardware platform used and the possibility of migrating the software system toward more economical platforms

if it does not add any value to the process services (AA1); the verification of whether the activity is or is not a bottleneck for the following activities (AA2) and, in this case, the consideration of its reengineering; the evaluation of the possibility that the adoption of techniques and tools for increasing the employees' competence (AA4) and/or benefits (AA8) can help in decreasing the time spent to produce the output, consequently, increasing the productivity; the evaluation of automatic solutions used for understanding their adequacy and planning their substitution and/or evolution (AA5); the introduction of a monitoring task for identifying the reasons why the productivity decreases (AA6); and so on.

Another example is the *allocation time of software resources* parameter. Its low value suggests the following kind of actions: analyze the software system supporting the activity in order to understand if it is adequate or if there is any need to evolve it (AA5); the introduction of the monitoring tasks (AA6) in order to understand if the software system is adequately used and beneficial for the human resources for promoting the usage of the electronic devise (AA8); review the allocation of the human resources (AA9); and so on.

The parameters values and the execution of the actions suggested by Tables 5 and 6 permit the identification of the activities that are affected by the evolution process and the process evolution requirements. Moreover, it leads to the identification of the information systems to be evolved and the definition of their evolution requirements,

Table 7: Software System Parameters and Actions.

		Improvement interventions								Transformation interventions						
		Reverse engineering	Redocumentation	Security mngt	Reformatting	Control restructuring	Data restructuring	Modularization	Data migration	User interface migration	Language migration	Platform migration	Architecture migration	Reengineering	Redevelopment	Encapsulation
Functionality	Suitability	L												L	L	
	Accuracy	L												L	L	
	Interoperability									L	L	L				
Usability										L						L
Maintainability	Changeability	L	L	L	L	L	L	L			L			L		
	Testability	L	L	L	L	L	L	L			L			L		
	Analyzability	L	L	L	L	L	L	L			L			L		
	Stability	L	L	L	L	L	L	L			L			L		
Portability						L	L		L		L	L	L	L		
Efficiency						L	L									
Reliability	Software Reliability													L	L	
	Hardware Reliability												L			
Quality in use	Effectiveness									L						
	Productivity									L						
	Safety			L												
Economic value	Redevelopment Cost	H	H	H	H	H	H	H								
	Maintenance Cost		H	H	H	H	H	H	H	H	H	H	H	H	H	H
	Future Utility									H		H				H
Data value							H		H				H			
Obsolescence	SW Obsolescence										H		H		H	
	DB Obsolescence								H		H		H		H	
	OS Obsolescence											H			H	
	HW/SW Infrastructure Obsolescence											H	H		H	

which can regard the addition, modification or deletion of functionalities. The effective implementation of the identified information system evolution requirements necessitates the information system assessment and identification of evolution strategy activities in the system evolution layer.

Software system can be assessed by considering the parameters listed as row headings in Table 7. They are identified on the basis of the standard ISO/IEC 9126 (ISO, 1999). The cited standard considers the following six characteristics: *functionality, usability, maintainability, portability, efficiency* and *reliability*. Moreover, the following other parameters are considered related to the software system: the *quality in use* helps to establish the system quality from the user's point of view; and the *data value* establishes whether the system keeps the organizational knowledge, which represents a very important source of information; finally, the *obsolescence* expresses the aging of a software asset, caused by the failure to meet changing needs, and corresponds to what Parnas (1994) considers as one of the two types of software aging. The values assumed by the parameters give the possibility of deciding which alternative evolution strategies should be adopted. The strategies can be deduced from the list of action categories described in Table 7 and can be identified taking into consideration the techniques presented in Table 1. In Table 7 each parameter is cross-referenced with the actions that may affect it.

As an example, migration interventions or redevelopment should be executed if the system obsolescence is high. Reverse engineering, restructuring, and modularization are proposed for improving the maintainability. Reverse engineering, reengineering or redevelopment can be performed for improving the functionality. Migration interventions are also suggested for improving the value of a software asset. For example, a data migration can be proposed to improve the data value, while a user interface migration can improve software usability.

Of course, Table 7 provides only coarse-grained indications, while each intervention will have to be more precisely specified and designed according to the exigencies of the maintenance organization.

The subsequent task for evaluating alternative actions identified on the basis of Tables 5, 6 and 7, has to be performed in order to determine the evolution strategy. Factors such as business constraints, risks, costs, and benefits of each alternative will all play a part in the decision making process, and decision rules will be defined to solve the problem in the most cost-effective and beneficial way.

Measurement Framework

The measurement framework is the toolkit component that can be used for measuring the parameters indicated in Tables 5, 6 and 7. It has been defined in terms of metrics, mechanisms of data collection, and guidelines to use the collected data. Various approaches can be used for defining a measurement framework. Our approach is defined on the basis of the Goal-Question-Metric (GQM) paradigm (Basili & Weiss, 1984), which considers three abstraction levels (Basili et al., 1994):

- *Conceptual level*, consisting of the goals to be achieved by the measurement activity. It is related to the object to be evaluated from various points of view and relative to a particular environment.
- *Operational level*, consisting of a set of questions dealing with the way the assessment/achievement of a specific goal is addressed.
- *Quantitative level*, identifying a set of metrics to be associated to each question in order to answer it in a quantitative way.

In particular, the focus of the measurement framework of the toolkit is the assessment of business processes and supporting software systems. On the basis of some of the characteristics introduced in Tables 5, 6 and 7, some goals have been identified. For example, and in the interests of brevity, only two goals are presented in detail: one refers to the information systems itself, in particular to its *quality in use*; and the other concerns the business process with reference to *efficiency*. The considered goals are the following:

- *GOAL-1*. Analyze a business process with the aim to evaluate its efficiency from the manager's point of view. It is necessary to identify the resources involved in the process and quantify them. In particular, for each activity of the process it is possible to measure the cost, the critical level, the amount and quality of the output produced, and the factors impacting on the output of the process.
- *GOAL-2*. Analyze a software system with the aim to evaluate its quality from the point of view of the end user. On the basis of the reference standard ISO/IEC 9126, the software product quality is evaluated in terms of functionality, reliability, usability and efficiency, while the quality in use is measured by considering the efficiency, productivity, security and satisfaction.

Table 8: Questions and Metrics of GOAL-1.

ID	Metric Identifier	QUESTIONS AND METRICS
Q1		**How many activities compose the process?**
M1.1	n^A	No. of activities composing the process
Q2		**What are the resources involved in the process?** *(Question proposed for each activity of the process)*
M2.1		List of type of human resources
M2.2	n_j^H	No. of type of human resources in activity *j*
M2.3	n_{ij}^H	No. of human resources of type *i* in activity *j*
M2.4		List of supporting software system
M2.5	n_j^{SW}	No. of different software system supporting activity *j*
M2.6	n_{ij}^{SW}	No. of licences of software system *i* supporting activity *j*
M2.7		List of used hardware resources
M2.8	n_j^{HW}	No. of different hardware resources used in activity *j*
M2.9	n_{ij}^{HW}	No. of hardware resources *i* used in activity *j*
M2.10		List of other types of resources used
M2.11	n_j^{Or}	No. of kinds of other types of resources used in activity *j*
M2.12	n_{ij}^{Or}	No. of other resources *i* used in activity *j*
Q3		**What are the costs of the resources used in the process?** *(Question proposed for each activity of the process)*
M2.1	c_{ij}^H	Cost of human resources of type *i* working in activity *j*
M2.2	c_{ij}^{SW}	Cost of the software resources of type *i* supporting activity *j*
M2.3	c_{ij}^{HW}	Cost of the hardware resources of type *i* used in activity *j*
M2.4	c_{ij}^{Or}	Cost of the other resources of type *i* used in activity *j*
Q3		What is the allocation time for each resource? *(Question proposed for each activity of the process)*
M3.1	t_{ij}^H	Allocation time of the human resources of kind *i* in activity *j*
M3.2	t_{ij}^{SW}	Allocation time of the software resources of kind *i* in activity *j*
M3.3	t_{ij}^{HW}	Allocation time of the hardware resources of kind *i* in activity *j*
M3.4	t_{ij}^{Or}	Allocation time of the other resources of kind *i* in activity *j*
Q4		**What are the outputs produced?** *(Question proposed for each activity of the process)*
M4.1		List of output categories produced by activity *j*
M4.2	n_out_j	No. of output categories produced by activity *j*
M4.3	n_out_{ij}	No. of output of category *i* produced by activity *j*
Q5		**What is the complexity of the output produced?**
M5.1	$compl\_out_{ij}$	Complexity of the output of category *i* produced by activity *j*
Q6		**What is the production time of the output?** *(Question proposed for each activity of the process)*
M6.1	t_out_{ij}	Production time of the output of category *i* produced by activity *j*

As Table 6 indicates, the efficiency of a business process is evaluated by considering *cost, time* and *productivity*. Table 8 shows the questions and the metrics referred to in GOAL-1. As can be noted, the proposed fragment of the measurement framework evaluates the efficiency characteristic by considering each single component involved in the process, which is the individual activity and the used resources. In order to make

Table 9: Variation Factors for GOAL-1.

Code	QUESTIONS AND METRICS
Q7	**How many dependences affect the productivity of each activity?**
M7.1	List of activities and artefacts affecting the current activity
M7.2	List of dependences blocking the current activity
Q8	**How many constraints affect the productivity?**
M8.1	List of constraints affecting the current activity
Q9	**How many external interfaces affect the productivity?**
M9.1	List of external interfaces affecting the current activity
Q10	**Do procedures exist that formalize the activity execution?**
M10.1	List of activities that are formalized by a procedure
M10.2	Percentage of the activities that are formalized by a procedure
M10.3	Percentage of the activities supported by electronic tools

the required measurements, it is necessary to correctly perform the process analysis and the assessment activity of the process layer cited in Figure 1. In particular, it is necessary to perform the process modelling before executing the assessment. To reach this objective, the used formalism is the UML language (Rational Software, 1997a, 1997b). The use cases, activities and class diagrams are used (Aversano & Tortorella, 2003). It may be necessary to refine the process model and modify the measurement framework when it is not possible to gather all needed data because they are not available in the current process model. This situation can require new interviews with the application domain experts and imply the progressive refinement of the measurement framework.

Besides the questions and related metrics, the first column of Table 8 contains the code associated with each question and related metrics, and the second column includes the identifiers of the metrics. The measures to be assigned to some metrics are mainly numeric, while other evaluations produce lists of items, singularly considered in the measurement of other metrics.

To abstract useful information from the collected data, a set of formulas are defined.

Table 10 contains the formulas defined to identify the values related to the process efficiency. The formulas are defined in terms of metric identifiers introduced in Table 8. It can be noticed that the process cost is evaluated in terms of costs of the human resources, software systems, hardware components and other resources. On the other hand, the process productivity is defined on the basis of productivity of the single activity. The productivity of an activity is evaluated in terms of outputs it produces, their complexity and the time needed to produce them. A formula has not been elaborated for evaluating the time measures, as the values involved are singularly considered in the process evaluation. The amount and quality of the produced output can be influenced by a set of variation factors regarding the activities. They consist of a critical level of the resources, dependencies, constraints, interfaces, and eventual formalization procedures. Table 9 presents a specific set of questions that are included in the framework with reference to GOAL_1 with the aim to discover critical points in the business process. The table presents only a subset of all the considered aspects.

Table 11 presents the section of the measurement framework related to GOAL_2.

The aim is to evaluate the quality characteristics of a software system, as a user can perceive it. The characteristics considered are introduced in Table 7.

Table 10: Formulas for GOAL_1.

CHARACTERISTIC	NAME	CALCULATION
COST	Total cost of the process	$C = \sum_{j=1}^{n^A} (C_j^H + C_j^{SW} + C_j^{HW} + C_j^{Ot})$
	Total cost of the human resources for the activity *j*	$C_j^H = \sum_{i=1}^{n_j^H} c_{ij}^H n_{ij}^H t_{ij}^H$
	Total cost of SW resources for the *j*-activity	$C_j^{SW} = \sum_{i=1}^{n_j^{SW}} c_{ij}^{SW} n_j^{SW} t_{ij}^{SW}$
	Total cost of the HW resources for the activity	$C_j^{HW} = \sum_{i=1}^{n_j^{HW}} c_{ij}^{HW} n_{ij}^{HW} t_{ij}^{HW}$
	Total cost of the other types of resources for the *j*-activity	$C_j^{Or} = \sum_{i=1}^{n_j^{Or}} c_{ij}^{Or} n_{ij}^{Or} t_{ij}^{Or}$
PRODUCTIVITY	Productivity of the process	$P = \frac{\sum_{j=1}^{n\_act} P_j}{n^A}$
	Productivity for the *j*-activity	$P_j = \frac{\sum_{i=1}^{n\_out_j} P_{ij}}{n\_out_j}$
	Productivity of the output of category *i* for the *j*-activity	$P_{ij} = \frac{n\_out_{ij}}{t\_out_{ij}} compl\_out_{ij}$

The metrics of Table 11 are at a high level of abstraction. Their values are derived from simpler measures. For example, the *adequacy level of the information system to the user requirements*, f_r, can be calculated by comparing the user requirements with those satisfied by the information system, while the *accuracy level of the output of the system*, a_o, is evaluated on the basis of the structure of the output automatically produced, and the one needed in the e-business process. These metrics can assume a value within a range representing the possible acceptance levels, while other metrics such as the ones associated to question Q40 in Figure 11 are numeric. In addition, some other metrics are defined as Boolean values. In any case, some of the measurements made in this context are subjective. This kind of information is difficult to be interpreted and should be avoided.

The operands expressed in the formulas are the metrics introduced in Table 11.

- Functionality is the capability of the software system to provide functions meeting stated and implied needs when the software is used under specified conditions. It is evaluated by the following formula:

$$F = f_r a_o i_s$$

Table 11: Questions and Metrics of the GOAL_2.

ID	RIF. FORMULA	QUESTIONS AND METRICS
Q39		**Is the software system functionally adequate?**
M39.1	f_r	Adequacy level of the software system to the user requirements
M39.2	a_o	Accuracy level of the output of the system
M39.3	i_s	Interoperability level of the system
Q40		**Is the software system reliable?**
M40.1	t_{mf}	Mean time between failures
M40.2	t_{mr}	Mean time to repair a failure
Q41		**Is the software system usable?**
M41.1	u_1	Attractiveness of the user interface
M41.2	u_2	Existence of a graphical user interface
M41.3	u_3	Existence of an adequate training in the use of the system
M41.4	u_4	Visibility of the status of the software system
M41.5	u_5	Visibility of the action currently performed by the user
M41.6	u_6	Presence of 'undo' and 'redo' functionalities to recover default conditions
M41.7	u_7	Existence of an *interrupt* command to suspend an elaboration to be later recovered
M41.8	u_8	Understanding level of the user interface language
M41.9	u_9	Existence of icons associated to the system commands
M41.10	u_{10}	Existence of a short description of the commands when they are used (tool tip)
M41.11	u_{11}	Use of a significant title for each window and/or screen
M41.12	u_{12}	Use of selection lists favouring the use of adequate values in a correct form
M41.13	u_{13}	Consistence of the language and/or graphics in the working environment
M41.14	u_{14}	Coherence in the presentation of the information
M41.15	u_{15}	Existence of the online help for each command
M41.16	u_{16}	Number of accesses to the online help and/or manuals
M41.17	u_{17}	Simplicity level of use of the online help and/or manuals
M41.18	u_{18}	Comprehensibility level of the online help and/or manuals
M41.19	u_{19}	Effectiveness level of the system documentation to solving problems
M41.20	u_{20}	Background colour
M41.21	u_{21}	Foreground colour
Q42		**Is the software system efficient?**
M42.1	r	Adherence to the hardware requirements of the system
M42.2	V	Speedy level of answers of the system
Q43		**Is the software system effective?**
M43.1	n_o	Number of the system outputs
M43.2	n_i	Number of the process outputs
M43.3	Q_o	Mean quality value of the system output
Q44		**Is the software system productive?**
M44.1	t_{oj}	Production time for each output of activity *j*
M44.2	C_{aj}	Complexity for each output produced by the system in activity *j*
Q45		**Does the software system satisfy the expectations of the user?**
M45.1	S	User satisfaction level
Q46		**Is the software system safe?**
M46.1	s_1	Operative system used
M46.2	s_2	Presence of network
M46.3	s_3	Modality of access to the computers
M46.4	s_4	Modality of access to the software system
M46.5	s_5	Modality of access to database
M46.6	s_6	Management of the user profiles
M46.7	s_7	Availability of a computer for each user
M46.8	s_8	Access of unauthorized people
M46.9	s_9	Existence of a backup policy
M46.10	s_{10}	Installing of an antivirus
M46.11	s_{11}	Frequency of antivirus updating
M46.12	s_{12}	Presence of firewall
M46.13	s_{13}	Existence of courses and/or informative brochures on the computer safety

- Reliability represents the capability of the software system to maintain a specified level of performance when used under specified conditions. It can be calculated as:

$$A_s = t_{mf} + t_{mr}$$

- Usability is the capability of the software system to be understood, learned and used by a user and attractive to the user when used under specified conditions. It is measured considering the heuristics proposed in Nielsen (1994, 1999), in which the usability is defined as a measure of the quality of the experience of a user interacting with any type of system such as a Website, a traditional software system and so on. The formula applied is:

$$U = \sum_{i=1}^{19} u_i + f(u_{20}, u_{21}),$$

where $f(u_{20}, u_{21})$; it is a function that assumes different values for different combination of the text color and background color.

- Efficiency is the capability of the software product to provide appropriate performance, relative to the amount of resources used, under stated conditions:

$$\eta_s = rv$$

- Effectiveness is the capability of the software product to enable users to achieve specified goals with accuracy and completeness in a specified context of use. It can be defined as:

$$E_s = \frac{n_o}{n_t} Q_o$$

- Productivity is the capability of the software product to enable users to expend appropriate amounts of resources in relation to the effectiveness achieved in a specified context of use. It is calculated by the following formula:

$$P_s = \frac{n_o}{t_o}$$

- Safety is the capability of the software product to achieve acceptable levels of risk of harm to people, business, software, property or the environment in a specified context of use.
- Satisfaction is the capability of the software product to satisfy user needs in a specified context of use. The formula applied is:

$$S_c = Sg(s_4 s_5 s_6 s_{11} s_{12} s_{13}) \sum_{i=1}^{15} s_i ,$$

where *Sg( )* is the sign function.

As already stated, on the basis of its experience, the enterprise can provide, for each presented parameter, a threshold above/below that at which the value assumed by the parameter is not acceptable and can set in motion the interventions presented in Tables 5, 6 and 7.

CASE STUDY

In order to evaluate the effectiveness of the approaches discussed in the previous sections, a pilot study was conducted with some users to test the applicability of the approach. In particular, a peripheral Department of the Public Administration (a small

Figure 2: Activity Diagrams of the ICI Process Before and After the Reengineering.

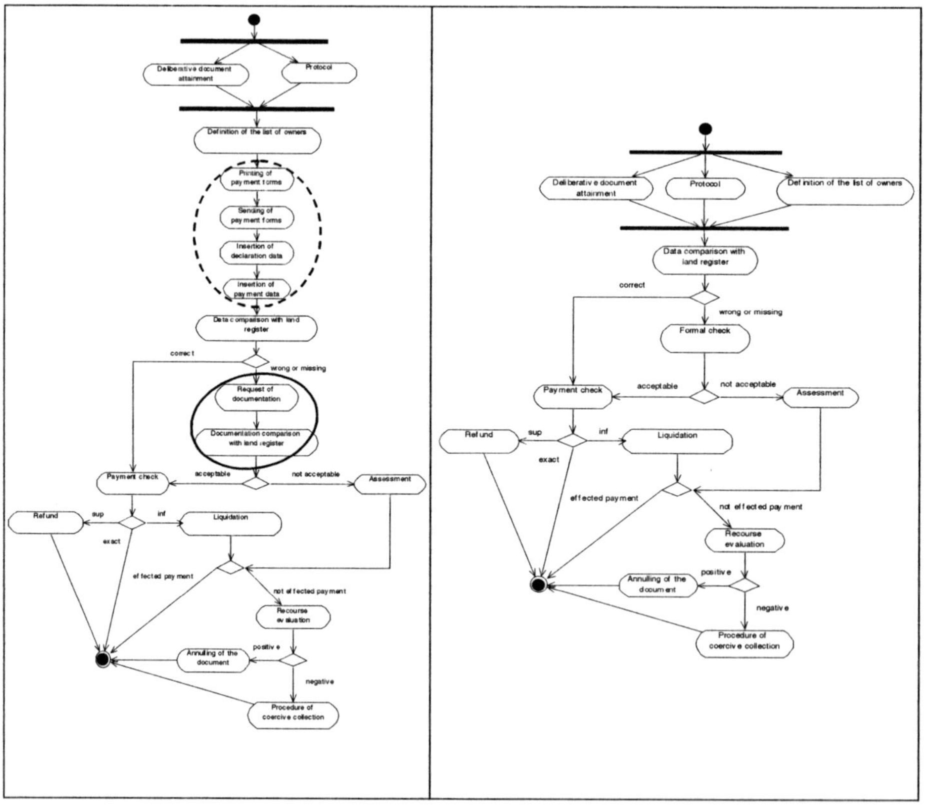

(a) (b)

Figure 3: Use case Diagrams of the ICI Process Before and After the Reengineering.

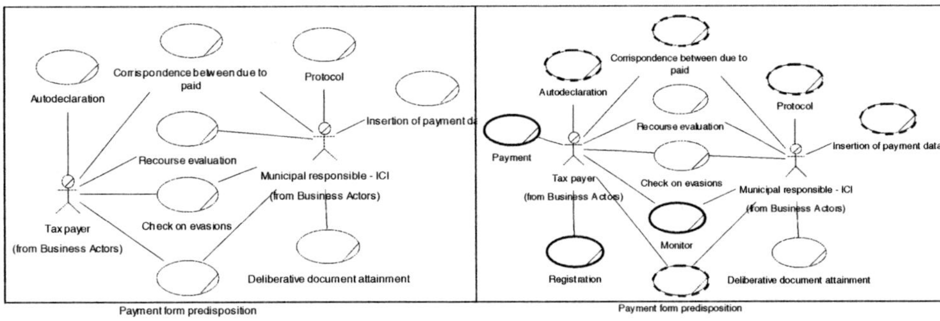

(a) (b)

town in the district of Benevento in Italy) agreed to participate in the pilot project as a customer. The business and process activities were conducted by interviewing the department managers for identifying the business needs and the processes to be analyzed for improvement. They highlighted that the main need of a public administration body is to increase citizen satisfaction and, on the other side, improve the effectiveness of the employees' tasks.

In order to identify the process to be analyzed, the administrative manager was interviewed and, at a first level of abstraction, three subprocesses were chosen:

- Payment of the land tax.
- Payment of the city refuse tax.
- Payment for occupation of public ground.

In particular, in the first stage, only the first process was considered. In the following, it will be indicated with the acronym ICI – **I**mposta **C**omunale sugli **I**mmobili. The process activities are graphically depicted by using a UML activity and use case diagrams in Figures 2a and 3a, respectively.

From the analysis of the measures collected at process level and presented in Table 12, it emerged that the parameters presenting a critical value are:

- Online interaction level with the users is 0, because there are not any online services, while the expected value that has been defined with the managers is the maximum; that is, 4.
- Sequential execution degree of the process activities is 0.75, achieved by the activity diagram, shown in Figure 2a, while the expected value defined with the managers is 0,5.

Therefore, the actions to be performed on the basis of Table 5 are: PA3, PA7, PA14, PA15, PA17, PA18.

At the activity level, the metrics and characteristics presented in Table 6 have been evaluated and some results are presented in Table 12. Table 12 contains the results

Table 12: ICI Process Data.

Activity	Allocation time of human resources (min)	Allocation time of specific SW (min)	Allocation time of HW (min)	Activity productivity	Cost of specific SW %	Cost of HW %	Cost of human resources %	Other costs %	Number of output	Automation level	Interaction with user	Actions
Deliberative document attainment	*15,00*	*0,00*	*0,00*	*0,040*	*0*	*0*	*0,061*	*0*	1	Non-automatable	Low	-
Protocol	*253,33*	*190,00*	*190,00*	*0,137*	*0,137*	*0,116*	*0,949*	*0*	65	50%	Low	AA3, AA5, AA7, AA11
Definition of the list of owners	*40,00*	*30,00*	*30,00*	*0,020*	*0,022*	*0,021*	*0,150*	*0,095*	1	90%	Very low	-
Printing of payment forms	*48,00*	*180,00*	*180,00*	*6,667*	*0,130*	*0,273*	*0,180*	*0,013*	2000	90%	Very low	AA1, AA2, AA7, AA11
Sending of payment forms	*360,00*	*0,00*	*0,00*	*1,111*	*0*	*0*	*1,349*	*0,132*	2000	Automatable	High	AA1, AA2, AA3, AA4, AA5, AA6, AA7, AA11
Insertion of declaration data	*650,00*	*650,00*	*650,00*	*0,020*	*0,470*	*0,398*	*2,436*	*0*	65	30%	Very low	AA1, AA2, AA3, AA4, AA5, AA6, AA7, AA8, AA9, AA11
Data comparison with land register	*433,33*	*65,00*	*65,00*	*0,002*	*0,047*	*0,043*	*1,624*	*0*	1	90%	Very low	-
Request of documentation	*200,00*	*0,00*	*100,00*	*0,067*	*0*	*0,107*	*0,750*	*0,006*	50	Non-automatable	Low	-
Insertion of payment data	*6000,00*	*6000,00*	*6000,00*	*0,067*	*4,340*	*3,678*	*22,486*	*0*	2000	30%	Low	AA1, AA2, AA3, AA4, AA5, AA6, AA7, AA8, AA9, AA10, AA11
Documentation comparison with land register	*1000,00*	*75,00*	*75,00*	*0,013*	*0,054*	*0,046*	*3,748*	*0*	50	50%	Very low	-
Assessment	*2666,67*	*2000,00*	*2000,00*	*0,040*	*1,447*	*1,498*	*9,994*	*0,013*	200	90%	High	-
Liquidation	*2666,67*	*2000,00*	*2000,00*	*0,040*	*1,447*	*1,498*	*9,994*	*0,013*	200	90%	Low	-
Recourse evaluation	*106,67*	*0,00*	*0,00*	*0,030*	*0*	*0*	*0,400*	*0*	4	Non-automatable	High	-
Annulling of the document	*266,67*	*20,00*	*20,00*	*0,060*	*0,014*	*0,012*	*0,999*	*0*	20	30%	Low	-
Procedure of coercive collection	*40,00*	*6,00*	*6,00*	*0,027*	*0,004*	*0,006*	*0,150*	*0*	1	90%	High	-
Refund	*400,00*	*0,00*	*60,00*	*0,040*	*0,043*	*0,064*	*1,499*	*0,004*	20	50%	Low	-
Payment check	*13,33*	*10,00*	*10,00*	*0,040*	*0,007*	*0,009*	*0,050*	*0*	1	90%	Very low	-
Total	*15159,67*	*11226*	*11386*									
Total cost of process				*7594,19*								
Process productivity				*0,495*								

regarding the *allocation time* and the *costs for human*, *software* and *hardware resources*, and the *productivity* for each process activity evaluated on the basis of the measurement framework in Table 8 and related formulas in Table 10. In Table 12 the critical values for each activity are highlighted with a background.

Also, the data collected at the activity level have been considered for identifying actions, with the support of Table 6. Indications of the actions to be performed have been extracted from the analysis of the data collected and listed in the last column of the Table 12. For example, the activity *protocol* presents a critical value for the *automation level*; therefore the actions to be performed for improving it are the AA3, AA5, AA7 and

Table 13: External E-Business Legacy System Requirements.

E-business **requirements**	**Legacy system evolution requirements**
To give the possibility to citizens to register themselves by using Internet.	• To migrate the legacy user interface to the Web. • To migrate the legacy system from a single user version to a multi-user version.
To give to citizens the possibility to monitor the current status of their registration.	• To migrate the data components of the system. • To implement new functionalities supporting the management of the user profiles.
To give the possibility to the citizens to perform the online payment.	• To evolve the existing user interfaces in order to collect and/or show new data to the user. • To integrate the existing legacy system with external components responsible to manage the payment.

AA11. In particular, the activity AA5 entails the analysis of the software systems supporting the activity to identify the possibility to introduce new functionalities and Web-based technology. Moreover, the activity *printing of payment forms* presents a critical value for the *number of output*; therefore the actions to be performed are AA1, AA2, AA7, and AA11. In this case the activity quality has been improved, reducing the production of paper documents (AA7). Performing these actions, the requirements for the evolution of the business process have been defined and listed in Tables 13 and 14.

In particular, the requirements for the process improvement were defined from two different perspectives:

- *External*, in which the improvement goals concerning the citizen were considered and e-business requirements were identified from the citizen's point of view. The new e-business process aims at facilitating the interaction of the user with the system, permitting checking of the status of their registration, paying the tax online, and receiving online communications from the public administration body.
- *Internal*, the improvement goal concerning the employees participating in the process, was taken into consideration for identifying other business requirements. The aim is to improve the process by increasing the process automation level and decreasing the manual operations.

The first columns of Tables 13 and 14 list some of the external and internal requirements of the process evolution, respectively, to move towards *e-business*. The satisfaction of these requirements led to the re-engineering of the ICI process. The requirements for evolving the legacy application and the implementation of new functionalities were identified considering the impact of the process evolution. The second columns of Tables 13 and 14 lists each *e-business* requirement of the requirements set of the legacy system evolution process. The tables show that many requirements concern the migration of the legacy component to Web technologies, or the implementation of new functionalities characteristic of the Web applications, such as security and user authentication. In particular, the introduction of the Web technologies through the evolution of the legacy systems favours the active participation of the citizen (Tax Payer actor) to the *e-business* process.

Table 14: Internal E-Business Legacy System Requirements.

Process reengineering requirements	Legacy system evolution requirements
To check automatically the amount to be paid by the citizens and the effective payment performed.	• To implement new functionalities that automatically check the correctness of the payment.
To update the tax percentage.	• To implement and integrate with the existing data model of new functionalities usable to change the tax percentage.
To optimize the tasks' effectiveness in terms of resources and time spent.	• To implement new functionalities that automatically check the internal data with the data obtained from other Public Administration.

Figures 2b and 3b depict the model of the evolved ICI process on the basis of the requirements in Tables 13 and 14. Figure 2a highlights the greater number of activities that are grouped in new activities in Figure 2b, with the reduction of the process complexity. The grouping was made possible by the legacy system evolution and the introduction of new functionalities. Figure 3b shows the impact of the process evolution on the interaction of both external and internal actors with the process components. The interactions of external and internal actors have been highlighted in the figure with, respectively, solid and dotted circles.

The considered parameters at software system level were evaluated by the measurement framework application and are the following:

- Functionality value is evaluated as Medium, as most of the user requirements are satisfied by the software system that is specific to support the process;
- Reliability assumes value High, as the interviewed employees affirmed that the system did not present any significant failure or fault from the moment they began to use it, and it was not possible to provide a quantitative value;
- Usability is calculated in terms of 84% and considered High for the user-friendly interface, and the availability of comprehensive online help and documentation;
- Efficiency amounts to 80%, which is High, for the short time required by the system to make elaborations and provide results;
- Effectiveness is Medium, as not all the outputs required by the process are produced by the software system;
- Productivity evaluates a Medium, reflecting the medium complexity of the produced outputs;
- Safety results are Very Low due to the lack of firewall, antivirus, and possibility to access the system and data without user identification;
- Evaluation of the Satisfaction from the users' point of view is High, also due to the fact that few people need to access the process and, then, the system.

At this point, using the obtained results and considering the identified evolution requirements, Table 7 can be applied for identifying the strategies for the evolution of the legacy system. They are the following: user interface and platform migrations. Other requirements regarding the data migration aimed at the interaction of all the modules of the evolved system, resulting from the evolution process, with a unified database.

CONCLUSIONS

The trend towards e-business calls for changes in the fundamental concepts of business process innovation and reengineering. Indeed, traditional views of process innovation and reengineering have focused on the internals of the enterprise with the aim of redesigning the business processes. Moreover, nowadays it is important to react to the central role that the Internet is playing in the definition of new business relationships within and among enterprises. The emerging of virtual and distributed organizational models, and the richness of the communication channels between customers and enterprises leads to a wider view of BPR. The view goes beyond the enterprise to involve both customers and business partners. Therefore, the process innovation cannot be performed without a careful evaluation of the impact of process changes on existing legacy systems and the introduction of innovative technologies. The adoption of new software systems to satisfy the new business evolution requirements is not a practical solution. Economic and technical constraints in most cases encourage the evolution of the existing legacy systems rather than the development of new systems from scratch. This means that a balance must be achieved between the constraints imposed by the existing legacy systems and the opportunities offered by the reengineering of the business processes. In other words, the requirements for the legacy system evolution must be extracted from the requirements of the evolution of business toward e-business.

In this chapter a strategy has been proposed to support the identification of the legacy system evolution requirements in the context of the business innovation. The chapter also proposed a supporting toolkit including decision table and a measurement framework. The measurement framework is based on the Goal-Question-Metric paradigm for assessing business processes and supporting software systems from both quantitative and qualitative points of view. It is generally applicable to any business process and supporting software systems after its instantiation to the specific context. The decision tables support the identification of the actions to be performed in the evolution activities on the basis of the assessment results. The strategy presented has been experimented within two different application domains concerning public administrations, even if just one context has been presented. The first activities of the case study aimed at investigating the practical applicability of the approaches and verifying the efficiency of the support offered by the identified parameters in the extraction of the requirements for the evolution of the legacy systems. Indeed, the process innovation in the analyzed peripheral public administration is characterized by the fact that there are few critical legacy systems, but the rules governing the processes tend to be very rigid, and the redesign of the processes must be coherent with the current laws.

Some of the lessons learned referred to the necessity to formalize as rigorously as possible the tools used in the assessment activities. In fact, the rough definition implies a continuous interaction with the process owners that can misunderstand the proposed questions. Moreover, the interviewed employees should not have any possibility to provide information deriving from their ideas and sensations. This can be avoided by formulating the questions in such a way to list the possible metric values and favouring the objective interviewed employees' answers.

In addition, the continuous meetings necessary to evaluate the metrics in the measurement framework can be avoided if a software environment exists facilitating the interaction and the data entry through the Internet. The environment should also support the evaluation of the formula and the proposal of the suggested actions. The authors are involved in the implementation of such a tool that will be used in the next applications of the strategy.

Finally, an instrument, in order to be successfully used with early adopters of BPR methodologies, needs to be tested in various contexts in order to be refined on the basis of the various needs and feedbacks received. For this reason, the proposed measurement framework and software tool that is being implemented will be experimented with in both *in vitro* and real contexts.

ACKNOWLEDGMENTS

The authors would like to thank Professor Gerardo Canfora for the stimulating discussions and the anonymous referees whose constructive suggestions have enabled the improvement of the chapter. Finally, many thanks are due to Ms. Antonietta Luongo for her precious support as technical writer.

REFERENCES

Ammarguellat, Z. (1992). A control-flow normalization algorithm and its complexity. *IEEE Transactions on Software Engineering, 18*(3), 237-251, IEEE Computer Society Press.

Antón, A.I. (1996, April). Goal-based requirements analysis. *Second IEEE International Conference on Requirements Engineering,* Colorado Springs, Colorado, IEEE Computer Society Press.

Aversano, L., & Tortorella, M. (2003). Evolving legacy systems towards eLegacy in eBusiness context. *Proceedings of the 7th European Conference on Software Maintenance*, Benevento, Italy, IEEE Computer Society Press.

Basili, V.R., & Mills, H.D. (1982). Understanding and documenting programs. *IEEE Transactions on Software Engineering, SE-8*, 270-283, IEEE Computer Society Press.

Basili, V.R., & Weiss, D.M. (1984, November). A methodology for collecting valid software engineering data. *IEEE Transactions on Software Engineering, 10*(6), 728-738, IEEE Computer Society Press.

Basili, V.R., Caldiera, G., & Rombach, H.D. (1994). The goal question metric approach. *Encyclopedia of Software Engineering.* Wiley Publishers.

Batini, C., & Santucci, G. (1999, August). *Sistemi informativi per la pubblica amministrazione: Metodologie e tecnologie.* Scuola Superiore della Pubblica Amministrazione.

Beck, J., & Eichmann, D. (1993, May). Program and interface slicing for reverse engineering. *Proceedings of the 15th International Conference on Software Engineering,* Baltimore, Maryland, USA, IEEE Computer Society Press.

Behm, A., Geppert, A., & Dittrich, K. (1997, December). On the migration of relational schemas and data to object-oriented database systems. *Proceedings of the 5th International Conference on Re-Technologies for Information Systems,* Klagenfurt.

Bennett, K.H. (1995, January). *IEEE Software Special Issue on Legacy Systems, 12*(1), IEEE Computer Society Press.

Bennett, K.H., Ramage, M., & Munro, M. (1999, June). Decision model for legacy systems. *IEE Proceedings Software, 146*(3), 153-159, News & Archive Press.

Bernd, J., & Clifford T.Y.T. (1992). *Business process reengineering and software systems strategy. Anwendungen in der Wirtschaft*. Frankfurt am Main.

Berztiss, A.T. (2001). Reengineering and processes. *Handbook of software engineering and knowledge engineering*. World Scientific Press.

Biggerstaff, T.J., Mitbander, B.G., & Webster, D.E. (1994). Program understanding and the concept assignment problem. *Communications of the ACM, 37,* 72-82.

Brodie, M.L., & Stonebaker, M. (1995). *Migrating legacy systems - Gateways, interfaces & incremental approach*. San Francisco: Morgan Kaufmann Publishers, Inc.

Canfora, G., & Cimitile, A. (1997, May). *A reference life-cycle for legacy systems*. Proceedings of the ICSE - Workshop Migration Strategies for Legacy Systems, Boston, MA (Technical Report TUV-1841-97-06). Technical University of Vienna, Information Systems Institute.

Chiang, R., Barron, T., & Storey, V. (1994, March). Reverse engineering of relational databases: Extraction of an EER model from a relational database. *Journal of Data and Knowledge Engineering, 12*(2), 107–142.

Chikofsky, E.J., & Cross, J.H. II (1990). Reverse engineering and design recovery: A taxonomy. *IEEE Software, 7*(1), 13-17, IEEE Computer Society Press.

Cifuentes, C., Simon, D., & Fraboulet, A. (1998, November). Assembly to high-level language translation. *Proceedings of the International Conference on Software Maintenance,* Bethesda, Maryland, IEEE Computer Society Press.

Claßen, I., Hennig, K., Mohr, I., & Schulz, M. (1997, March). CUI to GUI migration: Static analysis of character-based panels. *Proceedings of the 1st Conference on Software Maintenance and Reengineering,* Berlin, Germany, IEEE Computer Society Press.

Cowan, D.D., German, D.M., Lucena, C.J.P., & von Staa, A. (1994, September). Enhancing code for readability and comprehension using SGML. *Proceedings of the International Conference on Software Maintenance,* Victoria, British Columbia, Canada, IEEE Computer Society Press .

Csaba, L. (1997, March). Experience with user interface re-engineering: Transferring DOS panels to Windows. *Proceedings of the 1st Conference on Software Maintenance and Reengineering,* Berlin, Germany, IEEE Computer Society Press.

Dardenne, A., van Lamsweerde, A., & Fickas, S. (1993). Goal-directed requirements acquisition. *Journal of Science of Computer Programming, 20*(1),3-50, Elsevier Publication.

Darwen, P.J., & Yao, X. (1997). Speciation as automatic categorical modularization. *IEEE Transactions on Evolutionary Computation, 1*(2), 101-108, IEEE Computer Society Press.

De Lucia, A., Fasolino, A.R., & Pompella, E. (2001, November). A decisional framework for legacy system management. *Proceedings of the International Conference on Software Maintenance,* Florence, Italy, IEEE Computer Society Press.

Deng, Y., Kothari, S., & Namara, Y. (2001, May). Program slicing browser. *Proceedings of the 9th International Workshop on Program Comprehension,* Toronto, Ontario, Canada, IEEE Computer Society Press.

Dershowitz, N., & Jouannaud, J.-P. (1990). Rewrite systems. In J. van Leeuwen (Ed.), *Handbook of theoretical computer science* (*B*(6), pp. 243- 320). Elsevier.

Fletton, N., & Munroe, M. (1988, October). Redocumenting software systems using hypertext technologies. *Proceedings of the International Conference on Software Maintenance,* Phoenix, Arizona, IEEE Computer Society Press.

Hainaut, J.L. (1991, October). Database reverse engineering, models, techniques and strategies. *Proceedings of the 10th Conference on Entity-Relationship Approach,* San Mateo, CA, E/R Institute.

Hammer, M., & Champy, J. (1993). *Reengineering the corporation: A manifesto for business revolution.* NY: HarperCollins.

ISO. (1999). *Information technology - Software product quality, ISO/IEC.*

Jacobson, I., Ericsson, M., & Jacobson, A. (1995). *The object advantage: Business process reengineering with object technology.* ACM Press, Addison-Wesley.

Kelly, S., Holland, C., Gibson, N., & Light, B. (1999). Focus issue on legacy information systems and business process change: A business perspective of legacy systems. *Communications of the Association for Information Systems, 2*(7), 1-27.

Lamsweerde, A. van (2001, August). *Goal-oriented requirements engineering: A guided tour.* Invited Paper for RE'01 - 5th IEEE International Symposium on Requirements Engineering, Toronto, Canada, IEEE Computer Society Press.

Laubacher, R.J., & Malone, T. (n.d.). *Two scenarios for 21st Century organization: Shifting network of small firm or all-encompassing virtual countries.* Working Paper 21C WP 001 MIT.

Merlo, E., Girard, J.F., Kontogiannis, K., Panangaden, P., & De Mori, R. (1993, May). Reverse engineering of user interfaces. *Proceedings of the First Working Conference on Reverse Engineering,* Baltimore, Maryland, IEEE Computer Society Press.

Moore, M., & Rugaber, S. (1993, November). Issues in user interface migration. *Proceedings of the 3rd Software Engineering Research Forum,* Orlando, Florida.

Mylopoulos, J., Chung, L., & Yu, E. (1999, January). From object-oriented to goal-oriented requirements analysis. *Communications of the ACM, 42*(1), 31-37, ACM Press.

Nielsen, J. (1994, October). *Usability engineering.* Morgan Kaufmann Publishers.

Nielsen, J. (1999, December). *Designing Web usability: The practice of simplicity.* New Riders Publishing.

Oman, P.W., & Cook, C.R. (1990). The book paradigm for improved maintenance. *IEEE Software, 7*(1), 39-45.

Parnas, D.L. (1994, May). Software aging. *Proceedings of the International Conference on Software Engineering,* Sorrento, Italy, IEEE Computer Society Press.

Pigoski, T.M. (1997). *Practical software maintenance - Best practices for managing your software investment.* New York: John Wiley & Sons.

Presidenza del Consiglio dei Ministri, Dipartimento per l'Innovazione e le Tecnologie, Allegato n. 1. *Front office e servizi di egovernment per cittadini e imprese.* Available: *http://www.pianoegov.it/*

Ramshaw, L. (1988). Eliminating goto's while preserving program structure. *Journal of the ACM, 35*(4), 893-920.

Rational Software. (1997a). *UML notation guide versione1.1.* Available: *http://www.rational.com/uml/resources/documentation/media/ad970805UML11_Notation2.pdf*

Rational Software. (1997b). *UML extension for business modeling versione 1.1*. Available: *http://www.rational.com/media/uml/resources/media/ad970807_UML11_Business.pdf*

Richardson, R., O'Sullivan, D., Wu, B., Grimson, J., Lawless, D., & Bisbal, J. (1997, March). Application of case based reasoning to legacy systems migration. *Proceedings of the 5th German Workshop on Case-Based Reasoning Foundations, Systems, and Applications,* Centre for Learning Systems and Applications, Dept. of Computer Science, University of Kaiserslautern.

Rishe, N. (1992). *Database design: The semantic modeling approach*. McGraw-Hill.

Rugaber, S., Ornburn, S.B., & LeBlanc R.J., Jr. (1990). Recognizing design decisions in programs. *IEEE Software, 7,* 46-54, IEEE Computer Society Press.

Sieber, P., & Griese, J. (1999, September). Organizational virtualness and electronic commerce. *Proceedings of the 2nd International VoNet Workshop, 1*(1), Special Issue of *The Electronic Journal of Organizational Virtualness and Electronic Commerce.*

Sneed, H.M. (1995). Planning the reengineering of legacy systems. *IEEE Software, 12*(1), 24-34, IEEE Computer Society Press.

Sneed, H.M. (1999). Risks involved in reengineering projects. *Proceedings of the 6th Working Conference on Reverse Engineering,* Atlanta, GA, IEEE Computer Society Press.

Sneed, H.M. (2000). *Business reengineering in the age of the Internet*. Technical Report, Case Consult, Wiesbaden, Germany.

Steven, A., Judy, S., Ein-Dor, P., Vessey, I., & Markus, M.L. (2002). Does the trend toward e-business call for changes in the fundamental concepts of information systems? A debate. *Communications Of Association of the Information Systems, 5*(10), ACM Press.

Vergugo, G. (1988). Portfolio analysis - managing software as an asset. *Proceedings of the Sixth International Conference Software Maintenance/Management,* New York, DPMA Education Foundation.

Williams, M., & Ossher, H. (1978). Conversion of unstructured flow diagrams into structured form. *The Computer Journal, 21*(2), 161-167, British Computer Society.

Wong, K., Tilley, S.R., Müller, H.A., & Storey, M.-A.D. (1995, January). Structural redocumentation: A case study. *IEEE Software, 12*(1), 46-54, IEEE Computer Society Press.

Wu, B., Lawless, D., Bisbal, J., Grimson, J., Richardson, R., & O'Sullivan, D. (1997, October). Legacy system migration: A legacy data migration engine. *Proceedings of the 17th International Database Conference,* Brno, Czech Republic, IEEE Computer Society Press.

Yadav, S.B. (1990, January). Control and definition modularization: An improved software design technique for organizing programs. *IEEE Transaction on Software Engineering, 16*(1), IEEE Computer Society Press.

Yu, E. (1995). *Modelling strategic relationships for process reengineering*. PHD Thesis, University of Toronto.

Yu, E.S.K. (1993, January). Modeling organizations for information systems requirements engineering. *Proceedings 1st IEEE International Symposium on Requirements Engineering,* San Diego, California, USA, IEEE Computer Society Press.

Chapter XIV

Business Oriented Systems Maintenance Management

Malin Nordström, Linköping University and På AB, Sweden

Tommy Welander, På AB, Sweden

ABSTRACT

In the introduction to this chapter, we discuss some of the common problems in maintenance. In order to solve these problems, we find it necessary to think in a new way, including the relationship of businesses to the system maintenance. The world outside organisations changes continuously, and the business processes and functions must change with it. However, if we only maintain information technology (IT) and do not co-manage the business changes accordingly, IT will not change at the same pace as the business changes. It would result a gap between the business needs and services provided by the IT product. In that case, IT systems would not be able to provide sufficient business value. The main part of this chapter contains a management model for solving these problems, based on theoretical research and practical experience. The central theme of the model is the connection between the business needs and systems maintenance. This is achieved by maintaining maintenance objects rather than the systems, establishing micro-organisations for each maintenance object where business processes as well as the system are represented. Our proposed model is widely used in more than 50 organisations in Sweden. In conclusion, some future trends and central concepts of the model are discussed.

INTRODUCTION

Systems maintenance is about handling change, continuous change in businesses as well as IT systems (Bergvall, 1995). The world around us changes all the time, and thus businesses and IT systems must adjust to the changing conditions. But there is a delusion that a business' need for IT systems could be "downplayed" by emphasising the procurement of IT systems either purchased or developed in-house that would handle all future needs. Some enterprise managers are often surprised to find later that systems maintenance needs more than what is required for the development of the system. And there are still some who believe that a new technology is the solution to the poorly functioning maintenance process.

Systems maintenance is often acknowledged as a problem in the field of practice (e.g., Parikh, 1988; Kitchenham et al., 1999; Pigoski, 1997). It is described as being costly, low status activity, and unclear process definition (Pigoski, 1997; Kajko-Mattson, 2001; Nordström & Welander, 2002). Maintenance is frequently viewed from a developmental perspective, and thus positioned in relation to development in some kind of life cycle perspective (e.g., ISO/IEC, 2002). Furthermore, maintenance is often assigned lower priority than the development process, even though the time and costs for maintenance and development respectively are usually distributed according to the 80:20 rule (Parikh, 1988).

Based on our experiences from the industry and our research on the area (Berntsson & Welander, 1991; Bergvall, 1995; Nordström & Welander, 2002), we find that many of these problems and attitudes originate from the way in which maintenance is organised and managed. How to make maintenance manageable, and why it is so important to see the whole picture of maintenance—not just IT—is described in this chapter. This means that the focus area of this chapter lies in the intersection between business and technology,that is, how to achieve maintenance that effectively contributes to fulfilling the business objectives.

BACKGROUND AND PROBLEM AREA

We have found three important areas in which the improvement of systems maintenance could be better addressed: what should really be maintained, what can be gained from viewing maintenance as business exchange, and how to organise maintenance optimally.

In systems maintenance literature, systems maintenance is often described as a general activity in the organisation; it is seldom described in connection to any specific system or object. In the background discussions and the model descriptions in this chapter, we describe systems maintenance in relation to a specific situation, or maintenance object, in order to make the descriptions and definitions more detailed and applicable in practice.

What is to be Maintained?

There is a question that is rarely asked in maintenance, a question that we find to be vital in making maintenance efficient and manageable: what is to be maintained? Studies of literature in the maintenance field show that the common view of what is to be maintained is the ITsystems (e.g., Pigoski, 1997; Kemerer & Slaughter, 1987; Longstreet, 2001; Kajko-Mattsson, 2001). Further, in the international standard IEEE, maintenance is defined as "modification of a software system or component after delivery to correct faults, to improve performance or other attributes, or to adapt the software system or component to a changed environment" (IEEE, 1990). In other words, the focus is on the

Figure 1: Object Model (Nordström & Welander, 2002).

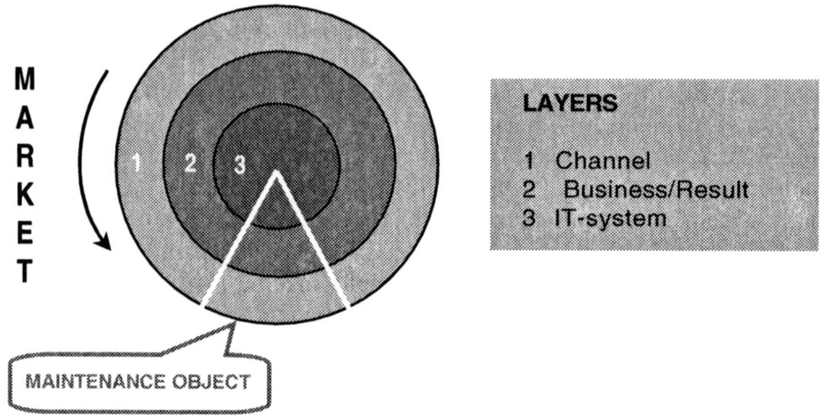

activities that the IT developers must perform. However, as early as in 1987, Bendifallah and Scacchi (1987) investigated systems maintenance from a business perspective and reached the conclusion that in order to understand the problems related to maintenance, one must understand the surrounding business needs, the users, and the system maintainers. Our studies and experiences in the field of practice support this view (Berntsson & Welander, 1991; Bergvall, 1995).

The reason for this is that maintenance that only focuses on the IT systems can, in the longer run, lead to unsatisfactory business value provided by the systems. In software development, enough studies are typically conducted in order to elicit the business requirements of the system. However, over time, businesses change and it is not at all certain that the IT systems change at the same pace – and thus, the business is left lacking IT support. It is also common to see that the IT system over time is being used for something different than the original purpose. If the *maintenance object* is not well defined, then the maintenance organisation would probably only support some parts of the original purpose, which may lead to a low business value. We will illustrate the discussion about the importance of maintaining the system along with the business needs with an object model cited in Figure 1.

If one cuts a slice of the "cake" that is the *object model* in Figure 1, this may illustrate what we call a *maintenance object* in an organisation. A maintenance object should consist of all three layers in the model. This is the fundamental interface channel of an organisation to the market. When the market changes, the channels and businesses/ results must adjust to satisfy the market demands. However, it is not obvious that the IT systems always follow this, as illustrated in Figure 2. To ensure that the business does not end up with unsatisfactory business value from the IT systems, a *maintenance object* must be seen as a whole.

It is important to be understood by the organisations that an IT system should be regarded as an integrated part of the organisational business. However, the boundaries between business and IT systems are not at all as clear as they may seem (Goldkuhl, 1993).

Figure 2: Consequence of IT-Focused Maintenance (Nordström & Welander, 2002).

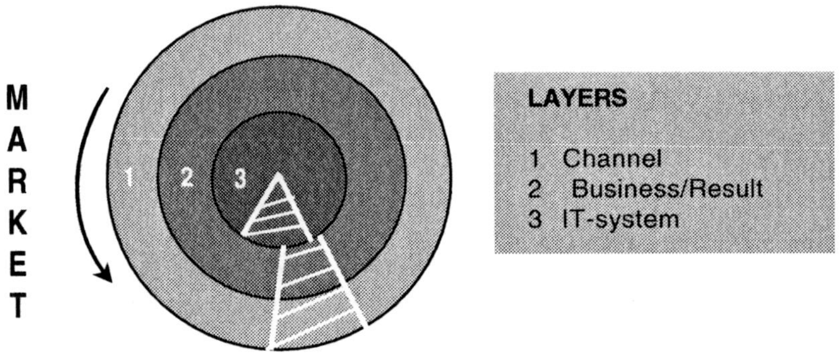

The trend that we see today in many large organisations is unfortunately leading in the other direction. As businesses become evermore dependent on technology, the management of ITsystems is increasingly separated from the organisational business needs, instead of integrating them together. How to define a maintenance object is further discussed in the section "Identify the maintenance object".

Business Orientation

Systems maintenance is, as mentioned above, a very complex phenomenon from an organisational and managerial perspective. A way of handling this complex situation is to view it as an agreement between two parties, namely the business that uses the IT systems, and the IT supplier that keeps them running (Berntsson & Welander, 1991; Bergvall & Welander, 1996; Nordström & Welander, 2002). This is the fundamental basis of applying a business-oriented perspective on systems maintenance.

Business orientation means focusing not only on the main business of the organisation, but also on the internal business agreements and exchange that take place daily between organisational roles, functions and units. Both parties in maintenance, business and IT, have a collective responsibility for the maintenance. Examples of how the business-oriented perspective works in practice are given in the description of the model Business-Oriented Maintenance Management below.

Organising Systems Maintenance

Systems maintenance is commonly regarded as line operations, a concern for the IT department (Pigoski, 1997), as opposed to, for instance, system development. One of the characteristics of the line organisation is that each employee has one manager (Bruzelius & Skärvad 1989; Handy, 1999). In practice, this creates a problem in systems maintenance, since for individual employees this means that their organisational line manager and the manager of the department that needs maintenance activities often are different people, and may have different goals and priorities.

The problem can be further clarified by studying the relationship between two concepts: *business* and *organisation*. Here, the concepts are related to each other according to the following; an organisation conducts business. This means that the business is what is being done, that is, actions and activities (Goldkuhl & Röstlinger, 1998), while the organisation is social structures with various forms of management, created to achieve a certain goal (Scott, 1998). This is, of course, a very simplified image of the business and organisation concepts, but sufficient for the discussions in this chapter. In systems maintenance these two phenomena are not consistent with each other. The maintenance organisation conducts a business that is managed by several organisational units (the IT supplier and the organisational units where the users of the systems work), and thus, conflicts of interests and prioritisations may occur.

The communication in the IT department usually evolves around maintenance as a product, fixing bugs, and so forth, instead of focusing on the service that the customers need (Niessink & van Vliet, 2000). Thus, when using the line organisation as control structure for maintenance, one has not taken into account the characteristics of maintenance, such as handling changes, and the need for several types of competences and skills. Our conclusion is that the line organisation is not powerful enough for the purpose of conducting effective systems maintenance. By using the line organisation, one loses the possibility of making maintenance manageable, since the line organisation focuses on hierarchical structures, not vertical ones (Bruzelius & Skärvad, 1989). One of the most important ways to make an organisation effective is to choose the right organisation and management structures (Robbins, 1990).

Central Concepts of the Chapter

In the continued discussions in this chapter, there is a need to clarify the different meanings of the word "business", since it is one of the key words in the model. "Business" may signify organisational action, as in the passage above. It may also be used in a more specific sense, meaning the exchange of value that takes place between buyer and seller, with or without financial involvement (Grönroos, 2000). Where needed, we will use the term "business exchange" to clarify this.

Another central term for the chapter is IT systems, with which we mean the computer-based information system. When the information is consumed, handled, and exchanged by the people, we use the term business. This means that IT systems are parts of businesses and perform actions in businesses (Goldkuhl, 1992).

MODEL FOR BUSINESS-ORIENTED MAINTENANCE MANAGEMENT

In this section, a model for business-oriented maintenance management is described. The model is designed to give simple but powerful solutions to the maintenance management problems discussed above. It has been constructed in the intersection between theory and empirical experience. The model is normative and thus states what is needed to make a maintenance situation manageable. By business orientation we mean to make good maintenance business exchange. Creating the best solution of a problem in practice demands a mixture of model management and situational management. Figure 3 shows the relations between model, method, tools and result.

As shown in Figure 3, an implementation of the model on a specific maintenance object results in a maintenance plan. This is a governing document that describes the

Figure 3: Relations between Model and Method in Business Oriented Maintenance Management (Nordström & Welander, 2002).

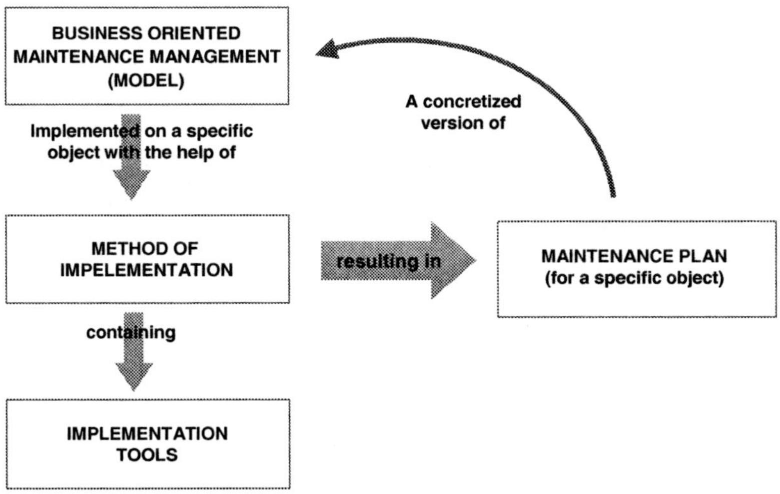

maintenance work for the object for the coming period of time. More on the maintenance plan is found in the section "Maintenance plans". The maintenance plan can then be complemented with the agreements between identified business parties. The maintenance model is based on the business-oriented perspective and consists of four success factors:

- Identify the maintenance object.
- Define the systems maintenance activities.
- Create forms of management.
- Organise the systems maintenance business.

Below, the model is described from these four success factors. The model is implemented on approximately 200 objects in more than 50 organisations and is continuously developed through consultancy work and research.

Identify the Maintenance Object

Defining maintenance objects is an important factor in making maintenance efficient and manageable. A business probably has several IT systems to support its activities. Experience shows that defining the IT system that supports specific business activities or functions is usually relatively easy. A much greater difficulty, however, lies in defining businesses. After the intense process mappings of later years, it has become easier, however, since these activities have helped organisations/employees become more aware of business actions. Thus, layer two in the object model (Figure 4) contains the process/functions and/or the results thereof, that is, the products/services. If one

Figure 4: An Example of a Maintenance Object.

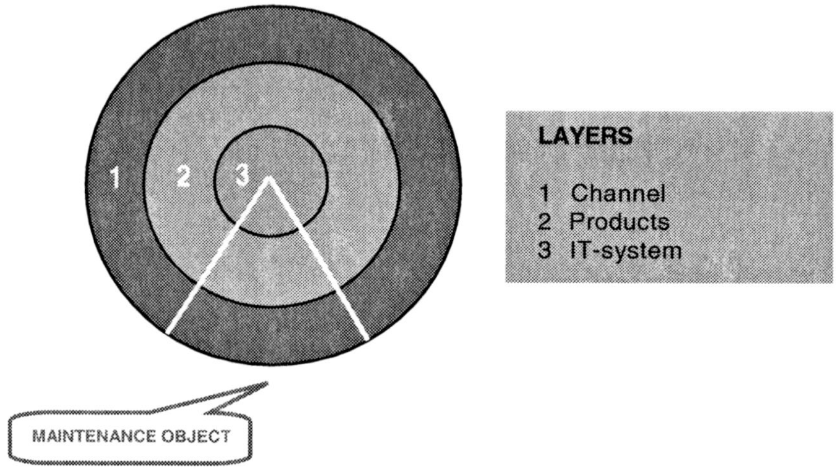

imagines doing it the other way around, that is, start with a defined part of the business (such as a function or process) and then define the maintenance object, what would this lead to? Since there seldom is a one-to-one relationship between IT systems and products/functions, this would probably not be any better in the long run. Our proposal, therefore, is to *define optimal maintenance* objects that can take into account the business perspective as well as the IT perspective. The layers in the object model serve as guidance and must be translated for each organisation, sometimes for each object.

Figure 4 shows one of the maintenance objects in an insurance company for example. The object is called *Child Insurance* and handles all maintenance that is needed for the company's child insurance products to work efficiently.

In the maintenance object in Figure 4, the channel layer (the outer layer) consists of the local representatives of the company that meet customers face to face. It also contains customer services via a telephone service line and mail contacts. Further, it contains the content of certain pages on the company's Website (but only the content of the child insurance information pages; the Website itself is another maintenance object). The product layer contains the back office functions that develop and maintain the insurance products, handle legal issues, support the local representatives in specifically complicated issues, and so forth. The IT system layer contains the IT systems that are needed to produce Child Insurance. Some other systems that Child Insurance shares with the rest of the company, like the Intranet, the Website, the IT systems for book-keeping and personnel, and so forth, are other maintenance objects and this object only delivers its specific demands and needs to the maintenance of these objects.

Business Parties in Maintenance: The "Who" Perspective

The maintenance object also contains a "who" perspective. For the purpose of mapping out which functions/roles in the organisation are involved in the maintenance of a specific object, a map of business parties has been developed (Nordström &

Figure 5: Business Parties in Systems Maintenance.

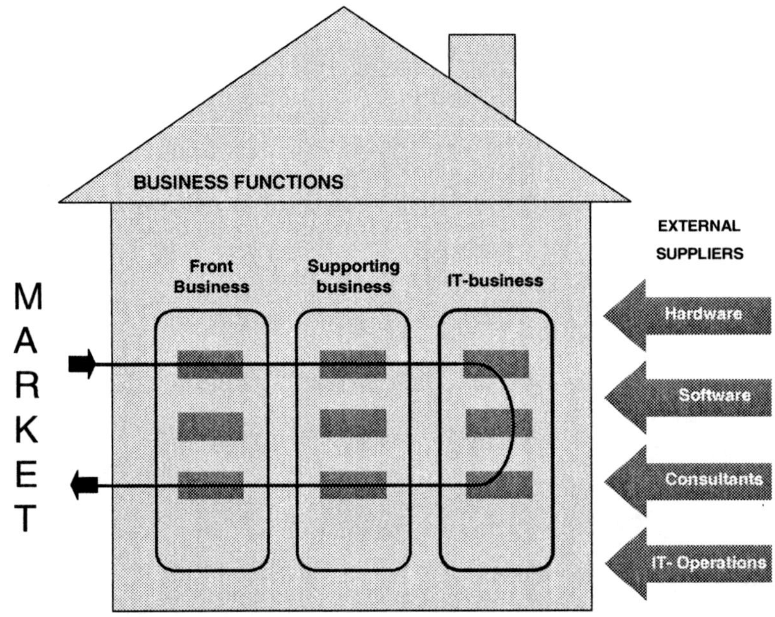

Welander, 2002). The map of business parties (Figure 5) shows the main business parties in a maintenance business, and it can be used at different levels of detail.

The market needs that form the starting point for the internal business process are shown in Figure 5. The market makes demands on the front business, which in turn makes demands on the support functions of the organisation, which in turn make demands on the IT business.

As discussed in the previous section, systems maintenance almost always has elements of internal business exchange, and thus the exchange between the business parties in a specific maintenance object is often unexplored. The map of business parties is meant to be of help in clarifying who makes business with whom from a maintenance point of view. The functions in a specific maintenance object can be identified and then drawn on to the map. This, in turn, helps in finding the right people to fill the roles in the maintenance organisation for the object.

Define the Systems Maintenance Activities

What is maintenance, in essence? We have earlier quoted the IEEE definition that limits the systems maintenance work to four different types of change activities. However, through our own studies of maintenance, we have found that maintenance often includes other activities, such as different types of user support and, especially, activities of managerial nature (Bergvall, 1995). In this, and following studies, we have also clarified the dependency between systems maintenance and IT operations. Because

Figure 6: Definitions of Maintenance Activities.

Maintenance Activity	Definition
Maintenance Management	Activities with the purpose of reaching the agreed upon goals and objectives concerning the maintenance object.
Support	Activities to support users in problem situations and activities to prevent problems.
Change Management	Activities from the occurrence of a need for change until the change is implemented and the object functions in the way it was intended.
IT operations	Activities for the continuous handling of technical infrastructure and IT systems for the purpose of making the IT system accessible to its users.

of this, our definitions of systems maintenance also include IT operations, in order to make the whole object work in practice.

Our definition of systems maintenance is thereby; "the work of continuously managing, changing and supporting maintenance objects where IT systems are integral parts, for the purpose of securing the intended business value and accessibility".

The definition of maintenance can, in practice, vary between two objects in the same organisation. We therefore suggest a specific definition for each object, based on the necessary activities needed in that object. The most important thing, however, is that all who are involved in the maintenance of an object share the view of which maintenance activities are needed for a particular object. The activities in Figure 6 occur in the majority of the objects we have studied.

Other activities from those described in Figure 6 may also be included; for example, marketing, handling of texts and images, handling of security solutions, and so forth, depending on the character of the object. The activities above can then be "packeted" into a number of task types, such as emergency tasks, tasks that can be planned, and specific projects. Thereby, one has defined the scope of the maintenance business at an activity level.

Create Forms of Management

One may encounter the view that maintenance cannot be planned nor managed, since changes occur so often nowadays. But that is the very reason why maintenance is more important than ever before. The maintenance must function optimally if the organisation is to be able to handle the increasing pace of change and thus continue to support the business. And to obtain efficient maintenance, one must manage it with well-defined objectives, budget and clear time limits.

Through literary studies (e.g., Bruzelius & Skärvad, 1989; Robbins, 1990; Pigoski, 1997; Handy, 1999) and practical work, we have identified three different means of control that may be used for maintenance:

- Models and procedures
- Maintenance plan
- Maintenance agreements

Models and Procedures

In some cases, development models and methods are used in maintenance work (Pigoski, 1997). Since systems maintenance often means "small" change, as opposed to a development project, these models and methods are often perceived as heavy and difficult to use. Furthermore, development models must often be supplemented with project management models, and thus, development models are considered insufficient for this purpose. Why are project management models not used in maintenance? They sometimes are, when it comes to larger changes or when a number of changes have been packed into so-called releases, but they are not seen as the solutions of the problem of continuous change.

These needs are the starting points for the creation of the Business-Oriented Maintenance Management model. Thus, for all the activities that are defined as maintenance, procedures must be created. Procedures ensure the standardisation of work processes (Robbins, 1990). The maintenance procedures should describe how, when and by whom the activity is to be carried out. Examples of graphical descriptions of procedures can be found in Figure 7 and Figure 8.

Maintenance Plans

Systems maintenance does not really suffer from too few goals; the problem is rather the opposite - there are several overlapping goals and objectives for different parts of the organisation that may lead to goal conflicts in maintenance. By dividing the life of the maintenance object into periods, it is easier to obtain an overview of the goals that are specific for maintenance. These must be based on, or related to, the other present organisational goals and objectives and thereby potential goal conflicts can be sorted out. This also facilitates a follow-up of the quality and customer value of maintenance. Since most business plans and budgets are done on a yearly basis, it is suitable to divide the maintenance period in one-year segments. Figure 7 shows a procedure for strategic maintenance management.

As shown in Figure 7, strategic maintenance management starts with examining the relevant governing documents that apply to the maintenance object (the ones shown in Figure 7 are examples of such documents). These form the basis for the strategic maintenance planning. When the present situation and the relevant organisational goals are described, new objectives for the maintenance object in the coming year are formed. The objectives should be measurable, realistic and clear. The objectives should then form the basis for the total object budget. The result is documented in a maintenance plan that is the governing document for the planned maintenance period. The maintenance plan is then complemented with the necessary agreements with the internal and external suppliers. The maintenance plan also forms the basis for the day-to-day management during the maintenance period.

Figure 8 shows the daily management of the object, as well as the cooperation between the decision-making groups during the maintenance period. In the maintenance object and its surroundings, demands for changes and needs for training and support

Figure 7: Procedure for Planning Systems Maintenance Work (Nordström & Welander, 2002).

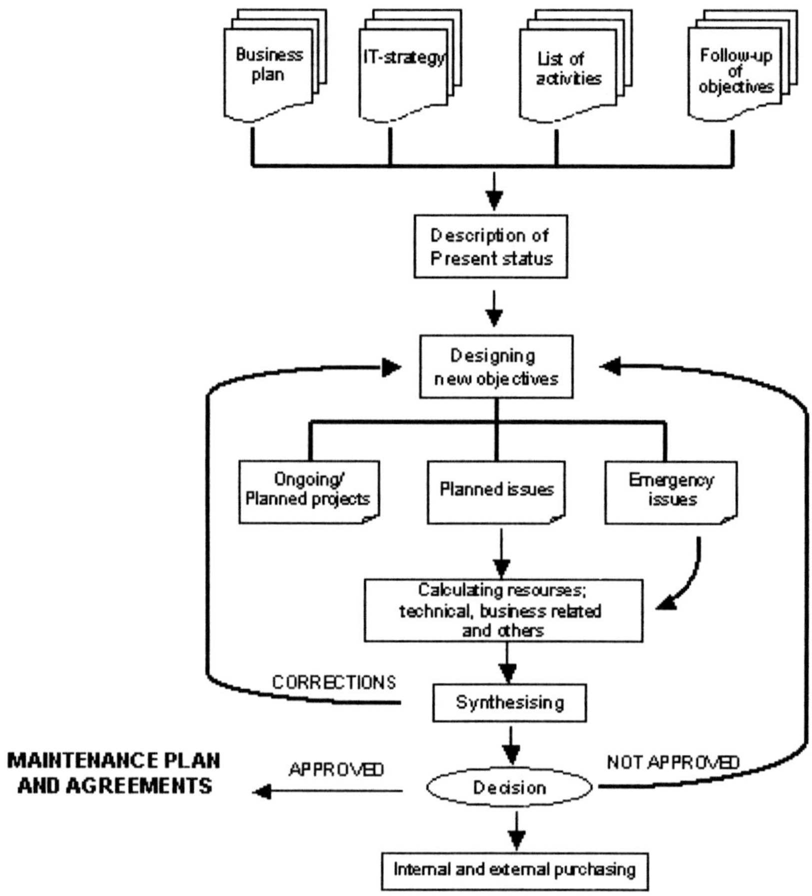

arise. These demands and needs are taken care of by the maintenance group (containing representatives from IT as well as business sections in the organisation) according to the plan. The group classifies, prioritises and decides the required actions. The demands and needs are turned into activities and when they have been taken care of, they are brought back into the maintenance object. In this way, the daily maintenance work "flows" as current. Sometimes, however, demands arise on bigger changes, outside the limits given in the plan. The maintenance group then prepares a decision memo for the steering committee to decide upon. If they choose to carry out the change, new resources must be added, or existing resources reprioritised. After the realisation, the result of the change is implemented in the maintenance object and the maintenance group takes over the responsibility for the changed maintenance object.

Figure 8: Management Principles for the Operative Systems Maintenance Work (Nordström & Welander, 2002).

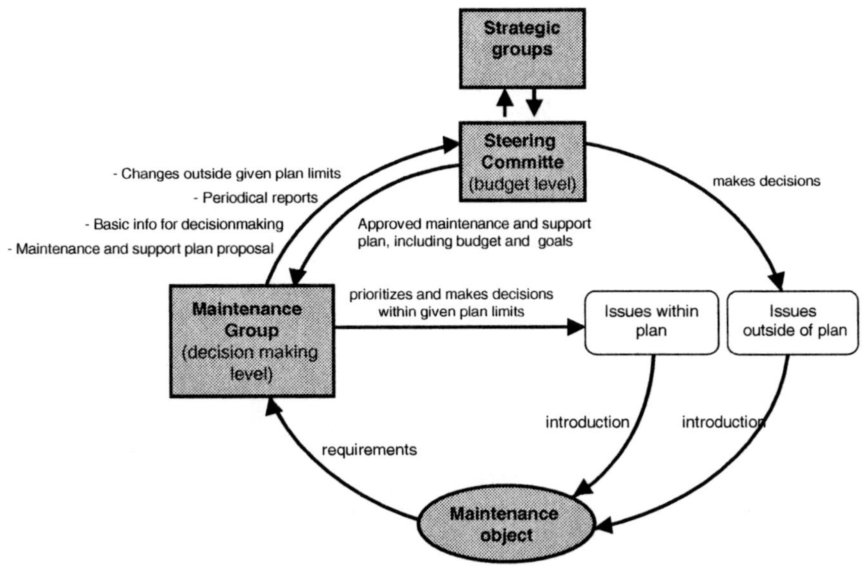

When the result does not turn out as planned, it has become common to change the plan instead of noting changes, taking measures and planning again. If the plan is changed too often during the maintenance period, there is nothing to follow up against at the end of the period, and thereby an important control factor is lost.

Maintenance Contracts/Agreements

The means of control that are used most in maintenance are contracts or agreements between the business and internal and/or external IT suppliers. Unfortunately, the agreements are not always the management instruments for the maintenance business that they ought to be. It is common that the agreements focus on fines, that is, what will happen if one does not agree, rather than focusing on what is actually to be achieved together. In order for an agreement to be considered business-oriented, it should:

- Be described in a measurable, realistic and clear manner.
- Be processed by the involved parties.
- Contain the commitments of the buyer as well as the supplier.

It is important to note that buyer and supplier agree on what the business involves, and describe this in the agreement. Sometimes, however, this seems to be the argument as to why the business exchange is not described. What should be kept in mind when making agreements is the importance of writing the agreements in such a way that they allow a gradual refinement of the business deal, since maintenance business often changes over time. Furthermore, the involved parties should process the agreement themselves, not professional negotiators who often write agreements or contracts in an abstract way.

For individual maintenance objects, there is often a need for additional agreements on different levels, on an overall business level as well as a delivery level per object, for example, development, operations and maintenance.

Organise the Systems Maintenance Business

As mentioned earlier, systems maintenance is often seen as line operations. Since it is most often the IT systems that are maintained, the maintenance organisation is built around these. Based on the characteristics of systems maintenance in which parties from business as well as IT are involved, we believe that a team-based organisation structure is better suited for systems maintenance than the line organisation. The team-based organisation structure makes it possible to combine various expertises, since a team is defined as a number of individuals with different skill levels that work together to reach certain goals (Lind & Skärvad, 2000).

A project organisation, put together for a specific task with a well-defined objective and dissolved when the objective is reached, may be the purest form of the team-based organisation structure (Handy, 1999). However, the element of continuity in systems maintenance makes the pure project organisation less suitable for systems maintenance. The continuity of systems maintenance is better provided for in the matrix organisation, which aims for flexibility by combining two or more organisational structures (Bruzelius & Skärvad, 1989; Gummesson, 1999). The most distinct characteristic of the matrix is that it breaks the basic bureaucratic (line organisational) principle that one single person has the final responsibility. It aims for increased communication, joint problem solving and joint responsibility for results (Bruzelius & Skärvad, 1989; Robbins, 1990).

The Maintenance Organisation

The principle for the maintenance organisation is that it is team-based, and formed on the basis of responsibility and roles. We can see that organisations sometimes try to create a single maintenance organisation for the entire organisation, but this becomes too abstract and impossible to manage efficiently. For each maintenance object that is identified in an organisation, a maintenance organisation should be created (Nordström & Welander, 2002). According to the discussion above, this makes it possible to gather the necessary competences for each specific maintenance object. Figure 9 shows the structure of maintenance organisations. Since we advocate business orientation, in which maintenance is regarded as a form of internal business exchange within the organisation, the maintenance organisation must consist of two parties. Each role in the team must have a role at the same level in the maintenance organisation to make business with. This organisation structure demands maturity from the managers; they must take joint responsibility and make joint decisions with their counterpart at the same level. Any conflicts and disagreements between the holders of these roles cannot be ignored; they must be dealt with and solved (Bruzelius & Skärvad, 1989).

The role names in the maintenance organisation can vary from object to object. The ones mentioned in Figure 9 are only examples; the name of the role should correspond with the content of the role. When an object is identified, it becomes natural to find the role names. If the object contains a process, the budget level roles may be called Process

Figure 9: Maintenance Organisation.

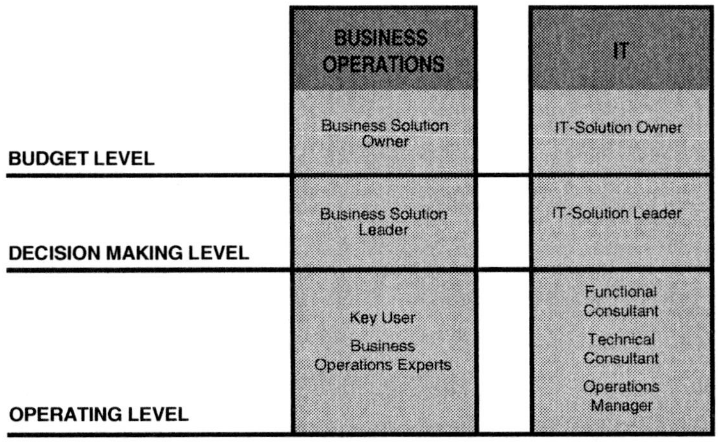

Owner and IT Process Owner, for instance. It is important that physical persons fill the roles, not functions or groups, and the responsibilities of the roles are defined and known. In order to ensure the right entities for the roles in the maintenance organisation, it is important to define the maintenance object, and identify the business parties that are involved in the object (see the map of business parties in Figure 5).

Role Descriptions

The roles are regulated with the help of role descriptions. Between Business Solution Owner and IT Solution Owner, business-oriented agreements are made that settle how maintenance should be conducted. In order for a maintenance organisation to be manageable, the following must apply:

- The maintenance business parties are identified.
- There is clarity about the added value of each business party.
- Each role holder in the maintenance organisation has somebody to make business with.
- All involved business parties are represented in the decision-making and work groups.

The responsibilities of the roles are clarified in role descriptions. These are based on the maintenance activities that have been defined for the maintenance object. The table in Figure 10 shows the overall responsibility for the roles on their respective levels.

On all levels of the maintenance organisation, there are two roles that make business. This is one of the ways of securing the manageability in maintenance, as well as the quality. Both parties on each level must use their competence in their specific area to strive towards the common goals and objectives in the maintenance plan. Because of this, roles on the decision-making or budget levels in the maintenance organisation should neither be added nor removed. On the operating level, however, roles can be

Figure 10: The Overall Responsibility of the Roles.

	DESCRIPTION
BUDGET LEVEL	On the budget level, the roles are of a controlling character. They approve of maintenance plans and sign agreements and contracts. They also decide about increased or decreased work resources. Budget level role holders take part in the Steering Committee.
DECISION MAKING LEVEL	Role holders on the decision making level have the executive responsibility to ensure that the maintenance object functions according to the maintenance plan. Within given limits, the role holder has the main responsibility to prioritize and carry out changes in order to reach the goals. The Maintenance Group is manned by role holders on the decision making level.
OPERATING LEVEL	On the operating level, the work is concentrated on operative maintenance and support. This includes activities such as carrying out changes, giving support, handling IT-operation activities and managing texts and images where necessary.

added as needed. There may also be a need for a strategic layer in the model. The important thing is that the business exchange is well defined, and that coordinating roles are not appointed. One should avoid adding "third parties" in the maintenance organisation; it is usually enough to have one business party and one technical party. The fact that these come from different organisations, or parts of the organisation, is handled by business-oriented agreements between those responsible in the line organisation. The principle is the same as in a project.

Filling the Roles

The people best suited to reach the goals should fill the roles. The best decision-making and work groups are the ones put together on the basis of experience, competence and personality, not because they belong to any particular line organisation (Mohrman et al., 1995). This is the strength of the maintenance organisation — and at the same time its weakness, since it may be hard to plan the work with the line function that the person belongs to. Resource contracts may be one method to use if it is difficult to free resources from the line organisation to maintenance. The resource contract is signed between one of the role holders on the budget level in the maintenance organisation and the line manager who is in control of the desired personal resource.

The filling of the roles in a maintenance organisation is very important. An organisation with roles held by the wrong people cannot fulfil its commitments in the maintenance plan. The following principles should be taken into account when filling the roles in a maintenance organisation, in order to secure the business orientation:

- The role holders must always be physical persons and not groups of people.
- The roles on the budget- and decision-making levels can never be held by the same person; for example, Business Solution Owner (BSO) and Business Solution Leader (BSL) can never be the same person.

- The roles on the budget- and decision-making levels can never be held by several people, for example, there can not be more than one BSL in the same object.
- The role of Business Solution Owner should always be placed on the business side of the organisation and be held by a person who is in control of the necessary resources.
- The roles on the operative level can usually be outsourced, but one should be more careful about outsourcing the IT Solution Owner and the IT Solution Leader, since these roles in an outsourcing situation often are responsible for coordinating several suppliers.

Decision-Making Groups

The teamwork is done in decision-making groups. The two most important are the steering committee and the maintenance group. The budget layer in the maintenance organisation forms the steering committee and the decision-making layer forms the maintenance group. One positive effect of the team structure is that a role holder in the maintenance organisation can have one authority in the maintenance organisation, but does not necessarily need to have the same authority in the line organisation. This requires that there is a maintenance plan, or an equivalent governing document, that describes what is to be done and how. Figure 8 showed the principles for the operative management.

FUTURE TRENDS

The definition of optimal maintenance objects is a central theme in the model that is presented and discussed in this chapter. When the business becomes part of the maintenance object, problems may arise concerning how to draw the boundary between what is systems maintenance and what is usage of the maintenance object. This is especially evident in maintenance objects that constitute processes or functions in a business. One of the authors of this chapter is currently involved in a research project that defines factors that clarify these boundaries and delimit maintenance objects. The project also defines different types of maintenance objects, so-called object classes, as well as principles for how to manage and organise these objects in the intersection between the organisational line and team-based work.

The model described in this chapter focuses on singular maintenance objects. In the research project, the multiple maintenance objects in an organisation are also dealt with.

SUMMARY

The description of Business Oriented Maintenance Management has contained a number of central concepts. In Figure 11, the relationships between them are modelled. Like the model, this graph is normative.

The model can be summarised as follows: An optimal maintenance object consists of business(es) as well as IT systems, as shown in Figure 11. The optimal maintenance object is handled by business parties. A business-oriented maintenance team, which is

Figure 11: The Relations between Concepts of the Model.

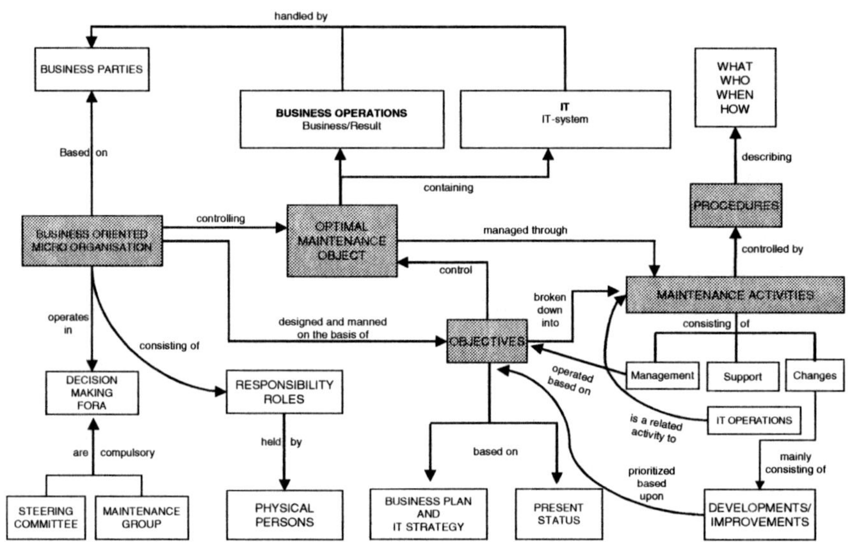

based on the business parties, works in decision groups that manage the optimal maintenance object. The steering committee and the maintenance group are compulsory decision-making entities. The team is built from responsibility roles that are held by physical persons. The team is built and the roles in it are created from objectives that are based on business plans and descriptions of the present state. The optimal maintenance object is handled through maintenance activities that are often broken down into maintenance management, support and change management. Change management mainly consists of development and improvement work that is prioritised from the objectives. In order to make maintenance work in practice, IT operations should also be co-planned with maintenance activities. The maintenance activities are managed at an action level with the help of procedures that describe what, when, where and how.

Furthermore, in this section, documents such as maintenance plans and agreements have been discussed. In the maintenance plan that is the result of a maintenance implementation, all the success factors for a specific object are documented.

The biggest development potential in the above mentioned model lies in the theories about the maintenance objects and their delimitations. Thus, this will be the focus in the continued research and development of Business Oriented Maintenance Management.

REFERENCES

Bendifallah, S., & Scacchi, W. (1987). Understanding software maintenance work. *IEEE Transactions on Software Engineering, SE-13*(3)

Bergvall, M. (1995). *Systems maintenance in practice –A qualitative study concerning central concepts, activities and roles.* IDA, Linköping University, (In Swedish).

Bergvall, M., & Welander, T. (1996). *Business oriented systems maintenance.* Dataföreningens Förlag AB, Stockholm, (In Swedish).

Berndtson, O., & Welander, T. (1991). *Functioning systems maintenance.* Dataföreningens förlags AB, Stockholm, (In Swedish).

Bruzelius, L H., & Skärvad, P.-H. (1989). *Integrated organisation studies.* Studentlitteratur, Lund, (In Swedish).

Goldkuhl, G. (1992). From HUMOR to VITS. IDA, Linköping University, (In Swedish).

Goldkuhl, G. (1993). *Business develop data systems*, Intention, Linköping, (In Swedish).

Goldkuhl, G., & Röstlinger, A. (1998). *The practice concept – A practice generic model as a basis for theory development and business development*, CMTO, Linköping University, (In Swedish).

Grönroos, C. (2000). *Service management and marketing. A customer relationship management approach.* Chichester, England: John Wiley & Sons.

Gummesson, E. (1999). *Total relationship marketing. Rethinking marketing management: From 4 Ps to 30 Rs.* Butterworth-Heinemann.

Handy, C. (1999). *Understanding organisations.* London: Penguin Books Ltd.

IEEE. (1990). *IEEE standard glossary of software engineering terminology* (IEEE Standard 610.12). New York: Institute of Electrical and Electronics Engineers Inc.

ISO/IEC. (2002). *Systems engineering – System life cycle processes,* 15288.

Kajko-Mattsson, M. (2001). Taxonomy of problem management activities. *Proceeding of the Fifth Conference on Software Maintenance and Reengineering, CSMR 2001*, Lisbon, Portugal, IEEE Computer Society.

Kemerer, F.C., & Slaughter, S.A. (1997). Determinants of software maintenance profiles: An empirical investigation. *Journal of Software Maintenance: Research and Practice*, *9*(4), Wiley Inter Science.

Kitchenham, B.A. et al. (1999). Towards an ontology of software maintenance. *Journal of Software Maintenance: Research and Practice*, *11*(6), Wiley InterScience.

Lientz, B., & Swanson, E.B. (1980). *Software maintenance management.* Reading, MA: Addison – Wesley.

Lind, J-I., & Skärvad, P.-H. (2000). *New teams in the wrganisational world.* Liber AB, Malmö, (in Swedish).

Longstreet, D. (2001). *Software metrics – Applied software economics.* Available: *http://www.ifpug.com/020927*

Mohrman, S.A. et al. (1995). *Designing team-based organizations. New forms for knowledge work.* San Francisco: Jossey-Bass Inc.

Niessink, F., & van Vliet, H. (2000). Software maintenance from a service perspective. *Journal of Software Maintenance: Research and Practice*, *12*(2), Wiley InterScience.

Nordström, M., & Welander, T. (2002). *Business oriented maintenance management - A reference model for (system) maintenance*, Dataföreningen Kompetens, Stockholm, (in Swedish).

Parikh, G. (1988). *Techniques of program and systems maintenance*. QED Information Sciences, Wellesley.

Pigoski, T.M. (1997). *Practical software maintenance*. New York: John Wiley & Sons.

Robbins, S.P. (1990). *Organization theory structure designs and applications*. New Jersey: Prentice Hall, International Editions.

Scott, W.R. (1998). *Organizations – Rational, natural and open systems* (4th ed.). New Jersey: Prentice Hall.

Chapter XV

Reducing IS Maintenance by Improving the Quality of IS Development Processes and Practices

Evan W. Duggan, University of Alabama, USA

ABSTRACT

The correlation between the quality of information systems (IS) development practices, the products they shape, and systems maintainability has been well established. Several organizations have expended large amounts of money on ineffective software that have attracted high maintenance activities, which consume a disproportionate share of IS development resources. The IS quandary is how to reverse this trend, and free up resources for more productive organizational endeavors. This chapter presents a review of a variety of IS quality-oriented approaches (based on research findings and dispassionate practitioner accounts) and an indication of their advantages and weaknesses, and the development environments and contexts for which they are most suited. These techniques are available to software developers to be used individually or in synergistic combinations to confront the prevalent problem of poor software quality and reduce its unfavorable impact on software maintenance.

INTRODUCTION

Organizations invest in information systems (IS) to apply information technology (IT) in support of their business processes against the backdrop of the extremely short half-life of IT and typically volatile business environments. The goal of IS maintenance, therefore, is to preserve some measure of stability (during the longest period of a system's life cycle) by keeping the application in congruence with the business operations it enables (Floyd, 1987). All systems (including IS) may degrade because of atrophy—the propensity of entities to deteriorate for lack of sustenance, or entropy—impairment due to natural decay. IS stability is directed at preventing the former and delaying the latter to leverage an organization's IS investment over a longer period.

Maintenance activities have progressively consumed a larger share of systems development budgets (Banker et al., 1998; Pressman, 2000; Swanson & Beath, 1989): approximately 40 percent in the 1970s; 60-70 percent in the 1980s; and up to 80 percent in the 1990s (Hoffer et al., 2002). But beyond this high resource allocation, organizations bear at least two other often overlooked systems maintenance costs: the direct cost of systems downtime, estimated by the Standish Group at $10,000 per minute for mission-critical applications (Schaider, 1999) and the opportunity cost of resources devoted to software maintenance, which could be invested in more productive organizational pursuits (Banker & Slaughter, 1997; Keil, 1995).

Consequently, several researchers (Banker et al., 1991; Dishaw & Strong, 1998; Prechelt et al., 2001; Ramanujan et al., 2000) have focused on understanding this phenomenon of escalating IS maintenance and have prescribed improvements to the maintenance process. They have analyzed the effects of factors such as software complexity, size, age, documentation, user population, program structure, capability of the maintenance group, and the stability of the business environment on maintenance practices.

Others, such as Banker et al. (1993), Banker and Slaughter (1997) and Boehm (1981) have concentrated on maintenance economies and cost-reducing mechanisms. Yet a third group of researchers (Banker et al., 1991, Dekleva, 1992; Gibson & Senn, 1989; Ghods & Nelson, 1998, Swanson & Dans, 2000; Vessey & Weber, 1984; Zagal et al., 2002) have explored the downstream effect of the quality of IS development practices and delivery processes on system maintainability and the maintenance experience. System maintainability has been defined as the ease and speed with which systems can be understood and modified to correct errors, adapt to changing business environments, and improve performance (Bandi, Vaishnavi & Turk, 2003; Oman & Hagemeister, 1994; Pressman, 2001; Zhuo et al., 1993). The discussion in this chapter extends the latter theme and describes a set of quality-focused, IS delivery approaches that could induce maintainability as a de facto software development goal.

There is empirical confirmation of the proposition that mature systems delivery processes and effective methods produce high quality systems (Harter et al., 1998; Kalifa & Verner, 2000; Ravichandram & Rai, 1996). Similarly, there is enormous support among researchers for a multivariate attack on the problem of poor software quality with deliberate and focused combinations of available methods, matched specifically to the software application context (Broady et al., 1994; Fitzgerald, 1998; Hocking, 1998; Jaakkola & Drake, 1991; Korac-Bosvert & Kouzmin, 1995; Lee & Xia, 2002; Meso & Medo, 2000; Saberwal & Robey, 1995; Vessey & Glass, 1998; Vlasblom et al., 1995). However, the allure has not necessarily caught on in practitioner communities, where several false alarms of silver bullets have left a great deal of ambivalence about the legitimacy of some approaches.

In this chapter, I synthesize elements of these streams of research to make three important contributions to the theme of managing software maintenance in organizations. First, I provide an extensive review of the literature on IS quality, maintenance practices, and information systems development approaches with implications for software maintainability. Second, I provide an analysis of researcher and practitioner accounts of several IS delivery approaches and the development contexts in which they may be applicable for improving systems quality and ultimately reducing the maintenance burden. These objectives support the third contribution, which is to provide some guidance to pre-development analyses and selection decisions about relevant alternatives and appropriate approaches (or combination of methods) within particular development settings.

In the rest of this chapter, I elaborate on IS quality problems, define accepted software quality requisites, and describe several available approaches that have been employed to focus on the quality of the software development process, the quality of the delivered product, and their implications for software maintainability. The essential thesis and the dominant message is that the upstream investment in the selection of a context-relevant mix of development methods can provide the software process improvement needed to deliver higher quality IS products and contribute to the reduction of the maintenance burden and costs downstream.

INFORMATION SYSTEMS QUALITY PROBLEMS

Software developers have failed to capitalize on the convergence of information and communications technologies (and the innovations they have enabled) to establish high quality organizational systems (Brynjolfssen, 1993; Gibbs, 1994). Consequently, software development woes have been a persistent concern for several years. There have been accounts of runaway projects (Mousinho, 1990), low quality applications (Niederman et al., 1991), severe software failures (KPMG in Computerworld, April 25, 1994), and high IS failure rate among Fortune 500 companies (the Standish Group International Inc., 1998). The well-publicized failure of the Denver airport baggage handling system is not atypical (Gibbs, 1994); recently, CIOs have expressed general dissatisfaction with the quality of their organizations' business software (CIO Magazine, June 2001).

Yet many systems developed in the last 25 years have outlasted the century; indeed, systems typically outlive the tenure of the people who develop, maintain, and use them by a long way (Swanson & Dans, 2000). The global spotlight on theY2K maintenance predicament dramatically underscored the long-term implications of IS development quality on maintenance, particularly when, as desired, systems experience longevity. Beyond the long-term cost impact of poorly developed systems, two morale issues bear emphasis: It is virtually impossible to establish developers' accountability for subsequent maintenance problems (Ghods & Nelson, 1998) and despite its prevalence, systems maintenance is still considered less rewarding than original development and perhaps even demotivating (Swanson & Beath, 1989; Zagal et al., 2002).

Brooks (1987) suggested that the essential difficulties of software development are instigated by uncontrollable factors such as its inherent complexity, requisite tractability (adaptability and conformity), and that, unlike physical products, software remains invisible during construction. These systems development hazards have, in fact, increased over time (Al-Mushayt et al., 2001). Software continues to conform to organizational characteristics and adapt to volatile business processes. We have not yet created visual models of software design products, and quality is primarily experienced through utilization. The increased organizational reliance on IS to apply progressively more sophisticated IT innovations to enable strategic priorities and enhance operational efficiencies have further delineated an increasing intolerance for the disruptions that system failures cause.[1]

The need for high-quality software is glaring. But what constitutes software quality? Palvia et al. (2001) offered two perspectives on this question: IS software quality is discernible in the features and characteristics that bear on the satisfaction of perceived needs and the delivery of expected benefits; its determination is conditioned, however, by the varied perceptions of developers, managers and users. Further, they claim, there is an often ignored but important socio-technical dimension of IS quality that reflects the symbiosis of human and machine in the accomplishment of system tasks.

Several scholars (Erikkson & McFadden, 1993; Grady, 1993; Hanna, 1995; Hough, 1993) have contributed further to the elucidation of the characteristics of IS quality. Systems should produce reliable features that are easy to access and use with a high probability of correct response and consistently acceptable response times. The delivery ought to be timely so that the solution remains relevant beyond deployment and the overall benefits should outstrip life cycle costs. Quality software should be maintainable: Defects discovered in field use should be amenable to correction and their sources ascertainable with normal effort; the software should be scalable so as to incorporate unforeseen functionality and accommodate additional users. The garbage heap of unused information systems is strewn, however, with brilliantly conceived, technical masterpieces because, according to Newman and Robey (1992), systems success is also determined by the affective and behavioral responses of stakeholders. This has prompted other scholars to include actual usage as a desirable requisite of software quality (Lyytinen, 1988; Markus & Keil, 1994).

It is generally acknowledged that organizations engage in four categories of software maintenance (Ramanujan et al., 2000): Corrective maintenance contends with fixing errors delivered with the software; adaptive maintenance is primarily about preserving the systems utility and relevance in changing business environments; perfective maintenance is concerned with enhancing functionality; and preventive maintenance refers to preemptive changes to forestall future problems. There is the view that excellent software merely alleviates corrective maintenance, which accounts for only a small proportion of software support (Cornelius et al., 1989). However, the combined definition of software quality belies this notion. Surely, high-quality systems that deliver the requisite functionality originally may attract other categories of maintenance later because they are extended beyond their normal lifetime, but in general, high-quality systems also provide the scalability to facilitate enhancements and are more amenable to easy comprehension (Bandi et al., 2003; Banker et al., 1998).

IMPROVING IS QUALITY

IS development involves a combination of social and technical processes in which several stakeholders interact to influence technical considerations (Robey et al., 2001). The participating users, developers, and managers react to each other as well as to the development approaches that are invoked (Palvia et al., 2001). These may include socio-technical features (such as prototyping and joint application development), IS development process structure, IS delivery paradigms (commonly distinguishing features of a family of life cycle models, such as the waterfall model or iterative/interactive approaches), IS delivery methods (principles and objectives like rapid application development and extreme programming that motivate particular development techniques), and development tools—supporting features and technologies (Iivari et al., 2000-2001).

In order to explicate their potential contribution to the suggested method-mix required to produce high-quality systems, several of these approaches are described below with assessments of claimed benefits and their limitations in given contexts. However, space and time would not permit descriptions of the abundance of the systems development tools (e.g., CASE, data flow diagrams, use cases, etc.) that support IS development. Similarly, the traditional waterfall SDLC paradigm, which is very well known and has been widely discussed in the literature, will not be covered in this chapter.

Social Process of Information Systems Development

Many IS development problems can be traced to inadequate user-developer interaction, which results in miscommunication and misunderstanding of systems requirements (Holtzblatt & Beyer, 1995) and inadequate attention paid to the social implications of systems delivery (Newman & Robey, 1992). Socio-technical systems (STS) thinking recognizes that IS are embedded within complex social structures in organizations. It seeks therefore to balance the human, organizational, and technical elements of the implementation environment (Al-Mushayt et al., 2001; Palvia et al., 2001) and co-generate social and technical requirements that influence systems quality (Doherty & King, 1998; Fox, 1995; Shani & Sena, 1994), which eventually determines the effort that must be devoted to systems maintenance.

Several user-centered themes, such as prototyping, joint application development, participatory design, and quality function deployment help to incorporate STS objectives in IS development. They provide the opportunity for attaining user involvement in software development (Barki & Hartwick, 1994); users meaningfully involved in system-building identify with system goals and often demonstrate commitment to system success (Borovits et al., 1990; Dodd & Carr, 1994; Hough, 1993). Involvement enhances the importance users attach to their systems development roles (Barki & Hartwick), which lays the foundation for improved systems quality and maintainability.

Prototyping

Prototyping involves close user-developer interaction to generate a series of progressively refined models of an intended system in order to simulate actual usage experience and progressively demonstrate the system's appearance and behavior. The initial model is seeded by partially defined requirements, and successive prototypes expand the concept based on users' feedback. The process progresses toward the discovery of the requirements (Boar, 1984; Davis, 1994; Dekleva, 1992; Weinberg, 1991). Prototyping may also be used to isolate and discover design problems, to obtain a more realistic sense of the proposed solution (proof of concept), and to uncover system malfunction during deployment. Non-procedural languages have provided the programming productivity to ensure the viability of this approach by enabling rapid production of succeeding versions. Two classes of prototypes are typically developed: a "throwaway" model, which is discarded at the end of the discovery process, and an "evolutionary" model, which is expanded to full functional form.

This technique is recommended to reduce the risk of failure of complex systems, for which requirements cannot be rigorously pre-specified (Weinberg, 1991). Prototyping permits an early assessment of the impact of the system on the user environment, which may also facilitate more effective change management (Adamopoulos et al., 1998). User-designer rapport, another of its key benefits, helps to moderate both quality-related and usage failure factors (Baskerville & Stage, 1996). However, prototyping has been known to overemphasize aesthetics (such as format of screens and reports) at the expense of performance reliability issues (Korac-Boisvert & Kouzmin, 1995). The opportunity for repeated revisions may also induce scope creep (Wetherbe, 1991), and counter-productivity because of over-analysis.

Joint Application Development (JAD)

JAD emphasizes effective communication and interaction among system users and developers (Liou & Chen, 1993-94). It was introduced in the 1970s as an alternative to the interviewing technique for generating information systems requirements. The formal structure consists of five phases[2] (Wood & Silver, 1995), including a workshop—a series of facilitated meetings that lasts for three to five days, depending on the scope and complexity of the project. In these meetings, system developers, users, and managers pool their knowledge and perspectives to determine information requirements. JAD has contributed to more accurate and consistent requirements than those aggregated from several interviews, and has helped to reduce the cycle time for specifying requirements from months and years to weeks. The workshop also provides a vehicle for strengthening user involvement (Andrews, 1991; Wood & Silver).

However, JAD meetings are conducted under the freely interacting group structure, in which the social and emotional dynamics of group relationships often impede the accomplishment of task objectives. Facilitation excellence is therefore a pivotal JAD requirement to help overcome potential group problems such as destructive dominance, freeloading—inadequate participation due to unnecessary acquiescence to powerful and influential group members, or simply by election because group members contribute of their own volition, and groupthink—the fixation on preserving group harmony (Kettelhut, 1993). Kettelhut, and Wood and Silver (1995) have advanced several recommendations for addressing these problems.

Participatory Design (PD)

PD is a powerful user participation scheme that is mostly practiced in Scandinavia. Its objective is to empower workers to make technology adoption decisions that determine how to improve their work lives. While JAD exploits opportunities for user-developer teams to experience synergy during the technical specification and design of IS, PD stresses technical knowledge-sharing to enhance social interactions (Carmel et al., 1993). PD promotes mutual learning, empathy, and the cross-fertilization of knowledge and encourages users and developers to help each other understand their respective domains (Kjaer & Madsen, 1995). PD stimulates more informed decision-making, broader user commitment, better systems fit to organizational needs, and sometimes longer-term morale benefits (Mankin & Cohen, 1997). It requires total organizational commitment; some feel that it may not be practical outside of the protection of Scandinavia's codetermination laws, which mandate such worker participation (Muller et al., 1993).

Quality Function Deployment (QFD)

QFD has been used extensively in manufacturing to capture, quantify, and prioritize customer preferences and other quality requirements and monitor their delivery through product design and fabrication. The deliberate focus on the customer typically leads to better products and services and often produces process improvement opportunities. QFD employs many quality-tracking techniques, such as the house of quality matrix through which product performance requirements are mapped to design decisions, affinity diagrams, hierarchy trees, and relations diagrams for assimilating interrelationships, discovering priorities, and even unearthing associated but unexpressed requirements. Process decision program diagrams are sometimes used to study potential failure factors of proposed design solutions. When QFD is used in IS, it is referred to as software QFD or SQFD (McDonald, 1995).

With SQFD, user quality requirements are deliberately captured and explicitly articulated, prioritized, and mapped to measurable system features; the results are reviewed with the users, and systematically tracked throughout the development process (Erikkson & McFadden, 1993). Elboushi (1997) demonstrated its effectiveness in producing efficient, robust, and consistent requirements for customers with diverse needs in an object-oriented application. It is time consuming, however. Successful use requires a quality-focused organization culture, and the process has to be accompanied by excellent group decision-making techniques to accommodate divergent and conflicting requirements (Ho et al., 1999) and solve other problems related to team dynamics and behavior management (Martins & Aspinwall, 2001).

IS Process Management

The inverse relationship between high-quality systems and the extent and difficulty of maintenance is axiomatic. However, the growing acceptance that a mature IS delivery process is a pre-requisite for delivering high-quality systems (Harter et al., 1998; Kalifa & Verner, 2000; Ravichandram & Rai, 1996, 2000) may be responsible for the relatively recent systems development preoccupation with formal IS process management techniques. The main vehicle through which process management rigor is established is the systems development methodology but organizations have also been paying a great deal of attention to the formal assessment of IS process capability (CIO magazine, April 2001) as a precursor to process improvement decisions.

Systems Development Methodology

A systems development methodology (SDM) provides the blueprint for progressing through the systems development life cycle. It prescribes the inputs to each development phase, what, when and how activities are performed, the deliverables of each phase of the methodology and their quality standards, the roles of people, and the tools and techniques that are supported in each stage (Roberts et al., 1999). The aim of SDM is to provide consistent, stable, and repeatable protocols and procedures for structuring systems delivery. It is recommended that an organization adopts a single methodology and trains all developers in its use. This allows for consistent process management across different projects and permits deployment of project participants across multiple projects to minimize the risk of failures due to attrition. However, methodologies may also be burdensome and some development efforts may well be frustrated by onerous process structures (Fitzgerald, 2000; Flatten, 1992).

Process Assessment Instruments

The best-known process assessment method is the Capability Maturity Model (CMM), an introspective tool to help organizations devise strategies for moving their process capability to the next level, and eventually as far as they can go. It was the brainchild of the Software Engineering Institute (SEI) of Carnegie Mellon University. The instrument uses five levels[3] to assess the maturity and the degree of discipline of an organization's IS development process against a normative ideal.

Several organizations have claimed CMM benefits such as shorter development cycles, reduced rework, higher development productivity, higher quality systems, and unsolicited end-user feedback about improvement and cost-reduction opportunities (CIO Magazine, April 2001). Software Process Improvement Capability Determination (SPICE) is another assessment instrument that addresses process capability determination and process improvement. It was developed collaboratively by 14 nations under the auspices of the International Standards Organization. Others include Bootstrap, Software Evaluation Process Model (SEPRM), and Personal Software Process (PSP). The last three are not as well known as CMM and SPICE.

IS Development Methods

Besides traditional SDLC methods, Robey et al. (2001) distinguished between two development paradigms that have helped to improve systems quality by reducing cognitive and technical complexity: the iterative/incremental paradigm (used with agile development methods, and cleanroom software engineering) and the software reuse paradigm, which is embodied in object-oriented and components-based development methods. The former helps to produce manageable pieces of the system functionality iteratively and/or incrementally and secure early buy-in by producing usable system increments earlier. The latter includes development methods that focus extensively on abstracting manageable units of software functionality and developing modules for reuse (Bandi et al., 2003).

Reuse in third generation programming languages targeted programming productivity by providing subroutines for common functionality that are used in several programs. Object and component technologies, however, have extended the objective to also include systems building quality and the reduction of scale-related complexities (Szyperski, 1998).

Agile Development Methods

Agile development philosophies seek to minimize encumbrances to expeditious software development and deployment. Methods such as dynamic systems development methodology (DSDM), a rapid application development (RAD) derivative that is used extensively in the UK (Barrow, 2000; Beynon-Davies et al., 2000) and extreme programming (XP) have grown in popularity because of claims that they reduce software failure rates, especially in volatile business environments. Agile development is touted to be both fast and efficient and small and nimble: requirements determination is abbreviated, system features are delivered in small increments, and the development team is small and interacts closely with intended system users.

RAD, for example, enables faster delivery of functional parts of an application (Hough, 1993) by segmenting a large development into smaller, more manageable modules that are developed in a parallel and evolutionary process. RAD embraces other user-centered design techniques such as JAD and prototyping. These help to blend analysis, design, and construction during the systems development life cycle and accelerate systems delivery. RAD begins with preliminary, high-level requirements that are used to produce an initial system model. The process involves intense user-developer interactions to alternate between modeling and evolutionary prototyping and progresses toward a fully documented, deployment-ready system (Hanna, 1995).

RAD is typically used with smaller, more easily partitioned systems that have clearly defined user groups (Beynon-Davies, 1998). It contributes to the reduction of the development cycle (average delivery times ranging from three to six months), which helps to reduce development costs while ensuring system-business fit. However, RAD sometimes sub-optimizes on speed of development and may forfeit desirable quality features for the compressed development cycle. For example, design rigor may be sacrificed in favor of quick business value (Bourne, 1994), and project delays are sometimes avoided by reducing requirements rather than postponing and rescheduling deadlines (Redding, 1995). Both could contravene system maintainability objectives. If the system is required for a long time RAD should probably not be the method of choice.

XP is also a radical systems delivery method, which helps small, co-located development teams use evolutionary deployment strategies to quickly produce small-scale systems (Beck, 2000). It uses highly interactive customer-developer sessions to produce requirements, and two-person programming teams (pair programming) to design and construct system modules in a series of small releases. Planning, analysis, design, and construction activities are collapsed into a single phase. First, users generate and prioritize "story cards" of features they require and developers classify them according to implementation risk and estimate their implementation time. Users then select the feature(s) to be developed and deployed next and developers distribute the workload among two-member implementation teams, who construct, test, deploy, and integrate new functionality into the overall system.

A great deal of skepticism surrounds the authenticity of this technique and its lack of process rigor (Glass, 2001). Proponents of the approach admit that it is "process-light," but deliberately so. They attest to its efficacy particularly in stabilizing systems quality and developing applications rapidly in environments of high volatility, in which business processes change frequently (Paulk, 2001). Like RAD, this approach could win the race for systems delivery ahead of business process changes, but this, conceivably, may only postpone the problem, which again breaches software design-for-maintainability objectives.

Object-Oriented Development (OOD)

OOD represents a major paradigm shift from traditional systems-building approaches, under which the independence of data and program procedures was almost sacrosanct. Object-orientation embraces exactly the opposite concept: Information systems are modeled and designed as collections of interacting objects about which organizations keep data. Objects encapsulate[4] (package and hide) data attributes and methods (also called behavior or operations), the only program procedures that are allowed to manipulate the attributes.

One complexity-reducing feature of object-oriented models is the similarity between notional objects and the physical or conceptual artifacts they represent (Brown, 2002). However, reusability (with or without modification) in applications other than the one for which they were created is the major benefit (Schmidt & Fayad, 1997). The focus on reuse also forces more disciplined design approaches, which enhances system reliability (Johnson et al., 1999) and results in more flexible systems that are easier to maintain (Agarwal et al., 2000). OO approaches have been accepted very slowly due to resistance from both developers and managers, presumably because of the steep organizational learning curve (Brown). The initial inability to integrate object-based modules with legacy systems (Bordoloi & Lee, 1994; Johnson et al., 1999), and the unavailability of familiar analytical models were also problematic (Fichman & Kemerer, 1992). Both have been rectified.

Component-Based Development (CBD)

CBD accommodates the assembly of prefabricated, platform-neutral "packages" of software functionality (components) that are reusable across multiple applications. It involves three steps—provisioning, inventorying, and assembling—in which software components are created by developers, registered with component repositories, and made available for application assembly, respectively. The granularity of these components may range from self-contained objects and subroutines to entire applications that deliver cohesive software functionality. There are infrastructural components, domain components of specific business application logic, or wrapped components to accommodate pre-existing functionality from legacy systems; all may provide presentation, data, and application logic services. Components are provisioned independently of immediate need and may be acquired or accessed to construct fully functioning systems (Szyperski, 1998).

The CBD approach contributes to delivery speed and eliminates unnecessarily repetitive analysis, design, and programming steps to produce commonly used applications infrastructure. Component costs are lower because they are amortizable over multiple applications (Szyperski, 1998). Importantly, CBD assemblers need not be system developers; thus entire systems solutions may be provided by non-technical domain experts (Robey et al., 2001). CBD addresses system maintainability directly, because components are replaceable; individual units that are either obsolete or deficient may be upgraded independently (Szyperski, 1998). The absence of agreed upon interoperability standards (Sparling, 2000) and the lack of a critical mass of component repositories have been the most important restrictions on the wider applicability of CBD.

Defect Prevention and Detection in IS

The IS development approaches discussed earlier addressed software maintainability indirectly by describing quality-oriented, software development behaviors that may increase the probability of delivering better software products and ultimately reduce the maintenance burden. The two techniques to be discussed next, cleanroom software engineering (CSE) and orthogonal defect classification (ODC) though philosophically opposing concepts (with regard to their approach to treating software defects), target system maintainability directly by focusing specifically on preventing and detecting defects, respectively. Like the preceding approaches, they may be used in combination with other techniques, and although both have been available for some time, they are not yet widely used.

Cleanroom Software Engineering

CSE has as its major focus the prevention instead of the detection of software defects. This method was borrowed from the semi-conductor industry where contaminant-free rooms were established to prevent defects during the production of silicon chips. Its objective is to produce high-quality software with certified reliability for failure-free performance in field use. CSE systems are generated incrementally in small delivery units by small development teams, under statistical quality control to better manage the evolution of product quality. Each increment of functionality is peer-reviewed to increase the probability of delivering error-free code. After construction, a subset of all possible use cases of the module is sampled, and inferential statistics used to determine whether defects in that module are above pre-established thresholds. If so, the module is abandoned and reconstructed.

Several high-quality, cleanroom applications have been delivered (Agrawal & Whittaker, 1993; Hausler et al., 1994; Head, 1994; Trammell et al., 1996) with significantly increased development productivity (Gibbs, 1994), and greatly reduced errors per line of code (Jerva, 2001; Spangler, 1996). The reduction of software failure in field-use results in lower maintenance effort and cost, and longer product life. Opponents of the cleanroom technique have mainly attacked the method's philosophical aversion to software verification by traditional inspection and testing methods (Beizer, 1997); in CSE, defective modules are redeveloped instead of modified.

Orthogonal Defect Classification

It is axiomatic that the last software error will never be caught before systems deployment, and sometimes not even after. Unfortunately, this notion is sometimes used to short-circuit system verification in order to expedite delivery. Among the many useful testing techniques that exist, ODC is isolated and described in this chapter because of the insights it provides to the development exercise: It removed the quandary organizations faced with the unidirectional flow of information between software development and maintenance; according to Banker et al. (1998), this had obscured lessons software developers might have gleaned from the maintenance problems they helped to create. ODC insights on the nature of the defects encountered is instructive for the development process.

ODC is a root cause analysis technique for evaluating software defects during testing. Its goals are to (1) extract key information from defects encountered in process to enable their identification and classification into orthogonal (all-inclusive and non-redundant) categories, which describe different error dimensions, and (2) provide enough information to indicate to developers and managers where in the process the problem occurred and where the defect was injected into the system (Butcher et al., 2002). ODC tracks two attributes of a defect: type, which categorizes defects by the semantics of the repair needed to remove them from the system; and trigger, which identifies the particular condition that caused the defect to surface (Chillarege et al., 1992). ODC thus provides dual insights into development and verification processes with in-process feedback to enable cause-effect determination for immediate corrective action as well as indications of scenarios to avoid in future IS projects.

IMPLICATIONS FOR IS MAINTAINABILITY

The preceding discussion of alternative IS development practices and approaches was intended to substantiate the central theme of this chapter that to maximize systems maintainability and reduce maintenance effort, developers need to understand the contextual capabilities of the range of methods that are available to them in order to select those most suitable for the particular problem domain. The judicious selection of a development approach comprising socio-technical schemes, IS process management techniques, IS delivery methods, and software verification schemes can help to improve system quality and ultimately reduce system maintenance. It is noteworthy that some development methods are associated with particular IS delivery paradigms. However, any of the process support techniques, socio-technical concepts, or systems development tools may be used with any IS development method (Iivari et al., 2000-2001).

The techniques selected for elaboration were typical precursors of a family of similar approaches with some name recognition and acknowledged strengths in particular development contexts. They were not presented as individual "silver bullets", but as potential infrastructural components of a quality-focused development environment. They should be assessed as candidates for the method-mix that is recommended to improve the quality of the IS process and the resulting product, contingent on their fit with the particular development context. In several cases, there is no general agreement about their worth; equivalent claims of their usefulness and ineffectiveness coexist in the literature, and this strengthens the signal for context-method fit evaluations.

The relationship between sound software processes, their products, and eventual maintenance effort not only has intuitive appeal but also enjoys the credence of empirical support. It is recognized that poor information systems quality is not the sole contributor to the extremely high allocation of IS development resources to systems maintenance. But the theme and dominant message of this chapter is that a well-considered blend of IS delivery process strategies can overcome the essential difficulties of systems development and help generate high-quality systems. This is expected to lead to the reduction of systems operations and maintenance costs and release human and financial resources to concentrate on more productive organizational activities.

Inferring logically coherent relationships among constructs from several related research streams, as I have done in this chapter, can provide useful insights. However, the conclusions drawn must necessarily be subjected to empirical verification. In this regard, further research is needed to provide greater insights into contingency considerations for the adoption of effective combinations of systems development methods and process-structuring approaches, and suitable criteria for grouping methods to maximize systems maintainability. It would also be useful to determine how different approaches impact the various categories of IS maintenance.

CONCLUSIONS

Developers will never get it right the first time regardless of the systems delivery approach they adopt. However, many maintenance problems result from inadequate software development practices, which result in low-quality systems and undoubtedly contribute to systems maintenance pressure. There are huge incentives to reduce the burden of this necessary evil, which is absolutely necessary to perpetuate systems to business-process relevance, but adverse in its resource exaction and generally regarded as the least interesting IS development activity. But the quest to reduce systems maintenance requires analytical effort way in advance of systems deployment; it should begin with the selection of appropriate, quality-enhancing systems delivery practices.

IS quality improvement ranks high among the objectives of organizations because IS development is on the critical path of enabling strategic priorities through value chain efficiencies (Ravichandran & Rai, 2000). Low quality systems eventually siphon organizational resources (for allocation to maintenance activities), which presumably reduces the allotment available for deployment in new developments and to research and assess technical and behavioral opportunities for improving IS productivity and quality in order to reduce the maintenance burden. This is a dangerous cycle. This chapter emphasizes the critical need to break such a cycle by judiciously selecting the right blend of existing and emerging quality-oriented IS delivery strategies that intrinsically target systems maintainability. These should be geared toward establishing the highest capability for improving the quality of IS processes and products and maximizing the probability of reversing the trend of low-quality, high-maintenance information systems.

Organizations need to steer clear of subjective allegiance to particular methods and over-hyped claims by enthusiastic proponents of the next silver bullet. There is no value in projecting alternative approaches as competitors and being forced to align with "the winner"; no method is inherently better than another in all situations. A focused pre-development analysis of available systems delivery techniques is required to objectively exploit potentially synergistic combinations of approaches that best fit the situational characteristics of the development effort. In that way we may be able, eventually, to adjust the imbalance of IS resources absorbed by maintenance activities in comparison to new developments; for while maintenance activities continue to consume a larger share of available effort, demand for new developments is simultaneously increasing.

REFERENCES

Adamopoulos, D.X., Haramis, G., & Papandreou, C.A. (1998). Rapid prototyping of new telecommunications services: A procedural approach. *Computer Communications, 21,* 211-219.

Agarwal, R., De, P., Sinha, A.P., & Tanniru, M. (2000). On the usability of OO representations. *Communications of the ACM, 43*(10), 83-89.

Al-Mushayt, O., Doherty, N., & King, M. (2001). An investigation into the relative success of alternative approaches to the treatment of organizational issues in systems development projects. *Organization Development Journal, 19*(1), 31-48.

Andrews, D.C. (1991). JAD: A crucial dimension for rapid applications development. *Journal of Systems Management, 42*(3), 23-27, 31.

Bandi, R.K., Vaishnavi, V.K., & Turk, D.E. (2003). Predicting maintenance performance using object-oriented design complexity metrics. IEEE *Transactions on Software Engineering, 29*(1), 77-87.

Banker, R.D., & Slaughter, S.A. (1997). A field study of scale economies in software maintenance. *Management Science, 43*(12), 1709-1725.

Banker, R.D., Dater, S.M, & Kemerer, C.F. (1991). A model to evaluate variables impacting the productivity of software maintenance projects. *Management Science, 17*(1), 1-18.

Banker, R.D., Dater, S.M., Kemerer, C.F., & Zweig, D. (1993). Software complexity and maintenance costs. *Communications of the ACM, 36*(11), 81-94.

Banker, R.D., Davis, G.B., & Slaughter, S.A. (1998). Software development practices, software complexity, and software maintenance performance: A field study. *Management Science, 44*(4), 433-450.

Barki, H., & Hartwick, J. (1994). Measuring user participation, user involvement, and user attitude. *MIS Quarterly, 18*(1), 59-82.

Barrow, P.D., & Mayhew, P.J. (2000). Investigating principles of stakeholder evaluation in a modern IS development approach. *Journal of Systems and Software, 52*(2-3), 95-103.

Baskerville, R.L., & Stage, J. (1996). Controlling prototype development through risk analysis. *MIS Quarterly, 20*(4), 481-504.

Beizer, B. (1997). Cleanroom process model: A critical examination. *IEEE Software, 14*(2), 14-16.

Beynon-Davies, P., Mackay, H., & Tudhope, D. (2000). It's lots of bits of paper and ticks and post-it notes and things: A case study of a rapid application development project. *Information Systems Journal, 10*(3), 195-216.

Boar, B.H. (1984). *Application prototyping*. New York: John Wiley & Sons.

Bordoloi, B., & Lee, M. (1994). An object-oriented view: Productivity comparison with structured development. *Information Systems Management, 11*(1), 22-30.

Borovits, I., Ellis, S., & Yeheskel, O. (1990). Group processes and the development of information systems. *Information & Management, 19*(2), 65-72.

Bourne, K.C. (1994). Putting the rigor back in RAD. *Database Programming & Design, 7*(8), 25-30.

Brooks, F.P., Jr. (1987). No silver bullet: Essence and accidents of software engineering. *IEEE Computer, 20*(4), 10-19.

Brown, D.W. (2002). *An introduction to object-oriented analysis*. New York: John Wiley & Sons, Inc.

Brynjolfssen, E. (1993). The productivity paradox of information technology. *Communications of the ACM, 36*(12), 67-77.

Butcher, M., Munro, H., & Kratschmer, T. (2002). Improving software testing via ODC: Three case studies. *IBM Systems Journal, 41*(1), 31-34.

Carmel, E., Whitaker, R.D., & George, J.F. (1993). PD and joint application design: A transatlantic comparison. *Communications of the ACM, 36*(6), 40-48.

Chillarege, R., Bhandari, I.S., Chaar, J.K., Halliday, M.J., Moebus, D.S., Ray, B.K., & Wong, M. (1992). Orthogonal defect classification—A concept for in-process measurements. *IEEE Transactions on Software Engineering, 18*(11), 943-956.

Cornelius, B.J., Munro, M., & Robson, D.J. (1989). An approach to software maintenance education. *Software Engineering Journal, 4*(4), 233-236.

Dekleva, S.M. (1992). The influence of the information systems development approach on maintenance. *MIS Quarterly, 16*(3), 355-372.

Dishaw, M.T., & Strong, D.M. (1998). Supporting software maintenance with software engineering tools: A computed task-technology fit analysis. *The Journal of Systems and Software, 44*(2), 107-120.

Dodd, J.L., & Carr, H.H. (1994). Systems development led by end-users. *Journal of Systems Management, 45*(8), 34-40.

Doherty, N.F., & King, M. (1998). The consideration of organizational issues during the systems development process: an empirical analysis. *Behavior & Information Technology, 17*(1), 41-51.

Elboushi, M.I. (1997). Object-oriented software design utilizing quality function deployment. *The Journal of Systems and Software, 38*(2), 133-143.

Erikkson, I., & McFadden, F. (1993). Quality function deployment: A tool to improve software quality. *Information & Software Technology, 35*(9), 491-498.

Fichman, R.G., & Kemerer, C.F. (1992). Object-oriented and conventional analysis and design methodologies. *IEEE Computer, 25*(10), 22-39.

Fitzgerald, B. (2000). Systems development methodologies: The problem of tenses. *Information Technology & People, 13*(3), 174-182.

Flatten, P.O. (1992). Requirements for a life-cycle methodology for the 1990s. In W.W. Cotterman & J.A. Senn (Eds.), *Challenges and strategies for research in systems development*, (pp. 221-234). New York: John Wiley & Sons.

Fox, W.M. (1995). Socio-technical system principles and guidelines: Past and present. *The Journal of Applied Behavioral Science, 31*(1), 91-105.

Ghods, M., & Nelson, K.M. (1998). Contributions to quality during software maintenance. *Decision Support Systems, 23,* 361-369.

Gibbs, W. W. (1994). Software's chronic crisis. *Scientific American, 271*(3), 86-95.

Gibson, V.R., & Senn, J.A. (1989). Systems structure and software maintenance performance. *Communications of the ACM, 32*(3), 347-358.

Glass, R.L. (2001). Extreme programming: The good, the bad, and the bottom line. *IEEE Software, 8*(6), 111-112.

Grady, R.B. (1993). Practical results from measuring software quality. *Communications of the ACM, 36*(11), 62-68.

Hanna, M. (1995). Farewell to waterfalls? *Software Magazine, 15*(5), 38-46.

Harter, D.E., Slaughter, S.A., & Krishnan, M.S. (1998). The life cycle effects of software quality: A longitudinal analysis. *International Conference on Information Systems,* 346-351.

Hausler, P.A., Linger, R.C., & Trammell, C.J. (1994). Adopting cleanroom software engineering with a phased approach. *IBM Systems Journal, 33*(1), 89-109.

Head, G.E. (1994). Six-Sigma software using cleanroom software engineering techniques. *Hewlett-Packard Journal, 45*(3), 40-50.

Ho, E.S., Lai, Y.J., & Chang, S.I. (1999). An integrated group decision-making approach to quality function deployment. *IIE Transactions, 31*(6), 553-567.

Hoffer, J.A., George, J.F., & Valacich, J.S. (2002). *Modern systems analysis and design.* New Jersey: Prentice Hall.

Hough, D. (1993). Rapid delivery: An evolutionary approach for application development. *IBM Systems Journal, 32*(3), 397-419.

Iivari, J., Hirschheim, R., & Klein, H.K. (2000-2001). A dynamic framework for classifying information systems development methodologies and approaches. *Journal of Management Information Systems, 17*(3), 179-218.

Jerva, M. (2001). Systems analysis and design methodologies: Practicalities and use in today's information systems development efforts. *Topics in Health Information Management, 21*(4), 13-20.

Johnson, R.A., Hardgrove, B.C., & Doke, E.R. (1999). An industry analysis of developer beliefs about object-oriented systems development. *The DATA BASE for Advances in Information Systems, 30*(1), 47-64.

Keil, M. (1995). Pulling the plug: Software project management and the problem of project escalation. *MIS Quarterly, 19*(4), 421-447.

Kettelhut, M.C. (1993). JAD methodology and group dynamics. *Information Systems Management, 14*(3), 46-53.

Kjaer, A., & Madsen, K.H. (1995). Participatory analysis of flexibility. *Communications of the ACM, 38*(5), 53-60.

Korac-Boisvert, N., & Kouzmin, A.K.N. (1995). IT development: Methodology overload or crisis. *Science Communication, 17,* 81-88.

Liou, Y.I., & Chen, M. (1993/4). Using group support systems in joint application development for requirements specifications. *Journal of Management Information Systems, 10*(3), 25-41.

Lyytinen, K. (1988). Expectation failure concept and systems analysts' view of information system failures: Results of an exploratory study. *Information & Management, 14*(1), 45-56.

Mankin, D., & Cohen, S.G. (1997) Teams and technology: Tensions in participatory design. *Organizational Dynamics, 26*(1), 63-76.

Markus, M.L., & Keil, M. (1994). If we build it they will come: Designing information systems that users want to use. *Sloan Management Review, 35*(4), 11-25.

Martins, A., & Aspinwall, E.M. (2001). Quality function deployment: An empirical study in the UK. *Total Quality Management, 12*(5), 575-588.

McDonald, M.P. (1995). Quality function deployment - introducing product development into the systems development process. *Seventh Symposium on Quality Function Deployment*, Michigan.

Mousinho, G. (1990). Project management: Runaway! *Systems International, 6,* 35-40.

Muller, M.J., Wildman, D.M., & White, E.A. (1993). Taxonomy of PD practices: A brief practitioner's guide. *Communications of the ACM, 36*(4), 26-27.

Newman, M., & Robey, D. (1992). A social process model of user-analyst relationships. *MIS Quarterly, 16*(2), 249-266.

Niederman, F., Brancheau, J.C., & Wetherbe, J.C. (1991). Information systems management issues for the 1990s. *MIS Quarterly, 15*(4), 474-500.

Oman, P., & Hagemeister, J. (1994). Constructing and testing polynomials predicting software maintainability. *Journal of Systems and Software, 24*(3), 251-266.

Palvia, S.C., Sharma, R.S., & Conrath, D.W. (2001). A socio-technical framework for quality assessment of computer information systems. *Industrial Management & Data Systems, 101*(5), 237-251.

Paulk, M. (2001). Extreme programming from a CMM perspective. *IEEE Software, 8*(6), 19-26.

Pressman, R.S. (2001). *Software engineering: A practitioner approach.* New York: McGraw Hill.

Ramanujan, S., Scamell, R.W., & Shah, J.R. (2000). An experimental investigation of the impact of individual, program, and organizational characteristics on software maintenance effort. *The Journal of Systems and Software, 54*(2), 137-157.

Ravichandran, T., & Rai, A. (1996). Impact of process management on systems development quality: An empirical study. *Proceedings of the Americas Conference on Information Systems.*

Ravichandran, T., & Rai, A. (2000). Quality management in systems development: An organizational system perspective. *MIS Quarterly, 24*(3), 381-416.

Roberts, T.L., Gibson, M.L., & Fields, K.T. (1997). Systems development methodology implementation: Perceived aspects of importance. *Information Resources Management Journal, 10*(3), 27-38.

Robey, D., Welke, R., & Turk, D. (2001). Traditional, iterative, and component-based development: A social analysis of software of software development paradigms. *Information Technology and Management, 2*(1), 53-70.

Schaider, E.D. (1999) TCO in the trenches: The Standish group study. Available: *SoftwareMag.com*

Schmidt, D.C., & Fayad, M.E. (1997). Lessons learned building reusable OO frameworks for distributed software. *Communications of the ACM, 40*(10), 85-87.

Shani, A.B., & Sena, J.A. (1994). Information technology and the integration of change: Sociotechnical system approach. *The Journal of Applied Behavioral Science, 30*(2), 247-270.

Spangler, A. (1996). Cleanroom software engineering: Plan your work and work your plan in small increments. *IEEE Potentials, 15*(4), 29-32.

Sparling, M. (2000). Lessons learned through six years of component-based development. *Communications of the ACM, 43*(10), 47-53.

Swanson, E.B., & Beath, C.M. (1989). Reconstructing the systems development organization. *MIS Quarterly, 13*(3), 293-307.

Swanson, E.B., & Dans, E. (2000). System life expectancy and the maintenance effort: Exploring their equilibrium. *MIS Quarterly, 24*(2), 277-297.

Szyperski, C. (1998). *Component software, beyond object-oriented programming.* New York: Addison-Wesley.

Trammell, C.J., Pleszkoch, M.G., Linger, R.C., & Hevner, A.R. (1996). The incremental development process in cleanroom software engineering. *Decision Support Systems, 17*(1), 55-71.

Vessey, I., & Glass, S.A. (1998). Strong vs. weak approaches to systems development. *Communications of the ACM, 37*(5), 102-112.

Vessey, I., & Weber, R. (1984). Research on structured programming: An empiricist's evaluation. *IEEE Transactions on Software Engineering, 10*(4), 397-407.

Weinberg, R.S. (1991). Prototyping and the systems development life cycle. *Information Systems Management, 8*(2), 47-53.

Wetherbe, J.C. (1991). Executive information requirements: Getting it right. *MIS Quarterly, 15*(1), 51-65.

Wood, J., & Silver, D. (1995). *Joint application development.* New York: John Wiley & Sons.

Zagal, J.P., Ahués, R.S., & Voehl, M.N. (2002). Maintenance-oriented design and development: A case study. *IEEE Software, 19*(4), 100-106.

Zhuo, F., Lowther, B., Oman, P., & Hagemeister, J. (1993). Constructing and testing software maintainability assessment models. *Proceedings of First International Software Metrics Symposium,* IEEE.

ENDNOTES

[1] In 1999, the U.S. market for quality-enhancing software development tools and techniques was estimated at $900 million and steadily growing (Information Week, July 3, 2000).

[2] JAD Phases:

1. *Project definition.* Facilitator works with system owners and sponsors to determine management perspectives on purpose, scope, and objectives.
2. Background research into the current business processes and related computer systems.
3. Extensive planning, training, and preparation for the workshop, the logistics, of the scribe.
4. The JAD workshop, where the neutral facilitator guides the session toward the accomplishment of its goals.
5. Preparation of the final document containing the decisions and agreements.

[3] CMM Levels

- *Level 1.* The "initial" stage is characterized by the absence of and formal procedures - a state of near chaos, in which project planning and control are non-existent.
- *Level 2.* The "repeatable" stage, in which basic project management capability exists but process management discipline is lacking. Several stylistic approaches are supplied by the various project leaders.
- *Level 3.* The "defined" stage, which uses a common, institutionalized process management method (systems development methodology) for all its IS projects, which produces consistent, stable, and predictable outcomes.
- *Level 4.* The "managed" stage, in which the organization collects detailed measures of process and product quality to learn each development experience.
- *Level 5.* The "optimized" stage in which the metrics from level 4, acknowledged best practices, and the results of controlled experiments and pilot studies are used to adjust the process to achieve continuous process improvement.

[4] Important OO notions include:

- Encapsulation, which makes an object self-sufficient by abstracting and isolating its attributes and procedures, as in a "capsule", and protecting them from other objects; objects, however, interact by exchanging messages that request information or the activation of particular procedures.
- Inheritance is supported by the structure of classes (generic groupings) or instances (specific concrete invocation of an example in application) and enabled by defining special cases, subclasses, which share the common

attributes, procedures, and relationships of a more general class (superclass), but may have their own peculiar attributes and procedures. Existing objects may also be augmented with additional procedures to create new classes with enhanced functionality.

- Polymorphism exploits the hierarchy of object classification to apply the same named procedure in different ways depending on the characteristics of the object class in which it is invoked.

About the Editors

Khaled M. Khan is a senior lecturer in the School of Computing and Information Technology at the University of Western Sydney, Australia. His major research interests include software maintenance, security of software components, software architecture, software metrics and systems quality. He has taught computer science and information systems at various universities in Europe, Africa and Asia for more than 15 years. He received his undergraduate and postgraduate degrees both in Computer Science and Informatics from the University of Trondheim, Norway.

Yan Zhang is an associate professor in the School of Computing and IT, University of Western Sydney, Australia. He received his PhD in Computer Science from Sydney University in 1994. His research interests include knowledge update, logic programming, model checking, descriptive complexity theory, and information security. Dr. Zheng has published many research papers in top international conferences and journals in his areas. He has also succeeded in obtaining national competitive research grants since he joined UWS in 1996.

About the Authors

Lerina Aversano received the Laurea degree in Computer Engineering from the University of Sannio, Italy, in 2000 and a PhD degree in Computer Engineering from the University of Sannio, Italy, in 2003. She is currently an assistant researcher at the RCOST - Research Centre on Software Technology of the University of Sannio. Her research interests include process and information system modelling, workflow management, document management, business process reengineering, software reengineering and migration.

Rafael Capilla is an associate professor at the Universidad Rey Juan Carlos (Madrid, Spain) and was previously an associate professor at the Universidad Politécnica de Madrid. He worked for a telecommunications company for two years and later as a UNIX system manager for eight years in the Faculty of Computing at the University of Seville. He participated in the European ESPRIT IV FLEX, and now his current work is in developing under the Biodiversidad project, partially funded by the Spanish Ministry of Environment. He is an author of more than 20 papers in the field of software engineering and co-author of a book of Web applications programming. He is a member of IEEE CS.

Zeljka Car received her BSc, MSc and PhD degrees in Electrical Engineering from the University of Zagreb, Croatia in 1993, 1996 and 2001, respectively. Since 1993 she has been affiliated with the Faculty of Electrical Engineering and Computing of the University of Zagreb, where she currently works as a teaching assistant at the Department of Telecommunications. Her educational activities are comprised of the following: telecommunication software design, diagnostics and reliability and concurrent systems. Her research interests are software engineering, especially software process modelling and development and maintenance of telecommunication software systems.

Ned Chapin is an information systems consultant with InfoSci Inc., USA. His decades of experience include all phases of the software life cycle and cover industrial, business, financial, non-profit, and governmental organizations. He has also served in roles from lecturer to professor of Information Systems at various universities. Dr. Chapin's interests include software maintenance and evolution, database technology, systems analysis and design, and software management. He is a member of the ACM, ACH, AITP, IEEE Computer Society, and Sigma Xi—Scientific Research Society. Dr. Chapin is a registered professional engineer and a certified information systems auditor. His MBA is from the Graduate School of Business of the University of Chicago, and his PhD is from Illinois Institute of Technology. Dr. Chapin currently is co-editor of the *Journal of Software Maintenance and Evolution*. He can be contacted at: NedChapin@acm.org

Darren Dalcher is a professor of Software Project Management at Middlesex University (UK) where he leads the Software Forensics Centre, a specialised unit that focuses on systems failures, software pathology and project failures. He gained his PhD in Software Engineering from King's College, University of London. In 1992, he founded and has since continued as chairman of the Forensics Working Group of the IEEE Technical Committee on the Engineering of Computer-Based Systems, an international group of academic and industrial participants formed to share information and develop expertise in failure and recovery. Professor Dalcher is active in a number of international committees and steering groups. He is heavily involved in organising international conferences, and has delivered numerous keynote addresses and tutorials. He is editor-in-chief of *Software Process Improvement and Practice.*

Juan C. Dueñas is an associate professor at the Universidad Politécnica de Madrid, Spain, in the Telecommunications School, where he was awarded the prize of the best PhD thesis in software engineering. Since then, he has participated in several European IST and ESPRIT (IPTES, IDERS, ARES, ESAPS, CARTS, CAFÉ, FAMILIES) consortia, in the roles of technical development and technical management of real-time, software engineering and architectural engineering projects. He has written more than 30 papers on international congresses and workshops in the field of software engineering, software evolution and maintenance. He is a member of IEEE CS.

Evan W. Duggan is an assistant professor of MIS in the Culverhouse College of Commerce & Business Administration at the University of Alabama (USA). He obtained PhD and MBA degrees from Georgia State University and a BSc from the University of the West Indies, Jamaica. He has over 25 years of IT experience in industry. His research interests involve the management of information systems (IS) in corporations with reference to IS success factors and quality, sociotechnical issues, and systems development and project management methodologies. He has publications (or articles forthcoming) in the *International Journal of Industrial Engineering,* the *Journal of International Technology and Information Management, Information Technology & Management,* the *Journal of End User Computing,* the *Information Resources Management Journal, Human-Computer Interactions* and *Information & Management.* Dr. Duggan has taught MIS and Decision Sciences courses at the graduate and undergraduate levels, including executive MBA programs, in several U.S. and international institutions.

Raffaele Esposito is a research assistant at the Research Centre on Software Technology of the University of Sannio, Italy. He graduated in electronic engineering at the University of Naples "Federico II", Italy. His research interests include software maintenance and evolution, software reengineering, business process reengineering, software quality, and verification and validation.

George T. Heineman is an associate professor in the Computer Science Department of Worcester Polytechnic Institute (WPI) in Worcester, USA. He founded the Software Engineering Research Group (SERG) at WPI and has received funding from DARPA and the National Science Foundation, including a prestigious CAREER award. Together with Bill Councill, he co-edited the 2001 Addison-Wesley publication *Component-Based Software Engineering: Putting the Pieces Together.* He has served on a variety of workshop and conference program committees and has numerous academic publications on the topics of software engineering and component-based software engineering.

Mira Kajko-Mattsson has a PhD in Software Engineering. Presently, she works as a senior lecturer and researcher in the Department of Computer and Systems Sciences at Stockholm University and Royal Institute of Technology in Stockholm in Sweden. Her research interests include software maintenance, life cycle processes, and software quality. Dr. Kajko-Mattsson was involved in three research projects, of which two were in co-operation with industry (Ericsson and ABB). She is the author of more than 30 international publications. Kajko-Mattsson is the author of *Corrective Maintenance Maturity Model (CM^3).*

Kostas Kontogiannis obtained his PhD from McGill University, School of Computer Science. He is an associate professor in the Department of Electrical and Computer Engineering, University of Waterloo (Canada), where he is leading the Software Re-engineering group. His research focuses on the design and implementation of tools and techniques that allow for large legacy software systems to be re-engineered and integrated in distributed and Network-Centric environments. He is the recipient of a Canada Foundation for Innovation Award and of three IBM University Partnership Program Awards.

Teresa Mallardo is a research assistant at the Research Centre on Software Technology of the University of Sannio, Italy. She graduated in computer science at the University of Bari, Italy. Her research interests include software inspections, global software development, software reengineering and business process reengineering, and software quality.

As chief technology officer, **Alok Mehta** is currently in charge of technology research and development at AFS (USA) (www.afs-link.com), specializing in Internet application development. He also leads the software development team to maintain, enhance and develop existing software products. Dr. Mehta joined AFS in 1990. He holds a PhD in Computer Science from Worcester Polytechnic Institute and an MBA from Plymouth State College. Dr. Mehta has publications in prestigious academic conferences, such as the International Conference on Software Engineering, and developer magazines, such as *MSDN* and *Advisor.* In addition to his professional and academic pursuits, he is a highly competitive racquetball player, winning a gold medal in the 2003 U.S. National Racquetball Tournament.

Frank Niessink is a principal consultant at the Software Engineering Research Centre (SERC) in Utrecht, The Netherlands. His research interests are software measurement, software maintenance and process improvement. Before joining SERC in 2001, he had been an assistant professor of Computer Science at the Vrije Universiteit Amsterdam, division of Mathematics and Computer Science and a quality advisor at ASZ (Automatisering Sociale Zekerheid/Automation Social Security). Dr. Niessink received a PhD in Computer Science, a MSc in Computer Science and a MSc in Economics from the Vrije Universiteit Amsterdam.

Malin Nordström has her background in the academic world, working and researching at the University of Östersund (Mitthögskolan). She started På (Sweden) in 1997 with Tommy Welander. Previously, she was the Managing Director of På, and now, she is responsible for research and development. Together with Tommy Welander, Dr. Nordström creates models, methods and tools for systems maintenance management, and she is the author of two books about systems maintenance. Apart from her managing role in På, she has also been strategically responsible for the design and quality of large-scale systems maintenance management projects in a number of organisations. Dr. Nordström is currently doing research towards a doctoral dissertation at the University of Linköping, which will be presented in June 2004. She is a much sought-after lecturer on "Business Oriented Maintenance Management".

Kamran Sartipi is an assistant professor in the Department of Computing and Software at McMaster University, Canada. Dr. Sartipi obtained a BSc degree and a MSc degree in Electrical Engineering from the Department of Electrical and Electronic Engineering, University of Tehran, Iran, and a PhD degree in Computer Science (Software Engineering) from the School of Computer Science, University of Waterloo, Canada. He has been involved in research and teaching in both hardware and software engineering. In recent years, his research has included different aspects of software architecture such as software architecture views, recovery, and evaluation. He has designed and developed techniques and tools for pattern-based software architecture recovery and evaluation. This research has produced several publications in international journals and conferences. Dr. Sartipi's research was funded by IBM Canada Ltd. Laboratory, Center for Advanced Studies (Toronto), the Consortium for Software Engineering Research (CSER), and the Institute for Robotics & Intelligent Systems (IRIS).

Alexandru C. Telea received his PhD in Computer Science in 2000 from the Eindhoven University of Technology in The Netherlands, where he currently is an assistant professor in the field of scientific visualization and computer graphics. During his four years as a member of the scientific computing group of the mathematics faculty, his interests focused on designing object and component oriented architectures for numerical simulation and visualization software. Currently, his research focus is on developing visualization methods and algorithms for a wide range of data types, such as software structures, data hierarchies, scientific, and numerical. He is also involved in research on geometric surface and image processing, computer vision, and image synthesis. He has co-authored over 30 papers on the above topics and has been actively involved in conferences such as IEEE Visualization and IEEE VisSym.

Maria Tortorella is an assistant professor of the Engineering Faculty at the University of Sannio. She is a research leader at the RCOST – Research Centre on Software Technology of the University of Sannio (Italy). Her research interests include reverse engineering, maintenance, software comprehension, business process re-engineering, business process and software system evaluation. She received a BS degree in Computer Science at the University of Salerno, a MSc in Computer Science at the University of Durham, and a PhD in Electronic Engineering and Computer Science at the University of Naples.

Tommy Welander worked as a marketing director and market strategist for many years before founding På in 1997 together with Malin Nordström. Today, he is the managing director for the company, which works with several of the largest public authorities and a number of market-leading companies in Sweden. Together with Malin Nordström, he creates models, methods and tools for business oriented systems maintenance management and he is also the author of three books on systems maintenance management. Apart from being the managing director of På, he has also been the main project leader in several major projects concerning maintenance management and business orientation in large organisations. In addition, he is often invited to hold seminars and lectures about "Business Oriented Maintenance Management".

Limin Xiang received a BS in 1982, a ME in 1988, and a PhD in 1999, all degrees in Computer Science, from Nanjing University, the University of Electronic Science and Technology of China, and Kyushu University, respectively. He is currently an associate professor of information science at Kyushu Sangyo University, Japan. His research interests include algorithm design and analysis and parallel computation.

Uwe Zdun is an assistant professor in the Department of Information Systems at the Vienna University of Economics. He received his MS and PhD degrees from the University of Essen (1999, 2001). Dr. Zdun's research focuses on various software engineering topics, including software patterns, scripting, object-orientation, software architecture, reengineering, distributed object frameworks, and Web engineering. He is co-author of the object-oriented scripting language Extended Object Tcl (XOTcl), the active Web object and mobile code system ActiWeb, the conference management system Lorien, and numerous other freely available software systems. He worked also on many commercial software systems, as a consultant for industry companies, and in various research projects.

Jianjun Zhao received a BS and PhD in Computer Science from Tsinghua University, China in 1987 and Kyushu University, Japan in 1997. He is an associate professor of Computer Science at Fukuoka Institute of Technology, Japan. His research interests include program analysis and compiler, software architecture analysis, ubiquitous computing environment, and aspect-oriented software development. He is a member of ACM and IEEE.

Ying Zou obtained her PhD from University of Waterloo, Department of Electrical and Computer Engineering. She is an assistant professor in the Department of Electrical and

Computer Engineering, Queen's University (Canada). Her research focuses on Web centric software migration and integration, object oriented migration, quality driven software transformation, program comprehension, source code representation and source code analysis.

Index

A

B

C

D

E

F

G

H

I